The Art of Leadership

The Art of Leadership

Fourth Edition

GEORGE MANNING
Northern Kentucky University

KENT CURTIS
Northern Kentucky University

McGraw-Hill
Irwin

McGraw-Hill Irwin

THE ART OF LEADERSHIP, FOURTH EDITION

Published by McGraw-Hill, a business unit of The McGraw-Hill Companies, Inc., 1221 Avenue of the Americas, New York, NY 10020. Copyright © 2012 by The McGraw-Hill Companies, Inc. All rights reserved. Previous editions © 2009, 2007, and 2003. No part of this publication may be reproduced or distributed in any form or by any means, or stored in a database or retrieval system, without the prior written consent of The McGraw-Hill Companies, Inc., including, but not limited to, in any network or other electronic storage or transmission, or broadcast for distance learning.

Some ancillaries, including electronic and print components, may not be available to customers outside the United States.

This book is printed on acid-free paper.

1 2 3 4 5 6 7 8 9 0 QDB/QDB 1 0 9 8 7 6 5 4 3 2 1

ISBN   978-0-07-802908-0
MHID   0-07-802908-2

Vice President & Editor-in-Chief: *Brent Gordon*
Vice President EDP/Central Publishing Services: *Kimberly Meriwether David*
Editorial Director: *Paul Ducham*
Managing Developmental Editor: *Laura Hurst Spell*
Associate Marketing Manager: *Jaime Halteman*
Project Manager: *Erin Melloy*
Buyer: *Nicole Baumgartner*
Design Coordinator: *Brenda A. Rolwes*
Cover Designer: *Studio Montage, St. Louis, Missouri*
Cover Image: *© Royalty-Free/ CORBIS*
Media Project Manager: *Balaji Sundararaman*
Compositor: *Aptara®, Inc.*
Typeface: *10/12 Times Roman*
Printer: *Quad/Graphics*

All credits appearing on page or at the end of the book are considered to be an extension of the copyright page.

Library of Congress Cataloging-in-Publication Data

Manning, George.
   The art of leadership/George Manning, Kent Curtis.—4th ed.
     p. cm.
   Includes bibliographical references and index.
   ISBN 978-0-07-802908-0 (alk. paper)
   1. Leadership.   2. Management.   I. Curtis, Kent, 1939- II. Title.
   BF637.L4M26 2012
   158′.4—dc22

                          2011005534

www.mhhe.com

Dedication

We dedicate this book to our families:

Nancy and Page, Larry, and Heather

Mary and Lisa, Denise, and Craig

Contents in Brief

Contents

Preface

The word *leader* first appeared in the English language in the 1300s, coming from the root word *leden* meaning "to travel" or "show the way." The term *leadership* followed some five centuries later. Today the study of leadership is multidisciplinary with contributions from history, philosophy, psychology, political science, business, and education.

The fourth edition of *The Art of Leadership* combines behavior theory with business practice to teach central concepts and skills in leadership. The book is made more valuable and the impact greater by the self-evaluation questionnaires and practical exercises that are used for personal development and class involvement. *The Art of Leadership,* fourth edition, is more than a textbook; it is a "learning" book that actively involves the reader in the learning process.

The fourth edition teaches leadership in a way that is appropriate for both new and experienced leaders, as well as for the everyday person who must influence others to get things done. Our goal is for you to use this book to develop your full potential as a leader, to *become the kind of leader you always wanted to have,* and to help you become a good, and perhaps even a great leader.

The fourth edition of *The Art of Leadership* adds theoretical foundation as well as learning exercises to personalize the subject. Topics include leadership trait and behavior theories, charismatic and transformational leadership, leadership ethics and values, human relations and the empowerment of people, the team concept and group dynamics, leader as coach and developer of people, cultural diversity and the global economy, stress in the workplace and adaptive capacity, and performance management and organizational success.

We have revised each part of the book based on comments provided by students and colleagues who used the first three editions and on formal reviews submitted by a cross-section of instructors from community colleges, four-year schools, and universities with graduate programs in leadership. We have attempted to tighten up the writing, expand on real-world examples, and broaden coverage to areas that have emerged more recently on the leadership scene. Using an evidence-based management approach, the book is thoroughly referenced with classic and current citations. The number of references has increased from 722 to 840.

We have retained the most popular features from previous editions and have added new material in the following areas :

- **Part 1:** leadership failure, leadership intelligence, followership
- **Part 2:** workplace culture, leadership vision, organizational alignment
- **Part 3:** moral behavior, leadership values, organizational ethics
- **Part 4:** servant leadership, the quality imperative, civil work climate
- **Part 5:** employee morale, virtual leadership, leading teams
- **Part 6:** employee engagement, emotional intelligence, cross-cultural leadership, women in leadership, generational differences
- **Part 7:** leadership personality and leadership skills
- **Part 8:** leading change, work–life balance, leadership coaching, employee retention
- **Part 9:** performance management, innovation, sustaining discipline

Video cases with questions for discussion are included to enhance each part of the text. Web sites are identified for additional information.

Central Ideas of This Book

This book is based on two ideas. The first is that leadership will take place to the extent the leader cares about the work to be done. Equally important, the leader must care about people. Neither of these qualities is sufficient without the other, and neither can be false. People know when the leader cares. When the leader is committed to the task and is concerned about people, these qualities serve as magnets and motivators to followers, and their potential for achievement becomes enormous.

The second premise of the book is that leadership is an art that can be developed through mastery of nine key areas of success. The successful leader must possess knowledge and skills in the following areas: understanding leadership variables, the power of vision, the importance of ethics, the empowerment of people, leadership principles, understanding people, multiplying effectiveness, developing others, and performance management.

Who Should Read This Book?

The fourth edition of *The Art of Leadership* is written for students in leadership development and other management-related courses, such as leadership principles, contemporary leadership, and managerial skills. It is appropriate for leadership courses in business, education, psychology, communication, health care, criminal justice, military, and public administration.

The Art of Leadership, fourth edition, is appropriate for use at the university level as well as in corporate university programs. It is ideally suited for undergraduate degree–completion students and organization-based education, where there is an emphasis on developing leadership competency. No prior coursework in business or management is required.

The level of material is appropriate for both emerging and experienced leaders. Emerging leaders can use this book to prepare themselves to meet the demands of being a leader. Having a vision of what should be done, effectively using authority, motivating people to perform at their best, and solving tough personnel problems— discussed in Parts 2, 4, 6, and 9—are challenges all leaders must face.

Experienced leaders can use this book to address workplace issues, taking leadership skills to new levels of effectiveness. Matching leadership style with the needs of followers, leading by values and ethical principles, raising employee morale, delegating work effectively, and helping people through change—discussed in Parts 1, 3, 5, 7, and 8—are important areas for leaders to address.

By understanding leadership and its challenges, appreciating the importance of caring leadership, and developing the skills required for effective leadership, readers will (1) be more effective at work, (2) gain knowledge and skills, and (3) have the ability to lead others when the opportunity occurs.

Approach and Style of the Book

The difference between most other leadership texts and *The Art of Leadership,* fourth edition, can be compared to the difference between a lecture and a seminar. Although both are good educational vehicles, the lecture is better for conveying large amounts of information, while the seminar is better for developing skills and attitudes. A good lecture is interesting and builds knowledge, while a good seminar is stimulating and builds competency. Without sacrificing either theoretical foundation or important content, the fourth edition of *The Art of Leadership* emphasizes the interactive, seminar approach to learning.

Reviewers of the book identify its major strengths to be clarity of writing and user-friendly exercises. The writing style is personal and conversational, with minimal professional jargon. True-life examples clarify points under consideration. Concepts are supported by facts and figures, as well as by stories and anecdotes that are meaningful and easy to remember. Each unit includes learning activities to bridge the gap between theory and on-the-job practice. Our goal has been to include material that is interesting to read, practical to use, and personalized to the reader's own concerns.

Supplemental Information and Instructional Aids

Instructional aids have been significantly enhanced for *The Art of Leadership,* fourth edition. The **Online Learning Center (OLC)** at www.mhhe.com/manning4e includes password-protected instructor and student supplements. The instructor's center includes a revised and robust Instructor's Guide that contains learning objectives, discussion questions, PowerPoint presentations, notes and anecdotes, suggested films and videos (annotated), extensive bibliography, suggested articles, interactive cases, applications and exercises, and suggested Web sites. All chapters have updated testbank questions and PowerPoint slides. The Instructor's Guide includes 19 new exercises, 25 new applications, and 12 new cases.

Student content includes learning objectives, fill-in-the-blank summaries and answer keys, learning exercises and questionnaires, testbank items, and premium content. **Premium Content** (printed card ISBN 0077424646 or for eCommerce purchase from the OLC) includes Test Your Knowledge, Self-Assessments, and Manager's Hot Seat exercises. Manager's Hot Seat is an interactive, video-based software that puts students in the manager's hot seat where they have to apply their knowledge to make decisions on hot issues such as ethics, diversity, working in teams, and the virtual workplace.

The **Organizational Behavior Video DVD Vol. 1** (ISBN 0073337285) contains a collection of videos featuring interesting and timely issues, companies, and people related to organizational behavior and leadership.

How to Use This Book

The fourth edition of *The Art of Leadership* integrates current knowledge, skill development, and personal insight about leadership. It can be used as a textbook for teaching others, a workbook for personal development, and a desk book for ready reference in the area of leadership. The material is arranged in a logical sequence for learning. The best approach is to *interact* with the material. Read the narrative, complete the questionnaires, examine the interpretations, and review the principles and techniques. Then ask: How does this apply to me? How can I use this concept or information to improve my leadership effectiveness? Then *take action.*

To increase interest and improve overall learning, try the following:

1. Use the Learning Objectives and Reflection Points included in each part of the book to focus your reading, improve comprehension, and increase retention of the material.

2. Share questionnaires and exercises with family, friends, and co-workers, especially those who are interested in leadership development. In this way, you can make tangible use of what you learn and may even help others.

3. Think of the best leader you have ever had. What qualities did this individual possess? In what ways did he or she demonstrate the art of leadership? Use the material in this book to develop your own leadership effectiveness.

4. Write in the book. Follow the advice of Yale professor William Phelps: "Books are for use, not for show; you should own no book that you are afraid to mark up." You may want to use two markers to highlight information—one for personal development and one to help others. Use the margins, underline, write your own ideas. Personalize the material.

5. Visit the text's online Web site for more information: www.mhhe.com/manning4e.

Good luck in your learning!

We want your suggestions. If you have questions or see a way to improve this book, please write. Thank you.

George Manning
Kent Curtis
Northern Kentucky University, Highland Heights, Kentucky 41099
E-mail: manningg@nku.edu
       curtisk@nku.edu

Acknowledgments

The last words written in a book are the acknowledgments, and they are placed in the beginning, as they should be.

Special thanks go to Sharyn Cerda, Mary Curtis, Amanda Dole, Jessica Dyer, and Barbara Thomes for their tireless efforts in researching, editing, and preparing the multiple manuscript revisions for publication.

We are especially grateful to those whose work has helped shape and guide our ideas. Many of these prominent thinkers are mentioned in this book. Although the others are too numerous to list, we are no less indebted to them for their contributions to the field. Every effort has been made to locate the sources of the numerous quotes and references we cite, with an eye toward keeping the book both historically rich and up to date. From time to time, such information may shift. We welcome any corrections or changes.

Appreciation also goes to the following colleagues and supporters who have provided substantive help in manuscript review and research:

Shamima Ahmed, Northern Kentucky University

William Attenweiler, Northern Kentucky University

Mark Berry, Delta Airlines

Melanie Bingham, Perfetti-Van Melle, USA

Anthony Blair, Eastern University

Mendy Blair, Baptist Healthcare System

Bruce Blaylock, Radford University

Coulter R. Boyle, American Electric Power

Kimberley Breitenbecher, Northern Kentucky University

Rick Brockmeier, Northern Kentucky University

Timothy Burt, University of Durham (England)

Alan Burton, Cianbro Companies

Mike Campbell, American Electric Power

Bob Caplon, IBM

Margaret Casarez, Unbound Consulting

Ruth Cash-Smith, Ottawa University

Dennis Chandler, Measured Progress

Jeanetta Chrystie, Southwest Minnesota State University

Mike Daly, Ft. Thomas City Government

Mary Deville, Pulaski Technical College

Jeanne Dexter, Southwestern College

Mark Donaghy, RTA

Charles Drubel, Muskingum College

Mark Fulford, University of Central Missouri

Gail George, Great American Insurance Company

Fred Gilliam, Capital Metro

Kerry Gillihan, Cardinal Hill Healthcare System

Sharon Glazer, San Jose State University

Wade Graves, Grayson County College

Ronald Green, Johnson & Johnson

Dan Gregorie, V2E Consulting

David Hall, Saginaw Valley State University

William Harbour, Longwood University

Loretta Harper, University of Utah

Ray Henschen, SMG, Limited

Chuck Hewett, The Jackson Laboratory

Pat Hinckley, State of Maine

Larry Hitch, Ford Motor Company

Martha Hunt, NH Technical Institute

Terri Iacobucci, Northern Kentucky University

Jill Isaacs, Western & Southern Financial Group

Deloris James, University of Maryland

Ray Jones, The Citadel

Peter Jordan, Radisson Hotels

Dan Keefe, Great American Insurance Companies

Anne Kilpatrick, Medical University of South Carolina

Chris Kleymeyer, Kentucky Department of Corrections

Michael Koshuta, Purdue University

Cathy Kramer, Association for Quality and Participation

Denny Krause, Great American Insurance Company

David Krings, Hamilton County Government

Dennis Kripp, Roosevelt University

Mae Landesman, The Jackson Laboratory

Niaz Latif, Purdue University

Charles Leffler, North Carolina State University

Catherlyn Lewis-Brim, Warner Southern College

Bill Lindsay, Northern Kentucky University

Kathleen Magee, Anna Maria College

Charles Mambula, Langston University

Steve Martin, The Huber Company

Barbara Mathews, Baptist Healthcare System

Steve McMillen, Tennesee Valley Authority

William McQueen, University of Mississippi

Laban Miller, Cardinal Hill Healthcare System

Atul Mitra, University of Northern Iowa

Philip Moberg, Northern Kentucky University

Nancy Monday-Yates, Butler County Community College

Nassar Nassar, Bethel College

Joe Ohren, Eastern Michigan University

Rhonda Palladi, Georgia State University

Joe Petrick, Wright State University

Paul Quealy, Cincinnati Milacron

David Richeson, Mannesmann-Stabilus, USA

Dan Ronay, Indiana Department of Corrections

Tony Ross, Fidelity

Joseph Santora, Essex County College

Kraig Schell, Angelo State University

Vince Schulte, Northern Kentucky University

Angel Scott, University of Durham (England)

Matthew Shank, University of Dayton

Art Shriberg, Xavier University

Jennifer Skinner, TriHealth

Jeffrey Smith, Northern Kentucky University

Betty Jo Sproull, Ohio Valley Medical Center

Terri Stewart, Just the Basics

Christian Strong, La Rosa's Inc.

Robert Thomas, Georgia Institute of Technology

Marius Van Melle, Van Melle, Inc.

Claus Von Zychlin, Mt. Carmel Health Care System

Jeff Walter, Great American Insurance Companies

John Waltman, Eastern Michigan University

Earl Walz, The Urology Group

Beverly Watts, Tennessee Commission on Human Rights

Susan Wehrspann, University of Colorado Hospital

Angela Woodward, University of Kentucky

Jim Youngquist, Arkansas State University

With deep appreciation, we would like to thank the talented and dedicated book publishing team of McGraw-Hill/Irwin: Editorial Director—Paul Ducham; Managing Editor—Laura Hurst Spell; Development Editor—Libby Rubenstein; Marketing Manager—Jaime Halteman; Editorial Assistant—Jane Beck; Senior Account Manager—John Douglass; Project Manager—Erin Melloy, Manish Sharma/Aptara; Copyeditor—Rich Wright; Proofreader—Susan Higgins; Senior Production Supervisor—Nicole Baumgartner; Designer—Brenda Rolwes; Producer, Media Technology—Balaji Sundararaman. Each of you has made the writing of this book enjoyable and the quality of the book immeasurably better.

Most of all, we would like to thank our wives, Nancy and Mary, for their love, encouragement, and never-ending support.

About the Authors

George Manning is professor of psychology at Northern Kentucky University. He is a consultant to business, industry, and government, serving such clients as the AMA, AT&T, General Electric, IBM, the United Auto Workers, Young Presidents' Organization, the U.S. Navy, and the National Institutes of Health. He lectures on economic and social issues, including quality of work life, workforce values, and business ethics. He maintains an active program of research and writing in organizational psychology. His current studies and interests include the changing meaning of work, leadership ethics, and coping skills for personal and social change.

Kent Curtis is professor at Northern Kentucky University (NKU). He has examined the collegiate tutorial system as a visiting Fellow at the University of Durham in England, and has designed numerous employee and management development programs serving such clients as Texas Medical Center, Wendy's International, Procter & Gamble, and American Electric Power. He developed the NKU online leadership degree. His current research includes leading teams and teaching leadership via distance learning.

The Art of Leadership

art (ärt), noun. 1. Skill acquired by experience or study. 2. a system of rules to facilitate performance; the use of skill and imagination in applying such rules (the art of building, the art of persuasion). 3. endeavor requiring special knowledge and ability (fine arts, practical arts). 4. the product or result of artistic faculty (body of work).

leadership (lēd-er-ship), noun. 1. Showing the way or direction; the course of action. 2. influencing or causing to follow by words and deeds. 3. guiding the behavior of others through ideas, strength, or heroic feats. 4. the position or function of one who leads (the king led his people). 5. the ability to lead (she displayed leadership skill).

The Importance of Leadership: Setting the Stage

ALL OVER THE WORLD in corporations and government agencies, there are millions of executives who imagine their place on the organization chart has given them a body of followers. And of course it hasn't. It has given them subordinates. Whether the subordinates become followers depends on whether the executives act like leaders.

—John Gardner

Learning Objectives

After studying Chapter One, you will be able to:
- Define *leadership* and discuss its importance.
- Know where leaders learn to lead and what people want in a leader.
- Identify the satisfactions and frustrations of leadership.
- Describe the elements of caring leadership.

Leadership is a concept that is both current and timeless. In one form or another, the leadership process has been central to human interaction since the dawn of society. Excellence in leadership requires the ability to attract capable people, motivate them to put forth their best efforts, and solve problems that arise. These are difficult tasks, which helps explain why effective leadership is rare and why we respect those who excel.

To personalize the subject, consider these questions: Have you ever been the victim of a poor leader? How do you feel about the good leaders you have known? If you have experienced both types of leaders, you know firsthand the importance of good leadership. No other factor is more important for work morale and job performance.

There are millions of people who know what it is like to work for a boss who

- Takes all the credit for work done by others.
- Is selfish and rude.
- Makes mistakes and blames others.
- Is tyrannical and cruel.
- Cares only about self-preservation.
- Is threatened by competence.
- Is dishonest and unfair.

All these examples are real, all these factors diminish people's lives at work, and none is necessary. We are convinced that the weakest link in business, industry, and government today is leadership. It is not technology; it is not tools or equipment; it is not facilities; it is not the skills of employees; it is not systems and procedures. It is leadership. Leadership failure rates range from 40 percent to 60 percent, costing organizations millions of dollars each year.[1]

What Is Leadership?

Leadership is social influence. It means leaving a mark. It is initiating and guiding, and the result is change. The product is a new character or direction that otherwise would never be. By their **ideas** and **deeds,** leaders show the way and influence the behavior of others.[2]

To understand the importance of ideas, consider the legend of King Arthur, who led the Knights of the Round Table with his vision of chivalry:

My teacher Merlyn, who always remembered things that haven't happened better than things that have, told me once that a few hundred years from now it will be discovered that the world is round—round like the table at which we sat with such high hope and noble purpose. If you do what I ask, perhaps people will remember how we of Camelot went questing for right and honor and justice. Perhaps one day men will sit around this world as we did once at our table, and go questing once more . . . for right . . . honor . . . and justice.[3]

To understand the importance of deeds, consider the storyteller Homer's account of Achilles, who led Greek warriors by his heroic feats:

So saying, he plunged once more into the fight and man after man fell before his sword and before his spear. He raged among the Trojans like a whirlwind that drives the flames this way and that when there is a forest fire along the dry slopes of the mountains.[4]

History holds countless examples of ideas and acts that have determined human destiny. Consider the events put in motion and the impact on the world when 56 leaders signed the Declaration of Independence, a Unanimous Declaration of the Thirteen United States of America, in Congress July 4, 1776.[5]

The Importance of Leadership

Upon every wave of political history has been a Caesar, an Elizabeth, a Napoleon, or a Saladin. In every lull, leadership has been absent. Consider the period of approximately AD 800 to 1000:

Europe lapsed into utter decentralization, and lost for centuries the administrative unity that the reign of Charlemagne promised. A heavy blow was dealt at the slowly developing culture that the eighth century produced. It was not without justice that the ninth and tenth centuries have been called "the Dark Ages." The internal history of continental Europe became a dismal record of tiresome local feuds and private wars.[6]

Leadership is important not only in government, but in other areas of life as well. Social conscience and conduct have been influenced by reformers such as Martin Luther King and Susan B. Anthony:

Susan B. Anthony was a passionate advocate, who saw "the vote" as the symbol of women's emancipation and independence as well as the indispensable condition of a true government. . . . Although still voteless, she declared, "The world has never witnessed a greater revolution than in the status of women during the past half century."[7]

The fates of nations have been determined by military figures such as Alexander the Great and Joan of Arc:

Alexander the Great opened a new era in the history of the world and, by his life's work, determined its development for many centuries. The permanent result of his life was the development of Greek civilization into a civilization that was worldwide.[8]

Civilization has been shaped by philosophers such as John Stuart Mill and Adam Smith:

John Stuart Mill was one of England's greatest philosophers, hardly surpassed by thinkers of the highest order. Mill taught that a popular representative government (democracy) inevitably makes for progress.[9]

The initiative of leaders has a formative place in history. At times their eloquence, like Churchill's, may be worth a thousand regiments; their skill, like Napoleon's, may win battles and establish states. If they are teachers or prophets, like Muhammad, wise in insight, their words may inspire good deeds.

Three Types of Leaders

There are many ways to lead, and indeed, we are influenced by some people even centuries after they are gone. Some leaders are **teachers,** who are rule breakers and value creators; some are **heroes,** responsible for great causes and noble works; and some are **rulers,** motivated principally to dominate others and exercise power. Consider how the ideas and deeds of the teachers, heroes, and rulers in Table 1–1 have influenced the world.[10]

Table 1–1
Types of Leaders in History

Teacher	Hero	Ruler
Aquinas	Beethoven	Alexander
Aristotle	Columbus	Akbar
Augustine	Curie	Charlemagne
Buddha	da Vinci	Elizabeth I
Confucius	Darwin	Frederick II
Ghandi	Edison	Genghis Khan
Jesus	Einstein	Hitler
Lao-tzu	Ford	Isabella I
Luther	Galileo	Julius Caesar
Marx	Gutenberg	Louis XIV
Moses	Hippocrates	Mao Tse-tung
Muhammad	Michelangelo	Napoleon
Paul	Newton	Ramses II
Plato	Pasteur	Saladin
Rumi	Shakespeare	Washington
Socrates	Watt	Yoritomo

How Many Leaders Are There?

Are we led by a few, or are there many who lead? Words such as *emperor, king,* and *chief* differentiated leaders from others in earlier times. There were few powerful positions, books were rare, and mass education was unknown. Today information is everywhere, ideas are free, and self-expression is encouraged. It is a different world, as evidenced by the 65th edition of *Who's Who in America, 2011,* which contains entries for more than 95,000 people. Each of these individuals, by ideas or deeds, has influenced the lives of others; each has been a teacher, hero, or ruler.

There is a changing perception of who can be a leader today. The response is heard over and over: Everyone can be a leader. Leadership is shifting from an autocratic, hierarchical model toward an empowering, participatory model. The new definition recognizes the potential and unique contributions of everyone. As former secretary of labor Robert Reich says, "Everyone has a leader inside." No longer is leadership viewed as a combination of charisma and expertise possessed by only a few people at the top of an organizational pyramid. Today it is viewed as the challenge and responsibility of every individual with potential to make a difference.[11]

Consider the example of Rosa Parks, whose courage helped determine the course of civil rights in American society:

It was December 1, 1955, when a white passenger aboard a Montgomery, Alabama, bus asked Rosa Parks to yield her seat. Her refusal to move to the back of the bus ended in her arrest, but began the nonviolent protest movement for civil rights in the United States. A year-long boycott of the Montgomery bus system, led by Martin Luther King, forced the issue of the South's Jim Crow laws to the forefront of America's consciousness. The Supreme Court's 1956 decision to declare segregation laws unconstitutional signaled a victory for Parks, of whom King said "she had been tracked down by the Zeitgeist—the spirit of time."[12]

In meaningful ways, leadership is provided by the multitude of people who influence their families, friends, work groups, and organizations. These leaders are parents, supervisors, officers, and other leadership figures. Think of your own experiences. Have you not at some time provided leadership to others, either by your ideas or by the example you set?

How Qualities of the Individual and Environmental Factors Influence the Leadership Process

The leadership scholar James MacGregor Burns once called leadership one of the most observed and least understood phenomena on earth. Questions frequently asked are, Which is more important—the individual or the environment? Are leaders born or made? In his book *Leadership,* Burns concludes that leadership is fired in the forge of both personal ambition and social opportunity.[13]

Qualities of the Individual

Historically, leadership has been attributed to the individual. This view is sometimes called the "great man theory." Reflecting this view, the Scottish philosopher and historian Thomas Carlyle believed that among the undistinguished masses are people of light and learning, individuals superior in power, courage, and understanding. Carlyle saw the history of the human race as the biographies of these leaders, its great men and women: "Their moral character may be something less than perfect; their courage may not be the essential ingredient; yet they are superior. They are followed, admired, and obeyed to the point of worship."[14]

Ralph M. Stogdill, one of the most distinguished scholars on leadership, has found certain traits of the individual that correlate positively with leadership:

> The leader is characterized by: a strong drive for responsibility and task completion; vigor and persistence in pursuit of goals; venturesomeness and originality in problem-solving; drive to exercise initiative in social situations; self-confidence and sense of personal identity; willingness to accept consequences of decision and action; readiness to absorb interpersonal stress; willingness to tolerate frustration and delay; ability to influence other persons' behavior; and capacity to structure social interaction systems to the purpose at hand.
>
> It can be concluded that the cluster of characteristics listed above differentiate leaders from followers, effective from ineffective leaders, and higher echelon from lower echelon leaders. In other words, different strata of leaders and followers can be described in terms of the extent to which they exhibit these characteristics. These characteristics considered individually hold little diagnostic or predictive significance. In combination, it would appear that they interact to generate personality dynamics advantageous to the person seeking the responsibilities of leadership.[15]

Environmental Factors

More recently, leadership has been viewed as an acquired competency, the product of many forces, not the least of which are environment and circumstance. In this sense, leadership is seen as a social phenomenon, not an individual trait. This school of thought helps explain why leaders who are successful in one situation (for example, building a bridge) may not be successful in another (such as directing a play or a research team).[16] The same individual may exert leadership in one time and place and not in another. Stogdill explains:

> It should be noted that to a large extent our conceptions of characteristics of leadership are culturally determined. The ancient Egyptians attributed three qualities of divinity to their king. They said of him, "Authoritative utterance is in thy mouth, perception is in thy heart, and thy tongue is the shrine of justice." This statement would suggest that the Egyptians were demanding of their leader the qualities of authority, discrimination, and just behavior.
>
> An analysis of Greek concepts of leadership, as exemplified by different leaders in Homer's *Iliad,* showed four aspects were valued: (1) justice and judgment—Agamemnon; (2) wisdom and counsel—Nestor; (3) shrewdness and cunning—Odysseus; and (4) valor and action—Achilles. All of these qualities were admired by the Greeks. Shrewdness and cunning are not as highly regarded in our contemporary society as they once were (although justice, judgment, wisdom, valor, and action remain in high esteem).[17]
>
> The patterns of behavior regarded as acceptable in leaders differ from time to time and from one culture to another; thus, the establishment of educational institutions and curricula to impart and reinforce knowledge, skills, and attitudes deemed to be important by a society or group.[18]

Probably the most convincing support for leadership as a social phenomenon is the fact that throughout history, male leaders have outnumbered female leaders to a significant degree. Even the definition of the word *leader* is a social phenomenon. Consider the case of "President" Edith Wilson, leader in all but name during the incapacitating illness of her husband, President Woodrow Wilson. It is Woodrow, however, whom history credits as leader, as president, even during the period of his inability to govern. Public recognition of Mrs. Wilson's influence would not have been in line with the norms of the times.

Interaction between the Individual and the Environment

Evidence shows that both the **qualities of the individual** *and* **environmental factors** are important elements in the leadership equation. Leadership results from the inextricable interaction between the two. Findings from sociobiological studies of other animal species support this view. For example, biologist Richard Borowsky has discovered spontaneous growth among male fish. Young males remain small and sexually underdeveloped until the adult population in the group is reduced. Then, size and sexual maturation accelerate dramatically. Clearly, biological and sociological systems are closely related.[19]

Similar signs of sudden maturation are found in human beings. Leaders may emerge spontaneously in social crises after filling essentially anonymous roles for years. Consider the transformation of Poland's Lech Walesa from shipyard worker to national labor leader during the 1980s. Some people seem to have innate abilities that unfold under certain conditions—external circumstances and internal qualities interact to create a sudden and dramatic spurt of performance.

Where Leaders Learn to Lead and What People Want in a Leader

In the most extensive study ever done on leadership, the U.S. Chamber of Commerce sought to answer two questions: (1) Where do leaders learn to lead? and (2) What do people want in a leader?[20]

The number one place people say they learn to lead is from **experience.** They are thrown in the water and expected to sink or swim. Common Cause founder John W. Gardner identifies his arduous experience as a Marine during World War II as the "learning crucible" in which his own leadership abilities emerged.[21] Ask yourself how much of your leadership approach and skill you have learned from experience.

The second most-cited place people learn to lead is from **examples** or models. They watch Bill or Jill lead and it seems to work out, so they do the same. They watch Sarah or Sam lead and it doesn't work out, so they resolve never to use those methods or techniques. Who have been your models or examples in the practice of leadership?

The third most-cited place people say they learn to lead is from **books and school.** Formal education, learning seminars, and professional reading can provide valuable information and insight. What book, theory, or class has helped in the development of your leadership skills?

Even more interesting, especially for leaders, is to know what people want in a leader. Desired qualities change across culture and time, but what people say they want most in American society is **integrity.** When people are asked to define *integrity,* the word they mention most frequently is *honesty.* The leader with integrity always tells the truth as he or she believes it to be. Think about the best leader you have ever had; she or he probably had integrity. First and foremost, people want a leader they can trust. Ask yourself whether you have a reputation for integrity.

The second most-cited quality people want in a leader is **job knowledge.** This quality ranges from knowing what direction to take (abstract visioning) to knowing how to solve problems (practical ability). Again, think about the best leader you have ever had; it is likely that this person had a purpose, a plan, and the skill to succeed. Moreover, truly great leaders keep job knowledge current. They know what it takes to be effective in the leadership position—they are good but not complacent, and they continually strive to improve. How do you currently rate on the job knowledge scale?

The third most-cited quality people want in a leader can be summarized as **people-building skills.** This quality includes the ability to assemble and develop a winning team, and it involves a variety of important skills: performance planning, performance coaching, and correcting poor performance; effective delegation; effective discipline; and the ability to motivate. People want an empowering leader who will be a mentor and developer of others. Do you have the interest, ability, and patience required to motivate and develop others?[22] (See Exercise 1–1.)

**Exercise 1–1
Personalizing
Leadership**

1. Where have you learned your leadership skills? Describe each pertinent learning area.

   ■ Personal experience _____

   _____

   _____

   _____

   _____

   ■ Examples or models _____

   _____

   _____

   _____

   _____

   ■ Books and school _____

   _____

   _____

   _____

   _____

2. Do you possess the qualities people want in a leader? Support your response.

   ■ Integrity (honesty)—resulting in trust _____

   _____

   _____

   _____

   _____

   ■ Job knowledge—resulting in confidence _____

   _____

   _____

   _____

   _____

   ■ People-building skills—resulting in motivation and teamwork _____

   _____

   _____

   _____

   _____

Satisfactions and Frustrations of Leaders

Approximately 1 out of every 10 people in the American workplace is classified as a supervisor, administrator, or manager.[23] Management author Andrew DuBrin identifies seven satisfactions and seven frustrations that individuals in leadership roles typically experience. If you are a leader, make note of the ones that relate to you.

Satisfactions of Leaders

1. *A feeling of power and prestige.* Being a leader typically grants one power and a sense of importance.
2. *A chance to help others.* A leader works directly with people, often teaching them job skills, serving as a mentor and an advisor.
3. *High income.* Leaders, in general, receive higher pay than nonleaders, and executive leaders typically earn substantial incomes.
4. *Respect and status.* A leader is typically respected by group members and enjoys a higher status than people who are not occupying leadership roles.
5. *Opportunities for advancement.* Once one becomes a leader, advancement opportunities usually increase.
6. *A feeling of being in a position of knowledge.* A leader typically receives more information than do nonleaders.
7. *An opportunity to control money and other resources.* A leader is typically in the position of determining budgets and authorizing expenses.

Frustrations of Leaders

1. *Too much uncompensated work time.* People in leadership positions typically work longer hours than nonleaders. During periods of high demand, working hours can surge to 80 hours per week and more.
2. *Too many problems.* A leader is subject to the universe of problems involving people and things. The leader is expected to address problems and get them solved.
3. *Not enough authority to carry out responsibility.* People in leadership positions may be held responsible for outcomes over which they have little control.
4. *Loneliness.* The higher one rises as a leader, the more lonely it can be. Leadership limits the number of people in whom one can confide.
5. *Too many problems involving people.* A frustration facing a leader is the number of people problems requiring action. The more employees one has, the more problems one is likely to face.
6. *Organizational politics.* The leader must engage in political byplay from three directions: below, sideways, and above. Although tactics such as forming alliances and coalitions are a necessary part of a leader's role, it can be particularly frustrating if people purposefully work against each other within an organization.
7. *The pursuit of conflicting goals.* A major challenge facing leaders is navigating among conflicting goals. The central issue of such dilemmas is attempting to grant others the authority to act independently, yet still get them aligned and pulling together for a common purpose.[24]

At this time, do the satisfactions of leadership outweigh the frustrations you may have, or is the opposite the case? Consider the pros and cons of your leadership position.

Caring Leadership

Whether one leads by word or deed; whether a leader is teacher, hero, or ruler; whether leadership is inborn or formed; no matter where one learns to lead; no matter the arena where leadership occurs; no matter the level of satisfaction or frustration a leader may feel; there is an essential ingredient necessary for success. The leader must *care.* Only when the leader cares will others care. Only when the leader cares will there be focus and energy for the work to be done.

There are two aspects of caring leadership: First is **commitment to a task;** second, and equally important, is **concern for people.** Theodore Roosevelt captures the spirit of the caring leader with a task to achieve:

> The credit goes to the man
> who is actually in the arena,
> whose face is marred with
> sweat and dust and blood;
> who strives valiantly;
> who errs and comes short again and
> again; who knows the great
> enthusiasms, the great devotions,
> and spends himself in a worthy
> cause; who at the best knows
> the triumph of high achievement;
> and who, if he fails,
> at least fails while daring greatly.
> Far better it is to dare mighty things,
> to win glorious triumphs,
> even though checkered by failure,
> than to take rank with those cold and timid souls
> who live in the gray twilight that knows not
> victory nor defeat.[25]

With fervor and eloquence, Roosevelt blasts a life of ease and advocates a strenuous life of engagement and meaning. For the caring leader, this means personal commitment to accomplish a goal. The goal may be a one-time endeavor or a life's work. The goal may be a tangible product, such as the creation of a business, or it may be an idea or a cause, such as stamping out tyranny. In any case, the leader's commitment becomes contagious, igniting the emotions of all who are present.

Caring leadership also means caring about people. The caring leader is unselfish, ready and eager to hear the other person's story. The caring leader will dedicate her- or himself in service to others. Concern for others results in loyalty to the leader and dedication to the leader's goals.[26] Jan Carlzon, former chairman and CEO of Scandinavian Airlines, explains the importance of caring leadership in the work setting: "In my experience, I have learned there are two great motivators in life. One is fear. The other is love. You can manage people by fear, but if you do, it will diminish both them and you. The path to success begins in the heart."[27]

James Autry, former CEO of the Meredith Corporation, reminds us that caring leadership must come from the heart, from within, not from policy books. Sharing the wisdom of years of experience in his wonderful volume *Love and Profit,* Autry states, "If you don't truly care about people, you should get out of leadership; it will save a lot of people a lot of trouble and maybe even a heart attack." He captures the spirit of the caring leader in a poem entitled "Threads."[28]

Threads

Sometimes you just connect, like that,
no big thing maybe, but something beyond
the usual business stuff. It comes and goes
quickly so you have to pay attention,
a change in the eyes when you ask about
the family,
a pain flickering behind the statistics about
a boy and a girl in school, or about seeing them
every other Sunday.
An older guy talks about his bride,
a little affection after 25 years.
The hot-eyed achiever laughs before you want
him to.
Someone tells you about his wife's job
or why she quit working to stay home.
An old joker needs another laugh on the way
to retirement.
A woman says she spends a lot of her salary on
an au pair and a good one is hard to find but
worth it because there is nothing more important
than the baby.
Listen. In every office you hear the threads of
love and joy and fear and guilt, the cries for
celebration and reassurance, and somehow you
know that connecting those threads is what you
are supposed to do
and business takes care of itself.

Both commitment to a goal and concern for others must be present for caring leadership to occur. Without commitment there is no passion, and without concern there is no loyalty. Caring leadership cannot be legislated, and it cannot be an act. It is either present or not. When the leader cares, others become focused and energized. It is at this point that direction and momentum develop and great achievements are made.

Leadership in the Work Setting

Leadership is an important and difficult task, and it is the cornerstone of organizational success. Management author John Kotter describes the need for effective leadership at work, saying that too many organizations are overmanaged and underled. Too much emphasis on order and control, and not enough emphasis on motivation and creativity can reduce vitality and lead to failure. What is needed is development of leadership capacity at all levels of responsibility. With good selection, training, and encouragement, many more people can play valuable leadership roles.[29]

The question is often asked, What is the difference between leadership and management? These are terms that are often used interchangeably. Management involves four functions or processes first identified by Henri Fayol in 1916: planning, organizing, directing, and controlling, all of which are essential for organizational success. The term *leadership* is popularly used to describe what takes place in the first three of these functions—**establishing a direction** (planning), **aligning people and resources** (organizing), and **energizing people to accomplish results** (directing). These processes require insight, decisiveness, courage, strength, resolve, diplomacy, and other important leadership qualities to be successful.[30]

Another way to describe the difference between management and leadership is to say that management denotes formal authority and accountability is delegated, while leadership is the ability to influence the activity or behavior of people. The primary purpose of management is to provide order and consistency, a bottom-line focus; the primary function of leadership is to produce change and movement, a top-line focus. Successful organizations have excellent management and great leadership. If an organization has strong management without leadership, the result can be reliable accomplishment of the wrong things. If an organization has strong leadership without management, the result can be inconsistent performance.

The political theorist Karl Marx observed that the manner in which a society does its work shapes most of the other things the society believes and does. This belief only adds to the importance of leadership in the work setting. Principles and practices on the job are repeated and have impact in the home and larger community.

Nine Key Areas of Leadership

The successful leader must master the art of leadership, with nine key areas for success. If people cannot decide which course of action to take or if they are not making satisfactory progress along a chosen path, breakdown occurs. Breakdown can be traced to deficiency in one or more of these areas:

The leadership equation—understanding the influence of leadership qualities, characteristics of followers, and the nature of situations.

The power of vision—establishing a clear and compelling direction and a plan to succeed.

The importance of ethics—leading by moral principles, goodness of character, and personal courage.

The empowerment of people—fostering a high-performance culture through participative leadership and service to others.

Leadership principles—demonstrating human relations skills, managing morale, and developing a winning team.

Understanding people—comprehending human motivation, the art of persuasion, and the value of diversity.

Multiplying effectiveness—using delegation skills and dealing effectively with different kinds of people.

Developing others—understanding the role of the leader as teacher, helping people through change, and developing adaptive capacity.

Performance management—achieving organizational success through personal humility, fierce resolve, and sustained discipline.

Each key area is discussed in the following pages. Also included are principles and techniques to improve leadership effectiveness, along with questionnaires and learning exercises for personalizing the concepts.

Chapter One Summary

After reading Chapter One, you should know the following key concepts, principles, and terms. Fill in the blanks from memory, or copy the answers listed below.

Leadership is social influence. By (a) _____ and _____, leaders light the path and influence the behavior of people. Types of leaders include (b) _____, _____, and _____. Two basic factors that influence the leadership process are (c) _____, and _____. People learn to lead primarily from (d) _____, _____, and _____. The three qualities people want most in a leader are (e) _____, _____, and _____. Satisfactions of being a leader include (f) _____, _____, and _____; frustrations of being a leader include (g) _____, _____, and _____. The two essential elements of caring leadership are (h) _____ and _____. Leadership, in essence, is (i) _____, _____, and _____.

Answer Key for Chapter One Summary

a. **ideas, deeds,** page 2

b. **teachers, heroes, rulers,** page 3

c. **qualities of the individual, environmental factors,** page 4

d. **experience, examples, books and school,** page 6

e. **integrity, job knowledge, people-building skills,** page 7

f. (any three) **a feeling of power and prestige, a chance to help others, high income, respect and status, opportunities for advancement, a feeling of being in a position of knowledge, an opportunity to control money and other resources,** page 9

g. (any three) **too much uncompensated work time, too many problems, not enough authority to carry out responsibility, loneliness, too many problems involving people, organizational politics, the pursuit of conflicting goals,** page 9

h. **commitment to a task, concern for people,** page 10

i. **establishing a direction, aligning people and resources, energizing people to accomplish results,** page 11

Part 1 Leadership Variables

2. **The Leadership Equation**
3. **Leadership Qualities, Characteristics of Followers, and Situational Factors**

THE EAR OF THE LEADER must ring with the voices of the people. Together they rise to the challenge of the day.

—Woodrow Wilson

Learning Objectives

After studying Part One, you will be able to:
- Describe the variables that determine leadership effectiveness.
- Assess 10 qualities that distinguish a leader.
- Know how susceptible you are to leadership influence.
- Identify situations in which you are likely to lead.
- Know your natural kind of intelligence and leadership strength.

CHAPTER

2

The Leadership Equation

For years, researchers have been trying to answer the questions, What does it take to be a successful leader? and What is the most effective leadership style? The *Encyclopedia of Leadership* identifies more than 40 theories or models of leadership that have influenced the study and practice of leadership.[1] Early studies were based on two main theories—**trait theory,** focusing on qualities of the leader, and **behavior theory,** focusing on leadership actions.

Leadership Trait Theory

Sir Francis Galton is credited with being one of the earliest leadership theorists, mentioning the trait approach to leadership for the first time in his book *Hereditary Genius,* published in 1869. In keeping with the general thinking of the period, Galton believed that leadership qualities were genetic characteristics of a family. Qualities such as courage and wisdom were passed on—from family member to family member, from generation to generation.[2]

How did Steve Jobs, a college dropout, become an iconic leader of the technology world? What enabled George Patton, who did so poorly at West Point that he had to repeat a year, to become a four-star general and hero of World War II? How could John L. Lewis, a coal miner with no formal education or leadership training, either energize or shut down an entire industry? Do individuals such as these share unique leadership traits?

The trait theory of leadership makes the assumption that distinctive physical and psychological characteristics account for leadership effectiveness. Traits such as height, attractiveness, intelligence, self-reliance, and creativity have been studied, and lists abound, from *The Leadership Traits of the U.S. Marine Corps* to the *Leadership Principles of the U.S. Army.* Almost always included in these and other lists of important leadership traits are (1) basic **intelligence,** (2) clear and strong **values,** and (3) high level of personal **energy.**[3]

One of the most widely reported studies of leadership traits was conducted by Edwin Ghiselli, who evaluated over 300 managers from 90 different businesses in the United States. Ghiselli identified six traits as being important for effective leadership:

1. *Need for achievement*—seeking responsibility; working hard to succeed.

2. *Intelligence*—using good judgment; having good reasoning and thinking capacity.

3. *Decisiveness*—making difficult decisions without undue hesitation.

4. *Self-confidence*—having a positive self-image as a capable and effective person.

5. *Initiative*—being a self-starter; getting jobs done with minimal supervision.

6. *Supervisory ability*—getting the job done through others.[4]

To personalize the concept of trait theory, evaluate yourself (or a leader you know) on Ghiselli's six traits for leadership effectiveness. (See Exercise 2–1.)

**Exercise 2–1
Six Traits of
Leadership**

Rate yourself (or a leader you know) on the following six traits for leadership effectiveness by circling a number from 1 to 10 (1 is low; 10 is high).

1. Need for achievement

| 1 | 2 | 3 | 4 | 5 | 6 | 7 | 8 | 9 | 10 |

2. Intelligence

| 1 | 2 | 3 | 4 | 5 | 6 | 7 | 8 | 9 | 10 |

3. Decisiveness

| 1 | 2 | 3 | 4 | 5 | 6 | 7 | 8 | 9 | 10 |

4. Self-confidence

| 1 | 2 | 3 | 4 | 5 | 6 | 7 | 8 | 9 | 10 |

5. Initiative

| 1 | 2 | 3 | 4 | 5 | 6 | 7 | 8 | 9 | 10 |

6. Supervisory ability

| 1 | 2 | 3 | 4 | 5 | 6 | 7 | 8 | 9 | 10 |

Scoring and Interpretation:

Add all the circled numbers to find the overall trait score: _____

High	**Individual Trait Score**	**Overall Trait Score**	**Evaluation**
↑	9–10	54–60	Very good
↓	7–8	42–53	good
Low	1–6	6–41	Needs improvement

Trait Theory Applied

An interesting application of trait theory was practiced by Paul von Hindenburg, war hero and second president of post–World War I Germany. Von Hindenburg used a form of trait theory for selecting and developing leaders. He believed that leadership ability was determined by two primary qualities—intelligence (bright versus dull) and vitality (energetic versus lazy). He used a box (see Figure 2–1) to evaluate potential military leaders on these two dimensions.

**Figure 2–1
Dimensions of Leadership**

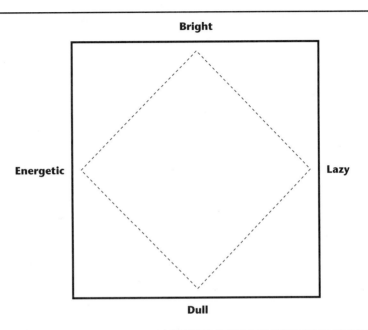

If an individual was deemed to be bright and energetic, he was developed as a field commander, because it takes judgment and gumption to succeed as a leader on the battlefield. If the individual was deemed to be energetic but dull, he was assigned to duty as a frontline soldier, because as a leader, he could actively lead his command in the wrong direction. If the individual was believed to be bright but lazy, he was assigned to be a staff officer, because intelligence is important for developing a creative strategy that others may implement. If the individual was judged to be lazy and dull, he was left alone to find his own level of effectiveness.[5]

Leadership Behavior Theory

During the 1930s, a growing emphasis on behaviorism in psychology moved leadership researchers in the direction of the study of leadership behavior versus leadership traits. A classic study of leadership behavior was conducted at the University of Iowa by **Kurt Lewin** and his associates in 1939. These researchers trained graduate assistants in behaviors indicative of three leadership styles: **autocratic, democratic,** and **laissez-faire.** The *autocratic* style was characterized by the tight control of group activities and decisions made by the leader. The *democratic* style emphasized group participation and majority rule. The *laissez-faire* leadership style involved very low levels of any kind of activity by the leader. The results indicated that the democratic style of leadership was more beneficial for group performance than the other styles. The importance of the study was that it emphasized the impact of the behavior of the leader on the performance of followers.[6]

By the 1940s, most research on leadership changed focus from leadership traits to leadership behaviors. Behavioral leadership theories assume that there are distinctive actions that effective leaders take. In 1945 **Ralph Stogdill** and others at Ohio State

University developed an assessment instrument known as the Leader Behavior Description Questionnaire (LBDQ).[7] Respondents to the questionnaire described their leaders' behaviors toward them in terms of two dimensions:

1. **Initiating structure**—the extent to which leaders take action to define the relationship between themselves and their staff, as well as the role that they expect each staff member to assume. Leaders who score high on initiating structure establish well-defined channels of communication and ways of getting the job done. Five assessment items measuring initiating structure are as follows:

   a. Try out your own new ideas in the work group.

   b. Encourage the slow-working people in the group to work harder.

   c. Emphasize meeting deadlines.

   d. Meet with the group at regularly scheduled times.

   e. See to it that people in the group are working up to capacity.

2. **Showing consideration**—the extent to which leaders take action to develop trust, respect, support, and friendship with subordinates. Leaders who score high on showing consideration typically are helpful, trusting, and respectful, and have warm relationships with staff members. Five questionnaire items that measure showing consideration are as follows:

   a. Be helpful to people in the work group.

   b. Treat all people in the group as your equals.

   c. Be willing to make changes.

   d. Back up what people under you do.

   e. Do little things to make it pleasant to be a member of the group.

At about the same time the Ohio State studies were being conducted, the University of Michigan's Survey Research Center started leadership studies under the direction of Rensis Likert, who gave special attention to the impact of leaders' behaviors on worker motivation and the performance of groups.[8] The Michigan studies identified two similar dimensions of leadership behavior:

1. *Job-centered*—same as initiating structure.

2. *Employee-centered*—same as showing consideration.

In 1964 Robert Blake and Jane Mouton developed a managerial grid reflecting the Ohio and Michigan dimensions of initiating structure (job-centered) and showing consideration (employee-centered).[9] This model identifies the ideal leader as having *a high concern for production and a high concern for people.* It has been used extensively in organizational development and leadership consulting throughout the world. See Figure 2–2.

The horizontal axis of the grid represents concern for production, and the vertical axis represents concern for people. Each axis is on a scale of 1 through 9. Lowest concern is 1, and highest concern is 9. The managerial (leadership) grid has 81 possible combinations, but identifies five major styles:

■ (1,1) *The Impoverished Manager*—has low concern for production and low concern for people. The leader is uninvolved in the work and withdraws from people.

■ (9,1) *The Sweatshop Manager*—has high concern for production but low concern for people. The leader is results driven, and people are regarded as tools to that end.

■ (1,9) *The Country Club Manager*—has high concern for people and low concern for task accomplishment. The leader focuses on being agreeable and keeping human relations smooth.

■ (5,5) *The Status Quo Manager*—has medium concern for both production and people. The leader emphasizes work requirements to a moderate degree and shows moderate consideration for the needs of people.

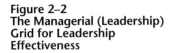

Figure 2–2
The Managerial (Leadership)
Grid for Leadership
Effectiveness

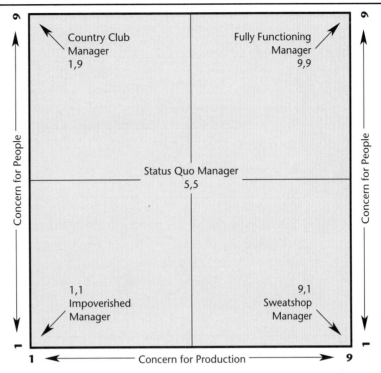

■ (9,9) *The Fully Functioning Manager*—has high concern for both production and people. The leader cares intensely about task accomplishment and cares deeply about people.

In recent years, two additional styles have been seen with such frequency that they are now listed as major styles:

1. *The Paternalistic Manager*—uses high concern for production (9,1) combined with use of rewards (1,9) in exchange for compliance and loyalty.

2. *The Opportunistic Manager*—uses whichever style will best promote his or her advancement (1,9 to please subordinates; 5,5 in interactions with peers; and 9,1 to gain favor with bottom-line-focused bosses).

To personalize leadership behavior theory, use Exercise 2–2 to evaluate yourself (or a leader you know) on two dimensions of leadership effectiveness—concern for production and concern for people. Note that concern for production is analogous to the terms *job-centered* and *initiating structure,* while concern for people is analogous to the terms *employee-centered* and *showing consideration.*

**Exercise 2–2
Two Dimensions
of Leadership**

Rate yourself (or a leader you know) on the two dimensions of leadership effectiveness indicated in the graph below (1 is low; 10 is high). Then mark the point where *concern for people* and *concern for production* intersect.

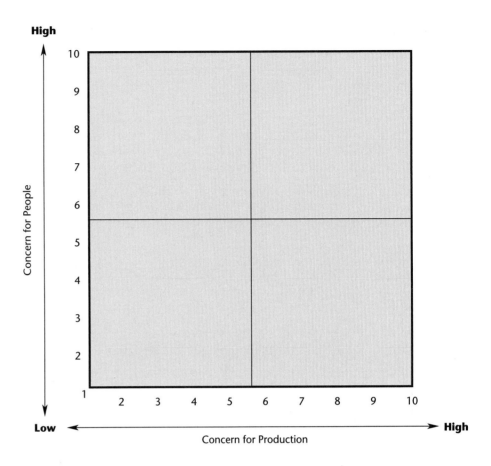

Scoring and Interpretation:

The higher the score on both axes, the higher the expectation for overall leadership effectiveness. To find the overall score, multiply the scores for the two dimensions. The best possible score is 100 (10 × 10). The ideal leader is a caring leader who focuses on job tasks and results, and is simultaneously concerned with the welfare of employees.

Behavior Theory Applied

In *Shackleton's Way: Leadership Lessons from the Great Antarctic Explorer,* Margot Morrell presents a detailed account of Ernest Shackleton's endurance expedition and the leadership lessons to be learned from it. The book is based on primary sources—on the actual comments of the men who were led by Shackleton. She uses diaries, letters, and interviews to understand Shackleton's leadership behavior. Morrell believes that even today we can look to his behaviors as a source of inspiration and education. The four cornerstones of Shackleton's leadership behavior are leading by example, communicating a vision, keeping up morale, and maintaining a positive attitude. Morrell concludes from her research of Shackleton and leadership: "If you look closely at any successful leader, you will find [he or she is] executing on these four points."[10]

Leadership Contingency Theory

Both the trait theory and the behavioral theory of leadership were attempts to identify the one best leader and the one best style for all situations. By the late 1960s, it became apparent that there is no such universal answer. Leadership **contingency theory** holds that the most appropriate leadership qualities and actions vary from situation to situation. Effectiveness depends on leader, follower, and situational factors. Forces in the leader include personal values, feelings of security, and confidence in subordinates. Forces in the follower include knowledge and experience, readiness to assume responsibility, and interest in the task or problem. Forces in the situation include organizational structure, the type of information needed to solve a problem, and the amount of time available to make a decision.[11]

Matching Qualities of Leaders, Characteristics of Followers, and the Nature of the Situation

In the past 60 years, more than 65 classification systems have been developed to define the dimensions of leadership, and more than 15,000 books and articles have been written about the elements that contribute to leadership effectiveness. The usual conclusion is that the answer depends on leader, follower, and situational variables. A leader in a bank and a leader on the farm will need different interests, values, and skills. Experienced followers and new followers will have different leadership needs. Situational factors include the job being performed, the culture of the workplace, and the urgency of the task.

No single element explains why leadership takes place. Leadership results when the ideas and deeds of the leader match the needs and expectations of the followers in a particular situation. The relationship between General George Patton, the U.S. Third Army, and the demands of World War II resulted in leadership; however, the same General Patton probably would not have much influence on the membership and goals of a PTA meeting today. Even if there were agreement about goals, disagreement over style probably would interfere with the leadership process.

A modern example of matching qualities of the leader, characteristics of followers, and the nature of the situation would be Nelson Mandela, the first black president of South Africa.[12] A negative example, but one of historic significance, is that of Adolf Hitler, the German people, and the period 1919 to 1945:

Hitler generated his power through the skillful use of suggestion, collective hypnosis, and every kind of subconscious motivation that the crowd was predisposed to unleash. In this way, the people sought out Hitler just as much as Hitler sought them out. Rather than saying that Hitler manipulated the people as an artist molds clay, certain traits in Hitler gave him the opportunity to appeal to the psychological condition of the people.

Seen in this light, Hitler was not the great beginner, but merely the executor of the people's wishes. He was able to feel the character and direction of the people and to make them more conscious of it, thereby generating power that he was able to exploit. This is not due to his personal strength alone. Isolated from his crowd, Hitler would be with reduced potency.

Hitler had many personal weaknesses, but as one who sensed the character and direction of the group, he became the embodiment of power. No doubt his strength came through his claiming for himself what actually was the condition and achievement of many.[13]

Ultimately, the leader, the followers, and the situation must match for leadership to take place. One without the other two, and two without the third, will abort the leadership process.[14]

Case Study:

Mr. Black, Ms. Blue, and Mr. White[15]

Recently you were promoted from the job of first-level supervisor to that of middle management, and you now have under your supervision several of your former equals. You get along well with them, and there is no resentment about your advancement because they recognize that you are the best person available for the job.

You know from past associations that you will have to straighten out three of these subordinates; the rest are all right. The three are Black, Blue, and White. Black has always been against the organization, Blue has always been snowed under by work, and White has always been a permissive supervisor.

Black, the anticompany supervisor, always sides with his subordinates against the organization and sympathizes with them when things go wrong. He wants conditions to be perfect and is always pointing out the defects in the company and finding fault with the way the organization is run. (Conditions, while not perfect, are above average.) Black does his job grudgingly and does not get along well with the other people in the organization.

Blue, on the other hand, is snowed under by her work; she carries the whole load of the department on her shoulders. Her subordinates take no initiative, and she is continually correcting their mistakes. Blue sees that whatever little work comes out of her section is letter-perfect even if she has to have her employees do their jobs over and over again and she has to put on the finishing touches herself. Often her subordinates are standing around waiting for her to get around to checking their work. They know their jobs but wait for Blue to make all the decisions.

Finally, there is White, the permissive supervisor. Instead of running his employees, he is letting them run him. His subordinates do their jobs in any manner they wish. They do not respect White's authority, and they raise so many objections that he lets them do whatever they want. Often they boast of how they tell him off.

All the other supervisors under your jurisdiction are doing a good job. You would like to take the easy way out and fire Black, Blue, and White, but they have been with the company for quite a while. Besides, you feel that if you can lick these problems, you will receive quite a bit of recognition from upper management.

Questions

1. How would you help Black become an effective supervisor?

_____

_____

_____

2. How would you help Blue become an effective supervisor?

_____

_____

_____

3. How would you help White become an effective supervisor?

_____

_____

_____

Transformational Leadership

Some people have an extraordinary ability to inspire others and bring forth loyalty. A person who has such a personality is said to have charisma. The German sociologist Max Weber explains in his *Theory of Social and Economic Organization:* The term 'charisma' applies to a certain quality that causes one to be set apart from ordinary people and to be treated as endowed with superhuman, or at least exceptional, powers or qualities. In this sense, charisma is a gift or power of leadership.[16]

In 1976 R. J. House published a theory of charismatic leadership that has received a great deal of attention by researchers. He traces the influence of the charismatic leader to a combination of personal characteristics and types of behavior. The characteristics of charismatic leaders include being dominant, ambitious, and self-confident, as well as having a strong sense of purpose.

Charismatic leaders also demonstrate specific types of behaviors: (1) They are role models for the beliefs and values they want their followers to adopt. For example, Gandhi advocated nonviolence and was a role model of civil disobedience. (2) They demonstrate ability that elicits the respect of followers. Leaders in art, science, religion, business, government, and social service influence followers through their personal competence. (3) They have ideological goals with moral overtones. Martin Luther and Martin Luther King both employed this type of charismatic behavior. (4) They communicate high expectations for their followers and show confidence in their ability to meet those expectations. Military history is replete with examples of charismatic war leaders. (5) Charismatic leaders ignite the motives of their followers to take action. Motives and tasks fall broadly into three areas—affiliation, power, and achievement.[17]

The psychologist David McClelland describes the nature of charismatic leadership:

We set out to find exactly, by experiment, what kinds of thoughts the members of an audience had when exposed to a charismatic leader. They were apparently strengthened and uplifted by the experience; they felt more powerful, rather than less powerful or submissive. This suggests that the traditional way of explaining the influence of leaders has not been entirely correct. The leader does not cause followers to submit and go along by intimidation and force. In fact, the leader is influential by strengthening and inspiring the audience. The personality of the leader arouses confidence in followers, and the followers feel better able to accomplish whatever goals they share with the leader.[18]

In every walk of life, an individual with charisma may emerge. When this happens, the person is recognized as a leader. See, for example, the account by Willie Davis, all-pro lineman for the Green Bay Packers, which shows how Vince Lombardi exercised tremendous influence in the field of sports because of his charismatic personality. Men played their hearts out for Lombardi. Their goal was to please him, to be equal to their understanding of his values and goals.

The example of Lombardi shows how an individual can generate the respect and following of others through personal charisma. According to Willie Davis, how did Lombardi do this?

■ First, he *cared.* No one was more committed to achieving the goal and winning the game.

■ Second, he *worked hard.* No one worked harder and more diligently to prepare.

■ Third, he *knew the right answers.* He knew the game of football, he knew the teams, and he had a plan to succeed.

■ Fourth, he *believed.* He believed in himself and his players, and that made them believers as well.

■ Fifth, he *kept the bar high.* He had uncompromising standards that raised the pride of his team as they rose to the challenge.

■ Sixth, he *knew people.* He knew how to motivate each of his players, each in his own way.

He Made Me Feel Important

Willie Davis

Football is a game of emotion, and what the old man excels at is motivation. I maintain that there are two driving forces in football; one is anger and the other is fear, and he capitalized on both of them. Either he got us so mad we wanted to prove something to him, or we were fearful of being singled out as the one guy who didn't do the job.

In the first place, he worked so hard that I always felt the old man was really putting more into the game on a day-to-day basis than I was. I felt obligated to put something extra into it on Sunday; I had to, just to be even with him. Another thing was the way he made you a believer. He told you what the other team was going to do, and he told you what you had to do to beat them, and invariably he was right. He made us believe that all we had to do was follow his theories on how to get ready for each game and we'd win.

Probably the best job I can remember of him motivating us was when we played the Los Angeles Rams the next-to-last game of 1967. We had already clinched our divisional title, and the game didn't mean anything to us, and he was worried about us just going through the motions. Before the game, he was trembling like a leaf. I could see his leg shaking. "I wish I didn't have to ask you boys to go out there today and do this job," he said. "I wish I could go out and do it myself. Boy, this is one game I'd really like to be playing in. This is a game that you're playing for your pride."

How about the day we beat the Rams 6–3 in Milwaukee in 1965? We'd broken a two-game losing streak, and we were all kind of happy and clowning around, and he came in and you saw his face and you knew nothing was funny anymore. He kicked a bench and hurt his foot, and he had to take something out on somebody, so he started challenging us. "Nobody wants to pay the price," he said. "I'm the only one here who's willing to pay the price. You guys don't care. You don't want to win."

We were stunned. Nobody knew what to do, and finally Forrest Gregg stood up and said, "My God, I want to win," and then somebody else said, "Yeah, I want to win," and pretty soon there were forty guys standing, all shouting, "I want to win." If we had played any football team in the world during the next two hours, we'd have beaten them by ten touchdowns. The old man had us feeling so ashamed and angry. That was his greatest asset—his ability to motivate people.[19]

In his book *Leadership*, political sociologist James MacGregor Burns states that the term *charisma* has taken on a number of different but overlapping meanings: leaders' magical qualities; an emotional bond between the leader and the led; dependence on a powerful figure by the masses; assumptions that a leader is omniscient and virtuous; and simply popular support for a leader that verges on love.[20]

The term **transformational leadership** can be used to describe the leadership of individuals such as Vince Lombardi. These leaders use optimism, charm, intelligence, and a myriad of other personal qualities to raise aspirations and transform individuals and organizations into new levels of high performance.[21]

Although transformational leadership was first discussed by J. V. Downton in 1973, its emergence as an important theory of leadership can be traced to Burns, who distinguished two kinds of leadership: *transformational* and *transactional*. Transactional leaders focus on exchanges between leaders and followers. An example would be a manager who exchanges pay and promotion for work performed. In contrast, transformational leaders focus on the potentialities of the relationship between the leader and followers. This leader taps the motives of followers to better reach the goals of both. Burns uses Gandhi as an example of transformational leadership because he not only raised the hopes and demands of millions of his people, but in the process was also changed himself.[22]

In contrast to transactional leaders, who emphasize exchanging one thing for another, such as jobs for votes and rewards for favors, transformational leaders engage the full person of the follower. The result is elevation of the potential of followers and achievement beyond previous expectations.[23] It is important to note that transformational leadership can occur at all levels of an organization and transformational leaders can emerge in both formal and informal roles.[24]

Leadership Qualities, Characteristics of Followers, and Situational Factors

Certain qualities belong potentially to everyone, but leaders possess these qualities to an exceptional degree. The following is a discussion of 10 qualities that mark a leader and help influence the leadership process—vision, ability, enthusiasm, stability, concern for others, self-confidence, persistence, vitality, charisma, and integrity.[25]

■ **Vision.** *The first requirement for a leader is a strong sense of purpose.* A vision of what could and should be is a basic force that enables the leader to recognize what must be done and to do it. Vision inspires others and causes the leader to accept the duties of leadership, whether pleasant or unpleasant. A sense of vision is especially powerful when it embodies a common cause—overcoming tyranny, stamping out hunger, or improving the human condition.

Native Americans believe that the leader should look to the seventh generation when making decisions today, and this will ensure that a vision is sound and just. Antoïne de Saint-Exupéry once commented on the imaginative nature of vision, saying, "A rock pile ceases to be a rock pile the moment a single man contemplates it, bearing within him the image of a cathedral."[26]

Examples of leadership vision and its power can be seen in computer pioneer Steve Jobs, who foresaw a computer on every desktop and in every home, and in business entrepreneur Bill Gates, who asked the optimistic and compelling question, Where do you want to go today? Jobs of Apple and Gates of Microsoft have altered business and society in irreversible ways.

If you are the leader of a work group or an organization, you should ask, Do I have a plan? What is my vision of what this department or organization should be?

■ **Ability.** *The leader must know the job—or invite loss of respect.* It helps if the leader has done the job before and done it well. Employees seldom respect the individual who constantly must rely on others when making decisions, giving guidance, or solving problems. Although employees usually show a great deal of patience with a new leader, they will lose faith in someone who fails to gain an understanding of the job within a reasonable period of time. Also, the leader must keep job knowledge current. Failure to keep up leads to lack of confidence and loss of employee support. Finally, a leader must have a keen mind to understand information, formulate strategies, and make correct decisions.[27]

Leaders should ask, How competent am I? Am I current in my field? Do I set an example and serve as a resource for my employees because I keep job knowledge current? Mentally, are my perceptions accurate, is my memory good, are my judgments sound?

■ **Enthusiasm.** *Genuine enthusiasm is an important trait of a good leader.* Enthusiasm is a form of persuasiveness that causes others to become interested and willing to accept what the leader is attempting to accomplish. Enthusiasm, like other human emotions—laughter, joy, happiness—is contagious. Enthusiasm shown by a leader generates enthusiasm in followers. As Harry Truman once said, "The successful man has enthusiasm. Good work is never done in cold blood; heat is needed to forge anything. Every great achievement is the story of a flaming heart."[28]

If you are a leader, you must ask, Do I care personally and deeply about what I am doing? Do I show this to my employees? Does my enthusiasm ignite others to take action?

■ **Stability.** *The leader must understand her or his own world and how it relates to the world of others.* One cannot solve the equation of others when preoccupied with the equation of self. Empathy for employees cannot be developed if the leader is emotionally involved with personal problems. Problems with alcohol, problems with money, and problems with relationships are fertile fields for emotional instability. A display of emotional instability places the leader in a precarious position with regard to employees, because they will question the leader's objectivity and judgment. Leaving personal problems at home allows the leader to think more clearly and to perform more effectively on the job. One can see the consequences of loss of stability with examples ranging from the fall of Alexander the Great to the fall of Captain Queeg in *The Caine Mutiny.*

The leader must ask, Do I possess objectivity? Do I convey stability to my employees? Do they trust that personal problems will not interfere with my judgment?

■ **Concern for others.** *At the heart of caring leadership is concern for others.* The leader must not look down on others or treat them as machines—replaceable and interchangeable. The leader must be sincerely and deeply concerned about the welfare of people. The character of caring stands in clear contrast to the character of bullying. The caring leader never tears down, belittles, or diminishes people. The leader must also possess humility and selflessness to the extent that, whenever possible, others' interests are considered first. Concern for others requires patience and listening, and the result is trust, the bedrock of loyalty. Loyalty to followers generates loyalty to the leader; and when tasks become truly difficult, loyalty carries the day.

Leaders must question, Do I truly care about my employees as people, or do I view them more as tools to meet my goals? Do I ever demean people, or do I always lift them up? If I value my employees, do they know it?

■ **Self-confidence.** *Confidence in one's ability gives the leader inner strength to overcome difficult tasks.* If leaders lack self-confidence, people may question their authority and may even disobey orders. Researchers at the Center for Creative Leadership have found that successful leaders remain calm and confident even during intense situations. By demonstrating grace under pressure, they inspire those around them to stay calm and act intelligently. According to football quarterback Roger Staubach, the key to self-confidence is how hard the leader works: "Confidence comes from hours, days, weeks, and years of preparation and dedication. When I'm in the last two minutes of a December playoff game, I'm drawing confidence from windsprints I did the previous March. It's just a circle: work and confidence."[29]

A leader must ask, What is my self-confidence level? Do I show confidence in my actions? Have I done the homework and preparation needed to build self-confidence?

■ **Persistence.** *The leader must have drive and determination to stick with difficult tasks until they are completed.* According to Niccolò Machiavelli, "There is nothing more difficult to take in hand, more perilous to conduct, or more uncertain as to success, than to take the lead in the introduction of a new order of things."[30] Israeli prime minister Golda Meir referred to the quality of persistence when she advised that things do not just occur in one's life. She encouraged people to *believe,* be *persistent,* and *struggle* to overcome life's obstacles.[31] Leaders from Walt Disney to Ray Kroc, founder of McDonald's, have shown the importance of persistence for business success, and military leaders from Ulysses Grant to George Patton have proved its importance on the battlefield. However, no better example exists to show the importance of fierce resolve as a leadership quality than that of Winston Churchill. Historians agree that this leader, with his bulldog will, was a determining element in the success of the Allied nations in defeating the Axis powers in World War II. In the face of impossible odds and seemingly certain defeat, Churchill rallied his people. Simply, he would not give in; he would not give up.[32]

If you are the leader, ask, Do I have self-drive and unflagging persistence to overcome adversity even when others lose their strength and their will?

■ **Vitality.** *Even if the spirit is willing, strength and stamina are needed to fulfill the tasks of leadership.* Effective leaders are typically described as electric, vigorous, active, and full of life, no matter how old they are or if they are physically disabled. Consider Franklin Roosevelt, who had polio, and Helen Keller, who was blind and deaf. It is interesting to note that at one point in recent history, the American President Ronald Reagan, the Roman Catholic Pope John Paul II, and the Ayatollah Khomeini of Iran were all over 70 years of age—and more vital than many people half their age. At all ages, leaders require tremendous energy and stamina to achieve success. The caring leader must have health and vigor to pursue his or her goals. Physical checkups and physical fitness are commonsense acts.

Leaders must ask, Am I fit for the tasks of leadership? Do I have sufficient energy? Am I doing everything I can to keep physically strong?

■ **Charisma.** *Charisma is a special personal quality that generates others' interest and causes them to follow.* Napoleon makes the point that great leaders are optimists and merchants of hope.[33] Optimism, a sense of adventure, and commitment to a cause are traits found in charismatic leaders. These are qualities that unleash the potential of others and bring forth their energies. Charisma is a Greek word that means "divinely inspired gift." The result is admiration, enthusiasm, and the loyalty of followers. Charismatic leaders in history include Julius Caesar, Charlemagne, and Elizabeth I.

As a leader, ask yourself, Do I possess a positive outlook and commitment in my demeanor that transforms followers to new levels of performance as well as personal loyalty to me?

■ **Integrity.** *The most important quality of leadership is integrity, understood as honesty, strength of character, and courage.* Without integrity there is no trust, the number one element in the leader–follower equation. Integrity leads to trust, and trust leads to respect, loyalty, and ultimately, action. It is trust coming from integrity that is needed for leading people from the boardroom, to the shop floor, to the battlefield.[34] A model of integrity was George Washington, about whom it was written:

Endowed by nature with a sound judgment, and an accurate discriminating mind, he was guided by an unvarying sense of moral right, which would tolerate the employment only of those means that would bear the most rigid examination, by a fairness of intention which neither sought nor required disguise, and by a purity of virtue which was not only untainted but unsuspected.[35]

Washington's abilities, his determination, and even his image all furthered his achievements, but his greatest legacy was his integrity. He was respected by everyone. He refused ostentatious titles, insisting that in a republican country, he should be called simply "Mr. President." When Washington died in 1799, Americans mourned the loss of the man known as "the father of his country."[36]

As a leader, ask, Do my people trust me? Do they know that I seek the truth and that I am true to my word? Do they see that I possess strength of character and the courage of my convictions?

How do you rate on the 10 qualities of leadership: vision, ability, enthusiasm, stability, concern for others, self-confidence, persistence, vitality, charisma, and integrity? Do you have the qualities that inspire others to follow? Exercise 3-1 will help you evaluate yourself (or a leader you know).

Exercise 3–1
Ten Leadership Qualities—How Do You Rate?

Evaluate yourself (or a leader you know) on the following leadership qualities by circling a number from 1 to 10 (1 is low; 10 is high).

1. **Vision:** a sense of what could and should be done

   1   2   3   4   5   6   7   8   9   10

2. **Ability:** job knowledge and expertise to achieve results

   1   2   3   4   5   6   7   8   9   10

3. **Enthusiasm:** personal commitment that invigorates and motivates people

   1   2   3   4   5   6   7   8   9   10

4. **Stability:** emotional adjustment and objectivity

   1   2   3   4   5   6   7   8   9   10

5. **Concern for others:** service to followers and interest in their welfare

   1   2   3   4   5   6   7   8   9   10

6. **Self-confidence:** inner strength that comes from preparation and competence

   1   2   3   4   5   6   7   8   9   10

7. **Persistence:** determination to see tough tasks through to completion

   1   2   3   4   5   6   7   8   9   10

8. **Vitality:** strength and stamina

   1   2   3   4   5   6   7   8   9   10

9. **Charisma:** magnetic ability to attract people and cause them to follow

   1   2   3   4   5   6   7   8   9   10

10. **Integrity:** honesty, strength of character, and courage that generates trust

   1   2   3   4   5   6   7   8   9   10

Scoring and Interpretation:

Add all the circled numbers to find the overall score: _____

Score	Evaluation
100–90	Excellent; exceptional
89–80	High; very good
79–70	Average; needs improvement
69–60	Low; much work needed
59 and below	Deficient; poor

Researcher Barbara Kellerman states valuable insights can be gained by examining qualities of ineffective leaders. Her analysis has uncovered six negative behaviors or flaws:

1. *Incompetence.* The leader lacks will or skill (or both) to sustain effective action.
2. *Rigidity.* The leader is closed-minded to new ideas, new information, or changing times.
3. *Intemperance.* The leader lacks self-control in personal habits and conduct.
4. *Callousness.* The leader is uncaring and unkind, discounting the needs of others.
5. *Corruption.* The leader puts self-interest ahead of public interest, and is willing to lie, cheat, or steal.
6. *Cruelty.* The leader commits atrocities inflicting physical and/or emotional pain on others.[37]

Similar findings are reported by Morgan McCall and Michael Lombardo in *Off the Track: Why and How Successful Executives Get Derailed,* published by The Center for Creative Leadership. Derailed leaders

1. Use a bullying style that is intimidating and abrasive.
2. Are viewed as being cold, aloof, and arrogant.
3. Betray personal trust.
4. Are viewed as self-centered, overly ambitious, and thinking of the next job.
5. Have specific business performance problems.
6. Overmanage and are unable to delegate or build a team.[38]

To personalize the subject, consider individuals who have failed or derailed as leaders as the result of negative behaviors or flaws. What were the consequences?

Characteristics of Followers

The word *follower* is rooted in the Old German word *follaziohan,* which means to help, serve, and assist. Two characteristics of followers that influence the leadership process are **respect for authority** and **interpersonal trust.** People who respect authority figures and have a trusting nature are led more easily than people who disregard authorities and are suspicious of others. (Exercise 3–2, evaluates susceptibility to follow, based on the trust you have in others.)

A general decline is evident in the level of trust employees have in leadership personnel in American society. The tendency to withhold trust and be self-guarded can be traced to a number of factors: (1) breakdown of the traditional family structure; (2) decline of a wide range of social structures, such as schools, churches, and neighborhoods; (3) lack of shared values and a sense of community as the society has focused on individual advantage and self-absorption; and, perhaps most important, (4) case after case in which highly visible and influential leadership figures are discovered putting self-interest over the public good—clear evidence that too many leaders violate the trust that they have been given.[39]

Attitudes toward authority have been changing in Western society, and effective leadership today requires adjustment to the ideas and expectations of a new generation of followers. In the past, the leader in the work setting typically was a taskmaster who ruled with a strong arm and forced employees to obey or face the consequences. If employees failed to show respect or follow orders, they were threatened with dismissal or other punishment. Over the years, employees have developed defenses to protect themselves. They have organized unions to represent their interests, and labor legislation has been created to protect workers from arbitrary firing or mistreatment. In addition, management has learned that people who feel oppressed usually respond in negative ways—slowing down production, producing poor-quality work, and being uncooperative.[40]

Today's effective leaders do not use the power tactics of the past. Modern managers find that the practice of threatening employees is usually counterproductive. Instead, they view their task as one of motivating employees to do their best. In adopting this approach, leaders function as facilitators and teachers as opposed to enforcers and disciplinarians, believing that trust and respect should be earned, not demanded. With this approach, the response of the good follower is in the tradition of the apprentice, disciple, and student—one of reliable effort and loyalty to the leader.[41]

Effective leaders and effective followers have many common qualities—integrity, ability, commitment, and so on. Two qualities that are necessary for organizational success are high involvement and critical thinking. Leaders and followers who care deeply and think well make a powerful team.[42]

The Importance of Trust

Management authors Stuart Levine and Michael Crom write about building trust in the workplace. They identify six principles of trust for leadership effectiveness:

1. *Deal openly with everyone.* Hidden agendas will erode people's trust in you, while also showing that you don't trust them.

2. *Consider all points of view.* See situations from the other person's perspective. Show that although you may not agree with them, you do respect the views of others.

3. *Keep promises.* Never say you will do one thing and then do another. If you can't do what you have promised, explain why; don't try to hide the fact that you couldn't keep your word.

4. *Give responsibility.* As a leader, you have bottom-line expectations. Explain your expectations to employees; then let them use their talent, education, and experience to achieve results.

5. *Listen to understand.* Situations may arise that at first appear as though someone is untrustworthy. Missed deadlines, unreasonable expenses, and deviations from standard practices are examples. By simply asking what is happening instead of assuming the worst, you will build a trusting relationship.

6. *Care about people.* This principle will have a major impact on how people react to you and to situations. If they know you care about them, they will be honest with you and will do all they can to meet your expectations.[43]

**Exercise 3–2
Interpersonal Trust
Scale**[44]

The following is a survey of a number of work and social issues. Respond to each item on the basis of your own experience and judgment in dealing with people. Many views are represented in this survey. You may find yourself agreeing strongly with some of the statements, disagreeing with others, and perhaps being undecided about others. Whether you agree or disagree with any statement, you can be sure that many people feel the same as you do. Circle the response that shows the extent to which you agree or disagree with each statement.

1. The best way to handle people is to tell them what they want to hear.
   a. Strongly disagree
   b. Disagree
   c. Undecided
   d. Agree
   e. Strongly agree

2. It is hard to get ahead without cutting corners here and there.
   a. Strongly disagree
   b. Disagree
   c. Undecided
   d. Agree
   e. Strongly agree

3. Anyone who completely trusts someone else is asking for trouble.
   a. Strongly disagree
   b. Disagree
   c. Undecided
   d. Agree
   e. Strongly agree

4. When you ask someone to do something for you, it is best to give the real reasons for the request rather than giving reasons that might carry more weight.
   a. Strongly disagree
   b. Disagree
   c. Undecided
   d. Agree
   e. Strongly agree

5. It is safest to assume that all people have a vicious streak and that it will come out when they are given a chance to use it.
   a. Strongly disagree
   b. Disagree
   c. Undecided
   d. Agree
   e. Strongly agree

6. One should take action only when sure it is morally right.
   a. Strongly disagree
   b. Disagree
   c. Undecided
   d. Agree
   e. Strongly agree

7. Most people are basically good and kind.
   a. Strongly disagree
   b. Disagree
   c. Undecided
   d. Agree
   e. Strongly agree

8. There is no valid reason for lying to someone else.
   a. Strongly disagree
   b. Disagree
   c. Undecided
   d. Agree
   e. Strongly agree

9. Most people forget more easily the death of their father than the loss of their property.
   a. Strongly disagree
   b. Disagree
   c. Undecided
   d. Agree
   e. Strongly agree

10. Generally speaking, people won't work hard unless they are forced to do so.
    a. Strongly disagree
    b. Disagree
    c. Undecided
    d. Agree
    e. Strongly agree

Scoring:

Complete Steps 1 and 2.

Step 1:

In the following key, circle the score that corresponds to your answer for each item of the questionnaire:

1. a. 5	2. a. 5	3. a. 5	4. a. 1	5. a. 5
b. 4	b. 4	b. 4	b. 2	b. 4
c. 3	c. 3	c. 3	c. 3	c. 3
d. 2	d. 2	d. 2	d. 4	d. 2
e. 1	e. 1	e. 1	e. 5	e. 1
6. a. 1	7. a. 1	8. a. 1	9. a. 5	10. a. 5
b. 2	b. 2	b. 2	b. 4	b. 4
c. 3	c. 3	c. 3	c. 3	c. 3
d. 4	d. 4	d. 4	d. 2	d. 2
e. 5	e. 5	e. 5	e. 1	e. 1

Step 2:

Add your scores; then divide the total by 10:
Total score _____ ÷ 10 = _____

Interpretation:

Scores on the Interpersonal Trust Scale, which range from 1.0 to 5.0 (see Figure 3–1), show your tendency to trust people. Typically, the higher the score on the scale, the more trust you have in the inherent decency of others. A high score may also reflect susceptibility to suggestion from others. The lower the score on the scale, the less trusting you would be expected to be of others. A low score may also reflect a tendency to manipulate others in accomplishing goals.

Figure 3–1
Interpersonal Trust Scale

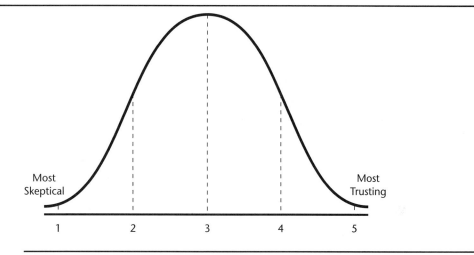

Reprinted with permission from *Psychology Today Magazine,* copyright 1970, Sussex Publishers, Inc.

Score	Characteristics
1.0–2.0	This person believes that most people seek personal advantage, even at the expense of others; thus, the best course of action is self-protection. The 1.0–2.0 individual may manipulate others in interpersonal relations and avoid making personal commitments. Such a person is often difficult to lead.
2.0–3.0	This person is generally suspicious of the motives of others and tends toward skepticism and self-reliance rather than seeking assistance or direction. The 2.0–3.0 individual will usually act independently, rather than ask for help or delegate, believing the best way to get something done is to do it oneself.
3.0–4.0	This person has confidence in the basic decency of others, combined with an evaluation of the merits of the situation. The 3.0–4.0 individual will usually trust others temporarily, yet reserve final judgment.
4.0–5.0	This person believes that people are essentially good and therefore readily trusts others. Such a person may not look below the surface of things. The 4.0–5.0 individual is easily persuaded and should be encouraged to look at all sides of an argument before making a decision.

Review your interpersonal trust scores. What is your tendency? Do you lean toward suspicion and self-reliance? Do you tend to be trusting and suggestible? Or are you, like most people, somewhere in the middle? Given your level of trust, are you typically easy or difficult to lead?

Situational Factors

In addition to qualities of the leader and characteristics of followers, many situational factors influence the leadership process. The following is a discussion of important situational factors, including the size of the organization, the social and psychological climate, patterns of employment, and the type, place, and purpose of work performed. Also included is a discussion of leader–follower compatibility.

■ *Size of the organization.* Studies show that the size of an organization demands a certain type of leadership skill. A small organization needs a leader who is both a salesperson and a production manager. Outside the organization, the leader is the organization's chief advocate, personally meeting with clients and winning their loyalty. On the inside, the leader organizes the work, assigns tasks, coaches employees, and evaluates progress. In contrast, the leader of a large organization devotes efforts primarily to the organization's public image and its investment and growth plans. Leaders of large organizations think in broad terms about the community and the marketplace, considering how the organization can be placed best in both.[45]

■ *Social and psychological climate.* Social and psychological factors such as confusion, anxiety, and despair can also influence the leadership process. Consider pre–World War II Germany, where a great depression and the inactivity of the people seemed intolerable:

The streets of German towns were full of millions of unemployed waiting for the dole, which was scarcely sufficient to provide for the indispensable needs of daily life. These observations were common to everyone who lived in Germany during the years preceding Hitler's advent to power. The lack of such an important educational factor as compulsory military service on the one hand, and the plague of unemployment on the other, produced their inevitable consequences in the slope of a deplorable moral relaxation and in a not less deplorable decrease of patriotism. In these circumstances that were ripe for leadership, Adolf Hitler came to power.[46]

■ *Patterns of employment.* In his book *The Age of Unreason,* management author Charles Handy describes how contemporary patterns of work are changing in fundamental ways. He describes the "shamrock" organization, in which there are three workforces supporting an organization, but only one leaf of the shamrock is permanent and full-time; the other two are (1) part-time or temporary or both, and (2) independent workers and contractors who form alliances with the organization to perform specified tasks. Handy describes how the seemingly unusual work assignments of our day— working at home, flextime, independent contractors, networks of professionals, associations, virtual offices and companies, and the like—are part of a new pattern of work that adds to the challenge of leadership.[47]

■ *Type, place, and purpose of work.* The type of work to be done is an important factor in the leadership process. Leadership studies show that, in general, when the work to be done is clear-cut, routine, or monotonous, a nondirective and supportive approach is best. If work duties are defined loosely, a directive and task orientation is needed until roles, responsibilities, and relationships are clarified.[48]

Also important is the context of place and purpose. Where is the setting, and what is the goal? Is the place the farm, the factory, or the lab? Is the purpose selling or serving? Is the task shipbuilding or singing? What is the challenge—starting a business or minding the store? All these factors of the situation have tremendous influence on who will light the path and how bright the light will be.

Different Kinds of Intelligence

Intelligence is multidimensional. *Crystallized intelligence* represents one's lifetime of intellectual attainments, as shown by vocabulary, accumulated facts about the world, and ability to solve problems within one's area of expertise. It includes comprehension of information and the ability to communicate in oral and written forms. Crystallized intelligence can be increased over time. *Fluid intelligence* involves mental flexibility, as shown by the ability to process information rapidly, as in solving problems in new areas of endeavor. People draw upon fluid intelligence in novel situations or when conventional solutions fail. It includes reasoning, creative thinking, and memory. One can imagine an ancient mariner who is both sea-wise (crystallized) and people-smart (fluid).[49]

Although intelligence is positively related to leadership effectiveness, different situations require different kinds of intelligence.[50] Once Henry Ford was asked who should lead the band. His answer was, "The one with rhythm." Exercise 3–3, based on the work of Keith Rogers, Robert Sternberg, and Howard Gardner, measures multiple intelligences that are combinations of both crystallized and fluid mental abilities. This exercise can be used to answer the questions, What kind of intelligence do you possess? In which situations are you likely to lead, and in which are you likely to follow? What is your natural leadership strength?

**Exercise 3–3
Indicator of Multiple
Intelligences[51]**

For each statement, indicate your most accurate response by placing a check mark in the appropriate space. Think about your knowledge, beliefs, preferences, behaviors, and experiences. Decide quickly and move on. There is no right or wrong, no good or bad, no expected or desirable response. Focus on the way you really are, not on the way someone else may think you ought to be.

	Rarely 1	Occasionally 2	Sometimes 3	Usually 4	Almost Always 5
1. I am careful about the direct and implied meanings of the words I choose.	_____	_____	_____	_____	_____
2. I appreciate a wide variety of music.	_____	_____	_____	_____	_____
3. People come to me when they need help with math problems or any other calculations.	_____	_____	_____	_____	_____
4. In my mind, I can visualize clear, precise, sharp images.	_____	_____	_____	_____	_____
5. I am physically well coordinated.	_____	_____	_____	_____	_____
6. I understand why I believe and behave the way I do.	_____	_____	_____	_____	_____
7. I understand the moods, temperaments, values, and intentions of others.	_____	_____	_____	_____	_____
8. I confidently express myself well in words, written or spoken.	_____	_____	_____	_____	_____
9. I understand the basic precepts of music, such as harmony, chords, and keys.	_____	_____	_____	_____	_____
10. When I have a problem, I use a logical, analytical, step-by-step process to arrive at a solution.	_____	_____	_____	_____	_____
11. I have a good sense of space and direction.	_____	_____	_____	_____	_____
12. I have skill in handling objects such as scissors, balls, hammers, scalpels, paintbrushes, knitting needles, and pliers.	_____	_____	_____	_____	_____
13. My self-understanding helps me make wise decisions for my life.	_____	_____	_____	_____	_____
14. I am able to influence other individuals to believe and/or behave in response to my own beliefs, preferences, and desires.	_____	_____	_____	_____	_____
15. I am grammatically accurate.	_____	_____	_____	_____	_____
16. I like to compose or create music.	_____	_____	_____	_____	_____
17. I am rigorous and skeptical in accepting facts, reasons, and principles.	_____	_____	_____	_____	_____
18. I am good at putting together jigsaw puzzles, and reading instructions, patterns, or blueprints.	_____	_____	_____	_____	_____
19. I excel in physical activities such as dance, sports, or games.	_____	_____	_____	_____	_____

	Rarely 1	Occasionally 2	Sometimes 3	Usually 4	Almost Always 5
20. My ability to understand my own emotions helps me decide whether or how to be involved in certain situations.	___	___	___	___	___
21. I would like to be involved in the helping professions, such as teaching, therapy, or counseling, or to do work such as political or religious leadership.	___	___	___	___	___
22. I am able to use spoken or written words to influence or persuade others.	___	___	___	___	___
23. I enjoy performing music, such as singing or playing a musical instrument for an audience.	___	___	___	___	___
24. I require scientific explanations of physical realities.	___	___	___	___	___
25. I can read maps easily and accurately.	___	___	___	___	___
26. I work well with my hands, as would an electrician, plumber, tailor, mechanic, carpenter, or assembler.	___	___	___	___	___
27. I am aware of the complexity of my own feelings, emotions, and beliefs in various circumstances.	___	___	___	___	___
28. I am able to work as an effective intermediary in helping other individuals and groups solve their problems.	___	___	___	___	___
29. I am sensitive to the sounds, rhythms, inflections, and meters of words, especially as found in poetry.	___	___	___	___	___
30. I have a good sense of musical rhythm.	___	___	___	___	___
31. I would like to do the work of people such as chemists, engineers, physicists, astronomers, or mathematicians.	___	___	___	___	___
32. I am able to produce graphic depictions of the spatial world, as in drawing, painting, sculpting, drafting, or mapmaking.	___	___	___	___	___
33. I relieve stress or find fulfillment in physical activities.	___	___	___	___	___
34. My inner self is my ultimate source of strength and renewal.	___	___	___	___	___
35. I understand what motivates others even when they are trying to hide their motivations.	___	___	___	___	___

	Rarely 1	Occasionally 2	Sometimes 3	Usually 4	Almost Always 5
36. I enjoy reading frequently on a wide variety of topics.	____	____	____	____	____
37. I have a good sense of musical pitch.	____	____	____	____	____
38. I find satisfaction in dealing with numbers.	____	____	____	____	____
39. I like the hands-on approach to learning, when I can experience personally the objects that I'm learning about.	____	____	____	____	____
40. I have quick and accurate physical reflexes and responses.	____	____	____	____	____
41. I am confident in my own opinions and am not easily swayed by others.	____	____	____	____	____
42. I am comfortable and confident with groups of people.	____	____	____	____	____
43. I use writing as a vital method of communication.	____	____	____	____	____
44. I am affected both emotionally and intellectually by music.	____	____	____	____	____
45. I prefer questions that have definite right and wrong answers.	____	____	____	____	____
46. I can accurately estimate distances and other measurements.	____	____	____	____	____
47. I have accurate aim when throwing balls or in archery, shooting, golf, and the like.	____	____	____	____	____
48. My feelings, beliefs, attitudes, and emotions are my own responsibility.	____	____	____	____	____
49. I have many good friends.	____	____	____	____	____

Scoring:

In the Scoring Matrix on the next page, the numbers in the boxes represent the statement numbers in the preceding survey. You made a rating judgment for each statement. Now place the numbers that correspond to your ratings in the numbered boxes. Then add the columns, and write the totals at the bottom to determine your score for each of the seven intelligence categories.

Once you have calculated your total score for each kind of intelligence, consult the section "Interpretation" to determine the intensity level that corresponds to each total score. Record that number in the final section of the Scoring Matrix.

Scoring Matrix

	Verbal-Linguistic	Musical-Rhythmic	Logical-Mathematical	Visual-Spatial	Bodily-Kinesthetic	Intrapersonal	Interpersonal
	1	2	3	4	5	6	7
	8	9	10	11	12	13	14
	15	16	17	18	19	20	21
	22	23	24	25	26	27	28
	29	30	31	32	33	34	35
	36	37	38	39	40	41	42
	43	44	45	46	47	48	49
Total							
Intensity of knowledge, beliefs, preferences, behaviors, and experiences: (3) equals low, (2) equals moderate, and (1) equals high							

Interpretation:

To some degree, everyone possesses all seven kinds of intelligence, and all can be enhanced. We are each a unique blend, however, and we differ in the degree to which we prefer and have competence to use each of the intelligences. Presented below are interpretations for the total scores for each kind of intelligence. Intensity levels range from (3) low, to (2) moderate, to (1) high.

Score	Intensity of Knowledge, Beliefs, Preferences, Behaviors, and Experiences
7–15	*Tertiary preference (3): Low intensity. You tend to avoid activities in this area.* Unless you are unusually motivated, gaining expertise would be frustrating and would likely require great effort. Keep in mind, however, that all intelligences, including this one, can be enhanced throughout your lifetime.
16–26	*Secondary preference (2): Moderate intensity. You could take or leave the application of this intelligence.* Although you accept it, you do not necessarily prefer to use it. On the other hand, you would not typically avoid using it. Gaining expertise in this area would be satisfying, but would require attention and effort.
27–35	*Primary preference (1): High intensity. You enjoy using this intelligence.* You are excited and challenged by it, perhaps even fascinated. Given the opportunity, you will usually select it. Becoming an expert in this area would be rewarding and fulfilling, and would probably require little effort compared with the effort required for intelligence in a moderate or low area of preference.

The following are the specific characteristics of each of the seven kinds of intelligence:

1. If you have *verbal-linguistic intelligence*, you enjoy reading and writing, and have a good memory for names and places. Like the playwright William Shakespeare, you like to tell stories, and you are good at getting your point across. You learn best by seeing, saying, and hearing words. People whose dominant intelligence is in the verbal-linguistic area include poets, authors, speakers, attorneys, politicians, lecturers, and teachers.

2. If you have *musical-rhythmic intelligence*, you are sensitive to the sounds in your environment, enjoy music, and prefer listening to music when you study or read. Like the composer Ludwig van Beethoven, you appreciate pitch and rhythm, and learn best through melody and music. Musical intelligence is obviously demonstrated by singers, conductors, and composers, but also by those who enjoy, understand, and use various elements of music.

3. If you have *logical-mathematical intelligence*, you like to work with numbers, perform experiments, and explore patterns and relationships. Like the scientist Marie Curie, you enjoy doing activities in sequential order and learn best by classifying information, engaging in abstract thinking, and looking for basic principles. People with well-developed logical-mathematical abilities include mathematicians, biologists, geologists, engineers, physicists, researchers, and other scientists.

4. If you have *visual-spatial intelligence,* you are likely to engage in imagining things, sensing spatial changes, and working through mazes and puzzles. Like the artist Michelangelo, you like to draw, build, design, and create things. You learn best by looking at pictures, watching videos or movies, and visualizing. People with well-developed visual-spatial abilities are found in professions such as sculpting, painting, surgery, and engineering.

5. If you have *bodily-kinesthetic intelligence,* you process knowledge through bodily sensations and use your body in skilled ways. Like the warrior Achilles, you respond best in situations that provide physical activities and hands-on learning experiences, and you are able to manipulate objects with finesse. People who have highly developed bodily-kinesthetic abilities include carpenters, soldiers, mechanics, dancers, gymnasts, swimmers, and other athletes.

6. If you have *intrapersonal intelligence,* you are a creative and independent thinker. Like the philosopher Spinoza, you are comfortable focusing inward on thoughts and feelings, following personal instincts, and pursuing goals that are original. You may respond with strong opinions when controversial topics are discussed. Pacing your own work is important to you. People with intrapersonal abilities include both philosophers and entrepreneurs.

7. If you have *interpersonal intelligence,* you enjoy being with people, like talking with others, and engage in social activities. Like Eleanor Roosevelt, you have the ability to understand people, and people often come to you for help. You learn best by relating, sharing, and participating in cooperative group environments. People with strong interpersonal abilities are found in public service, sales, consulting, community organizing, counseling, teaching, or one of the other helping professions.

Intelligence is complex and multidimensional. You may find that you have strengths in several different areas. When needs for leadership arise in your areas of strength, you can capitalize on these aptitudes for success.

The concept of multiple intelligences is relevant to successful leadership. Leadership effectiveness is in direct proportion to strength of commitment; commitment comes from passion; and passion comes from within the person. Consider examples such as Walt Disney in entertainment and Steve Jobs in technology.

Although there are many models and ways to describe and express human talent, the idea that there are seven kinds of intelligence is interesting and useful. The force of an idea or action is greatly determined by the style of intelligence of the leader.

Styles of Leading

An important factor in the leadership process is leader–follower compatibility based on styles of leading. Exercise 3–4 is designed to evaluate your preferred style of leading—directive, participative, or free-rein.[52]

**Exercise 3–4
What Is Your
Leadership Style?**

Answer the following questions, keeping in mind what you have done, or think you would do, in the situations described.

	Yes	No
1. Do you enjoy the authority leadership brings?	___	___
2. Generally, do you think it is worth the time and effort for a leader to explain the reasons for a decision or policy before putting the policy into effect?	___	___
3. Do you tend to prefer the planning functions of leadership, as opposed to working directly with your employees?	___	___
4. A stranger comes into your work area, and you know the person is a new employee. Would you first ask, "What is your name?" rather than introduce yourself?	___	___
5. Do you keep employees up-to-date on a regular basis on developments affecting the work group?	___	___
6. Do you find that in giving out assignments, you tend to state the goals, leaving the methods up to your employees?	___	___
7. Do you think leaders should keep aloof from employees, because in the long run familiarity breeds lessened respect?	___	___
8. It comes time to decide about a company event. You have heard that the majority prefer to have it on Wednesday, but you are pretty sure Thursday would be better for all concerned. Would you put the question to a vote rather than make the decision yourself?	___	___
9. If you had your way, would you make communication sessions employee-initiated, with personal consultations held only at the employee's request?	___	___
10. Do you favor the use of audits and performance evaluations as a way of keeping work standards high?	___	___
11. Do you feel that you should be friendly with employees?	___	___
12. After considerable time, you determine the answer to a tough problem. You pass along the solution to your employees, who poke it full of holes. Would you be annoyed that the problem is still unsolved, rather than become upset with the employees?	___	___
13. Do you agree that one of the best ways to avoid problems of discipline is to provide adequate punishment for violation of rules?	___	___
14. Your way of handling a situation is being criticized by your employees. Would you try to sell your viewpoint, rather than make it clear that, as supervisor, your decisions are final?	___	___
15. Do you generally leave it up to your employees to contact you, as far as informal, day-to-day communications are concerned?	___	___
16. Do you feel that everyone in your work group should have a certain amount of personal loyalty to you?	___	___
17. Do you favor the practice of using task force teams and committees, rather than making decisions alone?	___	___
18. Some experts say that difference of opinion within a work group is healthy; others say it indicates basic flaws in the management process. Do you agree with the first view?	___	___

Scoring:

In the Scoring Matrix below, place a check mark next to each question you answered *yes*. Add the check marks for each column to find the totals for the leadership styles you prefer.

Scoring Matrix

Directive	Participative	Free-Rein
1. _____	2. _____	3. _____
4. _____	5. _____	6. _____
7. _____	8. _____	9. _____
10. _____	11. _____	12. _____
13. _____	14. _____	15. _____
16. _____	17. _____	18. _____
Total _____	Total _____	Total _____

Interpretation:

Your highest score indicates your preferred style of leading. A description of each style is presented in Figure 3–2.

Figure 3–2   Continuum of Leadership Styles[53]

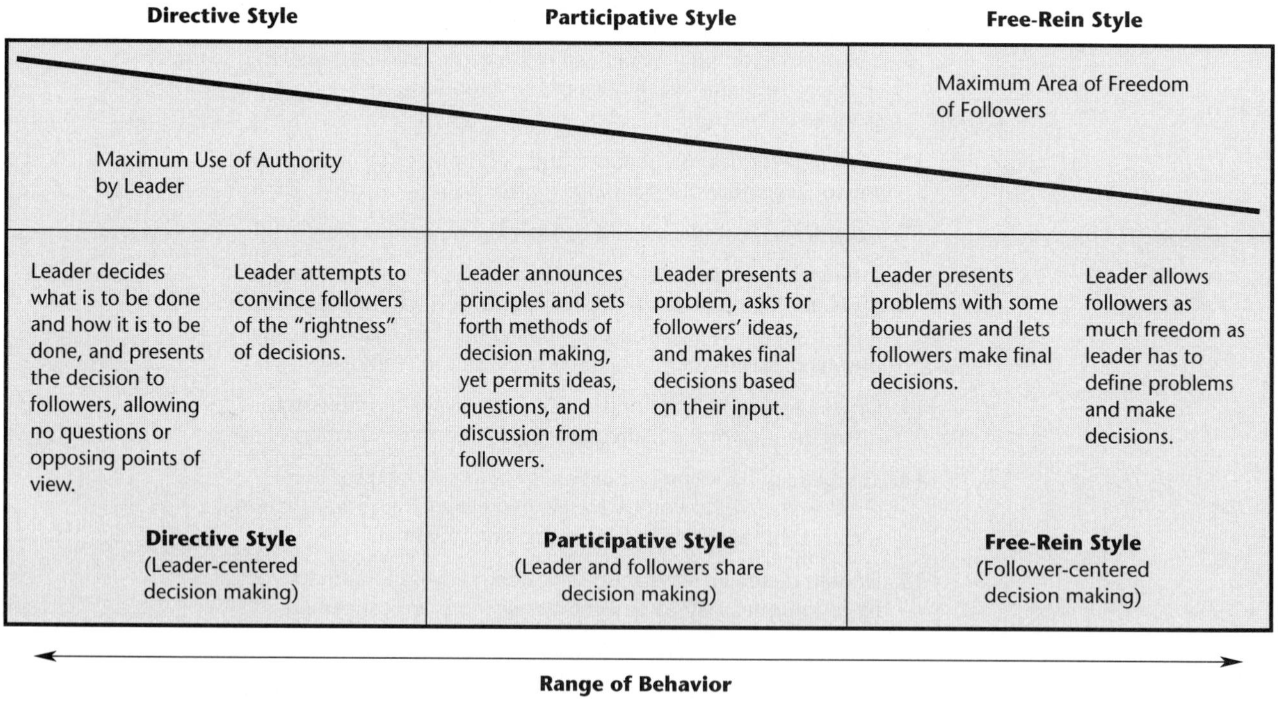

Directive Style		Participative Style		Free-Rein Style	
Maximum Use of Authority by Leader				Maximum Area of Freedom of Followers	
Leader decides what is to be done and how it is to be done, and presents the decision to followers, allowing no questions or opposing points of view.	Leader attempts to convince followers of the "rightness" of decisions.	Leader announces principles and sets forth methods of decision making, yet permits ideas, questions, and discussion from followers.	Leader presents a problem, asks for followers' ideas, and makes final decisions based on their input.	Leader presents problems with some boundaries and lets followers make final decisions.	Leader allows followers as much freedom as leader has to define problems and make decisions.
Directive Style (Leader-centered decision making)		**Participative Style** (Leader and followers share decision making)		**Free-Rein Style** (Follower-centered decision making)	

Range of Behavior

Figure 3–3 shows the different emphases in the use of power for the three styles of leadership.

**Figure 3–3
Emphasis in the Use of Power**[54]

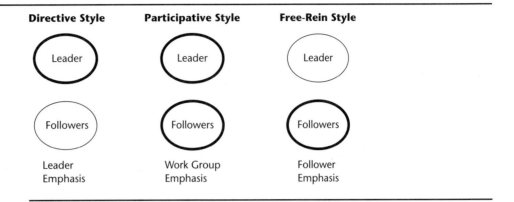

According to the ideas of Hollander, Vroom, and Yetton; Tannenbaum and Schmidt; Hersey and Blanchard; Daniel Goleman; and others, there are five points to remember about styles of leading:[55]

1. People develop preferred styles by modeling others, going through formal training, and learning from personal experience.

2. An individual usually prefers the same style of leading and style of following. Confusion results when this is not the case. General George Patton was a directive leader and a free-rein follower, causing mixed signals and much controversy in his relations with commanders and soldiers.

3. Leaders have been successful along all points of the continuum: Elizabeth I was directive in her style; Thomas Jefferson chose participative leadership; Dwight Eisenhower preferred the free-rein style. It is interesting to contrast Italian political philosopher Niccoló Machiavelli (1469–1527), who advocated being directive to the point of believing that the ends justify the means, to sixth-century BC Chinese philosopher Lao-tzu, who prescribed nondirective leadership to the point of believing in total selflessness: "Of a good leader when his work is done and his aims fulfilled, all will say, 'we did it ourselves.'"

4. There is no universally effective style of leading. Sometimes it is best for the leader to tell employees what to do; sometimes it is best for leaders and subordinates to make decisions together; and sometimes it is best for employees to direct themselves. The best style of leadership depends on qualities of the leader, characteristics of the followers, and the nature of the situation.

Increasingly, the American workplace is becoming faster paced, more culturally diverse, and more global in nature. See Table 3–1, which shows a general shift from

**Table 3–1
The Changing Character of Work Culture and Changing Focus of Effective Leadership**[56]

	Directive		
Decade	Nature of Work Culture		Focus of Leadership
Pre-1950	Hierarchy		Command and control
1950s	Organization		Supervision
1960s	Systems		Administration
1970s	Strategy		Management
1980s	Innovation		Entrepreneurship
1990s	Diversity		Team building
Post-2000	Community		Relationship management
	Free-rein		

directive (command and control) to free-rein (relationship management) focus of leadership, and a shift from a hierarchy to a community nature of work culture, as innovative products, quick reaction time, and individual initiative are requirements for success.

5. If styles of leading and styles of following conflict, extra patience and communication are needed, especially in the following areas:

■ *Decision making.* Directive leaders may be upset by free-rein followers who insist on challenging decisions and behaving independently. These leaders must remember that free-rein followers usually do their best work on special assignments and independent projects. They respond best to individual treatment and personal freedom.

■ *Goal setting.* Directive followers may be upset by free-rein leaders who provide few details on how to do a job. These leaders must remember that directive followers usually do their best work when job duties are spelled out and direct orders are given.

■ *Communication.* Participative followers usually are upset by leaders who fail to have staff meetings, ignore the open-door policy, and show little concern for people's feelings. These leaders must remember that participative followers want open communication and active involvement in the decision-making process. They usually perform well on task forces, committees, and other work teams.

To understand the importance of leader–follower compatibility, consider your own experience. Have you ever had a leader who missed the mark in meeting your needs? Do you, yourself, have the range to meet the needs of all three styles—directive, participative, and free-rein?

Leadership Effectiveness Today

Because there is no universal formula for success, leadership is more **art** than science and more **skill** than knowledge. Above all, leadership is difficult. In "No Easy Task," management author and educator Douglas McGregor, originator of the terms *theory X* and *theory Y,* describes how difficult leadership can be.

No Easy Task

Douglas McGregor

I believed (before becoming President of Antioch College) that a leader could operate successfully as a kind of advisor to his organization; I thought I could avoid being a "boss." Unconsciously, I suspect, I hoped to duck the unpleasant necessity of making difficult decisions, of taking the responsibility for one course of action among many uncertain alternatives, of making mistakes and taking the consequences. I thought that maybe I could operate so that everyone would like me—that "good human relations" would eliminate all discord and argument.

I couldn't have been more wrong. It took a couple of years, but I finally began to realize that a leader cannot avoid the exercise of authority any more than he can avoid responsibility for what happens to his organization. In fact, it is a major function of the leader to take on his own shoulders the responsibility for resolving the uncertainties that are always involved in important decisions. Moreover, since no important decision ever pleases everyone in an organization, the leader must also absorb the displeasure, and sometimes the severe hostility, of those who would have taken a different course.[57]

The role of the leader in today's high-tech, fast-paced, and ever-changing workplace is increasingly difficult. In dealing with a wide variety of employees along a full range of skills, the leader must add new demands to traditional duties (see Table 3–2):

Table 3–2
Leadership Demands and Duties

Traditional Duties	New Demands
1. Give orders.	1. Empower people.
2. Implement plans.	2. Generate ideas.
3. Manage individuals.	3. Coach teams.
4. Do things right.	4. Do the right things.
5. Organize work.	5. Develop people.

The effective leader today must be a director *and* motivator, implementer *and* innovator, mentor *and* team builder, expert *and* moral force, organizer *and* developer of people. These are great challenges that bring both satisfaction and appreciation for caring leaders who are willing and able to meet them.

Part One Summary

After reading Part One, you should know the following key concepts, principles, and terms. Fill in the blanks from memory, or copy the answers listed below.

Historically, the study of leadership has emphasized (a) _____ theory, focusing on qualities of the leader, and (b) _____ theory, focusing on leadership actions. Almost always included as important leadership traits are (c) _____, _____, and _____. Leadership behavior theory has included styles of leadership—(d) _____, _____, and _____—studied by (e) _____, and others, as well as dimensions of leadership—(f) _____, and _____—studied by (g) _____, and others. Leadership (h) _____ theory holds that the most effective leadership qualities and actions vary from situation to situation, depending on qualities of leaders, characteristics of followers, and the nature of the situation. The term (i) _____ is used to describe the elevation of the performance of followers beyond previous expectations. Qualities that mark a leader include (j) _____, _____, _____, _____, _____, and _____. Characteristics of followers that influence the leadership process are (k) _____, and _____. Principles for developing trust in the workplace include (l) _____, _____, _____, and _____. Many situational factors influence the leadership process, including (m) _____, _____, _____, and _____. There is no universal formula for leadership success, so what is effective can change, case by case. Thus, leadership is more (n) _____ than science.

Answer Key for Part One Summary

a. **trait,** page 16

b. **behavior,** page 16

c. **intelligence, values, energy,** page 16

d. **autocratic, democratic, laissez-faire,** page 19

e. **Kurt Lewin,** page 19

f. **initiating structure, showing consideration,** page 20

g. **Ralph Stogdill,** page 19

h. **contingency,** page 25

i. **transformational leadership,** pages 27–28

j. (any six) **vision, ability, enthusiasm, stability, concern for others, self-confidence, persistence, vitality, charisma, integrity,** pages 30–32

k. **respect for authority, interpersonal trust,** page 35

l. (any four) **deal openly with everyone, consider all points of view, keep promises, give responsibility, listen to understand, care about people,** page 36

m. **size of the organization; social and psychological climate; patterns of employment; type, place, and purpose of work,** page 41

n. **art,** page 54

Reflection Points—personal thoughts on the leadership equation, leadership qualities, characteristics of followers, and situational factors

Complete the following questions and activities to personalize the content of Part One. Space is provided for writing your thoughts.

■ Critique the idea that leadership success requires effectiveness on two dimensions: (1) initiating structure—focus on the task and concern for production—as well as (2) showing consideration—employee support and concern for people. Evaluate an actual leader's effectiveness using these two dimensions.

_____

_____

■ Describe an incident or time when the qualities of the leader, the characteristics of followers, and the nature of the situation matched and leadership occurred. What took place, who was involved, and what were the results?

_____

_____

■ Consider the qualities that mark a leader—vision, ability, enthusiasm, stability, concern for others, self-confidence, persistence, vitality, charisma, and integrity. On the basis of these 10 qualities, discuss the best leader you have ever had.

_____

_____

■ How susceptible to leadership are you? Are you basically a trusting person or a suspicious person when it comes to following others?

_____

_____

■ What is your natural intelligence strength? When and where have you provided leadership based on your preferred intelligence area(s)?

_____

_____

■ Have you ever clashed with a supervisor or subordinate over leadership style? Discuss dynamics and results.

_____

_____

■ Discuss the influence of Oprah Winfrey in American society. What factors of Oprah, her followers, and the situation have resulted in her leadership influence?

_____

_____

■ Some think leadership is a born ability. Some think leadership can be learned. Some think leadership is the product of a need or challenge. What do you think? Cite experience or research to support your view.

_____

_____

Part One Video Case
Toying with Success: The McFarlane Companies

Todd McFarlane, president and CEO of the McFarlane Companies, is an entrepreneur who understands the importance of product development. Comics, sports, toys, and rock-and-roll have all benefited from his creativity. When McFarlane's dream to play major league baseball didn't happen, he fell back on another interest he developed as a teenager—drawing superheroes. He faced the same question faced by all other entrepreneurs: Could he make money pursuing his dreams? He sent his sketches to prospective employers, and after 300 rejection letters McFarlane got a job freelancing for Marvel Comics. Working many hours for low pay, he made a name for himself and by 1990 was the highest-paid comic book artist in the industry.

Frustrated over creative differences and his desire to own the rights to his characters, McFarlane quit, took six other artists with him, and started his own company. He went from artist to entrepreneur overnight. While industry experts predicted he would last less than a year, McFarlane didn't even think about the future. *Spawn,* his first comic, sold 1.7 million copies.

Entrepreneurship rewards individuals willing to take risks. In Todd McFarlane's case, the need to control his destiny drove his aspirations. His path is similar to that taken by many others: receiving training at a large company, then leaving when he decided he could provide a better product on his own.

Today's dynamic business environment has a tremendous effect on the success or failure of entrepreneurs like Todd McFarlane. Economics plays a key role at the McFarlane Companies. The firm must protect the many intellectual properties it creates and licenses. The business uses technology to support and spark creativity in developing new products. The competitive environment drives quality at McFarlane, which produces high-quality products even if they cost more, and thus McFarlane gains an edge over competitors. The CEO uses the Web to interact with his key demographic, or as he puts it, the freaks with long hair and cool tattoos. Spawn.com provides a place where fans can interact with each other and with the company. Finally, the global influence on business has an impact on all the other environments. Knowing he can't control the global environment, McFarlane focuses on managing what he can control.

Todd McFarlane's purchase of Mark McGwire's 70th home run ball for $3 million illustrates his willingness to take a risk and focus on what he controls. While many thought he was crazy, McFarlane saw an opportunity. He combined the ball with several others hit by McGwire and Sammy Sosa to create the McFarlane Collection, which was displayed in every major league stadium and garnered enormous publicity. A portion of the proceeds was donated to the Lou Gehrig Foundation. Most significant, McFarlane began a relationship with professional sports that led to his obtaining the exclusive rights to nearly every professional sports team toy license.

Questions for Discussion

1. What personality traits do leaders like Todd McFarlane possess that distinguish them from other individuals?

2. How have global competition and technology advances changed business conditions and leadership challenges?

For more information, see www.spawn.com.

Action Assignment

As a bridge between learning and doing, complete the following action assignment.

1. What is the most important idea you have learned in Part One?

2. How can you apply what you have learned? What will you do, with whom, where, when, and, most important, why?

Part 2 The Power of Vision

4. The Importance of Vision and the Motive to Lead
5. Organizational Climate

MOMENTUM COMES FROM HAVING A CLEAR VISION of what the organization ought to be, from a well-thought-out strategy to achieve that vision, and from carefully conceived and communicated directions and plans that let everyone participate and be accountable in achieving these plans. Momentum is vital and palpable. It is the feeling among a group of people that their lives and work are intertwined and moving toward a recognizable and legitimate goal.

—Max DePree
Leadership Is an Art

Learning Objectives

After studying Part Two, you will be able to:
• Know the role of vision for leadership success.
• Describe how a leader creates and implements a powerful vision.
• Understand the importance of alignment and prioritization.
• Know your motive for assuming the tasks of leadership.
• Develop an organizational climate that attracts and keeps good people.
• Describe the elements of true community.

CHAPTER

4

The Importance of Vision and the Motive to Lead

Management author Peter Drucker once said, "The best way to predict the future is to create it."[1] Most leaders agree with this statement completely. The leader wants to make a difference and strives to create a thing that never was before. This thing, this difference, constitutes a **vision.**

The most important function of a leader is to develop a clear and compelling picture of the future, and to secure commitment to that ideal. Consider the words of Henry Ford as he communicated his vision to make a car for the masses: "I will build a motor car for the great multitude . . . constructed of the best materials, by the best men to be hired, after the simplest designs that modern engineering can devise . . . so low in price that no man making a good salary will be unable to own one and enjoy with his family the blessing of hours of pleasure in God's great open spaces."[2]

Ford's leadership success began with a vision. To this, he added a **strategy** to succeed. Three great ideas that gave his vision life were (1) the moving assembly line; (2) paying workers not as little as possible but as much as was fair; and (3) vertical integration, which made Ford's River Rouge plant a marvel of the industrial world.

Ford believed that a vision should not be just to make money. He saw profit as the by-product of a vision achieved. Ford wrote: "A business ought not to drift. It ought to march ahead under leadership. The easy way is to follow the crowd and hope to make money. But that is not the way of sound business. The right way is to provide a needed product or service. Try to run a business solely to make money and the business will die. Profit is essential to business vitality. But a business that charges too high a profit disappears about as quickly as one that operates at a loss. Short-sighted businessmen think first of money, but the quality of a product or service is what makes or breaks a business. Without these, customers soon go elsewhere."[3]

In addition to developing a vision and a strategy to succeed, the leader must have intensity and **stamina** to see these through. As CEO at Johnson & Johnson, James Burke estimated that he spent 40 percent of his time communicating and reinforcing the company's vision. Much is said about the vision of leaders and about their creative strategies. However, the incredible energy they display as they face repeated challenges and even failures must not be overlooked. Leaders typically have substantial vitality, and they manage to transmit this energy to others. This is a force born out of deep convictions and passion for the work or goal. Such leaders breathe life into their organizations; hence the term *animator* is used to describe the leader.[4]

Examples of Powerful Visions

Consider the strong and all-embracing vision of Johnson & Johnson that has helped thousands of employees throughout the world understand that their first obligation is to the customer: "We believe our first obligation is to the doctors, nurses, and patients; to mothers and all others who use our products and services."[5]

Consider the moving vision of Collis Huntington, founder of Newport News Shipbuilding and Dry Dock Company in 1886:

We shall build good ships here.
At a profit—if we can;
At a loss—if we must.
But always good ships.[6]

And consider oil magnate J. Paul Getty who identified his vision as follows: "get up early, work hard, find oil."[7]

Table 4–1 is a vision of an organization that impacts every American.

Table 4–1
United States Central Intelligence Agency (CIA)

Vision

We will provide knowledge and take action to ensure the national security of the United States and the preservation of American life and ideals.

Mission

We are the eyes and ears of the nation and at times its hidden hand. We accomplish this mission by:

- Collecting intelligence that matters.
- Providing relevant, timely, and objective all-source analysis.
- Conducting covert action at the direction of the president to preempt threats or achieve United States policy objectives.

Values

In pursuit of our country's interests, we put Nation before Agency, Agency before unit, and all before self. What we do matters.

- Our success depends on our ability to act with total discretion and an ability to protect sources and methods.
- We provide objective, unbiased information and analysis.
- Our mission requires complete personal integrity and personal courage, physical and intellectual.
- We accomplish things others cannot, often at great risk. When the stakes are highest and the dangers greatest, we are there and there first.
- We stand by one another and behind one another. Service, sacrifice, flexibility, teamwork, and quiet patriotism are our hallmarks.

Source: CIA Web site accessed May 25, 2010, at www.cia.gov/information/mission.html.

What is the role of vision in helping organizations succeed? As Figure 4–1 shows, success begins with a clear, compelling vision, a picture in the minds of the members of the organization of how things should and could be. Without vision, there is confusion. Also required are other important ingredients: skills, incentives, resources, and an action plan.

Vision as an Ideal

The word *vision* evokes pictures in the mind. It suggests a future orientation, implies a standard of excellence or virtuous condition, and has the quality of uniqueness. These are the elements that give life and strength to vision. Vision is an ideal image of what could and should be. The leader must ask three questions to test his or her vision: (1) Is this the right direction? (2) Are these the right goals? (3) Is this the right time? Then, the leader must share this vision and have it supported. Turn to page 65 and read and feel the power of the words of Martin Luther King, Jr., as he delivered his vision of civil rights before the Lincoln Memorial on August 28, 1963.[8]

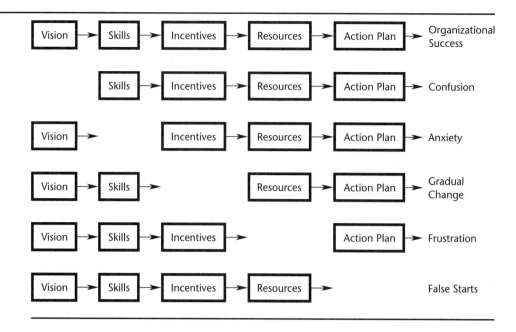

**Figure 4–1
Organizational Success[9]**

Leader as Visionary and Motivator of People

Management author Warren Bennis states that leaders must be clearly focused on a positive and future-focused goal or vision. Clarity of purpose provides guidance for making decisions about time and resources. Also required is constancy of effort. Passion and authority come to leaders who clearly know where they are going and have dedication to succeed. When leaders have passion and authority, others are inspired to follow.[10]

The role of leadership is to chart a direction that will motivate people. This is necessary at every level and walk of responsibility. Imagine a governor who says, "I can't create a vision till the president does," or a mayor who says, "I can't create a vision till the governor does," or a police chief who says, "I can't create a vision till the mayor does," or a captain who says, " I can't create a vision till the chief does." Every subordinate of every leader is thinking: And what about you? No matter how uncertain conditions are above the leader, the effective leader must create a clear and compelling vision of what should be done in his or her area of responsibility. Remember, if a vision is not clear in the leader's mind, it will be a perfect blur in the minds of subordinates.

Visions can be small or large and can exist at any organizational level. The important points are: (1) a vision is necessary for effective leadership; (2) a leader can develop a vision for any project, work group, or organization; and (3) many leaders fail because they do not have a vision—instead they focus on surviving on a day-by-day basis.[11]

Researchers Noel Tichy and Mary DeVanna describe how successful leaders help their organizations meet the challenge of change. The data from their interviews show that they use a three-act process: Act 1 is to recognize the need for change; act 2 is to create a clear and positive vision for the future; act 3 is to institute empowering structures and processes to achieve the vision.[12]

In a major study of leadership effectiveness, the Forum Corporation reports on the characteristics of successful leaders at middle to senior levels of responsibility. The study identifies three leadership qualities, analogous to Tichy and DeVanna's three-act process, that are needed for steering organizations through periods of change:

1. *Taking personal responsibility for initiating change.* A major function of the leader is to manage attention. The leader must be personally involved and committed to making a difference. Absolute identity with one's cause is the first condition of successful leadership.

I Have a Dream

Martin Luther King, Jr.

So I say to you, my friends, that even though we face the difficulties of today and tomorrow, I still have a dream. It is a dream deeply rooted in the American dream that one day this nation will rise up and live out the true meaning of its creed—we hold these truths to be self-evident, that all men are created equal.

I have a dream that one day on the red hills of Georgia, sons of former slaves and sons of former slaveowners will be able to sit down together at the table of brotherhood.

I have a dream that one day, even the state of Mississippi, a state sweltering with the heat of injustice, sweltering with the heat of oppression, will be transformed into an oasis of freedom and justice.

I have a dream my four little children will one day live in a nation where they will not be judged by the color of their skin, but by the content of their character. I have a dream today!

I have a dream that one day, down in Alabama, with its vicious racists, with its governor having his lips dripping with the words of interposition and nullification, that one day, right there in Alabama, little black boys and little black girls will be able to join hands with little white boys and little white girls as sisters and brothers. I have a dream today!

I have a dream that one day every valley shall be exalted, every hill and mountain shall be made low, the rough places shall be made plain, and the crooked places shall be made straight and the glory of the Lord will be revealed and all flesh shall see it together.

This is our hope. This is the faith with which I return to the South. With this faith we will be able to transform the jangling discords of our nation into a beautiful symphony of brotherhood. With this faith we will be able to work together, to pray together, to struggle together, to go to jail together, to stand up for freedom together, knowing that we will be free one day.

This will be the day when all God's children will be able to sing with new meaning, "My country 'tis of thee, sweet land of liberty, of thee I sing. Land where my fathers died, land of the pilgrim's pride, from every mountainside, let freedom ring."

And if America is to be a great nation this must become true.

So let freedom ring from the prodigious hilltops of New Hampshire.

Let freedom ring from the mighty mountains of New York.

Let freedom ring from the heightening Alleghenies of Pennsylvania.

Let freedom ring from the snow-capped Rockies of Colorado.

Let freedom ring from the curvaceous slopes of California.

But not only that.

Let freedom ring from Stone Mountain of Georgia.

Let freedom ring from Lookout Mountain of Tennessee.

Let freedom ring from every hill and molehill of Mississippi, from every mountainside, let freedom ring.

And when we let freedom ring, when we let it ring from every village and hamlet, from every state and city, we will be able to speed up that day when all of God's children—black men and white men, Jews and Gentiles, Catholics and Protestants—will be able to join hands and to sing in the words of the old Negro spiritual, "Free at last, free at last; thank God Almighty, we are free at last."

2. *Creating a vision and strategy for the organization.* The vision and strategy must be **leader-initiated, shared and supported by followers, comprehensive and detailed,** and above all, worth doing. The leader must create a vision that is **uplifting** and **inspiring to others.**

3. *Trusting and supporting others.* The leader must treat people with respect and dignity, expecting the best in effort and personal responsibility, and showing sincere appreciation for work performed. The leader combines individual incentive with group success as an important empowerment principle.[13]

Key findings of the Forum study are summarized as follows:

- *Leadership is important from the boardroom to the shop floor.* In a sense, the leadership chain is as strong as its weakest link. Without effective leadership at every level of responsibility, frontline employees and, ultimately, customers are bound to suffer.

- *Positions and titles have little or no relationship to leadership performance.* People are often skeptical of authority figures. New leaders have to earn the trust and respect of subordinates; otherwise, people will resist their efforts to lead. Indeed, workers with strong leadership skills can inspire their peers as well as any chief executive could.

- *Without leadership, organizations falter in times of change.* This situation is analogous to that of a car without an engine or a ship without a rudder. The organization will be dormant, or a terrible crash will occur as the group goes in the wrong direction.

- *Organizational leadership involves interdependence more than individualism.* The genius stroke of the independent contributor is important; but more important for organizational leadership are relationship skills, such as demonstrating concern for members of the work group, recognizing other peoples' contributions, and building enthusiasm about projects and assignments.

- *Leaders inspire others to take on the tasks of leadership.* Giving others the power and encouragement to make decisions frees the leader from the role of controller, liberating critical time and energy for charting and shaping the overall future of the organization.

- *Leadership is contextual.* Effective leadership requires an understanding of the forces and events that have shaped an industry, a company, or a work group; an assessment of organizational strengths, weaknesses, opportunities, and threats; and the development of a plan to meet current and future challenges. Understanding, assessment, and plans are specific to the organization and its environment.[14]

Leadership Effectiveness

The following questionnaire (Exercise 4–1) can be used to evaluate your leadership effectiveness (or the effectiveness of a leader you know).

**Exercise 4–1
Leadership
Assessment**[15]

The following 20 practices cluster into four distinct areas that correlate positively with leadership effectiveness. Using a scale from 1 to 10 (1 is low; 10 is high), evaluate yourself (or a leader you know) on each practice in the following four areas.

Getting the Facts

The effective leader gains insight into the realities of the world and into him- or herself. This process includes getting the facts and interpreting conditions affecting the group. Rate each item separately (from 1 to 10).

1. Determining the facts by seeking information from as many sources as possible—library, field, lab, and so on. _____
2. Learning the challenges facing the group, including internal strengths and weaknesses, as well as external opportunities and threats for meeting these challenges. _____
3. Knowing the capabilities and motivations of the individuals in the group. _____
4. Analyzing how well the members of the group work together. _____
5. Knowing the leader's own capabilities and motivations. _____

Add your ratings and divide by 5 for an overall score on *getting the facts.* Circle that score on the scale below.

1	2	3	4	5	6	7	8	9	10

Creating a Vision

The effective leader develops a vision and a strategy to give meaning to the group's work, thus providing purpose and clarity of direction. Rate each item separately (from 1 to 10).

1. Standing up for what is important, including basic principles or core values. _____
2. Involving the right people in developing the group's vision and strategy. _____
3. Creating a clear and positive picture of the future of the group. _____
4. Developing a strategy for the success of the group, including clarity of individual and group assignments. _____
5. Adjusting plans and actions as necessary based on changing conditions. _____

Add your ratings and divide by 5 for an overall score on *creating a vision.* Circle that score on the scale below.

1	2	3	4	5	6	7	8	9	10

Motivating People

The effective leader is a motivator, possessing the ability to mobilize individuals with different ideas, skills, and values to achieve a common mission. Rate each item separately (from 1 to 10).

1. Appealing to people's hearts and minds to accomplish a worthy endeavor. _____
2. Communicating clearly the high standards and performance results expected from others. _____
3. Demonstrating concern for members of the group. _____
4. Showing confidence in the abilities of others. _____
5. Letting people know how they are progressing toward the group's goals, including giving recognition when milestones are reached. _____

Add your ratings and divide by 5 for an overall score on *motivating people.* Circle that score on the scale below.

1	2	3	4	5	6	7	8	9	10

Empowering Others

The effective leader has the ability to increase effectiveness by sharing power, thus igniting the energy and liberating the talent of the group. Rate each item separately (from 1 to 10).

1. Recognizing the contributions of others, for example, through performance awards, letters of commendation, and personal appreciation. _____

2. Promoting the development of people's abilities, by providing training and challenging assignments. _____

3. Enabling others to feel and act like leaders. _____

4. Stimulating others' thinking and creativity by soliciting suggestions and ideas. _____

5. Building enthusiasm about projects and assignments, especially through personal involvement. _____

Add your ratings and divide by 5 for an overall score on *empowering others.* Circle that score on the scale below.

1	2	3	4	5	6	7	8	9	10

Scoring and Interpretation:

Add the overall scores for all four areas to determine your leadership effectiveness.

Total Score	Evaluation
37–40	Excellent; your leadership effectiveness is outstanding.
28–36	Very good; your effectiveness as a leader is high.
17–27	Average; you are neither high nor low in your overall leadership effectiveness.
8–16	Below average; your effectiveness as a leader is low.
4–7	Failing; much work is needed to improve.

A useful exercise is for the leader to compare his or her self-evaluation on the leadership assessment with the evaluations of constituents or colleagues. Points of agreement and disagreement can be explored, and actions can be taken to improve as needed.

The Concept of Visioning

The importance of *vision* is an old idea, first stated in the Bible: "Where there is no vision, the people perish" (Proverbs 29:18, King James Version).

Henry David Thoreau describes the importance of having a vision and striving to attain it: "If one advances confidently in the direction of his dreams, and endeavors to live the life which he has imagined, he will meet with a success unexpected in common hours."[16]

The concept of visioning as it is used in organizations today is credited to Ronald Lippitt, who, as early as 1949, began referring to "images of potential" rather than to "problems" as starting points for change.[17] Management author Stephen Covey identifies certain process, content, and application principles that have been found to be effective in creating a vision.

Visioning Process Principles

1. *Initiate and provide constant vigilance by leaders.* It is the proper role of leadership to begin the process, to discuss and articulate the basis for developing a vision, and to start drafting a document. This effort begins the top-down portion of the visioning process.

2. *Be challenging, yet realistic.* Set the mark high, but stay in touch with reality. A vision should stretch the abilities of the organization but not destroy its members.

3. *Seek significant early involvement by other members of the organization.* This aspect includes discussing, writing, and rewriting the vision. In this joint-effort phase, senior leaders, in effect, say, "We've begun—but we need your input. Your involvement is essential."

4. *Encourage widespread review and comment.* Include as many people as possible. This bottom-up period of review invites critical analysis. Here, leaders are saying, "We've worked hard on this and like it—but what do you think? Give us your ideas. We want this to belong to everyone." Be open and show appreciation for suggestions. Incorporate modifications and the best thinking of all respondents. Involvement fosters commitment.

5. *Keep communications flowing.* Don't assume everyone knows what is going on. Report on progress for developing the vision. Give acknowledgment and appreciation, and report on the adoption of elements of the vision—agreement on purpose, broad goals, core values, stakeholders, strategic initiatives, and so on. Provide feedback as achievements are made toward attaining goals.

6. *Allow time for the process to work.* People need time to think about and adjust to change, even positive change. The development of a vision may take longer than people expect. Top leaders may spend weeks on the original draft, months on the involvement and feedback process, and a year or more to finish the product.

7. *Demonstrate commitment, follow-through, and concurrent action by leaders.* Leaders must make reality match rhetoric. Any sincere effort to put words into action will lend credibility and will reinforce the actual attainment of the vision.

8. *Maintain harmony of subunits.* The content of the vision statements for subunits (such as divisions, plants, departments, and work teams) should be in harmony with the overall vision of the organization.[18]

Visioning Content Principles

Key elements of an overall vision or strategic plan typically include the following:

1. *Central purpose or mission (reason for existence).* This is a clear, compelling statement of purpose that provides focus and direction. It is the organization's answer to the question, Why do we exist?

2. *Broad goals to achieve the mission (enduring intentions to act).* These are process or functional accomplishments that must be met to achieve the mission.

3. *Core values to measure the rightness and wrongness of behavior (hills worth dying on).* Sometimes called operating principles, core values such as truth, trust, and respect define the moral tone or character of the organization.

4. *Stakeholders and what the attainment of the vision will mean to them (the human element).* These are the people who will be affected by what the organization does or does not do.

5. *Analysis of the organization and its environment, including internal Strengths and Weaknesses, as well as external Opportunities and Threats.* This is a **SWOT**

assessment of current conditions that must be both thorough and objective. Information that is unknown and facts that are denied will hinder and can even destroy an organization.

   6. *Strategic initiatives (sometimes called critical success factors).* These are short-term, intermediate, and long-term objectives necessary to achieve the goals and mission. They may be person- or group-specific, or may involve all members of the organization. They are strategic, measurable, action-oriented, realistic, and timely, with dates or numbers to measure accomplishment.

   7. *Tactical plans and specific assignments (projects and activities) to support strategic initiatives, broad goals, and the attainment of the mission.* These projects and activities serve as guides in performance planning for units and members of the organization, and constitute the plan of work.

   Elements 1 through 4 provide *general direction* for the organization. Adding elements 5 and 6 involves *strategic planning.* This gives definition to the vision and focuses people and resources on specific objectives that can be measured. Element 7, *tactical planning,* refers to projects and activities designed to implement strategy, the plays that drive the game to success. Tactical planning results in group- and person-specific assignments and concrete actions.[19]

   An important goal in the SWOT analysis is to identify core competencies in the form of special *strengths* the organization has or does exceptionally well. These can become sources of competitive advantage. Core competencies may be found in efficient manufacturing technologies, special product knowledge or expertise, or unique distribution systems, among many other possibilities. Another goal is to identify *opportunities* in the environment that the organization can act upon. Examples include new technologies, strategic alliances, and possible new markets for products and services. See Figure 4–2.

Visioning Application Principles

   1. *Honor and live the vision as the organization's constitution.* The values and principles of the vision, not the personal style of individuals, should govern organizational culture and behavior.

   2. *Encourage new-member understanding and commitment through early introduction.* Those not involved in the development process can identify with the vision

Figure 4–2
SWOT Analysis of Organizational Strengths and Weaknesses and Environmental Opportunities and Threats[20]

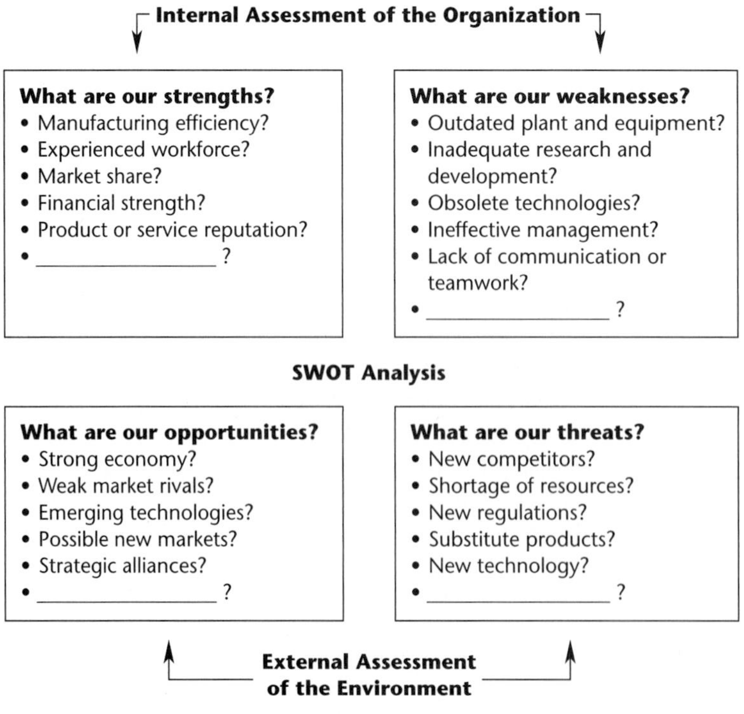

from the first association: "This is what we are all about; if you can embrace this mission and these values as your own, then we may join together." The vision should be the centerpiece of the orientation program for all new members.

3. *Make it constantly visible.* Express constancy of purpose through a written statement. The vision should be publicized to customers, employees, suppliers, owners—everyone.

4. *Create integrity through alignment and congruency.* Use the vision as a leadership tool and decision-making guide; as a checkpoint to test alignment of strategy, structures, systems, and member behavior; and as a means to track progress.

5. *Reinforce employee behavior that supports the vision.* This encourages similar behavior that helps the vision be achieved.

6. *Review the vision periodically, revising as appropriate to reflect changing conditions.* Even the U.S. Constitution has been amended over the long term. View the vision as a program with people as the programmers.[21]

The process of creating a vision must be tailored to each organization to be most effective. The process, content, and application principles are guidelines to achieve the required objective—agreement on direction and commitment to succeed.

The Importance of Alignment and Prioritization

Vision is important and execution is critical. Both are essential for organizational success. From vision to execution, the stories of great organizations (when they are great) are stories of alignment. Sam Walton aligned every resource of Walmart to support *the box* (his stores). Ray Kroc aligned every process at McDonald's to deliver *quality, service, cleanliness, and value*. Walt Disney aligned every practice of his company to bring *wholesome entertainment* to children and their families. Fred Smith aligned every structure and system of FedEx to *deliver the package on time*. These great leaders knew the attainment of their vision would require integrity through alignment and congruency.[22] Practically speaking, alignment means making sure organizational structure and employee behavior support the purpose and values of the organization. Ray Kroc was famous for saying, "If we've got time to lean, we've got time to clean," thus emphasizing a core McDonald's value.

The following story shows how important it is to set priorities:

When he was president of Bethlehem Steel, Charles Schwab called Ivy Lee, a consultant, and said, "Show me a way to get more things done with my time, and I'll pay you any fee within reason."

"Fine," Lee replied. "I'll give you something in twenty minutes that will step up your output at least fifty percent."

With that, Lee handed Schwab a blank piece of paper, and said: "Write down the six most important tasks that you have to do tomorrow, and number them in order of their importance. Then put this paper in your pocket, and the first thing tomorrow morning look at item one and start working on it until you finish it. Then do item two, and so on. Do this until quitting time, and don't be concerned if you have finished only one or two items. You'll be working on the most important ones first anyway. If you can't finish them all by this method, you couldn't have by any other method either; and without some system, you'd probably not even have decided which was the most important."

Then Lee said: "Try this system every working day. After you've convinced yourself of the value of the system, have your employees try it. Try it as long as you wish, and then send me a check for what you think it is worth."

Several weeks later, Schwab sent Lee a check for $25,000 with a note proclaiming the advice to be the most profitable he had ever followed. This concept helped Charles Schwab earn $100 million and turn Bethlehem Steel into the biggest independent steel producer in the world.

You may think Charles Schwab was foolish to pay $25,000 for such a simple idea. However, Schwab thought of that consulting fee as one of his best investments. "Sure, it was a simple idea," Schwab said. "But what ideas are not basically simple? For the first time, my entire team and I are getting first things done first."[23]

Use a to-do list to accomplish organizational goals. Write down what you want to accomplish in order of importance. The small amount of time you invest in doing this will repay you many times over. A point to remember: Make sure your to-do list is readily visible; it should be where you are—in the office or on the road.

Why Create a Vision?

Peter Drucker explains the importance of having a vision:

Because the modern organization is composed of specialists, each with his or her own narrow area of expertise, its purpose must be crystal clear. The organization must be single-minded, or its members will become confused. They will follow their own specialty rather than apply it to the common task. They will each define "results" in terms of their own specialty and impose its values on the organization. Only a focused and shared vision will hold an organization together and enable it to produce. Without agreement on purpose and values, the organization will soon lose credibility and, with it, its ability to attract the very people it needs to perform.[24]

Management authors James Collins and Jerry Porras report on the business benefits of having a vision. They asked a sample of CEOs from Fortune 500 and INC 100 companies to identify "visionary" organizations. For the 20 companies most frequently selected, they "invested" one dollar in stock in 1926 or whenever the firm was first listed. They found that, as a group, these visionary companies performed 55 times better than the general market. They also compared visionary companies with nonvisionary counterparts—companies that started at the same time—such as Motorola and Zenith, and Disney and Columbia. Again, vision-driven companies proved more successful, performing 8 times better than their competitors.[25]

Occupying center stage in explaining the importance of vision is author and educator Joel Barker. Barker's ideas are drawn primarily from three individuals—Frederick Polak, Benjamin Singer, and Viktor Frankl.[26]

Historian Frederick Polak asked this question: Is a nation's positive image of its future the consequence of its success, or is a nation's success the consequence of its positive image of the future? He concluded that the fates of nations and civilizations have depended primarily on their visions for the future. He cites examples in history of ancient Greece, Rome, Spain, England, and America to support this thought. Polak makes three main points: (1) Significant vision precedes significant success; (2) a compelling image of the future is shared by leaders with their followers, and together they strive to make this vision a reality; and (3) a nation with vision is enabled, and a nation without vision is at risk.[27]

Psychologist Benjamin Singer showed how children's lives are similarly shaped by positive self-concepts and expectations for the future. Children without vision become powerless, feeling no control over their own futures. Children with vision are focused and energized, and these are strong and positive agents in a self-fulfilling prophecy. Adults should always take seriously a child's dreams of what he or she wants to be. The interest and support shown communicates the message that the child is worthy and his or her future is important.[28] Consider the power of vision for one child, somehow conveyed by her father:

I was fourteen years old the night my daddy died. He had holes in his shoes but two children out of college, one in college, another in divinity school, and a vision he was able to convey to me as he lay dying in an ambulance that I, a young black girl, could be and do anything; that race and gender are shadows; and that character, self-discipline, determination, attitude and service are the substance of life.[29]

Barker believes that what is true for nations and what is true for children is especially true for organizations, because organizations have the ideal size and complexity to put vision's power into practice.

The third individual who influenced Barker was Viktor Frankl, author of *Man's Search for Meaning,* based on his experiences in the Nazi death camps of World War II. Frankl believed that everyone needs a purpose or meaning in life, something important yet to be done. Often this can be attained in the experience and achievements of one's work. Frankl also believed that everything we do goes down in history and, in this sense, is irretrievable. As *The Rubáiyát of Omar Khayyám* states:[30] The Moving Finger writes; and having writ, / Moves on: Nor all your Piety nor Wit / Shall lure it back to cancel Half a Line, / Nor all your Tears wash out a Word of it.

In Frankl's view, meaning that transcends oneself and extends to people and ideals beyond the individual is meaning on its highest and most human plane. Just as an airplane is most like an airplane when it rises from the runway and flies, so are we most human when we seek meaning in our lives, and commit to a purpose or mission that transcends the self.[31]

Requirements for an Effective Vision

The requirements for an effective vision are as follows:[32]

■ *First, a vision must be developed by leaders, those individuals with strength and influence to establish direction and mobilize the organization.* Leadership is dreaming a dream and then making it come true. Leaders create clear and worthy images that motivate the organization, and then create a climate so that ideas are transformed into deeds. Leadership is commitment to purpose along with persistence to see it through. The leader's vision should appeal to a common good and be believed passionately. Of six characteristics common to peak performers, management author Charles Garfield describes as the most important commitment to a mission that motivates.[33]

■ *Second, a vision must be communicated to followers and must be supported by them.* Leaders have to let others see, hear, taste, touch, and feel their vision. A picture in the mind of the general is merely that until it is understood in the minds and adopted in the hearts of the soldiers. Only then will hands and feet be activated and the vision be implemented in fact. It may take leadership to articulate and give legitimacy to a vision, but it takes the strength of an empowered people to get things done. In this regard, the vision of leaders must be in harmony with the nature and needs of the people. Authors James Kouzes and Barry Posner write, "Constituents want visions of the future that reflect their own aspirations. They want to hear how their dreams will come true and their hopes fulfilled."[34]

■ *Third, a vision must be comprehensive and detailed, so that every member of the organization can understand his or her part in the whole.* Roles and responsibilities must be well understood if the vision is to be fulfilled. Each person must know what is expected and the rewards that will accrue when the vision is achieved. Put yourself in the shoes of the soldier, who, upon hearing the vision and seeing the battle plan of the general, can't help wondering, Yes, but what about me? A clear line of sight between personal effort and personal reward is a major determinant of the ultimate fulfillment of the vision.[35]

■ *Fourth, a vision must be uplifting and inspiring.* It must be worth the effort; it must be big enough. Relating to Frankl's message that every person needs meaning in life and something important yet to be done, the organization's vision must be meaningful and important for the members to do.[36] Psychologist Abraham Maslow once remarked, "If you purposefully choose to be less than you can be, then you are surely doomed to be unhappy."[37] The same is true for organizations; the members of an organization must seek to achieve the organization's fullest potential.

Social Motives to Lead

Someone must provide the spark for action; someone must provide energy and purpose for leadership to occur. There are three basic motives for leadership: (1) **power**—the desire to have influence, give orders, and have them carried out; (2) **achievement**—the need to create and build something of value; and (3) **affiliation**—a heartfelt interest in helping others.

To understand the role of social motives at work, imagine three supervisors given the task of building a house: (1) The power-oriented leader focuses on how to organize the production of the house. She feels comfortable being in charge and enjoys being recognized as the powerful figure who causes the house to be produced. (2) The achievement-oriented leader obtains satisfaction from creating the house. Building a sound structure and completing the task on time is rewarding. (3) The affiliation leader enjoys working with his crew. He is concerned with human relations and strives to create a spirit of teamwork. Also, he is pleased to think of how much the home will mean to the family who lives in it.

Why would you want to be a leader? What would be your purpose for assuming the challenge of leadership? Do your job and personal life allow the expression of your social motives? The questionnaire in Exercise 4–2 will help you answer these questions. Remember three important points about scores on the questionnaire:

■ Although it is normal for everyone to have some of each social motive, a person usually will prefer one or two over the others. Preference depends on the values (power, achievement, or affiliation) promoted by one's culture and on personal traits and experiences.

■ People exert leadership to satisfy one or a combination of these three motives. All leadership can be said to be motivated by power, achievement, or affiliation.

■ As either leader or follower, a person will be most happy and productive in a situation that allows the expression of personal social motives. If an individual's work precludes this, morale and productivity can be expected to go down.

Exercise 4–2
Social Motives in the Work Setting[38]

This questionnaire consists of 12 statements. There are no right or wrong answers. For each statement, indicate which of the three alternatives—a., b., or c.—is most preferred by or most important to you by placing a 3 next to that choice. Place a 2 by your second choice and a 1 by the choice that is least preferred by or least important to you. Do not debate too long over any one statement. Your first reaction is desired.

1. In a work situation, I want to
   _____ a. be in charge.
   _____ b. give assistance to my co-workers.
   _____ c. come up with new ideas.

2. If I have ultimate responsibility for a project, I
   _____ a. depend on my own ability to accomplish tasks.
   _____ b. delegate work and oversee progress.
   _____ c. use teamwork to accomplish tasks.

3. My co-workers see me as
   _____ a. a competent person.
   _____ b. a considerate person.
   _____ c. a forceful person.

4. When I disagree with a decision, I
   _____ a. voice my disapproval immediately.
   _____ b. take into consideration other peoples' feelings and circumstances.
   _____ c. suggest alternatives based on logic.

5. In a group discussion,
   _____ a. I encourage others to express themselves.
   _____ b. I will change my view only if a better one is suggested.
   _____ c. my ideas generally prevail.

6. In a labor–management dispute, I would
   _____ a. keep human relations smooth.
   _____ b. maintain a position of strength.
   _____ c. work for a compromise.

7. I am most satisfied with my job when I
   _____ a. see progress being made.
   _____ b. have a strong voice in determining policy.
   _____ c. work with others to achieve results.

8. When disagreements arise, I usually
   _____ a. yield a point to avoid conflict.
   _____ b. stick to my guns.
   _____ c. use reasoning to seek the best solution.

9. As a leader, I would
   _____ a. permit flexibility, as long as the job gets done.
   _____ b. recognize that workers have good days and bad days.
   _____ c. insist on compliance with my rules and directions.

10. As a member of the board of directors dealing with a problem, I would most likely
   _____ a. try to get my ideas adopted.
   _____ b. solicit ideas from all members.
   _____ c. review the facts.

11. When hiring a new employee, I would
   _____ a. expect future loyalty to me.
   _____ b. hire the person who is technically best qualified.
   _____ c. take into consideration future relations with co-workers.

12. I am most happy in my work if I

_____ a. am the decision maker.

_____ b. work with good friends and colleagues.

_____ c. make significant achievements.

Scoring:

Step 1:

Scoring is done across the page, from left to right. For each question, put your a., b., and c. scores in the appropriate columns. Note that a., b., and c. scores do not remain in the same columns. Continue until all scores are filled in; then total the columns. (The grand total for the three columns should be 72.)

Column 1	Column 2	Column 3
1. a._____	1. c._____	1. b._____
2. b._____	2. a._____	2. c._____
3. c._____	3. a._____	3. b._____
4. a._____	4. c._____	4. b._____
5. c._____	5. b._____	5. a._____
6. b._____	6. c._____	6. a._____
7. b._____	7. a._____	7. c._____
8. b._____	8. c._____	8. a._____
9. c._____	9. a._____	9. b._____
10. a._____	10. c._____	10. b._____
11. a._____	11. b._____	11. c._____
12. a._____	12. c._____	12. b._____
Total _____	Total _____	Total _____

Step 2:

Mark the total scores for each column in the appropriate places in Figure 4–3. Shade in the areas as shown in the example, Figure 4–4.

Interpretation:

A high score in column 1 indicates social motives that are power-oriented. A power-oriented person strives for leadership because of the authority it brings. This person's goal is to influence people and events. Historical examples are Winston Churchill and Elizabeth I, who are recognized as outstanding leaders because of their mastery of power politics. Strength, assertiveness, and dominance are characteristics of power-oriented leaders. Positions involving the expression of power are manager, supervisor, and political officeholder.

A high score in column 2 indicates achievement-oriented social motives. This type of leader wants to discover, create, and build. Marie Curie and Tim Berners-Lee are good examples of achievement-oriented people, each succeeding in making valuable contributions to humankind in science and technology. Achievement-oriented leaders are described as successful, competent, skillful, and productive. Achievement-oriented people are often found in occupations such as science, business, and the arts.

A high score in column 3 indicates a strong concern for human welfare. Mother Teresa and Mahatma Gandhi would be such leaders. These individuals care about other people and desire to serve humanity. This type of leader is likely to have traits similar to those of Florence Nightingale and Albert Schweitzer in the field of medicine. Common characteristics of these leaders are helpfulness, unselfishness, and consideration of the condition and well-being of others. Occupations such as teaching and counseling allow the expression of this social motive.

The basic needs that motivate leaders serve to motivate the employees in a company as well. Consider how you as a leader can use an employee's primary need as a motivating force:

1. *The need for power.* These employees gain satisfaction from influencing others. They like to lead and persuade, and are motivated by positions of power. They are comfortable with argumentation and debate, and are not reluctant in advancing their views. Give them the opportunity to make decisions and direct projects.

2. *The need for achievement.* These employees want the satisfaction of accomplishing projects successfully. They want to exercise their talents to attain success. They desire unambiguous feedback on performance and recognition for their accomplishments. They are self-motivated if the job is challenging enough, so provide them with meaningful work assignments and they will consistently produce.

3. *The need for affiliation.* These employees gain satisfaction from interacting with others. They enjoy people and find the social aspects of the workplace rewarding. They actively support others and try to smooth out workplace conflicts. Motivate them by giving them opportunities to interact with others: team projects, group meetings, and so on.[39]

Figure 4–3
Your Social Motives

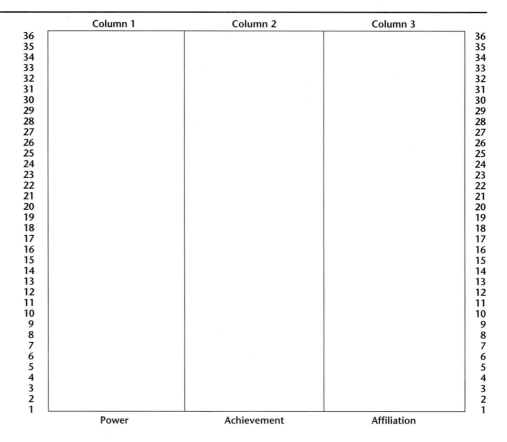

Figure 4–4
Example

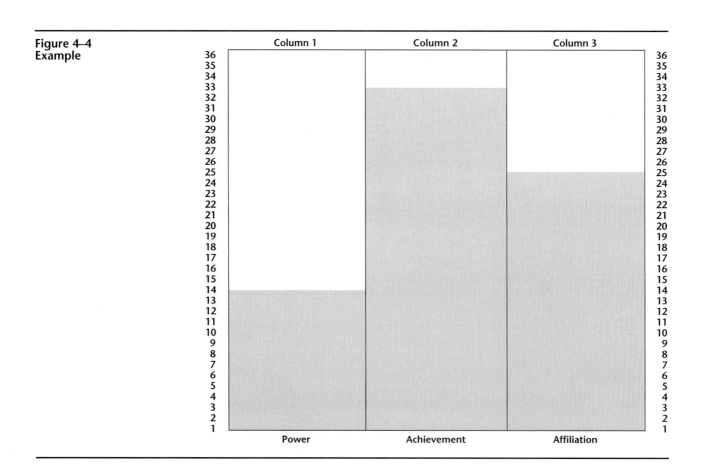

Organizational Climate

Most organizations resemble villages more than the finely honed, clearly focused structures they talk about in their annual reports—villages that are merging with other villages; villages that have become cross-cultural; villages that have richer and poorer parts of town. Organizations are like villages in that they have a certain pace and style of working and unspoken taboos. Organizations have social structures, pecking orders, and patterns of behavior, including habits governing dress, language, food, and the like. Established norms of behavior govern use of resources. Artifacts of the organizational village are its physical structures, rituals, stories, and legends, and these are based on shared and deeply held assumptions, beliefs, and values. An important element in the life of the organizational village is its psychological climate.[40]

Even if an organization has a vision that is leader-initiated, member-supported, comprehensive and detailed, and worth doing, it must be sustained by a supportive organizational climate. Important dimensions include the *reward system, organizational clarity, standards of performance, warmth and support,* and *leadership practices.* An evaluation of these and other dimensions of organizational climate can be used to determine whether that organization is exploitive, impoverished, supportive, or enlightened. Keep in mind the following points:

■ Just as sick societies can make people sick, so can an unhealthy work climate make employees sick. In contrast, a psychologically healthy work environment brings out the best in employee and organizational well-being.[41]

■ An organization is only as strong as its weakest link. An individual may have an excellent nervous system, sound muscular system, and good respiratory system, but if the circulation system is poor, ultimately, the whole organism will fail. Similarly, an organization may be strong in performance standards, organizational clarity, and warmth and support, but if the reward system is poor, the entire organization will ultimately suffer.

■ Organizational climate is important because it influences both the quality of work and the quality of work life of members. Depending on the nature of the group or organization, even life-and-death consequences can result.

Consider an exploitive or impoverished hospital: People who can find employment elsewhere will probably leave, and those may be some of the best personnel. People who remain may spend more time complaining about working conditions and management practices than actually doing their work, with the result being unattended patients, poor housekeeping, and medical and clerical errors. Exploitive and impoverished hospitals experience unnecessary mistakes due to human factors—untrained, unqualified, and uncommitted workers.

Now consider an enlightened or supportive hospital, where standards of performance are high, leadership is effective, goals and responsibilities are clear, warmth and support prevail, and the reward system reinforces good work. Given a choice, where would you want to be treated, and where would you want to work? Which type of organization provides the best quality of health care and the best quality of work life?

■ Enlightened and supportive organizations represent good investments because they attract excellent personnel, who usually outperform their demoralized counterparts in exploitive and impoverished organizations.

■ Organizations are composed of interdependent groups. The success of the total organization depends on conditions in each of its subgroups. As such, every division and unit should develop an enlightened or supportive climate.

You can evaluate the climate of your organization by completing the questionnaire in Exercise 5–1.

**Exercise 5–1
Organizational Climate
Questionnaire[42]**

For each dimension of organizational climate, circle the number on the scale that represents conditions in your organization (1 is low; 20 is high).

1. **Reward system**—the degree to which people are recognized and rewarded for good work, rather than being ignored, criticized, or punished when something goes wrong.

    1   2   3   4   5   6   7   8   9   10   11   12   13   14   15   16   17   18   19   20

    Rewards are not in line with   Effort and performance are
    effort and performance.   recognized and rewarded positively.

2. **Organizational clarity**—the feeling that things are well organized and that goals and responsibilities are clearly defined, rather than being disorderly, confused, or chaotic.

    1   2   3   4   5   6   7   8   9   10   11   12   13   14   15   16   17   18   19   20

    The organization is disorderly,   The organization is well organized, with
    confused, and chaotic.   clearly defined goals and responsibilities.

3. **Standards of performance**—the emphasis placed on quality performance and achievement of results, including the degree to which meaningful and challenging goals are set at every level of the organization.

    1   2   3   4   5   6   7   8   9   10   11   12   13   14   15   16   17   18   19   20

    Performance standards are low.   Performance standards are high.

4. **Warmth and support**—the feeling that friendliness is a valued norm and that people trust, respect, and support one another; the feeling that good relationships prevail in the day-to-day work of the organization.

    1   2   3   4   5   6   7   8   9   10   11   12   13   14   15   16   17   18   19   20

    There is little warmth and support   Warmth and support are
    in the organization.   characteristic of the organization.

5. **Leadership**—the extent to which people take leadership roles as the need arises and are rewarded for successful leadership; the willingness of people to accept leadership and direction from others who are qualified. The organization is not dominated by or dependent on just one or two individuals.

    1   2   3   4   5   6   7   8   9   10   11   12   13   14   15   16   17   18   19   20

    Leadership is not provided, accepted, or   Leadership is provided, accepted, and
    rewarded; the organization is dominated by rewarded based on expertise.
    or dependent on one or two individuals.

6. **Communication**—the degree to which important information is shared—up, down, and sideways. Communication channels are open and free-flowing between levels and areas of the organization.

    1   2   3   4   5   6   7   8   9   10   11   12   13   14   15   16   17   18   19   20

    Information is incorrect or unavailable.   Information is accurate and available.

7. **Innovation**—the extent to which new ideas are sought and used in all areas of the organization. Creativity is encouraged at every level of responsibility.

    1   2   3   4   5   6   7   8   9   10   11   12   13   14   15   16   17   18   19   20

    The organization is closed   The organization is innovative
    and unresponsive to new ideas.   and open to new ideas.

8. **Feedback and controls**—the use of reporting, comparing, and correcting procedures, such as performance evaluations and financial audits. Controls are used for tracking progress and solving problems, as opposed to policing and punishment.

    1   2   3   4   5   6   7   8   9   10   11   12   13   14   15   16   17   18   19   20

    Controls are used for policing   Controls are used to provide
    and punishment.   guidance and solve problems.

9. **Teamwork**—the amount of understanding, cooperation, and support demonstrated between different levels and groups in the organization.

1	2	3	4	5	6	7	8	9	10	11	12	13	14	15	16	17	18	19	20

Teamwork is low.   Teamwork is high.

10. **Involvement**—the extent to which responsibility for decision making is broadly shared in the organization. People are involved in decisions that affect them.

1	2	3	4	5	6	7	8	9	10	11	12	13	14	15	16	17	18	19	20

There is little participation   Participation in decision making is high.
in decision making.

Scoring:

Total the scores for all the dimensions; then divide by 10. Circle that number on the scale below.

Type of Organization

1 2 3 4 5	6 7 8 9 10	11 12 13 14 15	16 17 18 19 20
Exploitive	Impoverished	Supportive	Enlightened

Interpretation:

Results of this questionnaire can be used to reinforce strengths and improve weaknesses. High scores represent enlightened and supportive organizations. Low scores reflect exploitive and impoverished organizations.

Leaders and followers may have different views about the climate of a group or organization. People in upper levels of responsibility often evaluate conditions more favorably than do people in lower levels. See the example in Figure 5–1.

**Figure 5–1
Extent to Which Leaders and Followers Agree on Organizational Conditions[43]**

Behavior	Top Staff Self-Evaluation*	First-Line Supervisor Evaluation of Top Staff Behavior	First-Line Supervisor Self-Evaluation**	Employee Evaluation of First-Line Supervisor Behavior
Always tells subordinates in advance about changes that will affect them or their work	70%	27%	40%	22%
Nearly always tells subordinates	30%	36%	52%	25%
(grouped totals)	100%	63%	92%	47%
More often than not tells subordinates	—	18%	2%	13%
Occasionally tells subordinates	—	15%	5%	28%
Seldom tells subordinates	—	4%	1%	12%

*Top staff rated themselves 37% higher than they were rated by subordinates.
**First-line supervisors rated themselves 45% higher than they were rated by subordinates.

Patterns of Leadership

How do organizations become what they are? Who decides whether an organization will be enlightened, supportive, impoverished, or exploitive? Although members may have considerable influence, organizational climate is determined primarily by leaders. Those in charge establish the character and define norms of behaviors.

Management author Rensis Likert identifies four patterns of leadership that correspond to the four types of organizational climate. His conclusions are based on studies of thousands of leaders in widely different kinds of organizations, both inside and outside the United States. A description of each of the four patterns of leadership follows.[44]

Pattern I Leadership (Exploitive)

Exploitive leadership is autocratic and hierarchical, with virtually no participation by members. Leaders make decisions, and members are expected to comply without question. Leaders show little confidence or trust in others, and members do not feel free to discuss job-related problems with leaders. In a free social and economic order, Pattern I organizations rarely survive because people avoid them as much as possible. Where they do exist, they are characterized by a lack of loyalty and recurrent financial crises.

Pattern II Leadership (Impoverished)

Impoverished leadership makes some attempt to avoid being completely autocratic. Power remains at the top, but members are given occasional opportunities for participation in the decision-making process. Pattern II organizations fall into two categories that determine their relative success. Successful Pattern II organizations are benevolent autocracies in which leaders have genuine concern for the welfare of members. Failing Pattern II organizations are autocracies that do not consider the interests or ideas of members. Some organizations are founded by autocratic but benevolent leaders, who achieve good results. Then, as time passes and new leaders assume power, the autocratic style of leadership is maintained, but benevolence is not, and the organization fails.

Pattern III Leadership (Supportive)

Supportive leadership shows a great deal of interest and confidence in members. Power resides in leaders, but there is good communication and participation throughout the organization. People understand the goals of the organization, and commitment to achieve them is widespread. Members feel free to discuss job-related problems with leaders. This leadership pattern involves broad member participation and involvement in decision-making activities.

Pattern IV Leadership (Enlightened)

Enlightened leadership delegates power to the logical focus of interest and concern for a problem. People at all levels of the organization have a high degree of freedom to initiate, coordinate, and execute plans to accomplish goals. Communication is open, honest, and uncensored. People are treated with trust rather than suspicion. Leaders ask for ideas and try to use others' suggestions. Pattern IV leadership results in high satisfaction and productivity. Absenteeism and turnover are low, strikes are nonexistent, and efficiency is high.

Likert describes the Pattern IV organization as follows:

A Pattern IV organization is made up of interlocking work groups with a high degree of group loyalty among the members and favorable attitudes among peers, supervisors, and subordinates.

Consideration for others and skill in problem solving and other group functions are present. These skills permit effective participation in decisions on common problems. Participation is used, for example, to establish objectives that are a satisfactory integration of the needs of all the members of the organization.

Members of the Pattern IV organization are highly motivated to achieve the organization's goals. High levels of reciprocal influence occur, and a high level of coordination is achieved in the organization.

Communication is efficient and effective. There is a flow from one part of the organization to another of all the relevant information important for each decision and action.

The leadership in the Pattern IV organization has developed an effective system for interaction, problem solving, and organizational achievement. This leadership is technically competent and maintains high performance goals.[45]

Four principles should be followed to develop an enlightened, Pattern IV organization:

1. *View human resources as the organization's greatest asset.*
2. *Treat every individual with understanding, dignity, warmth, and support.*
3. *Tap the constructive power of groups through visioning and team building.*
4. *Set high performance goals at every level of the organization.*[46]

Likert recommends that all organizations adopt the enlightened principles of Pattern IV leadership. He estimates that U.S. organizations, as a whole, are between Pattern II and Pattern III, and that a shift to Pattern IV would improve employee morale and productivity by 20 to 40 percent, or more.[47]

Research supports Likert's ideas. Study after study shows that when an organization moves to Pattern IV leadership, performance effectiveness improves, costs decrease, and gains occur in the overall satisfaction and health of the members of the organization. In addition, research findings show that Pattern IV leadership is applicable to every size and type of organization, including private businesses, not-for-profit organizations, and government agencies.[48]

How important are organizational climate and enlightened leadership practices? Management author John Hoerr states: "We are in a global economy. To have world-class quality and costs and the ability to assimilate new technology, an organization must have world-class ability to develop human capabilities. This can't be a drag on the system; it has to be a leading variable."[49]

The Power of Stories

Storytelling has an almost innate appeal. When a teacher interrupts a class with the statement, "Let me tell you a story," attention in the room doubles. Stories can be used in a similar way to develop and reinforce a positive work climate. They serve as prescriptions of the way things should (or should not) be done. They have the greatest impact on an organization when they describe real people and are known by employees throughout the organization.[50]

More than a decade ago, Southwest Airlines introduced an ad campaign with the phrase "Just Plane Smart." Unknowingly, the Dallas-based airline had infringed on the "Plane Smart" slogan at Stevens Aviation, an aviation sales and maintenance company in Greenville, South Carolina. Rather than paying buckets of money to lawyers, Stevens's chairman Kurt Herwald and Southwest CEO Herb Kelleher decided to settle the dispute with an old-fashioned arm wrestling match at a run-down wrestling stadium in Dallas. A boisterous crowd watched the "Malice in Dallas" event as "Smokin" Herb Kelleher and "Kurtsey" Herwald battled their designates, and then each other. When Kelleher lost the final round to Herwald, he jested (while being carried off on a stretcher) that his defeat was due to a cold and the strain of walking up a flight of stairs. Stevens Aviation later decided to let Southwest Airlines continue to use its ad campaign, and both companies donated funds from the event to charities.

"Malice in Dallas" is a legendary story that almost every Southwest employee knows by heart. It is a tale that communicates one of the airline's core values—that having fun is part of doing business.[51]

Building Community in the Workplace

The word *corporation* conjures up images of authority, bureaucracy, competition, control, and power. The word *community* evokes images of democracy, diversity, co-operation, inclusion, and common purpose. The model under which an organization chooses to operate can determine its survival in a competitive and changing world. The idea of community at work is particularly satisfying to the makeup and challenges of today's diverse workforce.[52]

Community is experienced in two ways: as "a group of people" and as "a way of being." The first type of community is formed by bringing people together in place and time. The second is created when barriers between people are let down. Under such conditions, people become bonded, sensing that they can rely on and trust each other. When people experience a feeling of community, their potential for achievement becomes enormous.[53]

Thomas Carlyle, the Scottish philosopher, thought that each person wanted to be treated as a unique and valuable individual. He also believed we each have a simultaneous need to belong to something greater than self, something more than one alone can do or be.[54] For many people, feelings of self-worth and transcendence to something greater than self occur in the experience of community.

The benefits of interrelationship can be found everywhere in nature. If a gardener places two plants close together, the roots commingle and improve the quality of the soil, thus helping both plants grow better than if they were separated. If a carpenter joins two boards together, they will hold much more weight than the total held by each alone.

In the human sphere, our challenge is to apply the creative cooperation we learn from nature in dealing with those around us. The essence of this is to value differences, build on each other's strengths, transcend individual limitations, and achieve the full potential of community.

Writer and educator John Gardner states, "We are a community-building species." He goes on to describe the conditions necessary to experience true community:[55]

- *Shared vision.* A healthy community has a sense of where it should go, and what it might become. A positive and future-focused role image provides direction and motivation for its members.

- *Wholeness incorporating diversity.* A group is less of a community if fragmentation or divisiveness exists—and if the rifts are deep, it is no community at all. We expect and value diversity, and there is dissent in the best of groups. But true community requires facing and resolving differences.

- *Shared culture.* Success is enhanced when people have a shared culture—that is, shared norms of behavior and core values to live by. If a community is lucky, it has shared history and traditions as well. This is why developing communities must form symbols of group identity and generate stories to pass on core values, customs, and central purpose.

- *Internal communications.* Members of a well-functioning community communicate freely with one another. There are regular occasions when people gather and share information. There are opportunities and means for people to get to know and understand what others need and want. Communication is uncensored and flows in all directions within the community.

- *Consideration and trust.* A healthy community cares about its members and fosters an atmosphere of trust. People deal with one another humanely; they respect each other and value the integrity of each person.

- *Maintenance and government.* A fully functioning community has provision for maintenance and governance. Roles, responsibilities, and decision-making processes are conducive to achieving tasks while maintaining a supportive group climate.

- *Participation and shared leadership.* The healthy community encourages the involvement of all individuals in the pursuit of shared goals. All members have the opportunity to influence events and outcomes. The good community finds a productive balance between individual interests and group responsibilities as community tasks are accomplished.

- *Development of younger members.* Opportunities for growth are numerous and varied for all members. Mature members ensure that younger members develop knowledge, skills, and attitudes that support continuation of the community's purpose and values.

- *Affirmation.* A healthy community reaffirms itself continuously. It celebrates its beginnings, rewards its achievements, and takes pride in its challenges. In this way, community morale and confidence are developed.

- *Links with outside groups.* There is a certain tension between the community's need to draw boundaries to accomplish its tasks and its need to have fruitful alliances with external groups and the larger community of which it is a part. A successful community masters both ends of this spectrum.

In *Productive Workplaces,* Marvin Weisbord writes that we hunger for community and are a great deal more productive when we find it. If we feed this hunger in ways that preserve individual dignity, opportunity for all, and mutual support, we will harness energy and productivity beyond imagining.[56]

Community Building and the Role of the Leader

The plaque outside the two-family house at 367 Addison Street in Palo Alto, California, identifies the dusty one-car garage out back as the "birthplace of Silicon Valley." But the site, where Dave Packard and Bill Hewlett first set up shop, in 1938, is more than that. It's the birthplace of a new approach to management, a West Coast alternative to the traditional, hierarchical corporation. More than seven decades later, the methods of Hewlett and Packard remain the dominant DNA for tech companies—and a major reason for U.S. preeminence in the information age.

The partnership began when the pair met as students at Stanford University. Packard, an opinionated star athlete from the hardscrabble town of Pueblo, Colorado, had a commanding presence to match his 6-foot-5-inch frame. Hewlett, whose technical genius was obscured from teachers by undiagnosed dyslexia, favored dorm-room pranks and bad puns. While different in temperament, the two soon discovered a shared passion for camping and fishing—and for turning engineering theory into breakthrough products.

The result was one of the most influential companies of the 20th century. Hewlett-Packard Co. (they flipped a coin to decide whose name would go first) cranked out a blizzard of electronic tools that were crucial to the development of radar, computers, and other digital wonders. Still, the pair's greatest innovation was managerial, not technical. From the first days in the garage, they set out to create a company that would attract like-minded people. They shunned the rigid hierarchy of companies back East in favor of an egalitarian, decentralized system that came to be known as "the HP Way." The essence of the idea, radical at the time, was that employees' brainpower was the company's most important resource.

To make the idea a reality, the young entrepreneurs instituted a slew of pioneering practices. Starting in 1941, they granted big bonuses to all employees when the company improved its productivity. That evolved into one of the first all-company profit-sharing plans. When HP went public in 1957, the founders gave shares to all employees. Later, they were among the first to offer tuition assistance, flextime, and job sharing.

Even HP's offices were unusual. To encourage the free flow of ideas, employees worked in open cubicles. Even supply closets were to be kept open. Once, Hewlett sawed a lock off a closet and left a note: "HP trusts its employees." In Packard's own words, "The close relationship among people encouraged a form of participative management that supported individual freedom and initiative while emphasizing commonness of purpose and teamwork. We were all working on the same problems and we used ideas from wherever we could get them."

If HP's policies were progressive, there was nothing coddling about either man. Until his death in 1996, Packard was a fearsome paragon of corporate integrity. He was famous for flying to distant branches to make a show of firing managers who skirted ethical lines. Neither man would hesitate to kill a business if it wasn't hitting its profit goals. The result: HP grew nearly 20 percent a year for 50 years without a loss.

Today, the behavior of the two founders remains a benchmark for business. Hewlett, who died in 2001, and Packard, who died in 1996, expected employees to donate their time to civic causes. And they gave more than 95 percent of their fortunes to charity. "My father and Mr. Packard felt they'd made this money almost as a fluke," says Hewlett's son Walter. "If anything, the employees deserved it more than they did." It's an insight that changed corporate America—and the lives of workers everywhere.[57]

In *A World Waiting to Be Born,* Scott Peck identifies the leader within a group or organization to be a potential obstacle to creating community. Specifically, no matter how deeply those at the bottom or middle desire it, community will be difficult to achieve if those at the top are resistant. Conversely, if the leaders are the kinds of people who want community, they can probably have it. They may have to work hard for it. It may require time and resources. But if leaders want to achieve a positive and healthy human environment, it can be done under almost any circumstances.[58]

In an article entitled "The Brave New World of Leadership Training," Jay Conger describes *building community* as the most important task facing leaders today. He views this as a special assignment that combines two basic leadership competencies— visioning and empowerment—which are related, since vision itself must be empowering. The vision's purpose is not only to achieve a meaningful strategic or company goal, but also to create a dedicated community of people.[59]

The Mouse and the Web

What does *Charlotte's Web* have to do with the most famous research mouse in the world? It is a fascinating story of two remarkable men—one of science and one of literature.[60]

The Jackson Laboratory, the world's foremost mammalian genetics research center, was founded by Clarence Little in 1929. Little left his position as president of the University of Michigan to pursue his love of biological studies along the stern and craggy shores of Acadia in Bar Harbor, Maine.

Residents say that when Little met his neighbor, E.B. White, famous for his essays in the *New Yorker* and for his children's book *Charlotte's Web,* two minds ignited with ideas and insights.

White noted that the colored coats of the mice could explain deeper biological secrets, an observation that profoundly influenced Little's research.

For his part, the writer named a small mouse of his own, Stuart, after his good friend, Little. Their partnership and intellectual collaboration lasted more than 25 years.

What do Clarence Little and E.B. White have to do with building community in the workplace? The spark that was ignited more than 80 years ago lives on in the scholarship, creativity, and culture of the Jackson Laboratory today. Scientists throughout the world depend on Jackson Laboratory mice in their efforts to conduct the highest level of research, and the laboratory thrives as a center for genetic studies and scientific endeavors.

Today's leaders are committed to preserving the Jackson Laboratory culture and building on its record of achievement. Elements of true community are monitored, strengths are celebrated, and areas for improvement are addressed. It is whimsical, but true, to say that a dedicated community of people continues the spirit of the mouse and the web. Little and White would be pleased, indeed.

The Struggle to Stay Flat

An important element of organizational culture and climate is structure. As organizations grow in size, there is a need for layers and divisions of responsibility. Mid-level leaders are needed to guide work activities, coach subordinates, and manage organizational growth. Sufficient resources must be allocated to perform these functions well.[61] Past an optimum point, organizations can have too many layers of management with corresponding reduction in creativity and performance. The case of Nucor Corporation shows the value of being flat:

When Ken Iverson became CEO of Nucor Corporation in the mid 1960s, he insisted that the Charlotte, North Carolina, steelmaker have only three layers of management below him: Crew supervisors reported to their functional manager (production, shipping, and maintenance), who reported to a plant manager, who reported to Iverson. By allowing each plant to operate as an independent business, this flat structure was manageable even as Nucor grew to more than two dozen plants. But today Nucor is America's largest steelmaker in terms of shipments, employing 20,000 people at more than four dozen facilities worldwide. Managing 50 or more direct reports would be a full-time job, so Nucor's current chairman and CEO, Dan DiMicco, reluctantly added another layer of management (five executive vice presidents). "I needed to be free to make decisions on trade battles," says DiMicco, adding that he continues to stay involved by checking his own e-mail and meeting with staff at every opportunity. Even with five layers of hierarchy, Nucor is incredibly lean. Many other companies the same size have twice as many levels of management.[62]

There are strong arguments for being as flat as it is practical to be:

1. Tall organizational structures have higher overhead costs due to the cost of managers versus employees who actually make the product or supply the service.

2. Layers of hierarchy tend to slow down the transmittal of information and the speed of response even in today's e-business environment.

3. Tall structures tend to undermine employee satisfaction and organizational commitment because they focus power around managers rather than employees.[63]

Part Two Summary

After reading Part Two, you should know the following key concepts, principles, and terms. Fill in the blanks from memory, or copy the answers listed below.

The most important function of a leader is to develop a clear, compelling (a) _____ and to secure commitment to that ideal. In addition, the leader must have a (b) _____ to succeed. Finally, the leader must have (c) _____ to see these through. These three items are the requirements for leadership success. Four distinct areas that correlate positively with leadership effectiveness are (d) _____, _____, _____, and _____. An effective vision must be (e) _____, _____, _____, and _____. The three motives for assuming leadership responsibility are (f) _____, _____, and _____. The climate of an organization includes the (g) _____, _____, _____, _____, and _____. The climate of an organization is determined primarily by the quality of leadership. Leaders in the best organizations follow four enlightened principles: (h) _____, _____, _____, and _____.

Answer Key for Part Two Summary

a. **vision,** page 62

b. **strategy,** page 62

c. **stamina,** page 62

d. **getting the facts, creating a vision, motivating people, empowering others,** pages 67, 68

e. **leader-initiated, shared and supported by followers, comprehensive and detailed, uplifting and inspiring,** page 66

f. **power, achievement, affiliation,** page 74

g. (any five) **reward system, organizational clarity, standards of performance, warmth and support, leadership, communication, innovation, feedback and controls, teamwork, involvement,** pages 81, 82

h. **view human resources as the organization's greatest asset; treat every individual with understanding, dignity, warmth, and support; tap the constructive power of groups through visioning and team building; set high performance goals at every level of the organization,** page 84

Reflection Points—Personal Thoughts on the Importance of Vision, the Motive to Lead, and Organizational Climate

Complete the following questions and activities to personalize the content of Part Two. Space is provided for writing your thoughts.

■ Describe the vision of a successful leader you have known; discuss the role of stamina in achieving that vision.

_____

_____

■ Have you ever taken responsibility for initiating change? Have you ever created a vision and a strategy for success? Discuss.

_____

_____

■ Discuss Martin Luther King, Jr.'s, speech "I Have a Dream." Why is the speech so powerful? Consider the message, words that are used, images that are conjured up, feelings that are evoked, and repetition of key ideas.

_____

_____

■ The French philosopher Jean-Paul Sartre (1905–1980) believed every person needs a project in life, and the Austrian psychiatrist Viktor Frankl believed we each need a purpose. What is your project or purpose yet to be done?

_____

_____

■ Why would you want to be a leader—power, achievement, or affiliation? Does your work or personal life allow the expression of your social motives?

_____

_____

■ Evaluate the climate of an organization you know, including the reward system, organizational clarity, performance standards, warmth and support, leadership, and other dimensions. Discuss strengths and areas to improve.

_____

_____

Part Two Video Case
Andre Thornton

André Thornton, a retired professional baseball player, is no stranger to the business world, nor is he a stranger to being a minority businessman. Thornton is president and CEO of GPI Procurement Services, a small sourcing and procurement service company that provides its clients with a wide variety of promotional and incentive items as well as uniforms and hospital apparel.

Thornton became involved in this business after a successful run at managing a chain of Applebee's restaurants. He describes wealth as being distinctively different from money. Wealth, according to Thornton, is an assortment of assets, whereas money is just an asset to be used to make and acquire other assets.

After leaving the big leagues, Thornton and two other retired professional athletes decided to enter the restaurant industry. Their desire was to operate restaurant locations in swank areas in Florida, such as Orlando or Miami. Much to their dismay, the franchising company they were going to be working with, Applebee's, would provide the partners with a territory only in the St. Louis area. They decided to go for it and made the most of the situation, making their chain of stores very successful. In fact, the stores they managed were consistently ranked in the top 10 percent and frequently were in the top 5 percent of all the Applebee's locations. After a short period, the Applebee's company approached the partners with a buyout offer, and they took it.

Thornton left the restaurant industry with a wealth of knowledge and decided that there were plenty of ways he could capitalize on it in a business setting. Thornton put his knowledge to work at GPI. This has not been an easy road for him, especially because he is a minority businessman. He will be the first to tell you that being an entrepreneur is a tough task and selling in an open market requires tremendous perseverance—an attribute he developed during his professional baseball career.

Thornton was able to translate his knowledge of the restaurant industry into a sourcing and procurement company that serves the needs of both small and large clients in three business sectors—financial, health care, and business and industry. GPI not only provides promotional and incentive items to its clients, but also designs programs, sources products, and manages processes to assist in bringing cost efficiencies to its customers. And because of its size, GPI is able to be much more flexible than its larger counterparts in terms of pricing, customizing, and providing customer service.

GPI is a minority vendor in what Thornton describes as a restrictive and controlled industry, but according to Thornton, "diversity is here to stay." He acknowledges that because he is a minority businessman, many people won't accept him and feel that his business is "second-rate," or that he has inadequate financing or products. He states that he acknowledges that women and other minorities face the same issues. To combat these views, Thornton prepares presentations that dispel these myths.

According to Thornton, there is a correlation between business and sports. He feels that any time you have a group of people working toward a common objective, you have a team. As a result, we commonly hear sports analogies used to describe business. According to Thornton, "business pressures drive business, not likes and dislikes," especially in a global world that is rapidly changing demographically.

Questions for Discussion

1. How do Thornton's experiences in professional sports and in restaurant management assist him in running GPI? Does the fact that he is a minority help or hinder him personally in business?

2. What does GPI have to offer its clients? Does the fact that it is a minority vendor help or hinder the company?

For more information, see http://www.aswglobal.com/leadership/Andre-Thornton.htm.

Action Assignment

As a bridge between learning and doing, complete the following action assignment.

1. What is the most important idea you have learned in Part Two?
2. How can you apply what you have learned? What will you do, with whom, where, when, and, most important, why?

Part 3   The Importance of Ethics

6. Leadership Ethics
7. The Role of Values and Ethics at Work

UNTIL PHILOSOPHERS ARE KINGS, or the kings and princes of this world have the spirit and power of philosophy, and political greatness and wisdom meet in one, and those commoner natures who pursue either to the exclusion of the other are compelled to stand aside, cities will never have rest from their evils—no, nor the human race, as I believe—and then only will this our State have a possibility of life and behold the light of day.

—Plato (428–347 BC)
The Republic: An Ideal Commonwealth

Learning Objectives

After studying Part Three, you will be able to:
- Know the importance of ethics at work.
- Identify the levels and stages of moral development.
- Understand why leadership by values is important.
- Describe the values that guide you in moral dilemmas.
- Know the role of the leader in setting the moral tone and ethical climate of the workplace.

Leadership Ethics

With one after another high-profile scandal in business and government, interest in the nature of ethical leadership has grown proportionally.[1] Prominent scholars, including Ronald Heifetz, James MacGregor Burns, and Robert Greenleaf, have provided perspective on this important subject. A common theme is the need for leadership that is based on honesty, service to others, and moral courage.

For Heifetz, leadership involves the use of authority to help followers uphold important values in the workplace. Burns's theory of transformational leadership emphasizes the moral development of followers and maintaining high standards of ethical conduct. Greenleaf's approach to leadership has strong ethical overtones, with the central premise being that true leadership is service to others.[2]

Leaders must understand the subject of ethics—what it is and why it is important. Ethics is the branch of philosophy concerned with the intent, means, and consequences of moral behavior. It is the study of **moral judgments and right and wrong conduct.** Some human judgments are factual (the earth is round); others are aesthetic (she is beautiful); and still others are moral (people should be honest and should not kill). Moral judgments are judgments about what is right and wrong, good and bad.[3] The Spanish writer Cervantes wrote about ethics in *Don Quixote:*

I know that the path of virtue is straight and narrow, and the road of vice broad and spacious. I know also that their ends and resting places are different; for those of vice, large and open, end in death; and those of virtue, narrow and intricate, end in life; and not in life that has an end, but in that which is eternal.[4]

The word *ethics* is derived from the Greek word *ethos,* referring to a person's fundamental orientation toward life. Originally, *ethos* meant "a dwelling place." For the philosopher Aristotle, *ethos* came to mean "an inner dwelling place," or what is now called "inner character." The Latin translation of *ethos* is "mos, moris," from which comes the English word *moral.* In Roman times, the emphasis shifted from internal character to overt behavior—acts, habits, and customs.[5]

In more recent times, ethics has been viewed as an overall human concern:

One of the chief problems is to determine what the basis of a moral code should be, to find out what one ought to do. Is right that which is the word of God given to man in the Ten Commandments? Is it what is revealed to us by conscience and intuition? Is it whatever will increase the sum of human happiness? Is it that which is the most reasonable thing to do? Is it whatever makes for the fullness and perfection of life? Above all, is there any absolute right, anything embedded, so to speak, in the nature of the universe, which should guide our actions? Or are right and wrong simply relative, dependent on time and place and cultural pattern, and changing with environment and circumstance? What, in short, is the basis of our moral values? These questions are of vital importance in a day when intellectual power threatens to outrun moral control and thus destroy humankind.[6]

Ethical questions are important in all areas of life—work and personal. Put yourself in the shoes of the individuals in Exercise 6–1.

Exercise 6–1
Moral Dilemmas

In each dilemma, what would you do? Place a check mark by your response; then provide the rationale for your answer in the space provided.

1. *The citizen.* You are driving your car when you come upon the scene of an accident. One person will die without immediate medical care. You take the victim and speed to the hospital. The extra speed causes another accident, in which another person dies. How should you be judged? Was your act right because your motive was good, or was your act wrong because its consequences were bad?

    Check one: ☐ Right; motive was good   ☐ Wrong; consequences were bad   ☐ Alternative response

    Rationale: _____

    _____

    _____

    _____

2. *The salesperson.* You learn that your company is selling faulty equipment that could be dangerous. Your spouse needs medical treatment that costs a large percentage of your income. You have reason to believe that if you confront your employer, you will lose your job. What would you do?

    Check one: ☐ Confront employer   ☐ Avoid confrontation   ☐ Alternative response

    Rationale: _____

    _____

    _____

    _____

3. *The administrative assistant.* You are an executive administrative assistant who has been with the company for 20 years. You provide sole support for your family (boy, 12; girl, 10; mother, ailing). Your new boss, the company president, has made it clear to you that continued employment depends on occasional sexual favors. What would you do?

    Check one: ☐ Provide favors   ☐ Refuse to provide favors; risk losing job   ☐ Alternative response

    Rationale: _____

    _____

    _____

    _____

4. *The parent.* You have two daughters. One always complains when you send her on errands. The other doesn't like going either but usually goes without arguing. Typically, you send the daughter who does not complain more often than the one who does. Is this right or wrong?

    Check one: ☐ Right; continue to send noncomplaining daughter   ☐ Wrong; send both daughters equally   ☐ Alternative response

    Rationale: _____

    _____

    _____

    _____

5. *The firefighter.* It is World War II, and you are a firefighter in a city in Germany that is under constant bombing. One day, after an especially heavy attack, you leave the bomb shelter to go to your fire station. On the way, you decide to see whether your family is safe. Although your home is quite distant, you go there first. Is this right or wrong?

Check one: ☐ Right; check   ☐ Wrong; go to fire   ☐ Alternative response
                  family first   station first

Rationale: _____

              _____

              _____

              _____

6. *The friend.* You promise to keep your best friend's secret; then she tells you that her son is selling drugs and even has sold them at a nearby grade school. Your friend is upset but plans on taking no action. What would you do?

Check one: ☐ Notify   ☐ Keep friend's   ☐ Alternative response
                  authorities   secret

Rationale: _____

              _____

              _____

              _____

7. *The supervisor.* Your company is reducing the workforce, and you must dismiss one of your engineers. You have narrowed the choices to T. J., an older employee who has been coasting for years, but who is capable of outstanding performance, and Morgan, a new employee who tries his best, but who almost certainly will never perform at the same level as T. J. Who would you let go?

Check one: ☐ T. J.   ☐ Morgan   ☐ Alternative response

Rationale: _____

              _____

              _____

              _____

These dilemmas show the range of ethical questions that people face and the consequences moral judgments can have. As a human being, you are constantly making decisions about what is the best or right action to take with family, friends, and colleagues. For leaders, the number and gravity of dilemmas are intensified because of the role and influence they have.

No Easy Subject

Ethics is a difficult subject, forcing people to think about moral issues with elusive answers. This is true now more than ever before. Consider the questions that people are being faced with today:

- *The conscious creation of new forms of life.* What are the benefits and penalties of creating new forms of life through recombinant genetics? Should people be cloned? If so, who should be cloned?

- *Exploration and the use of outer space.* Should people be exploring space? Are the huge financial sums spent on space exploration justified in view of the human misery on earth?

- *Nuclear energy.* What should be done with our knowledge about atomic energy? Should we build bombs that can destroy life, or should we apply this knowledge to human welfare? What should be done, and who is to decide?

- *Information technology.* Should everything that *can* be known *be* known by anybody anytime? Should children see the surface of Mars on a computer screen before they feel the surface of the earth—its rocks, sand, water, and grass—firsthand, with their own bodies? What should we do in response to the admonition not to become tools of our tools?

Aside from moral issues created by developments in science and technology, there are many ethical problems common to the workplace—issues of quality, safety, property, and human relationships. It is the task of the leader to understand and make judgments on these difficult subjects.[7]

The Roots of Ethics

Ethics has both religious and secular roots. Religious ethics is based on a theistic understanding of the world. What is real, true, and good is defined by God. Secular ethics is based on a scientific understanding of the world. Reality, truth, and goodness do not depend on the existence of a god. Both religious and secular ethics may endorse many common values, such as the preservation of life and the importance of the Golden Rule. The primary difference is how values are justified.

The Secular Tradition

Aristotle (384–322 BC) was one of the first and perhaps most influential of all people to shape the ethics of Western civilization from a secular orientation. He believed that every type of animal has a common essence or nature, and that human beings are essentially, or by nature, rational. He viewed rationality as the central and most significant trait distinguishing humankind from other creatures. Further, Aristotle taught that the good person is the one who lives most rationally and whose moral judgments and social conduct are born of contemplation and reason, in contrast to spontaneity and emotionality. Today, when we address a moral dilemma by saying, Let us use reason; let us use logic; let us think rationally about this, we are being ethical in the Aristotelian secular tradition.[8] Consider the short essay on the next page by the Englishman Bertrand Russell (1872–1970), a modern philosopher whose views were secular.

The Religious Tradition

All the world's religions make prescriptions for moral behavior. St. Augustine (354–430), for example, who generally is agreed to have had a greater influence on Western religious thought than any other writer outside biblical scripture, maintained that the naturally evil inclinations of humanity could be overcome only by divine grace. St. Augustine synthesized Plato's philosophy with Christianity. He believed that if we allow ourselves through faith to be drawn to God, we will overcome our basic immoral nature and eventually be reconciled in the city of God in heaven.[9]

Another Christian philosopher, Thomas Aquinas (1224–1274), integrated the philosophy of Aristotle with Christian theology. Aquinas taught that all people are endowed with a natural desire to be good. He believed that this inclination could be dormant in an individual and could even be perverted. Nonetheless, he believed it

What I Have Lived For

Bertrand Russell

Three passions, simple but overwhelmingly strong, have governed my life: the longing for love, the search for knowledge, and unbearable pity for the suffering of mankind. These passions, like great winds, have blown me hither and thither, in a wayward course, over a deep ocean of anguish, reaching to the very verge of despair.

I have sought love, first, because it brings ecstasy—ecstasy so great that I would often have sacrificed all the rest of life for a few hours of this joy. I have sought it, next, because it relieves loneliness—that terrible loneliness in which one in shivering consciousness, looks over the rim of the world into the cold, unfathomable, lifeless abyss. I have sought it, finally, because in the union of love I have seen, in a mystic miniature, the prefiguring vision of the heaven that saints and poets have imagined. This is what I sought, and though it might seem too good for human life, this is what—at last—I have found.

With equal passion I have sought knowledge. I have wished to understand the hearts of men. I have wished to know why the stars shine. A little of this, but not much, I have achieved.

Love and knowledge, so far as they were possible, led upward toward the heavens. But always pity brought me back to earth. Echoes of cries of pain reverberate in my heart. Children in famine, victims of torture by oppressors, helpless old people a hated burden to their sons, and the whole world of loneliness, poverty, and pain make a mockery of what human life should be. I long to alleviate the evil, but I cannot, and I too suffer.

This has been my life. I have found it worth living, and would gladly live it again if the chance were offered me.[10]

to be present in all people and impossible to destroy. Aquinas taught that to resist God's pull is contrary to human nature and that if we allow ourselves to follow God, we will fulfill our nature and we will be purely good. Further, by acting out this goodness in our day-to-day lives, we will be moral and will experience the greatest meaning of which we are capable.[11]

The majority of people who have ever lived have been influenced by religions such as Christianity and individuals such as St. Augustine and Thomas Aquinas. Consider the example of Ben Franklin, who believed that the soul of man is immortal and will be treated with justice in another life respecting its conduct in this.[12]

Ethics, Humankind, and Other Animals

Whether based on religious belief or secular thought, ethics is a concern unique to humankind. People are the only creatures who combine emotion (feelings) with knowledge (information) and through abstract reasoning (thought) produce a moral conscience, or a sense of what should be.

Some ideas about right and wrong are of prehuman origin. Indeed, such social virtues as self-sacrifice, sympathy, and cooperation can be seen among many other species, such as elephants, porpoises, and lions. However, more than 40,000 years ago, the human race evolved into beings who could distinguish between what is and what ought to be, and it is this attribute that separates people from all other animals.[13]

In *The Descent of Man,* biologist and social philosopher Charles Darwin concludes of ethics, humankind, and other animals:

I fully subscribe to the judgment of those writers who maintain that, of all the differences between man and the lower animals, the moral sense of conscience is by far the most important.

It is summed up by that short but impervious word, ought, so full of high significance. It is the most noble of all attributes of man, leading him without a moment's hesitation to risk his life for the life of a fellow creature, or after due deliberation, impelled simply by the deep feeling of right or duty, to sacrifice it in some great cause.[14]

Moral Development

How is morality developed? The English philosopher John Locke, one of the most important philosophers of modern times, viewed the newborn child as a tabula rasa, or blank tablet, on which a life script would be written. He believed that experience and learning would shape the content, structure, and direction of each person's life. In this sense, the ethics of the infant are amoral—that is, there is no concept of good and bad or right and wrong that is inborn.

After birth, babies soon discover that they are rewarded for certain things and punished for others. As a result of this early programming, they develop an understanding of what the adult world considers good and bad. Thus a social conscience is begun, and this becomes the foundation for future moral development.[15]

Through modeling and socialization, the older community passes on ethics to young people. The words and actions of parents, teachers, and older companions teach and reinforce morality before children develop their own critical faculties. Ben Franklin's advice to "teach children obedience first so that all other lessons will follow the easier" captures the spirit in which moral values are taught.[16]

When practiced over time, ethical behavior becomes habitual and part of people themselves. By telling the truth, people become trustworthy; by serving others, people become kind; by being fair, people become just.[17]

On a societywide scale, the ethics of adults are similarly programmed. Swiss psychologist Jean Piaget writes that heteronomy (rules as sacred external laws laid down by authorities) is the unifying factor in adult societies, and that in every society there are leaders (governmental, religious, and educational) who believe in certain moral ideals, and who see their task to be one of imprinting these ideals on succeeding generations.[18]

Practically speaking, the three most important influences on character formation are:

- **Associations.** Family, friends, and role models help shape our future lives. The example and encouragement of some people may improve us, while that of others may pull us down. Whenever possible, avoid toxic people and keep company with agents of goodness.

- **Books.** The printed page and other media can poison us with wrong accounts and harmful thoughts, or can enlighten and lift up our lives with reason and spirit fundamental to a healthy person. Consider the influence of just one book, *Don Quixote,* a cultural landmark of the Spanish-speaking world and second only to the Bible in terms of total number of copies printed. Cervantes's courageous hero refuses to conform and seeks to right the wrongs of the world, providing inspiration to generations of people.

- **Self-concept.** When our thoughts and actions are not consistent, the result is dissonance that the mind cannot tolerate. We do what we do to be consistent with who we think we are. Our primary motivation is not self-preservation, but preservation of the symbolic self. Whoever considers him- or herself to be honest, brave, and worthy is likely to be so, as our outer lives are first decided in our inner hearts.[19]

Consider the ABCs of your own character development:

1. *Associations.* Who in your life has influenced your character development?

_____

_____

_____

2. *Books.* What books, films, and other media have helped you become a better person?

_____

_____

_____

3. *Self-concept.* What image of yourself has shaped your values and guided your life?

_____

_____

_____

Levels of Morality

A person's level of morality is one of the most important dimensions of leadership, determining whether people will trust and respect the leader. Regardless of the code of ethics a society teaches and regardless of one's personal values, on what basis does the individual make ethical decisions? What motive, goal, or frame of reference does the person bring to moral dilemmas? There are many ideas on this question, but the work of social psychologist Lawrence Kohlberg occupies center stage.[20]

Kohlberg explains that each person makes ethical decisions according to three levels of moral development—**preconventional, conventional,** and **postconventional.** Table 6–1 describes these levels, defines two stages within each level, and presents examples of moral reasoning at each stage. As you read the chart, evaluate your own ethics. At which level do you usually operate? At which level would you want leaders to behave?

Different people go through the six stages of moral development at different rates, and some people never reach the principled morality of stages 5 and 6. Individuals who remain at lower levels of morality experience arrested developmental integrity. The egocentric orientation of stages 1 and 2 is most characteristic of preadolescent children, whereas the community-oriented morality of stages 3 and 4 is common in teenagers and most adults. The self-direction and high principles of stages 5 and 6 are characteristic of only 20 percent of the adult population, with only 5 percent to 10 percent of the population operating consistently at stage 6.[21]

The case and analysis that follow show how levels of morality influence human conduct in the face of moral dilemmas:

The Stolen Drug

In Europe, a woman was near death from a rare kind of cancer. There was one drug that the doctors thought might save her. It was a form of radium that a druggist in the same town had recently discovered. The drug was expensive to make, but the druggist was charging ten times what the drug cost him. He paid $200 for the radium and charged $2,000 for a small dose of the drug.

The sick woman's husband, Heinz, went to everyone he knew to borrow the money, but he could only get together about $1,000, which was half of what it cost. He told the druggist that his wife was dying and asked him to sell it cheaper, or let him pay later. But the druggist said, "No, I discovered the drug and I'm going to make money from it." Heinz became desperate and broke into the man's store to steal the drug for his wife.[22]

When confronted with the moral dilemma of either letting his wife die or stealing the drug, Heinz stole the drug. Was he right or wrong? Table 6–2 presents examples of moral reasoning Heinz may have used at each stage of moral development.

Table 6–1   Levels, Stages, and Examples of Moral Development[23]

Level of Moral Development	Stage of Moral Development	Example of Moral Reasoning at Each Stage
Level I Preconventional morality. The individual is aware of cultural prescriptions of right and wrong behavior. Response is based on two concerns: Will I be harmed (punishment)? Will I be helped (pleasure)?	Stage 1 At this stage, physical consequences determine moral behavior. Avoidance of punishment and deference to power are characteristics of this stage.	I won't hit him because he may hit me back.
	Stage 2 Individual needs are the primary motives operating at this stage, and personal pleasure dictates the rightness or wrongness of behavior.	I will help her because she may help me in return.
Level II Conventional morality. Morality is characterized by group conformity and allegiance to authority. The individual acts in order to meet the expectations of others and to please those in charge.	Stage 3 The approval of others is the major determinant of behavior at this stage, and the good person is viewed as the one who satisfies family, friends, and associates.	I will go along with you because I want you to like me.
	Stage 4 Compliance with authority and upholding social order are primary ethical concerns at this stage. Right conduct is doing one's duty, as defined by those in authority positions.	I will comply with the order because it is wrong to disobey.
Level III Postconventional morality. This is the most advanced level of moral development. At this level the individual is concerned with right and wrong conduct over and above self-interest, apart from the views of others, and without regard to authority figures. Ethical judgments are based on self-defined moral principles.	Stage 5 Social ethics are based on rational analysis, community discussion, and mutual consent. There is tolerance for individual views, but when there is conflict between individual and group interests, the majority rules. This stage represents the "official" morality of the U.S. Constitution.	Although I disagree with his views, I will uphold his right to have them.
	Stage 6 At this stage, what is right and good is viewed as a matter of individual conscience, free choice, and personal responsibility for the consequences. Morality is seen as superseding the majority view or the prescriptions of authority; rather, it is based on personal conviction.	There is no external force that can compel me to do an act that I consider morally wrong.

Table 6–2   Heinz's Reasoning: Should I Steal the Drug?[24]

Moral Stage	Argument For	Argument Against
Stage 1: Orientation to punishment	It isn't wrong to take the drug. It is really worth only $200, and I probably won't get caught anyway.	It is wrong to take the drug. After all, it is worth $2,000. Besides, I would probably get caught and be punished.
Stage 2: Orientation to pleasure	If I don't want to lose my wife, I should take the drug. It is the only thing that will work.	I should not risk myself for my wife. If she dies, I can marry somebody else. It would be wrong for me to give up my well-being for her well-being.
Stage 3: Orientation to social approval	I have no choice. Stealing the drug is the only thing for a good husband to do. What would my family and friends say if I didn't try to save my wife?	I must not steal the drug. People won't blame me for not stealing the drug; it is not the kind of thing people would approve of.
Stage 4: Orientation to social order	When I got married, I vowed to protect my wife. I must steal the drug to live up to that promise. If husbands do not protect their wives, the family structure will disintegrate, and with it, our society.	Stealing is illegal. I have to obey the law, no matter what the circumstances. Imagine what society would be like if everybody broke the law.
Stage 5: Orientation to social rights and responsibilities	I should steal the drug. The law is unjust because it does not protect my wife's right to life. Therefore, I have no obligation to obey the law. I should steal the drug.	As a member of society, I have an obligation to respect the druggist's right to property. Therefore it would be wrong for me to steal the drug.
Stage 6: Orientation to ethical principles	The principle of the sanctity of life demands that I steal the drug, no matter what the consequences.	The principle of justice and the greatest good for the greatest number prevents me from stealing the drug, even for the good of my wife.

The following examples show the importance of levels of morality in history:

■ *Nazi death camps.* In April 1961, Adolf Eichmann, accused executioner of five million Jews in Nazi Germany during World War II, testified at his trial in Jerusalem:

In actual fact, I was merely a little cog in the machinery that carried out the directives of the German Reich. It was really none of my business. Yet what is there to "admit"? I carried out my orders.[25]

Level II, stage 4 moral reasoning is reflected in Eichmann's statement.

■ *Civil disobedience.* In March 1922, Mohandas Gandhi, the Indian spiritual and political leader, addressed a British court with these words:

Nonviolence is the first article of my faith. It is also the last article of my creed. But I had to make a choice. I had to either submit to a system that I considered had done irreparable harm to my country, or incur the risk. . . . I am here, therefore, to invite and cheerfully submit to the highest penalty that can be inflicted upon me for what in law is a deliberate crime and what appears to me to be the highest duty of a citizen.[26]

Level III, stage 6 morality is seen in the life and teaching of Gandhi. With similar moral reasoning, Socrates refused to admit social wrong in his farewell address to the Athenian people. Instead, he drank the lethal hemlock, setting an example of moral heroism that has inspired Western civilization for over 2,000 years.

To personalize the subject of levels of morality, consider these questions: At what level of moral reasoning do you operate? Are you stage 1 or 2 (egocentric), 3 or 4 (community-oriented), or 5 or 6 (principled) in your response to ethical dilemmas at work, in your community, and in your personal life? Think of the leaders you respect. At what level of morality do they operate?

Lessons in Obedience

In the 1960s, Stanley Milgram, a psychologist at Yale University, performed a series of experiments on obedience. Milgram demonstrated how a situation can overpower an individual's conscience. His findings have been used to explain the great atrocities of our time: the Holocaust, the My Lai massacre, the genocide in Rwanda, and Abu Ghraib in Iraq.

Milgram drew his subjects from all walks of life, including lawyers, firefighters, and construction workers. They all agreed to accept $4.50 per hour to participate in an experiment on learning and punishment. In the experiment, they were told by a doctor in a white coat to act as "teachers" by reading a list of associations to a "learner," who was out of sight but could hear in the next room. If the learner got an association wrong, the teacher was instructed to give him an electric shock, increasing the voltage after each incorrect answer. The first shock was labeled "Slight shock—15 volts." The last was labeled "Danger: severe shock—450 volts."

Of course, the real experiment was on the teachers to see how much punishment they would administer. At 180 volts, the learner, who was an actor, would cry out that he could not stand the pain; at 300 volts, he refused to participate; at 330 volts, there was silence. To Milgram's surprise, 65 percent of the teachers pushed on to the end, 450 volts, even if they were told the learner had a mild heart condition. Many of the teachers were seriously upset—sweating profusely, biting their lips—but with the prodding of the white-coated experimenter, they continued in spite of their moral qualms.

Milgram's research demonstrated how ordinary people could be induced to perform inhumane acts simply by the presence of an authority figure. Milgram also found that the more psychological distance the subjects had from the victim, the more likely they were to follow orders to the bitter end. If the teacher only read the questions but did not administer the shocks, 90 percent finished the experiment. However, if the teacher had to touch the learner to administer the shocks, then only 30 percent went up to 450 volts.

Milgram's studies have been replicated in Australia, Germany, Jordan, and other countries around the world, all with similar results. Milgram began his experiments because he wanted to prove William Shirer's theory advanced in *Inside the Third Reich,* that Hitler could happen only in Germany. His experiments at Yale and New Haven showed that Hitler could happen in America as well.[27]

Virtue: The Nature of Level III, Stage 6 Morality

Moral evolution has followed a path from preconventional (level I, stage 1) to post-conventional ethics (level III, stage 6). Increasingly, people as individuals versus people as society have become the basis of moral judgments. The sentiment that just because the majority of a group or society judges an act to be right or wrong does not make it so reflects this orientation toward individual conscience (personal principles), as opposed to collective thought (community standards) or self-service (egocentric morality).[28]

At level III, stage 6 morality, a person's view of right and wrong depends on the meaning she or he attaches to personal existence, and that meaning is based on self-discovered and self-accepted values. This is the orientation of German writer Hermann Hesse's young Siddhartha, even after he had listened to the teachings of Buddha Siddartha Guatama (Shakyamuni):

"Do not be angry with me, O Illustrious One," said the young man. "I have not spoken to you thus to quarrel with you about words. You are right when you say that opinions mean little, but may I say one thing more? I did not doubt you for one moment. Not for one moment did I doubt that you were the Buddha, that you have reached the highest goal that so many thousands of Brahmins and Brahmins' sons are striving to reach.

"You have done so by your own seeking, in your own way, through thought, through meditation, through knowledge, through enlightenment. You have learned nothing through teachings, and so I think, O Illustrious One, that nobody finds salvation through teachings. To nobody, O Illustrious One, can you communicate in words and teachings what happened to you in the hour of your enlightenment.

"The teachings of the enlightened Buddha embrace much, they teach much—how to live righteously, how to avoid evil. But there is one thing that this clear, worthy instruction does not contain; it does not contain the secret of what the Illustrious One himself experienced—he alone among hundreds of thousands.

"That is what I thought and realized when I heard your teachings. That is why I am going on my way—not to seek another and better doctrine, for I know there is none, but to leave all doctrines and all teachers and to reach my goal alone—or die. But I will often remember this day, O Illustrious One, and this hour when my eyes beheld a holy man."[29]

In 1884, Mark Twain wrote *The Adventures of Huckleberry Finn,* a moving story that appeals to readers of all ages. The novel centers on Huck's struggles to reconcile the dictates of society with his own feelings regarding slavery. In the end, Huck decides that a society's rules can be unjust and that his own sense of right and wrong must be followed.

The following example depicts level III, stage 6 morality in the world of work. It shows how important it is for people to determine their own moral principles, whether religious or secular, and to decide on ethical conduct in the light of the meaning they attach to their own lives. It also shows that an individual's actions are most virtuous when they proceed from the highest motives, utilize the best means, and achieve the best consequences. The absence of any one of these qualities will result in less than level III, stage 6 morality—and less than one's potential for moral virtue.[30]

Level III, Stage 6 Morality: A True-Life Case

Susan is an art student about to graduate from college. She is offered a position with a daily newspaper. The position pays well and she is interested in that type of employment, but to work on the newspaper staff, she must draw cartoons that express the sentiments of the paper's owners and managers, not her own sentiments or convictions. The paper is jingoistic and isolationist, whereas Susan wishes to promote international machinery for the peaceful settlement of disputes. The paper also stresses property rights, while Susan wishes to emphasize human rights. Should she accept the position?

How the Problem Is Handled

Susan is very pleased with the job offer. She feels that it is an honor and a compliment. But she does not accept at once. There are some questions in her mind that she wishes to think over. She begins to weigh the pros and cons. During this process, she talks with friends and consults a number of older people whose judgment she respects.

In favor of accepting the position, Susan reasons that it is a good position, it pays well, and she may not get another offer as good—in fact, no other position of this nature may be open in the near future. Furthermore, the position will give her experience and contacts, and she would like to take up this type of work as a profession.

When her friend, Donna, hears about the offer, she says, "Susan, you're in luck. Grab it while you can. Why in the world would you even hesitate?" Another friend adds, "What if you don't accept the position? Someone else will, so what's the difference?"

The older people with whom Susan talks are less simplistic in their advice. They suggest that she think the issue through carefully. While they are not all in agreement in the advice they offer, they do bring to light some aspects that Susan has not considered. Susan asks for an interview with the manager of the newspaper to gain more information about the position and what would be expected of her.

By this time, some of the arguments against accepting the offer are beginning to take shape in Susan's mind; most important is the fact that when working for the newspaper, she must express and promote sentiments opposite to her own. This means that she will be promoting social attitudes and movements in which she does not believe. She asks, What will this position do to me? Can I be successful in work that is promoting a cause in which I do not believe? Do I want my reputation and my influence to count on behalf of the issues I will be asked to promote?

As Susan weighs the relative merits of the two courses of action, certain convictions emerge. First, if she accepts the position, she may not be able to throw all of her mind and heart into the work. Consequently, she is not likely to be as creative as she would be if she were promoting causes in which she believed. Second, if she does manage to give her whole energy to the work, she will soon become a different type of person, with different sentiments and convictions. As her name becomes identified with causes and as she forms friendships in these circles, the possibility of breaking away will be increasingly difficult. Wouldn't it be better, she reasons, to accept another position with a lower salary if need be and retain her personal integrity?

After a few days of uncertainty, Susan declines the offer and asks the placement bureau to keep her name on the active list for new openings.

Analysis

Motives. Susan's motives undoubtedly are good. She wants to do the right thing if she can discover it. This is evident in her approach to the problem and in the questions she asks as she considers the alternatives. Also, her desire to get a good position so that she may be able to earn a living and practice her profession is commendable. The problem centers on the means to be chosen and the general consequences to her and to society of the use of these means.

Means. The problem is handled by Susan in a highly moral way: (1) She thinks about the problem before making a decision. She makes a genuine and intelligent attempt to discover all the relevant factors in the situation. As a result, her decision is made with more facts in mind than would have been the case otherwise. (2) She weighs the relative merits of the alternative possibilities. She judges the case on the basis of long-term considerations, not merely on the basis of immediate interests. (3) She takes into account the social effects of her decisions, not merely her personal interests. (4) She seeks advice from the people who she thinks may throw additional light on the problem. (5) The final decision is her own. It is made on the basis of principle and on the basis of her personal value system.

Consequences. The essence of level III, stage 6 morality is the ability and willingness to weigh all relevant facts in moral dilemmas and to base actions on the results of such reflection at the point of decision making. In Susan's case, time will tell the moral consequences of her decision. With the passage of time, the knowledge of the results of her actions may lead to new moral dilemmas and the necessity for new moral decisions.

In summary, level III, stage 6 morality begins with good motives, is affected by good means, and results in good consequences. At this level and stage of morality, the saying that the ends justify the means is no more acceptable than to say methods are most important, or that good intentions are all one needs to ensure good results. This is because any one of these qualities without the other two will result in lowered morality.

All three—motives, means, and consequences—are necessary ingredients of virtuous, level III, stage 6 moral leadership. We use these criteria to judge the character of a leader both in the instance and over the span of time. We have highest respect for those leaders who behave with honor over the course of their lives. Their records are known, and the verdict is given—these are the great leaders. When faced with a moral dilemma, they do not ask, Will I go to jail? (level I morality), or Will my reputation suffer? (level II morality), but What is the right thing to do? (level III morality). Virtuous leaders know the difference between reputation and character: the first is what people say about them; the second is what they do when no one is watching.

Ethics and the Legal Department

The philosopher Lou Marinoff gives practical advice about leadership and moral dilemmas: Everyone's ethical warning lights go off at different times. Although working will always involve compromises, it is important to know when an action may take you over a line you do not want to cross. In these situations, your conscience should guide you.[31]

In the world of work, ethics is typically the purview of the legal department. But being legal may or may not mean being moral. Legality includes everything the law permits or doesn't expressly forbid. Morality is an even older idea, predating even legislated laws.

By all means, you should do what the people in the legal department advise to abide by the law, but you must never lose your own moral compass. If something makes you morally upset, so much so that you know what you are doing is clearly wrong, don't let legality alone appease you. The argument that "I was only following orders" won't absolve you if you make a moral error. Remember, every society has laws, but not all laws are just.

So what is a person to do? The best advice is to follow the dictum "nonharm to sentient beings." This is the basis of every professional code of ethics and every moral society. If your actions cause harm to others, they are immoral. Systems of morality and the laws of a society can get complicated, but if you live by this basic requirement, you will have a clear conscience.[32]

The Role of Values and Ethics at Work

I n 1727 Benjamin Franklin formed the Junto, a forerunner of modern-day civic clubs. It was dominated by businessmen having goals of community fellowship and service. Charter members were a shoemaker, a surveyor, a woodworker, a glazier, and four young printers. Character was a significant concern of that organization. Franklin's own values included temperance, order, resoluteness, industry, sincerity, justice, moderation, cleanliness, and humility. Clearly, these are poles apart from current-day expressions such as one-upmanship, looking out for number one, and assertiveness, which have captured considerable public following.[33]

Some organizations view values as a fundamental requirement for success. James Burke, former chairman of Johnson & Johnson, states that J&J's credo, first articulated in 1945, was responsible for the company's rapid action in taking Tylenol off the market after poisoning incidents in which seven people died. To support the importance of values, he cites a study of the financial performance of U.S. companies that have had written value statements for at least a generation. The net income of those companies increased by a factor of 23 during a period when the gross national product grew by a factor of 2.5.[34]

For many organizations, values are a social glue. Global enterprises requiring long-distance management may use values to provide structure and stability for people of diverse backgrounds in far-flung locations. Jack Welch, former CEO of General Electric, sees management values as a primary source of corporate identity, adding to a sense of cohesion among GE's highly diverse business units. Also, values can provide guidance for members who function as independent decision makers— for example, the factory team with the power to stop production if a core principle is violated.[35]

It should be noted that value statements can mask hypocrisy. If a company espouses quality in its written vision or promotional literature, but sacrifices it for short-term profits, cynicism will prevail among customers and employees. To be meaningful, values must enter into the daily practices of the organization. Values must reflect enduring commitments, not vague notions and empty platitudes. Thus, leaders who seek to manage through values must examine their own value systems and put good intentions into concrete actions that others can witness.

An organization can have an abundance of values, but lack clarity and reinforcement of those that are the most important. A lack of agreement on core values that all members will live by will reduce the character and strength of the organization. Author Leon Wieseltier writes, "The contemporary problem in American society is not that people believe in too little, it is that they believe in too much. Too much of what too many people believe is too easily acquired and too thoughtlessly held." Wieseltier believes Americans are choking on identities. Not the lack of meaning, but the glibness of meaning is the trouble.[36]

How can an organization know if it needs to clarify or reinforce its values? Red flags are the following:

- Members lack clear understanding about how they should behave as they attempt to meet organizational goals.
- Different individuals and groups have fundamentally different value systems.
- Top leaders send mixed messages about what is important.
- Day-to-day life is disorganized, with the left hand and the right hand often working at cross-purposes.
- Members complain about the organization to neighbors, friends, and family.
- Like the person who has ears, but hears not, the organization has values, but does not practice them.

Management author Peter Drucker states:

Each organization has a value system that is influenced by its task. In every hospital in the world, health is the ultimate good. In every school in the world, learning is the ultimate good. In every business in the world, the production of goods and services that please the customer is the ultimate good. For an organization to perform at its highest level, its leader must believe that what the organization is doing is, in the last analysis, an important contribution to people and society, one that is needed or adds some value.[37]

In *A Business and Its Beliefs: The Ideas That Helped Build IBM,* Thomas Watson, Jr., explains the importance of values: (1) To survive and achieve success, an organization must have a sound set of values on which it premises all policies and actions; (2) the single most important factor in an organization's success is its leaders' faithful adherence to those values; and (3) if an organization is to meet the challenges of a changing world, it must be prepared to change everything about itself except its core values. The need is to be open to change in structure, tasks, technology, and people, but always guided by, and remaining true to, basic or core values.

Watson goes on to say that when IBM has been successful, it has been true to its three core values—respecting the individual, giving the best customer service possible, and performing every job with excellence. And when IBM has gone astray at times in its history, it is because it lost sight of—or deviated from—those three basic business values.[38]

The Starbucks Story

A good example of the importance of values for business success is Starbucks. In 1971, The Starbucks Coffee, Tea, and Spice store opened for business in Seattle, Washington. Today, Starbucks is a global enterprise with 11,000 stores in 37 countries and more than 100,000 employees. It averages 35 million customer visits each week and has customers who return an average of 18 times a month. Since 1992 its stock has risen 5,000 percent.

In *The Starbucks Experience,* Joseph Michelli describes five leadership principles that are the foundation of Starbucks' greatness—make it your own, everything matters, surprise and delight, embrace resistance, and leave your mark.

These principles are put into practice through the *Green Apron Book,* a pocket-size job-aid that describes partner (employee) "ways of being" in order to be successful— be welcoming, be genuine, be knowledgeable, be considerate, be involved. These are simple instructions provided in an appealing way that captures the essence of the company's culture.

Starbucks' ways of being are expected behaviors at every level of responsibility, and they form the basis for selecting, training, and promoting partners. It is interesting to note that Starbucks spends more money on training than it does on advertising.

To ensure that leaders are upholding the company's espoused values, all partners are encouraged to bring their concerns to a *Mission Review Committee* when they think policies, procedures, or leadership behaviors are straying from Starbucks' principles. The *Green Apron Book* and the *Mission Review Committee* have been instrumental in Starbucks' vision to be a value-based company that cares about coffee *and* cares about people.[39]

In 2008 Michael Gill wrote *How Starbucks Saved My Life*. It is a story about life and work with valuable leadership lessons.

Values and the Importance of Courage

Certain values are mentioned most often in the American workplace:

- **Honesty** in all dealings, as a foundation for all other values.
- **Respect** for others, as shown by consideration for their beliefs and needs.
- **Service** to others, guided by the principle of doing for others as you would have them do for you.
- **Excellence** in all work performed, reflecting the Greek ideal of excellence as a virtue, and resulting in both public admiration and personal pride.
- **Integrity,** having the courage to act and live by one's convictions.

When people define character, what they say is important, what they do is more important, but what they sacrifice for is most important. These are the layers of identity and character formation for individuals and groups. In its highest form, character is based on a value system that is known, cherished, stated, lived, and lived habitually. Caring to the point of personal sacrifice is the highest form of living by one's values.

Character and leading by values require **courage,** a superordinate quality of the person. Philosopher–psychologist Rollo May explains the importance of courage:

Courage is not a virtue or value among other personal values like love or fidelity. It is the foundation that underlies and gives reality to all other virtues and personal values. Without courage our love pales into mere dependency. Without courage our fidelity becomes conformism.

The word courage comes from the same stem as the French word coeur, meaning "heart." Thus just as one's heart, by pumping blood to one's arms, legs, and brain enables all the other physical organs to function, so does courage make possible all the psychological virtues. Without courage, other values wither away into mere facsimiles of virtue.

An assertion of the self, a commitment, is essential if the self is to have any reality. This is the distinction between human beings and the rest of nature. The acorn becomes an oak tree by means of automatic growth; no courage is necessary. The kitten similarly becomes a cat on the basis of instinct. Nature and being are identical in creatures like them. But a man or woman becomes fully human only by his or her choices and his or her commitment to them. People attain worth and dignity by the multitude of decisions they make from day-to-day. These decisions require courage.[40]

Many leadership situations are characterized by ambiguity, uncertainty, and even danger. The leader must be able to act in spite of these factors. Many decisions will require overcoming fear, gritting one's teeth, and doing what must be done. True leadership requires courage to act and live by one's convictions.

Traditional Definitions of *Good*

The English philosopher Alfred North Whitehead wrote, "We are in the world, not the world in us."[41] He explains that while a concern for right and wrong may be universal to all people, what is considered right and wrong depends on the universe and a person's place in it. We are evolving creatures in an evolving world, and human ethics are changing as well.

In the history of Western civilization, what *ought to be* has had different meanings in different times and circumstances. Generally, the cultures of the Western world condemn such practices as slavery, witchcraft, and dueling today, even though these were once considered acceptable.

There have been many definitions of the ethical person in Western culture. *Good* and *right* have been defined in terms of power, personal integrity, natural simplicity, will of God, pleasure, greatest good for the greatest number, pragmatism, and duty and right action. As you read the following, evaluate your own ideas on these central concepts of good.[42]

Power

If life is a struggle for survival and human beings are fundamentally selfish and greedy, then the best individuals are those who adapt to these market forces and become masters of manipulative relations. So believed Niccolò Machiavelli, (1469–1527), an Italian diplomat and political writer. Machiavelli argued for winning and retaining power in a world containing extensive political factionalism and lust for dominion. He maintained that flattery, deceit, and even murder may be necessary if a person is to win and retain power. He stated that a person should never cultivate private virtues that in public life can prove politically suicidal; instead, one should develop vices if these will help perpetuate one's rule. Machiavelli believed that ends justify means and taught that might makes right.[43]

Personal Integrity

The German philosopher Friedrich Nietzsche (1844–1900) believed that human resoluteness, born of independent judgment, was the highest good. Nietzsche was a champion of individualism and encouraged the individual to be independent in thought and strong in conviction, even in the face of group pressure and government authority. Nietzsche believed that nature is filled with conflict spilling over into society, and the best human beings are those who exhibit moral virtue—wisdom, justice, courage, and other ideals—regardless of personal loss or gain.[44]

In this vein, Martin Heidegger (1889–1976), the German existential philosopher, pointed to the Greek ideal of nobility and taught the importance of freely and resolutely adhering to personal principles rather than succumbing to social pressures to conform. Personal integrity, he believed, is inherently good regardless of the results. Practicing personal integrity, though, means that one may not comfortably coexist with everyone, so each person must choose his or her lifestyle and commitments carefully.[45]

Natural Simplicity

In the eighteenth century, the Frenchman Jean-Jacques Rousseau (1712–1778) wrote that nature in essence is good, and because humanity is part of nature, human beings too are naturally good. It follows that to achieve the highest good, one must strive to be most purely natural. Rousseau also held that corruption comes only with civilization, and that children should be raised in a state of simplicity.[46]

Writer–philosopher Henry David Thoreau (1817–1862) wrote in a spirit of natural-ness and simplicity in *Walden,* "I went to the woods because I wished to live deliber-ately, to front only the essential facts of life, and see if I could not learn what it had to teach, and not, when I came to die, discover that I had not lived. Every morning was a cheerful invitation to make my life of equal simplicity, and I may say innocence, with Nature herself."[47] Thoreau believed in developing one's inner self while leaving the exterior environment pristine. In *Economy from Walden,* he wrote that most of the luxuries, and many of the so-called comforts of life, are not only dispensable, but positive hindrances to the elevation of mankind. In this same spirit, many people to-day resist technological changes, complex lifestyles, and artificial creations.

The French writer Vauvenargues summarizes the importance of naturalness: "Naturalness gets a better hearing than accuracy. It speaks the language of feeling, which is better than that of logic and rationality, because it is beautiful and appeals to everyone."[48]

Will of God

Religious leaders announce visions and make moral judgments, drawing on the authority of a supreme being (or many gods). Saying, "It is the will of Allah," the prophet Muhammad (about 570–632) decreed the "five pillars" of Islamic faith: (1) the repetition of the belief, "There is no God but Allah, and Muhammad is the prophet of Allah," (2) prayer five times daily, (3) the 30-day fast of Ramadan, (4) alms giving, and (5) pilgrimage to Mecca. These beliefs and the religious and moral teachings of the *Quran,* the holy book of Muslims, are held most sacred by over 723 million Muslims today. Similarly, nearly three billion adherents of many other religions define the ethical good as the "will of God."[49]

No other body of thought has been embraced by so many people, nor has any been so influential in history, as has Christianity. At the core of Christian character formation are the life and teachings of Jesus of Nazareth. The ethic Jesus taught was to love God and to love humanity: "Thou shalt love the Lord thy God with all thy heart, and with all thy soul, and with all thy mind. This is the first and great commandment. And the second is like unto it, Thou shalt love thy neighbor as thyself. There is no other commandment greater than these."[50] Whether based on Christian teaching or not, a belief in love is the ethical ideal of millions of people.

Pleasure

The idea that pleasure, broadly interpreted as physical enjoyment and avoidance of pain, is the highest state of goodness dates back at least to Aristippus (about 435–366 B.C.). This pupil of the philosopher Socrates believed that experiencing pleasure and avoiding pain should be the goals of human existence, and that definite pleasure of the moment should not be postponed for uncertain pleasure of the future.[51] To understand the importance of this belief, consider the wars that have been fought because of passion between man and woman, the steps people take to avoid discomfort and pain, and the value people place on self-satisfaction in day-to-day affairs. In *Reflections and Maxims,* Vauvenargues wrote:

The indifference we display toward moral truth is due to the fact that we determine to indulge our passions in any event, and that is why we do not hesitate when action becomes necessary, notwithstanding the uncertainty of our opinions, to satisfy desire. It is of little consequence, say men, to know where truth lies, if we know where pleasure lies.[52]

Greatest Good for the Greatest Number

Two of the principal architects of the belief that "what is best brings the greatest good for the greatest number" were the nineteenth-century political philosophers Jeremy Bentham (1748–1832) and John Stuart Mill (1806–1873).[53] Their moral philosophy, utilitarianism, reflects the official ethics of both American democracy and Marxist communism. Bentham wrote, "The greatest happiness of all those whose interest is in question is the right and proper, and the only right and proper and universally desirable, end of human action.[54] When we weigh the consequences of moral behavior by considering the best interests of everyone involved, we are being ethical according to utilitarian ideals.

Pragmatism

Pragmatism is a philosophical belief that originated in the United States with the work of Charles Sanders Peirce (1839–1914), William James (1842–1910), and John Dewey (1859–1952). Many regard pragmatism to be America's most original contribution to philosophy. Many also see it as a reflection of a superficial society. Pragmatists maintain that what is true must be based on evidence, and that philosophical beliefs should be evaluated in terms of the role they play in solving life's practical problems. For pragmatists, the term *practical* applies to all aspects of life, including social, political, economic, and religious. Ideas and actions are considered good to the degree they help us solve life's problems. Pragmatism is summarized in this saying: "That which is good is that which works."

Duty and Right Action

In *Criticism of Practical Reason* (1788) and *Fundamental Principles of the Metaphysics of Morals* (1785), the German philosopher Immanuel Kant (1724–1804) detailed a view of right and wrong that has had significant influence on the thinking of Western civilization. Kant believed that people must be their own lawgivers, freely choosing their obligations, and that these, in turn, become their duty. Because people are free to determine ethical beliefs and have free choice in moral dilemmas, all people must be responsible for their own actions.

Kant believed that a person with character will choose duty to conscience and will not succumb to base or expedient desires. Further, he believed that if an individual acts from a good motive and a sense of duty, the act is good regardless of the consequences. Thus, if a person seeks to help another, but because of unforeseen circumstances the result is a worsened condition for the other, the helper is nonetheless a good and ethical person. On the other hand, if a person seeks to harm another, but in doing so actually helps the other, this act is nonetheless immoral.[55]

The importance of personal conscience and duty can be seen in the words of Israeli stateswoman Golda Meir: "I can honestly say that I was never affected by the question of the success of an undertaking. If I felt it was the right thing to do, I was for it, regardless of the possible outcome."[56]

In the face of ethical questions, a person with character tries to sort out right from wrong. In this effort, traditional definitions of *good* have guided Western culture. As you consider the subject of character, what is your moral ideal? Are your values reflected in both your personal life and your public life? Individuals must remember the truth of the saying, "People must stand for something; otherwise, they will fall for anything."

Honesty as a Leadership Value

Honesty is the most important leadership value. It is the single most important ingredient in the leader–follower relationship. The effective leader holds truth as a central value and foundation for all other values.[57] This is a message as old as the Bible— "Know the truth and it will set you free."[58] It is the message of Shakespeare, who advised, "this above all: to thine own self be true, and it must follow as the night the day, thou canst not then be false to any man."[59] And it is the message of successful leaders today. Herb Kelleher, former CEO of Southwest Airlines, was admired for both his business success and his basic honesty. When asked, What is the secret to building a great organization; how do you create a culture of commitment? Kelleher's answer was: Be yourself.[60]

The Bible, Shakespeare, and Kelleher agree that character begins with truth, that truth is inside the person, and that the leader must be true to his or her values. This is what Thomas Jefferson meant when he wrote: "In matters of style, swim with the currents; in matters of principle, stand like a rock. Character is what you are. It is different than reputation which is from other people. True character is in you."[61]

In his book *The Ethical Imperative,* John Dalla Costa makes the point that being honest means more than not deceiving. It also means not making promises you cannot keep, not misrepresenting facts and data, not hiding behind half-truths and evasions, not avoiding accountability for your actions. The leader must live by the principle of honesty and must reward honest behavior in others.[62]

Full-Swing Values

There is a concept in ethics that can be used to assess the strength of one's values. It is especially important for people in leadership positions. This concept is **full-swing values.** Think about the sport of baseball, in which a full swing is needed to hit a home run. An arrested swing will result in less success—a triple, double, single, or foul ball. The same is true for questions of right and wrong, and good and bad: In ethical dilemmas, a values home run results only when one completes a full swing and does not suffer axiological arrest. Axiology is the branch of philosophy dealing with values, and ethics is applied axiology.[63]

A full swing comprises five points, from beginning through completion:[64]

- Point 1 is to *know* one's values.
- Point 2 is to *cherish* one's values.
- Point 3 is to *declare* one's values.
- Point 4 is to *act* on one's values.
- Point 5 is to *act habitually* on one's values.

Consider the cases of Jim, Jane, Jack, Jill, and John, each facing an ethical dilemma (such as what to do about safety, what to do about taxes, what to do about quality):

- Jim knows what he values but has not examined other alternatives. His is an unthinking stance with little or no personal commitment. He hits a foul ball.
- Jane knows what she values and cherishes this privately. She experiences self-satisfaction with her values. She hits a single.
- Jack knows what he values, cherishes this personally, and declares his values. He hits a double.
- Jill knows what she values, cherishes this personally, declares her values, and acts on her value system. She takes action and accepts the consequences. She hits a triple.
- John knows what he values, cherishes this personally, declares his values, acts on them, and does this habitually. John hits a values homerun, demonstrating maximum strength of values conviction.

See Table 7–1 for a depiction of the cases noted above.

Table 7–1
Full-Swing Values

Points on the Swing	Jim	Jane	Jack	Jill	John
Knows values	X	X	X	X	X
Cherishes values		X	X	X	X
Declares values			X	X	X
Acts on values				X	X
Acts habitually on values					X

To personalize the subject of values strength, evaluate your own values—freedom, responsibility, love, justice, and so forth. Consider an ethical dilemma—for example, discrimination according to gender, race, or religion—in which your values play a part. Ask yourself, Are your values full-swing, or do you experience axiological arrest?

In every field—science, art, government, business, service, religion—the highest level of leadership is full-swing. At this level of leadership, the leader is impelled to act because the act itself is deemed good, and for no other reason—not self-gain or public acclaim, but only because conscience dictates that the act is the right thing to do. The quality of doing the right thing for the right reason is called integrity, and it is possessed by all truly great leaders.

An ideal example of the importance of values and the power of full-swing leadership is that of Clara Barton, founder of the American Red Cross:

When the U.S. Civil War broke out in the 1860s, Clara Barton was working as a clerk in the U.S. Patent Office. Her compassion for soldiers on the battlefield drove her to get involved by organizing and undertaking supply deliveries to the front lines. Once there, the couldn't leave. She acted as a nurse to Union field surgeons, earning her the nickname "The Angel of the Battle-field." After the war, she heard about the International Red Cross while on a visit to Switzerland. It took her 13 years of lobbying Congress for funding before she was able to establish the American Red Cross in 1882. She ran the agency for 22 years, fulfilling the promise of a Red Cross that would serve Americans in war and peace.

Leadership and Values

Why is it important for an organization to have values, and what is the role of the leader in establishing and enforcing values? There are many ideas on these questions, but few are as influential as those of the philosopher Plato.

Plato answers these questions as he lays the groundwork for his book *The Republic*. He retells the myth of Gyges and the invisible ring: A young shepherd stumbles upon a magic ring that has the power to make the wearer invisible. Immediately, he takes advantage of the ring to do things he could never do before—eavesdrop, steal, trespass—and in a short time, he amasses wealth, kills the king, seduces the queen, and rules the land.[65]

The moral of the story is that, given power without accountability, an individual may do terrible deeds that are harmful to others. People need the values of a just society and the oversight of wise leaders to govern their actions; otherwise, they may engage in selfish and destructive behavior.

Plato's Allegory of the Cave

See human beings as though they were in an underground cave-like dwelling with its entrance, a long one, open to the light across the whole width of the cave. They are in it from childhood with their legs and necks in bonds so that they are fixed, seeing only in front of them, unable because of the bond to turn their heads all the way around.[66]

In this allegory, people trapped in the cave represent the world's ignorant masses. They see only representations of objects, the sights and sounds that can be discerned by the physical senses. The individual who escapes the cave to witness the true nature of things is the philosopher. Using intellect, philosophers are able to discern forms—abstract, immutable truths that are the real foundation of the universe. The philosopher who escapes the cave knows the true nature of reality.

The Republic is ultimately concerned with the question of justice. Plato believed that to establish justice, one must know what is good. Therefore, philosophers who understood the form of the good should rule as kings. The rest of society should be organized to fulfill those rulers' demands.[67]

Plato believed that, for the good of all individuals, a republic is needed, administered by philosopher–kings. The argument can be made that, in a similar way, every workplace needs high ethical values upheld by strong and caring leaders.

It must be recognized that a leader may have false or harmful values that are injurious to others. The examples of Hitler, Stalin, and many other tyrants in history can be cited. These cases only point more clearly to the need for caring leaders who are both good and strong.

We need to keep in mind that culture shapes the leader's values, which influence his or her actions. For example, woven into the fabric of African society is the concept of *ubuntu*. *Ubuntu* represents a collection of values, including harmony, compassion, respect, human dignity, and collective unity. It is "that profound African sense that each of us is human through the humanity of other human beings," explains former South African President Nelson Mandela. *Ubuntu* is often described through a Zulu maxim: "*umuntu ngumuntu ngabantu.*" Archbishop Desmond Tutu offers this translation: "We believe that a person is a person through other persons; that my humanity is caught up and bound up inextricably in yours."[68]

How Leader Behavior Influences Employee Conduct and Organizational Reputation

Studies show that people who excel in leadership have a sense of purpose, a deep commitment, and a feeling that what they do has meaning and contributes to a worthwhile cause. Their actions are deeply rooted in values. Leading with an understanding of who you are and what is important can be termed leading from within or managing by values.[69]

People will forgive the leader who fails to manage by objectives, or is inefficient in the use of time, or fails to achieve the smoothest human relations; but they find it difficult to forgive the leader who is immoral and nonprincipled. Such a person lacks moral authority and is not trusted or respected. Even as important as vision is to leadership success, more important are values, because the values of the leader will determine the rightness and wrongness of all that he or she does.

What a leader says and does regarding values has enormous influence on others. More than any memo, directive, or brass band, the **actions** of the leader communicate. The leader's actions set the tone for people's behavior toward one another and for performance on the job. An effective leader accomplishes, through personal example, the building of individual commitment and group cooperation toward accomplishment of the task or mission. The leader who is honest, unselfish, and dedicated in his own actions helps the group succeed.[70]

When Warren Buffett took over as interim chairman of Salomon after the Treasury auction crisis, his first action was to instruct senior managers to report "instantaneously and directly" any legal violations or moral failures by Salomon employees. He told the firm's assembled personnel: "Lose money for the firm, I will be very understanding; lose a shred of reputation for the firm, I will be ruthless." Executives like Buffett understand instinctively what researchers have documented—a commitment to basic values such as honesty and responsibility is crucial for building trust, and trust is the bedrock of organizational survival and growth over the long term.[71]

Although historically negligent, it is interesting to note that more and more business schools are teaching basic principles of ethical leadership. Almost half of all business schools now require one or more courses in ethics, and business ethics doctoral programs have been established at the University of Pennsylvania's Wharton School and the University of Virginia's Darden School of Business.[72]

It is safe to say that a leader's value system will be known. It won't be a secret because it will reveal itself in the policies and decisions she makes, the way she spends her time, and for what she sacrifices. In general, a leader's belief or value system will determine her success. The following are six values of caring leaders in every field and level of responsibility:

1. *Honesty*—knowing oneself and being honest in all dealings with others.

2. *Consideration*—doing unto others as you would have them do unto you.

3. *Responsibility*—taking the attitude that life is what you make it and choosing to make a difference.

4. *Persistence*—being determined; if at first you don't succeed, try, try again.

5. *Excellence*—living by the motto, Anything worth doing is worth doing well.

6. *Commitment*—viewing the great essentials of life as someone to love and something to do.[73]

The overall value of the caring leader is to serve guided by the *Golden Rule* of treating others as one would like to be treated. In the business world, this means service to four groups of people. The caring leader focuses on the welfare of (1) *customers*—anticipating their needs and providing state-of-the-art products; (2) *employees*—providing a healthy work environment, treating them with fairness, and helping them achieve their professional potential; (3) *shareholders*—maintaining a strong growth rate and return on investment; and (4) *community*—exemplifying the highest standards of ethical behavior and contributing to the well-being of society.[74]

Values are important elements of leadership character because they affect everything a person does or is. The more you understand your values, the clearer you can be in your ideas about life, the more confident you can be in your actions, and the more developed you will be as a leader. Because of the ability to influence moral behavior, the leader should address two questions: (1) What values or principles do I wish to promote? (2) Are my actions helping accomplish that goal?

Personal Values

All aspects and institutions of society require leaders who are competent, caring, and value-based—committed to certain ideals and goals. A useful model and tool that addresses this issue is *The Study of Values* by Gordon Allport, Phillip Vernon, and Gardner Lindzey, based on Eduard Spranger's *Types of Men*. Complete Exercise 7–1 to discover your own value orientation.

Exercise 7–1
Personal Values—What Is Important to You?[75]

Each of the following questions has six possible responses. Rank these responses by assigning a 6 to the one you prefer the most, a 5 to the next, and so on down to 1, the least preferred of the alternatives. Sometimes you may have trouble making choices, but there should be no ties; you should make a choice.

1. Which of the following branches of study do you consider most important?
   _____ a. philosophy
   _____ b. political science
   _____ c. psychology
   _____ d. theology
   _____ e. business
   _____ f. art

2. Which of the following qualities is most descriptive of you?
   _____ a. religious
   _____ b. unselfish
   _____ c. artistic
   _____ d. persuasive
   _____ e. practical
   _____ f. intelligent

3. Of the following famous people, who is most interesting to you?
   _____ a. Albert Einstein—discoverer of the theory of relativity
   _____ b. Henry Ford—automobile entrepreneur
   _____ c. Napoleon Bonaparte—political leader and military strategist
   _____ d. Martin Luther—-leader of the Protestant Reformation
   _____ e. Michelangelo—sculptor and painter
   _____ f. Albert Schweitzer—missionary and humanitarian

4. What kind of person do you prefer to be? One who
   _____ a. is industrious and economically self-sufficient
   _____ b. has leadership qualities and organizing ability
   _____ c. has spiritual or religious values
   _____ d. is philosophical and interested in knowledge
   _____ e. is compassionate and understanding toward others
   _____ f. has artistic sensitivity and skill

5. Which of the following is most interesting to you?
   _____ a. artistic experiences
   _____ b. thinking about life
   _____ c. accumulation of wealth
   _____ d. religious faith
   _____ e. leading others
   _____ f. serving others

6. In which of the following would you prefer to participate?
   _____ a. business venture
   _____ b. artistic performance
   _____ c. religious activity
   _____ d. project to help the poor
   _____ e. scientific study
   _____ f. political campaign

7. Which publication would you prefer to read?

_____ a. *History of the Arts*

_____ b. *Psychology Today*

_____ c. *Power Politics*

_____ d. *Scientific American*

_____ e. *Religions Today*

_____ f. *The Wall Street Journal*

8. In choosing a spouse, whom would you prefer? One who

_____ a. likes to help people

_____ b. is a leader in his or her field

_____ c. is practical and enterprising

_____ d. is artistically gifted

_____ e. has a deep spiritual belief

_____ f. is interested in philosophy and learning

9. Which activity do you consider more important for children?

_____ a. scouting

_____ b. Junior Achievement

_____ c. religious training

_____ d. creative arts

_____ e. student government

_____ f. science club

10. What should be the goal of government leaders?

_____ a. promoting creative and aesthetic interests

_____ b. establishing a position of power and respect in the world

_____ c. developing commerce and industry

_____ d. supporting education and learning

_____ e. providing a supportive climate for spiritual growth and development

_____ f. promoting the social welfare of citizens

11. Which of the following courses would you prefer to teach?

_____ a. anthropology

_____ b. religions of the world

_____ c. philosophy

_____ d. political science

_____ e. poetry

_____ f. business administration

12. What would you do if you had sufficient time and money?

_____ a. go on a retreat for spiritual renewal

_____ b. increase your money-making ability

_____ c. develop leadership skills

_____ d. help those who are less fortunate

_____ e. study the fine arts, such as theater, music, and painting

_____ f. write an original essay, article, or book

13. Which courses would you promote if you were able to influence educational policies?

_____ a. political and governmental studies

_____ b. philosophy and science

_____ c. economics and occupational skills

_____ d. social problems and issues

_____ e. spiritual and religious studies

_____ f. music and art

14. Which of the following news items would be most interesting to you?

_____ a. "Business Conditions Favorable"

_____ b. "Relief Arrives for Poor"

_____ c. "Religious Leaders Meet"

_____ d. "President Addresses the Nation"

_____ e. "What's New in the Arts"

_____ f. "Scientific Breakthrough Revealed"

15. Which subjects would you prefer to discuss?

_____ a. music, film, and theater

_____ b. the meaning of human existence

_____ c. spiritual experiences

_____ d. wars in history

_____ e. business opportunities

_____ f. social conditions

16. What do you think the purpose should be for space exploration?

_____ a. to unify people around the world

_____ b. to gain knowledge of our universe

_____ c. to reveal the beauty of our world

_____ d. to discover answers to spiritual questions

_____ e. to control world affairs

_____ f. to develop trade and business opportunities

17. Which profession would you enter if all salaries were equal and you felt you had equal aptitude to succeed in any one of the six?

_____ a. counseling

_____ b. fine arts

_____ c. science

_____ d. politics

_____ e. business

_____ f. ministry

18. Whose life and works are most interesting to you?

_____ a. Madame Curie—discoverer of radium

_____ b. Katherine Graham—businesswoman

_____ c. Margaret Thatcher—British prime minister

_____ d. Mother Teresa—religious leader

_____ e. Martha Graham—ballerina and choreographer

_____ f. Harriet Beecher Stowe—author of _Uncle Tom's Cabin_

19. Which television program would you prefer to watch?

_____ a. _Art Appreciation_

_____ b. _Spiritual Values_

_____ c. _Investment Opportunities_

_____ d. _Marriage and the Family_

_____ e. _Political Power and Social Persuasion_

_____ f. _The Origins of Intelligence_

20. Which of the following positions would you like to have?

_____ a. political leader

_____ b. artist

_____ c. teacher

_____ d. theologian

_____ e. writer

_____ f. business entrepreneur

Scoring:

Step 1:

For each lettered response to each question, insert your score in the appropriate space in the following chart. Note that the letters are not always in the same column.

Example: a. _2_   b. _6_   c. _4_   d. _5_   e. _3_   f. _1_

	I	II	III	IV	V	VI
1.	a. ____	e. ____	f. ____	c. ____	b. ____	d. ____
2.	f. ____	e. ____	c. ____	b. ____	d. ____	a. ____
3.	a. ____	b. ____	e. ____	f. ____	c. ____	d. ____
4.	d. ____	a. ____	f. ____	e. ____	b. ____	c. ____
5.	b. ____	c. ____	a. ____	f. ____	e. ____	d. ____
6.	e. ____	a. ____	b. ____	d. ____	f. ____	c. ____
7.	d. ____	f. ____	a. ____	b. ____	c. ____	e. ____
8.	f. ____	c. ____	d. ____	a. ____	b. ____	e. ____
9.	f. ____	b. ____	d. ____	a. ____	e. ____	c. ____
10.	d. ____	c. ____	a. ____	f. ____	b. ____	e. ____
11.	c. ____	f. ____	e. ____	a. ____	d. ____	b. ____
12.	f. ____	b. ____	e. ____	d. ____	c. ____	a. ____
13.	b. ____	c. ____	f. ____	d. ____	a. ____	e. ____
14.	f. ____	a. ____	e. ____	b. ____	d. ____	c. ____
15.	b. ____	e. ____	a. ____	f. ____	d. ____	c. ____
16.	b. ____	f. ____	c. ____	a. ____	e. ____	d. ____
17.	c. ____	e. ____	b. ____	a. ____	d. ____	f. ____
18.	a. ____	b. ____	e. ____	f. ____	c. ____	d. ____
19.	f. ____	c. ____	a. ____	d. ____	e. ____	b. ____
20.	e. ____	f. ____	b. ____	c. ____	a. ____	d. ____
Totals	____	____	____	____	____	____

Step 2:

Add the scores for each column, and record the total in the appropriate space.

Step 3:

Mark the total for each personal value column in the appropriate place in Figure 7–1. Connect the scores with straight lines to form a profile of your overall value orientation. See the example in Figure 7–2.

Interpretation:

A description of each personal value follows:

Theoretical. The primary interest of the theoretical person is the discovery of truth. In the laboratory, field, and library, and in personal affairs as well, the purpose of the theoretical person is to know the truth above all other goals. In the pursuit of truth, the theoretical person prefers a cognitive approach, one that looks for identities and differences, as opposed to the beauty or utility of objects. This person's needs are to observe, reason, and understand. Because the theoretical person's values are empirical, critical, and rational, this person is an intellectual and frequently is a scientist or philosopher. Major concerns of such a person are to order and systematize knowledge and to understand the meaning of life.

Economic. The economic person is interested in what is useful. Based originally on the satisfaction of bodily needs and self-preservation, the interest in usefulness extends to the practical affairs of the business world—the production and marketing of goods, and the accumulation of wealth. This type of person is enterprising and efficient, reflecting the

**Figure 7–1
Your Personal Value
Orientation**

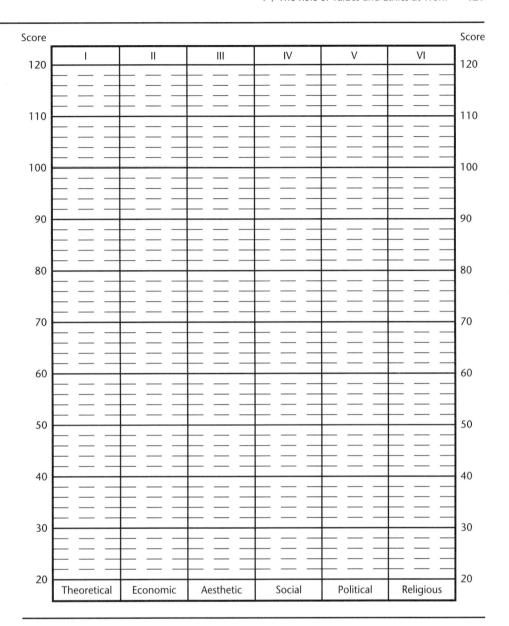

stereotype of the average businessperson. Economic values sometimes come into conflict with other values. The economic person wants education to be practical and regards unapplied knowledge as wasteful. Great feats of engineering and application result from the demands economic people make on people in science. Economic values may conflict with aesthetic values, such as in the advertising and promotion of products and services, except when art meets commercial ends. In relationships with people, the economic person is more likely to be interested in surpassing others in wealth than in dominating them politically or in serving them socially.

Aesthetic. The aesthetic person finds highest satisfaction in form, harmony, and beauty. The value of each single experience is judged from the standpoint of grace, symmetry, and fitness. The aesthetic person regards life as a procession of events, with each impression to be enjoyed for its own sake. An aesthetic person may or may not be a creative artist; the aesthetic person finds chief interest in the artistic episodes of life. Unlike the theoretical person, the aesthetic person usually chooses, with the poet John Keats, to consider truth as equivalent to beauty, or agrees with H. L. Mencken that to make a thing charming is a million times more important than to make it true.[76] In the economic sphere, the aesthetic person often sees the process of manufacturing,

Figure 7–2
Example: Personal Value
Orientation

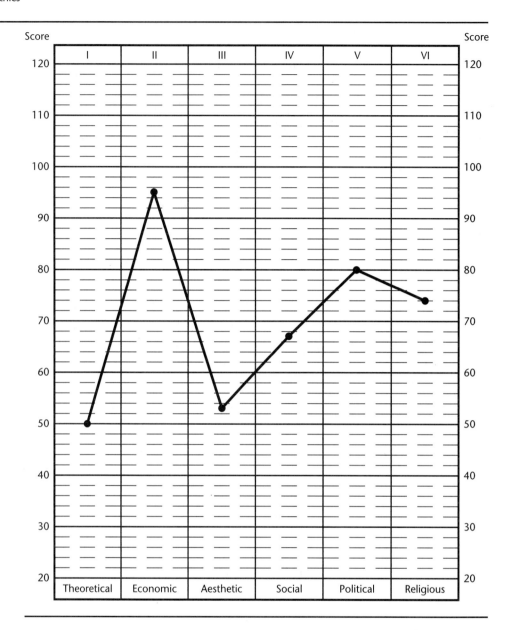

advertising, and trade as a destruction of important aesthetic values. In social affairs, the aesthetic person may be said to be interested in people, but not necessarily in their welfare. The aesthetic person tends toward individualism, self-sufficiency, and idealism in personal relations.

Social. The highest value for this type of person is love. The altruistic or philanthropic aspect of love is the interest of the social person. Humanistic by nature, the social person prizes other people as ends in and of themselves, and not as tools or means to other goals. Therefore, the social person is kind, sympathetic, and helpful toward others. Such a person may find the economic and political values to be cold and inhumane. In contrast to the political type, the social person regards love instead of power as the most suitable form of human relationship. In purest form, social values are totally unselfish.

Political. The political person is interested in power and influence, although the person's activities may not fall within the narrow field of politics. Whatever the vocation, the political person seeks to be a *Machtmensch,* an individual who is powerful. Leaders in any field usually will have a high interest in power and status. Because competition and struggle play a large part in all of life—between the sexes, between groups, between nations, and between individuals—many philosophers have viewed power as the most universal and most fundamental of human motives. In certain people, however, the desire for direct expression of power is uppermost, and their primary values are social influence and the exercise of authority.

Religious. The highest value of this type of person is spiritual peace. A religious person may or may not belong to an organized religion; people are religious if they but seek to comprehend the cosmos as a whole and to relate themselves to its embracing totality. Religious people have as their goal the creation of the highest and most satisfying value experience. Some people who are religious focus on events, people, and experiences in this world; that is, they experience meaning in the affirmation of life and active participation therein. With zest and enthusiasm, they see something divine in every event. On the other hand, some religious people are transcendental mystics, seeking to unite themselves with a higher reality by withdrawing from life. This type is ascetic, and like the holy men of India, finds inner peace and unity through self-denial and meditation. In many individuals, the affirmation and negation of human existence alternate to yield the greatest value satisfaction.

In evaluating your personal values, remember the following points:

■ All six values on the questionnaire are positive. The questions do not measure negative values, such as greed or violence.

■ Culture influences personal values. Through the processes of imprinting, modeling, and socialization, people learn to place higher importance on some values over others. Thus, the prestige afforded the monarch, priest, businessperson, scientist, artist, and teacher depends on the values promoted by each society. In the Pygmy culture, for example, the male with the greatest social esteem usually is not the strongest, wealthiest, most spiritual, most artistic, or most intelligent; rather, he is the one who shares most generously. Consider American society: What are the primary values for people in the United States today? Are they the same for men and women? Do they reflect your personal values?

■ By forcing choices among six personal values, the questionnaire provides an overall value orientation. This means that your lowest personal value may be more important to you than the highest personal value of another individual. Similarly, your highest may be less important to you than the lowest of another individual. The questionnaire measures the relative strength of six personal values, so that you obtain a picture of *your* overall value orientation, or an understanding of what is most important to you.

■ Ideally, a person's life will allow maximum expression of personal values. This helps explain the achievements and satisfactions of "theoretical" Albert Einstein, "economic" John D. Rockefeller, "aesthetic" Leonardo da Vinci, "social" Jane Addams, "political" Elizabeth I, and "religious" Martin Luther.

■ Basic value systems are fairly firm by the time most people reach adulthood. Ideas about what is important are well established and are unlikely to change unless a significant emotional event takes place. For most people, few experiences are significant or emotional enough to disrupt basic values formed during childhood and adolescence. As a rule, if a person changes basic values during the adult years, it is only because a situation is experienced that previous values cannot resolve.[77]

■ Different organizations reflect and endorse different values, and each organization's success depends on having people in it, especially leaders, who promote its value system. Some people may be ideally suited for *theoretical* organizations such as universities, *economic* organizations such as corporations, *aesthetic* organizations such as performing groups, *social* organizations such as human service agencies, *political* organizations such as political parties, or *religious* organizations such as churches, synagogues, and mosques. Mismatches can be stressful for both the individual and the organization. Examples include the social person who gives away the store, the individual who uses religious position for personal power, and the art curator whose priority is profit. Consider your own values. What type of organization, if any, would be most appropriate for you?[78]

Remember, the personal values questionnaire does not measure other important factors, such as aptitude, personal interests, and individual temperament, nor does it measure levels of morality, a critical element in leadership and human relationships. Finally, remember that different values can actually enrich a group or an organization. In this spirit, use the following thought as a guide: "Our errors and our controversies in the sphere of human relations often arise from looking on people as though they could be altogether bad, or altogether good."[79]

Exercise 7–2 can be used to clarify individual and organizational values.

**Exercise 7–2
Values Auction**

We are not born with values, but we are born into cultures and societies that promote, teach, and impart their values to us. The process of acquiring values begins at birth. But it is not a static process. Our values change continually throughout our lives. For example, as children, our highest value might have been play; as adolescents, perhaps it was peer relationships; as young adults, our highest value may be raising children or the work we do. For many older people, service to others is the highest value. We are formed largely by the experiences we have, and our values form, grow, and change accordingly.[80]

Because values are important in an individual's personal, social, and occupational adjustment, it is important to understand basic value patterns. This exercise will help you

- Determine those life values that are of greatest importance to you.
- Explore the degree of trust you have in the group.
- Examine how well you compete and cooperate.
- Consider how your values affect your decisions regarding personal and professional life goals.

Auction Rules:

During this values auction, you will have the opportunity to buy, and thus own, any of the values listed—if your bid is highest. Owning a value means you have full rights and privileges to do with the value whatever you choose at the conclusion of the exercise. Follow these rules:

1. Gather in a group for the purpose of having an auction for the 20 values listed on the Values Auction Sheet.
2. Choose one person to be the auctioneer.
3. Each person should receive 10 tokens valued at $100 each to be used for bidding. Only these tokens will be accepted as payment for any value purchased.
4. You may elect to pool your resources with other group members in order to purchase a particularly high-priced value. This means that two, three, four, or more people may extend a bid for any one value. You are allowed to participate, and win, in such a pool *one time only.* If you pool, but lose, you are allowed to pool again.
5. The auctioneer's task is to collect the highest number of tokens possible in the course of the auction. After the auction has begun, no further questions will be answered by the auctioneer. Allow 5 to 10 minutes for participants to budget desired amounts for preferred values. Notice that these amounts may change during the course of the auction. Use the Values Auction Sheet to record budgeted amounts and to keep a record of winning bids.
6. Begin the auction.

Values Auction Sheet

	Amount I Budgeted	Highest Amount I Bid	Top Bid
1. All the food and drink you want without ever getting fat	_____	_____	_____
2. Freedom to be and do what you want in life	_____	_____	_____
3. A chance to direct the destiny of a nation	_____	_____	_____
4. The love and admiration of good friends	_____	_____	_____
5. Travel and tickets to any cultural or athletic event as often as you wish	_____	_____	_____
6. Complete self-confidence with a positive outlook on life	_____	_____	_____
7. A happy, healthy family	_____	_____	_____
8. Recognition as the most desirable person in the world	_____	_____	_____
9. A long life free of illness	_____	_____	_____
10. A complete library with all the time you need to enjoy it	_____	_____	_____
11. A deep and satisfying religious faith	_____	_____	_____
12. A lifetime of financial security and material wealth	_____	_____	_____
13. A lovely home in a beautiful setting	_____	_____	_____
14. A world without prejudice and cruelty	_____	_____	_____
15. A world without sickness and poverty	_____	_____	_____
16. International fame and renown for your achievements	_____	_____	_____
17. An understanding of the meaning of life	_____	_____	_____
18. The chance to be a contestant on a *Survivor* TV episode	_____	_____	_____
19. The highest success in your chosen profession	_____	_____	_____
20. A deep and satisfying love with someone	_____	_____	_____

Discussion:

At the conclusion of the values auction, consider the following questions:

1. What values did you win that are truly important to you? What values did you miss?

2. How competitive and cooperative were you during the values auction? Does this suggest a need to be more aggressive if you are going to achieve what is important to you? Does this indicate a need to be more cooperative and open to strategic alliances?

3. Are you living your life in line with your values? Do your work, community, and personal life conditions support your value system?

After completing the values auction, people can discuss and agree upon core values, usually three, for the organization or group. These values should be the stars that guide members of the organization in all moral dilemmas. They should be the "hills worth dying on," or the principles worth losing one's position or membership to uphold.

Disputes can often be avoided if people will discuss their value systems and find points of common interest and agreement. This situation is pictured in Figure 7–3.

Figure 7–3
Core Values Are Points of Common Interest

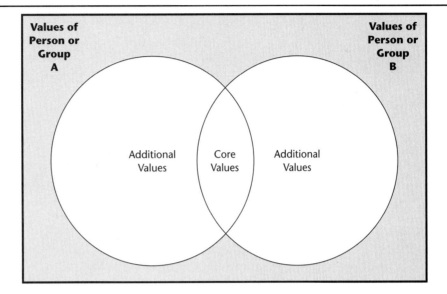

Through discussion, shared values—those that define the basic character of the group, tribe, or family—can be emphasized. For example, shared values may represent the Catholic church, the Cherokee tribe, the Smith family, or a particular business organization. Additional individual values at the fourth, fifth, and sixth levels can serve to enrich a community, especially if there is tolerance and appreciation of diversity.[81]

Organizational Ethics

In his book *Management: Tasks, Responsibility, Practices,* Peter Drucker suggests that once an organization reaches the size of 1,000 employees, work rules should be developed to maximize efficiency and serve as a guide for employee conduct. Such a code of conduct can be important in determining the nature, reputation, and success of the organization.[82] The best work rules meet the following criteria: They reflect the ethical ideals of the ownership, or, in the case of public organizations, the public trust; they are reviewed periodically for needed revisions; they are few in number; they are stated clearly; they are communicated to all employees; and they apply equally to all employees, regardless of level of authority or nature of duties.

A comprehensive code of ethics for an organization includes guidelines in each of the following areas:

- *Government relations.* How does the organization pay its taxes and obey national and international law?

- *Employee relations.* How does the organization deal with employee welfare and grievances?

- *Business relations.* How does the organization deal with suppliers and competitors?

- *Production.* What are the standards of quality for the organization's products and services?

- *Consumer relations.* How does the organization price and advertise its products and services?

- *Community and environmental relations.* What are the effects of the organization on its social and physical environment?

For example, Procter & Gamble has an ethical community and environmental quality policy, as follows:

Procter & Gamble is committed to providing products of superior quality and value that best fill the needs of the world's consumers. To carry out this commitment, it is Procter & Gamble's policy to

- Ensure our products, packaging, and operations are *safe* for our employees, consumers, and the environment.

- Reduce or prevent the *environmental impact* of our products and packaging in their design, manufacture, distribution, use, and disposal whenever possible.

- Meet or exceed the requirements of all environmental *laws and regulations*.

- Continually assess our environmental technology and programs, and *monitor* programs toward environmental goals.

- Provide our consumers, customers, employees, communities, public interest groups, and others with relevant and appropriate *factual information* about the environmental quality of P&G products, packaging, and operations.

- Ensure every employee understands and is *responsible and accountable* for incorporating environmental quality considerations in daily business activities.

- Have operating policies, programs, and resources in place to *implement* our environmental quality policy.[83]

The misdeeds of organizations such as Enron, Arthur Andersen, WorldCom, and others have moved ethics to center stage in American Society.[84] Responding to a series of corporate scandals, the U.S. Congress passed the Sarbanes-Oxley Act in 2002 to improve and maintain investor confidence. The law requires companies to have more independent boards of directors, to adhere strictly to accounting rules, and to have senior managers personally sign off on financial results. Violations result in heavy fines and criminal prosecution. The time and money costs of compliance are high, but efforts to meet the requirements can reduce the likelihood of misdeeds.[85]

Organizational ethics is an issue that concerns virtually everyone—customers, employees, owners, and citizens at large. In his influential book *Vanguard*

Management, James O'Toole identifies the key characteristics of ethical and successful organizations:

■ They try to satisfy all their constituencies—customers, employees, owners, suppliers, dealers, communities, and governments. They subscribe to the utilitarian ideal—the greatest good for the greatest number.

■ They are dedicated to high and broad purposes. Profit is viewed as an essential means to a higher end—human service and quality of life.

■ They are committed to learning, investing enormous resources and effort to remaining current and responsive to change. They view employee growth and development as a critical foundation of business success.

■ They try to be the best at whatever they do. Their performance standards rise continually. Excellence in product and service is an organizationwide commitment and source of pride.[86]

One of the most influential guidelines for ethics at work comes from Rotary International. Many generations of leaders from all areas of the world have been taught to test their actions against four basic questions:

1. **Is it the truth?**
2. **Is it fair to all concerned?**
3. **Will it build goodwill and better relationships?**
4. **Will it be beneficial to all concerned?**[87]

Why Are Ethics at Work Important to Leaders?

The following are five good reasons to be concerned about leadership ethics:

■ Bernard Ebbers, former CEO of WorldCom, is serving a 25-year prison sentence for fraud and conspiracy.

■ Jeffrey Skilling, former CEO of Enron, is serving a 24-year prison sentence for securities fraud and insider trading.

■ John Rigas, former CEO of Aldelphia Communications, is serving a 12-year prison sentence for conspiracy and bank fraud.

■ Dennis Kozlowski, former CEO of Tyco, is serving an 8-year prison sentence for grand larceny and falsifying business records.[88]

■ Bernard Madoff is serving a 150-year prison sentence for his "Ponzi scheme" against investors.

In her excellent book *Value Shift,* Lynn Sharp Paine cites a variety of motives linking leaders and ethics at work: (1) One executive believes high ethical standards and business success are positively related; (2) another sees ethical commitment as a basis for building customer trust; (3) another believes a reputation for integrity will help attract and keep the best employees; (4) another wants his company to be a role model for society; (5) another wants to avoid any conflict with the law; and (6) another answers succinctly and pragmatically, "*60 Minutes.*" Misconduct threatens leaders at all levels of responsibility; even those who are not personally involved can suffer reputational and financial damage.[89]

The social and economic costs of ethical misconduct can include: (1) loss of customers and sales; (2) increased turnover and loss of good employees; (3) demoralized and cynical managers and workers; (4) loss of ownership equity; (5) high operating costs due to misspent energy and poor execution; (6) additional legal expenses and possible fines, penalties, and settlement costs; (7) high funding costs imposed by lenders and investors; (8) loss of public trust and goodwill; and (9) loss of financial viability and ultimate failure of the enterprise.[90]

For some leaders, the concern for ethics at work is less about defensive measures and damage control and more about principled leadership. These leaders adhere to high standards of moral reasoning and value ideals such as truth, trust, and respect as the building blocks of a successful organization. With these leaders, there is little discussion about risk prevention and public opinion. Their behavior is about responsibility and doing what is right *because it is right.* The result is employees who take pride in their organization and engage in discretionary behavior beyond the defined requirements of the job.[91]

Ethical Climates of Organizations

In dealing with moral dilemmas regarding people, products, prices, and profits, organizations typically reflect one of three ethical climates: (1) profit-maximizing; (2) trusteeship; or (3) quality-of-life management. Each climate provides different levels of organizational support for ethical decision making.[92]

Exercise 7–3 presents a description of each climate on 14 ethical dimensions. As you complete the exercise, you will see how different ethical climates influence moral judgments and result in different experiences for employees, customers, and citizens. As you read the descriptions, ask yourself what type of organization you respect; what type of organization you have; and what you can do to influence the ethics of your organization.

Exercise 7–3
Organizational Ethics[93]

Evaluate your organization by circling the appropriate description of the prevailing climate—profit-maximizing, trusteeship, or quality-of-life management—for each of the 14 ethical dimensions listed in the first column.

Ethical Dimension	Profit-Maximizing	Trusteeship	Quality-of-Life Management
1. Social definition of *good*	What is good for me is what counts.	What is good for my organization is what counts.	What is good for humankind is good for my organization and ultimately is best for me.
2. Democracy at work	I am a rugged individualist and will do as I please.	I am an individualist, but I recognize the value of employee participation in the decision-making process.	Democratic management is fundamental to a successful organization.
3. Attitude toward profit	I seek as much profit as the market will bear.	I want a substantial profit.	Profit is necessary, but not to the exclusion of other considerations that influence human welfare.
4. Attitude toward wealth	My wealth is more important than other people's feelings.	Money is important, but so are people.	Other people's needs are more important than my wealth.
5. Labor relations	Labor is a commodity to be bought and sold.	Labor has certain rights that must be recognized.	It is essential to preserve employee dignity, even if profit is reduced.
6. Consumer protection	Let the buyer beware.	Let us not cheat the customer.	Consumer welfare comes first; satisfaction is guaranteed.
7. Self-interest versus altruism	My interest comes first.	Self-interest and the interests of others are considered.	I will always do what is in the best interest of all concerned.
8. Employee relations	Employee personal problems must be left at home.	I recognize that employees have needs and goals beyond economics.	I employ the whole person and am concerned with achieving maximum employee welfare.
9. Management accountability	Management is accountable solely to the owners.	Accountability of management is to the owners, customers, employees, and suppliers.	Accountability of management is to owners, customers, employees, suppliers, and society in general.
10. Attitude toward technology	Progress is more important than people's feelings.	Technology is important, but so are people.	Human needs are more important than technology advances.
11. Minority relations	Minorities have their place in society, but not with me.	Some people are more important than others, and they should be treated accordingly.	Everyone—regardless of age, color, creed, or sex—should be treated equally.
12. Attitude toward government	Government is best when it stays out of my way.	Government is a necessary evil.	Business and government should work together to solve society's problems.
13. Human–environment interface	The environment exists for economic ends.	People should control and manipulate the environment.	People must preserve the environment for the highest quality of life.
14. Aesthetic values	Aesthetic values are a low priority.	Aesthetic values are OK, but not to the exclusion of economic needs.	Aesthetic values must be preserved, even if economic costs are increased.

Scoring:

Assign a score of 1 to each *profit-maximizing* response, 2 to each *trusteeship* response, and 3 to each *quality-of-life management* response. Add the scores and enter the total here: _____ .

Interpretation:

The terms *profit-maximizing, trusteeship,* and *quality-of-life management* correspond with Kohlberg's levels of morality—I, II, III. *Profit-maximizing* reflects preconventional morality. In this case, the organization's focus is on self-gain and avoidance of punishment. *Trusteeship* reflects conventional morality. The organization behaves to conform to the expectations of others and to satisfy higher authorities. *Quality-of-life management* reflects postconventional morality. Here, the ethical climate of the organization is to do what is right, over and above self-interest and apart from the influence of others. With this climate, ethical conduct is based on the highest moral principles. Use your total score to determine your organization's overall climate and level of morality.

Scores	Level of Morality
14–23	Profit-maximizing—level I, preconventional
24–32	Trusteeship—level II, conventional
33–42	Quality-of-life management—level III, postconventional

The following is an example of a *quality-of-life management–level III* company credo:

We will be honest and trustworthy in all our dealings. We will treat every individual with respect and dignity. We will follow the Golden Rule in all matters. We will strive for excellence in all work performed. We will obey the laws of our land in fact and in spirit. We will always do the right thing in every situation to the best of our abilities. If we fail in abiding by these principles, we will do whatever is needed to make amends.

Although many organizations have a code of ethics, far fewer have a comprehensive ethics program that includes training, procedures for reporting violations, and discipline for violations. Only 43 percent include ethics in performance reviews and 23 percent have a comprehensive ethics and compliance program.[94] Maintaining consistent ethical behavior by all employees is an ongoing challenge. What are danger signs that an organization may be allowing or even encouraging unethical behavior?

1. Failure to establish a written code of ethics.
2. Failure to include ethical conduct as part of performance appraisal.
3. Unwillingness to take an ethical stand that may impose financial cost.
4. Consideration of ethics solely as a legal issue or public relations tool.
5. Lack of clear procedures for handling ethical problems.
6. Condoning unethical leadership practices.[95]

What is the central solution for maintaining an ethical work environment? Leaders at all levels are selected and rewarded for their performance in meeting both integrity and business standards, and if violations occur, even leaders who were otherwise successful are held accountable and disciplined, sending a powerful message that ethical behavior is valued and will be upheld in every instance.[96]

The question may be asked, Won't quality-of-life management organizations fail in competition with rough-riding, profit-maximizing organizations? Research does not bear this out. Data show a positive and significant relationship between the ethical climate of organizations and the level of profit. The higher the ethical climate, the higher the level of profit when computed over a period of years. In contrast, examples from Enron to Worldcom show the negative consequences of unprincipled, profit-maximizing morality.[97]

Increasingly, organizations are being held to high standards in both moral and financial dimensions. Corporate reputation rankings, employee morale surveys, customer satisfaction records, and quality performance reports are used as measures of success that have bottom-line financial impact. The best organizations are those that satisfy both the social and financial expectations of their constituencies.[98]

Lynn Sharp Paine argues that "ethics counts" is a better slogan than "ethics pays," which casts ethical commitment as only a servant to financial interests. "Ethics counts" embraces values and morality as full partners in the quest for outstanding performance. This philosophy of business recognizes the intrinsic worth of other human values, and takes moral considerations seriously in their own right, over and above material gain.[99]

The Tylenol Story

There is no better example to show how "ethics counts" than the Johnson & Johnson Tylenol crisis. When CEO James Burke and other executives of the company were unable to solve the mystery of seven deaths linked to the company's popular Tylenol capsules, they took the dramatic and unprecedented action of immediately removing 31 million bottles of the pain reliever from stores and inventory out of concern for the safety of the public and to avoid any further deaths associated with the product. At that time, Tylenol was Johnson & Johnson's most important brand name, accounting for 8 percent of annual sales and 16 percent to 18 percent of net profit. Had Johnson & Johnson's motives been viewed as purely monetary and selfish, the reputation and ensuing positive financial consequences of its actions would have been very different. The Johnson & Johnson Tylenol crisis demonstrates clearly how the well-being of society and the well-being of an organization are inextricably related.[100]

The WorldCom Case

In contrast to the Tylenol story, consider the role of ethics in "The Rise and Fall of WorldCom."

Bernie Ebbers built WorldCom, Inc. (now part of Verizon, Inc.) into one of the world's largest telecommunications firms. Yet he and chief financial officer (CFO) Scott Sullivan have become better known for creating a massive corporate accounting fraud that led to the largest bankruptcy in U.S history. Two investigative reports and subsequent court cases concluded that WorldCom executives were responsible for billions in fraudulent or unsupported accounting entries. How did this mammoth accounting scandal occur without anyone raising alarm? Evidence suggests that Ebbers and Sullivan held considerable power and influence that prevented accounting staff from complaining, or even knowing, about the fraud.

Ebber's inner circle held tight control over the flow of all financial information. Ebber's group also restricted distribution of company-level financial reports and prevented sensitive reports from being prepared at all. Accountants didn't even have access to the computer files in which some of the largest fraudulent entries were made. As a result, employees had to rely on Ebber's executive team to justify the accounting entries that were requested

Another reason why employees complied with questionable accounting practices was that CFO Scott Sullivan wielded immense personal power. He was considered a "whiz kid" with impeccable integrity who had won the prestigious "CFO Excellence Award." Thus, when Sullivan's office asked staff to make questionable entries, some accountants assumed Sullivan had found an innovative- and legal-accounting loophole. If Sullivan's influence didn't work, other executives took a more coercive approach. Employees cited incidents where they were publicly berated for questioning headquarters' decisions and intimidated if they asked for more information. When one employee at a branch refused to alter an accounting entry, WorldCom's controller threatened to fly in from WorldCom's Mississippi headquarters to make the change himself. The employee changed the entry.

Ebbers had similar influence over WorldCom's Board of Directors. Sources indicate that his personal charisma and intolerance of dissension produced a passive board that rubber-stamped most of his recommendations. As one report concluded: "The Board of Directors appears to have embraced suggestions by Mr. Ebbers without question or dissent, even under circumstances where its members now readily acknowledge they had significant misgivings regarding his recommended course of action."[101]

The examples of Tylenol and WorldCom show it is not enough to merely create a values statement, distribute a code of conduct, and exhort employees to high standards; leaders must model and reinforce the values of the organization. The role of the leader is paramount in establishing the moral tone and ethical climate of the organization. With power to set policy and make decisions, the leader can create a place that attracts and rewards the best in both ethical conduct and business performance.

Author Carol Cooper summarizes the need for values-based and principled leadership: The world needs more people who do not have a price at which they can be bought; who do not borrow from integrity to pay for expediency; who are as honest in small matters as they are in large ones; who know how to win with grace and lose with dignity; whose handshake is an ironclad contract; who are not afraid to go against the grain of popular opinion; who are occasionally wrong and always willing to admit it. In short, the world needs *leaders*.[102]

Case Study:

Wendy Kopp—The Recruiter

Sitting in a lunchroom at Columbia University with the school's star students—the senior class president, the student council VP, the premed triple major, and 15 other superachievers—Wendy Kopp is begging them to shelve their career plans to teach in America's most troubled public schools. "This problem has to be this generation's issue," she tells the future grads. "We know we can solve it if we get enough true leaders."

Kopp is talking with prospective recruits for Teach for America, the Peace Corps-like program that she dreamed up when she was a senior at Princeton. As she speaks, she frequently covers her mouth with her right hand, a nervous gesture. But the students, too, are nervous about the job Kopp is asking them to do. Seniors who compete to be Teach for America corps members must endure hours of interviews and tests designed to assess their organizational skills, perseverance, and resiliency—critical traits since recruits receive only five weeks of teacher training (albeit grueling) before they get plopped into a classroom in the South Bronx or some other impoverished locale. As the students voice their qualms about TFA—"What if I fail? Won't poor kids reject Ivy League teachers?"—Kopp doesn't sugarcoat the obstacles: "It can be really overwhelming and depressing," she warns. "We all have bad days, and people who teach in Teach for America probably have more bad days than most."

Kopp's pitch is part challenge and part cautionary tale, yet the combination has been a winning one. [In 2006], 19,000 college students—including 10 percent of the senior class at Yale and Dartmouth, 9 percent at Columbia, and 8 percent at Duke and the University of Chicago—applied to Teach for America. (While local school districts cover the salaries of TFA teachers, TFA screens and trains them—and requires a two-year commitment.) "We recruit insanely aggressively," says Kopp, 39, who accepted 2,400 of those 19,000 applicants this year. That makes Kopp's nonprofit one of the largest hirers of college seniors, according to CollegeGrad.com—bigger than Microscoft, Procter & Gamble, Accenture, or General Electric.

Kopp, in fact, has built such a mighty recruiting machine that corporations are angling to work with TFA to buff their own images on campus. "One of the few jobs that people pass up Goldman Sachs' offers for is Teach for America," says Edie Hunt, Goldman's co-COO [chief operating officer] of human-capital management. (First-year pay at Goldman averages $65,000, about twice what a TFA corps member makes.)

Wendy Kopp never wanted to be a corporate role model. She just wanted to reform public education. Growing up in Dallas (where her parents owned a travel-guide business), she moved from parochial school to public school in sixth grade and went on to be valedictorian of her high school. Her interest in the failures of America's public schools began at Princeton, where she helped organize a conference on education reform during the fall of her senior year. Her senior thesis was entitled "A Plan and Argument for the Creation of a National Teacher Corps," and she wrote a letter to then-President George H. W. Bush, urging him to establish such a two-year service program. "I received a job-rejection letter in response," she recalls.

Rejection spurred her on. Failing to land a job after college (she was turned down by Morgan Stanley, Goldman, McKinsey, Bain, and P&G), she decided to launch the teaching corps herself. Though she describes herself as "very shy," Kopp drummed up the courage to cold-call scores of CEOs and foundation leaders. A Mobil executive named Rex Adams agreed to give her a seed grant of $26,000, and Dick Fisher, then-CEO of Morgan Stanley (and a Princeton alum), donated office space. A letter to the chairman of Hertz got her six cars for TFA's skeleton crew of recruiters (who included Richard Barth, now Kopp's husband). Other early believers—Merck, Union Carbide, Apple Computer, Young & Rubicam, and fellow Texan Ross Perot—chipped in, building her first-year budget to $2.5 million. That was enough to recruit, train, and place 500 teachers.

Kopp wants to continue the success of TFA. "We're trying to be the top employer of recent grads in the country," she says. "Size gives us leverage to have a tangible impact on school systems." [And this she has done.][103]

Questions

1. How would you describe Wendy Kopp's success based on what you have learned in this chapter?

_____

_____

_____

2. Would you apply for a TFA job? What are the ethical implications of your answer?

_____

_____

_____

Part Three Summary

After reading Part Three, you should know the following key concepts, principles, and terms. Fill in the blanks from memory, or copy the answers listed below.

Ethics is the branch of philosophy concerned with (a) _____. The most important influences on character formation are (b) _____, _____, and _____. The three levels of moral development are (c) _____, _____, and _____, with the highest level being characteristic of only 20 percent of the adult population. Value ideals include (d) _____, _____, _____, _____, and _____. (e) _____ is the foundation that underlies and gives life to all other virtues and values. A concept in ethics that can be used to assess the strength of one's values is (f) _____. Fully ethical individuals know, cherish, declare, act on, and act habitually on their values. The leader's (g) _____ are critical in establishing the values and moral tone of an organization. One of the most influential codes of ethical conduct in the workplace is provided by Rotary International, which asks leaders to measure all actions against four questions: (h) _____, _____, _____, and _____.

Answer Key for Part Three Summary

a. **moral judgments and right and wrong conduct,** page 94

b. **associations, books, self-concept,** page 99

c. **preconventional, conventional, postconventional,** page 100

d. **honesty, respect, service, excellence, integrity,** page 109

e. **courage,** page 109

f. **full-swing values,** page 112

g. **actions,** page 115

h. **Is it the truth? Is it fair to all concerned? Will it build goodwill and better relationships? Will it be beneficial to all concerned?** page 132

Reflection Points—Personal Thoughts on Leadership Ethics, the Role of Values, and Ethics at Work

Complete the following questions and activities to personalize the content of Part Three. Space is provided for writing your thoughts.

■ Cite examples of the influence of leadership on the ethical behavior of a work group, an organization, or a society. Use personal or historical examples.

_____

_____

■ Discuss levels of morality in the workplace today. Give examples of leadership actions that are preconventional, conventional, and postconventional.

_____

_____

■ What values are important to you? How strong is your value system? Do you exhibit full-swing values and courage of conviction in ethical dilemmas?

_____

_____

■ If you were the president of a company, what values would you promote? What values would guide you in dealing with people, products, prices, and profits?

_____

_____

■ Develop a code of ethics for an organization. The code should be between one and five pages in length. Present and defend this code of ethics before an audience of interested people.

_____

_____

■ Discuss organizations with differing ethical climates. What is it like to work in profit-maximizing, trusteeship, and qualify-of-life management organizations?

_____

_____

■ A committed person with a good heart and a good idea can make a difference in the world. Based on your values, what could you do to improve the lives of others? How can you engage and serve society?

_____

_____

Part Three Video Case
Patagonia

Yvon Chouinard began climbing as a 14-year-old member of the Southern California Falconry Club. At the time, the only available pitons (spikes used in mountain climbing) were made of soft iron, used once, and left in the rock. In 1957 Chouinard bought a used coal-fired forge to make reusable iron pitons; the word spread and soon he was in business. From climbing equipment to apparel, his company, Patagonia, has evolved into a highly successful private firm with annual revenues of $250 million. Chouinard has kept it private so that he can continue to pursue his mission: earth first, profits second.

According to CEO Michael Crooke, Patagonia is a very special company with a set of core values that is more than the bottom line. Because of the basic values, employees come to work every day with the attitude that they are making a difference. For each new hire, Patagonia receives 900 résumés. To understand the firm's success in satisfying employees, one need only look at a catalog. Not many companies place such significance on environmental and social issues. From the start, Yvon Chouinard advocated a purer, equipment-light approach to making climbing hardware in order to preserve the environment. The philosophy has continued. A recent catalog featured an essay entitled, "Do You Need This Product?" The message? If you don't need another shirt or jacket, don't buy it. Patagonia's management believes that this honest approach, while rare, creates loyal customers and dedicated employees.

To many environmentalists, corporations are the enemy. Patagonia takes a different approach. The company's goal is to make a difference; to do so, it must use its power to work from within the system. Patagonia is a successful company socially, environmentally, and financially. The success starts with great products and great people. Product quality and guarantees assure that the products meet high expectations at any store no matter the location in the world.

In choosing employees, Patagonia looks for people who are passionate about an interest or cause. Over the years, many workers with similar causes and values have joined the company. The culture is based on commitment to environmental, moral, ethical, and philosophical causes. Patagonia employees derive true meaning from work, family, and health, rather than money and status. The goal is psychological success, achieved through a protean career.

Patagonia spends little on recruiting. The firm experiences very low turnover, about 4 percent annually. Each year, *Fortune* magazine rates the company as one of the best to work for. Why have workers found so much satisfaction with their jobs at Patagonia? Four reasons:

- *Let My People Surf.* The philosophy of Yvon Chouinard, not only an accomplished climber but also a passionate surfer, is that you have to surf when the surf's up. At Patagonia, workers set their own schedules; when they need to work, they get their jobs finished. To develop great products, you need to be users of the products. You can't develop great surfboards if you don't surf.

- *Environmental Internship.* After employees have completed a year, the company pays up to 60 days' salary for each individual to intern for an environmental group. The only requirement is that employees present a slide show when they return. Some employees have left Patagonia after the internships to become full-time activists. That's fine with the firm. Patagonia recently joined with several other apparel companies and six leading anti-sweatshop groups to devise a single set of labor standards with a common factory inspection system.

- *Child Development Center.* Started in 1985, the child care facility is one of the first of its kind and an integral component of the company. Children are part of the campus all day, every day. The connection between work and family increases job satisfaction. Knowing their children are being well cared for onsite helps employees become fully committed.

■ *One Percent for the Planet.* In 1985, Patagonia started an "earth tax" and donates 1 percent of sales to grassroots environmental activists worldwide. Each group has its own budget for local activism. Patagonia employees serve on grant committees that fund proposals. Because of employee involvement, this program also contributes to worker satisfaction.

Questions for Discussion

1. What values are important at Patagonia?

2. How do values play an important role in attracting and retaining top employees?

For more information, see www.patagonia.com/web/us/home.

Action Assignment

As a bridge between learning and doing, complete the following action assignment.

1. What is the most important idea you have learned in Part Three?
2. How can you apply what you have learned? What will you do, with whom, where, when, and, most important, why?

Part 4   The Empowerment of People

8. Leadership Authority
9. Empowerment in the Workplace and the Quality Imperative

LEADERSHIP IS SERVICE, not selfishness. The leader grows more and lasts longer by placing the well-being of all above the well-being of self. Through service to others, the leader becomes strong.

—Lao-tzu

Tao-te Ching, sixth century BC

Learning Objectives

After studying Part Four, you will be able to:
- Describe the philosophy and practice of participative leadership.
- Understand leadership as a calling to serve.
- Know the sources and types of leadership power.
- Identify practical steps a leader can take to empower others and develop a high-performance workplace.
- Know the historical roots of the quality movement.
- Improve performance through quality initiatives.

Leadership Authority

There are two views of leadership authority—*top-down* and *bottom-up*.[1] The top-down view holds that leadership authority is based on position in a social hierarchy, and that power flows from the highest level to the lowest. The classical organizational pyramid has frontline workers supporting managers and supervisors, who, in turn, support top-level executives. This pyramid of authority serves as the basis of most classical organizational structures. See Figure 8–1.

Figure 8–1
Classical Organizational
Structure

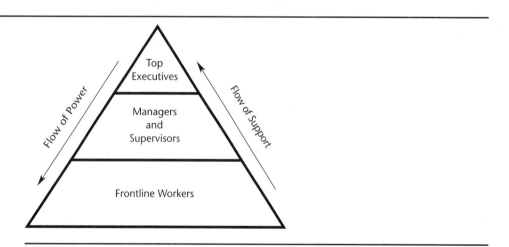

The first application of the organizational pyramid in the United States was made in the 1850s. David McCallum, general superintendent of the New York and Erie Railroad, prepared an organization chart for his company. Formalizing the position and status of all employees in a hierarchical structure was soon adopted by most other American companies.[2]

The top-down concept is well established, and it is the traditional view of leadership authority in the United States. The right of authority is derived from the right of private property, which is guaranteed in the Constitution. This guarantee gives owners of property the right to manage their affairs as they decide, as long as they do not violate the rights of others as determined by law. Owners may transfer power to a board of directors, which, in turn, may appoint top executives to manage the organization. These executives may delegate authority to managers and supervisors, who may empower employees to act in the interests of the organization. This transfer of authority is seen in Figure 8–2.

The bottom-up view of authority contends that power flows from below, because people can always reject a directive. By saying yes or no, the individual affirms or denies the authority of others.[3] This view of authority was first described by Chester

**Figure 8–2
Classical Transfer
of Authority**[4]

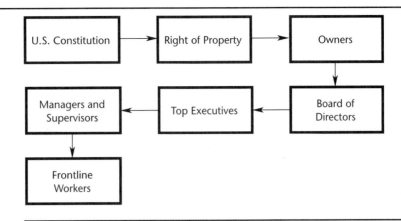

Barnard of AT&T. Barnard was a career executive (including president of New Jersey Bell Telephone Company and later, head of two foundations), who wrote several influential books on management and organizations including *The Functions of the Executive,* 1938. He emphasized that organizations depend on effective communication and that a manager's formal authority depends on the employee's willingness to accept that power. According to Barnard, people will accept an order if four conditions are met: (1) the person understands the order; (2) the person believes the order is consistent with the organization's goals; (3) the person believes the order is compatible with his or her interests; and (4) the person is mentally and physically able to comply with the order.[5]

Effective leaders make certain that their directives fall within their subordinates' zones of acceptance. Otherwise, orders may be met with resistance and even hostility, as the following story shows:

An agent of the Textile Workers Union of America likes to tell the story of the occasion when a new manager appeared in the mill where he was working. The manager came into the weave room the day he arrived. He walked directly over to the agent and said, "Are you Belloc?" The agent acknowledged that he was. The manager said, "I am the new manager here. When I manage a mill, I run it. Do you understand?" The agent nodded, and then waved his hand. The workers, intently watching this encounter, shut down every loom in the room immediately. The agent turned to the manager and said, "All right, go ahead and run it."[6]

Both the top-down and the bottom-up views of authority have merit. By accepting employment, employees acknowledge the authority of owners and managers to make decisions and give orders, as well as their own duty to comply and obey. Also, the successful manager is the first to acknowledge the power of employees to achieve both their own and organizational goals. A manager can govern most effectively with the consent of those being governed. This condition shows the interdependence common to most leader–follower relationships.[7]

An approach to leadership that recognizes both the top-down and bottom-up views of authority, and that effectively addresses the interdependent nature of the leader–follower condition, is **servant leadership.**[8]

Servant Leadership

Management author Robert Greenleaf states that servant leadership is a calling to serve. This calling begins with the feeling deep down inside that one cares about people and wants to help others. Then conscious choice causes one to aspire to lead. The great leader is a servant first, and that is the secret of his or her greatness.[9]

The servant leader is different from the individual who is motivated by selfish goals. Winston Churchill captured the spirit of servant leadership when he said,

"We make a living by what we get, but we make a life by what we give. What is the use of living if not to strive for noble causes and to make this muddled world a better place for those who will live in it after we are gone?"[10]

People do not trust the self-server, whose primary thoughts are for personal gain. Trust is given to the leader who works for the common good and has the interests of others at heart. The servant leader is the one people will choose to follow, the one with whom they will prefer to work.

Greenleaf coined the term *servant leadership* after reading *The Journey to the East,* by Herrmann Hesse. In this story, Leo, a cheerful and caring servant, supports a group of travelers on a long and difficult journey. His helpful ways keep the group's morale high and purpose clear. Years later, the storyteller comes upon a spiritual order and discovers that Leo is the group's highly respected leader. By serving the travelers unselfishly rather than trying to lead them for personal gain or prestige, Leo had helped ensure their survival and eventual success. This story represented a transformation in the meaning of leadership for Greenleaf. Servant leadership is not about personal ego or material rewards. It is about a true motivation to serve the interests of others.[11]

A sure sign of servant leadership is the leader who stays in touch with the challenges and problems of others. One good way to do this is to get out of the executive suite and onto the shop floor, out of headquarters and into the field, out of the ivory tower and into the real world.

One company has an active reception area: pickup, delivery, walk-in customers, and in-coming calls. To give receptionists a little relief, and to stay in touch with real customers, real employees, real products, and real problems, each top executive is on a duty roster giving two hours a month at the reception desk . . . including the president.[12]

Servant leaders do not view leadership as a position of power; rather they are coaches, stewards, and facilitators. They seek to create climates where others can do great work. Their approach is to ask, "How can I help?"[13]

Quint Studer, author of *Hardwiring Excellence,* identifies four questions servant leaders should ask all employees: (1) What is going right? (2) What can be improved? (3) Do you have what you need? (4) How can I help you achieve your goals? New employees should be asked: (1) How has your experience been compared to what you thought it would be? (2) What has worked well? What has not worked well? (3) You have a fresh pair of eyes. What ideas and suggestions do you recommend?[14]

Access, Communication, and Support

The servant leader is committed to people, and this commitment is shown through **access, communication,** and **support:**

- *Access.* People need to have access to their leaders, to be able to read their faces, to see recognition of their own existence reflected in their leaders' eyes. Management by objectives and other rational techniques of management do not alter fundamental human needs. People need contact and support, and effective leaders at all levels of responsibility recognize this as one of their primary tasks. The age of computers, information technology, and e-mail does not change the importance of the human moment at work.

- *Communication.* The effective leader knows the value of communication. As long ago as 59 BC, Julius Caesar kept people up-to-date with handwritten sheets and posters distributed around Rome. Communication in today's organizations is frequently discussed, but not always delivered. The suggestion that leaders meet with their people on a regular basis is often greeted with the response that there is not enough time. But such meetings provide valuable opportunities to share information, lay out the work, anticipate problems, and gather momentum. They also serve to reinforce a sense of cooperative helpfulness and mutual support. Meetings can serve as an opportunity to close the communication loop and see if frontline people are receiving information and hearing the leader's message.

■ *Support.* Even in routine operations, when there is no emergency or strategic crisis, people benefit from support in the form of feedback. As a rule, they do not get enough of it. One can ask people in almost any organization, "How do you know if you are doing a good job?" Ninety percent are likely to respond, "If I do something wrong, I'll hear about it." Too often this topic is discussed as if praise were the only answer; it is not. What people are saying is that they do not have sufficient discussion about performance and tangible support from their leaders to improve effectiveness. Successful leaders know that praise without support is an empty gesture.[15]

Servant leadership encourages trust, listening, and the ethical use of power and empowerment. A picture can be an excellent way to convey a concept. The servant leader uses the upside-down pyramid approach to leadership. See Figure 8–3.

Figure 8–3
The Upside-Down Pyramid Approach to Leadership

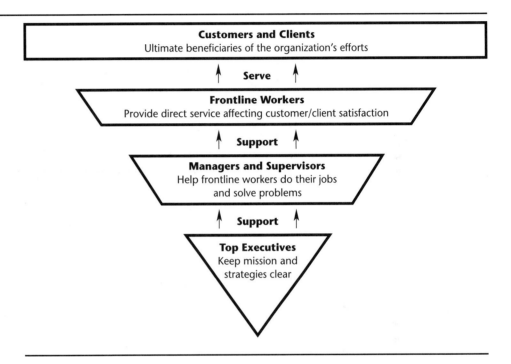

Frontline workers are near the top of the pyramid. They are supported in their efforts by leaders below them. The implications are dramatic for day-to-day work. From this perspective, each person provides added value. The whole organization is devoted to satisfying the customer, and this is made possible through the support of caring leaders.[16]

A Case of Servant Leadership

Brian Tierney was a young trader in the Commercial Operations Division of American Electric Power. His senior leaders saw important leadership qualities in Brian—he cared about people, cared about the company, kept job knowledge current, and, critically, he possessed integrity.

The company developed Brian's leadership skills through formal training, challenging stretch assignments, and counseling from senior members of management. When the time came to choose a new vice president of commercial operations, Brian got the call. Prior to this time, the trading floor was one level below the executive offices. On the day Brian was promoted, he moved his office to the entrance of the trading floor and opened the door. This concrete and visible action improved employee access, communication, and support, and resulted in significant improvement of performance of an already successful trading operation.

Brian was next promoted to senior vice president over three operating divisions of the company. In this position, he continued to practice the upside-down servant approach to leadership. Most recently, Brian became the chief financial officer of his company. Brian's case shows both the value and the rewards of servant leadership in today's workplace.

Max DePree, in his book *Leadership Is an Art,* describes the character of servant leadership:

> The first responsibility of a leader is to define what can be. The last is to say thank you. In between the two, the leader must become a servant and a debtor. That sums up the progress of an artful leader.
>
> In a day when so much energy seems to be spent on maintenance and manuals, on bureaucracy and meaningless quantification, to be a leader is to enjoy the special privileges of complexity, of ambiguity, of diversity. But to be a leader means, especially, having the opportunity to make a meaningful difference in the lives of those who permit leaders to lead.[17]

Can you think of a servant leader who embodies DePree's ideal? Consider her or his actions and impact on people. How do you fulfill this role?

Authentic Leadership

Closely related to servant leadership is the concept of authentic leadership, described by Bill George in his book by the same title. Authentic leaders have a genuine desire to serve others. They lead from core values, they have courage and self-discipline, they establish trusting relationships, and they are purpose driven. Consider the example of Nelson Mandela, the first black president of South Africa.

Mandela was a servant to all of the people, regardless of color. He knew who he was at his core, and his leadership actions reflected those values. He had courage and discipline to remain true to his conviction in the face of personal pain and hardship. He remained kind and trusting in his relationships, yet was unyielding in his mission to achieve justice and equality for all. Mandela was a role model for authentic leadership.

On trial in South Africa in 1963, Mandela said: "I have cherished the ideal of a democratic and free society in which all persons live together in harmony and with equal opportunities. It is an ideal I hope to live for and to achieve. But if need be, it is an ideal for which I am prepared to die." The verdict: life imprisonment. Mandela visualized the future of South Africa using the metaphor of a rainbow, a society tolerant of the color of others. This belief helped him survive 27 years of imprisonment.[18]

Military Leadership

Caring and servant leadership permeate the American military. The focus of the military is on the followers, their well-being and development. Leaders at all levels are taught to put the needs of their subordinates before their own and to lead by the principle, "Mission first, soldiers always." Consider the results: The world's best military force of 18-year-olds led by 20-year-olds led by 25-year-olds that the world has ever known.[19]

Participative Leadership Philosophy

How do you tap the constructive power of people? How do you create both a humanistic and a productive workplace? The answer is through participative leadership. The process begins with involving people, which is necessary to achieve understanding, which is necessary to achieve commitment. It is important to know the views and consider the interests of all who are affected when decisions are made.

To develop an empowered workplace that leads to high-quality products and services, leaders must adopt the kind of leadership philosophy promoted by the Japanese Union of Scientists and Engineers:

No matter how much factories are mechanized, as long as there are people still working there, they should be treated as human individuals. Those companies that do not give due consideration to humanity will lose their best people sooner or later. There can be no excuse for disregarding individual personality, slighting a person's ability, regarding people as machinery, and discriminating against them. People spend much of their lifetime at their working place. It would be much more desirable to work in a pleasant place where humanity is paid due respect and where people feel their work has some real meaning. That is what quality practices aim to achieve. A mechanized factory still requires control by a workshop of people.[20]

A concrete example of the participative leadership philosophy is Jack Stack, the CEO from Springfield, Missouri, who popularized open-book management in the 1980s. Open-book management involves sharing financial information with employees and encouraging them to recommend ideas that improve those financial results.[21]

An Open-Book Example

Employees at Artists' Frame Service in Chicago knew what the company charged customers, and knew their pay was only a fraction of that. The CEO wanted them to understand that the difference between invoice prices and their salaries wasn't all profit. So the employees were given a demonstration of the company's expenses, illustrated as portions of a hypothetical $100 order.

As the presenter explained where the money was going, different departments came forward to claim the proceeds of the sale. An oversized $5 bill, for example, was disbursed to cover the cost of the company's yellow page listing, which costs the company roughly 5 percent of its receipts. The pile of cash was whittled down as claims were made by rent, health insurance, and other fixed and operating expenses that many employees don't think about. When all the bills were paid, $5 remained.

The demonstration improved morale by giving workers an understanding of the company's expenses, and challenging them to look for ways to save the company money. When they understood how lean a company has to run to stay competitive, buyers began ordering in bulk and watching inventory carefully, and clerks began finding ways to handle orders more efficiently.[22]

Management authors Warren Bennis and Philip Slater identify the shift toward participative leadership as necessary if organizations are to survive under conditions of chronic change. They define participative leadership as **democratic,** not as permissive or laissez-faire, management. This type of management involves a system of beliefs and common values that govern behavior. These include:

- Full and free communication, regardless of rank and power.
- A reliance on consensus, rather than on traditional forms of coercion and compromise, to manage conflict.
- The idea that influence is based on technical competence and knowledge, rather than on the vagaries of personal whim or the prerogatives of power.
- An atmosphere that permits and even encourages emotional expression as well as task-oriented acts.
- A basically human bias, one that accepts the inevitability of conflict between the organization and the individual, but that is willing to cope with and mediate this conflict on rational grounds.[23]

Examples of work systems and techniques for employee participation in the United States and abroad can be arranged along a continuum, as shown in Figure 8–4. On the left part of this continuum, employees possess less power and are less involved in the decision-making process. Workers in industrial sweatshop systems exert less control over their work lives than do employees in industrial democracy systems.

Figure 8–4 explains much of the popularity and success of total quality management and other empowerment efforts. It shows quality improvement groups

**Figure 8–4
Continuum
of Empowerment**[24]

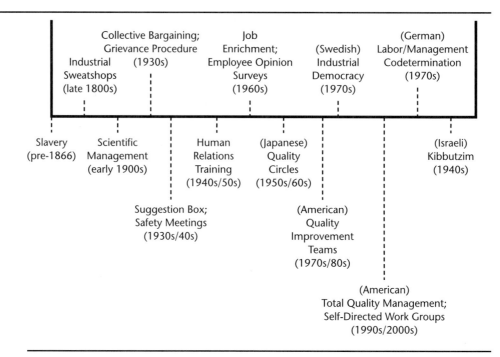

to the right of middle—satisfying needs for employee involvement, yet not so participative that owners and managers fear loss of power and ownership.

Participative leadership has been employed effectively by many supervisors and managers to build employee morale and achieve high performance. With roots in democratic ideals, participative leadership allows the leader to tap the constructive power of the group. In *Productive Workplaces,* Marvin Weisbord writes:

> The democratic process is the best procedure yet devised for promoting decision-making that is a part of all social living, and at the same time, safeguarding to each individual the conditions necessary for self-realization. The democratic process allows each individual to participate in making decisions that determine his or her conditions of life.[25]

The Leadership Position

Leadership is needed in all areas of society and at all levels of responsibility. Titles of leadership include *president, chief, captain, manager, director,* and *supervisor,* to name just a few. Both responsibility and power come with the office of leadership. The challenge is to meet the responsibility of the position without abusing its power.

An example of a leader using power effectively is Herb Kelleher, former CEO of Southwest Airlines. At one point in his career, he was recognized by *BusinessWeek, Fortune,* and *The Wall Street Journal* as America's most effective executive. He states:

> I started to get involved in the day-to-day operations. I got to know people in a personal way, and that was very enjoyable for me. You'd go over to maintenance and talk about how the planes were running. You'd talk to the flight attendants and get involved in such discussions as what their uniforms ought to be.
>
> You have to treat your employees like customers. When you treat them right, then they will treat the customers right. This has been a powerful competitive weapon for us at Southwest Airlines. You've got to take the time to listen to people's ideas. If you just tell somebody *no,* that's an act of power and, in my opinion, an abuse of power. You don't want to constrain people in their thinking.[26]

**Negative Consequences
in the Use of Power**

Abraham Lincoln once said, "Nearly everyone can stand adversity, but if you want to test a person's true character, give him power."[27] And T. S. Eliot wrote, "Half of the harm that is done in this world is caused by people who have power and want to feel important. They do not mean to do harm; they are simply absorbed in the useless struggle to think well of themselves."[28]

One interesting study reveals the tragic consequences of the negative use of power in the medical world. Researchers found a dramatic difference in performance results between intensive care units (ICUs) in which the staff unquestioningly followed the lead of an autocratic physician in charge and those ICUs that functioned as a team of colleagues, all of whom were free to make suggestions that might benefit the patient. The "obedient," power-oriented ICUs experienced higher staff turnover, lower efficiency, and twice the rate of patient deaths.[29]

The idea of using and not abusing the power that comes from leadership position is very old. The following quote is from Lao-tzu, the founder of Taoism, who was born in the village of Jhren, China, in 604 BC:

I have three precious things which I hold fast and prize. The first is gentleness; the second is frugality; the third is humility, which keeps me from putting myself before others. Be gentle and you can be bold; be frugal and you can be liberal; avoid putting yourself before others and you can become a leader.[30]

Taoism is one of China's ancient spiritual traditions that is viewed as both a philosophy and a religion. The *Tao-te Ching* is a book of virtue comprising only 5,000 words. It lays out the Tao, or "the Way," that is believed to be present in everything that exists in the world. It is seen as the continuity behind life's ever-changing forces. The Tao gives rise to the opposite but complementary forces of yin and yang, which are the source of the endless changes that the world endures.

Sources of Leadership Power

The successful leader masters the use of power to influence the behavior of others. John French and Bertram Raven developed the most cited and discussed typology of power. Table 8–1 shows sources and types of power used by leaders: One is based in the leadership position; the second is based in the leader's personal qualities. To personalize the concept of leadership power, complete Exercise 8–1.

Table 8–1
Sources and Types of Power Used by Leaders[31]

Power of the Position	Power of the Person
Based on what leaders can offer to others	Based on how leaders are viewed by others
Reward power is the capacity to offer something of value as a means of influencing others: "If you do what I ask, you will be rewarded."	*Expert power* is the capacity to influence others because of expertise—specialized knowledge or skill. Ability in an art, science, profession, or trade are examples.
Coercive power is the capacity to punish as a means of influencing others: "If you don't do what I ask, you will be punished."	*Referent power* is the capacity to influence others because of their desire to identify with the leader. Unselfish motives and virtuous character raise trust and respect.
Legitimate power is the capacity to influence others by virtue of formal authority or the rights of office: "Because I am the leader, you should do as I ask."	*Rational power* is the capacity to influence others because of well-developed reasoning and problem-solving ability. Intelligence increases power.
Information power comes from having access to data and news of importance to others: "I have important information, so you should do as I ask."	*Charisma power* is the ability to motivate and inspire others to action by force of personal traits, including optimism, sense of adventure, and commitment to a cause.

Abigail Johnson is a good example of a leader who effectively uses both the power of the position and the power of the person. As president of Fidelity, the financial services company with $1.4 trillion in mutual funds and other assets under management, she possesses the power of position. Although she is the granddaughter of the company's founder, she worked her way up through the ranks, beginning as a customer service telephone representative. Along the way, she developed expert power based on technical knowledge and referent power based on building strong internal and external networks.[32] Generally, power is given to leaders who get results and have good human relations skills. Similarly, power is taken from those who are incompetent and are callous or cruel.[33]

Exercise 8–1
What Type of Power Does Your Supervisor Use?[34]

Indicate how strongly you agree or disagree with the following statements as they describe your immediate supervisor. If you are not currently employed, evaluate a supervisor you have had in the past. For each statement, select the most appropriate response, using the following scale: 1 = strongly disagree; 2 = disagree; 3 = neither agree nor disagree; 4 = agree; 5 = strongly agree.

My supervisor

1. _____ Recognizes efforts and rewards accomplishments.
2. _____ Uses fear to control behavior.
3. _____ Shows appreciation for work well done.
4. _____ Manipulates others to gain compliance.
5. _____ Makes timely decisions to get things done.
6. _____ Stays abreast of job-related news.
7. _____ Exercises authority and power of position.
8. _____ Provides skill and advice to solve job problems.
9. _____ Maintains access to important facts and data.
10. _____ Keeps job knowledge current.
11. _____ Has high ideals and standards of conduct.
12. _____ Thinks clearly and explains things logically.
13. _____ Causes people to respect what he or she stands for.
14. _____ Creates a vision and strong sense of purpose.
15. _____ Gets the facts before making decisions.
16. _____ Motivates others and inspires them to action.

Scoring:

Power of the Position

1. Add the numbers assigned to statements 1 and 3. This is the *reward power* score.

   _____

2. Add the numbers assigned to statements 2 and 4. This is the *coercive power* score.

   _____

3. Add the numbers assigned to statements 5 and 7. This is the *legitimate power* score.

   _____

4. Add the numbers assigned to statements 6 and 9. This is the *information power* score.

   _____

Power of the Person

5. Add the numbers assigned to statements 8 and 10. This is the *expert power* score.

   _____

6. Add the numbers assigned to statements 11 and 13. This is the *referent power* score.

   _____

7. Add the numbers assigned to statements 12 and 15. This is the *rational power* score.

   _____

8. Add the numbers assigned to statements 14 and 16. This is the *charisma power* score.

   _____

Discussion:

The effective leader emphasizes the power of the person to accomplish goals. This involves maintaining knowledge and skill (expertise), having high moral character (referent power), demonstrating effective problem-solving ability (rational power), and motivating and inspiring people (charisma). The effective leader also uses the power of the position to reward efforts and accomplishments (rewards), make effective decisions (legitimacy), and keep people informed on important matters (information). The effective leader rarely if ever uses fear (coercion) as a form of power. Coercion involves threats, punishment, and negative rewards.

Psychological Size and Two-Way Communication

The concept of **psychological size** has special relevance for people in authority positions. The individual who determines careers, decides wages, and makes job assignments has considerable power over others, and this power can influence the communication process.

Employees are in a weaker position, dependent to some degree on the authority figure to protect them and watch out for their well-being. Some will deny this observation, but one has only to observe the typical work environment to see how differences in psychological size can affect relationships and determine the way things are done. Deference and paternalism are not uncommon.[35]

People in positions of authority are often surprised to discover that others may fear their power and inhibit behavior accordingly. A graphic representation of a leader with big psychological size and the one-way communication that can result is presented in Figure 8–5.

Figure 8–5
Abuse of Psychological Size

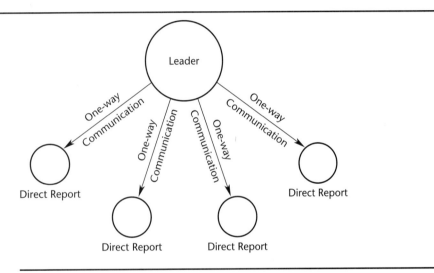

One-way communication presents three problems:

1. *People may be reluctant to say or do anything that might offend the powerful figure.* According to George Reedy in *The Twilight of the Presidency,* even people who had enjoyed two-way communication with Lyndon Johnson when he was in the Senate began to censure their behavior once he assumed the presidency.[36]

2. *People may become dependent on the leader to make all the decisions.* Unwilling to risk making a mistake and being criticized, people may fail to take initiative. The leader must then solve all the problems and make all the decisions. Dependency on the leader underuses direct reports and overburdens the leader.

3. *People may become resentful of the leader.* The leader is seen as autocratic and arrogant, and this perception may cause anger, hostility, and even rebellion. Consider the case of the infamous Captain Queeg in the film classic *The Caine Mutiny.* The captain's abusive behavior eventually led to tragedy for everyone.

How can leaders avoid the abuse of psychological size and develop the two-way communication that is necessary for both employee morale and job performance? First, they must recognize the factors that contribute to psychological bigness:

High-status position.

Use of terminal statements so that no disagreement is possible.

Formal, distant manner.

Know-it-all, superior attitude.

Commanding physical appearance.

Power to make decisions.

Use of sarcasm and ridicule.

Job competence.

Cruel and punishing remarks.

Ability to express oneself.

Interrupting and shouting at others.

Public criticism.

Some of the items on this list are distinctly positive. For example, job competence and the ability to express oneself are desirable traits. Additionally, some of the factors causing psychological bigness are attributes of the person or the office, and it may be difficult or undesirable to change them. For example, neither a leader's commanding physical appearance nor the power to make decisions should be changed. Similarly, the status of the position is most likely an unchangeable factor. The seven remaining factors of psychological bigness on the list above, however, serve no purpose except to alienate people and result in one-way communication.

■ Use of sarcasm and ridicule.

■ Use of terminal statements so that no disagreement is possible.

■ Formal, distant manner.

■ Cruel and punishing remarks.

■ Know-it-all, superior attitude.

■ Interrupting and shouting at others.

■ Public criticism.

As a rule, leaders should avoid any behavior that demeans or intimidates another person. The solution is to equalize psychological size. A picture of the proper use of psychological size and good two-way communication is presented in Figure 8–6.

Many leaders mistakenly think that the best way to equalize psychological size is to reduce their own size. In doing so, however, they may reduce their size so much that respect is lost and cannot be regained. Few individuals have the ability to go from large psychological size to small psychological size and back again without

Figure 8–6
Effective Use
of Psychological Size

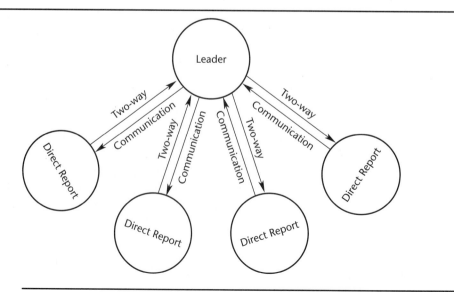

losing effectiveness. Therefore, the most effective approach is not for leaders to reduce their own psychological size, but to raise the size of others.

The effective leader is a very big circle with a very big reputation, but this leader never gets in the way of the growth of others. The best way to raise psychological size is to show genuine interest in people. Through attention to others and sincere **listening,** the leader shows that others are important. A proven technique is to give people a project, some work to "grow into." This approach builds pride and commitment, and increases the productivity of the group as a whole.

Leaders should keep in mind three important points in developing two-way communication. First, model an honest and open style of communication. Be direct and sincere in speaking. Second, be patient. It takes time and trust to create dialogue between people, and too rapid a change from one style of operating to another may be interpreted as insincerity or may confuse people. Third, make a sincere effort to draw people out without constantly evaluating their remarks. This will be seen as a demonstration of respect and will help create true dialogue. The following guidelines can help accomplish this goal:[37]

- *Stop talking.* You cannot listen to others if you are talking. Shakespeare wrote, "Give every man thine ear, but few thy voice."[38] We each have two ears and one mouth, and we should use these in proportion.

- *Put the talker at ease.* Help the other person feel free to talk. Provide a supportive environment or atmosphere. Sit or stand in a relaxed manner.

- *Show the person that you want to listen.* Look and act interested. Don't read your mail while the other person is talking. Maintain eye contact.

- *Remove distractions.* Don't doodle on, tap, or shuffle papers. Shut down the computer. Hold telephone calls. Will it be quieter if you close the door?

- *Empathize with the person.* Try to put yourself in the other person's place to understand the speaker's point of view.

- *Be patient.* Allow time. Don't interrupt. Don't walk toward the door or walk away while the other person is talking. Some people take longer than others to make a point.

- *Hold your temper.* An emotional person may misinterpret a message or may say something unintended. If you are angry, cool off before responding. Take a walk, or try counting to 10.

- *Go easy on argument and criticism.* Being judgmental puts the speaker on the defensive and may result in a blowup, or it may cause the person to shut down. Listen to understand, rather than to make judgments.

- *Ask questions.* This response encourages the speaker and shows you are listening. It also helps develop additional points. Few actions demonstrate respect as much as asking others for their opinion.

- *Encourage clarification.* When the speaker touches on a point you want to know more about, simply repeat the statement as a question. This technique will allow clarification and elaboration.

- *Stop talking.* This is the first and last point, because all others depend on it. You cannot do a good job of listening while you are talking. As Shakespeare wrote, "Give thy thoughts no tongue."[39]

Overall, a leader's use of psychological bigness and overbearance is effective for only a short period of time. After a while, dissatisfaction causes employees to rebel or escape. Effective leaders at all levels of authority understand this human relations principle.

Lessons from Gandhi

What can we learn from Gandhi, the Indian spiritual and political leader? We can learn what Gandhi learned from his wife Kasturbi during 57 years of marriage. When they were married in their teens, as was the custom in India, the young bridegroom was full of strong opinions and recommendations for his young wife to implement. Her usual approach was to listen and smile, but then to proceed with her own methods and at her own pace.

Later in life, Gandhi reported that he had learned the power of civil disobedience and the importance of patience from his wife. From her, he had learned a lifelong leadership message—most people, in the final analysis, will do what they personally choose to do, and no amount of coaxing or force can overcome an idea or principle that is personally believed. Great leaders guide and inspire—not command and control.[40]

Empowerment in the Workplace and the Quality Imperative

CHAPTER 9

In a report for the Brookings Institution, Steve Levine and Laura D'Andrea reviewed all major studies of empowerment in the workplace. Their findings: "If you sum it all up, employee participation has a positive impact on business success. It is almost never negative or neutral. Moreover, studies of employee-owned companies show that stock ownership alone doesn't motivate employees to work harder, while ownership combined with participation does."[41]

Federal Express, now known simply as FedEx, has remained the market leader in the industry it helped create 40 years ago. The name FedEx is synonymous with overnight delivery. Participative leadership and employee empowerment have been instrumental in the company's success. Fred Smith, Chairman of Federal Express, explains the importance of empowerment in the workplace:

Empowering people is the single most important element in managing our organization. Empowered people have the necessary information to make decisions and act; they don't have to wait for multiple levels of authorization. Empowered people identify problems and they fix them. They do what it takes to keep customers happy. Empowered people don't have time for turf battles, because when everyone shares power and a common goal, turf becomes irrelevant and teamwork becomes an imperative.[42]

To diagnose the need for empowerment in a group or organization, answer the following questions:

- Do people seem uninterested in their work?
- Are absenteeism or turnover rates too high?
- Do people lack loyalty and team spirit?
- Is there a lack of communication among individuals and groups?
- Is there a low level of pride?
- Are costs too high as a result of waste and inefficiency?
- Does the quality of product or quality of service need to be improved?

If the answer is "yes" to any of these questions, then empowering people can help.

A great deal of empowerment in the workplace is generated by efforts to improve performance. As companies are forced to compete in an increasingly global economy, they are finding that the path to success is long and winding. On that path are many boulders and pebbles that must be cleared. It takes the strength of management to remove the boulders—build a new plant, create a new product, and the like. And it takes the attention and effort of employees to cast away the pebbles—solve problems with products and meet customer needs. Everyone must work together.

A story is told about a worker at a Ford plant many years ago who suggested a manufacturing improvement that saved the company hundreds of thousands of dollars. Henry Ford himself rewarded the employee and asked him when he had thought of the idea. "Years ago," the employee said. Asked by an incredulous Ford why he didn't say anything earlier, the employee replied, "Nobody asked me."[43]

Today, just as yesterday, the task of the leader is to unleash and channel the power of people. When he was asked, "What is your job?" General Electric's Jack Welch said: "I have three things to do. I have to choose the right people, allocate the right number of dollars, and transmit ideas from one group to another with the speed of light. I am really a communicator and facilitator for the work of others."[44]

As one of the most widely admired and studied CEOs of his time, Welch enriched not only GE's shareholders but also the shareholders of other companies around the globe. His total economic impact is impossible to calculate, but his leadership had staggering influence on GE's performance during his tenure in charge. Under his leadership, the company's revenue grew from $27 billion to over $100 billion in 20 years.

Welch began by changing GE's goal, which previously had been simply to grow faster than the economy. Welch gave GE a new mission: to be the world's most valuable company. As the centerpiece of the plan was his declaration that every GE business must be number one or number two in its industry.

Welch believed that the best strategies would not work without the right leaders. So he selected, trained, and held leaders accountable to the four E's of leadership: high personal *energy,* the ability to *energize* others, the *edge* to make tough decisions, and the ability to *execute* strategy.

Welch then concentrated on reforming the practices and culture that determined day by day how the company worked. He began by burning GE's blue books, five thick volumes of guidance for every GE manager. His message to GE's managers was, "You own these businesses. Take charge of them. Think for yourself. Get headquarters out of your hair. Fight the bureaucracy. Hate it. Kick it. Break it."

If employees were surprised by the words, they were more surprised by the actions that followed. Welch wiped out entire layers of bureaucratic management, and he launched the famous *workout process,* in which employees at all levels of an operation gathered for "town meetings" with their bosses and asked questions or made proposals about how the place could run better—80 percent requiring some kind of response then and there.

The multiday workout sessions took huge chunks of wasted money and time out of GE's processes, but their more important effect was to teach people that they had a right to speak up and be taken seriously; those who advanced good ideas were rewarded, as were those who implemented them.

The next natural step was to spread good ideas across the company. Doing this sounds logical and obvious—but it hadn't been done before. Then a more radical move followed: borrowing good ideas from other companies. Welch advocated this one personally to show it was actually OK, and today he states that what GE learned about asset management from Toyota or about quick market intelligence from Walmart has been enormously important in the success of the company.

Welch implemented Six Sigma at GE, a program that sets the goal of 99.99 percent quality production outcomes, or only 3.4 defective products per million operations. He required managers to set "stretch" goals, which were the highest they thought they had a reasonable chance of achieving.

At least as important as these high-profile changes were Welch's behind-the-scenes people practices, which he says took more of his time than anything else. When a manager met with Welch, the exchange was candid, not scripted. There were arguments. There was shouting. The manager almost certainly had to do new thinking on the spot. Afterward, Welch would dispatch a highly specific written summary of commitments the manager had made, and when Welch followed up later—also in writing—he would refer to the previous summary. He did this with relentless consistency with scores of managers.[45] The empowerment tactics used by Jack Welch can be applied in all sizes and types of private, public, and not-for-profit organizations.[46]

Principles of an Empowered Workplace

Robert Cole, influential author and educator, identifies five principles of leadership that empower people. Implicit in these principles is the assumption that broad participation in the decision-making process is necessary for success.

- *Trust in people.* Assume they will work to implement organizational goals if given a chance.
- *Invest in people.* View people as the organization's most important resource, which, if cultivated, will yield positive returns.
- *Recognize accomplishments.* Symbolic rewards are extremely important. Show people that they are valued.
- *Decentralize decision making.* Put responsibility for making decisions where the information is and as close to the customer as possible.
- *View work as a cooperative effort.* Model and reinforce the idea that by working together, people accomplish more.[47]

Characteristics of an Empowered Workplace

People experience feelings of ownership in empowered organizations. This ensures that they will do everything they possibly can to create success. Not only are their egos invested in the organization, but their abilities are as well. In the end, the result is victory for the person and the organization. See Table 9–1.

Table 9–1
Workplace Empowerment[48]

Process	Unempowered	Out of Control	Empowered
Decision making	Check with leader on all decisions.	Check with nobody on decisions.	Check with those affected on decisions.
Performance planning	Leader writes performance plan and reviews with subordinates.	There is no performance plan.	Subordinate writes performance plan and reviews with leader.
Making policy	Leader decides policy.	People ignore policy.	Work with those responsible to develop policy.
Problem solving	Wait for "them" to fix problems.	Bypass "system" to work around problems.	Find out who "they" are and work together to fix problems.
Taking initiative	Never volunteer for anything—wait to be asked or assigned.	Many people work on the same thing without communicating.	Recognize what needs to be done; inform leader and others affected; start action to improve.
Defining roles	Roles and responsibilities are defined by leader.	Roles and responsibilities are conflicting and unclear.	Work together to define roles and responsibilities.
Setting standards	Perform to standards determined by others.	There is no concern with standards.	Work together to determine standards of employee effectiveness.

The following case shows the role of empowerment in facilitating change on a global scale.

Empowerment Facilitates Change

Nissan Motor Company was on the brink of bankruptcy when French automaker Renault purchased a controlling interest and installed Carlos Ghosn as the effective head of the Japanese automaker. Along with Nissan's known problems of high debt and plummeting market share, Ghosn (pronounced "gone") saw that Nissan managers had no apparent sense of urgency to change. "Even though the evidence is against them, they sit down and they watch the problem a little bit longer," says Ghosn.

Ghosn's challenge was to act quickly, yet minimize the inevitable resistance that arises when an outsider tries to change traditional Japanese business practices. "I was non-Nissan, non-Japanese," he says. "I knew that if I tried to dictate changes from above, the effort would backfire, undermining morale and productivity. But if I was too passive, the company would simply continue its downward spiral."

To resolve this dilemma, Ghosn formed nine cross-functional teams of 10 middle managers each and gave them the mandate to identify innovative proposals for a specific area (marketing, manufacturing, etc.) within three months. Each team could form subteams with additional people to analyze specific issues in more detail. In all, more than 500 middle managers and other employees were involved in the so-called Nissan Revival Plan.

After a slow start—Nissan managers weren't accustomed to such authority or working with colleagues across functions or cultures—ideas began to flow as Ghosn stuck to his deadline, reminded team members of the automaker's desperate situation, and encouraged teams to break traditions. Three months later, the nine teams submitted a bold plan to close three assembly plants, eliminate thousands of jobs, cut the number of suppliers by half, reduce purchasing costs by 20 percent, return to profitability, cut the company's debt by half, and introduce 22 new models within the next two years.

Although [they were] risky, Ghosn accepted all of the proposals. Moreover, when revealing the plan publicly on the eve of the annual Tokyo Motor Show, Ghosn added his own commitment to the plan: "If you ask people to go through a difficult period of time, they have to trust that you're sharing it with them," Ghosn explains. "So I said that if we did not fulfill our commitments, I would resign."

Ghosn's strategy for organizational change and the Nissan Revival Plan worked. Within 12 months, the automaker had increased sales and market share and posted its first profit in seven years. The company introduced innovative models and expanded operations. Ghosn, who received high praise throughout Japan and abroad, is now Chairman and CEO of Renault, Nissan Motor Company.[49]

The Importance of Communication

An essential element of an empowered workplace is good communication. One of the best ways to achieve effective communication is to recognize where most people prefer to get information, as opposed to where they actually receive it. Table 9–2 shows various types of communication and ranks them, both as actual and as preferred information sources.

Table 9–2
Where People Go for
Information[50]

Actual Rank	Source	Major Source for Employees	Preferred Rank
1	Immediate supervisor	55.1%	1
2	Grapevine	39.8	15
3	Policy handbook and other written information	32.0	4
4	Bulletin board(s)	31.5	9
5	Small group meetings	28.1	2
6	Regular, general member publication	27.9	6
7	Annual business report	24.6	7
8	Regular, local member publication	20.2	8
9	Mass meetings	15.9	11
10	Union	13.2	13
11	Orientation program	12.5	5
12	Top executives	11.7	3
13	Audiovisual programs	10.2	12
14	Mass media	9.7	14
15	Upward communication programs	9.0	10

The actual and preferred rankings of where people go for information show that people want accurate, timely, and complete information, and that their most preferred sources are the *immediate supervisor, small group meetings, top executives, policy handbook, orientation programs,* and *member newsletters.*

Effective leaders realize that it is impossible to *not* communicate, even when you are not speaking. For example, a closed office door can communicate a powerful message. Communication is the most important tool we have to get work done, and the best leaders are those who acknowledge this and work on communication ability and content.

Successful companies use creative mechanisms to ensure communication. Consider Mother's "work table—cross-pollination technique": The company's 100 employees perform their daily work around one giant table that extends 300 feet like a skateboard ramp around the entire floor. Every three weeks, employees are asked to relocate their workspace—laptop, portable phone, and other tools—and move to another area around the table between two new people. One week, you might be sitting between a finance person and a creative marketeer. The next, you might be sitting between a partner in the firm and someone from production. Why the muscial chairs exercise? It breaks down communication barriers and encourages cross-pollination of ideas.[51]

Managing the Grapevine

Cisco CEO John Chambers states: Every leader is challenged to both hear and be heard. How does Chambers address this never-ending and critical need? He uses a combination of hi-touch and hi-tech methods that work well for him.

1. Regularly getting out of the office and talking with small and large groups of employees.
2. Daily email because it gives the ability to send a clear message to large numbers of people.
3. Forty to 50 voicemails a day (on the way to and from work) because he is a voice person who likes to listen to emotions and speak with emotion, too.
4. Video on demand–his primary communication vehicle today–ten to fifteen videos a quarter that employees and customers can watch when they want.
5. A monthly CEO breakfast with anyone who has a birthday in that month–no directors or VPs in the room–to keep a finger on the pulse of what's working and what's not. Chambers says, "It is brutal, but it is my most enjoyable session."[52]

Filling the "Need to Know" Gap

There are many books and articles on how to communicate; the question is, What should be communicated? Employees from the executive suite to the shop floor have three "needs to know": (1) They need to know the grand plan—the purpose, values, and strategies for success for the organization; (2) they need to know what is expected of them personally, and why; and (3) they need to have feedback on individual performance, with recognition for their efforts.

One can see this must be a top-to-bottom process to be most effective; if things are fuzzy at headquarters, they will be even more fuzzy at the "doing" level. It is obvious, yet often ignored, that the never-ending task of leaders is to be sure these messages are clearly communicated and understood by every individual in the organization. Those who occupy leadership positions must be held accountable for doing so.[53]

The High-Performance Workplace

What practical steps can a leader take to develop a high-performance workplace? Management authors Eric Harvey and Alexander Lucia have identified 144 time-tested ways to increase leader effectiveness. Presented in Table 9–3 are 20 of the best. An effective approach is to review these 20 and pick five to implement. By concentrating on five, the leader can make a measurable difference in work morale and job performance.

Table 9–3   **Practical Tips for Developing a High-Performance Workplace[54]**

1. *Adopt an orientation to action and results.* Focus on results-oriented processes and outcomes that add value to the organization, rather than on staying busy with activities and events that merely consume time.

2. *Recognize and reward those who make improvements to products, processes, and services.* Remember: What gets celebrated gets repeated.

3. *Be customer-driven.* Build customer satisfaction by underpromising, overdelivering, and following up to be sure customers are satisfied. Solicit input on how your products and services can be improved.

4. *Maintain a commitment to self-development.* Become a continuous learning machine. Set a personal goal to learn something new about your job, your organization, or your professional discipline every week.

5. *Make timely and value-driven decisions.* Involve those who must implement decisions in the decision-making process. Consider the ideas and opinions of those who do the work, because they frequently have a great deal to contribute. In addition, they'll be more likely to support decisions they help make.

6. *Be flexible.* Understand and appreciate that others may not do things exactly as you would do them. Be open-minded—you might discover their way is even better than yours.

7. *Coach others to succeed.* Pay attention to "middle stars." Avoid the trap of focusing only on the "super stars" (those with exceptional performance) and the "fallen stars" (those with significant performance problems). Most people shine somewhere in the middle.

8. *Schedule a short meeting with each of your direct reports once every two or three weeks.* Discuss their work in progress, provide feedback on how they are doing, and ask how you and others can contribute to their success.

9. *Minimize obstacles.* Ask each member of your work group to identify the three most significant obstacles to his or her performance. Create a master list, and develop a strategy to eliminate the obstacles.

10. *Benchmark the best.* Study industries, organizations, and individuals that beat the competition by overcoming challenges and obstacles. Also, review case studies of those that did not—and lost.

11. *Address deficiencies.* Pay attention when someone has a performance problem. Unaddressed deficiencies can have a negative effect on every member of your team. By dealing with performance issues as early as possible, you can prevent them from growing more serious—and more distasteful for both you and the individual to face.

12. *Let your conscience be your guide.* Do the right thing no matter how inconvenient, unpopular, or painful it may seem. *That's* integrity!

13. *Enhance the work environment.* Ask fellow workers to submit three ideas for enhancing the quality of work life in your area. Create a master list of ideas, and start implementing the doable ones as quickly as possible.

14. *Spread the sparkle.* Get enthused about others who are enthusiastic—it's contagious and can snowball quickly. Recognize and reward those who help contribute to a culture of contagious enthusiasm.

15. *Display resilience.* It's not whether you get knocked down, it's whether you get up that counts. Take a hike—go on a 10-minute walk to calm down, reflect, and develop a bounce-back strategy.

Continued

Table 9–3 *Continued*

16. *Show concern for others.* Remember special occasions. Send cards with personalized messages to your fellow workers on special days, such as birthdays and anniversaries with the organization.

17. *Spend one-on-one time with each member of your team.* Open these get-togethers with a general question, such as "How are things going with you?" Then really listen to what the person has to say. Listening is an important way to demonstrate that you care.

18. *Manage meetings effectively.* Supply participants with a written agenda two to three days before a meeting. Make sure the agenda includes meeting objective(s), issues to be discussed, start/end times and location, and information regarding who will be attending, how participants should prepare, and what they should bring. End all meetings with a short review of the results. Discuss what was accomplished and what, if anything, needs to be done after the meeting.

19. *Be sure everyone who reports to you has clarity of assignment and tools to succeed.* Do they know the grand plan and their place in it? Do they have equipment and supplies to do their best work?

20. *Communicate effectively.* Think before you speak, and plan before you write. Understand your message before expecting others to. Target your communication to the intended audience by using terminology they are likely to understand. Consider pretesting important communications on individuals who will give you candid feedback.

Leadership Challenge

Ren McPherson, past president of Dana Corporation, states: "Almost everybody agrees, 'people are our most important asset.' Yet almost no one really lives it. Great companies live their commitment to people." It is an old truth that applies today: The human side counts. And it is no secret that the number one factor is the character and actions of empowering leaders.[55]

Colin Powell is known for his leadership ability. He is universally admired as an empowering and effective leader. In *My American Journey,* he identifies rules gleaned from his years of experience: (1) have a vision; (2) be demanding; (3) check small things; (4) share credit; (5) be calm and kind; and (6) remember that perpetual optimism is a force multiplier.[56]

In his work on servant leadership, Robert Greenleaf proposes that the world can be saved as long as three truly great institutions exist—one in the private sector, one in the public sector, and one in the nonprofit sector. He believes that these organizations will achieve success through a spirit of community, and that their success will serve as a beacon for the world. The key in every case is **caring leadership** and the **empowerment of people.**[57]

The Quality Movement

If there is a single most important factor in efforts to empower employees, it is the quality challenge faced by companies struggling to compete in a global marketplace. Simply, quality products and service are demanded by consumers, and providing them requires a talented, committed, and empowered workforce.

Joseph Jablonski writes in *Implementing Total Quality Management,* "This is a cooperative form of doing business that relies on the talents and capabilities of both labor and management to continually improve quality and productivity using teams."[58] Implicit in this definition are three essential ingredients: (1) participative leadership, (2) continuous process improvement, and (3) the use of groups.

The philosophy behind the quality movement is that the people closest to the work usually have the experience and knowledge needed to come up with the best solutions to work-related problems. Ren McPherson, former president of Dana Corporation and dean of business at Stanford University, points out:

Until we believe that the expert in any particular job is most often the person performing it, we shall forever limit the potential of that person in terms of contribution to the organization and in terms of personal development. Consider a manufacturing setting: Within their 25-square-foot area, nobody knows more about how to operate a machine, maximize its output, improve its quality, optimize the material flow, and keep it operating efficiently than do the machine operators, material handlers, and maintenance people responsible for it. Nobody.[59]

The following are examples of improving quality through employee involvement:

The department store Nordstrom puts the philosophy and spirit of the quality movement into practice. Posted in the employee handbook is a five-by-eight-inch card with the following words: Welcome to Nordstrom. We are glad you are here! Our number one goal is to provide outstanding customer service. Set your personal and professional goals high. We have great confidence in your ability to achieve them, so our employee handbook is very simple. We have only one rule: "Use your good judgment in all situations." There are no additional rules. Please feel free to ask your department manager, store manager, or human resource office any question at any time.

At Ritz-Carlton, every worker is authorized to spend up to $1,000 to fix any problem a guest encounters. Employees do not abuse the policy. "When you treat people responsibly, they act responsibly," states Patrick Mene, the hotel chain director of quality.

Sam Walton, founder of Walmart, was famous for tapping the ideas of frontline employees, the people closest to the customer, saying, "The key to our success is to get out into the stores and listen to what our associates have to say." It is interesting to note that when he died, Sam Walton was the richest man on the planet and also beloved by his employees and customers.

An example of "forgetting the consultant and asking the employee" comes from one of New York's leading cultural institutions. Before contracting with an expensive outside consultant to determine which of its many exhibits was the most popular with visitors, management got the idea to ask the janitor where he has to mop the most.[60]

W. Edwards Deming

The influence of one person, **W. Edwards Deming,** has been critical in the history of the quality movement. In 1947 he was recruited by American authorities in Japan to help prepare a census, and immediately he took an interest in the restructuring of the Japanese economy. In 1950, a 49-year-old Deming delivered a speech to the Japanese Union of Scientists and Engineers (JUSE) entitled "The Virtues of Quality Control as a Manufacturing Philosophy." This speech was to have a profound effect on Deming's audience. The Japanese believed in this teacher from the United States with his spartan dedication to work and Socratic teaching style, and they applied his ideas.[61]

Deming became a Japanese folk hero, and since 1951, the Deming Prize has been awarded annually in recognition of outstanding achievement in quality control. In an interview before his death in 1993, Deming said, "I think I was the only man in 1950 who believed the Japanese could invade the markets of the world, and would, within five years. They did this through a dedicated and sustained commitment to quality."[62]

The primary result of Deming's influence in Japan was that people at the production level were taught the statistical techniques of quality control, and then were delegated the task and the power to organize their work so that the quality of products could be improved. Also, Deming was able to convince top management of the necessity of personal involvement and commitment to building quality products.

In a lecture at the Hotel de Yama near Hakone, Japan, Deming produced a simple flow diagram to illustrate his concept of a quality system. That diagram, or a slight variation thereof, can be found in just about every Japanese corporation today. Essentially, Deming taught that the more quality you build into anything, the less it costs over a period of time.[63] He also taught the importance of designing a good system and process. To demonstrate this idea, Deming developed what he called the "Red Bead Experiment":

Ten people are picked and assigned jobs: six "willing workers," two "inspectors," one "chief inspector," and one "recorder." The objective is to show how a poorly managed system, not the workers, leads to defects and poor quality.

Deming explains that the "company" has received orders to make white beads. Unfortunately, the raw materials used in production contain a certain number of defects, or red beads.

With both the white and red beads in a plastic container, the six workers are given a paddle with fifty indentations in it and told to dip it into the container and pull it out with each indentation filled with a bead. They then take the paddle to the first inspector, who counts the red beads, or "defects." The second inspector does the same, and the chief inspector checks their tally, which the recorder then records.

Deming, playing the role of a misguided manager, acts upon the results. A worker drawing out a paddle with fifteen red beads is put on probation, while a worker with just six red beads gets a merit raise. In the next round, the worker who had six red beads now has eight, and the worker with fifteen has ten. In his "misguided manager" role, Deming thinks he understands what's happening: that the worker who got the merit raise has gotten sloppy—the raise went to his head—and the worker on probation has been frightened into performing better.

And so it continues—a cycle of reward and punishment in which management fails to understand that the defects are built into the system and that the workers have very little to do with it.

"We gave merit raises for what the system did; we put people on probation for what the system did," Deming says. "Management was chasing phantoms, rewarding and punishing good workers, creating mistrust and fear, trying to control people instead of transforming a flawed system and then managing it."[64]

Quality was Deming's message to the Japanese. They listened, they learned, and they practiced what Deming preached. Japanese manufacturers became profitable, well managed, and competitive. Deming describes a chain reaction for business success beginning with improving quality and resulting in jobs and more jobs. See Figure 9–1.

**Figure 9–1
The Deming Chain
Reaction**[65]

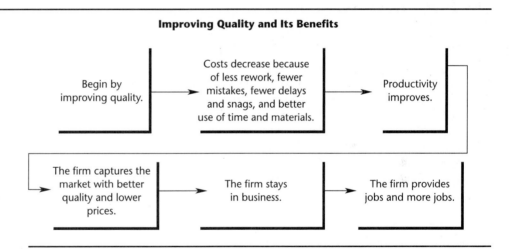

Improving Quality and Its Benefits

Begin by improving quality. → Costs decrease because of less rework, fewer mistakes, fewer delays and snags, and better use of time and materials. → Productivity improves.

The firm captures the market with better quality and lower prices. → The firm stays in business. → The firm provides jobs and more jobs.

Increasingly, American organizations—public and private, large and small—have followed the example of the successful Japanese in their efforts to improve quality. These organizations include General Electric, Motorola, Ford Motor Company, and the U.S. Army, Navy, and Air Force. Although quality improvement efforts were by no means universally successful, most organizations found their employees to be a valuable source of innovation and money-saving ideas. The following are typical examples:

In 1998, Boeing won the Malcolm Baldrige National Quality Award by achieving a 180-degree turnaround in quality with its C-17 military cargo jet. Using quality guidelines and improvement teams, Boeing cut the time it took to build a C-17 by 80% between 1994 and 1998. Productivity increased from $200,000 per employee to $327,000 per employee during this period of time.[66] In 2003, UBS PaineWebber brokers trained in team development generated 19 percent more revenues and 9 percent more assets than all other UBS PaineWebber advisers, whether they worked solo or on teams. The main reason for this improved performance is that properly trained teams offer clients better product and service development.[67]

Experiences such as these are now commonplace as the quality movement and employee empowerment have spread throughout American business, industry, and government.

No discussion about leadership, empowerment, and quality is complete without including Deming's 14 points for a successful workplace. These points or practices can be applied in both private and public organizations.

The Deming Way[68]

1. Create consistency and continuity of purpose. Plan products with an eye to the long-range needs of the company; don't succumb to the pressures of the quarterly report.
2. Set high standards. No company can compete in the world market until its management discards old notions about acceptable levels of mistakes, defects, and inadequate training and supervision.
3. Eliminate dependence on mass inspection for quality. Use statistical controls for incoming and outgoing goods.
4. Reduce the number of suppliers. Buy based on statistical evidence of quality, not price.
5. Recognize that there are two sources of quality problems: faulty systems (85 percent probability) and the production worker (15 percent probability). Strive to constantly improve the system.
6. Improve job training. Make continuous learning a way of life. Teach statistical techniques. The rudiments can be learned in a five-day intensive course.
7. Provide a higher level of supervision. Focus supervision on helping people to do a better job, and provide tools and techniques for people to have pride in their work.
8. Break down barriers between departments. Encourage problem solving through teamwork. Create a team consisting of design, research, sales, purchasing, and production personnel to eliminate errors and waste.
9. Stamp out fear by encouraging open, two-way communication.
10. Abolish numerical goals and slogans.
11. Use statistical methods for continuous improvement of quality and productivity.
12. Remove barriers to pride of work.
13. Institute a vigorous program of education and training to keep people abreast of new developments in methods, materials, and technologies.
14. Clearly define management's permanent commitment to quality and productivity.

Number 14 deserves special emphasis. Joseph Juran, a pioneering architect of the science of managing for quality, taught the importance of top management's ownership and participation. In the absence of visible commitment at the top, quality initiatives are doomed to failure.

Philosophical Roots of the Quality Movement

The following is a discussion of the philosophical roots of employee empowerment and the **quality movement.**

Beginning with Taylor

In 1911 Frederick W. Taylor wrote his famous book *Principles of Scientific Management,* which was eventually translated into dozens of languages. He developed one of the first monetary incentive systems to improve the productivity of workers who were loading pig iron onto railroad cars. His principles and incentive system were soon extended to many other industries, becoming the basis for a worldwide scientific management movement.

Taylor is recognized today as the father of modern management and of the industrial engineering discipline. His scientific management philosophy is summarized in four basic principles:

1. Develop a science for each element of an employee's work that replaces the old rule-of-thumb method.

2. Scientifically select, train, teach, and develop the worker. (In the past, the employee chose the job and was self-trained.)

3. Heartily cooperate with employees to ensure that all work is done in accordance with the principles of the science that has been developed.

4. Divide the work and responsibility between management and employee. Managers should take over all work for which they are better fitted than the worker. (In the past, the worker took almost all of the work and the greater part of the responsibility.)[69]

Taylor has been criticized for advocating an extreme division of labor, resulting in routine, repetitive, and boring jobs on assembly lines. When his scientific management philosophy is considered in the frame of reference of the early 1900s, however, it is logical and even participative in nature. He advocated a systematic approach to problem solving, cooperation between labor and management, training of employees, a fair reward system, and proper assumption of responsibility by both labor and management. These were revolutionary concepts for that time. If only slightly modified, they apply to the enlightened leadership practices of today.[70]

Scientific Management and the Model-T

Henry ford took a revolutionary approach to automobile manufacturing by using scientific management principles.

After much study, machines and workers in Ford's new factory were placed in sequence so an automobile could be assembled without interruption along a moving production line. Mechanical energy and a conveyor belt were used to take the work to the workers.

The manufacture of parts likewise was revolutionized. For example, formerly it had taken one worker 20 minutes to assemble a flywheel magneto. By splitting the job into 29 different operations, putting the product on a mechanical conveyor, and changing the height of the conveyor, Ford cut production time to 5 minutes.

By 1914 chassis assembly time had been trimmed from almost 13 hours to 1 1/2 hours. The new methods of production required complete standardization, new machines, and an adaptable labor force. Costs dropped significantly, the Model-T became the first car accessible to the majority of Americans, and Ford dominated the industry for many years.[71]

The Human Relations School

In the 1920s, Elton Mayo, Fritz Roethlisberger, and a team of researchers from Harvard University conducted a series of studies at the Hawthorne Plant of the Western Electric Company in a suburb of Chicago. These studies were to profoundly affect management theory and practice. The Hawthorne studies marked the beginning of what would later be called the human relations school.

When the Harvard team began their work, their goal was to determine how environmental conditions, such as lighting and noise levels, affected employee productivity. They soon discovered that social factors and group norms influence productivity and motivation much more than do the combined effects of physical conditions, money, discipline, and even job security. In 1939 Roethlisberger summarized these findings in his famous book *Management and the Worker.*[72]

In the 1950s and 1960s, the writings of Abraham Maslow, of "hierarchy of needs" fame, and Douglas McGregor, known for "theory X, theory Y," reinforced the human relations school of thought. Other behavioral scientists, including Rensis Likert (four systems of management), Chris Argyris (integrating the individual and the organization), and Frederick Herzberg (motivation hygiene theory), joined these influential figures to set the stage for many participative management experiments in the United States and abroad.

A Human Relations Pioneer

In 1837, William Procter, an English retailer, and James Gamble, son of a Methodist minister, formed a partnership in Cincinnati to make soap and candles. Both were known for their integrity, and soon their business was thriving.

By 1883, the business had grown substantially. When William Cooper Procter, grandson of the founder, left Princeton University to work for the firm, he wanted to learn the business from the ground up. He started working on the factory floor. "He did every menial job from shoveling rosin and soap to pouring fatty mixtures into crutches. He brought his lunch in a paper bag . . . and sat on the floor [with the other workers] and ate with them, learning their feelings about work."

By 1884, Cooper Procter believed, from his own experience, that increasing workers' psychological commitment to the company would lead to higher productivity. His passion to increase employee commitment to the firm led him to propose a scandalous plan: Share profits with workers to increase their sense of responsibility and job satisfaction.

Still, the plan was not complete. Cooper Procter recognized a fundamental issue for the workers, some of whom continued to be his good friends, was the insecurity of old age. Public incorporation in 1890 gave Procter a new idea. After trying several versions, by 1903 he had discovered a way to meet all his goals for labor: A stock purchase plan. For every dollar a worker invested in P&G stock, the company would contribute four dollars' worth of stock.

Finally, Cooper Procter had resolved some key issues for labor that paid off in worker loyalty, improved productivity, and an increasing corporate reputation for caring and integrity. He went on to become CEO of the firm, and P&G today remains one of the most admired corporations in the United States.[73]

Experiments in Participative Management

Some of the early pioneers in participative management included large firms, such as Texas Instruments, AT&T, General Foods, Boeing and Procter & Gamble, as well as smaller firms, such as Harwood Manufacturing and Lincoln Electric Company. These companies became famous for their innovative approaches to employee relations. Many of the participative management experiments they conducted in the 1950s and 1960s bear a close resemblance to employee empowerment and quality improvement practices of today.

Texas Instruments used work simplification training for line workers to help solve manufacturing problems and improve productivity. AT&T used job enrichment programs to increase motivation and employee output. General Foods designed a plant from the ground up around a team concept, in which workers were classified into skill categories and could progress to the top category by learning how to do all the jobs needed to run the plant. Procter & Gamble independently developed a concept of group work in the 1940s and 1950s. Many of these experiments were so successful that they are still in place today. Factors common to all successful experiments included the following:

- Management attitudes toward workers were positive; employees were viewed as important assets to the success of the company.
- Workers were given increased scope and control over job activities.
- Workers felt that the projects they undertook were important and doable, and had real-life applicability.
- Training in human relations, problem-solving, and decision-making skills was conducted through formal and informal means.

- Opportunities for advancement based on acquiring new skills and knowledge were provided.
- Productivity and morale increased during the period in which experiments were conducted.[74]

Quality Synthesis

As business schools and colleges expanded during the 1970s, old-line professors steeped in classical principles of management distilled from Frederick Taylor had to defend their theories against the onslaught of young behavioral scientists oriented toward human relations. Some time passed before both groups came to understand that there is no single best way to manage in a complex environment. Both the classicist and the behaviorist had to find that there was good in both points of view. During the 1970s, 1980s, and 1990s, the quality movement became the catalyst for joining these two management views. Here was one management technique that combined participative leadership practices with a problem-solving orientation, and it was being fervently employed in a real-world lab by the industrious Japanese as they outstripped competitors and set new standards of quality.[75]

The leadership philosophy behind quality improvement efforts such as total quality management (TQM) and continuous quality improvement (CQI) is both *hard,* based on scientific management, and *soft,* concerned with the human side of work. It is this balance or blend that helps account for its general acceptance across the broad spectrum of managers today. By focusing on quality goals and using problem-solving tools and methods, quality improvement activities satisfy the needs of managers whose values lie with Frederick Taylor, the management classicists, and quantitative analysis. Such "hard-nosed" managers are drawn to the "end product" benefits of better products and services.

Likewise, by focusing on employee empowerment and personal growth, and by using group process techniques, quality improvement activities satisfy the needs of managers who trace their philosophical roots to Elton Mayo, Kurt Lewin, Abraham Maslow, Douglas McGregor, Rensis Likert, and other figures in the human relations and behavioral science school. These "soft-hearted" managers are especially pleased with the "in-process" benefits of improved morale, quality of work life, and the experience of community. See Figure 9–2.

**Figure 9–2
The Leadership Philosophy behind Member Empowerment and the Quality Movement**

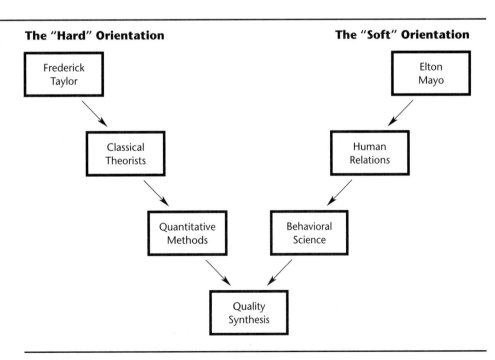

Improving Performance through Quality Initiatives

How effective is the quality movement? What results are experienced by participating organizations? A Government Accounting Office (GAO) report on American management practices shows U.S. companies experience good results using quality improvement efforts to improve business performance.[76]

Background

In recent years, a number of U.S. companies have found that they could not achieve world-class quality by using traditional approaches to managing product and service quality. To enhance their competitive position, American companies have reappraised the traditional view of quality and have adopted what is known as the total quality management model in running their businesses.

For many years the traditional way to achieve quality was through systematic final inspection. This approach is referred to as inspecting in quality. Intense foreign competition in general, and Japanese competition in particular, has led increasing numbers of U.S. companies to adopt total quality management practices that are prevention-based. This approach is often referred to as building in quality.

Results

- Companies that adopted quality management practices experienced an overall improvement in business performance. In nearly all cases, companies that used total quality management practices achieved better employee relations, higher productivity, greater customer satisfaction, increased market share, and improved profitability.

- Companies did not use a cookbook approach in implementing successful quality management systems, but common features that contributed to improved performance can be identified: Corporate attention was focused on meeting customer needs as a first priority; senior management led the way in building values into company operations; all employees were suitably trained, empowered, and involved in efforts to continuously improve quality and reduce costs; and systematic processes were integrated throughout the organization to foster continuous improvement.

- The diversity of companies studied showed that quality management is useful for small companies (500 or fewer employees) as well as large companies, and for service companies as well as manufacturers.

- Many different kinds of companies benefited from putting quality management practices into place. However, none of these companies reaped those benefits immediately. Companies improved their performance on average in about two and one-half years. Management allowed enough time for results to be achieved rather than emphasizing short-term gains.

Specific Findings

Specific findings revealed U.S. companies can improve performance through quality efforts.

- Better employee relations were realized. Employees experienced increased job satisfaction and improved attendance; employee turnover also decreased.

- Improved quality and lower cost were attained. Companies increased the reliability and on-time delivery of their product or service, and reduced errors, product lead time, and their cost of quality.

- Greater customer satisfaction was accomplished, based on the companies' survey results of their consumers' overall perceptions about a product or service, the number of complaints received, and customer retention rates.

For current information on improving performance through quality initiatives, see the Web site of the American Society for Quality (ASQ) (www.asq.org/) as well as the Web site for the Baldrige National Quality Program and National Quality Awards (www.quality.nist.gov), which are designed and managed by the National Institute of Standards and Technology (NIST).

Financial Benefits of Improving Quality

A report in *BusinessWeek* describes the financial impact of quality improvement efforts:

Total quality management (TQM) pays off handsomely. A study by the Georgia Institute of Technology and the College of William & Mary found that TQM award-winners posted 37% higher sales growth and 44% fatter stock prices, compared with a corporate control group. These results buttress similar findings for the stocks of 18 winners of the Malcolm Baldrige National Quality Award. They have outperformed the Standard & Poor's 500 stock index by over 100%.[77]

Implicit in the value system of the quality movement is the saying "If you always do what you have always done, you will always get what you have always gotten." This statement reflects the spirit of the childhood rhyme "Good, better, best. Never let it rest until the good gets better, and the better is the best," as well as the Greek ideal of *aretaic,* or excellence itself, as a virtue.[78]

Continuous Improvement Today

The quality movement is here to stay. Free markets and global competition combine to ensure competition for customers. Effective methods from Balanced Scorecard to Six Sigma are being used to help organizations rise to the challenge.[79]

- *Six Sigma Quality.* One of the most important developments in quality management has been the introduction of statistical tools to analyze the causes of product defects in an approach called Six Sigma Quality. Originating at Motorola in 1986, Six Sigma became popular in the 1990s after it was embraced by General Electric. The term is now widely used to describe a variety of performance improvement efforts (improving quality, increasing efficiency, cutting costs, and the like).

  In essence, Six Sigma seeks to remove variability from a process, thus avoiding errors and defects. Six Sigma quality is defined as having no more than 3.4 defects per million. At Six Sigma, a product or service is defect free 99.99966 percent of the time. The mantra of Six Sigma practitioners is DMAIC, standing for design, measure, analyze, improve, control for quality excellence.[80]

- *Lean Manufacturing.* An increasingly popular approach to improving business performance is *lean manufacturing,* developed by Toyota as a way of achieving quality, flexibility, and cost effectiveness. The essence of *lean* is commonsense management. It emphasizes the use of accurate data, insightful analysis, creative thinking to design work processes, the reliable measurement of important inputs and outputs, and the workforce discipline to do this without exception.

  In a *lean* operation, rejects are unacceptable, overhead and inventory costs are kept to a minimum, and emloyees are empowered to halt production to correct problems at their source so that future problems can be avoided. With a well-managed *lean* process, an organization can develop, produce, and distribute products with significantly less staff, space, tools, time, and overall costs.[81]

- *Checklist Procedures.* Physician Atul Gawande has an interesting prescription: Every professional should write—in her field or out, for others or herself, but by all means write. Taking his own medicine, Gawande has written a trilogy of books on medicine today (*Complication, Better,* and *The Checklist Manifesto*). Gawande's third book is a must-read for leaders and organizations challenged to get things done right, especially when tasks are complex and specialized knowledge and skills are required.

  Gawande identifies the lowly checklist—well conceived, communicated, and executed—as a tried and true answer that can be applied in the high-tech world of aviation, construction, finance, and medicine. This helpful book can be read cover to cover and then applied in a customized way to achieve high quality and reliable performance in any size or type of organization.[82]

- *ISO Standards.* The influence of the quality movement has become even more important with the emergence of ISO standards. ISO 9001 is a series of voluntary quality standards developed by the International Organization for Standardization, a network of national standards institutions in more than 150 countries. The number of companies receiving ISO 9001 certification continues to grow as hundreds of thousands of companies in manufacturing and service industries throughout the world are ISO certified. ISO 9001 standards of performance are set in eight areas:

1. *Customer focus*—learning and addressing customer needs and expectations.
2. *Leadership*—establishing a vision and goals, establishing trust, and providing employes with the resources and inspiration to meet goals.
3. *Involvement of people*—establishing an environment in which employees understand their contribution, engage in problem solving, and acquire and share knowledge.
4. *Process approach to work*—defining the tasks needed to successfully carry out each process and assigning responsibility for them.
5. *System approach to management*—putting processes together into efficient systems that work together effectively.
6. *Continual improvement*—teaching people how to identify areas for improvement and rewarding them for making improvements.
7. *Factual approach to decision making*—gathering accurate performance data, sharing the data with employees, and using the data to make decisions.
8. *Mutually beneficial supplier relationships*—working in a cooperative way with suppliers.[83]

The challenge to leaders and organizations today is to maintain predictability and reliability of current products and services, while simultaneously fostering innovation and creativity. Current success and future survival require mastering both ends of the quality spectrum. This is called avoiding the tyranny of the *or* and embracing the genius of the *and*. More academically, it is called organizational ambidexterity—being able to achieve multiple objectives at the same time. An example of organizational ambidexterity and business success is the story of Google, known for both innovation and reliability, stretch goals and incremental progress, core values and operational freedom, big thinking and bold action.[84]

The Toyota Way and the Starbucks Experience

For years, Toyota was a role model of improving quality by tapping the constructive power of employees. Toyota viewed themselves as a manufacturer, and viewed its employees as the company's most important asset. Toyota gave employees the training, tools, and encouragement to solve problems as they arose and head off new problems before they occurred. The company supported and rewarded the intellect of frontline people as its secret to success. The result was a relentless march to become the best and biggest automobile company in the world. The soul of the Toyota production system was a principle called *Kaizen*. The word is often translated as "continuous improvement," but its essence is that engineers, managers, and line workers collaborated continually to systemize production tasks and identify changes to make work go more smoothly.[85]

Starbucks is another example of a company that mastered both ends of the spectrum—business innovation as well as daily delivery of results. CEO and chairman Howard Schultz asked the question, How can you merge a quality coffee bean tradition with the charm of a European coffeehouse? The answer became the Starbucks experience, which transformed the ordinary to the extraordinary and created a brand name that became synonymous with the word *coffee*. At the doing level, Starbucks customers received consistent quality from store to store every day: "We have a basic line of deployment that we all understand, where person A is on the register, person B stays on the bar, and person C floats around making drinks if there is a long line. We also have checklists. Our brewed coffees, in theory, would be good for about five hours in the container in which they are made. But we brew a new container every hour to ensure that they are very fresh, very hot! It's the freshest coffee you can get.[86]

In the world of work, stories are written in the ink of the moment. Past performance is a predictor but not a guarantee of future success. Only as long as the quality of the product pleases the customer and the execution of service remains reliable will companies be role models for success. Focus and discipline helped Toyota and Starbucks rise to world prominence, but both brands have been tarnished in recent times. Recommitment and relentless adherence to time-tested principles are needed to regain their lofty posts. The leadership message is that quality performance and customer satisfaction are never-ending quests.

Malcolm Baldrige National Quality Award

In 1987 U.S. Congress established the Malcolm Baldrige National Quality Award to promote quality awareness, to recognize quality and business achievements of U.S. organizations, and to publicize these organizations' successful performance strategies. Now America's highest honor for performance excellence, the Baldrige Award is presented annually to U.S. organizations by the President of the United States. Awards are given in manufacturing, service, small business, education, and health care. In October 2004, legislation was passed to authorize the National Institute of Standards and Technology to expand the Baldrige award program to include nonprofit organizations. Awards are now given every year to companies and nonprofit organizations that have met specified standards of service in seven areas: (1) leadership; (2) strategic planning; (3) customer and market focus; (4) measurement, analysis, and knowledge management; (5) workforce focus; (6) process management; and (7) business results.[87]

Part Four Summary

After reading Part Four, you should know the following key concepts, principles, and terms. Fill in the blanks from memory, or copy the answers listed below.

Two kinds of leadership authority are top-down and bottom-up, both of which have merit. An approach to leadership that recognizes the value of both is (a)_____, emphasizing a commitment to people, as shown by (b)_____, _____, and _____. The essential character of leadership that involves people and gains their participation in decision making is (c)_____. The empowering leader raises the (d)_____ of others without lowering her or his own, primarily by (e)_____ to them, thus showing interest and respect. Three basic principles of an empowered workplace are to (f)_____, _____, and _____. Two of the top six places employees prefer to get information are (g)_____, and _____. Management author Robert Greenleaf believed that the world would be saved by having three truly great institutions as role models—one in each sector of society—private, public, and nonprofit. In each case, the secrets of success would be (h) _____ and _____. The central figure in the history of the quality movement has been (i)_____, primarily because of his influence first in Japan, then in the United States. The (j)_____ synthesizes the benefits of scientific management, most associated with Frederick Taylor, and behavioral science, associated with individuals such as Abraham Maslow and Douglas McGregor.

Answer Key for Part Four Summary

a. **servant leadership,** page 147

b. **access, communication, support,** page 148

c. **democratic,** page 151

d. **psychological size,** page 157

e. **listening,** page 159

f. (any three) **trust in people, invest in people, recognize accomplishments, decentralize decision making, view work as a cooperative effort,** page 163

g. (any two) **immediate supervisor, small group meetings, top executives, policy handbook, orientation programs, member newsletters,** page 165

h. **caring leadership, empowerment of people,** page 167

i. **W. Edwards Deming,** page 168

j. **quality movement,** page 170

Reflection Points—Personal Thoughts on Leadership Authority, Empowerment in the Workplace, and the Quality Imperative

Complete the following questions and activities to personalize the content of Part Four. Space is provided for writing your thoughts.

■ How do you rate as a servant leader? Discuss commitment to others as shown by access, communication, and support.

_____

_____

■ Describe a participative organization where leaders involve the people, gain understanding, and achieve good results. What do the leaders do? How do people react?

_____

_____

■ Discuss the use and abuse of leadership power. Is it necessarily true that power corrupts and absolute power corrupts absolutely? Cite examples of leaders who improved as a result of the responsibility of leadership.

_____

_____

■ Develop a five-point plan for organizational communication. What should be done to achieve the best communication possible—up, down, and sideways?

_____

_____

■ Implement one to five practical tips for a high-performance workplace. Discuss the results.

_____

_____

■ Critique "The Deming Way" as it applies to your workplace. Which points are present? Which are effective? Which points are missing? What are the results?

_____

_____

■ Use participative leadership to improve performance. Assemble a team, and discuss problems, bottlenecks, and opportunities. Select one and develop a recommendation. Follow up and evaluate.

_____

_____

Part Four Video Case
Pike Place Fish Market

Pike Place Fish is located in Seattle's historic, open-air Pike Place Market. Visitors from many parts of the world come not only to buy high-quality seafood and have it shipped home, but also to watch fishmongers throwing their wares and having fun. From a humble beginning as a small stand, Pike Place Fish has gained a big reputation. The change began when a young employee said, "Let's be world-famous," and the owner responded, "Why not?"

John Yokoyama worked at Pike Place Fish when the owner offered to sell him the business in 1965. Only 25, Yokoyama was reluctant to buy the struggling market, but after much thought he decided to give it a try. He knew nothing about managing people, and his management style was that of a tyrant: you do what I tell you or else. Pike Place Fish did not do well, and Yokoyama was close to failing. That's when Jim Bergquist entered the scene.

A consultant whose wife worked at the fish market, Bergquist approached Yokoyama with a proposition: Give me three months and I'll improve your business or else I'll quit. They agreed. Then, when they were trying to decide their strategy, the young worker made his wild suggestion. At first the partners regarded the notion of becoming world-famous as a joke, but the idea began to grow on them. They adopted the idea of becoming "world-famous," added the words to the logo, and had them printed on shipping boxes.

What does it mean to be world-famous? That's what Yokoyama, Bergquist, and their crew had to figure out. They decided it means making a difference in the lives of customers and others with whom they come into contact. "For us it means going beyond just providing outstanding service to people," explains Yokoyama. "We're out to discover how we can make their day. We've made a commitment to have our customers leave with the experience of having been served. They experience being appreciated whether they buy fish or not."

Providing such an experience for customers requires total commitment. At Pike Place Fish there are no jobs; rather, there are positions available for those who make the team. You have to commit to the purpose—being world-famous—or you won't even want to be on the team. New employees sometimes take three months to understand the distinction—*being* world-famous rather than merely wanting to be or believing you are—and become productive team members.

A big change for John Yokoyama was to share responsibility and power with workers. Yokoyama found the best way to manage the type of team he needed was to stay out of employees' way and let them be creative and manage themselves. Inspirational management is the preferred style. Pike Place Fish creates a context for personal growth and development. For instance, someone who wants to master the art of filleting fish will be coached to reach that goal. Anyone can be a coach, and everyone is allowed to coach others. The intention is for the coach to empower the other person to achieve. When coaching is needed, everyone has the responsibility to step up and contribute.

The best-selling book *Fish!* has popularized the workplace philosophy at Pike Place Fish. This book identifies four principles, based on the fishmongers at the Seattle market, for creating a fun-filled environment: play, make their day, be there, and choose your attitude. Pike Place Fish uses these principles to create a culture where employees are creative and mix well with customers. Sales, customer satisfaction, and employee retention have increased steadily since the "fish" philosophy has been introduced. Other companies, including Sprint and Marriott, also have adopted the principles.

Questions for Discussion

1. How does Pike Place Fish create an environment for workers to reach their maximum potential?

2. What roles do socialization and mentoring play in creating and nurturing this atmosphere?

For more information, see www.pikeplacefish.com.

Action Assignment

As a bridge between learning and doing, complete the following action assignment.

1. What is the most important idea you have learned in Part Four?

2. How can you apply what you have learned? What will you do, with whom, where, when, and, most important, why?

Part 5 Leadership Principles

10. Effective Leadership and Human Relations
11. The Team Concept

THE BOSS DRIVES; the leader coaches.

The boss wants power; the leader, good will.

The boss creates fear; the leader builds pride.

The boss says "I"; the leader says "We."

The boss places blame; the leader solves the problem.

The boss knows how; the leader shows how.

The boss uses people; the leader serves others.

The boss preaches; the leader teaches.

The boss takes credit; the leader gives credit.

The boss commands; the leader asks.

The boss says "Go"; the leader says "Let's go."

—William J. Stewart
Author and educator

Learning Objectives

After studying Part Five, you will be able to:
- Apply the principles and practices of effective leadership.
- Develop a high-morale, high-performance workforce.
- Understand the importance of good human relations in the work setting.
- Demonstrate the art of effective listening.
- Identify the elements of an enlightened workplace.
- Describe the characteristics of a high-performance group.
- Know what the leader can do to develop communication, teamwork, and a one-team attitude.

Effective Leadership and Human Relations

P art 5 addresses the role of the leader in creating a high-morale and high-performance workplace. Topics include work satisfaction, human relations, and team leadership. Chapter 10 begins with principles and practices for effective leadership.

How do you go about being an effective leader? Author and educator Warren Bennis provides a short-course answer distilled from years of study and experience:

Be yourself. Figure out what you are good at. Hire only good people who care. Treat people the way you want to be treated. Focus on one or two critical objectives. Ask your co-workers how to get there. Listen well. Call the play. Get out of their way. Cheer them on. Count the gains. Start right now.[1]

No individual has been more influential than Peter Drucker in the study and practice of effective leadership. His books are classics on the subject, and his advice has helped six generations of leaders. Drucker's conclusions about leadership include the following:

1. There may be "born leaders," but these are few. Effective leadership can be learned.

2. Without followers, there can be no leaders. Trust is the glue that binds the two.

3. Leadership is not rank, privilege, or title. Leadership is responsibility.

4. Popularity is not leadership; nor is it style or personality. Leadership is results.[2]

When Drucker died in 2005, *Fortune, BusinessWeek*, and *The Wall Street Journal* declared him to be the greatest management thinker and writer of all time. His ideas influenced Winston Churchill, Bill Gates, Jack Welch, and the Japanese business establishment, citing a famous few out of millions. Francess Hesselbein, past editor of the *Harvard Business Review* and CEO of the Girl Scouts of the USA, describes the influence of Peter Drucker: "In his 65 years of work, Peter Drucker redefined the social sector, redefined society, redefined leadership and management—and gave mission, motivation, and values powerful meanings that have changed our lives." Drucker's influence endures today especially in the booming economies of Asia where old school values like integrity and humility fit well with Confucian heritage.[3]

Certain principles of leadership have optimum positive influence on followers. Consider Amos Alonzo Stagg, Knute Rockne, Joe Paterno, Eddie Robinson, and Paul "Bear" Bryant in the field of sports. Although their styles were different, each followed universal principles of leadership that brought out the best in the pride and performance of people. These principles constitute leadership by competence. They apply at all levels of leadership and in all fields of work.[4]

For an evaluation of your competence as a leader (or an evaluation of your leader's competence), complete Exercise 10–1 and read the rationale that follows each question. Note that this questionnaire is an assessment of leadership behaviors, as opposed to personality traits. Followers are unable to read the minds of their leaders and can go only by what they see them do; therefore, it is important to consider how well you are *practicing* the principles of effective leadership.

**Exercise 10–1
Leadership Report
Card[5]**

Circle the appropriate number for each response, and read the accompanying rationale. If you are evaluating your leader, substitute *he* or *she* for *I,* and *his* or *her* for *my.*

A. I have a clear understanding of my responsibilities in order of priority.

  1. I haven't the foggiest.

  2. Things are vague.

  3. There is some confusion.

  4. Generally speaking, yes.

  5. Exactly.

Rationale:

■ If the leader is confused about personal goals and duties, how can the leader guide the behavior of others? The leader won't know in which direction to lead them.

B. All my people know what their job duties are in order of priority.

  1. None do.

  2. Some do.

  3. Most do.

  4. Almost all do.

  5. All do.

Rationale:

■ Job expectations must be understood and agreed upon for maximum job satisfaction and work performance.

■ Not knowing what is expected of you is a major cause of stress at work.

■ Manage by the Marine Corps "rule of three"—most people can efficiently handle three key responsibilities.

C. The jobs my people have are satisfying to them.

  1. Not really.

  2. Some are.

  3. So-so.

  4. More than most.

  5. Definitely yes.

Rationale:

■ A person's work is an important part of personal identity in Western society.

■ Work must be personally satisfying if high morale and productivity are to be achieved.

D. My people know whether they are doing a good job or if they need to improve.

  1. No, it's best they don't.

  2. Some do.

  3. I try to get to most of them.

  4. Practically all do.

  5. Yes, it's rare if they don't.

Rationale:

■ Not knowing how you are doing causes worry and anxiety and dissipates energy.

E. I recognize and reward good performance.

  1. The paycheck is enough.

  2. Sometimes.

  3. More often than not.

  4. Almost always.

  5. Always.

Rationale:

■ Appreciation for a job well done reinforces good work.

■ Ignoring a job well done reduces commitment. The employee begins to think, If they don't care, why should I? People need psychic, social, and economic reinforcement at work.

- Glorify the lower levels of the organization. Celebrate their successes and take pride in their performance. Most of an organization's critical tasks are accomplished by frontline leaders and their teams.

- Recognition techniques that build morale include (1) personal thanks; (2) year-end celebrations; (3) courtesy time off; (4) traveling trophy; (5) money.

F. I have criticized an employee in the presence of others.

   1. I believe in making an example.

   2. Occasionally.

   3. Almost never.

   4. Once.

   5. Never, not once.

Rationale:

- Public criticism embarrasses, alienates, and ultimately outrages not only the employee being chastised, but all who are present as well.

- As Ralph Waldo Emerson said, "Criticism should not be querulous and wasting, all knife and rootpuller; but guiding, instructive and inspiring—a south wind, not an east wind."[6]

G. I care about the personal well-being of my people, and they know it.

   1. Honestly, no.

   2. Some of them, yes.

   3. Usually.

   4. Almost all of them, yes.

   5. Totally.

Rationale:

- People resent being treated as unimportant; they want leaders to care about them and show respect for their interests, their problems, and their needs. Whether by personal hospital visits when they are ill, or by providing the best equipment and working tools available, or by sharing in the trials of battle and the rewards of victory, the effective leader shows consideration for others. Plutarch in *Lives* has this to say about the Roman leader, Julius Caesar:

  Caesar implanted and nurtured high spirits in his men: (1) first by gracious treatment and by bestowing awards without stint, demonstrating that the wealth he amassed from wars was a carefully guarded trust for rewarding gallantry, with no larger share for himself than accrued to the soldiers who merited it; and (2) secondly by willingly exposing himself to every danger and shrinking from no personal hardship of battle faced by his fellow soldiers.[7]

- A leader's ability to remember aspects of followers' personal lives (names of children, favorite hobbies, etc.) creates a bond that causes followers to admire and support the leader.

H. I have policies and procedures for employee development and cross-training.

   1. There is no need for this.

   2. I plan to someday.

   3. On occasion, for some employees.

   4. Yes, generally speaking.

   5. It is a major commitment I have.

Rationale:

- Employee training does six important things: builds skills, raises morale, cuts avoidable turnover and absenteeism, raises loyalty, reduces mistakes, and increases productivity.

I. I have given assignments to people without first considering the availability of their time and the competence they possess.

   1. Often.

   2. Occasionally.

   3. Rarely.

   4. I almost never do this.

   5. Never.

Rationale:

- Assigning work that is over a person's level of skill creates undue stress and is likely to result in a costly error.
- Assigning more work than is possible to accomplish in the time available creates frustration, low morale, resentment, and lower performance in the long run.

J. **I have been accused of favoritism regarding some of my employees.**

   1. Often.

   2. More than most.

   3. At times.

   4. Rarely.

   5. Never.

Rationale:

- The values of equality and fair treatment are widely shared in Western society; favoritism runs directly counter to these values.

K. **I take personal responsibility for the orders I give and never quote a superior to gain compliance.**

   1. Never.

   2. Rarely.

   3. Usually.

   4. Almost always.

   5. Always.

Rationale:

- Leaders who violate this principle lose the respect of their direct reports, upper management, and ultimately themselves as they become merely "paper leaders."
- The effective leader agrees with Harry Truman, who said, "The buck stops here" and "If you can't stand the heat, get out of the kitchen."
- When a leader refers to higher managers as "they," he or she drives a wedge between the employees and the organization, failing senior managers and employees as well.
- Karl Menninger's definition of loyalty can be helpful here:

  Loyalty doesn't mean that I agree with everything you say, or that I believe you are always right, or that I follow your will in blind obedience. Loyalty means that we share the same values and principles, and when minor differences arise, we work together, shoulder to shoulder, confident in each other's good faith, trust, constancy, and affection. Then together, we go forward, secure in the knowledge that few day-to-day matters are hills worth dying on.[8]

L. **I do not promise what cannot be delivered, and I deliver on all promises made.**

   1. I have dropped the ball often.

   2. I have failed occasionally.

   3. Usually.

   4. Almost without exception.

   5. Always.

Rationale:

- Broken promises lower employee confidence and respect for the leader.
- Disappointments deflate employee morale and performance, especially when they come from the leader.

M. **My people understand the reasoning behind policies and procedures.**

   1. Rarely.

   2. Occasionally.

   3. Sometimes.

   4. Usually.

   5. Always.

Rationale:

- Not knowing the purpose of a policy or procedure can result in mistakes.
- The following story shows the importance of understanding *why:*

   The members of a crew on a submarine were about to take battle stations, and the ship's Captain was worried about a young seaman whose job it was to close the water-tight doors between certain compartments. The young man didn't seem to realize the purpose of his job, so the Captain undertook to impress him. He told him that if he failed his job, the ship would be lost. Not only that, some of the men aboard were specialists and it cost thousands to train each of them; they might be drowned. The Captain stated: "So you see how important it is that you do your job . . . this is a very expensive ship, and these men are very valuable." The young crewman replied: "Yes sir, and then there's me too." The Captain stopped worrying.[9]

- Uncertainty about policies can lead to paralysis.

N. The rules we live by are discussed and modified as needed.

   1. Rarely.

   2. Sometimes.

   3. Usually.

   4. Almost always.

   5. Always.

Rationale:

- People are more likely to follow a rule they help set.
- People need to know the appropriate limits of behavior and guidelines for conduct.
- Rules should be periodically reviewed for appropriateness; some rules may no longer be necessary or desirable.

O. I encourage my people to express disagreement with my views, especially if I'm dealing in a controversial area.

   1. Never.

   2. Rarely.

   3. Sometimes.

   4. Fairly often.

   5. Always.

Rationale:

- People have the need to express themselves on emotional issues without fear of reprisal.
- Good ideas can come from constructive disagreement.
- Remember Harry Truman's advice: "I want people around me who will tell me the truth as they see it. You cannot operate if you have people around you who put you on a pedestal and tell you everything you do is right. Because that can't be possible."[10]

P. My people know and feel free to use a right of appeal, formal and informal.

   1. There is no procedure for appeal.

   2. There is a procedure, but it is not widely known.

   3. Some do.

   4. Most do.

   5. All do.

Rationale:

- Not all decisions are good ones, and some should be reversed.
- Every rule must have an exception, and a review or appeal process can facilitate this.
- An appeal process is a defense against arbitrary and capricious treatment, and it meets the need for a sense of fairness.

Q. The last time I listened closely to a suggestion from my people was:

   1. I can't remember.

   2. Two months ago.

3. A month ago.

4. Last week.

5. Within the past two days.

Rationale:

■ Not listening shows disrespect, and people shut down when they do not feel respected.

■ Important information and ideas may be lost unless two-way communication prevails.

■ Ben Jonson's words make the point well: "Very few men are wise by their own counsel; or learned by their own teaching. For he that was only taught by himself had a fool to be his [teacher]."[11]

■ One of the best ways to keep communication lines open is to be available. The simple act of placing your office in a position near the lobby, parking lot, or hall is a time-tested way to stay informed of employee needs and suggestions.

R. I encourage my people to participate in decisions affecting them unless compelling reasons prevent it.

1. Rarely.

2. Sometimes.

3. Usually.

4. Almost always.

5. Always.

Rationale:

■ Democracy is a political value taught in our society. It should come as no surprise when employees want to be involved in decisions that affect them.

■ Participation leads to understanding; understanding leads to commitment; and commitment leads to loyalty.

■ Peter Drucker makes the point: Good leaders know how to *tell;* great leaders know how to *ask.*[12]

S. I have mastered both the job knowledge and technical skills of my work.

1. I am totally out of my element.

2. I need much improvement.

3. I am OK.

4. I am very good.

5. I am excellent.

Rationale:

■ Job knowledge helps the leader gain the respect and loyalty of people.

■ Job expertise helps solve critical problems.

■ Effective leaders are teachers and developers of people; this role requires keeping job knowledge current.

T. I have lost control of my emotions or faculties in the presence of my people.

1. Often.

2. Occasionally.

3. Rarely.

4. Almost never.

5. Never.

Rationale:

■ Emotional stability in the leader can be an anchor of strength for others.

■ Past a certain point, as emotionality increases, objectivity and the ability to make good judgments decrease.

U. I set a good example for my people in the use of my time at work.

1. If they did what I do, we'd be in trouble.

2. I waste significant amounts of time.

3. Sometimes yes, sometimes no.

4. Usually.

5. I wish they would use me as a model.

Rationale:

- Because people are influenced primarily by the example the leader sets, leaders must follow effective time management practices.
- Effective time-management results in efficiency and smooth operations in the work setting.

Scoring:

Add the numbers you circled for all 21 questions; record your total score here: _____

Interpretation:

Check the following list for an evaluation of your (or your leader's) competence as a leader.

Score	Evaluation
95–105	You should go to the head of the class. Your leadership practices can serve as a model for others. Your behavior concerning employee communication, rewards, decision making, assignment of work, and the example you set are ideal.
84–94	You are on solid footing as a leader. You understand and employ the basic principles of effective leadership, regardless of the level and field of work. People should be happy under your direction, and the quality of their work can be expected to be high.
63–83	You are doing some things right, and you are making mistakes in other areas. Go back to the test, determine where your strengths are, and capitalize on those areas. Also, work diligently to raise your low scores. For example: Do you have good two-way communication with your people? Are you following the principles of effective motivation? Are you setting a good example by your own work habits and the use of your time?
62 and lower	Because of lack of training, lack of application, or lack of aptitude, you are not practicing the principles of good leadership. To diagnose the problem, answer these three questions: (1) Have you been reading the wrong book or following the wrong models of leadership? (2) Do you know the right answers but have been inattentive to practicing them? (3) Are you cut out for leadership, or do you feel more comfortable working alone—being responsible for your own work, as opposed to assigning, coordinating, teaching, coaching, and facilitating the work of others? Whatever the cause of your low scores, for the benefit of your employees and the quality of work of your group, you should address the problem and solve it. The best way to do this is to read the rationale for the correct answers and then make every effort to exhibit the correct behavior on the job.

Work Morale

The importance of morale has been recognized by all great leaders. Napoleon once wrote: "An army's success depends on its size, equipment, experience, and morale . . . and morale is worth more than all of the other elements combined."[13] Meta-analyses of research studies show positive relationships between employee morale and organizational commitment, job performance, organizational citizenship, and retention.[14]

A person's morale can be diagnosed according to the percentage of time spent on the job in each of three states—work, play, and hell. Consider your own job. What percentage of your time is spent doing *work* (drudgery)? What percentage is spent at *play* (enjoyable, uplifting activities)? What percentage is *hell* (pain and torture)? Record your percentages below to assess your morale.

State	Percentage of time
Work	_____
Play	_____
Hell	_____
Total	100%

If less than 20 percent of your job is enjoyable, your interest, commitment, and ultimately your performance will go down. There is not enough satisfaction in your job. If more than 20 percent of your job is hell, your attitude, performance, relationships, and even your health may be affected. More than a day of your week is spent in a miserable state. An acceptable work (drudgery) quotient depends on the work ethic you have developed. Because of either Western world or Eastern world socialization, some people have a higher degree of self-discipline and tolerance for tedious labor.

The single best way to achieve high morale is to get the right person in the right job in the first place. As a job aid in doing this, career counseling can be helpful. To find out what people actually do in a variety of jobs, what the salaries and working conditions are, and what the current and future job prospects are, see the *Occupational Outlook Handbook,* compiled by the U.S. Bureau of Labor Statistics. It can be found online at http://www.bls.gov/oco/. See also O*NET at http://online.onetcenter.org/.

Raising Employee Morale

Some policies and techniques for maximizing morale seem to work with the majority of employees in most cases. A review of 550 studies published since 1959 shows nine areas in which management can take action that will have positive effects on employee satisfaction and job performance. Following are the nine areas and possible actions:

- *Pay and reward systems.* **Introduce a group bonus.**
- *Job autonomy and discretion.* **Allow workers to determine their own work methods.**
- *Support services.* **Provide service on demand from technical support groups.**
- *Training.* **Provide training and development for all employees.**
- *Organizational structure.* **Reduce the number of hierarchical levels.**
- *Technical and physical aspects.* **Break long production and assembly lines into smaller work units.**
- *Task assignments.* **Assign whole tasks,** including preparatory and finishing work.
- *Information and feedback.* **Solicit and utilize direct feedback from users—** clients, customers, other departments.
- *Interpersonal and group processes.* **Increase the amount and types of group interaction.**

Research shows that positive results can be obtained by using one or more of these techniques. Costs go down, and the quality of work and quality of work life improve.[15]

The Measurement of Morale

Robert Levering, in his best-selling book *A Great Place to Work,* describes high morale as having pride in what you do (the job itself), enjoying the people you are working with (the work group), trusting the people you work for (management practices), and gaining economic rewards (wage and benefits). One of the best ways to understand the importance of morale is to evaluate your own level of morale in these four key areas. Complete the following exercise (Exercise 10–2).

Exercise 10–2: Morale Survey—What Is Your Level of Morale?[16]

The following survey addresses a number of work-related issues. Answer each question as it relates to your own experience. Circle the appropriate response.

Job

1. At this point in my job, I am doing the things I feel are important.

Strongly Disagree	Disagree	Undecided	Agree	Strongly Agree

2. When it comes to challenge, the job I am doing is demanding.

Strongly Disagree	Disagree	Undecided	Agree	Strongly Agree

3. As things are now, I have a sense of accomplishment in the work I am doing.

Strongly Disagree	Disagree	Undecided	Agree	Strongly Agree

Group

4. When it comes to pride in the work of my co-workers, it is high.

Strongly Disagree	Disagree	Undecided	Agree	Strongly Agree

5. I like the people with whom I work.

Strongly Disagree	Disagree	Undecided	Agree	Strongly Agree

6. There is teamwork between my co-workers and me.

Strongly Disagree	Disagree	Undecided	Agree	Strongly Agree

Management

7. Management strives to be fair.

Strongly Disagree	Disagree	Undecided	Agree	Strongly Agree

8. I understand and agree with the goals of management.

Strongly Disagree	Disagree	Undecided	Agree	Strongly Agree

9. Management shows concern for employees.

Strongly Disagree	Disagree	Undecided	Agree	Strongly Agree

Economics

10. My wages are satisfactory.

Strongly Disagree	Disagree	Undecided	Agree	Strongly Agree

11. My fringe benefits are satisfactory.

Strongly Disagree	Disagree	Undecided	Agree	Strongly Agree

12. The opportunity for advancement is satisfactory—if I desire to pursue it.

Strongly Disagree	Disagree	Undecided	Agree	Strongly Agree

Scoring:

What does the Morale Survey tell you about your own work situation? To find your level of satisfaction in four important areas—the job itself, relations with co-workers, practices of management, and economic rewards—complete the following three steps.

Step One:

For each question, score 1 for "Strongly Disagree," 2 for "Disagree," 3 for "Undecided," 4 for "Agree," and 5 for "Strongly Agree."

Step Two:

Add the total scores for each section of the questionnaire, divide by 3, and enter the averages in the appropriate spaces below.

Job	**Group**	**Management**	**Economics**
_____	_____	_____	_____
Average for items 1, 2, and 3	Average for items 4, 5, and 6	Average for items 7, 8, and 9	Average for items 10, 11, and 12

Step Three:

Make a three-dimensional picture of your morale at work, using Figure 10–1. Circle the appropriate number on each edge of the box, and connect the circles with straight and dotted lines as shown in the example (Figure 10–2).

Figure 10–1
Your Levels of Morale

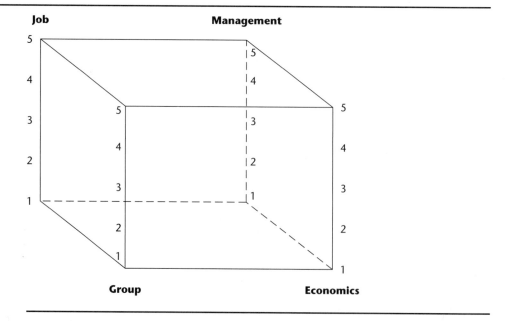

**Figure 10–2
Example of Levels
of Morale**

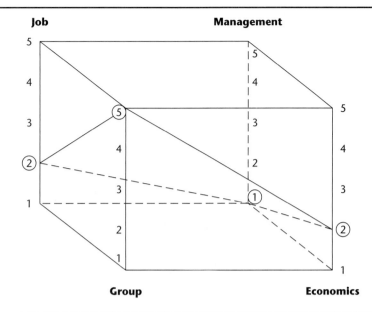

Interpretation:

Score	Description	Meaning
1.0–2.5	Low Morale	Scores from 1.0 to 2.5 on any one or a combination of the four edges of the box—job, group, management, and economics—indicate a low level of morale. If you are doing a good job, you are doing so because of personal qualities, not because of environmental support.
2.6–3.4	Wait-and-See Attitude	Scores between 2.6 and 3.4 on any one or a combination of the four edges indicate a wait-and-see attitude. It is likely that your morale is neither helping nor hurting your job performance at this point. However, you lack a sense of full satisfaction and do not feel complete commitment to your work. Your current condition can be likened to running in place or treading water.
3.5–5.0	High Morale	Scores between 3.5 and 5.0 on all four edges indicate a high level of morale. You are fortunate in that you receive much satisfaction from your work. You are striving to do the best job possible, and with training and practice your level of performance could be expected to be high.

Employee Morale and the Role of Management

Managing morale is the task of management. Meeting this responsibility requires a willingness to listen to employees and the ability to read between the lines of what they say and do. In this process, the morale of each person should be considered individually. Although the elements of morale are the same for everyone—job, group, management, and economic rewards—each element may be more or less important to different people at different times.

- The nature of the job itself may not be as important to the individual who views work as a temporary source of income while going to school as it is to the person in midcareer who foresees many more years in the same line of work.

- Typically, wages and the opportunity for advancement are of primary importance to younger workers, while older employees are more interested in fringe benefits for their retirement years. All three—wages, benefits, and advancement—are usually important to workers in their middle years, when the financial demands of raising a family must be met, security for sickness and retirement must be considered, and social needs for status and responsibility can be great.

- Relations with co-workers and practices of management probably would be less important to the inventor, who works alone, than to factory and office employees, who spend a significant amount of time in the company of co-workers and who are subject to a supervisor's orders.

In summary, when an employee has an attitude problem that is work-related, stress levels rise and performance goes down. It may be discovered that management is part of the problem. Occasionally, the problem is caused by other employees. Often, the problem is caused by the employee her- or himself. In any case, management's potential to help is enormous. If you are a manager and have an employee attitude problem, you should be concerned for the sake of the individual and the good of the organization.[17]

Work Morale and the Role of the Leader

Does morale make a difference, and does leadership count? Yes and yes, say Robert Levering and Milton Moskowitz in *The 100 Best Companies to Work for in America,* identifying Southwest Airlines as number one and quoting an enthusiastic employee: "Working here is an unbelievable experience. They treat you with respect, pay you well, and ask you to use your ideas to solve problems. They encourage you to be yourself. I love going to work!"[18]

Although he downplays his role in the success of the company, former CEO **Herb Kelleher** personifies the honest and caring leader who is committed to his people and who cares about their morale. As CEO, Kelleher spent his business day making sure employees believed in themselves and their company, and he did this in his own unique way. He smoked, arm-wrestled, drank Wild Turkey, rapped in music videos—and he loved it. His employees loved him, too. Kelleher states, "You can't just lead by the numbers. We've always believed that business should be enjoyable as well."[19]

Kelleher's attention to morale paid big dividends for Southwest Airlines. When he became CEO in 1982, the airline had just 27 planes, $270 million in revenues, 2,100 employees, and flights to 14 cities. By the time of his retirement in 2001, Southwest had become a $5.7 billion business with 30,000 employees and was flying to 57 cities. At $14 billion, Southwest's market capitalization was bigger than American's, United's, and Continental's combined. Most astounding of all was that, since the company first earned a profit in 1973, it never lost a penny. In an industry plagued by fare wars, oil crises, and other disasters, this is an amazing accomplishment—traced primarily to a caring leader who cared about his people.[20]

Does job satisfaction help customer satisfaction as well? "Indeed so," says Virgin Group founder Richard Branson. "It is common sense that happy employees make happy customers. At Virgin Group, our front line makes our bottom line."[21] The business case linking employee satisfaction with customer service is well documented. Research shows employees in a good mood display friendliness and positive interactions more naturally and frequently, and this causes customers to experience positive emotions and loyalty. Also, satisfied employees are less likely to quit their jobs, so they have better knowledge and skills to serve their customers. Lower turnover also enables customers to have the same employees serve them, so there is more consistent service.[22]

Practical Leadership Tips

The task of leadership is to manage morale, which means making sure people (1) feel they are given the opportunity to do what they do best every day; (2) believe their opinions count; (3) sense their fellow employees are committed to doing high-quality work; and (4) have made a direct connection between their work and the company's mission. By focusing on these key factors and by adhering to the following proven tips for being an effective leader, the leader can keep morale high and performance up in the work group or organization.[23]

1. **Be predictable.** One good rule for leading people is: Be consistent. If you give praise for an act today and criticism for the same act tomorrow, the result will be confusion.

2. **Be understanding.** Try to see things from the other person's view. How can you appreciate what another person is going through if you have never been there or at least listened?

3. **Be enthusiastic.** The atmosphere you create determines whether people will give their best efforts when you are not present. Why would *they* care if *you* do not?

4. **Set the example.** It is difficult to ask others to do something (for example, be at work on time—8:00 A.M.) if you, yourself, aren't willing to do it.

5. **Show support.** People want a leader they can trust in times of need and a person they can depend on to represent their interests. Care about your people and they will care about you. Mutual loyalty is an important force for getting things done, especially in emergencies and adverse conditions.

6. **Get out of the office.** Visit frontline people with your eyes and ears open. Ask questions, understand their concerns, and gain their support. This has to be done often enough to show that you care about their problems and their ideas.

7. **Keep promises.** When you make promises, keep them faithfully. One key to being an effective leader is credibility. Credibility is the formation of trust, and trust is an essential quality employees want in a leader.

8. **Praise generously.** Never let an opportunity pass to give a well-deserved compliment. Don't forget to show appreciation for effort as well as accomplishments, and do so in writing whenever possible.

9. **Hold your fire.** Say less than you think. Cultivate a pleasant tone of voice. How you say something is often more important than what you say. Most important, ask people, don't tell them. Discuss, don't argue.

10. **Always be fair.** Show respect, consideration, and support for all employees equally, but differentiate rewards based on performance. Reward good performers in a similar fashion, and nonperformers in a similar fashion, but don't reward good performers and nonperformers in the same fashion. Doing so is a sure way to demotivate good performers and lower the quality of work for all.

Psychological Health and the Concept of Flow

Research supports the importance of work as a central activity in people's lives. When asked, "If you had enough money to live as comfortably as you would like for the rest of your life, would you continue to work, or would you stop working?" 70 percent of Americans say they would continue to work.[24]

A satisfying work experience is important for emotional well-being. The Russian writer Fyodor Dostoyevsky expressed this when he wrote, "If it were considered desirable to destroy a human being, the only thing necessary would be to give his work a climate of uselessness."[25]

Thomas Jefferson believed it was neither wealth nor splendor, but tranquillity and occupation, which give happiness.[26] Along these lines, University of Chicago psychologist Mihaly Csikszentmihalyi coined the term **flow** after studying artists who could spend hour after hour painting and sculpting with enormous concentration. The artists, immersed in a challenging project and exhibiting high levels of skill, worked as if nothing else mattered.[27]

Flow is the confluence of challenge and skill, and it is what the poet Joseph Campbell meant when he said, "Follow your bliss." In all fields of work, from accounting to zookeeping, when we are challenged by something we are truly good at, we become so absorbed in the flow of the activity that we lose consciousness of self and time. We avoid states of anxiety, boredom, and apathy, and we experience flow. See Figure 10–3.

Figure 10–3
The Experience of Flow Combines High Challenge and High Skill

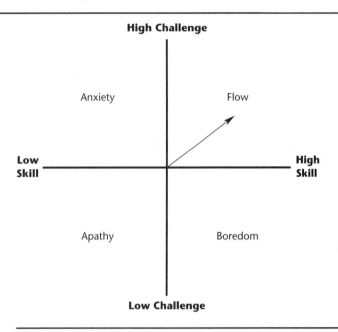

Note that low skill + low challenge = apathy and diminished work life; low skill + high challenge = anxiety and low self-esteem; high skill + low challenge = boredom and low creativity; high skill + high challenge = the experience of flow and work fulfillment.

What is it like to be in a state of flow? Csikszentmihalyi, in his book *The Evolving Self,* reports that over and over again, people describe the same dimensions of flow:

- A clear and present purpose distinctly known.
- Immediate feedback on how well one is doing.
- Supreme concentration on the task at hand as other concerns are temporarily suspended.
- A sense of growth and being part of some greater endeavor as ego boundaries are transcended.
- An altered sense of time that usually seems to go faster.[28]

At this point in time, where are you in your work and professional life: Are you in a state of apathy, anxiety, boredom, or flow? If you are not now in a state of flow, what would it take to get you there?

Forty years ago, Peter Drucker recognized that leaders are more effective when they focus on strengths rather than weaknesses. They capitalize on their own strengths and the strengths of their employees.[29] Yet research shows that only 20 percent of employees in large organizations say they have an opportunity to perform tasks they do best.[30] The untapped potential of people is the main message in the "concept of flow." Effective leaders will take action to be sure no employee stays long in a state of apathy, anxiety, or boredom; but instead is challenged to perform in his or her area of strength and gain the satisfaction of the experience of flow.

Job Design and Work Satisfaction

The works of Adam Smith and C. Babbage serve as the foundation for contemporary work design.[31] The design of good jobs and work satisfaction remain central concerns in today's workplace.[32]

What constitutes a good job? One of the best models of job design and work satisfaction shows intrinsic and extrinsic factors that are necessary for a rich job.[33] Intrinsic factors are:

1. **Variety and challenge**—including the use of different skills and talents.
2. **Opportunity for decision making**—including task identity and autonomy.
3. **Feedback and learning**—including evaluation and suggestions from users.
4. **Mutual respect and support**—including responsive listening and teamwork.
5. **Wholeness and meaning**—including tasks of social and personal significance.
6. **Room to grow**—including development of new knowledge and skills.

The first three must be optimal—not too much, which can add anxiety, or too little, which produces boredom. The second three are open-ended. No one can have too much respect, growing room, or wholeness. Thus a rich job has optimal variety, responsibility, and feedback, and as much respect, growth, and meaning as possible.

The rich job also includes extrinsic conditions of employment:

1. **Fair and adequate pay.**
2. **Job security.**
3. **Benefits.**
4. **Safety.**
5. **Health.**
6. **Due process.**

With this model as a basis, consider the employees in your jurisdiction. What steps can be taken to improve or maintain high job satisfaction?

The Importance of Human Relations

Human relations are important to the individual and the society. As John Donne, the seventeenth-century English poet, wrote, in the language of his time:

> No man is an Island, intire of its selfe;
> Every man is a peece of the Continent,
> A part of the maine;
> If a Clod be washed away by the Sea, Europe is the lesse,
> As well as if a Promontorie were,
> As well as if a Mannor of thy friends, or of thine owne were;
> Any man's death diminishes me,
> Because I am involved in Mankinde;
> And therefore;
> Never send to know for whom the bell tolls;
> It tolls for thee.[34]

In *The Different Drum,* psychiatrist Scott Peck writes: "We are all, in reality, interdependent. Throughout the ages, the greatest leaders of all of the religions have taught us that the journey of growth is the path away from self-love, and toward a state of being in which our identity merges with that of humanity."[35] Effective leaders understand this idea fully, and at a basic level feel connected with their fellow humans, care about the well-being of others, and relate effectively with people.

Consider the words of William Penn: "I expect to pass through this life but once; therefore if there be any kindness I can show or any good thing I can do for any fellow being, let me do it now, not defer or neglect it, for I shall not pass this way again."

Human Relations in the Workplace

Psychologist William Menninger explains the importance of human relationships in the world of work:

The only hope for man to be fulfilled in a world of work is that he get along with his fellowmen—that he try to understand them. He may then be free to contribute to their mutual welfare—theirs and his. Insofar as he fails this, he fails himself and society.[36]

The first empirical evidence of the importance of human relations in the workplace was provided by studies conducted at Western Electric's Hawthorne plant. The original purpose of the studies was to discover the effect of working conditions—noise, lighting, and the like—on employee performance. The final result was to demonstrate the critical role of human relations, particularly employee recognition and management support.[37]

The Hawthorne studies followed a period of American history marked by massive industrialization, exploitation of workers, and the use of scientific management to improve employee efficiency. As epitomized by Charlie Chaplin in the film *Modern Times,* the worker had been dehumanized in the pursuit of production and profit.

Among the findings commonly attributed to the Hawthorne studies are the following: (1) Productivity is affected by human relationships because the work environment is also a social environment; (2) a supportive leadership style and the amount of attention directed toward employees have positive influence on productivity; (3) there is a tendency for workers to set their own standards or norms for acceptable behavior and output.[38]

With the published results of the Hawthorne studies, the industrial community awakened to the fact that the worker must be treated as more than a machine, and that humanism in the workplace is good for both people and business. Participative work groups, enlightened leadership practices, and meaningful job assignments were recognized as important to prevent worker alienation, and a human relations movement began to take root.

Human relations are increasingly important in today's workplace for three reasons:

1. More people are employed in service occupations, where success depends on how well the customer is served. Writing in *Liberation Management,* Tom Peters states: "All business decisions hinge, ultimately, on conversations and relationships; all business dealings are personal dealings in the end."[39]

2. To build superior work teams, people need greater competence in human relations skills. In the 1980s, the National Science Foundation reported that Japanese companies of the period were more productive than American companies primarily because of collaborative work relationships.[40]

3. In his essay "Building Community," John Gardner describes the modern workforce as composed of a varied mix of personalities and cultures, thus the necessity—and challenge—of building strong human relations with all kinds of people. It is interesting to note that the most common cause of supervisory failure is poor human relations.[41]

Basic Beliefs about People

The quality of human relations in any workplace reflects its members', particularly its leaders', views of the essential nature and value of humanity itself.

■ *Human nature.* It makes a great deal of difference whether one views people in general as good or evil. If we assume that people are basically good, we can believe that misbehavior is a reactive response rather than a manifestation of character. This positive view of people will lead to a search for causes in experience rather than in nature. If, on the other hand, we assume that people are inherently bad, then we are prone to assume that misbehavior is caused by something within the person that cannot be altered directly. Accordingly, our attention will focus on limiting freedom to choose and act through external restrictions and controls.

■ *Human value.* What is the basic value of human beings? This is a question as old as written history and probably as old as society itself. It stems from the debate as to whether people are ends in themselves or merely means to ends. In simple terms, we treat people as ends when we allow them to establish their own purposes and to choose for themselves. When we view people as ends, we reflect a humanistic view. In contrast, when we treat people as means, we limit their choices and use them primarily as instruments for our own purposes.

■ *Where do you stand?* Personal history draws each of us toward some primary tendency that determines the general pattern of our relations with others. Small changes may occur to accommodate the various roles we play, but there seems to be a core pattern that represents our basic beliefs concerning human beings. Is your own view of people primarily positive or negative? What experiences and factors have influenced your view? As a result, what principles and practices do you follow in your relations with others?

Abuse and Physical Violence

Awareness and interest in workplace violence has increased in the past 25 years. It was in 1986 that Patrick Sherrill went on a rampage in the Edmond, Oklahoma, Post Office that resulted in the death of 14 of his co-workers before he took his own life. This event and others that followed resulted in the term *going postal* to describe episodes of violence at work.[42]

Bullying behavior and the escalation of abuse to the level of physical violence has become an increasingly important human relations issue in the workplace. Punching and shoving are becoming more common, and the extreme of violence, murder, is not unheard of. Men commit nearly 75 percent of the incidents, and women commit nearly a quarter of all threats and attacks.[43]

In an average work week in the United States, 10 employees are killed and 25 are seriously injured in assaults by current or former co-workers. Often the offender demonstrates clear warning signs of impending tragedy—revealing weapons, threatening co-workers, and talking about attacks. In many cases, employers ignore, downplay, or misjudge the seriousness of the threat.[44]

Paula Grubb, of the National Institute for Occupational Safety and Health, states that one out of four workplaces reports bullying and three out of five say uncivil behavior, such as berating employees and using "the silent treatment," occurs. From the professional office to the retail store to the factory floor, aggressive behavior is increasing personal injury, property damage, absenteeism, and turnover; and it is decreasing employee morale, productivity, and bottom-line profits of companies.[45]

Research shows that antisocial behavior can be influenced by the behavior of co-workers. Work groups can condone harmful behaviors, such as use of profanity, sexual abuse, damaging property, and threatening or bullying other employees. Codes of conduct, disciplinary action, offender counseling, and supervisory training are practical steps to deal with inappropriate behavior. It is essential for leaders to establish a work climate where ladies and gentlemen treat each other like ladies and gentlemen.[46]

The role of the leader is critical in preventing bullying behavior and dealing with workplace violence. It is important to establish a civil work climate and a no-violence code, and to back these up with quick and effective disciplinary action if violations occur. It is essential for the leader to model restraint and to avoid being a verbal or physical aggressor—behaviors that could be copied by employees.[47]

Studies of abusive leaders show that employees who face ridicule and verbal abuse develop anger and hatred toward their supervisors. Employee morale and work performance deteriorate until the supervisor is replaced or employees quit or are terminated. Abused workers are not happy, nor is the organization functioning at its most effective level.[48]

What to Do When People Complain

An important subject in human relations is how to handle complaints. If people think a mistake has been made, it is only natural for them to be upset, especially if the matter is important to them. When people complain, they want to be taken seriously and treated with courtesy. They also want to clear up the problem as soon as possible, so that it won't happen again. Management author Wendy Leebov recommends the following guidelines for handling complaints:

- *Keep cool, calm, and collected.* A polite and friendly manner works best, even with the most irritated people. A phrase to remember is: Maintain grace under pressure.
- *Listen patiently without interrupting.* Don't argue or become defensive; allow the person to vent emotions.
- *Accept and acknowledge the person's point of view.* Show empathy. Consider how you would feel if you were in the other person's shoes.
- *Ask questions to fully understand the problem and to fully understand what the person wants.* Don't jump to conclusions about how the problem should be resolved.
- *Fully discuss possible solutions.* Explain clearly what can and cannot be done.
- *Reach closure.* Don't leave the person hanging. If you can't solve the problem, find someone who can. Arrange a time and method for communicating the results.
- *Genuinely thank the person for speaking up.* Explain why you are glad that he or she pointed out a shortcoming. For example, " It gives me a chance to make things right," or "It helps us improve for the future."
- *Follow through.* Do what you say you will do when you say you will do it. Keep promises.

Handling complaints is everyone's responsibility. It is a practical and tangible demonstration of respect for people. If done effectively, it can help keep small irritations from becoming major problems and it can be an important asset in building and maintaining relationships.[49]

Trust and Respect in Human Relations

Today it is a recognized fact that people have greater satisfaction and produce more when they are involved in their work, when they feel they are doing something important, and when their work is appreciated. Both quality of work and quality of work life are greatest when people are treated with trust and respect.

Trust and respect are the key elements of all good relationships. Trust is expressed by an openness in sharing ideas and feelings. Respect is demonstrated by a willingness to listen to the ideas and feelings of others. Without trust and respect, human relations break down.

The rules for good relationships are to show respect by listening in a responsive manner and to show trust by expressing oneself honestly and openly. Exercise 10–3 provides an effective way to develop trust and respect, the foundation behaviors of good human relations.

**Exercise 10–3
The Dyadic
Encounter**[50]

Introduction:

A theme frequently thought and occasionally voiced when people meet or work together is, I'd like to get to know you, but I don't know how. This sentiment often is expressed in work groups and emerges in marriage and other dyadic (two-person) relationships. Getting to know another person involves a learnable set of skills and attitudes—self-disclosure, trust, listening, acceptance, and nonpossessive caring.

Through the dyadic encounter, a unique learning experience, people who need or want to communicate effectively can learn trust and respect by doing, as they build relationships and skills that can be applied both on the job and in the home.

The conversation that you are about to have is intended to result in more effective human relations. Tasks are accomplished more effectively if people have the capacity to exchange ideas, feelings, and opinions freely.

In an understanding, nonjudgmental manner, one person shares information with another, who reciprocates. This exchange results in a greater feeling of trust, understanding, and acceptance, and the relationship becomes closer.

Directions:

The following ground rules should govern this experience:

- Each partner responds to each statement before continuing to the next statement.
- Complete the statements in the order they appear, first one person responding and then the other.
- Do not write your responses.
- If your partner has finished reading, begin the exercise.

A. My name is . . . _____

_____

B. My hometown is . . . _____

_____

C. Basically, my job is . . . _____

_____

D. The reason I am here is . . . _____

_____

E. Usually, I am the kind of person who . . . _____

_____

F. The thing I like most is . . . _____

_____

G. The thing I dislike most is . . . _____

_____

H. My first impression of you was . . . _____

_____

I. On the job I am best at . . . _____

_____

J. My greatest weakness is . . . _____

_____

K. The best leader I ever had was . . . _____

_____

L. The worst leader I ever had was . . . _____

_____

M. I like people who . . . _____

_____

N. I joined this organization because . . . _____

_____

O. The next thing I am going to try to accomplish at work is . . . _____

_____

P. Away from the job, I am most interested in . . . _____

_____

Q. Society today is . . . _____

_____

R. What concerns me is . . . _____

_____

S. My most embarrassing moment was . . . _____

_____

T. I believe in . . . _____

_____

U. I would like to . . . _____

_____

V. What I like about you is . . . _____

_____

W. What I think you need to know is . . . _____

_____

X. You and I can . . . _____

_____

Y. During our conversation: _____

    a. your face has communicated . . . _____

_____

    b. your posture has conveyed . . . _____

_____

    c. your hands and arms have indicated . . . _____

_____

Z. Have a brief discussion of your reactions to this conversation. If time permits, you may discuss other topics. Several possibilities are projects at work, leadership practices, societal needs, and future goals. Or you may choose your own topics. _____

_____

_____

_____

The Art of Listening

Poor listening is a major cause of communication breakdown. The Roman philosopher Cicero wrote, "God gave us two ears and only one mouth. In view of the way we use these, it is a good thing this is not reversed."[51] More recently, psychologist Carl Rogers wrote, "The biggest block to personal communication is the inability to listen intelligently, understandingly, and skillfully to another person. This deficiency in the modern world is widespread and appalling."[52]

Poor listening is a problem that affects many people. Studies of listening effectiveness show that 40 percent of the average white-collar worker's day is spent in the listening process, yet listening comprehension typically is only 25 percent.[53] Most people would be upset if their pay were reduced by 30 percent (75 percent of 40 percent), yet the misunderstanding and mistakes resulting from inadequate listening can be critical (particularly in occupations with life-and-death consequences, such as medicine, transportation, justice, and the military), and this is precisely what would happen to a blue-collar laborer who produced poor-quality work.

What can be done to improve listening effectiveness? Ralph Nichols, pioneer and most recognized authority on the art of listening, outlines 10 principles of effective listening. These principles apply on the job, in the home, and in the greater community.[54]

Capitalize on Thought Speed

Most people talk at a speed of 125 words per minute. Yet people think at a much faster rate—around 500 words per minute.[55] It is difficult—almost painful—to slow down thinking speed. Therefore, you usually have about four times as much thinking time as you need for every minute you are in conversation. What you do with this extra thinking time depends on whether you are a poor listener or an effective listener.

If you are a poor listener, you usually start to listen to the speaker, then realize there is time to spare. So you briefly turn your thoughts to something else. These side trips of thought continue until you tarry too long on some enticing but irrelevant subject. When your thoughts return, you find the speaker is far ahead of you. At this point, the conversation is harder to follow, making it easier to take more mental side excursions. Finally, you stop listening entirely. The speaker is still talking, but your mind is in another world.

If you are a good listener, you will use thought speed to advantage—by applying spare thinking time to concentrating on what is being said. To capitalize on thought speed, you should

- Anticipate what the speaker is going to talk about on the basis of what has already been said. Ask: What is this person trying to get across?

- Mentally summarize what the speaker has been saying. What point, if any, has already been made?

- Weigh evidence by mentally questioning it. If facts, stories, and statistics are used, consider: Are they accurate? Am I getting the full picture? Is this person telling me only what will prove a point?

- Take a few helpful notes on major points. As an old saying goes, "The strongest memory is weaker than the palest ink." Research shows that you will gain 20 percent more retention if you take notes and 35 percent more if you put notes into a summary of how you will use what you have heard.[56]

- Listen between the lines. People don't put everything important into words. The changing tone and volume of the speaker's voice may have meaning; so may facial expressions, hand and arm gestures, and other body movements.

Listen for Ideas

Do you ever say, When I listen, I concentrate on details? If so, you may be a poor listener. Suppose someone is giving you information composed of points A through Z. The person begins to talk. You hear point A and think, Point A, point A, point A . . . I have to remember it. Meanwhile, the person is telling you about point B. Now you have two things to memorize. You are so busy memorizing point A and point B that you miss point C completely. And so it goes up to point Z. You catch some information, confuse other information, and completely miss the rest.

Good listeners focus on main ideas. As information is presented, weigh one point against the other. Try to find a relationship between them. The person talking usually will put several points together to develop or support a central idea. If you want to comprehend and remember the speaker's message, listen for main ideas, not for a series of memorized details.

Reduce Emotional Deaf Spots

Parallel to the blind spots that affect human vision are emotional deaf spots that impair one's ability to listen and understand. These deaf spots are the dwelling places of our most cherished notions, convictions, and complexes. Often, when a speaker invades one of these areas with a word or phrase, the mind turns to familiar mental pathways that crisscross the invaded area of sensibility. When emotional deafness occurs, listening efficiency drops rapidly to zero.

To show how emotional deaf spots work, suppose your tax accountant calls and says, "I have just heard from the Internal Revenue Service, and . . ." Suddenly, you breathe harder and think, Auditors. Can't they leave me alone? You have stopped listening. Meanwhile, your accountant is saying there is a chance you can save $3,000 this year. But you don't hear this, because the words "Internal Revenue Service" have created emotional deafness.

Emotional deaf spots are common to almost everyone. An ardent Republican, for example, may become temporarily deaf on hearing the names Jimmy Carter and Bill Clinton; and many Democrats quit listening when they hear the names Ronald Reagan and George Bush. Other red-flag words that cause emotional deafness include *tax increase, downsizing,* and *mother-in-law.*

For more effective listening, identify the words that bother you and analyze why they upset you. A thorough examination may reveal that they really shouldn't bother you at all.

Find an Area of Interest

Studies of listening effectiveness support the importance of being interested in the topic under discussion. Poor listeners usually declare a subject dry after the first few sentences. Once this decision is made, it serves to rationalize any and all further inattention. Good listeners follow different tactics. Although their first thought may be that the subject sounds boring, a second thought immediately follows, based on the realization that to get up and leave would be awkward. The final reflection is that, being trapped anyway, it would be good to learn if anything is being said that can be put to use.

The key to the whole matter of interest in a topic is the word *use.* Whenever you wish to listen carefully, ask yourself, What is the speaker saying that I can use? What worthwhile ideas are being expressed? Is the speaker reporting any workable procedures? Is there anything of value to me or anything I can use to make myself happier? Such questions help keep attention on the subject as you screen what is said in a constant effort to sort out elements of value.

Judge Content, Not Delivery

Many listeners justify inattention to a speaker by thinking to themselves, Who could listen to such a character? What an awful voice. Will the speaker ever stop reading from those notes? The good listener reacts differently. The good listener may well look at the speaker and think, This person has a problem. Almost anyone ought to be able to communicate better than that. But from this initial similarity, the good listener moves on to a different conclusion, thinking, But wait a minute. . . . I'm not interested in the speaker's personality or delivery. I want to find out if this person knows something that I need to know.

Essentially, people listen with their own experiences. Should a speaker be held responsible because a listener is poorly equipped to receive the message? Even if you cannot understand everything you hear, one way to improve communication effectiveness is to assume responsibility to be a good listener by judging content, not delivery. Can you remember a time when you withheld judgment of delivery and benefited by the content?

Hold Your Fire

Albert Einstein believed: If A equals success, then the formula is A equals X plus Y plus Z. X is work, Y is play, and Z is keep your mouth shut. Overstimulation is almost as bad as understimulation, and the two together constitute the twin evils of inefficient listening. The overstimulated listener gets too excited or excited too soon by the speaker. You must learn not to get worked up about a speaker's point until you are certain you thoroughly understand it. The secret is contained in the principle that you should withhold judgment until comprehension is complete.

Some people are greatly addicted to overstimulation. For them, a speaker can seldom talk for more than a few minutes without touching on a pet bias or conviction. Occasionally, they are aroused in support of the speaker's point, but often the reverse is true. In either case, overstimulation reflects the desire to enter into argument. This can be especially harmful if it occurs with family members, friends, and colleagues.

The aroused person usually becomes preoccupied by trying to do three things simultaneously: calculate the harm being done to personal ideas, plot an embarrassing question to ask the speaker, and mentally enjoy all the discomfort the speaker will experience once a devastating reply is launched. With these three things happening, subsequent passages go unheard.

Work at Listening

Listening is hard work. It is characterized by faster heart action, quicker blood circulation, and a small rise in body temperature. To be a good listener, you must be an active participant.

One of the most striking characteristics of poor listeners is their unwillingness to spend energy in a listening situation. People, by their own testimony, frequently enter school, community, or business meetings worn out physically, assume postures that only seem to give attention to the speaker, and then proceed to catch up on needed rest or reflect on purely personal matters.

Faking attention is one of the worst listening habits. It is particularly prevalent when you are listening to someone you know very well, such as family members or a friend. You think you know what the speaker is going to say anyway, so you just appear to tune in. Then, feeling conscience-free, you pursue any of a thousand mental tangents.

For selfish reasons alone, one of the best investments you can make is to give each speaker your full attention. You should establish and maintain eye contact and indicate by body posture and facial expression that the occasion and the speaker's efforts are of concern to you. When you do these things, you help the speaker express thoughts clearly, and you, in turn, profit by better understanding. This does not imply acceptance of the speaker's point of view or favorable action on the speaker's arguments. Rather, it is an expression of interest.

Resist Distractions

Ours is a noisy age. People are distracted not only by what they hear, but also by what they see. Poor listeners tend to be influenced readily by all types of distractions, even in an intimate face-to-face situation. Often they create distractions themselves by tapping feet, drumming fingers, and clicking pens.

A good listener fights distraction. Sometimes the fight is easily won—by closing a door, turning off the radio, moving closer to the person talking, or asking the person to speak louder. If distractions cannot be solved easily, then your task becomes one of concentrating.

Hear What Is Said

People often fail to hear what is said, even when spoken to directly. An employee may be ordered to improve performance or be released; or a supervisor may be criticized for poor leadership practices. Later, when the employee is discharged or the supervisor is relieved of leadership position, both may be surprised, claiming never to have known of impending trouble.

In such instances the mechanism of *denial* serves to shut out unfavorable messages. This poor listening habit is common to many people who use selective listening and hear only what they want to hear. Some people are masters of denial. Do you have a tendency toward selective hearing? What messages might you be blocking or denying?

Challenge Yourself

Perhaps the one word that best describes the poor listener is *inexperienced.* Although you may spend 40 percent of your day in the listening process, you may be inexperienced at hearing anything tough, technical, or expository; you may be conditioned to light, recreational material (television programs, radio shows, sports events, gossip, etc.). This problem can be significant because it lowers performance on the job and in the classroom.[57]

Inexperience can be difficult to overcome. It takes recognition of your weakness, a desire to improve, and effort. You are never too old to meet new challenges, particularly when the challenge is meaningful and the rewards are great. Seek opportunities to challenge your listening skills.

The Importance of Listening as a Leadership Skill

How important is effective listening as a leadership skill? Executive coach Marshall Goldsmith explains: One of the world's most respected research and development organizations had a problem—retaining young talent. The flaw was that during presentations members of senior management had the annoying habit of looking at their watches and checking their BlackBerries, motioning young scientists to move it along, and repeating over and over, "Next slide. Next slide." This annoying practice resulted in a serious company problem. The executives learned an important lesson as they watched talent walk out the door. People will leave (physically or mentally) when they do not feel respected.[58]

The Enlightened Workplace

Every so often, someone captures an important concept and expresses it in such a way that it penetrates and takes root in the society. Douglas McGregor and his book *The Human Side of Enterprise,* first published in 1960 and rereleased in 1985, stand like a lighthouse over the sea of literature on leadership. McGregor's book and his famous "Theory Y" speech, delivered at MIT's Alfred P. Sloan School of Management in 1957, changed the entire concept of organizational life for the second half of the twentieth century.[59] See Table 10–1 for the three propositions and five beliefs of Theory X in contrast to the four dimensions of Theory Y.

Table 10–1
Two Theories of Management—X and Y[60]

Theory X: Three Propositions and Five Beliefs

The conventional conception of management's task in harnessing human energy to meet organizational requirements can be stated broadly in terms of three propositions:

1. Management is responsible for organizing the elements of productive enterprise—money, materials, equipment, people—in the interest of economic ends.
2. With respect to people, this is a process of directing their efforts, motivating them, controlling their actions, and modifying their behavior to fit the needs of the organization.
3. Without this active intervention by management, people would be passive—even resistant—to organizational needs. They must therefore be persuaded, rewarded, punished, and controlled—their activities must be directed. This is management's task. We often sum it up by saying that management consists of getting things done through other people.

Behind this conventional theory there are five beliefs—less explicit, but widespread:

1. The average person is by nature indolent—working as little as possible.
2. The average person lacks ambition, dislikes responsibility, and prefers to be led.
3. The average person is inherently self-centered and indifferent to organizational needs.
4. The average person is by nature resistant to change.
5. The average person is gullible, not very bright, and the ready dupe of the charlatan and the demagogue.

Conventional organization structures and managerial policies, practices, and programs reflect these assumptions.

Theory Y: Four Dimensions

We require a different theory of the task of managing people based on more adequate assumptions about human nature and human motivation. The broad dimensions of such a theory are as follows:

1. Management is responsible for organizing the elements of productive enterprise—money, materials, equipment, people—in the interest of economic ends.

2. People are not by nature passive or resistant to organizational needs. They have become so as a result of experience in organizations.

3. The motivation, potential for development, capacity for assuming responsibility, and the readiness to direct behavior toward organizational goals are all present in people. Management does not put them there. It is a responsibility of management to make it possible for people to recognize and develop these human characteristics for themselves.

4. The essential task of management is to arrange organizational conditions and methods of operation so that people can achieve their own goals best by directing their own efforts toward organizational objectives.

This is a process primarily of creating opportunities, releasing potential, removing obstacles, encouraging growth, and providing guidance. It is a liberating and empowering process in contrast to a system of beliefs, policies, and practices that can best be described as "management by control."

McGregor married the ideas of social psychologist Kurt Lewin to the theories of Abraham Maslow. To these, he added his own perspective drawn from his experiences as a professor and practicing leader. The essence of McGregor's message is that people react not to an objective world, but to a world fashioned from their own perceptions and assumptions about what the world is like. Not content to merely describe alternative theories, McGregor went on to identify leadership strategies that could be used to create enlightened workplaces.[61]

McGregor emphasized the human potential for growth, elevated the importance of the individual in the enterprise, and articulated an approach to leadership that undergirds all types and forms of organization. McGregor's prescriptions for an enlightened workplace are as follows:[62]

- The practice of inclusion versus exclusion, based on democratic ideals; the active involvement of all concerned.

- Mutual satisfaction of individual needs and group goals through effective interpersonal relationships between leaders and followers.

- Leadership influence that relies not on techniques of coercion, compromise, and bargaining, but on openness, honesty, and working through differences.

- A conception of humanity that is optimistic versus pessimistic, and that argues for humanistic treatment of people as valuable and valuing, as opposed to objects for manipulation and control.

- A transcending concern for human dignity, worth, and growth, captured best by the phrase "respect for the individual."

- A belief that human goodness is innate, but that it can be thwarted by a dysfunctional environment, and that one's full potential can best be achieved in a healthy climate characterized by trust, respect, and authentic relationships.

- The importance of free individuals to have courage to act and accept responsibility for consequences.

To show the difference enlightened leadership can make, contrast conditions in two investment firms:

Firm 1. This firm refers to one-half of its staff as the professionals and the rest of the employees as office staff. While the office staff members, primarily secretaries, do not expect to earn the wages of college graduates with multiple degrees, they resent the inference that if one group is professional, it follows that everyone else is unprofessional. In this firm, morale is low, turnover is high, and work performance is reduced.

Firm 2. This firm considers its investment counselors and support staff to be directly associated. One or more counselors and a secretary form a team, and the company ties the secretary's bonus and other forms of recognition to the performance of the people he or she supports. Here, esprit de corps runs at stratospheric levels, performance is high, and the firm is prosperous.

Firm 2 puts into practice McGregor's prescriptions for inclusion, shared goals, respect for all people, and personal responsibility. Research exploring the relationship between managerial adjustment and attitudes toward subordinates shows managers with theory Y assumptions are better at accomplishing organizational objectives and better at tapping the potential of employees.[63]

Ricardo Sember of Semco, a Brazilian manufacturer of industrial products, shares the beliefs of a theory Y leader: "We simply do not believe our employees have an interest in coming in late, leaving early, or doing as little as possible. These are the same people who raise children, join the PTA, elect mayors and presidents. They are adults and at Semco they are treated like adults. We trust them. We get out of their way and let them do their jobs."[64]

The Evolving Context of Human Relations

Information technology has brought new human relations challenges. Virtual relationships are ones maintained at a distance, with the majority of interactions occurring through e-mail, fax, phones, Internet, intranet, video, and other communication technologies. Online technology allows geographic and time dispersement. The most recently developed tools for electronic communication generally fall into a category called Web 2.0, a set of Internet-based applications that encourage user-provided content and collaboration. The leader today finds herself in a web of virtual relationships with customers and co-workers.

The challenge is to maintain both a productive and humanistic work life in the face of virtuality problems such as these:

1. None of the technology of virtuality can currently carry a fraction of the whole range of communications that people use to relate to one another; intended meaning is lost.

2. Virtual communications tend to be brief and intermittent, while long-lasting relationships based on trust and respect usually take time to develop.

3. Virtual communications such as e-mail, teleconferences, and videoconferences may actually distract people from what is going on around them so they are neither fully here nor fully there.

4. Virtual communication works only when the party you desire to communicate with also uses it.

5. Many e-mail users are overwhelmed by hundreds of messages each week, many of which are either unnecessary or irrelevant to the receiver.[65]

It is important to remember that only 7 percent of what is communicated is with words; 38 percent is by sound (or tone), and 55 percent is by body language. More than 90 percent of communication is nonverbal, and this is lost without face-to-face contact.[66]

The successful leader recognizes the problems of virtuality but accepts the fact that electronic communication is a reality of modern organizational life and capitalizes on its strengths (speed, convenience, volume, cost, and so on). Effective leaders master changes in communication technology in the same manner that Franklin Roosevelt used the radio and John Kennedy used television. Senior executive Charles Cianchette of the Cianbro Companies explains: Networking technologies allow companies to run cohesive yet decentralized operations in a fast and efficient manner.

Currently, more than 40 percent of IBM employees work from home or on the road. This is an accelerating trend partly because of a new demographic of younger workers who cannot imagine a world without Google, smart phones, social networking, and instant messaging. No previous generation of employees has grown up understanding, using, and expanding on such a pervasive instrument as the computer. Many people today conduct business via virtual offices on the Internet, working off their computers from wherever they happen to be.[67]

HiWired co-president Singu Srinivas advises a balanced approach: He believes online communication tools, such as chat and e-mail, should be used to enhance face-to-face relationships rather than replace them.[68]

Although today's workplace has become more time pressured, more mobile, less dependent on geography, and more reliant on technological competence, the successful leader recognizes the importance of preserving the "human moment at work." This can be done three ways:

1. Maintain high standards of written and spoken communication, as great letter writers and public speakers have always done.

2. Engage in as much face time as possible to sustain satisfying and productive relationships. Exert the effort, pay the expense, and spend the time required.

3. Keep in mind these three don'ts: Don't hide behind technology, don't forget it's recorded, and don't use sarcastic or belittling statements.[69]

The Virtual World Hits Home

It is one thing to know about something and another to understand it. Understanding requires personal experience. We began writing textbooks in 1980. At that time, books were acquired, developed, and produced in one location. 2007 marked the publication of the third edition of this book: Acquired in New York, managed in Chicago, developed in Iowa, produced in Pennsylvania, with internal design from India, cover from California, copyedited in Greece, proofread in Ireland, printed in Canada, with an Instructor's Guide from North Carolina. This was a virtual stretch for two professors who began writing with yellow pads and pencils, and who were happy there. It took tremendous adjustment and the help of many patient people to work effectively in a virtual world. We were challenged to keep up, but willing to try.

The Team Concept

Sociologists Max Weber, Emile Durkheim, and George Simmel explain the role of groups in the human experience.[70] Whether preliterate or postindustrial, people have always used groups to satisfy important needs: For childbearing and intimacy, we use marriage and family; for our interest in the supernatural, we create religious sects and institutions; for social order and organization, we form governments; for education, we establish schools; for protection, we raise armies; for economic needs, we form work groups and organizations.[71]

The importance of group dynamics in the workplace and the role of the leader as team builder have a long history. The formal study of groups began in the human relations movement of the 1920s and 1930s, as collaborative efforts were featured to balance the individual efforts emphasized by scientific management theorists. In the 1940s and 1950s, the focus moved to sensitivity training and T-groups and the development of interpersonal skills. In the 1960s, an era of organizational development emphasized team and leadership effectiveness through interventions with ongoing work groups and organizations. In the 1970s and 1980s, competition from Japan and other countries resulted in an emphasis on participative management, employee involvement, and quality improvement through the use of teams. In the 1990s and 2000s, the focus shifted to high-performance teams to design products, serve customers, and improve quality to maintain a competitive advantage in a global economy. Leaders today rely on teams and new technology to enable communication across time and geographic distance. Leadership success requires an understanding of group behavior and the ability to tap the constructive power of teams.[72]

Teamwork Means Life and Death at Mayo Clinic

The Mayo Clinic, which employs more than 42,000 people at various locations, is an example of an organization that relies on teamwork to provide high-quality health care. Mayo hires at the top of the talent pool, but it also seeks people who view quality in medicine as a team endeavor. Mayo shuns the star system in favor of the team concept. Many excellent clinicians will not fit at Mayo, including those who lack interpersonal skills and a one-team attitude. States a Mayo physician: "The Mayo culture attracts individuals who see the practice of medicine best delivered when there is an integration of medical specialties functioning as a team. It is what we do best, and most of us love to do it. What is most inspiring is when a case is successful because of the teamwork of a bunch of docs from different specialties; it has the feeling of hitting a home run in baseball."[73]

Excellent Teams

The Russian writer Leo Tolstoy (1828–1910) opens his masterpiece *Anna Karenina* by saying, "All happy families are alike; each unhappy family is unhappy in its own way."[74] The same can be said for groups. Rather than a single thread, there is a tapestry of qualities that characterize all effective groups. The most important element of teamwork is commitment to a common purpose. The best teams also develop norms of behavior for working together to achieve their purpose. With a clear, motivating purpose and positive norms of behavior, people can pull together as a powerful force to achieve extraordinary results.[75] Fully functioning groups and excellent teams possess 12 key characteristics:

1. *Clear mission.* The task or objective of the group is well understood and accepted by all.

2. *Informal atmosphere.* The atmosphere is informal, comfortable, and relaxed. It is a working atmosphere in which everyone is involved and interested. There are no signs of boredom.

3. *Lots of discussion.* Time is allowed for discussion in which everyone is encouraged to participate, and discussion remains pertinent to the task of the group.

4. *Active listening.* Members listen to each other. People show respect for one another by listening when others are talking. Every idea is given a hearing.

5. *Trust and openness.* Members feel free to express ideas and feelings, both on the issues and on the group's operation. People are not afraid to suggest new and different ideas, even if they are fairly extreme.

6. *Disagreement is OK.* Disagreement is not suppressed or overridden by premature group action. Differences are carefully examined as the group seeks to understand all points of view. Conflict and differences of opinion are accepted as the price of creativity.

7. *Criticism is issue-oriented, never personal.* Constructive criticism is given and accepted. Criticism is oriented toward solving problems and accomplishing the mission. Personal criticism is neither expressed nor felt.

8. *Consensus is the norm.* Decisions are reached by consensus, in which it is clear that everyone is in general agreement and willing to go along. Formal voting is kept to a minimum.

9. *Effective leadership.* Informal leadership shifts from time to time, depending on circumstances. There is little evidence of a struggle for power as the group operates. The issue is not who controls, but how to get the job done.

10. *Clarity of assignments.* The group is informed of the action plan. When action is taken, clear assignments are made and accepted. People know what they are expected to do.

11. *Shared values and norms of behavior.* There is agreement on core values and norms of behavior that determine the rightness and wrongness of conduct in the group.

12. *Commitment.* People are committed to achieving the goals of the group.

Exercise 11–1 can be used to evaluate a group and improve both team spirit and team effectiveness on the basis of results. By reinforcing strengths and addressing deficiencies, people can take steps to build and sustain a high-performance group. When this is done, together everyone can accomplish more.

**Exercise 11–1
Characteristics of an
Effective Group**[76]

Consider each of the following characteristics. Evaluate your group as it is operating now (1 is the lowest rating; 10 is the highest).

1. Clear mission

| 1 | 2 | 3 | 4 | 5 | 6 | 7 | 8 | 9 | 10 |

2. Informal atmosphere

| 1 | 2 | 3 | 4 | 5 | 6 | 7 | 8 | 9 | 10 |

3. Lots of discussion

| 1 | 2 | 3 | 4 | 5 | 6 | 7 | 8 | 9 | 10 |

4. Active listening

| 1 | 2 | 3 | 4 | 5 | 6 | 7 | 8 | 9 | 10 |

5. Trust and openness

| 1 | 2 | 3 | 4 | 5 | 6 | 7 | 8 | 9 | 10 |

6. Disagreement is OK

| 1 | 2 | 3 | 4 | 5 | 6 | 7 | 8 | 9 | 10 |

7. Criticism is issue-oriented, never personal

| 1 | 2 | 3 | 4 | 5 | 6 | 7 | 8 | 9 | 10 |

8. Consensus is the norm

| 1 | 2 | 3 | 4 | 5 | 6 | 7 | 8 | 9 | 10 |

9. Effective leadership

| 1 | 2 | 3 | 4 | 5 | 6 | 7 | 8 | 9 | 10 |

10. Clarity of assignments

| 1 | 2 | 3 | 4 | 5 | 6 | 7 | 8 | 9 | 10 |

11. Shared values and norms of behavior

| 1 | 2 | 3 | 4 | 5 | 6 | 7 | 8 | 9 | 10 |

12. Commitment

| 1 | 2 | 3 | 4 | 5 | 6 | 7 | 8 | 9 | 10 |

Scoring:

Add all the circled numbers to find your overall score. Then see the following chart to find your group's effectiveness rating.

Score	Rating
108–120	Excellent
84–107	Good
49–83	Average
25–48	Poor
12–24	Failing

Interpretation:

Refer to the following discussion to interpret your group's rating. Note that each characteristic is important, so strive to improve low ratings, regardless of the overall total.

Excellent   *This is a top-notch group regarding communication and teamwork.* The atmosphere is warm and supportive. The focus of attention and effort is on the mission. Creativity is encouraged and success can be expected.

Good   *This is a strong group for morale and teamwork.* There is enthusiasm and an overall spirit of cooperation and dedication to accomplishing the mission. Such a group attracts and keeps good people; then these people work as a team to achieve success.

Average   *Conditions are neither all good nor all bad regarding group effectiveness.* As is, the group is average. If you are a member or leader of such a group, you are probably suffering from cognitive dissonance and won't be satisfied until conditions are in line with your ideals.

Poor   *This is a poor group environment.* Major work is needed to improve attitudes and performance. Without attention to team building, failure can be expected.

Failing   *Major change in group composition is in order.* Personal and social factors may exist that make staying together unacceptable. What is the answer? Separation and reorganization so that talented and dedicated individuals are not lost.

Positive versus Negative Group Member Roles

How do you develop a high-performance group? Success depends on the individual and what he or she chooses to do. It depends also on the example and direction of leaders. A high level of group performance can be achieved when formal leaders and influential members of the group model and reinforce positive versus negative group member roles. Roles that help build and sustain a high-performance group are as follows:[77]

- **Encourager.** This person is friendly, diplomatic, and responsive to others in the group. The encourager makes others in the group feel good and helps them make contributions to fulfill their potential. The encourager is a cheerleader, coach, and group advocate.

- **Clarifier.** The clarifier restates problems and solutions, summarizes points after discussion, and introduces new or late members to the group by bringing them up to date on what has happened. The gift of the clarifier is to create order out of chaos and replace confusion with clarity.

- **Harmonizer.** The harmonizer agrees with the rest of the group, brings together opposite points of view, and is not aggressive toward others. The harmonizer brings peace versus war, love versus hate, cooperation versus competition, and unity versus discord.

- **Idea generator.** The idea generator is spontaneous and creative. This person is unafraid of change and suggests ideas that others do not. Often these ideas are just what is needed to solve a problem. The idea generator is almost always a creative and unconventional thinker. Pose a problem, and ideas will flow. Idea generators are rich in ideas—half-baked or fully baked.

- **Ignition key.** This person provides the spark for group action, causing the group to meet, work, and follow through with ideas. The ignition key is often a practical organizer who orchestrates and facilitates the work of the group. In this sense, the ignition key plays a leadership role in group action.

- **Standard setter.** This person's high ideals and personal conduct serve as a model for group members. The standard setter is uncompromising in upholding the group's values and goals, and thus inspires group pride. The standard setter is often an expert, possessing knowledge and skills deemed important by the group.

- **Detail specialist.** This person considers the facts and implications of a problem. The detail specialist deals with small points that often have significant consequences in determining the overall success of a group project. A vigilant finisher, the detail specialist searches for errors and omissions and keeps the group on red alert. To understand the importance of the detail specialist, consider Benjamin Franklin's words:

  A little neglect may breed mischief: for want of a nail, the shoe was lost; for want of a shoe, the horse was lost; for want of a horse, the rider was lost; for want of a rider, the battle was lost; for want of a battle, the war was lost; for want of a war, the cause was lost. The cause could be something of great importance—life, liberty, the pursuit of happiness—lost for *want of a nail.*[78]

Group member roles that reduce group success are:[79]

- *Ego tripper.* This individual interrupts others, launches into long monologues, and is overly dogmatic. The ego tripper constantly demands attention and tries to manipulate the group to satisfy a need to feel important.

- *Negative artist.* This person rejects all ideas suggested by others, takes a negative attitude on issues, argues unnecessarily, and refuses to cooperate. The negative artist is pessimistic about everything and dampens group enthusiasm.

- *Above-it-all person.* This member withdraws from the group and its activities by being aloof, indifferent, and excessively formal, and by daydreaming, doodling, whispering to others, wandering from the subject, or talking about personal experiences when they are unrelated to the group discussion. The above-it-all person has a "don't care" attitude that detracts from group progress.

- *Aggressor.* This person attacks and blames others, shows anger or irritation against the group or individuals, and deflates the importance or position of the group and the members in it.

- *Jokester.* This person is present for fun, not work. The jokester fools around most of the time and will distract the group from its business just to get a laugh.

- *Avoider.* This person does anything to avoid controversy or confrontation. The avoider is dedicated to personal security and self-preservation, and is unwilling to take a stand or make a decision.

As a practical measure, consider your own work group or organization, and ask, Who is playing positive versus negative group member roles? Who is providing encouragement, harmony, new ideas? Take the time to let members know how important they are to the group's success, and how appreciated they are for their efforts. Be specific and be personal if you want to reinforce these helpful behaviors. Above all, be sure that your own actions are positive and constructive. For example, where a negative artist may complain about the wind, the effective leader adjusts the sails. This positive example is instructive and helpful for all.

Dealing with Problem Behavior

What do you do about the individual who reduces the effectiveness of the group? Psychologist Harry Levinson prescribes a nine-point plan for dealing with problem behavior:[80]

1. When an individual disrupts the group, talk it over in a calm and patient way. Recognize that the origins of negative behavior may be feelings of insecurity, need for attention, vulnerable self-image, and eagerness for perfection.

2. Report observations uncritically. Describe what happened, especially the behavior to which people reacted. Ask how the person thought others felt when she said or did what you describe. Was this the result desired? If not, discuss how the person can act in the future to get the response she wants.

3. Point out that you recognize the person wants to be successful but that to reach his goals, he must take others into account. Note also that usually there will be defeats and disappointments along the way.

4. If the person's behavior becomes irritating, avoid the impulse to attack or withdraw. Instead, report how he made you feel and how others must feel when he behaves this way. Let him know that you are annoyed, but you nevertheless value him as a person.

5. Ask why the person behaves as she does. For example, why does she attack people in situations that are not combative? Explain that being part of a critical discussion is one thing, but turning discussion into an argument or struggle for power is another.

6. If the person challenges, philosophizes, defends, or tries to debate your observations, don't counterattack. Keep your eye on *his* or *her* goal. People do what they do for their own reasons. What exactly does the person want, and how can participation in the group help accomplish his or her goals?

7. Help the person understand that compromise is not necessarily second best, that the all-or-nothing approach usually results in disappointment, and that cooperation with others can be rewarding. Expect to repeat this process again and again. In all discussions point out the legitimate achievements of which he can be proud.

8. A person may be closed-minded. Perhaps she is thinking of defensive arguments or is preoccupied with her own thoughts. Then she must be confronted with the facts and consequences of her negative group behavior.

9. If, despite your best efforts, the person does not respond, he needs to know in no uncertain terms that his behavior is unacceptable and will not be tolerated. Do not assume that he knows. He should be told repeatedly.

Designing Teams for Success

Over 50 years ago, Peter Drucker wrote: "Organizations years hence will bear little resemblance to the typical company, circa 1950. Traditional departments will serve as guardians of standards, as centers for training and assignment of specialists. They won't be where the work gets done; that will happen largely in task focused teams."

The team approach is being used more and more in organizational settings. Senior leaders may sponsor teams of five to eight individuals to work on projects related to the success of the company. Areas addressed include strategic planning, new markets, technology, product and service quality, safety, and "work life" issues.[81]

Types of teams include production, service, management, project, action, and advisory. The globalization of organizations and the changing nature of work have created the need for cross-cultural and virtual teams. The goal is to unlock slices of genius and tap the constructive power of teams of employees.[82]

Effective teams generate creative solutions to business problems, thus feeding innovation required for organization success. The example of Google makes the point. There is little in the way of corporate hierarchy. Innovation is achieved by creative and motivated employees working in teams.[83]

When a group approach is appropriate, the questionnaire in Exercise 11–2 can be used to construct teams for balance and diagnose existing teams for potential strengths and weaknesses. Note that the questionnaire evaluates **problem-solving styles,** not ability.

**Exercise 11–2
Problem-Solving
Styles—Darwin,
Einstein, Socrates, and
Henry Ford[84]**

There are 10 sets of phrases below. Rank each set by assigning a 4 to the phrase that is *most* like your problem-solving style, a 3 to the one *next most* like your style, a 2 to the one *next most* like your style, and a 1 to the phrase that is *least* like your problem-solving style. Be sure to assign a different number to each phrase in the set. There can be no ties. The example below shows how one person might rank the first set of phrases.

	E		**R**		**T**		**A**
Example: __2__	Following instincts	__1__	Weighing evidence	__3__	Developing thoughts	__4__	Accomplishing goals

E	**R**	**T**	**A**
_____Following instincts	_____Weighing evidence	_____Developing thoughts	_____Accomplishing goals
_____Relying on feelings	_____Considering facts	_____Considering potentialities	_____Trying things out
_____Being perceptive	_____Measuring effects	_____Thinking things through	_____Taking action
_____Emotional involvement	_____Impartial investigation	_____Rational analysis	_____Practical use
_____Being aware	_____Questioning details	_____Using reason	_____Performing deeds
_____Letting intuition guide	_____Recording information	_____Summarizing truths	_____Applying solutions
_____Present-oriented	_____Evaluation-oriented	_____Future-oriented	_____Achievement-oriented
_____Open to experience	_____Thorough observation	_____Conceiving ideas	_____Applying knowledge
_____Conscious of events	_____Studying data	_____Forming theories	_____Taking risks
_____Concrete experience	_____Unbiased inquiry	_____Abstract thinking	_____Producing results

Scoring:

When you have completed the questionnaire, find the total score for each column. Record that number in the appropriate space below:

_____	_____	_____	_____
Total for **E** column	Total for **R** column	Total for **T** column	Total for **A** column

Record your totals for E, R, T, and A on the appropriate axes in Figure 11–1, and connect the scores with straight lines to make a picture of your problem-solving style. The longest line of your four-sided figure indicates your preferred style—Charles Darwin, Albert Einstein, Socrates, or Henry Ford.

Interpretation and Discussion:

All problem solving involves having experiences (E), reflecting on results (R), building theories (T), and taking action (A). These processes or activities constitute four steps of the problem-solving cycle (see Figure 11–2). The following is a description of this cycle,

Figure 11–1
A Picture of Your Problem-Solving Style

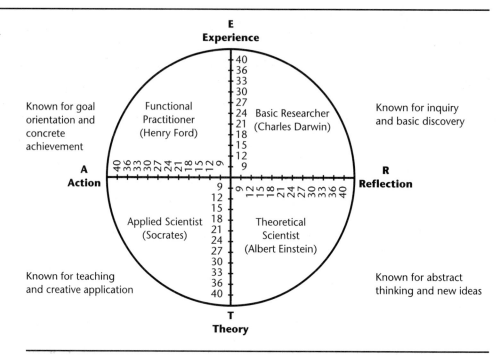

Figure 11–2
The Problem-Solving Cycle

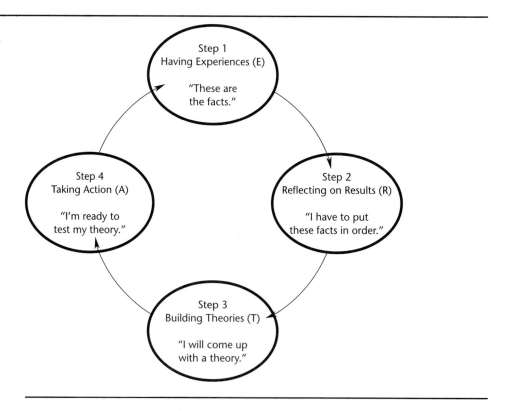

including the strengths and potential weaknesses of each style—Charles Darwin, Albert Einstein, Socrates, and Henry Ford.

Having experiences (step 1) is followed by reflecting on results (step 2). If the longest line of your four-sided figure is between E and R (see Figure 11–3), your preferred style of problem solving is like that of Charles Darwin (1809–1882), author of *On the Origin of Species by Means of Natural Selection* and *The Descent of Man and Selection in Relation to Sex.* At the age of 22, Darwin sailed the South Pacific on the HMS *Beagle.* His observations of plants and animals, most notably the rare creatures of the Galápagos Islands, were the basis for his theory of evolution. About himself, Darwin wrote, "My mind seems to have become a kind of machine for grinding general laws out of large collections of facts."[85]

Figure 11–3
The Charles Darwin
Problem-Solving Style

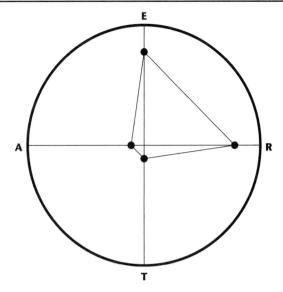

As a Darwin, your strengths are observing, recording facts, and identifying alternatives. Gathering data is enjoyable to you. By style, you are a basic researcher and you love the discovery process. Darwins are known in every field—social science, natural science, the arts, business, and the professions—for their thorough data collection and objective analysis. Carried to an extreme, however, the Darwin style of problem solving can lead to paralysis as each new fact becomes even more interesting than the last, resulting in indecision. It is important to look before leaping, but it is possible to look so long that one never leaps. Consider the case of Darwin himself, who had developed his theories of human evolution years before another scientist, Alfred Russell Wallace, came to similar conclusions and would have received credit for these theories had not Darwin at last published.

After the data are gathered, theory building takes place (step 3). At this stage, assumptions are developed and ideas are formulated. One moves from the world of experience into the world of theory, while remaining in the mode of reflecting rather than acting. If the longest line of your figure is between R and T (see Figure 11–4), your preferred style of problem solving is the same as the theoretical scientist Albert Einstein (1879–1955). Abstract conceptualization and blue-sky thinking are your forte. In 1905, known as Einstein's "year of miracles," he wrote four papers that are each regarded as works of genius. In his description of the world, Einstein wrote, "Physical concepts are free creations of the human

Figure 11–4
The Albert Einstein
Problem-Solving Style

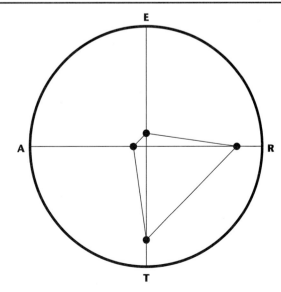

mind, and are not, however it may seem, uniquely determined by the external world."[86] When Einstein was asked how he would save the world in one hour, he replied 55 minutes should be spent thinking and 5 minutes doing. The Einstein style of problem solving is like that of the typical philosopher. Carried to an extreme, however, it can result in castles in the air with little practical value. This is the style of the husband whose wife says, "That's good, Albert, but when are you going to *do* something?"

After theories have been developed, they must be tested (step 4). If your longest line is between T and A (see Figure 11–5), your preferred style is that of the applied scientist. Your strength is not in collecting and analyzing data, but in translating ideas so that they can be put into action. As such, yours is the style of the teacher Socrates (470–399 BC):

We know Socrates as one of the greatest teachers in history, perhaps the greatest of the great men produced by Athens. . . . He wandered through the streets and down to the marketplace, or often he would go to the public gymnasium. Then he started business—the business of teaching. Socrates was the founder of moral philosophy. He was scoffed at for taking his examples from common life, but he did so to lead plain people to goodness, truth, and beauty.[87]

Figure 11–5
The Socrates Problem-Solving Style

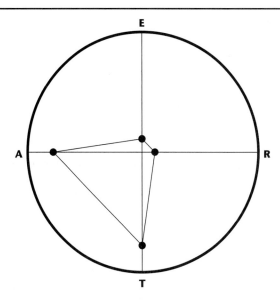

A more modern example of the Socrates problem-solving style is Thomas Alva Edison, a practical genius and America's greatest inventor, who said: "The only invention I can really claim as absolutely original is the phonograph. I'm an awfully good sponge. I absorb ideas from every source I can and then I put them to practical use. Then I improve them until they become of some value. The ideas that I use are mostly the ideas of other people who don't develop them themselves. None of my inventions came by accident. I saw a worthwhile need to be met and I made trial after trial until discovery came. What it boils down to is one percent inspiration and ninety-nine percent perspiration."[88]

Comfortable with ideas, but wanting to apply them, the applied scientist moves from a reflective to an active orientation. This person enjoys coordinating and problem-solving activities. When taken to the extreme, the Socrates style of problem solving may result in impressive, but incomplete, performance because these individuals dislike details. The Socrates-type person may give a beautiful speech, but fail to do thorough research.

Taking action automatically results in new experiences (step 1), so the problem-solving cycle never completely ends. In work, and in life, when one problem is solved, another arises. If your longest line is between A and E (see Figure 11–6), your style of problem solving is like that of Henry Ford (1863–1947), whose strength was achieving results. Upton Sinclair described Henry Ford, the functional practitioner, as follows:

Henry Ford was now fifty-five; slender, gray-haired, with sensitive features and a quick, nervous manner. His long, thin hands were never still, but were always playing with something. He was a kind man, unassuming, not changed by his great success, the world's first billionaire. Having had less than a grammar-school education, his speech was full of the peculiarities of the plain folk of the Middle

West. He had never learned to deal with theories, and when confronted with one, he would scuttle back to the facts like a rabbit to its hole. What Ford knew he had learned by experience, and if he learned more, it would be in the same manner.[89]

Figure 11–6
The Henry Ford Problem-Solving Style

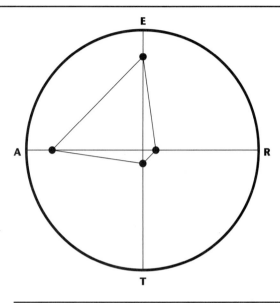

If the functional practitioner knows what needs to be done, the goal will usually be accomplished. This is a person of deeds and action, more than ideas and contemplation. But here, as with the other problem-solving styles, a strength may become a liability when carried to the extreme. If the functional practitioner does not have sufficient facts, or fails to work from a well-conceived plan, there may be tremendous accomplishment—of the wrong thing.

The versatile style of problem solving is represented by Figure 11–7. This individual is equally comfortable with each step of the problem-solving cycle—having experiences, reflecting on results, building theories, and taking action. As such, this person does not have structural strengths or weaknesses resulting from style preference.

Figure 11–7
A Versatile Style of Problem Solving

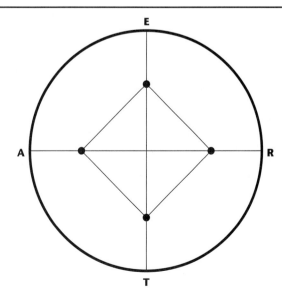

There are several important points to remember concerning styles of problem solving:

1. All problem solving involves four steps—having experiences, reflecting on results, building theories, taking action—and each step must be performed well for overall effectiveness. For example, an independent businessperson with a Socrates style must take extra care to consider details as well as concepts, and should remember to get the facts before making decisions, even if this does not come naturally.

2. It is possible to have preference for more than one style of problem solving. For example, a person may be equally comfortable as a Henry Ford and a Socrates. Such a person relates to the world in both an experiential and a theoretical sense. In either case, this person shows a bias for action.

3. When people with different styles of problem solving live or work together, **tolerance of differences** is required. A Henry Ford manager must be patient with the seeming lack of effort put forth by an Einstein employee, and a Socrates wife must try to understand her Darwin husband's preference for having experiences and reflecting on results over forming ideas and applying knowledge. Appreciation of the characteristics and needs of each type of person can go a long way toward improving relationships and increasing performance.

4. Most people have difficulty changing their styles of problem solving. This can be seen in school when a Henry Ford student fails or drops out. Often the cause is the nature of the curriculum and the style of instruction versus the ability of the student. The functional practitioner, who wants to apply knowledge and accomplish tangible results, may have difficulty relating to book reading and theoretical discussion.

An organization or group needs all four styles of problem solving. A balance of basic research, theoretical science, applied science, and functional practice helps maximize individual as well as group performance. Consider the following story:

Fred was a successful research chemist when he suffered a heart attack. During his stay in the hospital, his work was performed by younger employees. Like many large organizations, Fred's company was rich in talent, and others were qualified to do his job.

When Fred recovered and returned to work, he retained his title, his office was the same, and his income was unchanged. However, he had lost a significant part of his job—his duties were now make-work assignments, while important responsibilities and decision making were handled by others. Whereas Fred had been physically ill before, he now became depressed, and his overall health began to deteriorate. Fred had been placed on the shelf, and he knew it.

At that time, Fred's company began research and development on a new product, and the "Problem-Solving Styles" questionnaire was used to create a balanced team. On the team was a theoretical scientist, who could write formulas from wall to wall, but whom few could understand. This was the Einstein. Also on the team was an applied scientist, who could understand the Einstein's ideas and who knew how to bridge the gap between thinking and doing. The team had a Socrates. The team also had a Henry Ford, who was known for his practical nature. He was a goal-oriented person with the ability to produce results. What was missing on the new product team was a Charles Darwin, a basic scientist, who would be sure that all the facts were gathered and all the data were considered. Fred was chosen to be the team's Darwin.

Within a year, the team developed one of the company's most successful products. A year after that, Fred's wife phoned him at work. By accident, she reached his boss. She said: "Oh, Mr. Johnson, I have been wanting to talk to you for so long. I have wanted to thank you . . . for giving my Fred back to me."[90]

Fred's story shows how the needs of the individual and the needs of the organization are interwoven and how both can be met by creating a balanced team incorporating all four styles of problem solving.

Leader as Team Builder

Teamwork is essential for group success. The testimony of basketball star Michael Jordan, a superb individual contributor, is instructive for people in all fields of work: "One thing I believe to the fullest is that if you think and behave as a team, the individual accolades will take care of themselves. Talent wins games, but teamwork and intelligence win championships."[91]

Leaders in every endeavor know the power of the team concept for achieving results. Effective leaders value teamwork as a virtue, and they demonstrate this by their own efforts as team builders and champions of the group.[92]

A role model for team building and coaching to succeed is Pat Summit, head coach of Tennessee's women's basketball team since 1974, with six NCAA championships and the highest win percentage (.838) of any men's or women's college basketball program in history. Summit has both a love for the sport and a passion for developing others. She even says she enjoys practicing as much as the games because teaching is her "real passion."[93]

The Importance of Hiring and Developing Winners

The task of the leader is to recruit and develop team members who can perform successfully in the type of sport and level of league they are in. Winning performance is A and B levels, not C, D, or F, for every team member, as well as for the leader her- or himself.

This simple principle is employed by every successful athletic coach, yet it is too often overlooked by the leader in the workplace. The result is inadequate performance—loss of product, people, and profit—and, inevitably, replacement of the leader.

What can the leader do? The answer is to commit to excellence and model this ideal personally. The leader must follow the dictum: Hire the best and develop the rest. The successful leader hires the best talent available (A and B players), then trains and develops all other personnel to perform at A and B levels.

What happens to individuals who cannot or will not perform at A and B levels? For the sake of customers and co-workers and ultimately themselves, they are reassigned. The caring leader considers the interests of all, knowing effective performance is required and the individual may be better suited for another sport or league. As difficult or unpleasant as the task may be, action must be taken.[94]

A cautionary note is in order about the practice of labeling people in a group or organization as winners and losers and using a *required* distribution of ratings to reflect this. An example is Enron's "rank and yank" system of putting employees in one of five categories: 5 percent superior, 30 percent excellent, 30 percent strong, 20 percent satisfactory, and 15 percent need improvement. First, any inaccurate rankings can destroy motivation and reduce future performance. Second, *requiring* a percentage of group members to be rated lower than others in the group works against cohesion, teamwork, and, ultimately, effectiveness. Third, such ranking systems can lead to lawsuits. For example, employees with Microsoft, Ford, and Conoco have filed lawsuits claiming that ranking systems are biased toward some groups over others.

Most importantly, imagine how counterproductive a required distribution of performance rankings would be on any high-performance team in its era of greatness— Boston Celtics, Chicago Bulls, U.S. women's soccer team, for example. How long will the team be successful if certain percentages of its members are required to be labeled A, B, C, D, F, relative to each other regardless of individual performance? Leaders should evaluate performance case by case, using good judgment, rather than an artificial distribution of rankings.[95]

How to Create a High-Performance Team

Effective leaders understand that all the individual competence in the world will not result in a high-performance team. An essential component of success is the leader's ability to create a spirit of cooperation and a one-team attitude. Team leadership is important from the research lab to the fashion industry. A study of almost two thousand research publications shows the percentage of journal articles written by teams has increased substantially over the past five decades.[96] Executive Rose Marie Bravo of

Burberry, the London fashion house, explains the importance of teams: "It isn't one person. It is a whole group of people working cohesively towards a goal that makes something happen or not."[97] The best leaders develop successful teams by following 11 time-tested practices:

- Show enthusiasm for the work of the group. The leader's emotion ignites and energizes the team.
- Make timely decisions based on agreed-upon goals. In this way, leaders show decisiveness and consistency.
- Promote open-mindedness, innovation, and creativity by personal example and a conducive work climate.
- Admit mistakes and uncertainties, modeling honesty as a virtue.
- Be flexible in using a variety of tactics and strategies to achieve success.
- Have persistence and lasting power, never giving up on hope or effort.
- Give credit to others for the team's accomplishments, meeting people's needs for appreciation and recognition.
- Keep people informed about progress and problems, celebrating victories and fine-tuning efforts.
- Keep promises and follow through on commitments, earning the trust and confidence of others.
- Train for success; master fundamentals and practice for perfection.
- Put others first and self last, embodying the spirit of the caring leader.[98]

Research shows why some teams are successful and others are not. One study evaluated a number of high-performance teams, including national champion sports teams, heart transplant surgical teams, the crew of the *USS Kitty Hawk,* and others, to determine the characteristics that make them successful. Eight characteristics were always present:

1. A clear, elevating goal.
2. A results-driven structure.
3. Competent team members.
4. Unified commitment.
5. A collaborative climate.
6. Standards of excellence.
7. External support and recognition.
8. Principled leadership.

When any one feature is lost, team performance declines. The most frequent cause of team failure is letting personal or political agendas take precedence over clear and elevating team goals.[99]

Virtual Teams

The use of virtual teams is a growing trend. Virtual teams are teams whose members operate across space, time, and organizational boundaries and are linked through information technologies to achieve organizational tasks. Some virtual teams operate across a city; others operate across countries, cultures, and time zones. One reason why virtual teams have become so widespread is that information technology has made it easier than ever to communicate and coordinate with people at a distance.

Information technology makes virtual teams possible, but knowledge management and globalization make them increasingly necessary. Virtual teams operate best with structured tasks requiring only moderate levels of task interdependence. Complex and ambiguous tasks require an enormous amount of intense dialogue and are better suited to nonvirtual teams.[100]

Many teams use a combination of virtual and nonvirtual interaction. When IBM formed a virtual team to build a customer-access system for Shell, employees from both firms began with an "all hands" face-to-face gathering to assist the teamwork process. The two firms also made a rule that dispersed team members should have face-to-face contact at least once every six weeks throughout the project.[101]

A point to remember is that teams need meaningful face time even when doing virtual work across space and time. For example, at Lucasfilm Ltd., the creator of *Star Wars,* Lucas staffers across the board say the type of collaboration required wouldn't be possible if they hadn't been brought under the same roof. In an era of extreme telecommuting, when companies are rolling out expensive high-definition videoconferencing systems, even the highest-tech employees say there's no substitute for face-to-face interaction for their team-oriented projects if world-class work is the goal.[102]

Stages in the Life of a Group

Regardless of size or type, a group typically goes through predictable stages over the course of time. Figure 11–8 is an illustration of four stages in the life of a group, as described by Glenn Parker and Roy Lacoursiere.[103] By understanding these stages, including major issues, typical member behavior, and effective leadership actions at each stage, the leader can help a group move quickly to the high-morale–high-performance status of an effective team.

Figure 11–8
Stages in the Life of a Group

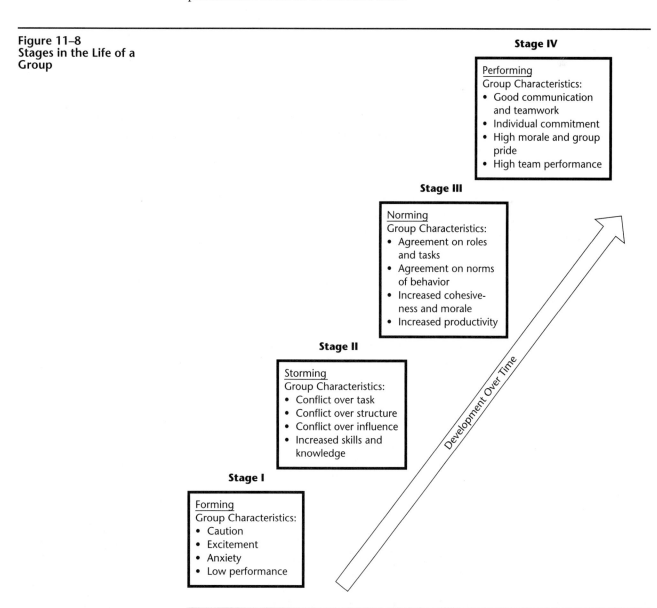

Stage IV

Performing
Group Characteristics:
• Good communication and teamwork
• Individual commitment
• High morale and group pride
• High team performance

Stage III

Norming
Group Characteristics:
• Agreement on roles and tasks
• Agreement on norms of behavior
• Increased cohesiveness and morale
• Increased productivity

Stage II

Storming
Group Characteristics:
• Conflict over task
• Conflict over structure
• Conflict over influence
• Increased skills and knowledge

Stage I

Forming
Group Characteristics:
• Caution
• Excitement
• Anxiety
• Low performance

Development Over Time

Table 11–1 **Forming**	**Major Issue Is Development of Trust, Including Answers to These Questions:**
	1. What is going to happen?
	2. Who is who in the group?
	3. Where do I fit in the group?
	4. How will I be treated?
	Member Behavior Is Characterized by
	1. Anxiety.
	2. Search for structure.
	3. Silence.
	4. Caution with leader and other group members.
	Leaders Can Reduce Uncertainty by
	1. Explaining purpose and goals.
	2. Providing time for questions.
	3. Allowing time for members to get to know each other.
	4. Modeling expected behaviors.

Stage I—**Forming.** In the start-up stage, the group is formed, but its purpose and members' expectations are unclear. This stage incorporates all the discomfort and apprehension found in any new social situation. It is characterized by caution and tentative steps to test the water. Individuals try to determine acceptable behavior and the nature of the group's task, as well as how to deal with each other to get work done. Interactions are superficial and tend to be directed toward the formal leader. Skills and knowledge as a team are undeveloped. See Table 11–1.

Stage II—**Storming.** The initial stage of forming is followed by a period of storming. In this stage, individuals react to what has to be done, question authority, and feel increasingly comfortable being themselves. This stage can be characterized by conflict and resistance to the group's task and structure, even as productivity begins to increase as skills and knowledge develop. Group members express concerns and frustrations, and feel fairly free to exchange ideas. Members learn to deal with differences to work together to meet the group's goals. A group that doesn't get through this stage successfully is marked by divisiveness and low creativity. See Table 11–2.

Stage III—**Norming.** The stage of storming is usually followed by a third stage in the life of a group, a period of norming. In this stage, norms of behavior are developed that are considered necessary for the group to accomplish its task. These norms can be explicit or implicit. In any case, a greater degree of order begins to prevail and a sense of group cohesion develops. Members now identify with the group and develop customary

Table 11–2 **Storming**	**Major Issue Is Increased Conflict from**
	1. Openly dealing with problems.
	2. Increasing group interaction.
	3. Power struggles for influence.
	4. Increasing independence from leader.
	Member Behavior Is Characterized by
	1. Confrontation with the leader.
	2. Polarization of team members.
	3. Testing of group tolerance.
	4. Fight-or-flight behavior.
	Leaders Can Reduce Conflict by
	1. Hearing all points of view.
	2. Acknowledging conflict as opportunity for improvement.
	3. Adhering to core values, such as truth, trust, and respect.
	4. Staying focused on the goal.

Table 11–3 Norming	**Major Issue Is Development of Norms for**
	1. Team member behavior.
	2. Decision-making processes.
	3. Resolving differences.
	4. Leadership behavior.
	Member Behavior Is Characterized by Shift from
	1. Power struggle to affiliation.
	2. Confusion to clarity.
	3. Personal advantage to group success.
	4. Detachment to involvement.
	Leaders Can Encourage Norm Development by
	1. Modeling listening skills.
	2. Fostering an atmosphere of trust.
	3. Teaching and facilitating consensus.
	4. Providing team-centered learning.

ways for resolving conflict, making decisions, and completing assignments. In this stage, members typically enjoy meetings and freely exchange information. Productivity continues to increase as group skills and knowledge further develop. See Table 11–3.

Stage IV—**Performing.** Stage III is usually followed by a fourth stage, performing. This is the payoff stage in the life of a group. People are able to focus their energies on the task, having worked through issues of membership, purpose, structure, and roles. The group is now focused on solving problems and completing tasks. Members take initiative, and their efforts emphasize results. As the group achieves significant milestones, morale goes up and people have positive feelings about each other and the accomplishments of the group. The group is no longer dependent solely on the leader for direction and support; instead, each member takes on leadership roles as necessary. At this stage, the group shows the characteristics of an effective team. See Table 11–4.

It is helpful to view each of the stages in the life of a group from two points of view. The first is *interpersonal relationships*. The group moves through predictable stages of testing and dependency (forming), tension and conflict (storming), building cohesion (norming), and finally, establishing functional role relationships (performing). Each stage focuses on problems inherent in developing relationships among group members.

Table 11–4 Performing	**Major Issue Is Group Performance, Including**
	1. Using a wide range of task and process behaviors.
	2. Monitoring and taking pride in group accomplishments.
	3. Focusing on goals as well as interpersonal needs.
	4. Maintaining the values and norms of the group.
	Member Behavior Is Characterized by
	1. Interpersonal trust and mutual respect.
	2. Active resolution of conflict.
	3. Active participation.
	4. Personal commitment to the success of the group.
	Leaders Can Help the Group Succeed by
	1. Being prepared for temporary setbacks.
	2. Focusing on task accomplishments *and* interpersonal support.
	3. Providing feedback on the work of the group.
	4. Promoting and representing the group.

At the same time, the group is struggling with *accomplishing tasks.* The initial stage focuses on task definition and the exchange of information (forming). This is followed by discussion and conflict over the task (storming). Next comes a period of sharing interpretations and perspectives (norming). Finally, a stage of effective group performance is reached (performing).[104]

Avoiding Groupthink

As important and effective as teams can be, there are also potential problems, the first of which is *social loafing.* Social loafers do not contribute to group effort because they do not feel they will reap individual rewards, nor will they have to suffer individual blame.[105] A second potential problem is *groupthink,* a term coined by William H. Whyte Jr. in 1952.

As a group settles on norms of behavior in stage III and into a mode of performance in stage IV, there is a risk of falling into a pattern of groupthink. This is a well-documented pitfall in group dynamics described by psychologist Irving Janis in *Victims of Groupthink.* Janis defined groupthink as "a mode of thinking that people engage in when they are deeply involved in a cohesive group, and when the members' striving for unanimity overrides their motivation to realistically appraise alternative courses of action." Groupthink is an important concept for a leader to understand.[106]

When people meet in groups, they are often under strong pressure to conform to the majority view. When they don't conform, they risk being isolated or cast aside. In such situations, people may make errors in judgment and conduct based on a desire to preserve group harmony and to continue to be accepted by the group and its leader.

Janis describes additional factors that, when combined with cohesiveness, can foster groupthink. These factors are a highly insulated group with restricted access to external information, and a stressful decision-making context, such as that brought on by budgetary crises, external pressure, or a history of recent setbacks. As a result of the trilogy of group cohesiveness, isolation, and stress, a group can arrive at decisions that are unsuccessful and possibly even catastrophic.[107]

Janis describes eight symptoms that can give a group early warning that groupthink may be present. The following is a description of these symptoms with cases in history to illustrate their effects:[108]

1. **Illusion of invulnerability.** A feeling of power and authority is important to any decision-making group. It gives members confidence that they will be able to carry through on any decisions reached. However, if they come to believe that every decision they reach will automatically be successful, then they become prey to an illusion of invulnerability. Janis showed that American military leaders had this illusion in choosing not to fortify Pearl Harbor more heavily prior to the disastrous attack by the Japanese that led to U.S. entry into World War II.

2. **Belief in the inherent morality of the group.** People want to believe in the rightness of their actions. In the extreme, this can lead to exhortations that "God is on our side." Such claims fulfill an important function—they relieve responsibility for justifying decisions according to rational procedures. People do this as a way to protect self-esteem.

3. **Rationalization.** When a final decision is reached, it is normal to downplay the drawbacks of the chosen course. The problem in a group arises when legitimate objections exist, but they are overshadowed by the perceived negative reaction to anyone who voices those objections. Key engineers in the NASA *Challenger* decision ultimately withdrew their objections to the ill-fated launch, not because of any correction in the admittedly problematic O-rings, but rather, because they rationalized the risk of catastrophic launch failure as only "possible," while the risk of censure and ostracism for continuing to speak out against the launch became a virtual certainty.

4. **Stereotypes of out-groups.** President Truman and his advisors fell victim to the temptation to falsely characterize enemy groups in 1950 with the decision to cross the 38th parallel, a line drawn by the Chinese Communists as a "line in the

sand" between North and South Korea. The decision was made despite repeated warnings from Communist China that to do so would be viewed as a declaration of war by the United States on China. How could Truman and his advisors have so seriously misinterpreted the Chinese warnings? The decision was based largely on a false stereotype of the Chinese Communists as being weak and dominated by Russia, who, it was believed, did not want war. The stereotype proved false, and the Korean "police action" became a resounding failure as the Chinese attacked with massive force.

5. Self-censorship. As one of the principles on which our country was founded, the ability to express oneself without censorship has always been highly valued. It has also been considered a healthy safeguard against group coercion in our work lives. But the fact is, the most common form of censorship is the one we commit on ourselves under the guise of group loyalty, team spirit, or adherence to company policy.

The decision by President Kennedy and his advisors to send a band of Cuban exiles into the Bay of Pigs has been ranked as the greatest foreign policy mistake of the Kennedy administration. The day after the Bay of Pigs fiasco, JFK said, "How could I have been so stupid?" The answer is that Kennedy and his advisors suppressed their doubts, censoring themselves to make the operative belief seem like the truth.

6. Direct pressure. Pressure on group members can surface in many forms. The net effect is the same: Group members are encouraged to keep dissident views to themselves. As one example, Janis reported that during Watergate, "Nixon time and again let everyone in the group know which policy he favored, and he did not encourage open inquiry." Another example involves the *Challenger* disaster. Several engineers made the recommendation to postpone the *Challenger* launch. According to the Rogers Commission report, certain group members responded with direct pressure on those engineers to alter their views, with statements such as "I'm appalled that they could arrive at the recommendation" and "At that rate, it could be spring before the shuttle would fly."

7. Mindguards. A bodyguard is someone charged with the protection of another person's physical well-being. In groupthink, a corollary entity may surface to protect the group from disturbing thoughts and ideas—a mindguard. Interestingly, such mindguards typically perform their function not within the group itself, but far from the confines of group discussion. Data, facts, and opinions that might bear directly on the group are deliberately kept out of the group's purview. Generally, this is done with a variety of justifiable intentions—time is running short, a regular member will summarize for the group, and not pertinent and perhaps saddest of all, the group has already made up its mind.

8. Illusion of unanimity. Finally, the rationalizations, psychological pressures, and mindguards have their effect—the group coalesces around a decision. Drawbacks are downplayed, and the invulnerability and morality of the final course are reinforced. Doubting group members may even feel that they have adequately put their own fears to rest. More likely, it is simply the sense of relief that the struggle has come to an end. An illusion of unanimity sets in.

In contrast to the destructive forces of groupthink, Janis describes a number of techniques that a leader can employ to help ensure a rational consideration of all available courses of action:

1. The leader should assign the role of critical evaluator to each member, encouraging the group to give open airing of ideas, including objections and doubts. This practice should be reinforced by the leader's acceptance of criticism of his or her own judgments.

2. When charging a group with a task, the leader should adopt an impartial stance instead of stating personal opinions and preferences. This approach will encourage open discussion and impartial probing of a wide range of policy and problem-solving alternatives.

3. The leader should set up outside evaluators to work on the same policy question. This tactic can prevent the group from being insulated from important information and suggestions.

4. When the agenda calls for evaluation of decision or policy alternatives, at least one member should play devil's advocate, functioning as a lawyer in challenging the testimony of those who advocate for a position.

5. After reaching a preliminary consensus about what seems to be the best policy or decision, the group should hold a "second chance" meeting, at which every member expresses as clearly as possible all residual doubts and rethinks the entire issue, before making a final decision.[109]

Team-Building Interventions and Techniques

There are many approaches to team building. The most common is for members of a group to develop and grow together over the normal course of time as the team responds to challenges and successfully performs its natural functions. Consider this example:

From time to time, the tribe gathered in a circle. They just talked and talked and talked, apparently to no purpose. They made no decisions. And everybody could participate. There may have been wise men or wise women who were listened to a bit more—the older ones—but everybody could talk. The meeting went on, until it finally seemed to stop for no reason at all and the group dispersed. Yet after that, everybody seemed to know what to do because they understood each other so well. Then they could get together in smaller groups and do something or decide things.[110]

Team building can be enhanced by experiential strategies and activities. Educational workshops in retreat settings are increasingly popular. This off-site format focuses on topics such as communication, teamwork, characteristics of effective groups, positive versus negative group member roles, and workshop/labs to improve team performance—goal setting, values clarification, problem solving, decision making, and the like.

Some organizations use adventure and challenge experiences that can be quite effective at building relationships, developing group identity, and increasing team pride. These interventions are usually conducted in field settings and involve a range of activities that include "ground" experiences, or low-course initiatives, to build team spirit and skills, and "ropes," or high-course challenges, that build individual confidence and pride. There are many varieties of challenges including rafting, rowing, and riding.

One of the best ways to develop and sustain team effectiveness is to meet in a conducive atmosphere, free of interruptions, and discuss important issues. Meaningful questions include:

- *Where have we been?* What forces and events have brought us to this point?
- *Where are we now?* What are our current "prouds" and "sorries"? What are our strengths, weaknesses, opportunities, and threats?
- *What is our purpose or mission?* What is our reason for existence?
- *What should be our goals?* What should we accomplish to fulfill our mission?
- *What are our values?* What principles should guide us in moral dilemmas?
- *Who are our stakeholders?* Who cares about our work and what will it mean to them when we are successful?
- *What should be our strategy?* What initiatives should we have to accomplish our goals and achieve our mission? What strategic, measurable, action-oriented, and timely projects and activities should we undertake?
- *What are the critical factors that define success?* How do we know what great performance looks like?
- *How should we work together to fulfill our potential?* What should we continue doing, start doing, or stop doing? How should we monitor progress? Who should do what by when?[111]

Exercise 11–3 is an easy-to-use and highly effective exercise for team building. It is a variation of Kurt Lewin's famous force field theory for improving team performance. A good approach would be to have individuals complete the exercise alone and then work as a group to develop and improve team effectiveness.

Exercise 11–3
Team Excellence[112]

Answer the following questions, first individually, then as a group.

To operate as a team, what do we *need?*

_____

_____

_____

_____

What should we *continue* doing?

_____

_____

_____

_____

What should we *start* doing?

_____

_____

_____

_____

What should we *stop* doing?

_____

_____

_____

_____

How should we *monitor* our progress?

_____

_____

_____

_____

Actions to be taken, including *who* should do *what* by *when,* are as follows:

_____

_____

_____

_____

_____

_____

_____

_____

_____

Appreciative Inquiry

A positive and popular approach to team building is appreciative inquiry, developed at Case Western Reserve University. This technique emphasizes building on strengths and gaining commitment through participation.[113] Appreciative inquiry typically uses a "Four-D" model or process. The first D is Discovery, or identifying the best of "What is." Positive experiences, success stories, and best practices are shared. The second D is Dreaming, or imagining "What could be." Open discussion and nonjudgmental listening are important. The third D is Designing, or "What should be." It includes collective dialogue and agreement on a direction and course of action. The fourth D is Delivering "What will be." It involves action steps to achieve specific objectives.[114] An example of using appreciative inquiry is provided by the British Broadcasting Corporation (BBC):

The British Broadcasting Corporation (BBC) needed more innovative programming to reverse declining audience numbers, but employees complained that the radio, television, and Internet broadcaster did not provide a creative work environment. To discover how to become more creative, the company sponsored an appreciative inquiry process of employee consultation, called Just Imagine. More than 10,000 employees (about 40 percent of BBC's workforce) participated in 200 meetings held over six months. At each meeting, employees were paired to ask each other three questions: (1) What has been the most creative/valued experience in your time at the BBC? (2) What were the conditions that made that experience possible? (3) If those experiences were to become the norm, how would the BBC have to change? The pairs then discussed their interview results in teams of 10 people, and the most powerful stories were shared with others at the meeting. These meetings produced 98,000 ideas, which boiled down to 15,000 unique suggestions and ultimately 35 concrete initiatives. The BBC's executive publicized the results and immediately implemented several recommendations, such as a job swapping and a newcomer orientation program. Greg Dyke, BBC's respected director-general at the time, commented that the appreciative inquiry process provided valuable guidance. "It gave me a powerful mandate for change," he stated. "I could look staff in the eye and say, 'This is what you told us you wanted.'"[115]

The Role of the Leader in the Team Concept

It is true that good teams can boost productivity and accomplish the seemingly impossible. It is also true that poor teams reduce effectiveness and generally create problems. Is there something that can be done to ensure team success? Research shows that success is enhanced if an organization understands and effectively manages five team processes:[116]

1. *Buy-in*—how the work of the team is legitimized and goals are set.
2. *Accountability*—how individual and team performance is managed and rewarded.
3. *Learning*—how performance is improved and skills developed.
4. *Infrastructure*—how the work of the team is systemized and resources accessed.
5. *Partnering*—how people interact and work together to achieve success on the team and across organizational units.

A key factor in all five team processes is **leadership.** Teams perform most successfully when they have a leader who facilitates the work of the group to accomplish buy-in—agreement on direction; accountability—clarity of assignments; learning—the development of members; infrastructure—allocation of resources; and partnering—a supportive work climate. The most effective team leaders are caring individuals who have a passion for the work and a concern for people.[117]

Organizations can empower their people and improve performance through the use of teams, but successful teams require effective leadership. For optimum results, a designated leader should coordinate the group, advocate for the team across the organization, access needed resources and processes, and ensure that results are supported by, and meaningful to, the organization.[118]

The Team Concept in Business Today: The Cisco Case

Over 100 years ago, businessman and philanthropist Andrew Carnegie wrote, "Teamwork is the fuel that allows common people to attain uncommon results." Today technology giant Cisco is actively and strategically applying this maxim.

As the Internet radically changed how people live and work, new opportunities were emerging in many areas. Cisco president and CEO John Chambers knew that the Internet's and Cisco's rapid growth had increased the difficulty for one top person to review new ideas, gather information, and make timely decisions. For Cisco to continue to grow, he reasoned, it needed to be more nimble and bring more products to market faster—in short, to innovate with speed.

Chambers saw collaborative teams as the solution and designed a new, broader, and more inclusive system in which decision-making responsibility is pushed deeper into the organization. The new configuration includes: An operating committee of 11 people—Chambers plus other top executives; several councils that manage $10 billion projects; boards that handle $1 billion opportunities; and working groups that support the councils and boards and perform other activities. The teams are cross-functional, interdepartmental, and even transnational. Each is organized around promising initiatives or product lines; other teams can spring up at the drop of a hat when needed. In the new company, to not share what you know is unacceptable, so few turn down an invitation to collaborate.

Chambers says collaborative technologies permit almost instant access to information and other people, providing new ways to interact. Cisco promotes all types of social networking: blogs, videos, and even an internal "My Cisco" system that employees use like an internal Facebook network. There employees can share what they have learned and provide details about their expertise.

Initially, not everyone embraced the new teamwork structure. The old Cisco sported a "cowboy culture," with leaders competing aggressively for resources. Nearly 20 percent of them left the company, deciding they couldn't work under Chambers's new setup. Leaders now share responsibility for each other's success. They are measured on how well they collaborate and are compensated on how well all businesses perform, not just their own unit.[119]

In 2009, author James Collins wrote a research-based book titled *How the Mighty Fall.* The contrast he describes between teams on the way down and teams on the way up provides excellent guidance for leading teams (see Table 11–5). Teams on the way up address the truth, use evidence-based problem solving, emphasize two-way communication, have a one-team attitude, show mutual respect, are cause-focused, are learning-centered, and accept responsibility.[120]

Table 11–5
Team Dynamics: On the Way Down Versus on the Way Up

Teams on the Way Down	Teams on the Way Up
People shield those in power from grim facts, fearful of penalty and criticism for shining light on the harsh realities.	*Address the truth*–People bring forth unpleasant facts—"Come here, look, man, this is *ugly*"—to be discussed; leaders never criticize those who bring forth harsh realities.
People assert strong opinions without providing data, evidence, or a solid argument.	*Use evidence-based problem solving*–People bring data, evidence, logic, and solid arguments to the discussion.
The team leader has a very low questions-to-statements ratio, avoiding critical input and/or allowing sloppy reasoning and unsupported opinions.	*Emphasize two-way communication*–The team leader employs a Socratic style, using a high question-to-statements ratio, challenging people, and pushing for penetrating insight.
Team members acquiesce to a decision yet do not unify to make the decision successful, or worse, undermine the decision after the fact.	*Have a one-team attitude*–Team members unify behind a decision once made and work to make the decision succeed, even if they vigorously disagreed with the decision.
Team members seek as much credit as possible for themselves yet do not enjoy the confidence and admiration of their peers.	*Show mutual respect*–Each team member credits other people for success yet enjoys the confidence and admiration of his or her peers.

Team members argue to look smart or to improve their own interests rather than argue to find the best answers to support the overall cause.

Are cause focused–Team members argue and debate, not to improve their personal position, but to find the best answers to support the overall cause.

The team conducts "autopsies with blame," seeking culprits rather than wisdom.

Are learning-centered–The team conducts "autopsies without blame," mining wisdom from painful experiences.

Team members often fail to deliver exceptional results, and blame other people or outside factors for setbacks, mistakes, and failures.

Accept responsibility–Each team member delivers exceptional results, yet in the event of a setback, each accepts full responsibility and learns from mistakes.

Part Five Summary

After reading Part Five, you should know the following key concepts, principles, and terms. Fill in the blanks from memory, or copy the answers listed below.

Leadership author Warren Bennis details advice to leaders based on years of study, including (a) _____, _____, _____, _____, _____, _____, and _____.

Research shows nine ways an organization can raise morale, including (b) _____, _____, _____, _____, _____, and _____. A master at building morale and achieving business success was (c) _____, who believed that you can't lead just by the numbers; business must also be enjoyable. Specific leadership actions that build morale include (d) _____, _____, _____, and _____. High morale and high performance result when a person is in a state of (e) _____, versus apathy, anxiety, or boredom. This state comes from the confluence of high challenge and high skill. The best (most rich) jobs are characterized by (f) _____, _____, _____, _____, _____, and _____. The key elements of good relationships are (g) _____, shown by listening in a responsive manner, and (h) _____, shown by expressing oneself honestly and openly. Douglas McGregor's book (i) _____ changed the entire concept of organizational life for the second half of the twentieth century. The characteristics of a high-performance work group and the need for positive versus negative group member roles are practical applications of McGregor's ideas. Positive roles include (j) _____, _____, _____, _____, _____, _____, and _____. In the design of teams for success, (k) _____ are important, as is (l) _____. Stages in the life of a group are (m) _____, _____, _____, and _____. There are potential pitfalls to effective group decision making, including (n) _____, _____, _____, _____, and _____.

Organizations can empower their people through the use of teams, but successful teams require effective (o) _____ to coordinate the group, advocate for the team, access needed resources or processes, and ensure that meaningful results are achieved.

Answer Key for Part Five Summary

a. (any seven) **be yourself, figure out what you are good at, hire good people, treat people fairly, focus on key objectives, ask your co-workers how to achieve the objectives, listen well, call the play, get out of the way, cheer them on, count the gains, start right now,** page 184

b. (any six) **introduce a group bonus, allow workers to determine their own work methods, provide technical support services, provide training, reduce the number of hierarchical levels, break production into small work units, assign whole tasks, gain direct feedback from users, increase group interaction,** page 191

c. **Herb Kelleher,** page 197

d. (any four) **be predictable, be understanding, be enthusiastic, set the example, show support, get out of the office, keep promises, praise generously, hold your fire, always be fair,** page 198

e. **flow,** page 199

f. **variety and challenge, opportunity for decision making, feedback and learning, mutual respect and support, wholeness and meaning, room to grow,** page 200

g. **respect,** page 204

h. **trust,** page 204

i. *The Human Side of Enterprise,* page 210

j. **encourager, clarifier, harmonizer, idea generator, ignition key, standard setter, detail specialist,** page 219

k. **problem-solving styles,** page 221

l. **tolerance of differences,** page 228

m. **forming, storming, norming, performing,** pages 232– 233

n. (any five) **illusion of invulnerability, belief in the inherent morality of the group, rationalization, stereotypes of out-groups, self-censorship, direct pressure, mindguards, illusion of unanimity,** pages 234–235

o. **leadership,** page 239

Reflection Points—Personal Thoughts on Effective Leadership, Human Relations, and the Team Concept

Complete the following questions and activities to personalize the content of Part Five. Space is provided for writing your thoughts.

■ How do you rate on principles of effective leadership? What are your strengths? What areas do you need to improve?

_____

_____

■ What is your level of morale? What practical steps can the leader take to keep morale and performance high in a work group or organization?

_____

_____

■ Have you ever been a member of a high-performance work group? Describe the conditions.

_____

_____

■ Discuss positive and negative group member roles. Which positive roles do you usually play when you perform at your best? Which negative roles do you need to eliminate?

_____

_____

■ What is your style of problem solving—Charles Darwin, Albert Einstein, Socrates, or Henry Ford? Does your career or current job allow you to capitalize on the strengths of your style—inquiry and discovery, abstract thinking, teaching and advising, execution of results?

_____

_____

■ What should a leader do to build a top-performing team? What policies and practices have worked for you? What have you seen work for others?

■ Use the "Team Excellence" exercise to develop and sustain team effectiveness. Discuss results.

■ A role-play exercise shows the importance of individual behavior in team dynamics: Gather in a group of 10 to 13 participants. Anonymously assign positive group member roles from page 219 to half the participants; assign negative group member roles to the remaining half. Charge each participant to play his or her role as the group plans the "Company Annual Employee Recognition and Appreciation Day." The budget is $120,000, and the time limit is 12 minutes. At the conclusion of the role-play exercise, discuss the importance for group success of modeling and reinforcing positive group member roles, as well as addressing and correcting negative group member roles.

Part Five Video Case
Hot Topic: Employees with Passion

Hot Topic Incorporated, located in City of Industry, California, is a retailer that licenses various products, such as T-shirts, clothes, and accessories geared toward alternative and pop culture with an emphasis on modern music trends. The average age of the employees at Hot Topic is 25 years old.

Hot Topic Incorporated reaches its customers through its two retail store lines—Hot Topic and its sister store, Torrid. Hot Topic offers a myriad of cultural items as well as accessories and clothing aimed at a younger market segment. Torrid is a fashion store offering modern, trendy clothing catering to plus-size women. This organization has been cited on the "Best Small Companies" and "Best Companies to Work For" lists many times over its 20-year history.

Betsy McLaughlin is the CEO of Hot Topic Incorporated. McLaughlin believes that the culture at Hot Topic is based on a passion for a concept. For Hot Topic, that passion is music, and for Torrid, it is fashion. McLaughlin says that the passion for the products and the inspiration behind them is what makes her company different from many others, and the passion that drives the culture is shared across all levels and positions of the organization. In fact, McLaughlin claims that music inspires not only the products they sell, but also store design and even the people they hire.

Hot Topic has a unique corporate culture but structurally does not differ tremendously from other organizations. Employees are fiercely loyal to the firm as a result of the great working environment where they feel they can "fit in" and be appreciated for what they contribute to the organization. One example of how Hot Topic encourages fitting in is its "concert reimbursement" program. Employees can attend a concert and bring someone with them, fill out an expense report, and be reimbursed for the cost of their tickets. The only requirement for this benefit is to submit a "fashion report." The culture also values collaboration, open communication, and empowerment, and is perpetuated by a lack of walls and doors in the corporate headquarters. Everyone works in one big room and shares space, taking emphasis off hierarchy and promoting collaboration and open communication. The employees are supported in risk-taking decisions when taking care of the needs of customers. This gives employees a feeling of inclusion and empowerment to make decisions.

Hot Topic has grown from 15 stores just 15 years ago to nearly 800 stores today. This provides a ready applicant pool to allow the company to hire for corporate jobs from within—a practice that has the worker bring her or his sense of the corporate culture to the new job. Employees are kept satisfied through such perks as cell phone discounts, on-site massages, health fairs, scholarship reimbursement, and "employee of the month" programs. Another interesting and no-cost perk offered to employees is the "9/80" program. This program allows employees to work 80 hours over 9 days—giving them a three-day weekend every other weekend.

McLaughlin talks to her employees and customers to learn in what direction they want Hot Topic to go. This along with all of the innovative ideas and programs provides Hot Topic with a unique culture that helps keep their employees and customers satisfied and loyal.

Questions for Discussion

1. What makes Hot Topic so successful as a retailer? What makes them so popular with their employees? How can they keep their success going?

2. How does the idea of no walls and no doors in the corporate headquarters encourage the culture Hot Topic is trying to perpetuate? Do you think you would like to work in such an atmosphere?

For more information, see www.hottopic.com.

Action Assignment

As a bridge between learning and doing, complete the following action assignment.

1. What is the most important idea you have learned in Part Five?

2. How can you apply what you have learned? What will you do, with whom, where, when, and, most important, why?

Part 6 Understanding People

12. Human Behavior and the Art of Persuasion
13. The Diversity Challenge

A FRIEND ASKED MICHELANGELO: "How's the work going at the Sistine Chapel?"

Michelangelo answered:

"About the same. You know, I really never should have started this thing. Four years, on and off, I've been at it. What I really wanted to do was a tomb for Julius II. But they made a decision and I'm stuck with it. The worst thing is that I had to start at the entrance of the chapel first, which I thought was a stupid idea. But they wanted to keep the chapel open as long as possible while I was working."

His friend inquired: "What's the difference?"

Michelangelo replied:

"What's the difference? Here I am trying to do a ceiling mural on the creation of man, right? But I have to start with the end of the whole scheme, and then finish with the beginning. Besides, I've never painted a ceiling before, and I'm not very experienced at murals either."

The friend sympathized: "Boy, that's tough."

Michelangelo went on:

"And on top of that, the scaffolding material I have to use is dangerous. The whole thing shakes and wiggles every time I climb up there. One day it's boiling hot, and the next day it's freezing. It's dark most of the time. Working on my back, I swallow as much paint as I put on the ceiling. I can't get any decent help. The long climb up and down the ladders will kill me yet. And to top everything, they are going to let the public in and show the thing off before it's even finished. It won't be finished for another year at least. And that's another thing, they are always nagging me to finish. And when I'm finished, what then? I've got no security. And if they don't like it, I may be out of work permanently."

The friend responded: "Gee, Michelangelo, that's tough. With no job security, such poor working conditions, irritating company policies, and inadequate subordinates, you must really be dissatisfied with your job. Are you ready to quit?"

Michelangelo replied:

"What? Quit? Are you crazy? It's a fascinating challenge. And I'm learning more and more every day about murals and ceilings. I've been experimenting and changing my style for these last few years, and I'm starting to get a lot of recognition from some very important people. You can see for yourself that it's going to be one of the finest achievements of all time. I'm the only one responsible for the design, and I'm making all of the basic decisions. It may bring me other opportunities to do even more difficult work.

"Quit? Never. This is a terrific job."[1]

The Sistine Chapel in the Vatican Palace was painted by Michelangelo between AD 1508 and 1512.

Learning Objectives

After studying Part Six, you will be able to:
- Understand why people do what they do.
- Tap the transformational power of human motivation.
- Achieve employee engagement.
- Assess your level of emotional intelligence.
- Know the power of words when spoken from the heart.
- Diagnose strengths and weaknesses in the art of persuasion.
- Know why diversity is an important subject for leadership effectiveness.
- Understand gender, age, and cultural diversity.
- Describe what the leader can do to achieve the benefits of diversity and avoid the pitfalls of prejudice.

Human Behavior and the Art of Persuasion

I wonder why she acts that way," "People! I'll never understand them." "We've met the enemy, and they are us." If you have ever had such thoughts as these, this chapter will be of interest to you. Understanding why people do what they do is important for employee morale and job performance. When the work is done, this understanding is important in dealing with family and friends.

Business leader Lee Iacocca prescribes a formula for success: "Effective leaders focus on three "p's—**people, products,** and **profit**—in that order." Mark McCormack, author of *What They Don't Teach You at Harvard Business School,* explains the importance of understanding people:

Whether it is a matter of closing a deal or asking for a raise, of motivating a sales force or negotiating one to one, of buying a new company or turning around an old one, business situations almost always come down to people situations. Those individuals with a finely tuned people sense, and an awareness of how to apply it, invariably take the edge.[2]

Psychological Forces

Physical and emotional needs are important determinants of human behavior, helping explain why people work, why they have certain personal goals, and what they want in their relationships with others. Psychologist Abraham Maslow divides human needs into five categories, progressing from basic needs for **survival** and **security,** to social needs for **belonging** and **respect,** to the complex need for **fulfillment.**[3] See Figure 12–1.

**Figure 12–1
Hierarchy of Human Needs**

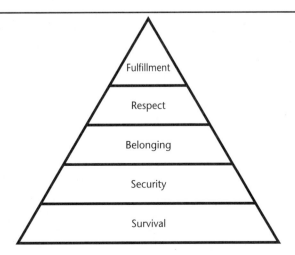

1. *Survival.* The needs that are taken as the starting point for motivation theory are the physiological, or basic body tissue, needs. Taking a breath of air and acting in self-defense are normal expressions of such needs. Survival needs are strong and natural forces within the person. Psychologist Viktor Frankl tells of his experiences in a Nazi concentration camp during World War II:

What did the prisoner dream about most frequently? Of bread, cake, cigarettes, and nice warm baths. During waking hours prisoners were concerned, above all else, with what they would get for their evening meal and how much would be available. When they received food, they were torn between whether they should consume all of it immediately, or save a part of it for that later time when their stomachs would hurt from hunger. In short, whether awake or asleep, their greatest concern was for the most basic physical needs—food and physical comfort.[4]

2. *Security.* Once survival needs are satisfied, security needs become important. Freedom from threat and protection from loss are major security goals, helping explain our interest in savings accounts, medical insurance, seniority rights, and burglar alarms. All ages and types of people experience the need for security. Both the child who is afraid of the dark and the worker who fears unemployment feel the need for security, and the drive to satisfy this need influences their actions.

3. *Belonging.* When survival and security needs are satisfied, the need for belonging emerges. This is true for people in all cultures, whether aggressive or peaceful, primitive or advanced. Every individual makes a distinct effort to belong to some aspired social group. If you have ever felt a need for love or a need to express love, you have experienced a natural need for belonging, and this has influenced your behavior.[5]

4. *Respect.* Once survival, security, and belonging needs are satisfied, people are motivated by the need for respect—the need to be considered favorably by self and others. The pursuit of fame, regardless of the field—business, government, the arts—can be explained only by the powerful need for respect. It is natural to want the recognition and honor of others. When this need is not satisfied, an individual feels inferior, weak, and discouraged. William James, American philosopher and founder of psychology as a discipline, writes:

We are not only gregarious animals, liking to be in sight of our fellows, but we have an innate propensity to get ourselves noticed, and noticed favorably, by our kind. No more fiendish punishment could be devised, were such a thing physically possible, than that one should be turned loose in society and remain absolutely unnoticed by all the members thereof.[6]

5. *Fulfillment.* After physical and social needs are satisfied, people are motivated by the need for fulfillment, which Maslow referred to as "self-actualization." These people may or may not please others by what they do, and their efforts may or may not result in the attainment of intended goals. Regardless of the consequences, if a person does something because it is valued personally, then the act itself is fulfilling.

The English author–philosopher Julian Huxley summarizes the need for fulfillment with the following observation:

Human life is a struggle—against frustration, ignorance, suffering, evil, the maddening inertia of things in general; but it is also a struggle for something. Fulfillment seems to describe better than any other single word the positive side of human development and human evolution—the realization of inherent capacities by the individual and of new possibilities by the race; the satisfaction of needs, spiritual as well as material; the emergence of new qualities of experience to be enjoyed; the building of personalities.[7]

In studying the characteristics of the fulfilled person, Maslow identified people he believed lived rich and fulfilling lives. Included were Albert Einstein, Eleanor Roosevelt, Ludwig van Beethoven, and Albert Schweitzer. Maslow found that these people shared 15 characteristics of self-actualization.[8] To evaluate your own development as a self-actualized person, complete Exercise 12–1.

Rate yourself on the following characteristics. Circle the number that best represents your current status (1 is low; 10 is high).

1. Acceptance of self and others

   1   2   3   4   5   6   7   8   9   10

2. Accurate perception of reality

   1   2   3   4   5   6   7   8   9   10

3. Close relationships

   1   2   3   4   5   6   7   8   9   10

4. Personal autonomy (independence)

   1   2   3   4   5   6   7   8   9   10

5. Goal-directedness; achievement orientation

   1   2   3   4   5   6   7   8   9   10

6. Naturalness (spontaneity)

   1   2   3   4   5   6   7   8   9   10

7. Need for privacy

   1   2   3   4   5   6   7   8   9   10

8. Orientation toward growth and new experience

   1   2   3   4   5   6   7   8   9   10

9. Sense of unity with nature

   1   2   3   4   5   6   7   8   9   10

10. Sense of fellowship with all people

   1   2   3   4   5   6   7   8   9   10

11. Democratic character

   1   2   3   4   5   6   7   8   9   10

12. Sense of justice

   1   2   3   4   5   6   7   8   9   10

13. Sense of humor

   1   2   3   4   5   6   7   8   9   10

14. Creativity

   1   2   3   4   5   6   7   8   9   10

15. Personal integrity (high principles)

   1   2   3   4   5   6   7   8   9   10

Scoring and Interpretation:

Add the numbers you circled to find your total score; then compare it with the corresponding description.

Score	Progress
15–45	Not great—should definitely improve
46–120	Just OK—needs work
121–150	Very good—keep going!

The characteristics I want to improve are:

_____

_____

_____

_____

_____

_____

Action steps I will take are:

_____

_____

_____

_____

_____

_____

Abraham Maslow's hierarchy of needs and characteristics of a self-actualized person are commonly taught in psychology, business, and leadership courses. He has influenced management theory and practice for over 50 years, including the works of Douglas McGregor, Rensis Likert, Warren Bennis, Ken Blanchard, and Peter Drucker.

In his book *The Farther Reaches of Human Nature,* Maslow prescribes five principles for developing one's full potential: (1) Experience life fully in the present rather than dwelling on the past or worrying about the future; (2) make choices in your life that will enhance growth by taking reasonable risks; (3) be honest with yourself and with other people; (4) strive to do your best in accomplishing tangible goals in line with your basic values; and (5) commit yourself to concerns and causes outside yourself.[9]

Motivation in the Workplace

To understand why people behave the way they do, one must consider motivation. Motivation has been a key interest to leaders since Hugo Munsterberg wrote *Psychology and Industrial Efficiency* almost 100 years ago. Today, C.G. Pinder's book *Work Motivation in Organizational Behavior* is one of the best overall sources on the subject. Motivation varies across and within individuals. It combines with ability and expectation to produce behavior and performance.[10]

The term *motivation* comes from the Latin word *movere* meaning "to move." Ancient scholars were fascinated by the fact that some objects in the world seem to be self-movers, while other objects remain stationary unless acted upon by some outside force. They assumed that motion was caused by a spirit inside the object—a "little man" of some kind—that pushed or impelled the object into action. Whenever the "spirit was moved," so was the object or body that the spirit inhabited.[11]

The effective leader must motivate people to accomplish tasks. This involves understanding the needs of others and arranging conditions so that individual needs can be met while advancing the organization. In this way, the little man, or *spirit* of the individual, is awakened and liberated. The performance that results can be tremendous.

For most employees, a few words of appreciation create renewed energy and job commitment. Of employees who leave a company, 5 to 10 percent do so because of money; of the remaining 90 to 95 percent, many leave because they don't feel they are being recognized. The importance of motivation is suggested in findings that most people believe they could give as much as 15 to 20 percent more effort at work than they now do with no one, including their own supervisors, recognizing any difference. Perhaps even more startling, these workers also believe they could give 15 to 20 percent less effort with no one noticing any difference.[12]

Exercise 12–2 evaluates motivation in the work setting. By completing this exercise, you will better understand the role of human needs in the world of work.

Exercise 12–2
Motivation at Work[13]

Rank your responses for each of the following questions. The response that is most important or most true for you should receive a 5; the next, a 4; and on down to the least important or least true, which should receive a 1.

Example: The work I like best involves

A   __4__   Working alone.

B   __3__   A mixture of time spent with people and time spent alone.

C   __1__   Giving speeches.

D   __2__   Discussion with others.

E   __5__   Working outdoors.

1. Overall, the most important thing to me about a job is whether or not

    A _____ The pay is sufficient to meet my needs.

    B _____ It provides the opportunity for fellowship and good human relations.

    C _____ It is a secure job with good employee benefits.

    D _____ It allows me freedom and the chance to express myself.

    E _____ There is opportunity for advancement, based on my achievements.

2. If I were to quit a job, it would probably be because

    A _____ It was a dangerous job, such as working with inadequate equipment or poor safety procedures.

    B _____ Continued employment was questionable because of uncertainties in business conditions or funding sources.

    C _____ It was a job people looked down on.

    D _____ It was a one-person job, allowing little opportunity for discussion and interaction with others.

    E _____ The work lacked personal meaning to me.

3. For me, the most important rewards in working are those that

    A _____ Come from the work itself—important and challenging assignments.

    B _____ Satisfy the basic reasons people work—good pay, a good home, and other economic needs.

    C _____ Are provided by fringe benefits—such as hospitalization insurance, time off for vacations, and security for retirement.

    D _____ Reflect my ability—such as being recognized for the work I do and knowing I am one of the best in my company or profession.

    E _____ Come from the human aspects of working—that is, the opportunity to make friends and to be a valued member of a team.

4. My morale would suffer most in a job in which

    A _____ The future was unpredictable.

    B _____ Other employees received recognition, when I didn't, for doing the same quality of work.

    C _____ My co-workers were unfriendly or held grudges.

    D _____ I felt stifled and unable to grow.

    E _____ The job environment was poor—no air conditioning, inconvenient parking, insufficient space and lighting, primitive toilet facilities.

5. In deciding whether or not to accept a promotion, I would be most concerned with whether

    A _____ The job was a source of pride and would be viewed with respect by others.

    B _____ Taking the job would constitute a gamble on my part, and I could lose more than I gained.

    C _____ The economic rewards would be favorable.

    D _____ I would like the new people I would be working with, and whether or not we would get along.

    E _____ I would be able to explore new areas and do more creative work.

6. The kind of job that brings out my best is one in which
   A _____ There is a family spirit among employees and we all share good times.
   B _____ The working conditions—equipment, materials, and basic surroundings—are physically safe.
   C _____ Management is understanding, and there is little chance of losing my job.
   D _____ I can see the returns on my work from the standpoint of personal values.
   E _____ There is recognition for achievement.

7. I would consider changing jobs if my present position
   A _____ Did not offer security and fringe benefits.
   B _____ Did not provide a chance to learn and grow.
   C _____ Did not provide recognition for my performance.
   D _____ Did not allow close personal contacts.
   E _____ Did not provide economic rewards.

8. The job situation that would cause the most stress for me is
   A _____ Having a serious disagreement with my co-workers.
   B _____ Working in an unsafe environment.
   C _____ Having an unpredictable supervisor.
   D _____ Not being able to express myself.
   E _____ Not being appreciated for the quality of my work.

9. I would accept a new position if
   A _____ The position would be a test of my potential.
   B _____ The new job would offer better pay and physical surroundings.
   C _____ The new job would be secure and offer long-term fringe benefits.
   D _____ The position would be respected by others in my organization.
   E _____ Good relationships with co-workers and business associates were probable.

10. I would work overtime if
   A _____ The work is challenging.
   B _____ I need the extra income.
   C _____ My co-workers are also working overtime.
   D _____ I must do it to keep my job.
   E _____ The company recognizes my contribution.

Scoring:

Place the values you assigned to A, B, C, D, and E for each question in the spaces provided in the scoring key on page 257. Notice that the letters are not always in the same place for each question. Then add each column to obtain a total score for each motivation level.

The five motivation levels are as follows (each will be discussed in the "Interpretation" section—see page 258):

Level I   Survival needs
Level II   Security needs
Level III   Belonging needs
Level IV   Respect needs
Level V   Fulfillment needs

Scoring Key

Motivation Level

I	II	III	IV	V
1. A _____	C _____	B _____	E _____	D _____
2. A _____	B _____	D _____	C _____	E _____
3. B _____	C _____	E _____	D _____	A _____
4. E _____	A _____	C _____	B _____	D _____
5. C _____	B _____	D _____	A _____	E _____
6. B _____	C _____	A _____	E _____	D _____
7. E _____	A _____	D _____	C _____	B _____
8. B _____	C _____	A _____	E _____	D _____
9. B _____	C _____	E _____	D _____	A _____
10. B _____	D _____	C _____	E _____	A _____
Totals _____	_____	_____	_____	_____

Next, make a graphic representation of your motivation at work on the motivation graph in Figure 12–2. Find the number on the scale that corresponds to each motivation level, and draw a line across that point in the column. Then fill in the area, creating a bar chart of your needs at work. See the sample motivation graph on page 258 (Figure 12–3).

The highest points of your motivation graph indicate the most important needs identified by you in your work. The lowest points show those needs that have been relatively well satisfied or de-emphasized by you at this time.

**Figure 12–2
Motivation Graph**

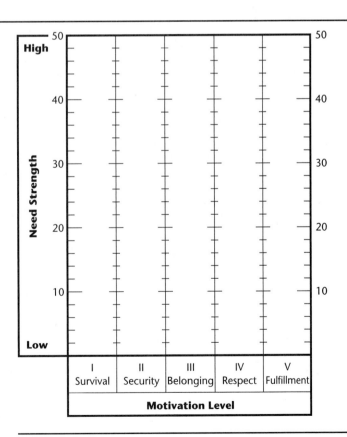

Figure 12–3
Sample Motivation Graph

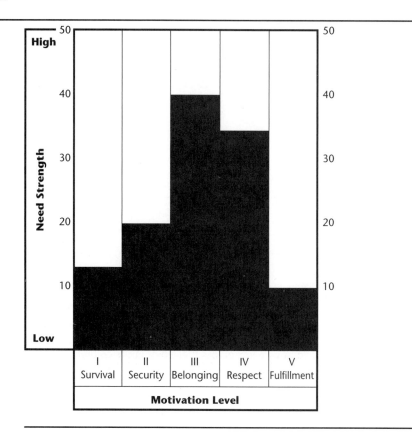

Interpretation:

The following is a description of the five motivation levels. Also included are policies and practices an organization should consider to help satisfy employee needs at each motivation level. In a real sense, the five best gifts to give employees are survival, security, belonging, respect, and fulfillment.

Level I: Survival Needs

People motivated at the first level are concerned with physical and economic survival. If they do not presently have a job, they feel the need to find one. If they do have a job, their goal is to keep it and to have a safe work environment. There is also concern for comfort and the avoidance of physical irritations such as inadequate space, inefficient equipment, and inconvenient parking, restroom, and eating facilities.

Physical needs may dominate the behavior of a person who has no job or who is in economic difficulty. Consider the plight of millions of people during the Great Depression, or that of an individual today who has lost a job, whose children need clothing, and whose dependent parents are ill. Consider Ma's words in John Steinbeck's masterpiece, *The Grapes of Wrath:*

But I like to think how nice it's gonna be, maybe, in California. Never cold. An' fruit ever'place, an' people just bein' in the nicest places, little white houses in among the orange trees. I wonder—that is, if we all get jobs an' all work—maybe we can get one of them little white houses. An' the little fellas go out an' pick oranges right off the tree. They ain't gonna be able to stand it, they'll get to yellin' so.[14]

An organization can meet the survival needs of its employees by providing:

- Sufficient pay.
- Safe working conditions.
- Safe equipment, tools, and materials.
- A supportive physical environment, with good lighting, heating, air conditioning, and restrooms.

Does your organization meet the survival needs of its employees? Evaluate on a scale of 1 to 10 (1 is low; 10 is high): _____

Level II: Security Needs

People motivated at the second level feel the need for security and predictability in their lives. They want assurance that their jobs are not subject to loss or change. As a result, there is a concern for benefits of a protective nature, such as health insurance, retirement income, and seniority rights. There is also a need for signs of stability from upper management.

The second motivation level, like the first, involves issues that are peripheral to the work itself; therefore, any job that provides economic protection and a dependable work environment will be valued by the person motivated at this level.

Security needs may erupt at all levels of responsibility and in all lines of work if business conditions are poor or if managers act in a threatening way. Think of how you would feel if you sensed that your job was in jeopardy; or imagine the concern you would feel if the equipment, supplies, and other resources required to perform your job were taken away.

An organization can meet the security needs of its employees by providing:

- Proper tools, equipment, and materials to do the job.
- Job aids, such as training manuals and technical assistance.
- Economic protection through insurance and retirement programs.
- Job security through career counseling, in-service training, and seniority systems.
- Confidence in management through stable and dependable actions of managers.

How well does your organization meet its employees' security needs? Evaluate on a scale of 1 to 10 (1 is low; 10 is high): _____

Level III: Belonging Needs

When belonging needs are the primary source of motivation, employees value work as an opportunity for establishing warm and satisfying human relationships. Jobs that allow them the opportunity to interact with people and to create friendships are likely to be valued, regardless of the nature of the work itself. A person motivated at this level may be more interested in human relations than job duties when considering which career to pursue or which company to join.

Employee needs for belonging are normal. How these needs are met (whether by counterproductive cliques and gripe sessions or by constructive work groups and employee meetings) can influence the success of an organization.

An organization can meet the belonging needs of its employees by providing:

- Communication sessions between employees and management (these are most effective when conducted in small groups).
- Celebration of holidays, birthdays, and special events.
- Expressions of consideration, such as notes of appreciation, hospital visits, and sympathetic understanding when employees have personal problems.
- Job participation vehicles, such as regular staff meetings, annual employee meetings, employee task forces, committees, and performance improvement teams.
- Communication outlets, such as employee newsletters, notices from management, bulletin boards, and annual reports.
- Most important, an open-door policy in which every employee feels free to share concerns and suggestions with every other employee, regardless of level of responsibility.

How well does your organization support the belonging needs of its employees? Evaluate on a scale of 1 to 10 (1 is low; 10 is high): _____

Level IV: Respect Needs

The fourth motivation level reflects a person's need for recognition. The respect of others for one's special traits or competencies is important. This is the first motivation level that is closely related to the nature of the work and depends on aspects of the job itself for satisfaction. Work that provides the opportunity to display skills that one feels others respect will be valued and will have motivation strength. The person who is primarily interested in self-image or reputation is motivated at the fourth motivation level.

An organization can meet its employees' needs for recognition by providing:

■ Individual incentives for high performance, such as achievement awards, worker-of-the-month honors, attendance awards, and recognition for suggestions.

■ Public acclaim for outstanding contributions at award banquets, retirement dinners, and annual meetings.

■ Opportunities to improve job status through training programs, job titles, and promotions.

■ Tangible rewards, such as increased pay, bonuses, commemorative plaques, letters of recognition, gifts, and privileges.

■ Most important, day-to-day recognition and praise for a job well done.

Does your organization provide recognition for employees' achievements? Evaluate on a scale of 1 to 10 (1 is low; 10 is high): _____

Level V: Fulfillment Needs

When a person is motivated at the fifth level, his or her primary concern is to fulfill personal values and to experience growth. There is a desire to demonstrate life values on the job. Writer Studs Terkel explains the motivation of employees at the fifth level:

It's about a search, too, for daily meaning as well as for daily bread, for recognition as well as cash, for astonishment rather than torpor; in short, for a sort of life rather than a Monday through Friday sort of dying.

There are, of course, the happy few who find a savor in their daily job: The Indiana stonemason who looks upon his work and sees it is good; the Chicago piano tuner who seeks and finds a sound that delights; the bookbinder who saves a piece of history; the Brooklyn fireman who saves a piece of life.

But don't these satisfactions, like Jude's hunger for knowledge, tell us more about the person than about the task? Perhaps. Nonetheless, there is a common attribute here: a meaning to their task well over and beyond the reward of the paycheck.[15]

Once people reach a certain level of material comfort and social needs are met, they care more about fulfillment; in plain English, they are more interested in what they actually do all day. Add a strong economy and a small labor pool, and the fifth motivation level is all the more important.

The nature of one's work is particularly critical for satisfying fulfillment needs, because the job itself must allow a good deal of freedom of expression and opportunity for experimentation. When the fifth motivation level is dominant, the individual channels more creative and constructive energy into the work activity than she or he would if motivated solely by the need for respect, belonging, security, or survival.

An organization can meet the fulfillment needs of its employees by:

■ Discussing organization values and goals in light of individual values and goals, and tailoring job duties to accomplish both.

■ Providing the opportunity for personal growth, through both on-the-job assignments and outside activities. For example, an organization may support an employee's involvement in community service activities or may support his or her continuing education efforts.

How well does your organization meet its employees' needs for fulfillment? Evaluate on a scale of 1 to 10 (1 is low; 10 is high): _____

Why People Do What They Do

There are nine points to remember about human motivation. With these in mind, you will better understand why people do what they do, both on the job and in their lives away from work. These points can also explain the complicated relationship between personal goals and work behavior.[16]

1. *A satisfied need is not a motivator.* It is not what people have that motivates behavior; it is what they do not have, or what they have done without. One person may be motivated by a need to never be hungry again; another, by a need to never be dependent again; another, by a need for love; another, by a need to be "somebody" someday; and yet another, by a need for self-expression. Each is motivated by a need that is not fully satisfied.

2. *Employee motivation and company success are related.* In his book *The Human Equation,* Jeffrey Pfeffer shows that profit is directly related to a company's effectiveness in motivating its workforce. He identifies seven practices that successful companies share: (1) employment security; (2) selective hiring of new personnel; (3) empowered teams and decentralization of decision making as the basic principles of organizational design; (4) comparatively high compensation, contingent on organizational performance; (5) extensive training; (6) reduced status distinctions and barriers, including dress, language, office arrangements, and wage differences across levels; and (7) extensive sharing of financial and performance information throughout the organization.[17]

This list shows that three of the practices—job security, above-average wages, and reduced wage differentials—address lower-level needs; and three practices—empowered teams, extensive training, and information sharing—address higher-level needs. The remaining practice, selective hiring, is made possible because these companies are desirable places to work. Pfeffer concludes that high performance requires both good pay and an enriched work environment.

3. *Psychological needs and social values are not the same.* Both Adolf Hitler and Mohandas Gandhi may have been motivated by the need for respect (the fourth motivation level), but their actions reflected different social values. Similarly, two employees may be motivated by fulfillment needs—both behaving for self-discovered, self-defined reasons. Yet the actions of one may be harmful to other people, while the actions of the other may help other people. The psychological forces are the same, but the values are not. Psychological needs explain human motivation; social values are the concern of ethics.

4. *The same act can satisfy any of the five motivation levels.* Consider that a person may work for any of the following reasons: (1) because there is no food to eat, thus meeting survival needs; (2) because job stability is in danger, thus meeting security needs; (3) to be an accepted member of a work group, trade, or profession, thereby meeting belonging needs; (4) to be recognized as important, skillful, or otherwise worthy of admiration, thus meeting respect needs; (5) for the personal satisfaction experienced doing the job, thereby meeting fulfillment needs.

Same Mile—Different Motives[18]

Level 1 or 2 Motivation
Michael Jazey (1965, 3:53): "I ran so I would not have to fight the war in Algeria."

Level 3 Motivation
Jim Ryun (1965, 3:51): "I ran to get a letter jacket, a girlfriend."

Level 4 Motivation
Noureddine Morceli (1993, 3:44): "I ran to be known as the greatest runner of all time."

Level 5 Motivation
Sebastian Coe (1981, 3:47): "I ran because I was meant to run."

5. *All people have the same needs, but to different degrees and accompanied by different wants.* *What* it takes to satisfy motivational needs and *how much* is required are unique to each person. To illustrate: (1) Sue's affection satisfies Bill's need for belonging, while Jim's belonging needs are satisfied by acceptance into his work group. (2) Jill's need for respect will be satisfied when she is recognized as a skilled actress, whereas Karen's need for respect is reflected in her goal to win an Oscar. Jill and Karen feel their needs to different degrees, showing that some people have a greater need for ego satisfaction.

6. *A person can be deficiency-motivated, bringing harm to self or others.* It is possible to have an extreme fixation on a natural need, so strong that it can lead to neurotic and even destructive behavior. For example, a person can be so hungry for love that the need becomes destructive. In the following passage, Gustave Flaubert describes Madame Bovary's relationship with her husband:

> She had to have her chocolate every morning, attentions without end. She constantly complained of her nerves, her chest, her liver. The noise of footsteps made her ill. When people went away, solitude became odious to her; if they came back, it was doubtless to see her die.
>
> When Charles returned in the evening, she stretched forth two long thin arms from beneath the sheets, put them around his neck, and having him sit down on the edge of the bed, began to talk to him of her troubles: he was neglecting her; he loved another; she had been warned she would be unhappy; and she ended by asking him for a dose of medicine and a little more love.[19]

No matter how much Charles showed his wife that he loved her, she was never satisfied, and in the end, her need for proof that she was loved ended in a diminished life and early death.

In contrast, the healthy individual is growth-motivated and reasons, I have satisfied this need; now I am ready to satisfy other needs. This point is important in interpersonal relations, especially leader–follower relationships. For example, when someone is deficiency-motivated and psychologically stuck at one of the need levels (except the fifth), direction from others is needed. In this case, help and advice from the wise would be appropriate. On the other hand, when someone is growth-motivated, the primary need is for understanding and nonpossessive caring. Those who want to help should listen in a nonjudgmental way as the person talks and discovers his or her own answers.[20] Good books that can be used to understand and deal with deficiency-motivated and growth-motivated people, respectively, are *The Road Less Traveled* by Scott Peck and *If You Meet the Buddha on the Road, Kill Him!* by Sheldon Kopp.

7. *Unsatisfied needs can harm your health, as surely as if you were physically stricken.* If you feel the need for recognition, but no one respects you; if you feel the need for love, but no one cares; if you feel the need for self-expression, but have no outlets, you can develop a motivation condition as harmful as physical illness. Consider the following case:

> Tim wanted to be an artist. He felt the need to express himself, and art was to be the means. The fact that no one else liked his work, and that he could not sell his paintings, mattered little to Tim; he was happy. Then Tim met Sarah. They fell in love and were married.
>
> A year later, twins were born to Tim and Sarah. With this change in his life, Tim's mind turned to food, clothing, and other needs for the children. Soon he went to work in an automobile factory as a production worker. Tim loved his family, and he was proud of himself for sacrificing his need for self-expression—his desire to paint—in the interest of his family.
>
> By the time four years had passed, Tim was experiencing poor physical health and recurrent depression. His inner need to paint, sidetracked because of the need to earn a living, would not be quieted. He felt incomplete and unhappy. Tim developed problems at work and became increasingly irritable.[21]

8. *Leadership is important in meeting employee needs and preventing motivation problems.* What a leader does will vary with the circumstances. Sample actions include improving job safety (survival needs), clarifying job assignments (security needs), offering a word of encouragement (belonging needs), providing praise for a job well done (respect needs), and offering new skills development (fulfillment needs). In any case, such leadership motivates employees and brings out their best in job performance. It is an example of enlightened and servant leadership.[22]

9. *The ideal is to integrate the needs of the individual with the goals of the organization.* If the needs of the individual can be satisfied while advancing the goals of the organization, the ultimate in employee morale and organization effectiveness will be achieved. Too many people are dissatisfied and perform below their potential because their jobs are not motivating. Many employees care more about off-the-job projects than on-the-job duties because these outside activities satisfy their psychological needs. The failure to integrate individual needs and organizational goals can represent a significant loss or brain drain for the organization.[23]

Jeffrey Pfeffer summarizes: "If you want to have great business results, you have to have customers who love your products and believe they are getting excellent treatment in the broadest sense of the word. To do that, you have to have employees who are motivated and using their talents to the utmost of their ability."[24] It must be added that the same relationship is found with employee motivation, job performance, and citizen satisfaction in public-sector organizations.[25]

Employee Engagement

When people discuss employee motivation, they often use the term *employee engagement. Engagement* involves both job satisfaction and organizational commitment.[26] The challenge facing leaders is to tap the performance potential of all employees. Studies show only one-fourth of American employees are highly engaged, 55 percent are somewhat engaged, and 20 percent have low engagement or are actively disengaged. Negative attitudes and disruptive behavior of actively disengaged employees can be harmful to an organization.[27]

The benefits of engagement are significant in improving organizational performance. British retailer Marks and Spencer reports that a 1 percent improvement in engagement produces a 2.9 percent increase in sales per square foot; and JCPenney calculates that stores with higher engagement produce higher sales. Research in both the private and public sector shows that employee engagement results in higher organizational citizenship and lower employee turnover.[28]

Jim Haudan, author of *The Art of Engagement,* provides an excellent framework for engaging the hearts and minds of people. Haudan identifies the roots of engagement, analyzes the causes and solutions to disengagement, and prescribes leadership actions or keys for achieving engagement in any organization. His premise is that organization success is not determined solely by the vision of leaders, but also by bringing these ideas to life in a way that is meaningful for all employees.

Roots of Engagement

The roots of engagement are in human motivation, the realization that people want survival and security, but they also want a sense of belonging, respect from others, and the opportunity to make a difference in the world. Employees have the need to be accepted. If they feel ignored, they slip into indifference. Employees want to be important. If they feel disregarded, they lose self-esteem. Employees want to live meaningful lives and accomplish something important. This is why the vision, mission, and values of an organization must be seen in the actions of its leaders.

Causes and Solutions to Disengagement

The causes and solutions to disengagement are as follows:

Cause 1: *Being overwhelmed with too many demands, too much confusion, and inadequate resources.* The solution is to prioritize and simplify the assignment of work and provide the systems, procedures, tools, and supplies to perform good work. Employees need a rational work environment.

Cause 2: *Not being relevant to customer needs because leaders are out of touch, self-serving, incompetent, or all three.* The solution is for leaders to set high standards of customer satisfaction and to require unrelenting adherence to these standards by all personnel, especially the leadership corps.

Cause 3: *Fear of being hurt personally can cause employee disengagement.* Employees do not want to risk economic security or personal well-being. The solution is to create a safe work environment where honesty, effort, and innovation are rewarded, and people feel free to be themselves.

Cause 4: *Not knowing the overall plan for the organization, including a strategy to succeed, and not understanding the importance of one's own role.* The solution is for every employee to understand the vision, mission, and values of the organization and his or her place in the plan, including performance expectations, accountabilities, and rewards.

Cause 5: *Lack of personal ownership causes disengagement.* The solution is to include all employees in both the success and failure of the organization. Performance and consequences must be shared in fair, proportional, and transparent ways as all boats rise and fall together. Executive and employee well-being must be tied together.

Cause 6: *Denial of reality and unwillingness to face the truth will result in employee disengagement.* The solution is for leaders to address the facts. Only when the truth is shared will employees let go of the past and focus on the future. Focus, traction, and momentum all begin with truth.

Keys of Engagement

The following are time-tested keys or leadership actions for achieving employee engagement. The goal is to engage people to get real work done.

1. *Keep people connected through stories and images.* Homer's *Iliad* and *Odyssey,* about the Trojan War, show the power of stories; and Aristotle said, "The soul doesn't think without a picture." A good way to communicate meaning is with a story, and a good way to tell a story is with pictures.

2. *Create pictures together that liberate the imagination.* The power of the notepad, pencil, and two or more heads together is enormous. The plan on a napkin, the project on a poster, and the story on the wall are icons of business innovation and achievement. Thinking together in pictures is a potent and creative engagement tool. Leaders and employees use data, anecdotes, and group dialogue to understand the past, diagnose the present, and decide the future.

3. *Gain employee trust through competence and integrity.* People give power to their leaders who must use their power well or they will take it away; or at least, they will withhold allegiance. Aristotle taught that leaders can maintain the trust of others through moral virtue, unselfish interest, and relevant skill. Engagement results when employees trust the integrity and competence of their leaders.

4. *Empower people to own business problems.* Both policy makers and action takers are personally committed in engaged companies. Engagement requires assigning meaningful tasks to achieve product and service excellence, holding people accountable for results, correcting mistakes that may occur, and rewarding success. This is the essence of performance management that all leaders must master.

There are many models for employee engagement. Jim Haudan's roots, causes, and solutions, and keys of engagement provide a practical guide that can be used to build high morale and high performance in any organization. Applying this guide can be done in a customized way by each leader, case by case.[29]

Emotional Intelligence

Management author Fred Fiedler writes, "Leadership is the use of influence to accomplish a task."[30] This point is supported in Working with Emotional Intelligence, a book that explains the importance of understanding and dealing with people. Author

Daniel Goleman explains that although technical skills are important, **emotional intelligence (EI)** is the essential and indispensable requirement for effective leadership. One person may call this practical wisdom, and another may call it commonsense leadership. No matter what label is put on the skill, leadership success requires the ability to understand and deal effectively with people.[31]

In the 1980s Howard Gardner proposed seven different kinds of intelligence. Two of these, interpersonal and intrapersonal, form the basis of emotional intelligence. Interpersonal intelligence is the ability to understand other people—what motivates them, how they work, and how to work cooperatively with them. Intrapersonal intelligence is a correlative ability turned inward. It is the ability to form an accurate model of oneself and to be able to use that model to operate effectively in life.[32]

The concept of emotional intelligence can be traced to an article published by E. L. Thorndike in 1920, "Intelligence and Its Use."[33] In 1973, R. E. Walker and J. M. Foley provided a review of research published on social intelligence during the 50 years following Thorndike's paper. They noted the two key elements of Thorndike's definition were the ability to understand the needs of others and the ability to behave wisely in respect to others.[34]

The following story is a practical example of emotional intelligence:

The owner of a fast-food franchise was having trouble with employee turnover. The majority of his employees were teenage students, and few would remain for an entire semester.

In an attempt to solve the problem, he sat down one day and wrote down everything he could think of about them. He noted the fact that they went to school; that most of them sought teacher approval and parental approval; that they liked money; that they were working to buy things, but were thinking about college. Most had pride in their school grades, were competitive, and were working to develop a work ethic. All sought recognition and some were worried about the future.

As he studied this list, the owner focused his attention on certain words: money, work ethic, pride in grades, teacher approval, parental approval, competitive, recognition, and college.

Then an idea hit him: a bonus plan based on grade-point averages. Any student who works for a whole semester and earns a 2.5 to 3.0 GPA would be awarded a 15-cent-per-hour bonus for all hours worked that semester. The ante would be upped to 25 cents per hour for students earning better than 3.0.

The cost was small—less than 5 percent of his payroll costs for the time period. The advantages were many:

Students were encouraged to work for the entire semester.

The bonus attracted better students, who tended to be better workers.

Guidance counselors and teachers did his recruiting for him, recommending his restaurant to students looking for work.

Parents encouraged their children to work at his place.

Great public relations for the restaurant—he received free newspaper and television coverage.[35]

A high-profile example of the importance of understanding and dealing effectively with people is the case of Louis V. Gerstner, Jr., former chairman and chief executive of IBM. By 1996, Gerstner was leading his company back to success, rebounding from nearly a decade of problems.[36] Business analysts and management authors would say that IBM had recommitted to its core values of service to the customer and performance excellence, as it took the efforts of literally thousands of talented and dedicated employees to create a resurgence of IBM. However, a particularly visible success factor was the *leader* Gerstner's personal ability to deal with people. In particular, Gerstner was effective in his personal appeals to major customers. A case in point was a visit to Toronto, where Gerstner held a conference with 20 top executives:

Seated at a horseshoe-shaped table, and dressed in shirtsleeves, the IBM top executive held forth for 90 minutes in a casual, but powerful presentation. There were no slides, no computerized overheads, and no prepared speech. Gerstner chatted about a wide range of subjects, including the changes that technology is bringing to business and society. Most of the CEOs in the room were impressed by the relevance of his discourse to their companies. In the words of the chairman and CEO of Rubbermaid, "He was able to connect." Lou Gerstner was filling a leader's quintessential responsibility—influencing key people to think and act in ways to benefit his organization.[37]

The legendary founder of Federal Express, Fred Smith, was a believer in using emotional intelligence to solve business problems. He tells about a situation where planes were getting backed up even though every control mechanism was tried. Smith realized the underlying cause was employees at the cargo terminal would run late because it meant more money for them. What was the solution? Align the interests of the employees with the needs of the company. Employees were given a minimum guarantee and told if they finished before a certain time they could go home. The results were remarkable—within about 45 days, the operation was ahead of schedule and the problem was solved.[38]

Goleman summarizes the character and ability of successful leaders with the phrase "nice guys finish first." The research on leadership success shows that the best commands, forces, and companies are run not by Captain Ahab types who terrorize their people, but by caring leaders with emotional intelligence to balance a people-oriented personal style with a decisive command role and willingness to make difficult decisions. These leaders do not duck the tough problems—technical or personnel. They are purposeful, decisive, and businesslike; but equally characteristic, they are positive, warm, and understanding with people. They are democratic in their character and show respect for all people regardless of position or status. They are appreciative, trustful, and even gentle in their dealings with people, although sometimes this trait is below the surface of a dignified and formal appearance. Goleman emphasizes that the successful leader is a caring leader who can understand people and deal with them effectively.[39]

There is much interest and ongoing research about emotional intelligence. Elements of emotional intelligence include self-awareness, impulse control, persistence, confidence, self-motivation, social awareness, empathy, social deftness, and relationship management. It is difficult to single out one trait as most important because different aspects of emotional intelligence come into play in different situations. One overall characteristic, however, is persuasiveness. Can you get buy-in for your ideas from the people around you? The most effective leaders have a finely honed ability to influence others. To evaluate your emotional intelligence in the workplace, complete Exercise 12–3.

A popular model organizes emotional intelligence into four dimensions representing the recognition of emotions in ourselves and in others, as well as the regulation of emotions in ourselves and in others. See Table 12–1.[40]

- *Self-awareness* is the ability to recognize and understand the meaning of one's own emotions.

- *Self-management* is the ability to regulate one's own emotions, keeping harmful impulses in check.

- *Social-awareness* is the abilitiy to understand another person's emotions and know his or her needs even though unstated.

- *Relationship management* is the ability to gain cooperation and inspire others as well as manage potentially dysfunctional emotions such as anger and fear.

Table 12–1 Dimensions of Emotional Intelligence		Yourself (Personal Competence)	Other People (Social Competence)
	Recognition of Emotions	Self-Awareness	Social Awareness
	Regulation of Emotions	Self-Management	Relationship Management

Sources: D. Goleman, R Boyatzis, and A. McKee, *Primal Leadership* (Boston: Harvard Business School, 2002), Chap. 3; and D. Goleman, "An EI–Based Theory of Performance," in *The Emotionally Intelligent Workplace,* ed. C. Cherniss and D. Goleman (San Francisco: Jossey-Bass, 2001), p. 28.

Exercise 12–3
What Is Your EI
at Work?[41]

The following 25 statements represent aspects of emotional intelligence. Using a scale from 1 to 4 (1 is low; 4 is high), estimate how you rate on each trait.

_____ I usually stay composed, positive, and unflappable, even in trying times.

_____ I can think clearly and stay focused on the task at hand under pressure.

_____ I am able to admit my own mistakes.

_____ I usually or always meet commitments and keep promises.

_____ I hold myself accountable for meeting my goals.

_____ I am organized and careful in my work.

_____ I regularly seek out fresh ideas from a wide variety of sources.

_____ I am good at generating new ideas.

_____ I can smoothly handle multiple demands and changing priorities.

_____ I am results-oriented, with a strong drive to meet my objectives.

_____ I like to set challenging goals and take calculated risks to reach them.

_____ I am always trying to learn how to improve my performance, including asking advice from people younger than I am.

_____ I readily make sacrifices to meet an important organizational goal.

_____ The company's mission is something I understand and can identify with.

_____ The values of my team—or of our division or department, or the company— influence my decisions and clarify the choices I make.

_____ I actively seek out opportunities to further the overall goals of the organization and enlist others to help me.

_____ I pursue goals beyond what is required or expected of me in my current job.

_____ Obstacles and setbacks may delay me a little, but they don't stop me.

_____ Cutting through red tape and bending outdated rules are sometimes necessary.

_____ I seek fresh perspectives, even if that means trying something totally new.

_____ My impulses or distressing emotions don't often get the best of me at work.

_____ I can change tactics quickly when circumstances change.

_____ Pursuing new information is my best bet for cutting down on uncertainty and finding ways to do things better.

_____ I usually don't attribute setbacks to a personal flaw (mine or someone else's).

_____ I operate from an expectation of success rather than a fear of failure.

Scoring and Interpretation:

Add your ratings for all 25 items: _____. A score below 70 indicates a need for improvement. Remember, however, that EI is not a permanent state. As Goleman notes in *Emotional Intelligence* and *Working with Emotional Intelligence:* "Emotional intelligence can be learned, and we can each develop it, in varying degrees, throughout our lives. Personal coaching, plenty of practice, and frequent feedback are particularly effective at developing EI. It is part of the process called maturity."[42]

Developing Emotional Intelligence in the Work Setting

Most jobs involve social interaction with co-workers and customers. Research shows that people with high EI are better at interpersonal relations and perform better in teams.[43] Human relations and teamwork can be improved through emotional intelligence training as the following case shows:

General Motors carefully selected staff for its new Holden production facility at Port Melbourne, Australia, but it wasn't long before the project unraveled due to infighting and interpersonal tensions. Consultants called in to analyze the problems offered the following solution: Employees need to improve their emotional intelligence. With this advice, the 30 plant design team members and more than 300 other employees completed a detailed assessment of their emotional intelligence. The automaker then introduced a variety of training modules targeting different aspects of emotional intelligence, such as effective self-expression, understanding others, and controlling emotions.

Some staff were skeptical about these touchy-feely seminars, so GM Holden evaluated the program to see whether employee scores improved and behavior changed. The company discovered that employee scores on the emotional intelligence test improved by almost 50 percent and that employees became much more cooperative and diplomatic in their behavior. "It has greatly improved communication within the team and with other teams outside the plant," says GM Holden quality systems engineer Vesselka Vassileva. Some employees also note that it has improved their interpersonal behavior outside the workplace. "I'm not so aggressive or assertive," says manufacturing engineer Alf Moore. "I feel better and it's helped me at home."[44]

The Art of Persuasion

The successful leader must master the elements of the art of persuasion including (1) **an understanding of people,** (2) **the effective use of words,** and (3) **the ability to manage conflict.**

An Understanding of People

Napoleon Bonaparte was a master of persuasion because he understood people. The secret of his leadership was simple: He first determined what people wanted most; then he did everything in his power to help them get it. Most of us take just the opposite tack: We first decide what we want; then we try to persuade others to want the same thing as badly as we do. Napoleon always keyed his plea to what his army wanted most at the moment:

When his army was half starved, Napoleon promised them food in exchange for victory. When they were homesick and thinking of deserting, he appealed to their pride by asking them how they wanted to return home: as conquering heroes or with their tails tucked between their legs? When they were fighting in Egypt under the pyramids, he appealed to their sense of history: "Forty centuries are looking down upon you," he told them. Helping others to achieve *their* goals—that is the essence of leadership.[45]

Contrary to myth, Napoleon was not exceptionally short. He was five feet six inches, slightly taller than the average Frenchman of his day. It was the English who alleged he was five feet two inches and seeking power to compensate for being short.

Understanding others requires sensitivity to their needs. The ability to see things from the other person's view is important in all human relations, especially leadership. Vince Lombardi was famous for his beliefs on coaching: "Coaches who can outline plays on a chalk board are a dime a dozen. Give me a leader who can get inside his players, find their talents, read their minds, and motivate them."[46]

America's thirty-sixth president, Lyndon Johnson, recognized that people do what they do for their own reasons, and he accomplished his goals by helping others achieve theirs. In her book *Lyndon Johnson and the American Dream,* historian Doris Kearns Goodwin describes how Johnson could usually persuade people to do what he wanted.

The Politics of Seduction

From facts, gossip, observation—a multitude of disparate elements—Lyndon Johnson shaped a composite mental portrait of every senator: his strengths and his weaknesses: his place in the political spectrum; his aspirations in the Senate, and perhaps, beyond the Senate; how far he could be pushed, in what direction, and by what means; how he liked his liquor; how he felt about his wife and his family; and, most important, how he felt about himself. For Johnson understood that the most important decision each senator made, often obscurely, was what kind of senator he wanted to be; whether he wanted to be a national leader in education, a regional leader in civil rights, a social magnate in Washington, an agent of the oil industry, a wheel horse of the party, or a President of the United States.

Johnson would, for instance, explain to a senator that, "Although five other senators are clamoring for this one remaining seat on the congressional delegation to Tokyo, I just might be able to swing it for you since I know how much you really want it. It'll be tough, but let me see what I can do." The joys of visiting Tokyo may never have occurred to the senator, but he was unlikely to deny Johnson's description of his desire—after all, it might be interesting, a relaxing change, even fun; and perhaps some of the businesses in his state had expressed concern about Japanese competition.

Johnson's capacities for control and domination found their consummate manifestation during his private meetings with individual senators. Face to face, behind office doors, Johnson could strike a different pose, a different form of behavior and argument. He would try to make each senator feel that his support in some particular matter was the critical element that would affect the well-being of the nation, the Senate, and the party leader; and would also serve the practical and political interests of the senator. From his own insistent energy, Johnson would create an illusion that the outcome, and thus the responsibility, rested on the decision of this one senator.

Then too, Johnson was that rare American man who felt free to display intimacy with another man, through expressions of feeling and also in physical closeness. In an empty room he would stand or sit next to a man as if all that were available was a three-foot space. He could flatter men with sentiments of love and touch their bodies with gestures of affection. The intimacy was all the more excusable because it seemed genuine and without menace. Yet it was also the product of meticulous calculation. And it worked. To the ardor and the bearing of this extraordinary leader, the ordinary senator would almost invariably succumb.[47]

The Effective Use of Words

Vocabulary, clarity, and eloquence can be used to persuade others to take action, especially in difficult times. Leaders can inspire with a phrase:

"Of the people, by the people, for the people"—Abraham Lincoln

"The only thing we have to fear is fear itself"—Franklin Roosevelt

"Ask not what your country can do for you—ask what you can do for your country"—John F. Kennedy

These motivational words are etched in the memories of most Americans.

In times of crisis, the conviction of a leader conveyed by his or her words can be a determining factor in the course of events. Consider the tenacity of the English people during World War II, inspired by a determined Winston Churchill who braced Britons to their task. Churchill told his people that even though all of Europe may fall to the German onslaught:

We shall not flag or fail. We shall go on to the end. We shall fight in the seas and oceans, we shall fight on the beaches, we shall fight on the landing grounds, we shall fight in the fields and in the streets, we shall fight in the hills; we shall never surrender.[48]

Churchill expressed his nation's gratitude to its airmen who, although outnumbered, fought bravely and defeated the German Luftwaffe, by saying, "Never in the field of human conflict was so much owed by so many to so few." Then Churchill declared:

Let us therefore brace ourselves to our duties, and so bear ourselves that, if the British Empire and its Commonwealth last for a thousand years, men will say, "This was their finest hour."[49]

About the importance of words and the power of persuasion, Churchill said, "If you have an important point to make, don't try to be subtle or clever. Use a pile driver. Hit the point once. Then come back and hit it again. Then hit it a third time a tremendous whack!"[50]

Churchill is among the select group of individuals whose name has become synonymous with historic, indeed heroic, leadership. His effective use of words cannot be overestimated.

The most recent edition of the *Oxford English Dictionary* contains 171,476 words in current usage, among the most of any language. But it is not the number of words you know that counts, it is how you use the words you know.

One of the best examples of the power of words to inspire people and persuade them to action is that of Patrick Henry, revolutionary and patriot, who proclaimed in 1775:

Is life so dear, or peace so sweet, as to be purchased at the price of chains and slavery? Forbid it, Almighty God! I know not what course others may take; but as for me, give me liberty, or give me death![51]

Day-to-day leaders are unlikely to face the magnitude of challenges that Winston Churchill did; nonetheless, they are still required to communicate their ideas and inspire their subordinates. They may not have the skill with words to the degree that Patrick Henry did, but they still must be convincing in conveying information and effective in generating emotion. Some ability to communicate can be learned in a good course on public speaking and developed further with practice. However, more important than technique is to *speak the truth* and *speak from the* **heart.** These two principles are required for credibility and trust, the fundamental elements of successful leadership. The best advice to the leader is to forget personal ego. Instead, concentrate on the audience. Consider what is important to them, and address their interests honestly, directly, and to the point.

The power of speaking from the heart is perfectly illustrated in the case of Civil War leader Joshua Lawrence Chamberlain, hero in the defense of Little Round Top during the Battle of Gettysburg in 1863. Michael Useem, author of *The Leadership Moment,* describes turning points in history when the actions of leaders have changed all that followed. Useem cites Gettysburg, Little Round Top, and the words of Chamberlain, recreated by Michael Shaara in *The Killer Angels,* to show the importance of "leadership moments."[52]

In September 1862, Joshua Lawrence Chamberlain left his family and a respected teaching position at Bowdoin College to serve in the Union Army during the American Civil War. He became the commander of the Twentieth Maine and would be the leader of this unit during one of the bloodiest battles of the war—Gettysburg.

The first few years of the war had not gone well for Union forces. They were now facing the second invasion of the North by Confederate troops. Morale was so low that some forces actually refused to follow orders. While moving into position for the battle, some of the mutineers from the Second Maine regiment were ordered to report to Chamberlain.

On July 2, 1863, Chamberlain's forces formed the southern flank of the Union army located on Little Round Top. If his troops could not hold their position, Confederate forces would then be able to cause the entire center of the Union army to collapse. The leadership shown by Chamberlain and the courage of his Maine troops proved to be a "turning point" in the battle, and therefore, the entire war.

Coming at the Twentieth Maine was a hardened Confederate regiment of 700 men under the command of William C. Oates. Oates's Fifteenth Alabama attacked and reattacked Chamberlain's defensive flank, with both sides gaining and giving. After two long hours and five attacks, the Union line remained unbroken.

When Oates pulled his regiment back to regroup a final time, the surviving soldiers of the Twentieth Maine had exhausted their ammunition. Chamberlain knew he could not withstand another attack, so he ordered his remaining force of 200 men to take the offensive with the only weapons they had available—bayonets. His command to charge stymied the Confederate army at Little Round Top. Oates would later write, "There never were harder fighters than the Twentieth Maine men and their gallant colonel."

A critical factor in the outcome at Little Round Top was the total number of men Chamberlain had in his command and the bravery they showed. Many of these men were formerly mutineers of the Second Maine; all of them responded to Chamberlain's leadership—his call to arms so compellingly made.

Chamberlain's Request of Maine Mutineers to Join His Twentieth Maine Regiment

This Regiment was formed last fall, back in Maine. . . . Some of us volunteered to fight for the Union. Some came in mainly because we were bored at home and this looked like it might be fun. Some came because they were ashamed not to. Many of us came because it was the right thing to do.

This is a different kind of army. If you look at history you'll see men fight for pay, or women, or some other kind of loot. They fight for land, or because a king makes them, or just because they like killing. But we're here for something new. This hasn't happened much in the history of the world. We're an army going out to set other men free.

Here you can be *something*. Here's a place to build a home. It isn't the land—there's always more land. It's the idea that we all have value, you and me, we're worth something more than the dirt. What we're fighting for, in the end, is each other.

I think if we lose this fight the war will be over. So if you choose to come with us I'll be personally grateful.[53]

A leader who spoke from the heart and built his vocabulary to be more persuasive was the African American ideological and religious leader Malcolm X.

The Autobiography of Malcolm X

Every book I picked up had sentences that contained anywhere from one to nearly all of the words that might as well have been in Chinese. When I just skipped those words, of course, I really ended up with little idea of what the book said. So I had come to the Norfolk Prison Colony still going through only book-reading motions. Pretty soon, I would have quit even these motions, unless I had received the motivation that I did.

I saw that the best thing I could do was get hold of a dictionary—to study, to learn some words. I was lucky enough to reason also that I should try to improve my penmanship. It was sad. I couldn't even write in a straight line. It was both ideas together that moved me to request a dictionary along with some tablets and pencils from the Norfolk Prison Colony school.

I spent two days just riffling uncertainly through the dictionary's pages. I'd never realized so many words existed! I didn't know which words I needed to learn. Finally, just to start some kind of action, I began copying. In my slow, painstaking, ragged handwriting, I copied into my tablet everything printed on that first page, down to the punctuation marks. I believe it took me a day. Then, aloud, I read back to myself, everything I'd written on the tablet. Over and over, aloud to myself, I read my own handwriting.

I woke up the next morning, thinking about those words—immensely proud to realize that not only had I written so much at one time, but I'd written words that I never knew were in the world. Moreover, with a little effort, I also could remember what many of these words meant. I reviewed the words whose meanings I didn't remember. Funny thing, from the dictionary's first page right now, that "aardvark" springs to my mind. The dictionary had a picture of it, a long-tailed, long-eared, burrowing African mammal, which lives off termites caught by sticking out its tongue as an anteater does for ants.

I was so fascinated that I went on—I copied the dictionary's next page. And the same experience came when I studied that. With every succeeding page, I also learned of people and places and events from history. Actually the dictionary is like a miniature encyclopedia. Finally the dictionary's A section had filled a whole tablet—and I went on into the B's. That was the way I started copying what eventually became the entire dictionary. It went a lot faster after so much practice helped me to pick up handwriting speed. Between what I wrote in my tablet, and writing letters, during the rest of my time in prison I would guess I wrote a million words.

I suppose it was inevitable that as my word base broadened, I could for the first time pick up a book and read and now begin to understand what the book was saying. Anyone who has read a great deal can imagine the new world that had opened. Let me tell you something: from then until I left prison, in every free moment I had, if I was not reading in the library, I was reading on my bunk. You couldn't have gotten me out of books with a wedge. Between Mr. Muhammad's teachings, my correspondence, my visitors—usually Ella and Reginald—and my reading of books, months passed without my even thinking about being imprisoned. In fact, up to then, I never had been so truly free in my life.

I have often reflected upon the new vistas that reading opened to me. I knew right there in prison that reading had changed forever the course of my life. As I see it today, the ability to read awoke inside me some long dormant craving to be mentally alive. Not long ago, an English writer telephoned me from London, asking questions. One was, "What's your alma mater?" I told him, "Books."[54]

Rhetoric in a Nutshell

Rhetoric is the use of language to influence others. It is the art of argument and the result is persuasion. The ancient Greeks considered rhetoric to be an essential skill of leadership, and they placed it at the center of education. Rhetoric taught them how to speak and write persuasively. After the Greeks invented it, rhetoric helped Roman orators like Julius Caesar and Cicero and even inspired Shakespeare. America's founding fathers studied rhetoric, and they used its principles in writing the Constitution.

The three issues of rhetoric (and persuasion) are blame, values, and choice, and these are time-graded in the past, present, and future. Blame is about who is responsible, values are about what is right, and choice is about deciding the future.

Aristotle identified three tools of rhetoric: Tool 1—*ethos*—is argument by character; tool 2—*logos*—is argument by logic; tool 3—*pathos*—is argument by emotion. *Ethos, logos,* and *pathos* appeal to the gut, brain, and heart of people. The gut tells us who and what we can trust, the brain sorts out the facts, and the heart makes us want to do something. These three tools form the essence of effective persuasion.

Effective leaders match the tools of rhetoric to the five senses of the audience. For *ethos* or character, they use mostly sight (seeing is believing). For *logos* or logic, they use mostly sound. For *pathos* or emotion, they use mostly smell, taste, and touch. They employ these tools and senses in the most advantageous sequence. A rule of thumb is: *ethos* first—gain their trust; *logos* second—gain their minds; *pathos* third—gain their hearts.

Effective leaders start by gaining the trust of the audience. They do this through shared values, good sense, and unselfish concern for the well-being of others. Then they state the facts and make the case for a course of action by proving points logically. Then they gain commitment through patriotism, anger, pride, or any other emotion that leads to action. This sequence can be done easily in 15 minutes and even as short as 2 minutes.

To review: Blame, values, and choice are the issues of rhetoric; ethos, logos, and pathos are the tools of rhetoric. The effective leader is a master of rhetoric to support his values and achieve his goals.[55]

The Ability to Manage Conflict

Conflicting purposes and personalities are inevitable in dealing with people, and they are part of the normal functioning of a healthy group. Without knowledge and skill in managing conflict, the leader will fail to achieve her or his full potential.[56] There are many strategies for dealing with conflict. The following points should be remembered:[57]

- Recognize that conflict is natural; indeed, nature uses conflict as an agent for change, creating beautiful beaches, canyons, and pearls.

- We can view conflict as either a problem or an opportunity. We can dwell on the negative or accentuate the positive. By choosing optimism over pessimism, we can be energized by events and focused in our efforts.

- Dealing with conflict effectively is rarely about who is right and who is wrong; it is more about what different people need and want. If everyone's needs are satisfied reasonably and everyone's wants are considered fairly, conflict can be a gift of energy that can result in a new and better condition for all.

- An important issue to address is, Do all parties want to resolve the conflict, and will all sides try with goodwill to settle their differences? If the answer is no, the best course is to agree to disagree, invite third-party resolution, and walk separate paths. Every student of history knows that war is the unacceptable alternative.

- If people want to resolve the conflict, it helps to reframe the problem. Reframing can be done by having each person see things from the other person's point of view. See things from the customer's standpoint, the employee's eyes, or the owner's perspective. In so doing, each party restates the problem from the other person's standpoint. This process often provides the breakthrough needed for constructive dialogue and the resolution of the problem.

The effective leader knows that conflict is an inevitable fact of human life, that no two people will see eye to eye on every issue all the time, and that what is needed is creative conflict, not destructive conflict.

In dealing with conflict, people fall into habits and patterns by placing different emphasis on cooperativeness and assertiveness. *Cooperativeness* is the desire to satisfy another person's needs and concerns; *assertiveness* is the desire to satisfy one's own needs and concerns. Figure 12–4 shows five styles of conflict that result from various combinations of cooperativeness and assertiveness.[58]

Figure 12–4
Styles of Conflict[59]

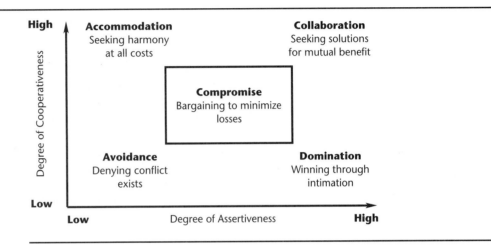

Avoidance—Being both uncooperative and unassertive, downplaying disagreement, withdrawing from the situation, and staying neutral at all costs. Avoidance pretends that a conflict doesn't really exist.

Accommodation—Being cooperative but unassertive, letting the wishes of others rule; smoothing over or overlooking differences to maintain harmony. Accommodation plays down differences and highlights similarities to reduce conflict.

Domination—Being uncooperative but assertive, working against the wishes of others, engaging in win–lose strategies, and forcing others through the exercise of authority. Domination uses force, skill, or authority to "win" a conflict.

Compromise—Being moderately cooperative and assertive, bargaining for acceptable solutions in which each party wins some and loses some. Compromise occurs when each party to the conflict gives up something of value to the other.

Collaboration—Being both cooperative and assertive, trying to satisfy everyone's concerns as fully as possible by working through differences, finding and solving problems so that everyone gains. Collaboration involves working through conflict differences and solving problems so that everyone wins.

The various styles of conflict can have very different outcomes. Conflict by avoidance and conflict by accommodation often create lose–lose situations. No one achieves one's true desires, and the underlying reasons for conflict often remain.

Conflict by domination and conflict by compromise tend to create win–lose situations. In extreme cases, one party achieves its desires to the complete exclusion of the other party's desires. Trust and goodwill are two common casualties.

Collaboration seeks to reconcile underlying differences. It results in win–win situations where issues are resolved to the mutual benefit of all parties. Collaboration offers the best chance of reaching mutually satisfactory solutions based on the ideas and interests of all parties, and of maintaining and strengthening relationships. Collaboration is the most preferred of the styles of conflict.[60]

To personalize the concept of styles of conflict, complete Exercise 12–4.

Exercise 12–4
Styles of Conflict[61]

Consider how you behave in conflict situations. In the space to the left of each statement, write the number that indicates how likely you are to respond in the manner indicated: 1 = very unlikely; 2 = unlikely; 3 = likely; 4 = very likely.

_____ 1. I am firm in pursuing my goals.

_____ 2. I try to win my position.

_____ 3. I give up some points in exchange for others.

_____ 4. I feel that differences are not always worth arguing about.

_____ 5. I try to find a position that is intermediate between the other person's and mine.

_____ 6. I am considerate of the other person's wishes.

_____ 7. I show the logic and benefits of my positions.

_____ 8. I consider the merits of all points of view.

_____ 9. I try to find a fair combination of gains and losses for both parties.

_____ 10. I try to achieve maximum benefit for all parties.

_____ 11. I try to avoid unpleasantness for myself or others.

_____ 12. I try to soothe the other person's feelings and preserve our relationship.

_____ 13. I attempt to get all concerns and issues out in the open.

_____ 14. I avoid taking positions that would create controversy.

_____ 15. I try not to hurt others' feelings.

Scoring:

Total the numbers assigned to items 1, 2, and 7 to find your _domination_ score: _____
Total the numbers assigned to items 8, 10, and 13 to find your _collaboration_ score: _____
Total the numbers assigned to items 3, 5, and 9 to find your _compromise_ score: _____
Total the numbers assigned to items 4, 11, and 14 to find your _avoidance_ score: _____
Total the numbers assigned to items 6, 12, and 15 for your _accommodation_ score: _____

Interpretation:

Research indicates that each style has a role to play in work situations but that the best overall approach is collaboration. Only collaboration can lead to problem solving that is most beneficial to all parties, resulting in true conflict resolution. You should consider any patterns that may be evident in your scores and think about how to best handle the conflict situations in which you become involved. Remember, collaboration involves working through differences and solving problems so that everyone wins.[62]

To exercise the art of persuasion, a leader must consider each person as an individual, learn what motivates that person, and then act to satisfy personal needs while at the same time accomplishing the goal. This process requires an understanding of people, the effective use of words, and the ability to manage conflict—essential skills of the leader who has developed emotional intelligence.[63]

CHAPTER

13

The Diversity Challenge

The character of U.S. culture has received much attention from historians, sociologists, and other scholars. Characteristics originally identified by anthropologists have been confirmed by large-scale empirical and cross-cultural studies. The U.S. mainstream culture is consistently described as being individualistic, egalitarian, pragmatic, hardworking, action-oriented, data-based, and amenable to change.[64]

If there is one additional word that characterizes America's culture, that word is *diversity*. People of Hispanic, African, and Asian heritage now constitute at least 35 percent of all new workers, and half of all new employees are women.[65] The U.S. workforce is composed of more minorities, recent immigrants, and women than ever before, and this pattern is expected to continue in the years to come. Currently, two-thirds of global migration is into the United States.

In addition, business has become increasingly global, so leaders are challenged to deal effectively with a wide variety of people and customs. The cross-cultural leader must be patient, understanding, willing to learn, and flexible. All these characteristics are part of **cultural sensitivity,** an awareness of and a willingness to investigate the reasons people of another culture act as they do.[66]

Researchers Adler and Bartholomew have identified five competencies needed by cross-cultural leaders: (1) understanding business, political, and cultural environments worldwide; (2) knowing the tastes, trends, and technologies of other cultures; (3) working simultaneously with people from many different countries; (4) adapting to living and traveling in foreign lands; and (5) learning to relate to people from other cultures on the basis of equality and mutual respect.[67]

Table 13–1 presents a sampling of appropriate and inappropriate behaviors in a variety of countries. It is important to emphasize the word *sensitivity* because cultural stereotypes do not always apply with every individual. The caring leader knows that each person must be considered as a unique individual, case by case.

Table 13–1	Protocol Do's and Don'ts[68]	
	Do's	**Don'ts**
	Europe	
Great Britain	DO hold your fork (tines pointed down) in the left hand and your knife in the right hand throughout the meal. DO say please and thank you—often.	DON'T ask personal questions. The British protect their privacy. DON'T gossip about royalty.
France	DO be punctual for appointments. DO shake hands (a short, quick pump) when greeting, being introduced, and leaving. Only close friends kiss cheeks.	DON'T expect to complete any work during the French two-hour lunch. DON'T try to do business during August—*les vacances* (vacation time).
Italy	DO write business correspondence in Italian for priority attention. DO make appointments between 10 A.M. and 11 A.M., or after 3 P.M.	DON'T eat too much pasta, as it is not the main course. DON'T hand out business cards freely. Italians use them infrequently.
Spain	DO write business correspondence in English, unless your Spanish is impeccable. DO take business lunches at 2:30 P.M. and dinner at 9 P.M. or 10 P.M. Be prepared to dine until midnight or later.	DON'T expect punctuality. Your appointments will arrive 20 to 30 minutes late. DON'T make the American sign for "OK" with your thumb and forefinger. In Spain, this sign is vulgar.

Continued

Table 13–1   *Continued*

Asia		
Japan	DO find a highly respected third party to act as your introducer to the lower-ranking person with whom you need to work.	DON'T attempt to get a deal going by directly approaching a target who is below the top level in the organization.
China	DO print your business cards and stationery without black borders.	DON'T use black borders because in China, black is associated with death.
Korea	DO say "yes," "perhaps," or "I will carefully consider your suggestion."	DON'T say "no." Koreans feel it is important to have visitors leave with good feelings.

Mexico and Latin America		
Mexico	DO meet two or three times before expecting to consummate a deal.	DON'T fly into a Mexican city in the morning and expect to close a deal by lunchtime.
Brazil	DO create a good impression by expressing an interest in the Portuguese language.	Don't attempt to impress Brazilians by speaking a few words of Spanish; Portuguese is the official language of Brazil.

Other cross-cultural don'ts inlcude: In Buddhist cultures, never touch someone's head, which is believed to be sacred; in Muslim cultures, never touch or eat with the left hand, which is thought to be unclean; in Germany or Switzerland, don't point your finger toward yourself—it insults the other person.

A Brief History of Diversity

Diversity is not a new issue in the American workplace. From the late 1800s to the early 1900s, most of the groups that migrated to the United States were from Italy, Poland, Ireland, and Russia. Members of these groups were considered outsiders because they did not speak English. They struggled, often violently, to gain acceptance in industries such as coal, steel, automobiles, insurance, and finance.

As late as the 1940s, and in some cases later than that, colleges routinely discriminated against immigrants, Catholics, and Jews, establishing strict quotas that limited education and employment prospects. It wasn't until the 1960s that the struggle for acceptance by the various white ethnic and religious groups had on the whole succeeded.

The most difficult struggle for equality has involved America's nonwhite minorities. Rigid segregation remained a fact of American life for 100 years after the Civil War, and racial discrimination in education, employment, and housing throughout the United States was a harsh, daily reality.

Then, in 1954, the unanimous *Brown v. Board of Education* Supreme Court decision declared segregation unconstitutional, setting the stage for the Civil Rights Act of 1964. Many rights all Americans take for granted today—equal employment opportunity, fair treatment in housing, the illegality of religious, racial, and sex discrimination—received their greatest impetus from the civil rights movement.

The traditional American image of diversity is one of assimilation. The United States is idealized as a "melting pot of the world," a place where religious, ethnic, and racial differences are blended into an American identity. As all Americans know, this journey is filled with challenges, setbacks, and, yes, victories too.[69]

Managing Diversity

Most large corporations today are multinational firms that maintain manufacturing, marketing, service, or administrative operations in many different countries. In fact, virtually all of the 500 largest U.S. industrial corporations maintain operations in more than one nation. Knowing the cultural tendencies of business partners, competitors, and customers is important for success. For example, for traditional Navajos, enculturated as collectivists, saving money is a dishonorable act of selfishness. A successful sales pitch for individual retirement accounts will be tailored to the benefits for the family, not for the individual.[70]

On the basis of common language, geography, religion, and history, 10 distinct cultural clusters emerge: Anglo, Latin Europe, Nordic Europe, Germanic Europe, Eastern Europe, Latin America, Middle East, Sub-Saharan Africa, Southern Asia, and Confucian Asia.

Leadership characteristics and the needs of followers vary across cultures in the areas of value-based leadership, team-oriented leadership, participative leadership, humane leadership, independent leadership, and self-protective leadership. The majority of U.S. employees prefer the first four and oppose the last two characteristics of leadership.[71]

Leadership itself is valued to different degrees across cultures. The Dutch place emphasis on egalitarianism and are skeptical of the value of leadership. Terms like *leader* and *manager* carry a stigma. If a father is employed as a manager, Dutch children are reluctant to admit it to their schoolmates.[72]

Although diversity is the new reality, many leaders are unprepared to handle it. Often their previous experiences have not covered the kinds of situations that arise in today's multicultural settings.[73] One short example gives diversity a human perspective, showing how difficult it can be for employer and employee as well:

An American nursing supervisor gave a directive to one of her Filipino nurses, and the supervisor wanted it to be done stat! For the supervisor, that meant now, immediately, before anything else. The Filipino nurse, meaning no disrespect but with a different time orientation, completed what she had been doing and then complied with the supervisor's request—five to ten minutes later than expected. To the nurse, stat meant soon. A few minutes delay was acceptable. She could complete her work in a short time, then take care of the supervisor's request. She certainly did not see her behavior as insubordinate. The supervisor saw this situation differently. The nurse was either casual about her duties or disrespectful of authorities.[74]

In addition to different perceptions about time, people can have different ideas about work habits, communication patterns, social roles, and a myriad of other workplace issues. For example, employee motivation practices continue to reflect white male experiences and attitudes. Some of these methods can be highly dysfunctional when applied to women or to African Americans, Asians, Hispanics, or Native Americans. Consider a few examples:[75]

■ A manager was pleased with a new breakthrough achieved by one of his Native American employees. Therefore, he recognized her with great fanfare and personal praise in front of all the other employees. Humiliated, she didn't return to work for days.

■ After learning that a friendly pat on the back would make employees feel appreciated, a manager took every chance to pat his subordinates. His Asian employees, who hated being touched, avoided him like the plague.

■ A new employee's wife, an Eastern European, stopped by the office with a bottle of champagne, fully expecting everyone present to stop and celebrate her husband's new job. When people merely said "hello" and then returned to work, she was mortified. Her husband quit within a few days.

An interesting finding is that some qualities are universally endorsed as characteristics of outstanding leaders, and some attributes are universally viewed as obstacles for effective leadership. Positive qualities include trustworthiness, intelligence/skill, and motivational ability. Negative qualities include dishonesty, incompetence, and egocentricity. Across all cultures, the qualities of integrity, knowledge, and interpersonal skill are valued.[76]

Dealing with diversity effectively means behaving in a way that creates trust and respect among people, and gains benefits from their differences. An analogy makes the point well: If you were planting a garden and wanted to have a variety of flowers, you would never think of giving every flower the same amount of sun, the same amount of water, and the same type of soil. Instead, you would cultivate each flower according to its needs. Neither the rose nor the orchid is more or less valuable because it requires unique or special treatment.[77]

Leaders of diverse work groups may wonder, How can I possibly learn about all these people? The answer is that although you can't learn all there is to know about every culture, the more you know, the more successful you will be. In addition, people will appreciate your efforts.

A Class Divided

It can be difficult to change the habits of people. Those in power have established or been rewarded by conditions as they are, so there is a tendency to resist efforts to change. A video that can raise consciousness, influence people to value diversity, and help build community is *A Class Divided*.

A Class Divided is a dramatic account of an experiment on prejudice performed by grade school teacher Jane Elliot, in which eye color becomes the basis for discrimination. This theme is played out in the adult world as well with live interaction in a prison institution. The two primary lessons are (1) to recognize the evil of discrimination, and (2) to realize the power of the self-fulfilling prophecy whereby beliefs can create reality. The prescription for the viewer is to adopt an *eyes-level approach* in all human dealings—never look up and never look down at anyone on the basis of age, race, sex, or any other physical attribute. Also, because people tend to fulfill the expectations of others and live up or down to their image, stack the cards and expect the best. On a scale of 1 to 10, this video is a 10 for impact, connecting on a human plane with all audiences.

In 2010, Jane Elliot reported on her 40-year quest to stamp out prejudice and cruelty in human relations: "spotty success in a never-ending battle." She points to the evils of racism, sexism, and nationalism that harm human beings throughout the world, saying it is a global problem. Elliot states that, "Too often, people judge others based on where they live and what they look like without knowing anything about them as individuals." She believes no one is born a bigot and there is no gene for racism. She believes all *isms* are learned responses and you have to be taught to hate someone. Her solution is education. She encourages us to remember the words of Nathan Rutstein, social justice advocate and author of *Healing Racism in America*, "Prejudice is an emotional commitment to ignorance."[78]

Diversity Prescription

Today, diversity refers to more than race, religion, gender, and ethnicity. It is a broad term that encompasses many differences, including age, disability status, military experience, sexual orientation, economic class, educational level, personality characteristics, and lifestyle. In the enlightened workplace, there is a philosophy of pluralism and a relentless effort to eliminate racism, sexism, ageism, and other discriminations. Where this occurs, all people have reason to believe that they are accepted and respected and that their voices will be heard. The prescription is to turn walls in our minds and hearts into bridges that join and make a structure that is stronger than its individual cells. The prescription is to value diversity as a strength. To that end, remember:

- All people should be treated with respect and dignity—we must have an *eyes-level* approach rather than an *eyes-up* or *eyes-down* approach in our dealings with people, regardless of social status.

- Every person should model and reinforce an essentially democratic character and humanistic approach to life.

- Valuing diversity provides strength and a positive advantage for organizations operating in multicultural environments.

In *The New Leaders: Guidelines on Leadership Diversity in America,* Ann Morrison reports the results of her study on diversity practices in U.S.-based private and public organizations. The practices considered most important are:

1. **Top management's personal involvement.**
2. **Targeted recruitment.**
3. **Internal advocacy groups.**
4. **Emphasis on Equal Employment Opportunity statistics.**
5. **Inclusion of diversity in performance evaluations.**
6. **Inclusion of diversity in promotion decisions.**
7. **Inclusion of diversity in management succession.**
8. **Diversity training groups.**
9. **Networks and support groups.**
10. **Work and family policies that support diversity.**[79]

Many companies have embraced the concept of diversity and have made enormous efforts to capitalize on the strengths of a diverse workforce. Consider the experiences of Apple Computer.

Apple Computer

Apple has been able to incorporate diversity at every level of the organization. Key components include:

- *Communication*—between employees and senior management about diversity issues. For example, African American employees meet with upper-level officers to discuss empowerment strategies, networking, and ways to assist the company in meeting its business goals.
- *Involvement*—with multicultural communities through company-sponsored and employee volunteer groups.
- *Celebration*—of multicultural holidays and events. Festivities are open to everyone, and these are held on the corporate campus.
- *Recruitment*—of talent from multicultural communities. Apple has formed ongoing relationships with minority, women's, and disability-oriented organizations.
- *Education*—about the meaning and benefits of diversity. Each manager is provided guidance that outlines what constitutes good management behavior from a multicultural perspective.

These programs and others have raised diversity as a highly visible issue at every level of the corporation.[80]

For the second time in three years, Verizon has ranked number one on *DiversityInc* magazine's Top 50 Companies for Diversity. Minorities make up 35 percent of Verizon's 230,000 employees and 38 percent of management positions. Magda Yrizarry, vice president of workplace culture and diversity, states, "As a company, we serve wide and diverse markets and people; so from our leadership to our frontline employees, we understand and value diversity." Verizon is a model employer and a reflection of the increasing diversity of people living in the United States and in many other countries.[81]

Benefits of Diversity

The following are benefits organizations receive by valuing and managing diversity as an asset: increase in workforce creativity; broader range of knowledge and skill; better decisions based on different perspectives; better services provided to diverse populations; ability to recruit excellent talent from the entire labor pool. Meta-analyses of the relationship between diversity and outcomes show that diversity can provide organizations with a competitive advantage when it is used in selecting and composing work teams. Far from being a stumbling block, diversity in the workplace can be a springboard for opportunity and excellence.[82]

Diversity Strategies and Techniques

The following are strategies and techniques that can help individuals and organizations manage diversity effectively.[83]

What Individuals Can Do

- Connect with and value your own culture. Assess how your background translates into your own lifestyle, values, and views.
- Think about how it feels to be different by remembering times when you felt that you were in the minority. Examine how you felt and the impact on your behavior.
- Try to understand each person as an individual, rather than seeing the person as a representative of a group.
- Participate in educational programs that focus on learning about and valuing different cultures, races, religions, ethnic backgrounds, and political ideologies.
- Make a list of heroes in music, sports, theater, politics, business, science, and so forth. Examine your list for its diversity.
- Learn about the contributions of older people and people with visual, hearing, or other impairments. Consider how their contributions have helped us all.
- Learn about other cultures and their values through travel, books, and films, and by attending local cultural events and celebrations.
- Continually examine your thoughts and language for unexamined assumptions and stereotypical responses.
- Include people who are different from you in social conversations, and invite them to be part of informal work-related activities, such as going to lunch or attending company social events.
- When dealing with people, try to keep in mind how you would feel if your positions were reversed.

What Organizations Can Do

- Include employees from a variety of backgrounds in decision-making and problem-solving processes. Use differences as a way of gaining a broader range of ideas and perspectives.
- Develop strategies to increase the flow of applicants from a variety of backgrounds. For example, if you commonly recruit students from college campuses, ensure that the student populations represent a diversity of backgrounds.
- Look for opportunities to develop employees from diverse backgrounds and prepare them for positions of responsibility. Tell them about the options in their present careers, as well as other career opportunities within the organization.
- Show sensitivity in the physical work environment. Display artwork and literature representing a variety of cultures, and make structural changes to ensure accessibility.
- Form a group to address issues of diversity. Invite members who represent a variety of backgrounds.

- Implement training programs that focus on diversity in the workplace—programs designed to develop a greater awareness and respect for differences.
- Pay attention to company publications such as employee newsletters. Do they reflect the diversity of ideas, cultures, and perspectives present in the organization?
- Evaluate official rules, policies, and procedures of the organization to be sure all employees are treated fairly.
- Develop mentoring and partnering programs that cross traditional social and cultural boundaries.
- Talk openly about diversity issues, respect all points of view, and work cooperatively to solve problems.

Exercise 13–1 can be used to develop understanding and appreciation of the rich variety of individuals in a group. It highlights the uniqueness of each person's experiences and the special talents each person has.

**Exercise 13–1
The Diversity Wheel**

Form discussion groups whose members reflect the diversity one might encounter in the workplace. Using the topics in the Diversity Wheel, group members, one at a time, may share information on a particular topic with other members. As each topic is discussed, members can learn to understand and respect others' points of view, backgrounds, and cultural differences.

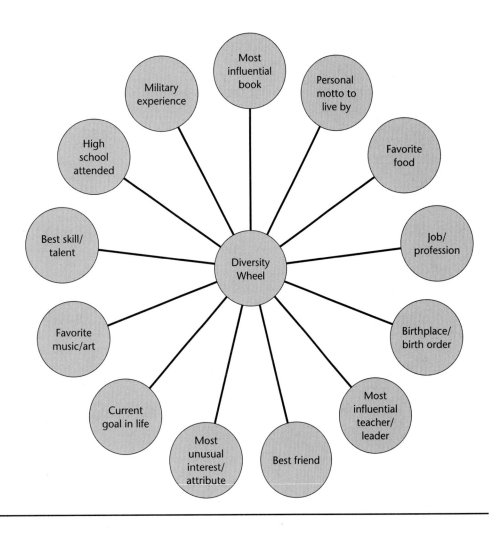

Why Tolerance Is Important

Tolerance is important because intolerance can lead to discrimination, and discrimination can have harmful effects. Put yourself in the shoes of writer–psychiatrist Alvin Poussaint:

A white policeman yelled, "Hey, Boy, come here." Somewhat bothered, I retorted: "I'm no boy." He then rushed at me, inflamed, and stood towering over me, snorting, "What d'ja say, Boy?" Quickly he frisked me and demanded, "What's your name, Boy?" Frightened, I replied, "Dr. Poussaint. I'm a physician." He angrily chuckled and hissed, "What's your first name, Boy?" When I hesitated, he assumed a threatening stance and clenched his fists. As my heart palpitated, I muttered in profound humiliation, "Alvin." He continued his psychological brutality, bellowing, "Alvin, the next time I call you, you come right away, you hear? You hear?" I hesitated. "You hear me, Boy?"[84]

Poussaint was humiliated and, in his words, "psychologically castrated." Frustration and powerlessness are burdens prejudiced people may intentionally or unknowingly place on others. Poussaint was the victim of discrimination born of intolerance.

For an example of the problem of prejudice, consider the experience of golfing champion Tiger Woods: "I became aware of my social identity on my first day of kindergarten. A group of sixth graders tied me to a tree, spray-painted the word "nigger" on me, and threw rocks at me. That was my first day of school. It was an eye-opening experience, being just five years old. We were the only minority family in all of Cypress, California."[85]

Most people would agree that the direction of progress is toward assimilation and multiculturalism (pluralism). For progress to occur, there truly must be social tolerance. The need for social tolerance is captured best in the following story:

The Cold Within

Alexander Pope

Six human beings were trapped one day
In black and bitter cold.
Each one possessed a stick of wood,
Or so the story's told.

With dying fire in need of logs,
The first one held hers back;
For of the faces around the fire,
She noticed one was black.

The next one looking across the way
Saw one not of his church,
And couldn't bring himself to give
The fire his stick of birch.

The third one sat in tattered clothes;
He gave his coat a hitch.
Why should he give wood to use
To warm the idle rich?

The richest man sat back and thought
Of the gold he had in store,
And how to keep what he had earned
From the lazy, shiftless poor.

The black man's face bespoke revenge
As the fire passed from his sight;
For all he saw in his stick of wood
Was a chance to spite the white.

And the last man of this forlorn group
Did naught except for gain.
Giving only to those who gave
Was how he played the game.

The logs held tight in death's still hands
Was proof of human sin.
They didn't die from the cold without;
They died from the cold within.[86]

Can People Change?

Once attitudes form, can people change? Is it possible to change behavior in the areas of tolerance and discrimination? Consider the story of Claiborne P. Ellis.

Attitudes Can Change

Claiborne P. Ellis describes his journey from childhood to becoming president of the Durham, North Carolina, chapter of the Ku Klux Klan to becoming the regional business manager of the International Union of Operating Engineers. The story illustrates a series of attitude changes. Ellis began by hating blacks, Jews, and Catholics, and ended by evaluating members of these groups based on their individual behavior.

Ellis was born in Durham, North Carolina. His family struggled constantly with poverty, and many of his early memories involve the economic depression of the 1930s. He was very close to his father, who worked during the week in a textile mill, but drank a great deal on weekends. When C.P. was around 17 years old, his father died. C.P. had to leave school to help support his family. He took a series of low-skilled jobs and eventually borrowed $4,000 to buy a service station. By then he had married and was working "my butt off and just never seemed to break even." Two months before the final loan payment was due, he had a heart attack. Despite his wife's efforts, the service station was lost. He had been taught "to abide by the law, go to church, do right and live for the Lord, and everything will work out." But it didn't work out. The continuing failure to lift his family into minimal economic security turned a smoldering bitterness into hatred. He wanted to blame something or someone for his failures and soon found a convenient group as a target.

While Ellis owned the service station, he was invited to join the Ku Klux Klan. It was an opportunity he seized eagerly because, "It gave me an opportunity to be part of something." Not only did he enjoy belonging to a group, but also his long-standing sense of inferiority began to disappear. His father had been a member of the Klan, and Ellis was well versed in their attitudes. The Klan hated blacks, Jews, and Catholics. And so did Ellis. He quickly rose through various offices to the presidency of the local chapter. Because the civil rights movement was becoming active in Durham at this time, Ellis's hatred was directed mostly at blacks. In particular, he despised a woman named Ann Attwater, who seemed involved in every boycott and demonstration he went to watch.

Although the Klan is notorious for protecting the anonymity of its members, Ellis unashamedly brought the local chapter out into the open. He began attending meetings of the city council and county commissioners to represent the Klan's point of view. He and his group had numerous confrontations with representatives of the black community at various board meetings.

Members of these boards would not publicly agree with the attitudes of the Klan, but many privately shared these views. The people who called to praise him also avoided him in public. While searching for an explanation for this inconsistency, Ellis began to reconsider his role. It struck him that he was being used. "As a result of our fighting one another, the city council still had their way. They didn't want to give up control to the blacks, nor to the Klan." It was at this point that Ellis recalled doing "some real serious thinkin'." Although he was becoming convinced of the correctness of his beliefs about being used, he could not persuade other Klansmen. He had to struggle with the inconsistency on his own, and it caused him many a sleepless night.

During this period, a critical event occurred. The state AFL–CIO received a federal grant to assist them in finding solutions to the racial problems in the public schools. To his amazement, Ellis was asked to join a citizens' panel to discuss these problems. As soon as he learned that members of the black community would also be invited, he refused the invitation by saying, "I am not going to be associated with those types of people." On a whim, however, he attended the first evening meeting. Many of the participants, including Ann Attwater, were familiar to him because of past confrontations. The moderator of the meeting was a black man who encouraged everyone to speak freely. During the meeting, Ellis did just that, repeating his extreme anti-black attitudes. To his surprise, some of the black members who did not agree with a single one of his attitudes praised him for his honesty in expressing his views. Ellis's involvement in the group began to grow. On the third night, with backing from some of the black participants, he was elected co-chairperson of the group along with Ann Attwater.

Despite mutual reluctance, Ellis and Attwater agreed to put aside their personal differences and to work together toward the common goal of finding solutions. Through their joint work, they began to see many similarities between themselves. Their efforts to recruit more panelists from among members of their respective groups were met with the same suspicion and rejection. Furthermore, the children of both had come home from school in tears. Ellis's child was ridiculed by his teacher for being the son of a Klansman, while Attwater's child was ridiculed by her teacher for being the daughter of an activist. The discovery of such commonalities and their joint work led Ellis to a feeling of respect and liking for Attwater. Through their leadership, the panel agreed on a number of resolutions. Although the school board did not implement all of them, the panel members had worked together effectively.

Ellis's attitudes did not change immediately. His initial justification for working on the panel was that school integration was the law and that all people should be law-abiding. In the hope of implementing the panel's recommendations, he ran for the school board. He was still associated with the Klan, but he did not campaign for Klan themes. His platform was simply that before making any decisions, he would listen to the voice of all of the people. The campaign brought him into contact with many blacks. At long last, he began seeing people as individuals. With this change came a sense of rebirth. He no longer had sleepless nights and enrolled in an evening program that resulted in his receiving a high school equivalency diploma. During this period, he helped to organize the first labor union at his place of employment. When the opportunity arose, he gladly switched his career to labor union work, where he felt he could help the poor, both black and white.[87]

Gender Diversity in the Workplace

Diversity takes many forms, and one of the most obvious is gender. The participation of women in the workplace continues to increase. Today's leaders must address the changing composition of the workforce and the special needs of women.

Of the approximately 150 million people employed in the United States, almost half (46.7 percent) are women.[88] With the changing role of women in American society from wife and mother, to wife and mother and career person as well, there has been a merging of the sexes in the workplace. This has brought the need for better understanding between men and women as work associates. Communication plays an important part in this equation.

Communication across Genders

In *You Just Don't Understand: Women and Men in Conversation,* linguist Deborah Tannen builds a strong case for her hypothesis that boys and girls grow up in different worlds of words. Tannen notes that boys and girls play differently, usually in same-sex groups, and that their ways of using language in their games are separated by a world of difference:

Boys tend to play outside, in large groups that are hierarchically structured. Their groups have a leader who tells others what to do and how to do it, and resists doing what other boys propose. It is by giving orders and making them stick that high status is attained. Another way boys achieve status is to take center stage by telling stories and jokes, and by sidetracking or challenging the stories and jokes of others. Boys' games have winners and losers and elaborate systems of rules that are frequently the subjects of arguments. Finally, boys are frequently heard to boast of their skill and argue about who is best at what.

Girls, on the other hand, play in small groups or in pairs; the center of a girl's social life is her best friend. Within the group, intimacy is the key, and differentiation is measured by relative closeness. In their most frequent games, such as jump rope and hopscotch, everyone gets a turn. Most of girls' activities, such as playing house, do not have winners or losers. Although some girls are certainly more skilled than others, they are expected not to boast about it, or show that they think they are better than the others. Girls don't give orders; they express their preferences as suggestions, and suggestions are likely to be accepted. Whereas boys say, "Gimme that!" and "Get outta here!" girls say, "Let's do this," and "How about doing that?" Anything else is put down as "bossy." They don't grab center stage—usually, they don't want it—so they don't challenge each other directly. Much of the time, they simply sit together and talk. Girls are not accustomed to jockeying for status in an obvious way; they are more concerned with being accepted and liked. Girls learn that by displaying differences, they jeopardize acceptance by their peers. They strive to appear the same as, not better than, their friends, thus creating power that is dead even. In contrast, boys, from the earliest age, learn that they can get what they want—higher status—by displaying differences, especially superiority, therefore favoring hierarchical power.[89]

Tannen believes differences developed in childhood cast a long shadow into adulthood. When men and women talk to each other about troubles, for example, there is a potential problem because each expects a different response. Men may ignore or avoid dealing with feelings and emotions, preferring instead to attack underlying causes. Women, expecting to have their feelings supported, may misconstrue men's aggressive approach and feel that they themselves are being attacked. In general, where men seek status, women seek connection.[90]

Tannen explains that from childhood, there is a tendency for men to use conversation to negotiate status; women talk to create rapport. The clash of the two styles can lead to frustration—in personal relations, of course, but in the office as well, from the female manager who feels she isn't heard in meetings, to the male executive who is baffled when his gruff orders spark resentment or anger.[91]

To the question, Who talks more, women or men? seemingly contradictory evidence is reconciled by differences between public speaking and private speaking. Men generally are more comfortable doing public speaking, whereas women usually feel more comfortable doing private speaking. Another way of capturing these differences is by using the terms *report talk* and *rapport talk.* For most men, report talk is primarily a means of preserving independence or negotiating and maintaining status in a hierarchical social order. To the man, talk is for information that can equate to power. For most women, the language of conversation is primarily a language of rapport. To the woman, talk is for interaction that can equate to love. Telling things is a way to show involvement, and listening is a way to show she is interested and cares.[92]

It is interesting to note how terms used in traditionally male sports permeate the language of the American workplace: When your *team* is on *offense,* you'll need a *strategy* to *score.* This may include an *end run* around the *opposition* and a *knockout punch.* When the *ball is in your court,* it's time to *step up to bat* and *hit a home run.* When you are playing *hardball,* you'll need a *game plan* to *get the ball rolling* so you can *get to first base.* You may have to *punt, pass the ball,* and *touch bases* with *teammates,* or *tackle* the problem yourself. Your goal may be the *whole nine yards,* but be careful not to *step out of bounds.* If you *strike out,* you may have to *throw in the towel;* but if you win, you can make it into the *big leagues.*

What should we do about differences in the way men and women communicate? Should women try to change to be more like men, or vice versa? Neither change is the answer. It is important to simply recognize that natural differences exist. When people don't know there are differences in communication styles, and that they are formed in the normal course of growing up, they end up attributing communication problems to someone's bad intentions or lack of ability.[93]

Women in Leadership Positions

Historically, women in high leadership positions have come from nonprofit organizations, educational institutions, and public office; increasingly, they come from the business world. Census data reveal that women constitute 15.7 percent of the corporate officer ranks of Fortune 500 companies. During the past decade, women have started businesses at twice the rate of men, and today 44 percent of small businesses in the United States are owned or operated by women. Women now constitute nearly half of the managerial workforce.[94] In government, women serve in a growing number of leadership capacities, including 12 percent of state governors, 17 percent of U.S. senators, and 16.8 percent of members of the U.S. House of Representatives.[95]

The Center for Creative Leadership has identified six success factors for women in high leadership positions:

- *Help from above.* Women in high levels of leadership have typically received the support of influential mentors.

- *A superior track record.* Held to high standards, executive-level women have usually managed effectively and have developed an excellent record of performance.

- *A passion for success.* Senior-level women have been determined to succeed. They worked hard, seized responsibility, and achieved their objectives.

- *Outstanding people skills.* Successful women executives typically utilize participative leadership, employee empowerment, and open communication to foster trust and high levels of morale among subordinates.

- *Career courage.* Successful women leaders have demonstrated courage to take risks, such as taking on huge responsibilities.

- *Mental toughness.* Senior-level women are seen as tenacious, demanding, and willing to make difficult decisions.[96]

Meta-analysis and individual studies show that women leaders tend to be more participative and less autocratic in leadership style than male leaders, and this approach is well suited to middle-management positions in twenty-first-century organizations. Analysis of leadership effectiveness shows that female and male leaders do not differ in overall effectiveness, although there remains a slight effectiveness advantage for male leaders in masculine domains and female leaders in feminine domains.[97] Comparison studies between men and women show essential similarity in motivation to be a leader, job satisfaction, and employee satisfaction. However, research shows women are less likely to promote themselves and initiate negotiation for opportunities, resources, and advancement.[98]

Although women have made progress in attaining and being successful in leadership roles, Figure 13–1 shows that each rung on the responsibility pyramid is progressively more difficult to climb. At each level, a higher percentage of women are sidetracked.[99]

**Figure 13–1
Long-Term Perspective on
Change: Few New Cracks
in the Glass Ceiling**[100]

Sources: U.S. Bureau of Labor Statistics, 2008 Catalyst,
Statistical Overview of Women in the Workplace, 2009.

Several factors can sidetrack women in the workplace. The "glass ceiling" is a catchphrase for the impediments women face as they seek top leadership positions. Sidetracking mechanisms include:

■ *Lack of encouragement.* Women are often ignored in the grooming of executives for senior-level jobs. Men are more often moved around and cross-trained within the company to learn about different aspects of the business.[101]

■ *Lack of opportunity followed by disillusionment.* In a national poll of middle-management women, 71 percent reported not having the same chances for promotion to top executive jobs as their male counterparts. Once there, unequal rewards can be a demotivator. At the managerial level, on average, for every dollar earned by white men, white women earn 74 cents, African American women earn 58 cents, Hispanic women earn 48 cents, and Asian and other women earn 67 cents.[102]

■ *Closed corporate culture.* Many women who enter the executive suite do so by modeling established behavior patterns and management customs. Those who do not conform find that the alternative is to leave the organization.[103]

■ *Women's ghettos and the feminization of jobs on the corporate staff.* Some women accept or are shunted into staff jobs that are difficult to exchange for line jobs, where salaries and responsibilities are usually greater. Many of these staff jobs are devoid of responsibility for finance and operations, two important disciplines for senior leaders to master.[104]

■ *Demands of parenthood.* In the majority of families, women are the first line of defense in raising children. When the school calls or a child is ill, it is usually the mother who responds. Women experience more career interruptions than men, largely because they assume more domestic responsibility. The demands of family life can require enormous energy and time that may interfere with business performance.[105]

■ *Double standards.* Women may have to be more competent than men to be accepted by the dominant group. This double standard can be seen when mistakes made by males are tolerated, but mistakes made by females are not tolerated, and when, to be selected or promoted, a woman must be clearly superior to every male candidate.[106]

An example of gender bias and a creative solution is seen in the evaluation of men and women auditioning for symphony orchestras. Traditionally male-dominated orchestras made one change: all applicants were required to audition while hidden behind a screen. This small change greatly increased the proportion of female musicians in symphony orchestras.[107]

Empirical data show that the numbers of women in the workforce and in leadership positions are growing. Gender stereotyping remains, however, and this often leads to biased judgment. Gender stereotypes can alter the perception and treatment of women in negative ways. Women with self-confidence in their abilities, commitment to achieve their goals, and the help of individuals in higher positions are increasingly successful in overcoming gender stereotypes.[108] The examples of CEO Anne Mulcahy and President Ursula Burns of Xerox are inspirational and instructive; see www.xerox.com.

For more information about women in the workplace, visit the Web site for the Women's Bureau of the U.S. Department of Labor: www.dol.gov/wb/. See also the Web site of the National Association for Female Executives: www.nafe.com.

Generational Differences

One important dimension of diversity is age difference. Leading, following, and working across generations is a challenge for people of all ages. It is difficult for older people to realize this about younger people: They do not know what *Sputnik* is; Tiananmen Square means nothing to them; they don't remember the 1960s, let alone the 1950s. It is difficult for younger people to realize this about older people: They grew up before MTV, AIDS, the microwave, and the iPod.

Many labels and time periods have been used to identify employees across generational cohorts since management author and speaker Morris Massey produced his influential and helpful video series in 1970, "What You Are Is Where You Were When," designed to bridge the gap between people of different ages. Today's cohorts and their different attitudes and expectations are: (1) *Baby boomers,* born between 1946 and 1964, seem to expect and desire more job security and are more focused on economic and social status than younger cohorts; (2) *Generation X* employees, born between 1965 and 1979, expect less job security and are motivated more by workplace flexibility, the opportunity to learn (especially new technology), and egalitarianism and "fun" organizations; (3) *Generation Y* employees, born after 1979, are noticeably self-confident, optimistic, multitasking, and more independent than even *Generation X* workers. These statements don't apply to everyone in each cohort, but they do reflect shifting values and expectations across generations in society today.[109]

In dealing with younger generations, older people should remember when their own behavior tested the tolerance and often the patience of their elders. Those who lived value-based lives of responsibility, courage, and justice, but were relaxed about such matters of style as music and dress, were role models for dealing with young people today.

For their part, young people should adopt the example of principled living and appreciation for generational differences shown by all enlightened people. The result will be social structures that enjoy the knowledge and wisdom of older people, as well as the spirit and vitality of younger generations. How can this happen? Not by legislation, edict, or force; but by the understanding and respectful behavior of each individual.

Leadership, Diversity, and Personal Example

Leadership plays a pivotal role in dealing with diversity. To be most effective, leaders should:

- *Empower others.* Share power and information, solicit input, and reward people on the basis of performance, without regard to race, gender, age, personality, job classification, and so on; encourage participation and share accountability.

- *Develop people.* Provide opportunities for growth, and then model and coach desired behaviors; delegate responsibility to those who have the ability to do the work; individualize training and development efforts.

- *Value diversity.* View diversity as an asset; understand diverse cultural practices; facilitate integration among people; help others identify their needs and options to be productive contributors.

- *Communicate.* Clearly communicate expectations, ask questions to increase understanding, and show respect through listening; develop communication across cultural and language differences; provide ongoing feedback with sensitivity to individual differences.[110]

The effective leader has an **integrative** approach. This involves bringing together people of different cultures, races, genders, personalities, and stages of development, and integrating them into a whole that is greater than the sum of its parts. This integration is not simply a melting-down process; rather, it is a building up in which the identity of the individual is preserved, yet simultaneously transcended. The effective team that results does not eliminate diversity. Instead, it welcomes other points of view, embraces opposites, and seeks to understand all sides of every issue.

As important as leadership is, in the final analysis, it falls on each person to do the right thing. In *The Measure of Our Success,* Marian Wright Edelman writes:

Remember that the fellowship of human beings is more important than the fellowship of race and class and gender. Be decent and fair and insist that others be so in your presence. Don't tell, laugh at, or in any way acquiesce to racial, ethnic, religious, or gender jokes, or to any practices intended to demean rather than enhance another human being. Walk away from them; stare them down; make them unacceptable. Through daily moral consciousness, face up to rather than ignore voices of division. Remember that we are not all equally guilty, but we are all equally responsible for building a decent and just society.[111]

Part Six Summary

After reading Part Six, you should know the following key concepts, principles, and terms. Fill in the blanks from memory, or copy the answers listed below.

Business leader Lee Iacocca's prescription for success focuses on
(a) _____, _____, and _____, with the emphasis on
(b) _____ as the most important aspect of the formula. Psychological
determinants of behavior include five human needs identified by Abraham Maslow—
needs for (c) _____, _____, _____,
_____, and _____. There are many principles of human
motivation, including (d) _____, _____, _____, and
_____. Leadership success requires the ability to understand people and
deal with them effectively, and this requires (e) _____, a term developed
by Daniel Goleman. Elements of the art of persuasion include (f) _____,
_____, and _____. Effective speaking requires speaking from
the (g) _____. Managing conflict most effectively requires
(h) _____, versus avoidance, accommodation, domination, and even
compromise. The American workplace is increasingly diverse and increasingly global;
thus leaders are challenged to deal with a wide variety of people and customs. Managing
diversity requires (i) _____, elements of which are patience, understanding,
willingness to learn, and flexibility. There are 10 practices that are most important in
tapping the constructive potential of diversity, including (j) _____,
_____, _____, _____, and _____. The
effective leader in a multicultural environment is (k) _____, embracing other
points of view and seeking to understand all perspectives of every issue, while
developing a whole that is greater than the sum of its parts.

Answer Key for Part Six Summary

a. **people, products, profit,** page 249

b. **people,** page 249

c. **survival, security, belonging, respect, fulfillment,** page 249

d. (any four) **a satisfied need is not a motivator; employee motivation and company success are related; psychological needs and social values are not the same; the same act can satisfy any of the five motivation levels; all people have the same needs; a person can be deficiency-motivated; unsatisfied needs can harm your health; leadership is important in meeting employee needs; the ideal is to integrate individual needs with organizational goals,** pages 261–263

e. **emotional intelligence,** page 265

f. **an understanding of people, the effective use of words, the ability to manage conflict,** page 269

g. **heart,** page 271

h. **collaboration,** page 275

i. **cultural sensitivity,** page 279

j. (any five) **top management's personal involvement, targeted recruitment, internal advocacy groups, emphasis on Equal Employment Opportunity statistics, inclusion of diversity in performance evaluations, inclusion of diversity in promotion decisions, inclusion of diversity in management succession, diversity training groups, networks and support groups, work and family policies that support diversity,** page 283

k. **integrative,** page 296

Reflection Points—Personal Thoughts on Human Behavior, the Art of Persuasion, and the Diversity Challenge

Complete the following questions and activities to personalize the content of Part Six. Space is provided for writing your thoughts.

■ What motivational needs do you feel in the workplace? Does your job allow the satisfaction of your motivational needs?

_____

_____

■ Discuss what a company should do to meet employee needs for (a) survival, (b) security, (c) belonging, (d) respect, and (e) fulfillment. What policies and practices would you recommend?

_____

_____

■ How important is emotional intelligence for leadership success? Do you know a leader who is a master at understanding and dealing with people?

_____

_____

■ Consider the elements of the art of persuasion in the leadership process. Evaluate yourself in the areas of understanding others, using words effectively, and dealing with conflict. Which areas are your strengths? Which do you need to improve?

_____

_____

■ Discuss the role of leaders in the U.S. Civil War in the context of position, power, and social influence. Examples are Lincoln, Davis, Lee, Grant, and Joshua Lawrence Chamberlain.

_____

_____

■ In the 1990s, South Africa experienced tremendous societal and governmental change without the level of violence that many anticipated. Efforts at reconciliation and building consensus were exemplary acts of leadership. Discuss the roles of Nelson Mandela, Desmond Tutu, and F. W. De Klerk in facilitating change, recognizing diversity, and leading courageously.

_____

_____

■ What experiences have you had in dealing with diversity? Have you ever witnessed firsthand the harmful effects of intolerance and discrimination?

_____

_____

■ Discuss gender diversity in the workplace, including the increasing numbers of women in the workforce and in leadership positions. If you have ever had an opposite-sex leader, discuss the pros and cons of your experience.

_____

_____

Part Six Video Case
Cirque du Soleil: A Truly Global Workforce

In 1984, Guy Laliberté left his home in Canada to make his way across Europe as a circus performer. There he and other artists entertained in the street. The troupe was called Cirque du Soleil—circus of the sun. It started with a simple dream: a group of young artists getting together to entertain audiences, see the world, and have fun doing it. Laliberté and company quickly found that their entertainment form without words—stilt-walking, juggling, music, and fire-breathing—transcended all barriers of language and culture. Though he understood that an entertainer could bring the exotic to every corner of the world, Laliberté did not envision the scope to which his Cirque du Soleil would succeed. Today, Cirque performs five permanent shows—four in Las Vegas and one in Walt Disney World—and five traveling shows. In 20-plus years of live performances, 44 million people have seen a Cirque show. Despite a long-term decline in the circus industry, Cirque has increased revenue 22-fold over the last 10 years. Growth plans include additional tours in Asia and permanent shows in New York, Tokyo, and London.

Cirque du Soleil is a family of more than 3,000 individuals—700 of whom are the shows' artists—from 40 different countries. Each of Cirque's employees is encouraged to contribute to the group. This input has resulted in rich, deep performances and expansion into alternative media outlets such as music, books, television, film, Web sites, and merchandising. The company's diversity assures that every show reflects many different cultural influences. Different markets will have an exotic experience at a Cirque show, regardless of which show is playing where. Cirque does target specific markets with products designed to engage a particular audience. Yet Cirque has little need to adapt its product to new markets; the product is already a blend of global influences. The result is a presentation of acrobatic arts and traditional, live circus with an almost indescribable freshness and beauty.

Cirque du Soleil's commitment to excellence and innovation transcends cultural differences and the limits of many modern media. Its intense popularity has made Cirque both the global standard of live entertainment and the place for talented individuals from around the world to perfect their talents. The extent of the diversity, however, does pose a host of unique challenges. Every employee must be well-versed in various forms and styles. To foster cultural enrichment, Cirque purchases and shares a large collection of art with employees and gives them tickets to different events and shows.

The performers work in the most grueling and intimate situations, with their lives depending on one another. The astounding spectacles they achieve on stage result from hours of planning, practice, and painstaking attention to detail among artists from diverse cultures who speak 25 different languages. Sensitivity, compromise, and hunger for new experiences are prerequisites for success at Cirque. The organization has learned the art of sensitivity and compromise in its recruiting. Cirque du Soleil has had a presence in the Olympics for a decade. It works closely with coaches and teams to help athletes consider a career with Cirque *after* their competitive years are over, rather than luring talent away from countries that have made huge investments in athletes. This practice has given Cirque a huge advantage in the athletic community, a source of great talent from all over the globe.

Guy Laliberté has not forgotten his humble beginnings as a Canadian street performer. Now that Cirque du Soleil has achieved an international presence and incredible success—the group earned over $1 billion in annual gross revenue in 2011—it has chosen to help at-risk youth, especially street kids. Cirque allocates 1percent of its revenues to outreach programs targeting youth in difficulty, regardless of the location in the world. Laliberté understands that to be successful in a world market, one must be a committed and sensitive neighbor. Cirque's Montreal headquarters is the center of an urban revitalization project that the company sponsors. Community participation and outreach bring international goodwill and help Cirque du Soleil prevent many of the difficulties global brands often face when spanning cultures.

Questions for Discussion

1. Why is Cirque du Soleil successful throughout the world? Why does the product transcend cultural differences between countries?

For more information, see www.cirquedusoliel.com.

Action Assignment

As a bridge between learning and doing, complete the following action assignment.

1. What is the single most important idea you have learned in Part Six?
2. How can you apply what you have learned? What will you do, with whom, where, when, and, most important, why?

Part 7 Multiplying Effectiveness

14. Effective Delegation and How to Assign Work
15. The Role of Personality

WHEN I WAS BUILDING MICROSOFT, I set out to create an environment where software developers could thrive. I wanted a company where engineers liked to work. I wanted to create a culture that encouraged them to work together, share ideas, and remain highly motivated.

—Bill Gates
Co-founder, Microsoft

Learning Objectives

After studying Part Seven, you will be able to:

- Multiply personal effectiveness by delegating authority.
- Know the rules for effective delegation.
- Know how to give orders.
- Know the types of skills needed at each level of management.
- Understand the importance of person–position fit based on personality types and job families.
- Deal effectively with different types of people.
- Know the strengths and needs of your own personality—traditional, participative, or individualistic.

CHAPTER

14

Effective Delegation and How to Assign Work

T he effective leader is an arithmetic artist, subtracting and dividing when less can be more, adding and compounding to achieve a greater good. In this way, the leader enlists the energies and improves the effectiveness of the group. Consider the case of Microsoft's **Bill Gates** and the ability he has shown to multiply his effectiveness through the efforts of others. See www.gatesfoundation.org.

Gates writes: "Develop your people to do their jobs better than you can. Transfer your skills to them. This is exciting but it can be threatening to a manager who worries that he is training his replacement. Smart managers like to see their employees increase their responsibilities because it frees the managers to tackle new or undone tasks."[1]

Successful leadership means picking the right people for the right assignments and developing them. These followers are not clones of the leader, but are people who have talents that may be dormant or underdeveloped.

In her wonderful book *Jesus CEO,* management author Laurie Beth Jones writes regarding targeted selection: "Who would pick someone who smells like fish and mud? Who would pick an unpopular tax collector? Who would pick leaders from filthy wharves and toil-filled fields? But He did, and together they changed the world."[2]

Effective leadership involves seeing qualities in others unknown to themselves and treating others in a way that brings out their best. The effective leader uses the multiplication key—the ability to **delegate**—to develop others and achieve more success than would otherwise be possible.

If you have doubts as to the importance of delegation, consider that the life span of most businesses is one and a half generations. The pattern is this: A person starts a business, and it lasts through his or her working lifetime. It takes successors only half a working generation to put the company out of business.[3]

The question is *why*? Surely the founder does not intend this result. The answer is failure to develop people because of failure to delegate power. By withholding authority, leaders guarantee that their companies will have short life spans. When the leader is unable or unwilling to develop others through effective delegation, no provision is made for continuation of the business and its lasting success.[4]

In today's downsized, fast-paced, and high-tech workplace, delegation is not only advisable but also necessary for success. All employees need to be involved if the full value of their skills is to be realized.

There are two ways of exerting leadership strength: One is pushing down through intimidation; the other is pulling up through delegation. Pulling up through delegation is infinitely more effective, and it is the chosen approach of the successful leader.

A role model for effective delegation was Thomas Alva Edison, the Wizard of Menlo Park and the greatest inventor of the modern age. By the end of his life, Edison was granted 1,093 patents for his inventions, one for every 11 days of his adult life. Edison gave credit for his success to the men he worked with, a mixed crew of dreamers, gadgeteers, and craftsmen who worked as a team. A story that is characteristic of him is one of delegation and trust: When Edison was working on improving his first lightbulb, to the astonishment of onlookers, he handed a finished bulb to a younger helper, who nervously carried it upstairs step-by-step to the vacuum machine. At the last moment, the boy dropped it. The whole team had to work another twenty-four hours to make the bulb again, but when Edison looked around for someone to carry it upstairs, he gave it to the same boy. The gesture probably changed the young man's life. Edison knew more than a lightbulb was at stake.[5]

Delegation Success Story

Think again of the famous success story of Herb Kelleher and Southwest Airlines—this time as an instance of truly effective delegation.

Herb Kelleher may have built Southwest Airlines from a doodle scratched on a cocktail napkin to the most successful airline in history, but he is the first to say he did not do it alone. Caring, competent and committed leadership may be required, but literally thousands of *turned-on* employees were also necessary. The triggering switch: effective delegation. Two notable examples are Jim Parker, general counsel for 15 years and now CEO, and Colleen Barrett, originally a secretary and now president of the company.[6]

There are many reasons leaders fail to delegate. Some do not know how. Others do not think their employees will do the job as well as they themselves will. Others do not trust their employees to follow through. Still others fail to delegate because they fear their employees will show them up by doing a better job.

Regardless of the cause, failure to delegate should be corrected for two important reasons:

1. Delegation gives the leader time to carry out important responsibilities in the areas of establishing direction, aligning resources, and energizing people.
2. Delegation helps prepare employees for more difficult tasks and additional responsibility. Employees who are bored and underused come alive when important jobs are delegated to them.[7]

Delegation is the key to multiplying the effectiveness of the leader and the group as a whole. Exercise 14–1 can be used to diagnose delegation strengths and areas for improvement. Complete the exercise based on yourself as a leader or based on a leader you know.

Exercise 14–1
Delegation Diagnosis[8]

Answer each of the following 25 questions. Do not debate too long over any one; go with your first reaction.

	Yes	No
1. Do you spend more time than you should doing work your employees could do?	_____	_____
2. Do you often find yourself working while your employees are idle?	_____	_____
3. Do you feel you should be able to answer personally any question about any project in your area?	_____	_____
4. Is your in-box usually full?	_____	_____
5. Do your employees take initiative to solve problems without your direction?	_____	_____
6. Does your operation function smoothly when you are absent?	_____	_____
7. Do you spend more time working on details than you do on planning and supervising?	_____	_____
8. Do your employees feel they have sufficient authority over personnel, finances, facilities, and other resources for which they are responsible?	_____	_____
9. Have you bypassed your employees by making decisions that were part of their jobs?	_____	_____
10. If you were incapacitated for an extended period of time, is there someone trained who could take your place?	_____	_____
11. Is there usually a big pile of work requiring your action when you return from an absence?	_____	_____
12. Have you ever assigned a job to an employee primarily because it was distasteful to you?	_____	_____
13. Do you know the interests and goals of every person reporting to you?	_____	_____
14. Do you make it a habit to follow up on jobs you delegate?	_____	_____
15. Do you delegate complete projects as opposed to individual tasks whenever possible?	_____	_____
16. Are your employees trained to their maximum potential?	_____	_____
17. Do you find it difficult to ask others to do things?	_____	_____
18. Do you trust your employees to do their best in your absence?	_____	_____
19. Are your employees performing below their capabilities?	_____	_____
20. Do you always give credit for a job well done?	_____	_____
21. Do employees refer more work to you than you delegate to them?	_____	_____
22. Do you support your employees when their authority is questioned?	_____	_____
23. Do you personally do those assignments that only you could or should do?	_____	_____
24. Does work pile up at any one point in your operation?	_____	_____
25. Do all your employees know what is expected of them in order of priority?	_____	_____

305

Scoring:

Give yourself 1 point for each *Yes* answer for numbers 5, 6, 8, 10, 13, 14, 15, 16, 18, 20, 22, 23, and 25: _____.

Give yourself 1 point for each *No* answer for items 1, 2, 3, 4, 7, 9, 11, 12, 17, 19, 21, and 24: _____ .

Record your total score here: _____.

Interpretation:

Score	Evaluation
20–25	You follow effective delegation practices that help the efficiency and morale of your work group. These skills maximize your effectiveness as a leader and help develop the full potential of your employees.
14–19	Your score is OK, but nothing special if you are striving for excellence in leadership. To improve your delegation skills, review the questions you missed and take appropriate steps so that you will not repeat those delegation mistakes.
13 and below	Delegation weakness is reducing your effectiveness as a leader. The overall performance of your work group is lower than it should be because you are either unable or unwilling to relinquish power to others. In addition, delegation mistakes may cause dissatisfaction among employees. At the minimum, they will not develop job interest and important skills unless you improve in this area. Remember Andrew Carnegie's admonition: "It marks a big step in a supervisor's development to realize that other people can be called upon to help do a better job than one can do alone."[9]

Steps and Rules for Effective Delegation

Figure 14–1 shows the steps for effective delegation.

**Figure 14–1
The Steps for Effective Delegation**

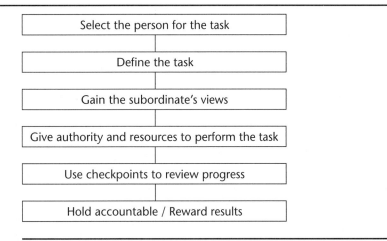

| Select the person for the task |
| Define the task |
| Gain the subordinate's views |
| Give authority and resources to perform the task |
| Use checkpoints to review progress |
| Hold accountable / Reward results |

The following rules for effective delegation apply to leading individuals as well as groups. Leaders who incorporate these rules will maximize the job performance and work morale of employees, and will increase the overall productivity of their work groups.[10]

- **Share power with employees.** Fight the natural fear, common to all leaders, of losing control. Remember, to hoard your power is to lose it. Only by delegating authority to others and holding them accountable for results will you accomplish more and greater work.

- **Don't delegate the bad jobs, saving the good ones for yourself.** Don't be like the supervisor who always calls on her or his assistant for the dirty work, late-night work, and disciplining, reserving for her- or himself all the easy assignments and the ones that bring reward.

- **Know your employees.** Effective delegation requires knowing the aptitudes and interests of all your employees. If all else is equal, assign social tasks to employees who enjoy dealing with people, fact-finding and report preparation to those who enjoy investigation and writing, and hands-on work to employees who like personal involvement. Include idea-oriented employees in brainstorming or in formulating policies. Capitalize on the special strengths of all your employees.

- **Use delegation as a development tool.** Improve the knowledge, skills, and attitudes of employees by delegating tasks that are meaningful and challenging and that raise their abilities to new levels.

- **Delegate work fairly among all employees.** Recognize the fact that some employees have higher capacity levels, but don't overburden those employees while underworking others. Delegation that is perceived as unfair lowers the morale and performance of both the overused and underused workers.

- **When you delegate authority, be sure to back your employees if that authority is questioned.** When all else is equal, support your employees. If someone has made a mistake, discuss the mistake privately; then let that person correct the problem him- or herself.

- **Let employees know what decisions they have authority to make and delegate decision making to the lowest possible level.** This approach improves effectiveness and efficiency by avoiding referrals through many departments and levels of an organization to solve a problem or receive an answer.

- **Delegate with consistency.** Don't go on delegation campaigns, overwhelming employees sometimes and underusing them other times.

- **Delegate whole tasks so that employees can see projects through to completion; allow sufficient time to get jobs done.** Avoid the "Zeigarnik effect," a term attributed to the Russian researcher Bluma Zeigarnik, in which employee morale, commitment, and performance deteriorate because employees are not able to finish tasks. Work that has not been started may or may not be a motivator, but unfinished tasks almost always demotivate.[11]

- **Insist on clear communication.** Obtain agreement to provide regular feedback on progress and problems. An effective technique is to post a visible calendar with assignment due dates marked. Clear communication and conscientious follow-up will ensure the success of delegated tasks.

- **Make good use of questions when delegating work.** Encourage employees to ask questions to clarify assignments. Also, ask what you can do to help them succeed.

- **Explain the importance of assignments.** Show employees how assigned tasks can satisfy important individual needs, as well as advance the goals of the organization.

- **Learn to live with work styles that are not like your own.** Establish high standards of performance and do not tolerate low-quality work; however, balance this requirement with the fact that no two people are exactly alike, and another person's approach to a task may not be the same as your own.

- **Avoid delegating tasks that are pets, personal, or petty.** Some tasks should not be delegated: (1) If an assignment is a *pet,* that is, one unique to your own interest or skill, you should do it; perhaps no one else will be able to do it as well; (2) if a task is private or *personal,* do it yourself; otherwise, it puts an unfair burden on your employees; (3) if a task is *petty,* never delegate it; to do so lowers self-respect and the respect of your employees.

- **Follow the three D's for all work—do it, delegate it, or ditch it.** *Do* assignments yourself; *delegate* work to competent employees as soon as possible; *ditch* unimportant tasks. In any case, don't let assignments pile up, as they will ultimately reduce the efficiency of your work group.

When people micromanage, they create a climate of distrust. This lowers morale and destroys creativity. The micromanager becomes a bottleneck in the flow of communication and decision making. By applying proven rules for effective delegation, leaders can multiply personal effectiveness, develop employee talents, have good leader–follower relations, and obtain the highest possible level of job performance.

Assigning Work Effectively

Meg Whitman, former CEO of eBay, walked into an online flea market and became inspired. She joined the company and was successful because she recognized opportunity, made a decision, and gave the orders to make it work. Whitman knew people she could depend on to get the job done, and she assigned work effectively. **Assigning work effectively** is one of the most important skills of the successful leader. The following is a list of proven principles for performing this leadership task:[12]

- **Consider the availability of the employee's time and whether this is the ideal person to do the job.** If the employee's schedule is heavily loaded, explain the priority level of the work. A common mistake is for the leader to assign a job to the one who can get it done, even if this is the same person over and over again. This practice creates three problems: (a) The overworked employee becomes resentful; (b) the overworked employee does not know the priority of many assignments; and (c) the abilities of underworked employees are wasted or never developed.

- **Use work assignments as a means of developing people.** If a task does not have to be done perfectly or within a certain time period, try giving it to an employee who has never done it before. Besides showing you have faith in the employee, you will be developing another person who will be familiar with the job if the regular performer is not available.

- **Know exactly what you want to communicate before giving an order.** Confusion on the leader's part creates doubt and lack of confidence in employees. If you are giving a speech to your employees, prepare and practice it so that what you say will be clear and understandable. If you are going to have a conference with your employees, make notes of the important points you want to cover and refer to them, if needed, during the meeting. If you are assigning a task, rehearse for clarity, and write it down if it is complex or has more than one part or step.

- **If many duties or steps are involved in an order, follow oral communication with a note, and keep a copy.** Keeping records of important conferences, orders, and rules can be helpful. As a reference, a note (short and to the point) can be an excellent memory aid. However, don't become memo crazy; this practice encourages defensive behavior and wastes both time and goodwill.

- **Ask rather than tell, but leave no doubt that you expect compliance.** This approach shows both courtesy and respect. The adage "You can catch more bears with honey than you can with vinegar" applies here. You can usually obtain more cooperation by asking for assistance than by commanding others to do a job.

- **Use the correct language for the employee's training level.** Recognize the fact that many people will not understand your words and terms as readily as you do. Most occupations and jobs have abbreviations, slang words, and technical language that the new or untrained person will not understand. What does "one BLT without, rush!" mean to a new employee, particularly if the person is from a foreign country? For such a person, understanding the English language may be difficult, even without acronyms and jargon.

- **Make assignments in a logical sequence, using clear and concise language.** People remember things best that are clearly stated. If you skip around and are vague, employees will miss the point of your message or will easily forget it.

- **Be considerate but never apologetic when asking someone to do a job.** Imagine that a water main breaks on a cold, snowy night and Bill, the foreman, says to Joe, the laborer: "Joe, I feel so sorry for your having to go down in that hole in this freezing weather. It's going to be like ice! Boy, am I glad I don't have to go . . . brrrr!"
  If Joe wasn't feeling sorry for himself before Bill started talking, he would be now. A better way for Bill to make the request would be: "Joe, I have some dry clothes for you in the truck, and a thermos of coffee will be ready when you come up. Good luck." The rule is: No apologies, just consideration.

- **Talk deliberately and authoritatively, but avoid shouting across a room or making an unnecessary show of power.** Save your power until it is needed. You reduce effectiveness and put people on the defensive if you are constantly forceful. The familiar statement, "She doesn't raise her voice very often, but when she does, everyone listens," exemplifies this principle.

- **Take responsibility for the orders you give.** Avoid quoting others to gain compliance or to relieve yourself of personal responsibility, as when a leader says, "Don't blame me. The boss says we have to do it." If you do not take personal responsibility for the orders you give, the results will be (a) loss of respect from your employees, (b) loss of confidence from your supervisor, and (c) reduced commitment to follow your orders.

- **Give people the opportunity to ask questions and express opinions.** This is a vital point because (a) employees may be confused by an assignment, and questions can help clarify instructions; (b) employees may have information or know something you do not; (c) when you encourage questions and self-expression, you demonstrate respect for employees; and (d) when you allow the opportunity to ask questions and express opinions, you will be rewarded with increased creativity and commitment from your employees.

- **Follow up to make sure assignments are being carried out properly, and modify them if the situation warrants.** Some leaders say, "I don't have time to follow-up; I am too busy giving orders." The folly here is that unless there is follow-up, an inappropriate order or assignment may be repeated. Without follow-up, one never learns from experience.

    If follow-up reveals that an order is a mistake, admit the error. A leader who has the attitude "right or wrong, that is my decision" does three things if the decision is wrong: (a) loses the opportunity to correct the mistake; (b) loses the respect of people who are concerned about the quality of work; and (c) sets an example of egotism and closed-mindedness.

Person–Position Fit

A good rule to follow in assigning work and selecting employees is PAP:

Performance. Can the person do the work at the level required? Will performance be high? The best indications are previous performance and current work samples.

Attitude. Does the person want to do the work? Will motivation be high to try one's best? The best indication is behavior itself. Measure commitment by actions, not words.

Psycho-social Fit. Will the work location, schedule, culture, and the like match individual and family needs? The best indication comes from full information exchange. This may require location and job visits.

When all three elements are present, a positive fit exists between the person and the position, and the payoff will be enormous in both high morale and work performance. Remember that once a person is hired and deployed, organizational structure, climate, resources, and processes must be present for that person to succeed.[13]

Job Families

Lance Morrow writes in *The Temping of America* that today's workforce must be fluid and flexible, always learning and growing. His message is that each person is on his or her own. For good or ill, today's employees have to continually develop and market themselves in an ever-changing work environment. Robert Schaen, former controller of Ameritech and currently a publisher of children's books, writes:

The days of the mammoth corporations and lifetime work contracts are coming to an end. People are going to have to create their own lives, their own careers, and their own successes. Some people may go kicking and screaming into the new world, but there is only one message there: You're now in business for yourself.[14]

Managing your career requires knowing your strengths. The concept of job families can help in this area. One of the best models comes from John Holland, who identifies six personality and occupational types[15] (see Figure 14–2).

Types most similar to each other are arranged next to each other, while those most dissimilar fall directly across the hexagon. No person is a pure type, and most people have a pattern of interests combining all six. The following are descriptions of each personality and occupational type, including general

**Figure 14–2
Holland's Model of
Personality and
Occupational Types**

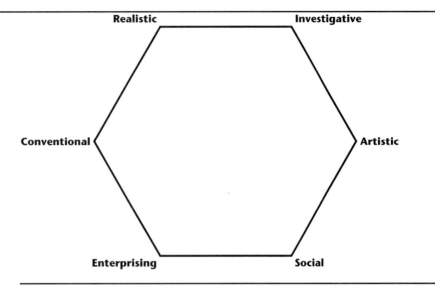

characteristics, personality traits, sample occupations, and a typical high-stress activity or situation:

- **Realistic** people like working outdoors and working with their hands. They prefer to deal with concrete physical tasks rather than with people. They are described as:

honest	natural	modest	strong
frank	practical	robust	rugged
humble	competent	stable	self-reliant

Sample occupations: engineer, surveyor, farmer, electrician, mechanic
Typical high-stress activity: making a speech

- **Investigative** people enjoy the research and discovery process. They are task-oriented and prefer working alone. They are described as:

analytical	independent	introverted	scientific
critical	intellectual	rational	scholarly
curious	methodical	reserved	cautious

Sample occupations: biologist, chemist, physicist, anthropologist, geologist
Typical high-stress situation: parties and small talk

- **Artistic** individuals thrive in artistic settings that offer opportunities for self-expression. They are described as:

creative	imaginative	intuitive	unique
emotional	impractical	nonconforming	idealistic
expressive	impulsive	original	aesthetic

Sample occupations: artist, writer, decorator, actor, composer
Typical high-stress activity: following rules and regulations

- **Social** people like to work with other people and are concerned with their welfare. They have little interest in machinery or physical exertion. They are described as:

friendly	helpful	responsible	tactful
generous	insightful	caring	concerned
kind	tolerant	understanding	supportive

Sample occupations: teacher, counselor, social worker, advisor, therapist
Typical high-stress activity: performing maintenance and repairs

■ **Enterprising** people enjoy leading, speaking, and convincing others. They are impatient with routine and detail work. They are described as:

adventurous	energetic	self-confident	enthusiastic
ambitious	optimistic	sociable	charismatic
variety-loving	pleasure-seeking	outgoing	dominant

Sample occupations: salesperson, business executive, producer, promoter, lawyer

Typical high-stress situation: restricted freedom of action

■ **Conventional** people prefer highly ordered activities, both verbal and numerical, that characterize detail work. They have little interest in artistic or physical skills. They are described as:

conscientious	dependable	organized	calm
careful	orderly	self-controlled	structured
conservative	neat	efficient	accurate

Sample occupations: accountant, assembler, banker, cost estimator, tax expert

Typical high-stress situation: ambiguity and clutter

There are many hundreds of professions and specialties in the world of work, and they are constantly changing. Holland's model of basic personality and occupational types is useful in considering avenues for peak performance throughout one's career. The best approach is to be what you are and do what you love. Success will follow.

Exercise 14–2 is based on Richard Bolles's excellent book *What Color Is Your Parachute?*[16] It provides a useful way to evaluate your own personality based on Holland's model of job families.

**Exercise 14–2
Understanding
Personality and
Occupational Types**

Presented below is a room in which a party is taking place. People with the same or similar interests have gathered in the corners of the room as described.

Realistic

People who have mechanical ability; prefer to work with objects, machines, tools, plants, or animals; or like to be outdoors

Conventional

People who like to work with data, have clerical or numerical ability, enjoy carrying things out in detail or following through on systems and procedures

Investigative

People who like the discovery process—to observe, learn, investigate, analyze, evaluate, and solve problems

The Party

People who like to work with people—influencing, persuading, leading, or managing others for organizational goals or for economic gain

People who have artistic, innovative, or intuitional abilities, and like to work in unstructured situations, using their imagination or creativity

Enterprising

Artistic

People who like to help people—to inform, enlighten, advise, train, develop, or cure them— and who are skilled with words

Social

1. Which corner of the room would you be drawn toward? Which group of people would you most enjoy being with for the longest time?

2. After a period of time, everyone in the corner you have chosen leaves the room. Of the groups that remain, which one would you most enjoy being with for the longest time?

3. After a period of time, everyone in the second corner you have chosen leaves the room. Of the groups that remain, which one would you most enjoy being with for the longest time?

Action Steps:

Consider the skills and activities of the people in each corner you have chosen. Do further research on vocations and work opportunities that require these skills and activities. Read the *Occupational Outlook Handbook,* available at all libraries and online (www.bls.gov/oc/home.htm), access O*NET Online!, U.S. Department of Labor, http://www.online.onetcenter.org, and interview successful people who are engaged in your areas of interest.

Management Roles and Skills

In 1955, Robert Katz wrote an important article in the *Harvard Business Review,* titled "Skills of an Effective Administrator." Many studies have been conducted since then showing that a leader's effectiveness depends on knowledge and skills in solving organizational problems. Further, the types of problems to be solved depend on the leader's role or level of responsibility.[17]

Top managers establish the organization's goals, overall strategy, and operating policy. These individuals officially represent the organization to the external environment.

Middle managers are responsible for implementing the policies and plans developed by top management and for supervising and coordinating the activities of lower-level managers. They can be significant sources of innovation and productivity when given the autonomy to make decisions affecting their operating units.

Front-line managers supervise and coordinate the activities of operating employees. They typically spend a large proportion of their time coordinating, facilitating, and supporting the work of subordinates.

Figure 14–3 shows the types of skills needed for effective performance at each level of management. The varying amounts of skills needed are represented by the different-sized blocks. Note that **relational skill,** the ability to understand and work effectively with people, is equally important at all levels of responsibility.

**Figure 14–3
Types of Skills Needed at Each Level of Management Responsibility[18]**

Management Level	Skills			Responsibilities
Top-Level Management	Conceptual Skills			Strategic Planning and Decision-Making
Middle-Level Management		Relational Skills		Coordination and Planning for Implementation
First-Level Management			Technical Skills	Implementation

A description of each type of skill follows:

Technical skill refers to having knowledge about and being proficient in a specific type of work or activity. It includes detailed job knowledge, hands-on expertise, and the specialized use of equipment, techniques, and procedures. Both the technical expert and the work group supervisor should have a high degree of technical skill. Examples include a computer specialist designing a program, a lawyer preparing a legal document, and a maintenance supervisor overseeing a repair job.

Relational skill refers to having knowledge about and being able to work with people. It includes the ability to motivate, coordinate, and advise other people, either as individuals or as a work group. Sensitivity in human relations and a willingness to help others are essential elements of relational expertise. Success at all levels of management—first, middle, and top—requires good human relation skills. Examples include an office supervisor handling an employee performance problem, a sales manager coordinating a sales force, and a plant superintendent solving a problem between the manufacturing and scheduling departments.

Conceptual skill refers to having knowledge about and being able to work with concepts and ideas. It includes the ability to think abstractly. Long-range planning, strategic decision making, and the weighing of ethical considerations in employee, customer, and government relations all require conceptual skills. Examples include a labor relations vice president evaluating a proposed labor agreement and a company president deciding whether to support a community service project.

The importance of these skills varies by managerial level. Technical skills are most important for first-level management. Conceptual skills become more important than technical skills as you rise higher in the organization. Relational skills are important throughout your career at every level of management.

Figure 14–4 shows the amount of time each level of management normally spends on the four processes or functions of management—planning, organizing, directing, and controlling. Note that the conceptual skills needed increase at each higher level of responsibility.

Figure 14–4
Normal Distribution of a Manager's Time[19]

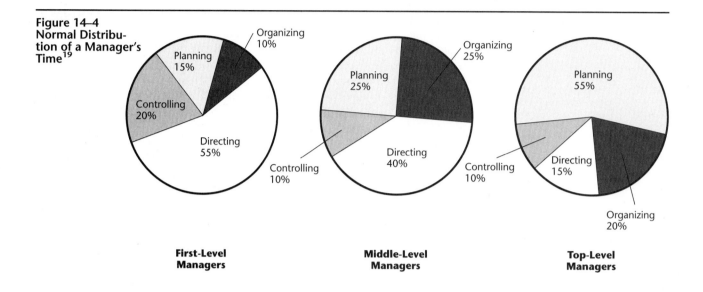

First-Level Managers

Middle-Level Managers

Top-Level Managers

Management Processes/Functions

Planning includes charting a direction, determining strategies to succeed, and making policy decisions.

Organizing involves aligning structure, people, and resources to achieve goals.

Directing entails supervising, facilitating, coaching, and developing people.

Controlling focuses on tracking progress against plans and making corrections.

To increase your understanding of the different functions of management at each level of responsibility, complete Exercise 14–3.

**Exercise 14–3
Functions and Levels
of Management—
In-Box Practice[20]**

Each of the individuals described below occupies one of three levels of management: first, middle, and top. Each is also involved in one of the four management functions: planning (P), organizing (O), directing (D), and controlling (C). Read the descriptions; then fill in the chart that follows.

Manager A of Wolverine World Wide has hired a market research company to investigate Asian markets for Wolverine shoes. If the market studies are promising, Manager A will set up a distribution network in Asia.

Manager B is responsible for cleaning the buildings and taking care of repairs for the county schools. He has spent the past weeks making a schedule, ordering equipment, and assigning work teams.

Manager C has trained her employees in the proper way to present the meal when the restaurant's customers order this evening's special.

Manager D is reviewing the company's three main sales goals for the current year. By next week, she will have a detailed progress report ready to present at the monthly meeting of the company's sales managers.

Manager E wants to use the company's surplus funds to buy a wholesale food distributor. However, the asking price for the distribution company is more than the amount of money on hand. So Manager E has contacted the bank about a 10-year loan to finance the purchase.

Manager F has decided that the human resources department needs an additional employee to interview job applicants. Manager F writes a help-wanted advertisement to place in the local newspaper.

Manager G has spent the morning resolving an argument among three of the company's clerical workers. The workers all want to take their lunch breaks at the same time, but one of the workers needs to remain in the office to answer the telephone.

Manager H is conducting a performance review of senior officers, focusing on quality of production, customer satisfaction, market share, employee morale, and financial performance.

Manager	Management Level First, Middle, Top	Management Function P, O, D, C
A		
B		
C		
D		
E		
F		
G		
H		

Answer Key:

A	Middle	P
B	First	O
C	First	D
D	Middle	C
E	Top	P
F	First	O
G	First	D
H	Top	C

The Vital Shift—Moving from Doer to Coordinator to Thinker

In the U.S. workplace, the reward for being an outstanding producer is often promotion into management. Success is measured by status in the organization, as blue-collar workers aspire to white-color jobs and first-line leaders strive to rise to executive levels. In much of the rest of the world, mobility is less the norm as people are hired into either blue- or white-collar jobs and are expected to remain there, and as management positions are typically filled on the basis of education or social standing. The opportunity to become a manager and rise in the organization is not as common elsewhere as it is in the United States.[21]

A promotion to supervisor can be more than a job change; for many people, it can be a culture shock. The progression through career stages and management levels is not always a smooth one. As seen in Figure 14–5, some of the most difficult times are the periods of vital shift, when a person leaves one type of work and moves to another.

Moving from a period of doing things, through a period of coordinating people, to a period of thinking about ideas can be difficult because different interests and skills are involved at each stage. When the transition is not made successfully, the result is the overpromotion syndrome popularized by author Laurence J. Peter. According to the **Peter Principle,** the individual may be dissatisfied because the new work is not interesting or may feel inadequate because needed skills are missing. At the same time, the organization and those it serves are harmed because the individual lacks competence in performing the tasks of the position. In effect, the individual has been promoted to his or her level of incompetence.[22]

Figure 14–5
Vital Shifts—Moving from Doer to Coordinator to Thinker[23]

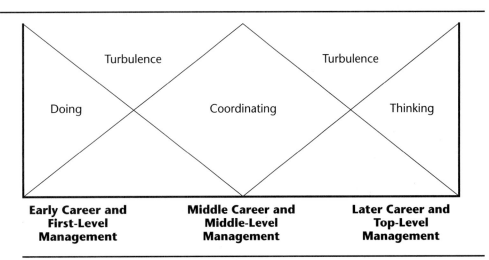

| Early Career and First-Level Management | Middle Career and Middle-Level Management | Later Career and Top-Level Management |

The New-Job Tryout

One of the best ways to successfully make a vital shift is to use the new-job tryout. This approach allows an individual to work at a different type of job or level of responsibility for an interim period of time to see if the work is agreeable and can be performed effectively. If either the person or the organization decides the employee should not continue in the new job, employee pride is easily preserved because the job was considered a two-way tryout. Without such a trial period, fear of embarrassment or an unwillingness to hurt people's feelings may result in a person's being retained in an unsuitable position, even when this harms the individual or the organization. The new-job tryout helps solve this problem. For example, before a permanent job assignment is made, the secretary may try out office management, the tradesperson may try out supervision, or the captain may try out the chief's position. Another way an individual can gain a realistic idea of a desired job role or level is by shadowing. The individual shadows the person in a role for a designated time period, providing the individual with the opportunity to ask questions and get a feel for the position before stepping into it.

The Role of Personality

Psalm 8 asks, "What is man, that thou art mindful of him?" The scientist answers, "Man is a product of internal and external forces." Each person is the result of interaction between biological heritage and cultural history. The kind of person you are and what you do depend on both raw material (heredity) and what is done with this raw material (how it is shaped and grown). We must eat to live; but whether we eat rice or meat, and whether we use fingers or utensils, is influenced by culture and experience.[24]

The Dutch philosopher Baruch Spinoza describes the *personal* nature of personality: "To be what we are and to become what we are capable of becoming is the ultimate end of life."[25] More than a century ago, Soren Kierkegaard emphasized that the most common despair is the unwillingness to be oneself and that the deepest form of despair is choosing to be other than oneself. "Even the richest personality is nothing before he has chosen himself. On the other hand, even what one might call the poorest personality is everything when he has chosen himself; for the great thing is not to be this or that, but to be oneself."[26]

Personality is also *social,* a series and integration of social roles. Shakespeare wrote:

> All the world's a stage,
> And all the men and women are merely players;
> They have their exits and their entrances,
> And one man in his time plays many parts,
> His acts being seven ages.[27]

Throughout our lives, we define ourselves as leaders, parents, citizens, and other social beings, adopting the goals, values, and characteristics of these roles. Social roles can be so important that the individual may break down when roles are changed. Imagine the successful businessman who, on losing his fortune and prestige, commits suicide. Or imagine the homemaking mother who, having raised her children, becomes depressed and physically ill.[28]

Leaders are more effective when they understand the personalities of their subordinates. Also, by gaining insight into the subject of personality, work group members can understand their reactions to the leader and to each other. The key is to remember that different personalities have different needs and ways of behaving. The wise, caring, and effective leader will value these differences and will strive to make the best use of the unique contributions of all types of people.[29]

The questionnaire in Exercise 15–1 measures **style of interpersonal relations,** an important element in dealing with people. As you complete the questionnaire and interpret the results, keep in mind that no questionnaire can capture the full flavor and uniqueness of a single human being. There is no one just like anyone else anywhere in the world. Each individual is biologically different because we are products of millions of ancestors, no two of whom were exactly alike. Additionally, each person is unique in his or her experiences, resulting in perceptions and judgments that are different from every other person's.

Also note that the following problems may exist with self-report questionnaires: (1) Answers may be inaccurate (e.g., an unemployed parent may feel justified in lying on an employment test); (2) the relationship between test scores and other behaviors may be unknown or lack dependability (e.g., there may be no correlation between test scores and job performance); and (3) the same test taken on different occasions may produce different results (e.g., a person's mood and recent experience may influence scores). Thus, no questionnaire should be used as a basis for decision making unless it has been proved valid and reliable.[30]

**Exercise 15–1
Interpersonal Style
Questionnaire**[31]

This questionnaire consists of 26 statements. There are no right or wrong answers. The best answers are your true opinions.

For each statement, indicate which of the three alternatives—*a, b,* or *c*—is *most true* or *most important* to you by circling *a, b,* or *c* in the "Most" column. Then choose the *least true* or *least important* of the two remaining alternatives, and circle its letter in the "Least" column. For example, if *a* is circled under "Most," then either *b* or *c* should be circled under "Least." For every statement, be sure you circle one alternative in each column.

Do not skip any questions, and do not debate too long over any one statement. Your first reaction is desired.

	Most			Least		
	T	P	I	T	P	I
1. When I enter new situations, I let my actions be guided by						
a. my own sense of what I want to do.						
b. the direction of those who are responsible.						
c. discussion with others.	b	c	a	b	c	a
2. When faced with a decision, I consider						
a. precedent and traditions.						
b. the opinions of the people affected.						
c. my own judgment.	a	b	c	a	b	c
3. People see me as						
a. a team player.						
b. a free spirit.						
c. a dependable person.	c	a	b	c	a	b
4. I feel most satisfied when						
a. I am working on personal goals.						
b. I do things according to standards.						
c. I contribute to a project.	b	c	a	b	c	a
5. I try to avoid						
a. not being myself.						
b. disappointing those in authority.						
c. arguments with my friends.	b	c	a	b	c	a
6. In my opinion, people need						
a. guidelines and rules for conduct.						
b. warm and supportive human relationships.						
c. freedom to grow.	a	b	c	a	b	c
7. Over time, I have learned						
a. no person is an island.						
b. old paths are true paths.						
c. you pass this way only once.	b	a	c	b	a	c
8. I want to be treated						
a. as a unique person.						
b. as an equal.						
c. with respect.	c	b	a	c	b	a
9. I avoid						
a. not meeting my responsibilities.						
b. compromising my personality.						
c. the loss of good friends.	a	c	b	a	c	b

	Most			Least		
	T	**P**	**I**	**T**	**P**	**I**
10. What the world needs is						
a. more people who think independently.						
b. more understanding among diverse people.						
c. more people who respect and abide by the law.	c	b	a	c	b	a
11. I am most happy when						
a. I am free to choose what I want to do.						
b. there are clear guidelines and rewards for performance.						
c. I share good times with others.	b	c	a	b	c	a
12. I am most responsible to _____ for my actions:						
a. family and friends						
b. higher authorities						
c. myself	b	a	c	b	a	c
13. To be a financial success, one should						
a. relax; money is not important.						
b. work in cooperation with others.						
c. work harder than others.	c	b	a	c	b	a
14. I believe						
a. there is a time and place for everything.						
b. promises to friends are debts to keep.						
c. the one who travels fastest travels alone.	a	b	c	a	b	c
15. I want the value of my work to be known						
a. soon after completion.						
b. with the passage of time.						
c. while I am doing it.	b	a	c	b	a	c
16. A group member should support						
a. the decisions of the majority.						
b. only those policies with which he or she personally agrees.						
c. those who are in charge.	c	a	b	c	a	b
17. I believe feelings and emotions						
a. should be shared with discretion.						
b. should be shared openly.						
c. should be kept to oneself.	c	b	a	c	b	a
18. The people I enjoy working with are						
a. free-thinking.						
b. well organized.						
c. friendly.	b	c	a	b	c	a
19. I value						
a. teamwork.						
b. independent thinking.						
c. order and organization.	c	a	b	c	a	b
20. I believe in the saying						
a. all work and no play makes Jack a dull boy.						
b. united we stand, divided we fall.						
c. there are no gains without pains.	c	b	a	c	b	a

	Most			Least		
	T	P	I	T	P	I

21. My workday goes best when I
   a. have freedom of operation.
   b. know what is expected of me.
   c. experience fellowship with good companions.   b   c   a   b   c   a

22. If I suddenly received a large sum of money, I would
   a. use most of it now for the things I want.
   b. invest most of it for the future.
   c. spend half of it now and save the rest.   b   c   a   b   c   a

23. I grow best by
   a. following established truths.
   b. interacting with others.
   c. learning from personal experience.   a   b   c   a   b   c

24. It is important that I
   a. plan a year or two ahead.
   b. live my life to the fullest now.
   c. think about life in a long-term way.   c   a   b   c   a   b

25. I am known for
   a. making my own decisions.
   b. sharing with others.
   c. upholding traditional values.   c   b   a   c   b   a

26. I work best
   a. with structure and organization.
   b. as a member of a team.
   c. as an independent agent.   a   b   c   a   b   c

Scoring:

Step 1:

Add the total number of circled letters for each of the six columns. Put these totals in the boxes below marked T, P, and I. Each "Most" and "Least" section total should be 26.

Most

T	P	I

(Total = 26)

Least

T	P	I

(Total = 26)

Step 2:

Determine your scores for T, P, and I by using the following formula:
Score = 26 + Most − Least. For example, if your T Most was 20 and your T Least was 12, your T score would be 26 + 20 − 12 = 34. Complete the following equations:

T Score = 26 + _____ − _____ = _____
              T Most   T Least

P Score = 26 + _____ − _____ = _____
              P Most   P Least

I Score = 26 + _____ − _____ = _____
              I Most   I Least

     (Your total should be 78.)   Total = _____

Interpretation:

The letters T, P, and I represent three styles of interpersonal relations:

> T = Traditional
>
> P = Participative
>
> I = Individualistic

If your highest score is T, you are **traditional.** You are known for your high standards and sense of tradition. If your highest score is P, you are **participative.** Caring about people and serving others are high values for you. If your highest score is I, you are **individualistic,** loving freedom and personal independence. If you are within 1 point of the same score for all three, you have built-in versatility for dealing with different types of people. If your two high scores are T and I, there are two opposite forces in your world asking you to act two different ways. One force is saying "be traditional," and the other is saying "be individualistic." Although this dichotomy can present problems, it can also be good if it allows you to accomplish your values and goals in life. Values and goals are more important than style of interpersonal relations. Note that occasionally it may be difficult for others to understand you because of the different signals you send.

Types of People and Types of Culture

One way to show that all styles of interpersonal relations have equal value is to identify people in history who represent distinctly different styles and who are each held in high esteem.

Traditional. When historians identify people who have had the most impact on humankind, the name of Moses always makes the top 10. As a leader and icon, Moses is the foremost individual in Jewish history. His leadership style exemplified traditional behavior. A woman in history who was traditional was the longest-reigning monarch of all the European monarchs. Indeed, a whole era or period of history was named after Queen Victoria, known for her moral strength and high standards of conduct.[32]

Participative. A woman in history who was participative was Eleanor Roosevelt. She was people-caring and people-serving. Always concerned with the welfare of others, she focused her life on the betterment of society.[33] Some of the best products of the United States have been the ideas and accomplishments of participative Benjamin Franklin. Indeed, without Franklin, the United States would not exist as we know it today.

There were few activities in which Benjamin Franklin did not excel. Philosopher, inventor, diplomat, printer, scientist—he was all of these and more. By his many achievements, including discovering electricity and helping to write the Constitution, Franklin left his mark upon the face of America and the world.[34]

Individualistic. One of America's most influential thinkers was the individualist Henry David Thoreau, who wrote:

> If a man does not keep pace with his friends,
> perhaps it is because he hears a different drummer.
> Let him step to the music he hears,
> however measured or far away.[35]

An example of a woman who was individualistic is Joan of Arc, who led the French people by her conviction and brave example. About Joan of Arc, Mark Twain wrote: [She is] easily and by far the most extraordinary person the human race has ever produced.[36]

If you were an employer, you would probably have trouble deciding which of these individuals to hire. Each has special qualities and would make valuable contributions. However, each is different in style of interpersonal relations, and each would require different treatment to be both happy and productive.

Personality and Culture

People are products of their culture—family, town, and country. Thus, style of interpersonal relations is influenced by how we are raised. Societies teach and reinforce behavior styles; just as individuals are traditional, participative, and individualistic, so are whole groups of people.[37]

Because personality is a social construct, it involves cross-cultural variations. Studies across cultures show that style of interpersonal relations is a basic dimension or characteristic.[38] Traditional social orientations put the needs and interests of the group above the individual. Individualistic social orientations involve separating the self from others. Participative social orientations seek a middle ground between individualistic and traditional styles with an emphasis on warm and supportive human relations.[39]

Traditional cultures tend to be formal and structured, such as those of England, Germany, and Spain. Many non-Western cultures, including those of Japan, China, and India, are traditional in nature.[40] Confucian ideals of filial loyalty and five right relationships—between father and son, ruler and subject, husband and wife, brother and sister, friend and friend—form the basis of much of East Asian culture. Participative cultures develop in melting pot societies: The United States is about 20 percent traditional, 60 percent participative, and 20 percent individualistic. Individualistic cultures include the French, Italian, and Greek. Indeed, the Greek civilization is based on individualism.

It is important to note that there are exceptions to these generalizations. For example, it is possible for an individual Frenchman to be more traditional than the most traditional German; and there may be a German who is more individualistic than the most individualistic Frenchman. It is also important to note that human traits vary in degrees, so that a person typically is a mixture of all three styles. While you may be primarily participative, you probably have a few traditional and individualistic characteristics as well.

Describing whole groups of people according to interpersonal style should not obscure the extensive diversity and variation that characterize each individual person. Also, it should be noted that certain qualities belong potentially to all people, such as basic honesty, concern for others, and open-mindedness.[41]

Understanding Others

Certain characteristics distinguish each style of interpersonal relations. As you read the following descriptions, think about the people with whom you live and work. The descriptions will help explain why some people are easy for you to understand, although you may not always agree with them (they are like you), and why other people are difficult for you to understand (they are different from you). Think also about the ways these different types of people should be treated to bring out their best.

Form of control. Traditionals are comfortable with rules, policies, and procedures. They believe that without such guidelines, social breakdown occurs. Participatives prefer interpersonal commitment as a form of control. The participative says, "I will do this. Will you do that?" Social ties are their preferred form of control. For individualists, *control* is a negative word. They dislike the idea of restricted freedom. In this spirit, Thoreau wrote, "The only obligation I have is to do at any time what I think is right."[42]

Basis of action. The basis of action for traditionals is direction from authorities in which they believe. These authorities may be parental, supervisory, governmental, or religious. In any case, traditionals believe those in charge should determine the course of action to be taken. Discussion and agreement with others are the basis of action for participatives. Democracy is their preferred form of government, and participative management is their favorite style of leadership. The basis of action for individualists is direction from within. The individualist has an internal compass to establish direction and a personal yardstick to measure the rightness and wrongness of behavior. A concept in psychology called locus of control asks, "Who is in charge, the world or me?" The individualist says "me."

To be avoided. Traditionals avoid deviation from authoritative direction. They appreciate job descriptions with responsibilities clearly defined. Business plans, life plans, and road maps for travel are important to them. Participatives avoid confrontation and strive to reach agreement if at all possible. Interpersonal conflict and misunderstanding are particularly painful. Abraham Lincoln, who had both traditional and individualistic moments, was mostly participative. In this fashion he wrote: "Am I not destroying my enemies when I make friends of them?" and, "A drop of honey catches more flies than a gallon of gall. So it is with men as well. If you would win a man to your cause, first convince him that you are his friend. It is a drop of honey that catches his heart, which, say what he will, is the high road to his reason."[43] Individualists avoid not being themselves. Congruency is important to them. They strive to be true to their essential nature. Individualists realize that life is a progression of social roles, but they insist on choosing their own parts.

Perception of responsibility. Traditionals believe highest allegiance should go to superordinate powers. These powers may be in the church, community, workplace, or home. Participatives feel responsibility to help others. They try not to disappoint family, friends, and colleagues. Participatives relate to the little boy who told Father Flanagan of Boys Town, "He ain't heavy, Father, he's my brother." They are the practicing humanitarians. They see themselves as their brothers' keeper. Individualists assign first responsibility for their own actions to their own conscience. "This above all: to thine own self be true, / And it must follow, as the night the day, / Thou canst not then be false to any man," advises Polonius, in *Hamlet*.[44] This is an individualistic principle.

Goals desired. Traditionals value organization and order. They believe the mission, goals, and objectives of an organization should be identified, and that each person's role should be made clear. Work plans and organization charts are helpful job aids for traditionals. Participatives value group consensus and smooth human relations. By interpersonal style, they make good personnel officers, counselors, and work group supervisors. Participatives are harmonizing agents. Individualists value independence and freedom. "Give me wings and let me fly" and "no rules for me" are interpersonal needs felt by individualists. They are especially uncomfortable with close supervision. Assignments that allow as much freedom as possible are ideal for individualists (assuming they have the ability and desire to accomplish the work). Consider Patrick Henry, the individualist, who said, "Give me liberty, or give me death." You may also recall that some people sought to kill him.

Basis for growth. Traditionals believe there is a time and place for everything, and the best way to grow is by following the established order. They value traditions in all areas of life—family, work, and religion. Philosophically, traditionals relate to Ecclesiastes 3:1–2: "To every thing there is a season, and a time to every purpose under the heaven: A time to be born, and a time to die; a time to plant, and a time to pluck up that which is planted." Participatives enjoy human interaction and prefer to grow in this manner. A participative would make a poor Robinson Crusoe—stranded on a deserted island. Participatives like to teach others and learn from them as well. Sharing is a basic interpersonal value. In the work setting, they especially appreciate group involvement activities. Staff meetings and collaborative work teams are seen as growth opportunities by participatives. Individualists prefer growth through introspection and self-analysis. It is important for them to get away occasionally and think, How do I feel about this; what is my philosophy on that, and what are my beliefs on this? Individualists grow best through personal experience and self-discovery. A sentiment that reflects their nature is expressed by the poet Robert Frost, who wrote "The Road Not Taken" in 1916:

> I shall be telling this with a sigh
> Somewhere ages and ages hence:
> Two roads diverged in a wood,
> And I—
> I took the one less traveled by,
> And that has made all the difference.[45]

Position in relation to others. Traditionals are comfortable as members of the hierarchy. Whether at the top, in the middle, or on the first rung of the ladder, they value structure and organizational clarity. Many people who are in top positions in organizations are traditionals. Note that George Washington was traditional in his style of interpersonal relations. Participatives are comfortable as members of the team. In fact, the *team* acronym, *together everyone accomplishes more*, is a participative concept. Participatives make good work group and committee members, because they enjoy working with and through others. Indeed, committees are creatures of the participative personality. They are tools not only to get the job done, but also to meet social needs. Individualists are most comfortable as separate people. For all their lives, they have seen the group go one way, and, almost instinctively, they have gone the other. By personality type, individualists are the pioneers of society—the first to do this and the first to go there. If Daniel Boone were to complete the "Interpersonal Style Questionnaire," he would be an individualist— as would Christopher Columbus, the explorer and navigator. Thoreau, the individualist, was famous for saying he could easily do without the post office. For their needs to be met, individualists must express themselves as the unique individuals they see themselves to be, not as members of a group or bureaucracy.

Material goods. The traditionals are excellent competitors. Witness the success of the Germans and Japanese in the international marketplace. And witness the New England Yankee, who came from Puritan stock and formed the basis of the American free market system. Participatives collaborate to get material goods. Teamwork comes naturally, as the participative says, "If we help each other, together we will accomplish more." Being involved in barn building, potluck suppers, and volunteer fire departments are participative activities. Individualists tend to take material goods for granted, thinking that everyone should have them. Compared with material wealth, personal independence is far more important.

Identification and loyalty. The traditional's first loyalty is to the organization—the U.S. Marine Corps, the FBI, the Roman Catholic Church. Pride in the organization is especially important to traditionals. This is the reason organizations need legends, logos, and other means to build "Yankee spirit" and achieve "Celtic pride." The participative's first loyalty is to the group—the shoulder-to-shoulder work group, team, or department. Inclusion and a sense of belonging are important values for participatives. Edwin Markham's short verse captures the essence of the participative personality:

> He drew a circle that shut me out,
> Heretic, rebel, a thing to flout;
> But Love and I had the wit to win—
> We drew a circle that took him in.[46]

Loyalty is not a major value for individualists, but when they have it, they have it intensely for the person or ideal they deem worthy.

To show how different personalities value loyalty in different ways, imagine three Marine Corps privates—traditional, participative, and individualistic. The traditional's highest loyalty will be to the corps and all it represents; the participative's first loyalty will be to his comrades in arms, the platoon; and the individualist's primary allegiance will be to those individuals and ideals who have earned his respect and support. Indeed, when thinking of patriotism, the traditional imagines an old Uncle Sam, finger pointing, saying, "I want you"; service for the participative is based on such ideas as "united we stand, divided we fall"; and the individualist's ideal is to preserve "the land of the free."

One can see these orientations surface when personalities clash. If you ever have an argument with a traditional, realize the importance placed on responsibility and duty. If you ever have an argument with a participative, know that what is valued is brotherhood and love. If you ever have conflict with an individualist, know that what is important is freedom and liberty. These differences explain why people can fail to communicate and still respect each other at a basic level. Participatives and individualists realize that traditionals uphold an important quality with commitment to responsibility, while traditionals and individualists recognize the universal value in the participative's commitment to love. Finally, traditionals and participatives see the importance of the individualist's dedication to freedom.

Time perspective. The time perspective for traditionals is the future. Because of this, they often have supplies, tools, and money when others do not. For participatives, the time perspective is the near future—tomorrow or next week; they can wait that long. The time perspective for individualists is the present—today. Don't talk to them about the past; they will say, "The past is gone." And don't talk to them about the future; they will say, "The future may never come." Individualists are primarily interested in here-and-now experience and living life fully in the moment.

It is interesting to see the influence of all three styles in American culture—traditional, participative, and individualistic. It can be argued that this diversity gives strength to the society. Consider the tenets that reflect each style. America is a nation of laws (traditional), conceived by and for people (participative), and dedicated to freedom and the rights of individuals (individualistic).

A summary of the styles of interpersonal relations is presented in Table 15–1.

**Table 15–1
Interpersonal Styles**

Behavior/Value	Traditional	Participative	Individualist
Form of control	Rules, laws, and policies	Interpersonal commitments	What I think is right or needed
Basis of action	Direction from authorities	Discussion and agreement with others	Direction from within
To be avoided	Deviation from authoritative direction	Failure to reach agreement	Not being oneself
Perception of responsibility	Superordinate powers	Colleagues and self	Self
Goals desired	Compliance	Consensus and smooth human relations	Individual freedom
Basis for growth	Following the established order	Human interaction	Introspection and personal experience
Position in relation to others	Member of hierarchy	Peer group member	Separate person
Material goods	Competition	Collaboration	Taken for granted
Identification and loyalty	Organization	Group	Individual
Time perspective	Future	Near future	Present

Dealing with Different Types of People

Differences in personality can result in perceptions and judgments that are poles apart. You have undoubtedly seen individuals and groups who should be working together smoothly but are not. An awareness of the nature and needs of different types of people is the first step in building relationships. This awareness can lead to new levels of cooperation and success.

Although each person is unique and should be treated according to individual makeup, the following guidelines are useful for meeting the needs of and bringing out the best in people with each style of interpersonal relations. Remember that most people have characteristics of all three styles but tend to develop a preference for one or two over the other(s). The most ardent individualist will have traditional moments, and vice versa.

- **Meeting the needs of traditionals.** Provide work rules and job descriptions with duties spelled out in priority order. Provide an organization chart showing reporting relationships; respect the chain of command. Respect traditions and established ways; appeal to historical precedent. Avoid changes when possible; if impossible, introduce changes slowly. Accentuate reason over emotion when handling problems. Mind your manners and language; be courteous. Establish a career plan with benchmarks for progress, rewards expected, and time frames. Provide tangible rewards for good performance, preferably money. Recognize good work with signs of status, such as diplomas, uniforms, medals, and titles. Reinforce company loyalty through service pins, award banquets, and personal appreciation. Communicate the mission, goals, and objectives of the organization, and provide an action plan. Keep work areas organized, clean, and safe. Finally, be clear and logical when giving orders.
- **Meeting the needs of participatives.** Include them in the decision-making process; use participative management. Provide opportunity for off-the-job social interaction—company picnics, recreation programs, and annual meetings. Emphasize teamwork on the job through task forces, committee projects, quality improvement teams, and other group involvement activities. Have regular, well-run staff meetings; provide ample opportunity for sharing ideas. Ask for opinions, listen to what is said, and then demonstrate responsiveness. Get to know the person—family makeup, off-the-job interests, and personal goals. Appeal to both logic and feelings when dealing with problems; emphasize a joint approach and talk with, not at, the person. Use communication vehicles such as bulletin boards, newsletters, focus groups, telephone hot lines, and the open-door

policy to exchange information. Allow people skills to shine in public relations, teaching, and mediation projects. Provide growth opportunities through in-service training and staff development programs. Finally, keep human relations smooth; consider personal feelings.

- **Meeting the needs of individualists.** Recognize independence and personal freedom; don't supervise too closely. Provide immediate reward for good performance; don't delay gratification. Talk in terms of present; de-emphasize past and future. Provide opportunities for growth through exploration and self-discovery. Keep things stimulating; keep things fun. Focus on meaningful personal experiences, satisfying interpersonal relationships, and important social causes. Provide individual job assignments, and assign work by projects when possible. Accentuate feelings as well as logic when handling problems. Reward good performance with personal time off and personal fulfillment activities. Keep things casual; minimize formality. Avoid rigid controls; allow for questions and creativity. Finally, treat the individualist as a separate person, not as a member of a group or organization.

The concept of interpersonal style is like being right-handed or left-handed. Although people are able to use either hand, they usually prefer one over the other. The preferred hand is generally better developed, making it more efficient and effective to use. You can demonstrate this for yourself by first writing your name as you normally would. Then change hands and sign your name. You can do it, even though it is difficult and feels unnatural.

Solving Personality Differences

Differences in personality can result in communication problems unless there is appreciation for the needs and contributions of different kinds of people. Unless the idea is accepted that it is OK to be different, misunderstanding can develop over any dimension of interpersonal style. When differences occur, there are four steps you can take to improve communication:

Step 1: Talk it out. Silence results in emotional wear and tear on everyone. At the same time, it prevents any possibility of solving problems. The silent treatment is a negative treatment; anyone can be negative. Use the positive approach and talk it out:

- *Where:* Talk it out in private so that all parties can communicate in an uncensored and honest way. Unless the truth is known, a problem will never be fully resolved.

- *When:* Talk it out when people are fresh. Otherwise, they won't be able to think clearly, much less express themselves clearly.

- *How:* Be sure every word spoken passes three important tests: Is it true? Is it necessary? Is it kind?

Step 2: Be understanding. Saint Augustine said, *Audi partem alteram*—Hear the other side. As a sioux Indian saying goes, "You can't understand another person until you have walked a mile in his shoes." So see things from the woman's point of view; see the man's side. See things from the boss's perspective; see them through the customer's eyes. See things from the different perspectives of traditionals, participatives, and individualists. Empathy can go a long way toward promoting understanding.

Also, try to understand the forces—past and present—in another person's life that may have influenced and helped shape her or his personality. You may understand Mary better if you know what it was like to be raised as an only child. You may understand John better if you know what it was like to be raised in a large family. Consider the differences between being brought up a Roman Catholic in Cleveland, Ohio; growing up Jewish in New York City; and being raised Baptist in Birmingham,

Alabama. If you do not know what it was like being a child in Mexico City, you may want to ask.

*Step 3: **Be flexible.*** Be willing to compromise. If people are frozen in different styles or points of view, no amount of talking will result in good relations. Remember, everyone must be flexible. If one party is always the one to compromise, a sense of fairness is violated and the relationship will ultimately deteriorate. People may stay in a relationship physically but leave it emotionally.

*Step 4: **Be tolerant.*** Benjamin Franklin once said: "Keep your eyes wide open before marriage and half shut afterwards." This idea applies in all human relationships. Recognize that differences in personality are unavoidable, that few people live or work with their identical twin, and that tolerance of different styles—traditional, participative, and individualistic—is necessary if communication, teamwork, and a one-team attitude are to be achieved.

Leadership Needs and Organizational Contributions of Different Styles

An important point to remember is that different types of people need different treatment to be satisfied and to achieve their full potential. The absence of planning and clear guidelines is particularly upsetting to traditionals. Conflict and impersonal relationships take an especially heavy toll on participatives. Strict rules and close supervision represent a hostile environment for individualists. The most effective leaders honor the needs of all three types of people. Each interpersonal style has positive qualities, and an organization with variety can benefit by a balance of styles.[47]

- *Traditionals* bring roots, stability, and discipline that every organization needs if it is going to grow and prosper. They provide systems and procedures that allow a lot of people to work together in an organized way.

- *Participatives* are interactive and friendly. They provide the glue that holds people together. As leaders, they are participative; as followers, they are good team players. Participatives are the harmonizing agents needed by every family, work group, and organization. Participatives provide warmth and support by their very nature.

- *Individualists* provide new ideas and creativity. They are independent and resist close supervision, but when personally motivated, they are dynamic and creative. An organization needs creativity within to remain vibrant and develop new markets, new products, and new initiatives, especially if it exists in a competitive environment.

Mixing Personalities to Strengthen the Group

In building a team, some leaders select members in their own image. They choose associates with personalities similar to their own. This approach can limit the potential of the group in meeting its goals. Leaders should instead consider what members with different styles can gain from each other. The following table shows how each style of interpersonal relations can add balance, flexibility, and overall effectiveness to a group or organization.

Strengths of Traditionals	Strengths of Participatives	Strengths of Individualists
■ Provide clarity of assignment.	■ Care about people.	■ Challenge the system.
■ Organize efforts.	■ Bring harmony and peace.	■ Find flaws in procedures.
■ Give attention to detail.	■ Teach and give counsel.	■ Tackle problems with zest.
■ Adhere to standards.	■ Give encouragement to others.	■ Provide reform where needed.
■ Appreciate traditions.	■ Instill team spirit.	■ Generate new ideas.
■ Remember facts and figures.	■ Persuade and motivate.	■ Focus energies on the present.
■ Give structure and order.	■ Are sensitive to others and aware of their needs.	■ Accentuate possibilities.
■ Provide consistency.	■ Provide warmth and support.	■ Celebrate the individual.

As an organization experiences greater diversity, there is a need for greater tolerance. With sufficient tolerance, the different positive qualities of traditional, participative, and individualistic types of people can help the organization achieve its full potential.

Table 15–2 provides an overall description of each style of interpersonal relations.

Table 15–2 An Overall Description of Each Style of Interpersonal Relations	Issue/Subject	Traditional	Participative	Individualistic
	Preferred social form	Formal organization	Group interaction	Individualism
	Leadership style	Organizer, director	Participative, inclusive	Entrepreneurial, creative
	Strategic emphasis	Stability and standards	Communication and teamwork	Innovation and change
	Behavioral norms	Rules, policies, procedures	Warmth and support	Independent effort
	Decision-making	Leader decides	Group decides	Individual decides
	Core value	Responsibility	Love	Freedom
	Public persona	Conservative, traditional	Collegial, flexible	Liberal, unconventional
	Leadership needs	Clarity, predictability, dependability	Encouragement, involvement, appreciation	Meaningful work and freedom to act
	Special characteristics	Prepares for the future	Needs to be needed	Lives life fully in the moment

Interpersonal Styles and Leadership Effectiveness

For a practical application showing that all three styles of interpersonal relations are important for organizational success, consider the case of five organization presidents:

- The first president was individualistic. He was a creative visionary whose genius was to found and physically create the organization. He was innovative and entrepreneurial.

- The second president was traditional, combining courtly ways with a basic goodness of character. His concern for people became a model and standard for others who would continue to serve the organization.

- The third president was participative, a master of diplomacy and persuasion. Gifted at finding the middle ground in disputes and the high ground in direction, he brought stability to the organization.

- The fourth president was versatile, with roughly equal amounts of all three styles. His administrative approach was traditional, or chain-of-command; his manner in dealing with people was participative; and his international initiatives were individualistic.

- The fifth president was a mixture of individualistic and participative. His creativity and ability to work with people were extraordinary, and he met the organization's traditional needs through excellent subordinates who provided needed structure and organization.

How can five people be so different, yet so effective? The answer is that as important as interpersonal style is, there are other factors that are even more important. These are character, leadership, and tolerance of diversity.

- *Character.* Each of the five presidents told the truth as he believed it to be, and in any moral dilemma, consideration of others came first. Think about it: We will forgive a person anything—odd dress, strange habits, even personality differences—when character is good.

- *Leadership.* All five presidents employed universal principles of effective leadership. Each had a vision and a plan. Each kept job knowledge current to solve problems and advance the organization. Each demonstrated a humanistic approach in dealing with people.

- *Diversity.* All five presidents showed understanding, responsiveness, and flexibility in relating to all types of people—young and old, black and white, male and female, and traditional, participative, and individualistic. Each was tolerant of differences and valued diversity as a strength.

In dealings with other people, the leader faces the challenges of understanding and valuing different types of people, and of being wise, caring, and flexible in meeting their needs. To the degree this challenge is met, individuals will be served and organizations will prosper by the gifts they bring.

What does it take to meet this challenge? First is a sincere belief that the greatest good for all individuals can best be achieved by working together. Second is the knowledge that diversity enriches individuals and groups. Third is the day-to-day practice of considering the interests and meeting the needs of others. Ask yourself how you are doing in these three key areas, and what you can do to improve.

Personality Consistency—The Big Five Personality Traits

Some aspects of personality change little over time. Researchers have identified five robust dimensions or traits, each of which shows considerable stability from one situation to another and over time, as well as across cultures: **openness to experience, conscientiousness, extroversion, agreeableness, and neuroticism.** (See Table 15–3.)

Table 15–3
The Big Five Personality Traits and Their Stability Over Time[48]

Trait	Quality of Individual High in That Trait	Stability Over Six Years 1.0 is the highest
Openness to experience	Imaginative, creative, original, curious, independent, adventurous, variety-loving	.83
Conscientiousness	Careful, reliable, hardworking, well-organized, punctual, persevering, dependable	.79
Extroversion	Sociable, talkative, fun-loving, outgoing, active, people-oriented, affectionate	.82
Agreeableness	Soft-hearted, trusting, generous, lenient, good-natured, courteous, considerate	.63
Neuroticism	Anxious, temperamental, self-conscious, worrying, emotional, vulnerable, highly strung	.83

R. McCrae, and P. Costa, "Personality Trait Structure as a Human Universal," *American Psychologist* 52 (1997): 509–516.

It is believed that neuroticism and extroversion are more strongly influenced by heredity than environment, while the other three dimensions are thought to be determined more by environment, although they also have a genetic component. All five factors of personality have been consistently observed in both Eastern and Western cultures.

An interesting example of personality consistency comes from David McClelland, who has been one of the major figures in personality research. McClelland describes his encounters over a period of years with a man originally known as Richard Alpert:

In the early 1960s, Richard Alpert was a psychologist at Stanford and Harvard, very verbal, charming, successful. He could hold classes spellbound. Alpert was ambitious, interested in influencing others, and had a strong need for power accompanied by guilt about wanting such power.

When he was a young faculty member, Alpert got involved with Timothy Leary, another Harvard professor who was experimenting with LSD and who advised young people of that time to "turn on, tune in, and drop out." Alpert did all three. He left Harvard, drifted about for a few years, then went to India, where he stayed at the ashram (study center) of a *guru*. Eventually Alpert came back to the United States with a new name—Ram Dass—and a new philosophy.

When I first saw Ram Dass again in the early 1970s he seemed like a completely transformed person. His appearance was totally different from what it had been. He was wearing long Indian style clothes with beads around his neck; he was nearly bald but had grown a long bushy beard. He had given away all his possessions, refusing his father's inheritance, carried no money on his person, and for a time lived as a nomad in a van which was all he had in the world. He had given up drugs, abandoned his career as a psychologist, no longer wanted even to save the world, and talked all the time as if he were "nobody special," although previously it had been clear to himself and others that he was somebody special.

Yet after spending some time with him, I found myself saying over and over again, "It's the same old Dick." He was still very intelligent, he was still verbally fluent, and he was still charming. At a somewhat less obvious level, Alpert was very much involved in high drama, just as he had always been. I would certainly conclude that he continues to have a strong interest in power. Furthermore he still feels guilty about being so interested in power.[49]

A meta-analysis of studies on personality and leadership supports the following generalizations:

- People high in openness to experience tend to be informative, creative, insightful, and curious. These qualities are important in jobs requiring imagination and unconventional thinking.[50]
- People high in conscientiousness tend to be thorough, organized, self-disciplined, and dependable. They are responsible, able to plan, and achievement-oriented. These qualities positively correlate with work success across a broad spectrum of occupations.[51]
- People high in extroversion tend to be active, outgoing, assertive, and sociable. These qualities are associated with jobs requiring high social contact and service to others.[52]
- People high in agreeableness tend to be good-natured, courteous, trusting, and nurturing. These qualities are helpful when tasks require getting along with others and dealing effectively with conflicts.[53]
- People high in neuroticism tend to be anxious, emotional, insecure, and worrying. People low in neuroticism perform well in work requiring a positive attitude and keeping things in perspective.[54]

Some experts suggest that high conscientiousness, high agreeableness, and low neuroticism represent a common underlying characteristic broadly described as "getting along"; while people who have high extroversion and high openness to experience share a common underlying factor called "getting ahead."[55]

Extroversion is the factor most strongly associated with leadership effectiveness. Conscientiousness is the second most associated factor. Openness to experience and low neuroticism are the next most related factors. Agreeableness is only weakly associated with leadership effectiveness. In summary people high in openness, conscientiousness, and extroversion, and low in neuroticism are more likely to emerge as leaders than their counterparts.[56]

The Big Five model of personality has its roots in the Lexical Hypothesis of Francis Galton, 1884. Galton believed that personality traits are captured in the words people use to describe each other and that are encoded in dictionaries.[57] During the 1930s, Gordon Allport and his associates at Harvard University expanded on Galton's work. The research task of personality theorists in the last half of the twentieth century was to reduce Allport's personality traits to a scientifically acceptable number of underlying factors.[58]

In 1949, D. W. Fiske was the first to identify five factors from "self" and "other" ratings of subject persons. In 1961, E. C. Tupes and R. E. Christal were the first researchers to identify a variant of what is now known as the Big Five.[59] In 1990, L. R. Goldberg identified these factors as openness to experience, conscientiousness, extroversion, agreeableness, and neuroticism. In 1992, P. T. Costa and R. R. McCrae developed a widely used personality inventory to measure the Big Five traits.[60]

At least some personality traits are strongly influenced by heredity. This helps explain why identical twins who are raised apart often show pronounced similarities in their personalities. Research shows that just as people inherit variations in physical appearance, they also inherit variations in body chemistry that influence how sensitive they are to different types of stimulation as well as the types of feelings they generally experience.[61]

A person highly sensitive to stress may have higher neuroticism than other individuals. A person with a high need for stimulation may be more extroverted and open to experience than others. A soft-hearted and considerate person may be more agreeable than others. And a person with a high need for order may be more conscientious than others. Personality is also formed by people's experiences in the world, not just by biology. Role models, social conditioning, and other environmental factors help shape personality traits.[62]

For an evaluation of yourself on the Big Five Personality Traits see Exercise 15–2.

Exercise 15–2 The Big Five Personality Test

How true is each of the following characteristics in describing you? Use the five-point scale below:

1 = Not at all true of me; I am almost never this way.

2 = Mostly not true of me; I am rarely this way.

3 = Neither true nor untrue of me; I can't decide.

4 = Mostly true of me; I am often this way.

5 = Almost always true of me; I am usually this way.

1.__Imaginative	13.__Fun-loving	25.__Emotional
2.__Careful	14.__Generous	26.__Adventurous
3.__Sociable	15.__Self-conscious	27.__Dependable
4.__Softhearted	16.__Curious	28.__People-oriented
5.__Anxious	17.__Well-organized	29.__Considerate
6.__Creative	18.__Outgoing	30.__Nervous
7.__Reliable	19.__Good-natured	31.__Variety-loving
8.__Talkative	20.__Worrying	32.__Responsible
9.__Trusting	21.__Independent	33.__Gregarious
10.__Temperamental	22.__Persevering	34.__Kind
11.__Original	23.__Active	35.__Highly strung
12.__Hardworking	24.__Courteous	

Scoring:

To compute your score, copy your answers below. Then total the column for each scale. There is a maximum of 35 points for each scale.

Scale O	Scale C	Scale E	Scale A	Scale N
1.	2.	3.	4.	5.
6.	7.	8.	9.	10.
11.	12.	13.	14.	15.
16.	17.	18.	19.	20.
21.	22.	23.	24.	25.
26.	27.	28.	29.	30.
31.	32.	33.	34.	35.
Total	Total	Total	Total	Total

Interpretation:

<u>Scale O</u>: Openness to Experience. People with high scores are described as adventurous, imaginative, and variety-loving.

<u>Scale C</u>: Conscientiousness. People with high scores are described as well-organized, responsible, and reliable.

<u>Scale E</u>: Extroversion. People with high scores are described as outgoing, sociable, and people-oriented.

<u>Scale A</u>: Agreeableness. People with high scores are described as good-natured, considerate, and kind.

<u>Scale N</u>: Neuroticism. People with high scores are described as anxious, emotional, and highly strung.

Part Seven Summary

After reading Part Seven, you should know the following key concepts, principles, and terms. Fill in the blanks from memory, or copy the answers listed below.

Business leader (a) _____ recommends developing others and delegating authority as a means of freeing up the leader to tackle new or undone tasks, thus multiplying the leader's effectiveness. In today's workplace, the ability to (b) _____ is not only desirable but also essential for organizational success, because all the talents of all employees need to be fully utilized. Established rules for effective delegation include (c) _____, _____, _____, _____, and _____. (d) _____ is one of the most important and useful leadership skills. Proven principles for assigning work effectively include (e) _____, _____, _____, _____, _____, and _____. Leaders should consider (f) _____, _____, and _____ when assiging work and selecting employees. (g) _____, the ability to work well in cooperation with people, is equally important at all levels of management responsibility. The (h) _____, popularized by author Laurence Peter, refers to being overpromoted to one's level of incompetency. Just as individuals are different, so are whole groups of people different in (i) _____. (j) _____ bring roots, stability, and discipline to the workplace. They respect the chain of command, and respond positively to high standards of work and conduct, as well as clear and logical orders. (k) _____ are warm and friendly, providing the harmony, peace, and teamwork that every work group needs. They respond positively to participative leadership and consideration in human interactions. (l) _____ are dynamic and creative when personally motivated. They avoid close supervision and respond positively to individual assignments requiring unconventional ideas and methods. When conflicts occur between different personalities, constructive steps are (m) _____, _____, _____, and _____. The "Big Five" personality traits that show stability over time are (n) _____, _____, _____, _____, and _____.

Answer Key for Part Seven Summary

a. **Bill Gates,** page 302

b. **delegate,** page 302

c. (any five) **share power with employees; don't delegate the bad jobs, saving the good ones for yourself; know your employees; use delegation as a development tool; delegate work fairly among all employees; be sure to back your employees if delegated authority is questioned; let employees know what decisions they have authority to make and delegate decision making to the lowest possible level; delegate with consistency; delegate whole tasks and allow sufficient time to get jobs done; insist on clear communication; make good use of questions when delegating work; explain the importance of assignments; learn to live with work styles that are not like your own; avoid delegating tasks that are pets, personal, or petty; follow the three D's for all work—do it, delegate it, or ditch it,** pages 307–308

d. **Assigning work effectively,** page 308

e. (any six) **consider the availability of the employee's time and whether this is the ideal person to do the job; use work assignments as a means of developing people; know exactly what you want to communicate before giving an order; if many duties or steps are involved in an order, follow oral communication with a note, and keep a copy; ask rather than tell, but leave no doubt that you expect** compliance; use the correct language for the employee's training level; make assignments in a logical sequence, using clear and concise language; be considerate but never apologetic when asking someone to do a job; talk deliberately and authoritatively, but avoid shouting or making an unnecessary show of power; take responsibility for the orders you give; give people the opportunity to ask questions and express opinions; follow up to make sure assignments are being carried out properly, and modify them if the situation warrants, pages 308–310

f. performance, attitude, psychosocial fit, page 310

g. **Relational skill,** page 315

h. **Peter Principle,** page 319

i. style of interpersonal relations, page 320

j. **Traditionals,** page 326

k. **Participatives,** page 326

l. **Individualists,** page 326

m. **talk it out, be understanding, be flexible, be tolerant,** pages 332–333

n. openness to experience, conscientiousness, extroversion, agreeableness, neuroticism, page 335

Reflection Points—Personal Thoughts on Effective Delegation, How to Assign Work, and the Role of Personality

Complete the following questions and activities to personalize the content of Part Seven. Space is provided for writing your thoughts.

■ Discuss the role of delegation in the leadership process. Do you know a leader with delegation weakness? Do you know a leader with delegation strengths?

_____

_____

■ Do you know a leader who is effective at assigning work and giving orders? What principles and techniques are used?

_____

_____

■ Have you developed the technical, relational, and conceptual skills appropriate for the work you do? Discuss.

_____

_____

■ Discuss the concept of the vital shift and the pros and cons of the new-job tryout. Give real-life examples.

_____

_____

■ Discuss the role of personality in your work experience. Are you primarily traditional, participative, or individualistic? Does your organization value your style of interpersonal relations? Is your supervisor wise, caring, and flexible in meeting your needs?

_____

_____

■ Complete the following exercise: Form a group consisting of a variety of personality styles. Discuss best practices (policies and actions) an organization can use to meet the needs and gain the special contributions of each style.

_____

_____

■ Imagine receiving job offers from three great employers: *Traditional* → FBI, *Participative* → Southwest Airlines, *Individualistic* → Pixar. Which culture is most appealing to you?

_____

_____

■ Here is a challenge: Write a six-word memoir that captures the essence of your personality and/or life story. Julius Caesar may have written, "I came, I saw, I conquered." Much can be learned from this self-reflective exercise.

_____

_____

Part Seven Video Case

Generation Next Changes the Face of the Workplace

In a report on changing generations in the workplace, Judy Woodruff of PBS uncovers some stark differences that will have drastic affects on the workplace in coming years. According to Jo Muse, the CEO of Muse Communications, Generation Y, those workers in their early 20s, want different things than did the Baby Boomers. Muse cites time as one major issue—Generation Y workers want time off sometimes as early as six months into their employment with a company and they don't care if its paid or not.

This is very different from the way work was viewed by the Baby Boomers who "paid their dues" or "put in their time" before expecting such perks. Muse feels that perhaps Generation Y wants the seniority system as we now know it to be "thrown out the door." Generation Y is an ambitious group who expects and strives for financial success by their 30s or 40s. According to one of Muse's Generation Y workers, everything they have had up to now was "microwaveable"—in other words, instantaneous—and they expect this with their careers as well.

According to Stan Smith who works for the Next Generation Initiative project for Deloitte-Touche, the generations all view work differently. Baby Boomers are all "Work. Work. Work" and Generation X would say "Work. Work. Wanna work some more? Let's talk about it." Generation Y however, would say "Work. Work. You want me to work even more? How lame!" Employers are trying to adapt to these younger worker preferences. They have no choice—due to basic supply and demand, as the Baby Boomers retire, there will be fewer and fewer workers to replace them.

Perhaps one of the biggest differences between the generations is the acceptance of technology. Generation Y is a very tech-savvy group, which influences their workplace expectations. According to Smith, for them, technology is an extension of how they relate to people, which changes how they work. Through technology, they can work anyplace anytime.

When talking with members of Generation Y, Woodruff found that this group describes themselves as being tech-savvy and some cited technology as being the biggest difference between them and their parents. For example, one Generation Y'er said his parents would pull out maps to plan a trip, where he would simply use Google Local. According to Jaclyn DeLammetres, a member of Generation Y, they feel they deserve jobs that are creative, interesting, and fast-paced where they can be their own bosses.

This group has been told they are smart, different, and special, and they bring these attitudes, along with their technology skills to the workplace. Smith's Next Generation Initiatives program at Deloitte provides young workers with confidential career counseling as well as online tools that allow them to learn about their strengths and weaknesses. Through the efforts of the Next Generation Initiatives program, Deloitte has retained over 700 employees who would have left, saving nearly $100 million in employee turnover costs. According to Smith, this worker trend is more than just a "phase of life" issue, and countering its effects is not an option, it's a reality.

Questions for Discussion

1. Why is addressing this issue so important? Shouldn't workers adjust to meet the needs of their employers?

2. What can employers who can't afford such extensive programs as the Deloitte organization do to address the changing preferences of their younger workers' wants and needs? What would you like to see your employer or prospective employer do to address your wants and needs to retain you?

For more information, see http://www.pbs.org/newshour/generation-next/index-old.html and http://pewresearch.org/millennials.

Action Assignment

As a bridge between learning and doing, complete the following action assignment.

1. What is the most important idea you have learned in Part Seven?

2. How can you apply what you have learned? What will you do, with whom, where, when, and, most important, why?

Part 8 Developing Others

16. **The Leader as Coach**
17. **Helping People through Change and Burnout Prevention**

THE BEST WAY OF EDUCATING PRINCES is to teach them to become intimate with all sorts and conditions of men. Their commonest handicap is that they do not know their people. People are always masked in their company because they are the masters. They meet many subjects, but no real people. Hence, bad choice of favorites and ministers that dims the fame of kings and ruins their subjects. Teach a prince to be sober, chaste, pious, generous, and you will teach him how to love his people and his kingly dignity; and you will implant in him every virtue at the same time.

—Marquis of Vauvenargues, 1715–1747
Maxims and Reflections of Luc de Clapiers

Learning Objectives

After studying Part Eight, you will be able to:
- Describe the role of the leader as coach and developer of people.
- Identify the conditions conducive to growth.
- Know how a leader can help people through change, including the importance of attitude and personal example.
- Identify where you are in the burnout process, including steps that can be taken for emergency, short-term, and long-term aid.
- Identify the characteristics of a hardy personality.
- Determine your level of adaptive capacity. Are you a stress-resistant person?

The Leader as Coach

The Native American totem for *teacher* is Wolf. As the moon rises every night, Wolf always finds something new to learn from it. Leaders, too, in exploring life may discover new truths to share with the rest of the clan, the human race. How does a leader show concern for others? An important way is by taking interest in people and by helping them grow to their full potential. The signs of caring leadership appear primarily among the followers. Are the followers engaged in their work and striving to do their best? Are they learning and growing in knowledge, skill, and attitude?[1]

Many leaders view **developing others** as the most relevant and rewarding of all their tasks. Effective leaders at all levels of responsibility—chief executive, middle manager, and frontline supervisor—are aware that the failure experienced by Roger in the following story can occur in the adult world of work as well.

Why Can't Roger Learn?

When Roger was first observed in the classroom, he was beginning to fail and to feel defeated, but he was trying. When the observers walked in, he was listening with obvious interest to a story his teacher was reading. He sat quietly for at least 15 minutes. After the story, the teacher wrote some letters of the alphabet on the blackboard and requested that the children copy them on a sheet of paper she passed out. Roger picked up the crayon and looked at his neighbor's paper to see what he was supposed to do; he then started to write. The teacher moved over to him, took the crayon out of his hand, and said firmly and with minor irritation, "Not a crayon, Roger; use a pencil."

Roger glanced at the little girl on his right, in obvious embarrassment. He wanted her to like him. He turned back to the teacher and said in a small voice, "I don't have a pencil." The teacher turned to the class and announced, "Some of us are not prepared. Who has a pencil to lend Roger?" Another child, eager to please the teacher, moved over to Roger and handed him a pencil. Roger was looking at the floor in embarrassment, but managed to thank him. In a few moments he again tried to find out how to do the assigned task. He watched his neighbor, but the child turned to him and said angrily, "Stop looking. Do your own stuff."

Finding no answer to his dilemma, Roger decided to escape by going up to sharpen his pencil. Another child was ahead of him, so Roger waited patiently for his turn. His smallness in comparison to the other children was very evident. Two other children came to sharpen their pencils and pushed Roger aside. He allowed the intrusion, because what can be done when others are so much bigger and aggressive? Another child came up and also attempted to push Roger aside. Anger flooded over his face. He had to show them that he had importance too. He attempted to push the intruder away saying, "It's my turn." The teacher noticed Roger pushing and said angrily, "Roger, take your seat, immediately." The teacher then glanced over at the observers, grimaced with distaste, and shook her head. She was sure that they shared insight into Roger's problems.

Roger walked dejectedly back to his seat. After a few moments of depressed staring at his paper, he leaned toward the girl on his left and whispered desperately, "How do you do it?" The girl frowned and said, "Shh-h," and hit him on the head with her pencil.

The teacher noticed difficulty again and assuming that Roger was responsible (after all, he is such a problem), said in exasperation, "Roger, will you please pay attention to your paper!"

Roger glanced around the room to see if everyone else was looking at him. He stared down at his shoe, his face red. He could have been saying, "What's wrong with me? Why can't I do anything right? Why does everyone hate me?" He still wanted to try; he had not reached the place where complete failure and hostility had taken over. Therefore, he attempted to do something about the hated paper before him. He made some marks; then, as though talking to himself, he said, "Is this good?" He glanced over at the paper of the boy on his right. As if in answer to his own question, he said, "Oh, ugh. Look at his." He wanted to think somebody was doing worse than he was. The boy stuck out his tongue at him, and Roger turned listlessly back to his paper.

The teacher was coming up the aisle again and paused at Roger's seat. "Roger, we are not writing our names, we are just practicing M's." She hurried over to the blackboard without showing him what to do and started moving through the next lesson. Several more letters were presented. Roger became restless. He didn't understand. He wiggled in his seat and then stood up. The children began to practice the letters again. Roger became very frustrated as he found he was unable to form them. He let his paper fall to the floor.

"Pass your papers to the end of the table," the teacher said. "Roger, get your paper," said the little girl next to him, "Roger, I'm telling. We have to pass them down." The angry voice of the teacher was once again heard. "Roger, get your paper off the floor." Roger complied, but he hit the paper with his pencil. He didn't like it. It was no good. He felt bad. He didn't want anyone else to see it.

The teacher gave all the children another piece of paper to continue the letter-making practice. Roger somehow found new determination and tried again. He followed the teacher's movements in the air, whispering to himself in concentration. The angry little girl leaned over to him and said, "Shh-h," and hit him on the head with her pencil again. Roger wanted her to like him, so he did nothing. But his frustration had to be expressed. He zoomed his pencil in the air, making a quiet airplane noise. He forgot the task. The teacher scolded him again and wearily exhorted him to pay attention.

The observation lasted only one hour. What happens over time to such a person, who experiences hour after hour of failure? Two months after the initial observation, Roger refused to try any learning task. He often crawled on the floor like an animal, making odd noises. He could not sit still for more than five minutes, and he hit his peers and yelled at them. His teacher became frantic. His mother was so worried that she came to school often and peered through the window of the schoolroom door. "He cries every day about school. He says everyone hates him," she explained.

Failure and a particular kind of punishment had distorted Roger. In many schools where administrators and teachers are unaware of the seriousness of allowing a child to fail or of using aversive techniques to change behavior, they still ask about such a child, "Why did it happen?" "Probably the parents," the accusing answer echoes down the school halls.[2]

Effective leaders know that Roger's failure wasn't necessary, that preventing such failure is important, and that their own ability to coach is often the key. It is a proven fact that expectation of failure can help bring about failure. Conversely, expectation of success can help bring about success. Children have been found to score from two to three points higher when an IQ test is administered by a teacher who conveys expectation for success than when the same test is given by a teacher who does not convey high expectations. This phenomenon is called the Pygmalion effect.[3]

Eugene Krantz, NASA Flight Director of *Apollo 13,* describes the role of the Pygmalion effect in the world of work. Expecting high performance is prerequisite to its achievement among those who work with you. Your high standards and optimistic anticipations will not guarantee a favorable outcome, but their absence will assuredly create the opposite.[4] Closely related to Pygmalion is the Galatea effect, when an individual's high self-expectation leads to high performance.[5]

The role of positive expectations and the strength of the self-fulfilling prophecy has been widely supported in the workplace. Research by J. Sterling Livingston confirmed and popularized the concept. A meta-analysis of 17 studies involving 3,000 employees shows the positive power of beliefs to influence results, including employees considered by management, and by themselves, to have low expectations.[6] It should be noted that the self-fulfilling prophecy works in the negative direction as well. Low expectation of success leading to poor performance is known as the Golem effect.[7]

Leadership author and educator John Gardner explains the importance of the leader as teacher and developer of people:

If one is leading, teaching, dealing with young people or engaged in any other activity that involves influencing, directing, guiding, helping or nurturing, the whole tone of the relationship is conditioned by one's faith in human possibilities. That is the generative element, the source of the current that gives life to the relationship.[8]

How do high-performance companies like Great American Insurance, Google, and others capitalize on the power of the Pygmalion and Galatea effects? Management educator Jeff Walter explains—the task is accomplished by using combinations of the following: (1) Treat all employees like top draft choices—expect success; (2) recognize that everyone has the potential to increase performance; (3) set high performance "stretch goals"; (4) provide the input and resources needed to achieve success; (5) provide constructive feedback and redirection when necessary; and (6) reward employees for hard work, dedication, team work, and jobs well done.[9]

The Development of Others

Motivation expert Zig Ziglar once observed that he had read a lot of birth announcements, all of them indicating that the newborn was a boy or a girl. None of them announced the arrival of a farmer, a doctor, an engineer, or a member of any other profession. There is an old saying—"If you ever see a turtle on a fence post, you know it didn't get there by itself." So it is with people: Performers in every field are developed, not born. Effective leaders recognize the importance of developing people. Like the productive farmer who plants good seeds and cares for them properly, effective leaders view developing others as an essential key to success.

Leading is like coaching in many ways. In basketball, for example, the coach cannot cross the line and move onto the playing court. She works in advance of playing time and on the side of the action. Before the game, she prepares her players by anticipating the problems they will face and by readying them to meet those problems. She trains, advises, and encourages, but she never touches the ball. The coach cannot do the players' work for them. Instead, she is a mentor and teacher.[10]

The leader as teacher is a concept that has been with us for centuries. The term *mentor* is derived from *The Odyssey,* in which Homer describes Ulysses as choosing his trusted friend, Mentor, to look after his son, Telemachus, as Ulysses begins his 10-year journey. Mentor gives Telemachus good counsel, and he cares for and protects him as his teacher. These attributes have been central to our modern concept of mentoring in the workplace.[11]

Types of Coaches/Leaders

Just as there is no single best way to lead, there is no one best way to develop others. Each leader brings unique personal experiences and talent to the task. The following list describes five types of coaches/leaders.[12] Keep in mind that not all types are appropriate for all learners in all circumstances.

- *Shamans* heal through the use of personal power. They focus the attention of their followers on themselves. When this approach is combined with unusual gifts and skills, shamans are charismatic. They have power, energy, and commitment that they use to energize others.

- *Priests* claim power through office. They are agents of omnipotent authority, and the people who follow them are taught to see themselves as set apart from others. Priests establish structure, order, and continuity—a past program and a plan for the immediate and distant future. Priests operate in a hierarchy with roles and duties in a hierarchical ladder.

- *Elected leaders* undergo trials, self-transformation, training, or some other rite to achieve their positions. Elected leaders derive power not only from their own experience, but also from the mandate of their followers. Consent of followers constitutes much of the power of these coaches/leaders.

- *Missionaries* are goal-directed. Usually, missions involve a utopian view of the future and a program for achieving reforms. Missionaries teach out of personal conviction, believing in certain ideals and seeing it as a duty to pass on these ideals to others.

- *Mystic healers* seek the source of illness and health in the follower's personality. Mystic healers try to discover the statue in the marble and seek, like Michelangelo, to find what can be created from the raw material. To be successful, these coaches/leaders require unselfish motivation and considerable sensitivity, as well as flexibility to vary treatment according to the nature and needs of each individual.

Much of contemporary leading and coaching incorporates the priestly, elected, and missionary types. The priest brings continuity and hierarchy to the task, as power is delegated by the most powerful, and people at each level, division, or unit are differentiated from others. The elected leader gains authority by election, and followership is by consent of the governed. Missionaries can be found in many organizations that have some kind of central mission—economic, religious, political, social service, or other. Shamans and mystic healers may or may not operate within the bounds or the dictates of an organization. Their approach to developing others tends to be individualistic and personalized.

Principles of Developing Others

Like pine trees that are stunted if they grow near the timberline, more fully developed if they grow farther down the mountainside, and tall and green if they grow in the valley, people also experience maximum development under certain conditions.

Personal conditions conducive to growth are the following:[13]

1. People grow when there is a felt need.
2. People grow when they are encouraged by someone they respect.
3. People grow when their plans move from general goals to specific actions.
4. People grow as they move from a condition of lower to higher self-esteem.
5. People grow as they move from external to internal commitment.

Organizational conditions conducive to growth are the following:[14]

1. Basic respect for the worth and dignity of all people is a cardinal value.
2. Individual differences are recognized, and a variety of learning experiences are provided.
3. Each person is addressed at his or her level of development and is helped to grow to fuller potential.
4. Good communications prevail—people express themselves honestly and listen with respect to the views of others.
5. Growth is rewarded through recognition and tangible signs of approval—commendation, promotion, income, and the like.

The *learning organization* is a familiar term for successful leaders and companies. Learning organizations use six ingredients to discover, create, and transfer knowledge and skills: (1) They search constantly for new knowledge and ways to apply it; (2) they carefully review both successes and failures; (3) they benchmark and implement best practices; (4) they share lessons learned; (5) they reward innovation; (6) experienced and new employees learn together.[15]

Principles to follow in developing others include the following:

1. *Have a respectful attitude.* Deep inside each person is the desire to achieve something, to be somebody. If you tap into that desire and demonstrate that you believe in the person, self-respect can be ignited. Ultimately, it is self-respect that fuels success. The effective leader agrees with W. B. Yeats, who said: "Education is not the filling of a pail, but the lighting of a fire."[16] Consider the story of the banker and the beggar:

There was a banker who would regularly drop a coin in a beggar's cup. Unlike most people, the banker would insist on receiving one of the pencils the beggar had with him. The banker would say, "You are a merchant, and I always expect to receive good value from the merchants with whom I do business."

One day the beggar was gone. Some years later, the banker walked by a concession stand, and there was the former beggar, now a shopkeeper. The shopkeeper said, "I always hoped you might come by some day. You are largely responsible for me being here. You kept telling me that I was a merchant. I started thinking of myself that way. Instead of a beggar receiving gifts, I started selling pencils, lots of them. You gave me self-respect and caused me to look at myself differently."[17]

2. *Build self-esteem.* The importance of developing self-esteem can be seen in the following story:

Thomas J. Watson, Jr. (1914–1993), son of the founder of IBM, initially had trouble living up to his father's charisma and achievements. Watson Sr. was one of the great entrepreneurs of the 20th century. He put IBM on the map and gave the world the motto THINK. In contrast, Watson Jr. even needed a tutor to get through the IBM sales school. "I had no distinctions, no successes," he writes in *Father, Son & Company.*

When Watson started taking flying lessons, however, something important happened. "What a feeling," he says. "I was good at flying, instantly good. I poured everything I had into this activity and gained a lot of personal self-confidence." This small success led to greater successes. Watson became an officer in the U.S. Air Force during WWII. It was in the Air Force that he discovered he had "an orderly mind, the ability to focus on what was important, and to put it across to others."

Watson eventually became the CEO of IBM and launched the company into the Computer Age. In 15 years, he multiplied IBM's earnings almost tenfold. By the time he retired, the IBM he shaped was the greatest success story of America's postwar boom, routing computer-industry rivals like General Electric, RCA, and Sperry-UNIVAC. During his tenure, IBM created more wealth for its shareholders than any other company in business history, an achievement that led *Fortune* magazine in 1987 to declare Watson, "The greatest capitalist who ever lived."[18]

3. *Use the correct medium or combination of techniques.* Consider whether one-on-one coaching, formal education, professional conferences, or on-the-job learning is the best method, or whether a combination of approaches would be most appropriate.

Sabbaticals in various forms are ideal ways to keep leaders fresh and motivated. They have long been a tradition in universities and can be equally effective in the business world. One example is the company with five leaders for every four turns or departments. By rotation, one person is available at any time to study and work on projects that otherwise would never be addressed. New products, markets, and enthusiasm are the by-products of such a system of working sabbaticals. This is a good way to combat the typical syndrome in which people get promoted, learn the job, then get bored, and pass the feeling on to others.

4. *Use coaching versus judging in developing people; consider—purpose, timing, focus, and process.*[19]

Purpose. Judging serves to label performance. Coaching serves to improve performance.

Timing. Judging is time-specific, such as a quarterly review. Coaching is ongoing and provided as needed.

Focus. Judging is standardized for all subjects. Coaching is tailored to each individual.

Process. Judging is unilateral, one-way. Coaching is interactive, two-way.

5. *Practice.* Practice builds proficiency. Most things people learn involve more than abstract thinking; they must be learned with the senses and muscles as well. By actually repairing a car, a person will learn more about automobile maintenance than by merely reading about it. As the Greek dramatist Sophocles said, "Knowledge must come through action." And as Confucius said, "I listen and I hear; I see and I remember; I do and I understand."[20]

Practice is especially important in the development of leaders. As leadership expert Henry Mintzberg explains: "The idea that you can take intelligent but inexperienced young people who have never managed anybody and turn them into highly effective leaders via two years of classroom training is unrealistic. This is the reason cooperative education, internships, and other learn-by-doing assignments are so important."[21]

Training in the Workplace

Management author Gary Hamel asks a challenging question: "Are you learning as fast as the world is changing?" It can be argued that the most successful organizations are masters of learning, and the most effective leaders are masters of teaching.[22]

Both the organization and the individual are helped if people have multiple skills, if they can move easily across functional boundaries, if they are comfortable switching between regular duties and special projects, if growth is valued, and if continuous learning is a way of life. In such organizations, there is an understanding that the employer and employee share responsibility for maintaining proficiency and achieving success. Employers give employees the chance to develop enhanced employability in exchange for better productivity and commitment to the company's purpose for as long as the employee works there.[23]

The American Society of Training and Development (ASTD) states that the overall U.S. commitment to training is approximately 2.34 percent of payroll ($1,103 per employee), with better employers providing substantially more—from 2.5 to 5 percent of payroll.

Annual training hours per employee average 32 hours, with leading employers providing 57 to 62 hours. Leadership development, technical procedures, and information technology are the three most-cited types of training. It should be noted that revenues and overall profitability are positively correlated with training expenditures. Evidence shows that training pays off in terms of higher net sales and gross profitability per employee.[24]

Employers spend $55 billion annually on formal training programs and another $180 billion on informal on-the-job instruction. It is interesting to note that training expenditures as a percentage of payroll are highest in Asia (3.8 percent).[25]

Through research on best practices, ASTD has developed a model of training that supports organizational effectiveness and contributes to individual productivity. Table 16–1 shows a model of highly effective training, including targeted training needs and types of training provided.

Table 16–1 Model of Highly Effective Training[26]	Targeted Training Need	Types of Training Provided
	Ensuring organizational performance	Executive development
		Management training and development
		Supervisory training and development
		Staff/employee training
	Meeting strategic goals	Strategic planning, team building, employee orientation, quality improvement
	Implementing new technology	Technical training
		Scientific and engineering training
		Technician training
		Craft and apprentice training
		Employee skill training
		Data processing and computer training
		Information systems training
	Engaging customers	Sales and marketing training
		Customer service training
	Protecting employees and communities	Health and safety training
		Regulatory compliance (e.g., meeting environmental standards)
	Ensuring job readiness	Basic skills training

Measurement of Learning Effectiveness

The measurement of learning effectiveness is an important issue in today's workplace. The clearest path through this maze continues to be *The Four Levels Approach*, outlined by Donald Kirkpatrick at the University of Wisconsin. Paraphrased, the levels are as follows:

1. *Satisfaction*—generally measured by participant approval ratings.
2. *Learning*—defined as measurable improvement in knowledge, skills, and attitudes.
3. *Application*—understood as on-the-job use of new concepts, principles, tools, and techniques.
4. *Impact*—as measured by improvement in bottom-line results such as sales, quality, customer satisfaction, safety, employee morale, turnover, costs, and profits.

The individual learner tends to be concerned about the first two levels, while managers focus on applications, and sponsors concentrate on impact.[27]

- At Level 1, data are usually gathered by questionnaires administered at the conclusion of a training program. They are a measure of participant satisfaction and typically evaluate content, delivery, and the like.
- At Level 2, learning is measured in terms of increased knowledge, skill, or attitude. Methods range from paper-and-pencil tests to complex job demonstrations.
- At Level 3, the question, "Are learners using new knowledge, skills, and attitudes back at work?" is answered. This can be determined through observation, surveys, and interviews.
- At Level 4, the focus is on business results. Assuming people have learned and are applying what they have learned, what difference does it make? Level 4 evaluation measures return on investment. Are the gains recorded greater than the expenditures for training?

Most training conducted in the United States is evaluated at Level 1, if at all. The next most-used level is Level 2. Levels 3 and 4 are used in the minority of cases, usually because of the time, cost, and skill involved in collecting, evaluating, and reporting the data. Table 16–2 is a sample format for evaluating Level 1 training effectiveness.

**Table 16–2
Four-Factor Training
Evaluation**

The following are four factors of training effectiveness—pace, relevance, value, and participation. On the basis of training you have attended, evaluate each factor on the scale provided.

	Poor		Fair		Average		Good		Excellent	

Pace If the pace of training was either too slow or too fast, indicate with a low evaluation; if the pace of training was just right, indicate with a high evaluation.

1 2 3 4 5 6 7 8 9 10
Too fast or too slow   Just right

Relevance If the subject matter was unimportant, indicate with a low evaluation; if the subject matter was important, indicate with a high evaluation.

1 2 3 4 5 6 7 8 9 10
Unimportant   Important

Value If the training experience was of low value, indicate with a low score; if the training experience was valuable, indicate with a high score.

1 2 3 4 5 6 7 8 9 10
Low value   High value

Participation If participants were not involved, indicate with a low score; if participants were actively involved, indicate with a high score.

1 2 3 4 5 6 7 8 9 10
Low participation   High participation

Comments/Suggestions:

Developing Leaders

Vince Lombardi is famous for saying: "Leaders are not born. They are made. They are made just like anything else, through hard work. That's the price you have to pay to achieve that goal or any goal."[28]

Organizations typically identify a leadership gap and then seek to fill the gap through training efforts. Competency and performance goals are usually set for achieving business results and developing people-building skills. Interventions include classroom instruction, seminars, assessment and feedback, performance coaching, mentoring, and action learning, or field activities. Are the results worth the effort? An example from sports shows the big dividends leadership development can pay.

In the book *Sacred Hoops,* coach Phil Jackson talks about his work with Michael Jordan. With such a gifted athlete, no coach could do much to improve his basketball play. So Jackson focused his efforts with Jordan on making the superstar a true leader of the team. And it worked. In 1989, five years after joining the league and the same year that Jackson became head coach of the Bulls, Jordan began to see his role not just as stealing balls and scoring points, but as a leader whose job also was to help raise the level of play of every other player on the team. It is this contribution, Jordan's ability to help his teammates be better players, more than his superb athletic talent, that made the Chicago Bulls the world's winningest basketball team.[29]

Robert Katz, in his book *Skills of an Effective Administrator,* explains that leadership is a learned skill. Although people possess varying amounts of aptitude to lead, their skills can be improved through training and practice. Furthermore, even those lacking strong innate ability can improve their performance through coaching and learning. This is the rationale for the establishment of leadership schools—Plato's Academy, 387 BC; Aristotle's Lyceum, 355 BC; Oxford University, AD 1117; Harvard University, AD 1636; and the U.S. military academies, as well as over 2,000 corporate universities found in American business, industry, and government by AD 2008.[30]

One good way to learn is by **studying the masters,** those who have gone before. If you observe carefully, you will note a trace of Jonathan Winters in Robin Williams. The Beatles learned from Chuck Berry. Matisse learned from Gauguin. The most effective performers are honest in appraising their current skills and humble enough to learn from others. They copy, adapt, and sometimes surpass the heroes who were the source of their inspiration. They take to heart Yogi Berra's famous slogan, "You can observe a lot by watching."[31]

Individuals who want to develop leadership effectiveness should identify superb leaders and learn from their example. They should observe their behavior and ask questions. Understanding the values and goals of successful leaders, the rationale for their decisions and actions, the principles underlying their skills and techniques, and the resources they use to solve problems and make decisions can serve as an excellent foundation for developing one's own leadership ability.[32]

It should be noted that leadership development is not always a top-down process. Many leaders have grown through the example, advice, and caring encouragement of direct-reports and peers. It must be said that for this to occur, all individuals involved (leaders, subordinates, and/or peers) must show a good deal of maturity and personal courage. Reverse mentoring can be a powerful process for keeping leaders current in both the technical and human aspects of work.

Although much of what is labeled as leadership development is classroom-based and is provided in courses, seminars, and lectures, important growth can come from on-the-job "stretch" experiences and, sometimes, the crucible of crisis. These experiences usually force people to rise to a challenge or endure a trial they have never faced before. Out of adversity, hardship, and even loss can come meaningful development that cannot be easily achieved in the classroom setting.

Experiences having developmental possibilities include early work experience, first-time supervision, responsibility for starting something from scratch or for fixing something (turnaround), expansion of job scope, special projects and task force assignments, and line to staff switch. As an example, an international assignment may help develop a leader to be more open-minded, appreciate different perspectives, improve communication effectiveness, and raise self-confidence.[33]

Coaching for Success

A popular approach to leadership development is individualized coaching to address areas for improvement—public speaking, product knowledge, financial management, computer skills, interpersonal effectiveness, and so on. Most leaders who have received coaching value their coaches' recommendations, and rate the process as useful to their career development. See the Web site of the International Coaching Federation with links to corporate coaching, small-business coaching, and career coaching—www.coachfederation.org. See also the Corporate Executive Board's resource, "Maximizing Returns on Professional Executive Coaching."[34]

Coaches use a variety of resources for developing leaders including helpful books. Examples include Peter Drucker's *Effective Executive,* Douglas McGregor's *The Human Side of Enterprise,* Ken Blanchard's *The One Minute Manager,* and Jim Collins's *Good to Great.* Books such as these provide valuable insight into concepts, principles, skills, and applications for effective leadership.[35]

Psychologist David Dunning explains how the rewards of effective coaching far outweigh the costs: (1) The organization is rewarded with the successful development of the next generation of leaders; (2) emerging leaders are rewarded with tremendous learning and growth opportunities; and (3) experienced leaders are rewarded with a profound satisfaction that comes from guiding and coaching others to achieve their potential.

Dunning describes the role of the coach as that of First Assistant. The First Assistant philosophy is best when it results in a total organizational culture of managers' developing their direct reports. The commitment of the First Assistant is as follows:

I will do everything in my power to help you be successful. I will share my knowledge and skills, disclose my value system, and assist you in every way for your professional and personal growth. I will not lower the bar of performance or excuse ineffective performance. If anything, I will raise the bar higher because I believe you are capable of stretching yourself and increasing your capabilities.

The First Assistant helps the individual develop learning and performance goals and action strategies to reach those goals, identify formal and informal training or learning opportunities, review progress and lessons learned, and keep focused. The following are some sample coaching challenges: a competent division manager needs to learn to manage anger and deal with conflict in more appropriate ways; a newly promoted project manager needs to develop better time management and delegation skills; and an associate who aspires to partnership wants to increase her leadership skills. For these individuals and countless others, coaching can provide invaluable assistance.[36]

Leadership Development for Organization Success

Noel Tichy, author of *The Leadership Engine,* states that great organizations—such as IBM, Intel, GE, and Walmart (when they are great)—don't have just one strong leader or a few here and there; they have many good leaders at all levels of the organization. They make leadership development and leadership excellence a strategic commitment and basis of success.[37]

The most effective leadership development efforts are *owned at the top* (including participation by senior leaders), *sustained over time* (versus one-time-only, flash-in-the-pan activities), *deemed strategically important* (to support mission and goals), and *based on behavior* (emphasizing on-the-job application of principles and practices).[38]

Developing the Leadership Pyramid

The business world is filled with dying organizations where people are paid at rates more than the value they contribute. There are also thriving organizations where people contribute over and above what they are being paid—and do so willingly. The central element of successful organizations is effective leadership and its development. Current leaders provide the engine for success, and a pipeline of emerging leaders provides the gas required to sustain success.

The example of Corrections Corporation of America (CCA) makes this point. The core competencies of the organization are *containment* and *humane treatment*—this is why CCA is hired. But the factor that most determines the quality of containment and quality of treatment is leadership effectiveness. CCA is fanatical about effective leadership and its development.

CCA has many caring leaders, but none more so than Jimmy Turner—once most happy on his horse, shotgun over the saddle, guarding the perimeter of a Texas prison, and now chief operations officer for CCA's 63 institutions. To quote Turner about corrections: "What we do is important, and we do it right." Turner describes CCA's approach to leadership development: "We don't delegate it to others—we have to develop too. And we don't delegate training either. Experts help us, but senior leaders provide training for new leaders. We are in this together."

The CCA model of leadership development has vice presidents and directors training wardens; directors and wardens training assistant wardens and captains; assistant wardens and captains training correctional officers—people at the "doing" level of containment and treatment. CCA doesn't miss a link in the leadership chain, and its business success shows it.[39]

The Employer–Employee Relationship

The employer–employee relationship is an important subject for both the individual and the organization, and it is especially important for people in leadership positions. The following is a discussion of what employers want in an employee and how to attract and keep good people.

What Employers Want in an Employee

The number one quality employers want in an employee is honesty. The need for trust is paramount because the employer relies on the employee to serve its customers, protect its property, and uphold its reputation. Employee honesty is essential.

Next, the employer wants someone who will take initiative and be a self-starter. The employee who is eager to serve is viewed as an asset. Specific skills are less important than the underlying qualities of self-motivation, desire to learn, and personal commitment.

Next, employers want employees with (1) technical knowledge; (2) communication skills; (3) the ability to get along well with others; (4) creative responses to setbacks and obstacles; (5) a high attitude–low maintenance approach to work; and (6) leadership potential.[40]

The shift from career dependence to career self-leadership is a reality in today's work environment.[41] The following are basic rules for succeeding in one's work:

Rule 1: **Put your best foot forward.** Ask what is expected of you and with whom you will be working; then exceed expectations. Build good working relationships from the beginning.

Rule 2: **Deliver results.** Be known for reliability and performance. Stay on task, and persevere in the face of challenge. Let your deeds speak louder than the words you use.

Rule 3: **Be considerate.** Work cooperatively to accomplish tasks. Lend a helping hand to others in need, and have a one-team attitude in dealing with people.

Rule 4: **Be creative.** Keep an open mind, and look for ways to improve your organization and the work you do. Be original and open to new ideas.

Rule 5: **Have integrity.** Remember, success comes from doing the right things for the right reasons in the right way. Keep your thinking cap on to *know* what is right. Keep your character strong to *do* what is right.

How to Attract and Keep Good People

Attracting and keeping good employees is an ever-increasing concern for today's employers. The investment in time, money, and energy to hire a good employee is high, and the cost in lost time, lost money, and psychic letdown if the company loses a good employee is even higher. Consider that the financial cost alone for turning over one semi-skilled employee after a 90-day probation period averages 30 percent of annual wages. The cost can be as high as 150 percent of yearly salaries for professional employees.[42] Based on a salary of $50,000, the cost of turnover would be $75,000. A company with 1,000 employees and a 10 percent turnover rate will pay an annual cost of $7.5 million.

It is important to know what attracts the best employees to a company and what makes them stay. These are two of the oldest issues in the business world, and maybe the most important.[43] Employers should meet employee needs in the following areas: **clarity of work assignment, good work tools and supplies, challenge in one's area of expertise, recognition for one's accomplishments, opportunity to grow, respect for one's opinions, a mission that motivates, feedback on performance, positive social interactions,** and **pride in one's group.**

As a leader, if you want to know what you should do to maintain a strong and productive work group, addressing these areas would be an excellent place to start. Three points should be noted: (1) None of these areas deals with employee wages; (2) in general, employees join organizations, but they leave supervisors; and (3) effective leaders possess a positive attitude and use an individualized approach in the development of people.[44]

Marcus Buckingham, author of *First Break All the Rules* and *Now Discover Your Strengths,* emphasizes the importance of point three. "There are as many styles of management as there are managers, but there is one quality that sets truly great managers apart from the rest. They discover what is unique about each person and then capitalize on it. Great managers know and value the special abilities and even the eccentricities of their employees, and they learn how to best use them for the highest performance."[45]

The Dream Manager by Matthew Kelly is a useful tool for managers and organizations who want to improve retention through caring leadership. Imagine a normal probability curve representing all leaders. The top 10 percent of this curve are exceptional leaders who are true gifts to their employees and organizations. The bottom 10 percent of the curve are good people, but their leadership beliefs and practices are harmful to others. The middle 80 percent will be awakened by The Dream Manager and will be nudged in the direction of effective leadership and the retention of good employees.

Peak Performance

Peak performance is important for the individual and the organization. It is hard to describe, but you know it when you see it.

A Perfectly Beautiful Laundress

When I was very young—five years old, as I remember it—I heard my mother say that she had engaged a perfectly beautiful laundress. I hid behind the kitchen sink to have my first look and my first disenchantment. My mother's

> laundress was less beautiful than the soap that she exercised on my jumpers, and her figure was, like that of her tub, round, stable, and very wide.
>
> That which was called beautiful was neither the laundress nor the objects of her laundering, but the performance to which these were machine and medium, a performance made express and visible in the comforting, crisp cleanliness of linens, pajamas, towels, and pillowcases.
>
> The work done was well done; the task and the process were perfectly mastered; the end was well attained, completely and without excess; and my mother, perceiving this unity of intention, method, and product, cast over all of these the aureole of beauty.[46]

The moral of this story is that whatever you are called to be in life you should perform your work so well that all the hosts of heaven will pause to say, here is a great baker, machinist, farmer, or chief, who does his or her work well.[47]

To personalize the concept of peak performance, answer the following questions:

1. Describe a time in your life when you performed at your personal best. When was it? Who was involved? What happened? What were the results?
2. As a result of your personal best, what did you learn about yourself? About other people? About excellence?
3. Based on your personal best and lessons learned, what are your plans for the road ahead? What goals do you have? What steps can you take to perform (again) at a peak-performance level?

Levels of Performance Effectiveness

In every endeavor, there are four levels of performance effectiveness, from novice to master. (See Figure 16–1.)

Figure 16–1
A Conscious-Competence Performance Model

	Level I	Level II	Level III	Level IV	
Novice Low Performance Effectiveness	Unconscious Incompetence	Conscious Incompetence	Conscious Competence	Unconscious Competence	**Master** High Performance Effectiveness

Level I. At the lowest level, one is unconsciously incompetent; one doesn't know what one doesn't know. One is a *novice*.

Level II. At the second level, one is conscious of one's incompetence; one knows what one doesn't know. This is the first step toward growth.

Level III. At the third level, one is conscious of one's competence; one knows what is required to be competent and is competent, in fact.

Level IV. At the highest level, one is unconsciously competent. The performance that results seems effortless, yet it is remarkable. One is a *master*.

The conscious-competence performance continuum can be seen in every art, science, profession, and trade. To personalize the subject, consider your own level of performance effectiveness. You should do the work you love and develop from novice to master through learning and practice. The result will be both personal happiness and professional success.[48]

Personal Performance   Although late bloomers and later-life success stories are not uncommon—showing personal performance is a lifelong concern—for most people the early career sets the stage for all that follows. No matter what field or profession you pursue, the following guide will be of help.[49] Before your middle years, do these things:

1. **Know yourself.** Know who you are and what is important to you. This will anchor you and make you efficient. The time and energy required to do this can be substantial, and these are best spent in your youth, not in midlife when the needs of others should be the focus of your attention.

2. **Become an expert.** Develop a body of knowledge and skills that people need and will pay you to do. Examples are carpentry, nursing, accounting, cooking, singing, writing, typing, and plumbing. In the final analysis, your ability to perform a wanted service is the best insurance you can have.

3. **Establish your style.** Whatever methods or tools you use—early riser, suit and tie, fresh flowers, thank-you cards, pickup truck—be sure they are both productive and comfortable for you. Do this when you are young. Adopt work habits that make you truly productive. Watch successful people in any line of work. Each has developed a distinctive and productive way of doing the craft, trade, or profession.

4. **Build a network.** This is usually done through personal interactions on the job, in the neighborhood, and in the family. It is best done by generous and gracious service to others—paid or unpaid. A web of trust, respect, and mutual support will build relationships and benefit all parties for years to come.

5. **Focus.** Cherish the past, plan for the future, but live in the moment. Only then will all of your faculties be functioning on the task at hand. By living life fully in the moment, you maximize all you have been and realize the full potential of which you are capable.

6. **Create a cushion.** Ideally, you don't want to be in your midlife years and unable to say, I quit. By this time you will know in your heart the hills worth dying on versus minor matters of opinion or style. When faced with such a hill, your conscience will cry out for expression, and it will help if you have economic strength to support it.

7. **Be true to your values.** Yogi Berra once said, "Everything is easy until it becomes difficult." This is where integrity comes in. Integrity requires honest assessment and action, and it requires courage to live by your convictions even at self-risk or sacrifice. Integrity is the foremost requirement for a successful career and life.

8. **Stay young, stay foolish.** In 2007, Steve Jobs addressed the graduating class of Stanford University with this advice: (1) Be who you are; (2) do what you love; (3) stay young, stay foolish. Jobs's challenge applies before your middle years, as well as after. See www.apple.com.

To help this list be more than words, respond to the challenge of the Latin phrase—*Carpe diem*—seize the day!

CHAPTER 17

Helping People through Change and Burnout Prevention

Nearly 2,500 years ago, the Greek philosopher Heraclitus noted that one can never cross the same river twice. In other words, change is a constant in life. In *Managing at the Speed of Change,* Daryl Conner writes that the volume, speed, and complexity of change are increasing in modern times. In our personal lives, we are constantly having to adjust to family changes, job changes, and health changes. In society at large, we face escalating changes in government, educational, religious, and other institutions.[50]

Change in the Workplace

Change is the label under which we put all the things that we have to do differently in the future. In general, people dislike change. It makes a blank space of uncertainty between what is and what might be. The four major types of change in the workplace are the following:[51]

1. *Structure.* Change in structure is often severely resisted. Mergers, acquisitions, right-sizing, and reengineering activities typically involve tremendous change.

2. *Tasks.* Changes in the environment, including products and processes, require changes in tasks. Driving forces include customer needs, productivity improvement, and quality initiatives.

3. *Technology.* Innovations in this area have dramatically increased the rate of change. No industry, trade, or profession is immune to change caused by technological advancements.

4. *People.* Change in any of the above variables can result in changing relationships—change in managers, employees, co-workers, and customers, and change within a given person, such as change in knowledge, attitude, and skills.

A particularly stressful change in the American workplace is the downsizing and reorganization activities resulting from reengineering business, reinventing government, and other management initiatives. Employees who are victims of job loss, particularly those in their middle years, face enormous economic, social, and personal stress. Employees who remain with an organization often experience the "survivor syndrome." They are afraid they will be part of the next round of cuts, and they feel sadness and guilt over their co-workers' fate. In addition, they often have more work to do personally if production demands do not reflect the reduced number of people to do the job.

Many lessons have been learned from studying organizational change, but four stand out: (1) People need to be flexible and willing to change to preserve important values and goals; (2) people need a positive attitude toward lifelong learning to remain viable in the workplace; (3) career education is a survival skill, since people must learn to manage their own careers; and (4) change can be expensive—consider that if 100 employees with an average annual salary of $24,000 go through a six-month change or transition resulting in two hours of distraction per day, the cost is $276,000.[52]

How prevalent is change in the workplace? A recent study found that 42 percent of the North American companies surveyed engaged in 11 or more change initiatives in a five-year period. In essence, the report describes a "change frenzy" that is creating cynical, demoralized employees and failing to produce meaningful improvements. The result is frontline workers who are overstressed by all the changes created by managers frantically searching for the next formula for success. Consider the following letter from an apologetic and enlightened management:[53]

Dear Employees:

For the last decade, we have been trying to change our organization. Because we are frightened for our economic future, we kept looking for—and finding—another program du jour. We've dragged you through quality circles, excellence, total-quality management, self-directed work teams, re-engineering, and God knows what else. Desperate to find some way to improve our profitability, we switched from change to change almost as fast as we could read about them in business magazines.

All of this bouncing from one panacea to the next gave birth to rampant bandwagonism. We forgot to consider each change carefully, implement it thoughtfully, and wait patiently for results. Instead, we just kept on changing while you progressed from skepticism to cynicism to downright intransigence because you realized that all of these changes were just creating the illusion of movement toward some ill-defined goal.

Now we've got a lot of burned-out workers and managers, tired of the change-of-the-month club and unlikely to listen to our next idea, no matter how good it might be. For our complicity in this dismal state of affairs, we are sincerely sorry.

The Management

Managing People through Change

Figure 17–1 depicts the all-too-common responses to change at various organizational levels.

Top management. Top leaders may underestimate the impact of change on lower levels of the organization. They expect employees to go along when a change is announced and blame middle managers if people resist or complain. They may be so insulated that they truly don't know the results of their decisions and programs.

**Figure 17–1
Organizational Response
to Change**[54]

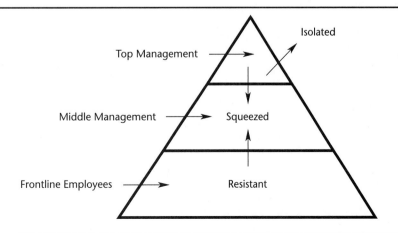

Middle management. Managers in the middle feel pressure to implement organizational change, but often lack information and top leadership direction to be successful. They may feel squeezed between resistant or withdrawn subordinates and demanding but out-of-touch superiors.

Frontline employees. Frontline people may feel threatened by changes announced by management and may respond with denial and resistance, leading often to worry and protective behavior. At this point, employees may shut down and be morale casualties. In this state, lack of willingness to take initiative and to be accountable is not uncommon.

People judge a change primarily on the basis of how it will affect *them.* If a change is personally disruptive, resistance can be great. Even computer professionals resist change when computerization has an impact on their own lives. Loss of control is one of the things people dislike most about change. Out of a need for control, they may choose dysfunction over uncertainty. Often the only way to get people to say good-bye to the past is to convince them that the price of holding on to it is too high and that change is the only way to survive.[55]

Rules to Guide Leaders in Implementing Change

When organizations have the right goals in mind—they want to be customer-focused, quality-conscious, empowered, and profitable—and the reason for change is accounted for by market competition, customer demands, and other forces, the question of how to implement or manage change should be addressed. Seven rules should guide leaders in all change efforts:

1. *Have a good reason for making a change.* Consider each change carefully against the following criteria: Will it support the organization's purpose and goals, and does it reflect the organization's basic principles and core values? If the answer is no, don't change. Change for the sake of change is a waste of precious resources, including people's time.

2. *Personalize change.* Let people know where you stand. Explain your commitment. Why is the change important to you? How will you be affected if the change is successful or if it fails? Why is this change important to them? What do they stand to gain or lose? People may resist or give lukewarm support to a change initiative unless they see how they will personally benefit.[56]

3. *Implement change thoughtfully.* Follow four proven principles: Involve the people who are affected by the change (if you want people in the landing, they have to be in the takeoff); go slow, giving people time to adjust (if you go too fast, you will have an empty train going down the tracks; sometimes you must slow down to carry more passengers); keep people informed through constant personal communication (however much you communicated before the change, raise the level by a factor of 10); be available (not just mentally, but physically as well).

4. *Put a respected person in charge of coordinating change.* Select someone who is trusted by all. Then tap the constructive power of the group through transition teams to plan, coordinate, and communicate change efforts. Provide training in new knowledge, attitudes, and skills to support change.

5. *Tell the truth.* When change is necessary, give the facts and rationale, not sugarcoated pep talks. Trust goes up when the truth is shared. Only after people know the truth and come to terms with negative feelings can they focus effectively on the future.

6. *Wait patiently for results.* It takes time for a seed to grow, and it takes time to realize benefits from change. Change that is too rapid can be destructive. Rush the process and reduce the results. The effective leader knows personal, political, and financial costs accompany any organizational change, and is willing to pay the price. To ensure success, install methods for tracking progress and stay personally involved.

7. *Acknowledge and reward people.* As change is made, take time to recognize people and show appreciation. Acknowledge the struggles, sacrifices, and contributions people have made. A word of thanks goes a long way.

In helping people through change, leaders must remember the different time and information perspectives of different levels of the organization. Senior leaders may be eager to implement changes that frontline personnel are just learning about. Listening, understanding, and being patient are necessary leadership actions for successful change to occur.

Social psychologist Kurt Lewin identified a three-step process for helping people through change: First, unfreeze the status quo; second, move to the desired state; third, live by conditions that become the new, but not rigid, status quo.[57]

- *Unfreezing* involves reducing or eliminating resistance to change. As long as people drag their heels about a change, it will never be implemented effectively. To accept change, people must first deal with and resolve feelings about letting go of the old. Only after people have dealt successfully with endings are they ready to make transitions.

- *Moving to the desired state* usually involves considerable two-way communication, including group discussion. Lewin advised that the person leading change should make suggestions and encourage discussion. Brainstorming, benchmarking, field study, and library research are good techniques for channeling the energies of the group. The best way to overcome resistance to change is to involve people in the changes that will affect them.

- *Living by new conditions* involves such factors as pointing out the successes of the change and finding ways to reward the people involved in implementing the change. Recognizing the contributions of others shows appreciation for their efforts and increases their willingness to participate in future change efforts.

Understanding Complex Organizational Change

Does this sound familiar? Senior leaders spend months coming up with a plan for moving the organization in a new direction. The board says, "Full speed ahead!" There is only one problem: The managers who actually run the place and the employees who actually do the work have no understanding of the plan, and are maybe even complaining about the newest "new thing" of senior management. The only way to move from boardroom discussion to on-the-job reality is to help managers and workers understand, share, and commit to a vision for change.[58]

There are many models for understanding organizational change. One of the best is an eight-stage process provided by John Kotter of Harvard University. Kotter's model summarizes the steps necessary to produce successful change. The first four steps unfreeze the status quo and energize the organization around a new vision. The remaining four steps help move the organization to the desired state, including implementing new practices and reinforcing changes in the organizational culture.[59] See Figure 17–2.

Kotter has identified common errors and their consequences in creating organizational change. These are presented in Figure 17–3.[60]

Organizational culture plays an important role in dealing with change. Imagine culture as an iceberg. Above the waterline are visible artifacts such as language, physical and social architecture, and customs for dealing with significant events. Below the waterline, and far more powerful, are deeply rooted assumptions, values, and beliefs. These strong forces must be appreciated when leading organizational change. Business history is replete with examples of merger failures traced to incompatible organizational cultures.[61]

Culture reflects the behavior and assumptions that are shared by members of a group. These give the group a unique character that can enrich its members and all who are affected by the group. Advancing the positive elements of culture (such as a tradition of service excellence) and eliminating the negative (such as an authoritarian management style) are the tasks of leadership, and it is this responsibility that is often the basis of change initiatives. To be successful, the leader must maintain a strong vision that serves as a source of purpose, exhibit strong values that serve as a guidance system, and display patience, understanding, and resolve when implementing needed change.[62]

Figure 17–2
The Eight-Stage Process
of Creating Major Change

1. Establishing a Sense of Urgency
- Examining the market and competitive realities
- Identifying and discussing crises, potential crises, or major opportunities

2. Creating the Guiding Coalition
- Putting together a group with enough power to lead the change
- Getting the group to work together like a team

3. Developing a Vision and Strategy
- Creating a vision to help direct the change effort
- Developing strategies for achieving that vision

4. Communicating the Change Vision
- Using every vehicle possible to constantly communicate the new vision and strategies
- Having the guiding coalition role-model the behavior expected of employees

5. Empowering Broad-Based Action
- Getting rid of obstacles
- Changing systems or structures that undermine the change vision
- Encouraging risk taking and nontraditional ideas, activities, and actions

6. Generating Short-Term Wins
- Planning for visible improvements in performance, or "wins"
- Creating those wins
- Visibly recognizing and rewarding people who made the wins possible

7. Consolidating Gains and Producing More Change
- Using increased credibility to change all systems, structures, and policies that don't fit together and don't fit the transformation vision
- Hiring, promoting, and developing people who can implement the change vision
- Reinvigorating the process with new projects, themes, and change agents

8. Anchoring New Approaches in the Culture
- Creating better performance through customer—and productivity—oriented behavior, more and better leadership, and more effective management
- Articulating the connections between new behaviors and organizational success
- Developing means to ensure leadership development and succession management

Reprinted by permission of Harvard Business School Press. From *Leading Change* by John P. Kotter, Boston, MA, 1996, p. 16. Copyright © 1996 by John P. Kotter; all rights reserved.

Figure 17–3
Eight Errors Common to Organizational Change Efforts and Their Consequences

> **Common Errors**
> - Allowing too much complacency
> - Failing to create a sufficiently powerful guiding coalition
> - Underestimating the power of vision
> - Undercommunicating the vision by a factor of 10 (or 100 or even 1,000)
> - Permitting obstacles to block the new vision
> - Failing to create short-term wins
> - Declaring victory too soon
> - Neglecting to anchor changes firmly in the corporate culture

> **Consequences**
> - New strategies aren't implemented well.
> - Acquisitions don't achieve expected synergies.
> - Reengineering takes too long and costs too much.
> - Downsizing doesn't get costs under control.
> - Quality programs don't deliver hoped-for results.

Reprinted by permission of Harvard Business School Press. From *Leading Change* by John P. Kotter, Boston, MA, 1996, p. 21. Copyright © 1996 by John P. Kotter; all rights reserved.

The empowerment of people is a key element for successful organizational change. Table 17–1 presents five principles leaders should follow for tapping the constructive power of all employees.

Table 17–1
Empowering People to Effect Change[63]

- **Communicate a clear, compelling vision to employees.** If employees have a shared sense of purpose, it will be easier to initiate actions to achieve that purpose.
- **Make structures compatible with the vision.** Unaligned structures block needed action.
- **Provide the training employees need.** Without the right skills and attitudes, people feel unempowered.
- **Align information and personnel systems to the vision.** Unaligned systems block needed action.
- **Confront supervisors who undercut needed change.** Nothing disempowers people the way a bad boss can. If managers fail to display commitment to a change, it is difficult for employees below them to be supportive.

The Role of the Individual

In dealing with change, employees are faced with uncertainty and lack of role clarity. Often there are more questions than answers. In such times, success belongs to the committed, to those who work from the heart and adjust quickly when change occurs. These individuals create role clarity for themselves. They chase down the information they need and align their efforts with the organization's larger purpose and goals. Then they attack the work to be done as best as they understand it to be. Two rules to follow are: (1) contribute more than you cost; and (2) make your customer your first priority.

Imagine a workforce that costs more than it contributes; this is a dying institution. Imagine a workforce that contributes more than it costs; this is a thriving, growing institution that meets the needs of employers and employees alike. The successful individual focuses on performance and results, not tenure, activity level, or good intentions. The successful employee contributes more than he costs.

The second rule is to put the customer first. Identify who you are supposed to serve—the customer (patient, passenger, guest, student, etc.), another department, a direct report. Then get close to this person or group. Anticipate special needs, know preferences, and develop a reputation for responsiveness. Make customer satisfaction your number one commitment. The successful individual makes the customer king.

To personalize the subject, consider yourself: Are your efforts aligned with your organization's purpose and goals? Do you contribute more than you cost? Who is your customer, and what evidence shows that his or her interests are your number one priority?

Myths and Realities in Dealing with Change

Historians have identified ages or periods of history—the Dark Ages, the Renaissance, the Age of Reason, and so on. An argument can be made that the current period is the Age of Change; further, the rate of change keeps picking up speed. In one way or another, people have always had to deal with change. What is different today is the pace and volume of change with diminishing time of the effectiveness of our responses.[64] Consider these facts: The top 10 jobs in demand in 2010 did not exist in 2004; the U.S. Labor Department estimates new college graduates will have on average 10 jobs by age 38; new technical information is doubling every 2 years; and one out of 8 couples married in the United States in 2008 met online.

Figure 17–4 shows the broad changes that are occurring in U.S. society today. These are drivers or themes that can result in significant pressure, conflict, and frustration. To personalize the subject, put a check mark next to those changes that affect you.[65]

Figure 17–4   **Changes in Today's World**

Technology is a major influence at work and at home.

_____All forms of work are affected by computerized systems.
_____New technology puts a premium on technical knowledge.

The pace of technological and social change is rapid and accelerating.

_____We expect things to change; some like it, but some resist the pace.
_____It is often easier to throw away objects and relationships than to repair them.

The speed of communication and access to information is increasing.

_____People are bombarded daily by information from a myriad of sources—print, electronic, and so on.
_____More available information poses more choices.

There is increasing reliance on self-help versus institutional help.

_____There is a trend toward empowering individuals.
_____There is greater need for continuing education and lifelong learning.

A dominant trend is greater diversity in the workplace.

_____Increasing numbers of women and minorities in the workforce means systemic change in family and social life.
_____Issues such as human dignity, mutual respect, and inclusion are important social concerns.

There is a greater variety of living arrangements.

_____More people are living in nontraditional families.
_____Young people increasingly are raised by nonrelated adults as less and less time is spent with natural parents and legal guardians.

There is greater variety of working arrangements.

_____Multiple careers and multiple employers are the norm.
_____Couples pursuing careers in different geographic locations is an increasing trend.

There is growth in population, including cultural and ethnic diversity.

_____The population of our planet didn't reach 1 billion until the 1860s, about the time of the Civil War; the U.S. Census Bureau predicts it will reach 10 billion by the year 2040.
_____Minority groups are affirming themselves as well as their rights to mainstream entitlements. Differing beliefs make it more difficult to know how to live.

There is globalization of world economies.

_____International competition in goods and services has an impact on the marketplace and employment patterns.
_____Globalization brings opportunities to exchange ideas and customs.

There is a trend toward breakdown of traditional values and social order.

_____Parents, teachers, and other leaders increasingly fail to live by high ethical standards.
_____People are increasingly exposed to crime and violence, both in person and through the media.

There are a number of myths and realities in dealing with change.[66] One myth is that change will go away, when the reality is that change is here to stay. If you have lived long enough, you have witnessed firsthand the truth of this statement as you have seen your own body change, your family change, your work change, and even your mind change.

Another myth is that you can just keep on doing things the way you have been, when the reality is that if your world is changing—home, work, and society—then you may have to change as well. For example, if the marketplace or technology or other external forces require doing business differently, you may not succeed if you are unwilling to make adjustments. Sometimes, to protect family, health, and other high-priority values, people have to make changes. As Charles Darwin wrote,

"It is not the strongest of the species that survive, nor the most intelligent, but the one most responsive to change."[67]

Overcoming Fear

In their book, *Working Scared,* Ken Wexley and Stan Silverman argue that stress associated with change causes many employees to work in a state of anxiety and fear. They identify eight major areas of change in organizations and provide helpful techniques for dealing with these stressors. (See Table 17–2.)[68]

Table 17–2
Organizational Changes That Lead to Stress

Organizational Change

A. *Less supervision:* As organizations downsize and cut back, managers have more subordinates—and less time for each.

B. *Team culture:* It's typical for employees today to work in a team environment, and being a team player can be difficult.

C. *Focus on quality:* Many employees are learning new methods and approaches to ensure that the organization is doing "quality" work.

D. *Downsizing:* Organizations feel the need to get "lean and mean," leaving many employees without jobs and others as layoff survivors.

E. *Mergers and acquisitions:* Companies are buying each other out; the result is very different companies—a situation that affects employees.

F. *Diversity:* As the workforce becomes more diverse, employees interact more with co-workers who have backgrounds different from theirs.

G. *International environment:* Companies are becoming more international, and employees often find themselves working in a different culture.

H. *Innovative pay strategies:* Employees are faced with different payment plans, such as gainsharing and bonuses.

Techniques for Dealing with These Stressors

A. Develop your own responsibilities and objectives. Seek high-quality feedback from co-workers and supervisors.

B. Be prepared for and accept empowerment. Improve your communication skills.

C. Don't wait for training; start learning on your own. Look for ways to improve your work—slowly, but steadily.

D. Be aware of rumors, but don't let them dominate your thoughts. Work hard and creatively to prove your worth to the organization.

E. Learn as much as possible about the other company. Be prepared and receptive to organizational changes.

F. Become more aware of your own values and prejudices. Consider the many benefits that come from diversity, including increasing productivity.

G. Be honest in considering whether an overseas assignment might work for you and your family. Expect six difficult months at first, with serious adjustments necessary on your part.

H. Understand the organization's new pay strategy. Ask for periodic performance reviews.

Figure 17–5 shows the relationship between morale and time in dealing with change. Figure 17–6 shows that the volume of change in the modern workplace increases the challenge.

**Figure 17–5
Change Process Starts**

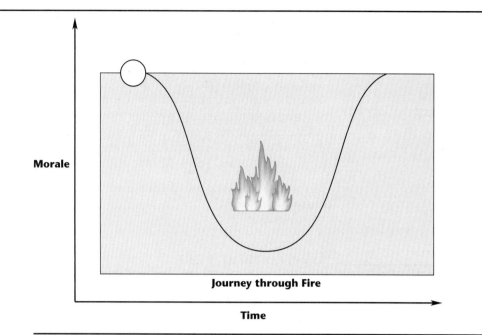

**Figure 17–6
The Changes Keep Coming**

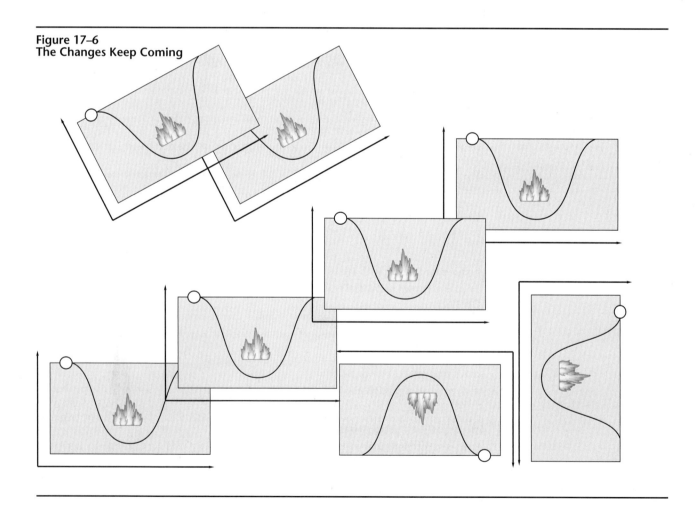

The Importance of Attitude

What a person does when change occurs depends on his or her attitude. At one extreme, the individual may shut down and declare, "I will never change." A more effective approach is to keep an open mind and say, "Let's consider the possibilities."

In all areas of life, attitude affects our happiness, effectiveness, and general well-being. Attitude can make or break your career, your relationships, and even your health. We have all known someone with an attitude problem.

Some people take the attitude of the victim when change occurs. This robs them of personal energy and makes them less appealing to others. In contrast, other people view change as a challenge and focus on the opportunities and benefits that change can bring.

The power of attitude to change people's lives is reflected in this statement: Life is 10 percent what happens to you and 90 percent how you react to it. If you change your attitude, your attitude will change you. Figure 17–7 shows an attitude curve in response to change.[69]

Figure 17–7   **Attitude Curve in Response to Change**

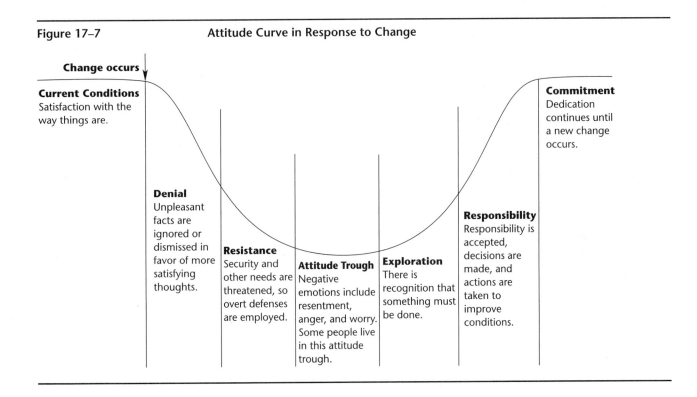

Figure 17–8 shows effective responses in dealing with change. Denial, resistance, and negative attitudes are avoided in favor of proceeding directly to states of **exploration, personal responsibility,** and **commitment.** This positive reaction is most likely to happen when people:

- Believe the change is the right thing to do.
- Have influence on the nature and process of the change.
- Respect the person who is championing the change.
- Expect the change will result in personal gain.
- Believe this is the right time for change.[70]

Figure 17–8   Effective Responses in Dealing with Change

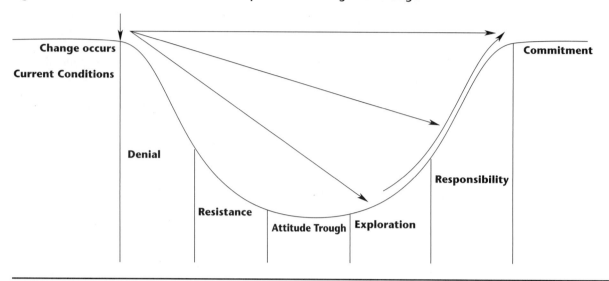

Strategies for Dealing with Change

Change often means loss—loss of security, confidence, relationships, direction, or possessions. Healthy coping means dealing with loss realistically and letting go of what must be given up in order to move on. You must adopt the belief that it is never too late to change your attitude and set your life on a new and positive course. At each phase of the attitude curve, there are strategies that can be taken to help you deal successfully with change.

	What the Individual Can Do	What Others Can Do
Denial	Remember the adage "He who drinks from the cup of denial will sleep in the inn of defeat." Live by the principle, "Know the truth and it will set you free."	Provide information. Answer questions. Communicate, communicate, communicate, ideally in person.
Resistance	State how you feel. Get it off your chest.	Listen and acknowledge feelings. Listening shows respect and may yield important and otherwise unknown information.
Attitude Trough	Say this is intolerable—enough is enough. Resolve to improve. Say good-bye to the past. Be willing to alter behavior.	Model and reinforce positive actions. Be patient.
Exploration	Have an open mind. Consider all possibilities. Coping includes fact-finding and visioning an ideal future.	Focus on possibilities. Channel energy in a helpful way. Brainstorm ideas and alternatives. Provide helpful training. Set short-term goals.
Responsibility	Have courage. Take action. Accept the consequences.	Encourage and expect the best. Help with planning and goal setting. Show support when decisions are made.
Commitment	Learn from the past. Enjoy the present. Plan for the future.	Acknowledge and celebrate accomplishments. Help prepare for future challenges.

Initiating Change

Thus far, our discussion about change has dealt with reacting healthfully and effectively to a changing world. What about initiating change? What if one's goal is to change others or improve conditions? These are admirable ambitions, but a word of advice from a Church bishop (name unknown) of Westminster Abbey (AD 1100) is worth remembering:[71]

> When I was young and free and my imagination had no limits, I dreamed of changing the world. As I grew older and wiser, I discovered the world would not change, so I shortened my sights somewhat and decided to change only my country.
>
> But it, too, seemed immovable.
>
> As I grew into my twilight years, in one last desperate attempt, I settled for changing only my family, those closest to me, but alas, they would have none of it.
>
> And now as I lie on my deathbed, I suddenly realize: *If I had only changed myself first,* then by example I would have changed my family.
>
> From their inspiration and encouragement, I would then have been able to better my country and, who knows, I may have even changed the world.

More modern, but similar, advice on this issue is provided by the Indian political and spiritual leader Mohandas Gandhi, who believed: If you would change the world, then you must be the way you want the world to be.[72]

Avoiding Burnout

Danger lurks in modern society, and the victim is often the dedicated and talented person. This danger is called burnout, and it can occur both on the job and in the home. The dictionary definition of *burn out* is "to fail, wear out, or become exhausted due to excessive demands on one's strength, resources, and energy."

In the human sphere, **burnout** is what happens when a person experiences physical, psychological, and spiritual fatigue and is unable to cope. Lack of energy and low vitality are characteristics of physical fatigue. Symptoms of psychological fatigue include depression and loss of sharpness in thinking and feeling. Spiritual fatigue is characterized by lack of interest and meaning in life, resulting in unhappiness and pessimism.[73]

Burnout can strike the businessperson with too many pressures and too little time, the homemaker with too much work and not enough appreciation, and the friend who is tired of being his or her "brother's keeper." The following are common types of burnout victims. Do any sound familiar to you?

- **Superpeople,** who want to do everything themselves because no one else can or will, and they have never let anyone down.
- **Workaholics,** who are driven to meet unreasonable demands placed on them (either by themselves or assigned by others).
- **Burned-out Samaritans,** who are always giving to others while receiving little help or appreciation in return.
- **Mismatched people,** who do their jobs well but who do not like what they are doing.
- **Midcareer coasters,** who may once have been high performers but whose enthusiasm is gone.
- **Overstressed students,** who are holding down full-time jobs and full course loads.[74]

Burnout was introduced to the scientific literature in the early 1970s by psychologists Herbert Freudenberger and Christina Maslach. The evocative image of their term has made it a popular topic in the print and electronic media since that time. Extensive research has also been carried out. A literature search of the *Psychological Abstracts* reveals 2,446 research articles and nearly 127 books on burnout.[75]

Burnout is a great equalizer. It is blind to age, sex, color, and creed. It is a condition that can affect both white- and blue-collar workers as well as those who work at home. Job burnout is widespread in modern society. It is hazardous, and it can be contagious. If left unchecked, it can harm individual health, human relationships, and organization effectiveness.

The result of burnout is that a company loses its best people at a critical point, or it leaves them so stressed that their attitude sabotages projects. The result for the individual can be even more tragic, as the following stories show.

We Buried Joe Today

People were surprised when Joe suffered a sudden fatal heart attack since he didn't seem ill or particularly out of condition. Joe was a salesman in his late 50s, who went into sales 30 years ago because he could sell anything. He was a great talker, people liked him, and he was known for his tremendous energy. One day, Joe accepted a position with a large corporation. He liked the idea of having a big product to push and wanted the security that working for a big company offered him.

Gradually, though, Joe found that what he had accomplished was under siege by younger people who had the kind of energy and enthusiasm that, after two decades on the job, Joe found hard to muster routinely. The facts before Joe were scary—his mortgage payments and living expenses were high, his children were in college, and the prospect of retirement loomed darkly before him. The benefits of his work—a larger home and more expensive toys—suddenly caused more worry than joy.

Joe became troubled over whether he could maintain the pace that he set for himself and his company expected him to meet. He began pushing himself harder and harder to perform, complaining almost daily that he was losing his touch, that his memory wasn't as sharp, that he couldn't make the number of sales calls he used to, and that he couldn't put in the hours he did 25 or 30 years ago.

Joe's fears led to increased irritability. He had trouble sleeping and found himself in a constant state of worry. He even began drinking to relax and to help him fall asleep. Trying to overcome his alcohol-induced sleep, he began drinking more and more coffee in the morning to lift the veil of drowsiness. Joe also kept his fears and concerns shielded from what was potentially his greatest support system—his wife and family.

Finally, Joe's boss called him into his office one day. Joe had been anticipating this particular call with extreme dread for weeks. He had seen the trend— his good accounts gradually were being siphoned to younger people, he no longer was invited to management meetings, and he sensed that people were talking behind his back. Even as Joe became more frantic and desperate, working harder and longer, his territory was dwindling around him. Joe was at the wrong end of a dangerous game of burnout. When the call came, Joe knew exactly what it meant. He never made it to his boss's office.[76]

A Tragic Story

The job was getting to the ambulance attendant. He felt disturbed by the recurring tragedy, isolated by long shifts. His marriage was in trouble. He was drinking too much. One night it all blew up.

He rode in back that night. His partner drove. Their first call was for a man whose leg had been cut off by a train. His screaming and agony were horrifying, but the second call was worse. It was a child-beating. As the attendant treated the youngster's bruised body and snapped bones, he thought of his own child. His fury grew.

Immediately after leaving the child at the hospital, the attendants were sent out to help a heart attack victim seen lying in the street. When they arrived, however, they found not a cardiac patient, but a drunk—a wino passed out. As they lifted the man into the ambulance, their frustration and anger came to a head. They decided to give the wino a ride he would remember.

The ambulance vaulted over railroad tracks at high speed. The driver took the corners as fast as he could, flinging the wino from side to side in the back. To the attendants, it was a joke. Suddenly, the man began having a real heart attack. The attendant in the back leaned over the wino and started shouting, "Die, you . . . ," he yelled. "Die."

He watched as the wino shuddered. He watched as the wino died. By the time they reached the hospital, they had their stories straight. "Dead on arrival," they said. "Nothing we could do."[77]

Joe and *the ambulance attendants* are tragic stories about stress and burnout. They are extreme but instructive, because they show the life-and-death consequences this subject can have. The following is a formula for the burnout process:

Too many demands on strength and resources over a prolonged period of time

+

High expectations and deep personal involvement in the work one does

+

Too few actions taken to replenish the energy consumed in meeting these demands

=

Burnout

Job burnout can be prevented and overcome. This effort requires self-understanding and the support of others. For a better understanding of the job burnout phenomenon, take the test in Exercise 17–1 to evaluate your own status (homemakers should evaluate conditions at home).

Exercise 17–1
Up in Smoke—Are You Burned Out?[78]

For each question, indicate your most accurate response by circling the number in the appropriate column.

Do you	Never	Rarely	Sometimes	Often	Always
Feel less competent or effective than you used to feel in your work?	1	2	3	4	5
Consider yourself unappreciated or "used"?	1	2	3	4	5
Dread going to work?	1	2	3	4	5
Feel overwhelmed in your work?	1	2	3	4	5
Feel your job is pointless or unimportant?	1	2	3	4	5
Watch the clock?	1	2	3	4	5
Avoid conversations with others (co-workers, customers, and supervisors in the work setting; family members in the home)?	1	2	3	4	5
Rigidly apply rules without considering creative solutions?	1	2	3	4	5
Become frustrated by your work?	1	2	3	4	5
Miss work often?	1	2	3	4	5
Feel unchallenged by your job?	1	2	3	4	5

Does your work	Never	Rarely	Sometimes	Often	Always
Overload you?	1	2	3	4	5
Deny you rest periods—breaks, lunch time, sick leave, or vacation?	1	2	3	4	5
Pay too little?	1	2	3	4	5
Depend on uncertain funding sources?	1	2	3	4	5
Provide inadequate support to accomplish the job (budget, equipment, tools, people, etc.)?	1	2	3	4	5
Lack clear guidelines?	1	2	3	4	5
Entail so many different tasks that you feel fragmented?	1	2	3	4	5
Require you to deal with major or rapid changes?	1	2	3	4	5
Lack access to a social or professional support group?	1	2	3	4	5
Involve coping with a negative job image or angry people?	1	2	3	4	5
Depress you?	1	2	3	4	5

Scoring and Interpretation:

Add all the circled numbers, and record your total: _____

Score	Category
94–110	Burnout
76–93	Flame
58–75	Smoke
40–57	Sparks
22–39	No fire

- *Burnout.* If your score is 94 to 110, you are experiencing a very high level of stress in your work. Without some changes in yourself or your situation, your potential for stress-related illness is high. Consider seeking professional help for stress reduction and burnout prevention. Coping with stress at this level may also require help from others—supervisors, co-workers, and other associates at work, and your spouse and other family members at home.

- *Flame.* If you scored from 76 to 93, you have a high amount of work-related stress and may have begun to burn out. Mark the questions on which you scored 4 or above, and rank them in order of their effect on you, beginning with the ones that bother you the most. For at least your top three, evaluate what you can do to reduce the stresses involved, and act to improve conditions. If your body is reflecting the stress, get a medical checkup.

- *Smoke.* Scores from 58 to 75 represent a certain amount of stress in your work and are a sign that you have a fair chance of burning out unless you take corrective measures. For each question on which you scored 4 or above, consider ways you can reduce the stresses involved. As soon as possible, take action to improve your attitude or the situation surrounding those things that trouble you most.

- *Sparks.* If your score is from 40 to 57, you have a low amount of work-related stress and are unlikely to burn out. Look over those questions on which you scored 3 or above, and think about what you can do to reduce the stresses involved.

- *No fire.* If your score is 22 through 39, you are mellow in your work, with almost no job-related stress. As long as you continue at this level, you are practically burnout-proof. A note to remember: Although you may currently have a low burnout score, others may not be as fortunate. Awareness, understanding, and support may be required.

Dealing with Burnout

Although you may be in a state of burnout, the "phoenix phenomenon" can occur. You can rise from the ashes to a new level of energy and commitment, depending on your use of corrective strategies. Strategies for dealing with burnout include **emergency aid, short-term actions,** and **long-term solutions.**[79]

Examples of *emergency aid* are doing deep breathing, engaging in positive self-talk, taking a physical retreat, and talking with a friend. Sample *short-term actions* are reducing workload, setting priorities, taking care of your body, and accentuating the positive. Important *long-term solutions* are clarifying values, renewing commitments, making lifestyle changes, and developing personal competencies.

For many people, both the job and the home represent potential sources for high stress and burnout. For this reason, having at least one safe haven is important. Ideally, if things are going badly on the job, rest and comfort can be found in the home. Similarly, if home conditions involve pressure, conflict, and frustration, having a satisfying work life helps. The person who faces stress on the job and stress in the home at the same time is waging a war on two fronts and is a prime candidate for burnout.

The Leader's Role in Burnout Prevention

Executives can institute the following 10 practices to prevent burnout in the workplace:

1. Clarify the mission, goals, and values of the organization, and *live* these personally.
2. Clearly communicate role expectations. People need to know their place in the plan.
3. Maintain a healthy work environment—meet physical, safety, and emotional health needs.
4. Manage work processes so that individuals and groups are neither overloaded nor underloaded.
5. Maintain an effective balance between continuity and change. While self-renewing change is vital for keeping up with shifting conditions, change should not occur at a pace so fast that it produces widespread stress.
6. Foster a spirit of belonging and teamwork throughout the organization through personal involvement, effective communication, and morale-building activities.
7. To the degree possible, allow people flexibility to work at the pace and manner that will ensure personal satisfaction while maintaining needed productivity.
8. Provide people opportunity for ongoing involvement in decisions affecting them.
9. Have career development policies and activities that help people achieve their full potential.
10. Provide assistance in times of stress. Services ranging from fitness programs to counseling centers can be provided within the organization, or referral networks can be established.[80]

In *Managing Stress for Mental Fitness,* Merrill Raber and George Dyck list 10 strategies for supervisors to follow in helping employees manage job stress:

1. Maintain a safe and organized work environment.
2. Clarify work unit goals and objectives.
3. Be sure individual job expectations and instructions are clear.
4. Evaluate workloads and deadlines. Are they reasonable?
5. Have regular reviews to provide accurate and timely feedback; give assurance that good work is appreciated.
6. Show patience, understanding, and support in dealing with employee problems.
7. Deal with personality differences directly and constructively.

8. Coach and develop employees to their full potential.

9. Involve people, as much as possible, in decisions that affect them.

10. Keep communication lines open with an open-door policy.[81]

Job Stress

Stress in the workplace is being encountered at ever-increasing rates. In 1983, 55 percent of people reported experiencing stress on a weekly basis. In 1996, almost 75 percent reported experiencing great stress on a daily basis.[82] Of the stress Americans experience, 82 percent say that work is their biggest source of stress. Thirty-five percent of American workers report their jobs negatively affect their physical or emotional well-being.[83] It is well documented that stressors in the work situation are positively related to intentions to quit the organization and to job search behavior.[84] The American Institute of Stress estimates that work stress costs U.S. industries $300 billion a year.[85]

Organizational stress is related to health problems and their associated costs, with costs 46 percent higher for employees who experience high levels of stress.[86] About half of all absenteeism is related to workplace stress, costing organizations billions of dollars per year.[87] There is consistent evidence that stressors at work have a causal effect on health and well-being.[88] A large-scale meta-analysis of more than 30 years of research shows that occupational stress can suppress the body's immune system, leaving the individual more vulnerable to disease with fewer physiological resources with which to combat it.[89]

Unwanted job loss can be especially distressful. Loss of social status, financial security, and personal control can lead to chronic physical problems and impaired emotional functioning. Distress can trigger the sensation of pain, thanks to a part of the brain called the anterior cingulated cortex. Interestingly, it does not distinguish between physical and emotional pain. It responds equally to a broken arm and to a broken heart.[90]

Stress in the Modern-Day Workplace

Michael Losey, past-president of the Society for Human Resource Management, describes the impact of stress on the individual in the modern-day workplace:

> The feverish pace most corporations have set for themselves is perhaps the largest contributor to workers' high stress levels. Fax machines, beepers, computers, cell telephones, and other products of the modern workplace have fueled the problem. Automation has left many workers virtually on call twenty-four hours a day. They feel a sense of "never punching out" and "no down time for rest." Clients and bosses can and do contact employees at home, in the car, at restaurants, during family outings—basically anywhere, at any time. As Henry David Thoreau once said, men have become the tools of their tools.[91]

Technology can offer great convenience and efficiency, but it can also fuel the flames of stress. Employees can reach a point when increasing demands simply become too much—a point at which family relations, personal health, and the quality of work itself are seriously threatened. Employers should not assume that by getting more hours out of their employees, they will necessarily increase productivity. Findings show that the more overworked employees feel, the more likely they are to make costly mistakes and the less committed they feel toward their employers.[92]

Surveys by the Families and Work Institute report that 44 percent of Americans say they are overworked, up from 25 percent who felt this way three years earlier. Work overload is an important factor in job burnout and can be a major cause of work–family conflicts. Overworked employees have insufficient time and energy to address nonwork responsibilities of being a parent, or a spouse, or other roles.

Juliet Schor, Harvard economist and author of *The Overworked American: The Unexpected Decline of Leisure,* sheds light on historical forces and events that have helped create the overstressed American worker:

> It all began with the Pilgrims who reduced leisure by dropping from the calendar more than 50 holidays enjoyed by the English since medieval times. Sunday was declared to be the only toil-free day. By the time the Industrial Revolution arrived in America, the Pilgrims' work ethic

was woven thoroughly into management's expectations; so much so that labor unions had to work for a century to secure eight-hour workdays with at least one day of rest.

With the end of World War II and the increased prosperity and leisure of the next twenty-five years, most unions reduced their vigilance. When the era of layoffs and vast cutbacks came to first one and then another industry and company during the '70s, '80s, and '90s, employees were unprepared to resist the side effects of "downsizing." Today companies routinely ask employees, including managers, to do the work of 1.3 people—for the same pay and with less time off. Overtime is at a modern-day high (an average of 4.7 hours a week) while in the last decade, the average yearly vacation and other paid absences decreased by 3.5 days. These are patterns that are expected to continue.[93]

A half century ago, social scientists predicted that technology would allow employees to enjoy a 15-hour work week at full pay by 2030. So far, it hasn't turned out that way.[94] More than 150 million Americans spend approximately one-third of their day on the job. Currently, five major forces or trends are sources of stress for increasing numbers of these people:

- **New technology.** Job skills and tasks are changing rapidly. No one can ignore the revolution in work caused by computer technology. Nearly every employee, from the frontline worker to the corporate executive, has been affected by the introduction of the computer in the workplace.[95] No longer can a person just walk in the door and be a decent citizen. Now it's walk in the door, be a decent citizen, and know how to run several computer programs. Millions of workers use computers every day, along with other products of modern technology—faxes, cell phones, e-mail, and instant messaging. This situation creates virtual offices for workers on the go, accelerating information transfer and changing the way products are developed and services provided.[96] Check here if new technology affects you. _____

- **Workforce diversity.** New members of the workforce are increasingly diverse and possess skill sets and value systems that are different from those of earlier generations. These differences, along with differences in race, gender, nationality, and creed, can result in a social mix that is highly stressful.[97] Check here if workforce diversity affects you. _____

- **Global competition.** The intensification of international competition brings pressure to perform and fear of failure. This phenomenon has been studied extensively in the case of Japan and the manufacture of automobiles, but it involves many other countries and a multitude of industries.[98] In the relatively sheltered era of the 1960s, 7 percent of the U.S. economy was exposed to international competition. That number grew to 70 percent during the 1980s, and it continues to climb higher with every passing year.[99] Check here if global competition affects you. _____

- **Organizational restructure.** The phenomenon of organizational restructuring—mergers, takeovers, reengineering, and rightsizing—is a continuing drumbeat reported in newspapers, magazines, and television. For an enormous number of people, these developments are sources of uncertainty, worry, and stress.[100] Displaced workers typically experience pay cuts, as downward mobility is the norm more than the exception. The reality for most people caught in organizational restructure is that spending power and standards of living decline.[101] Check here if organizational restructure affects you. _____

- **Changing work systems.** There is an emerging redefinition of work itself, with a growing disappearance of the job as a fixed bundle of tasks. In its place is an emphasis on fluid and constantly changing work assignments required to fulfill ever-increasing demands of customers. Change in how work is accomplished has become a way of life in the workplace, as many new concepts are tried, adapted, and discarded, only to be replaced by newer approaches. Quality teams, process improvement, and semiautonomous work groups are examples of trends in which traditional methods of hierarchical supervision are replaced by work teams and self-direction in a general shift from tier to peer.[102] Check here if you are affected by changing work systems. _____

Stress at Work and Public Policy

The good news is that the majority of U.S. workers are psychologically sound and are coping relatively well with work and with life in general. The bad news is that substantial numbers of people do not enjoy this condition, but are afflicted by the job stress syndrome. Some of these people are struggling with personal or family problems that often have repercussions on the job. Further good news, however, is that in recent years the mental health community and some governmental agencies have focused attention and resources on the subject of work and well-being.[103]

One product of collaboration between the National Institute of Occupational Safety and Health, the Association of Schools for Public Health, and experts from the American Psychological Association, labor, and industry is agreement on a blueprint for protecting the health and well-being of American workers. The four cornerstones of this blueprint are as follows:

- Well-designed jobs.
- Evaluation systems to detect psychological disorders and underlying risk factors.
- Education of workers and managers on the signs, causes, effects, and control of work-related psychological disorders.
- Improved mental health service delivery for workers.[104]

Stress across Cultures

Recognizing occupational stress to be more than just an American phenomenon, the World Health Organization has identified its prevalence in almost every occupation in every country, stating that it has become a "global epidemic."[105]

A report by the National Institute for Occupational Safety and Health states between 26 and 40 percent of all surveyed workers in the United States experience their work as very stressful. Similarly, 28 percent of the workers in the European Union report their work as stressful. In Japan, the percentage is even higher.[106] The Japanese word *Karoshi* means "death (shi) from overwork (Karo)." It is officially defined as a fatal mix of apoplexy, high blood pressure, and stress. *Karoshi* strikes primarily middle managers in their 40s and 50s who are characterized as being *moretsu sha-in* ("fanatical workers") and *yoi kigyo sen-shi* ("good corporate soldiers").

Karoshi is becoming more common in Japan as men and women struggle to meet the physical and emotional demands of modern Japanese life. Long working hours, little or no exercise, constant pressure to meet expectations, relentless traffic, little time for family, too much alcohol, too many cigarettes, increasing financial pressures, and a poor diet set the stage. The curtain comes down, not from an epidemic of some insidious virus, but from heart attacks, complications of high blood pressure, lung cancer, suicide, and the entire collection of degenerative diseases.[107]

Research conducted by Japan's Institute of Public Health identified five patterns of work behavior that lead to the fatal *karoshi* syndrome:

1. Extremely long hours that interfere with normal recovery and rest patterns.
2. Night work that interferes with normal recovery and rest patterns.
3. Work without holidays or breaks.
4. High-pressure work without breaks.
5. Extremely demanding physical labor and continuously stressful work without relief.[108]

Women, Work, and Stress

Many women do not work for wages, yet the stress in their lives can be fully as great as for those who do. The tasks required for maintaining a home and raising children may result in overload or underload, depending on the person and the situation. For those who choose or are required to hold down a job and raise a family at the same time, significant levels of stress can result. The amount of pressure these women face, the conflict they experience, and the frustration they feel can be enormous. Interviews with children of working mothers indicate that they do not object to their mothers working, but they do object to how stressed their mothers are when they return home.

Sociologist Arlie Hochschild describes the working mother's plight in her book *The Second Shift*. After working a full day on the job, she then puts in a full shift at home. In fact, women work an average of 15 hours a week more than their husbands do when a single child enters the picture. In a family with three or more children, working women spend an average of 90 hours on paid (workplace) and unpaid (household) work combined, while men spend an average of 60 hours.[109]

The Center for Work and Family at Boston University reports that the fastest-growing segment of the American workforce is women with young children. The typical problem unfolds like this: Wanting to be a model mother and a wonderful wife, as well as a perfect professional, the modern woman is increasingly overcommitted and overstressed. Consider the following description of a working mother's day.

A Day in the Life of a Working Mother

She is up at 6:00 A.M. has a shower and her makeup on by 6:30, at which time she wakens her husband and kids. She makes breakfast and everyone eats by 7:15. Everyone needs something—lunch money, a doctor's note, or a newspaper tucked under the arm—on the way to the door.

As she drives to work, she makes three stops: drops off Jessie at day care, picks up dry cleaning, and buys donuts for the monthly office meeting. It is 7:55 when she swings into the parking lot. She grabs her high-heel shoes (because she's supposed to dress great, too) and dashes across the drive and into the door at 8:00 sharp.

She no longer feels fresh as a daisy as she confronts her desk and the to-do list ahead. By 8:15 and with a kickoff coffee, she is focused and in the work groove. Her pace is steady as she moves efficiently through the day, from meeting to memo to meeting again. Her energy holds up as she maintains a high level of production, pausing just once for a personal break. She loves her work and is proud of her company, so her job is not a negative.

Lunchtime is used for errands, the normal pattern for most workdays. She buys a card for her friend who has just had surgery and has lunch while she drives, including a soda from the cooler that she keeps in the car.

From 1:00 P.M. on, the day goes crazy. A supplier slips up, a customer complains, a co-worker has problems, and then she gets the message she most hates to hear—"Your son's school called." She handles them all and still finishes the key account report by the end of the day.

As she straightens her office and prepares to go home, she thinks of the day and what it has meant. She is relieved that her son's school problem was easily handled, but she is also thankful that she could have called on her husband if the problem had required a trip to school. It was work as normal, but what does that mean? It was money for the family, but was it enough? It was time, which is life, and was it well spent?

These are good questions for the future, but more important is the flurry of activity that lies ahead. First is day care pickup of little Jessie, then a swing by school for Billy. Both of these are must-hits and they are always eventful, with progress reports, funny stories, laughter, and sometimes tears.

She arrives home at 5:45 but can't sit down or even start dinner because Susie is standing in the driveway and needs to be at her dance lesson by 6:00.

> While she waits for Susie, she uses the time productively to outline the talk she has to give the next day. The company believes in employee involvement and her team presentation has to go well.
>
> She's off again by 7:30, but now it's so late she decides to zip by the fast-food drive-through rather than cooking the meal she had planned. At 8:00 she is ready to set the food out, talk with the kids, and meet her husband.
>
> Dinner goes well, but as with most things, it seems a little late and a little rushed, plus dishes, homework, and laundry are yet to be done.
>
> At 10:00 she has a choice: do the family bills, check the news, return her mom's call, sew Billy's pants, write her friend's card, or talk with her husband. She wants to talk with Fred, but he is concentrating on Billy's Cub Scout project. She does 1 through 5, and then it's time for bed.
>
> She is too tired to fall asleep, plus she is waiting on Fred. She thinks about the family, each one in turn—their health, their happiness, and what they need. She then thinks about herself. She is tired but happy. She knows she is spending her chips, but she wouldn't change if she could. Her only question is, Can I keep it up? And how do others do it who don't have a husband?

As women have moved more and more into paid employment, there has been little reduction in home responsibilities. Some employers have responded with help for working mothers, offering flexible work schedules, job sharing, telecommuting, personal leave, and child-care facilities.[110]

The Executive Monkey Studies

Whether yours is a high-stress field, such as law enforcement, or a low-stress profession, such as library science, if you feel the responsibility of office, yet you feel out of control, then the case of the "executive monkey" and related research will be of interest to you.

"Executive monkeys develop ulcers" was the conclusion of a study Joseph Brady did in 1958.[111] In this study, Brady placed pairs of monkeys in an environment where both received electric shocks. A red light signaled the shock period. However, the monkeys were not shocked if one of them operated a lever that prevented the flow of electric current. See Figure 17–9.

**Figure 17–9
The Executive Monkey
Studies**

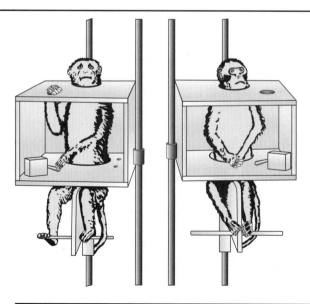

In each pair of monkeys, the executive monkey (so named because of the analogy to human executive situations) was the one having access to an operational lever and was able to learn the relationship between the light, the lever, and the shocks. The other, nonexecutive, monkey had a nonoperational lever and therefore was unable to learn any way to prevent the flow of electric current. The only thing this monkey knew was that every once in a while there was a shock, but the monkey didn't know why.

In this study, the executive monkeys, who were responsible for saving their partners and themselves, developed ulcers and died, while the uninformed, nonexecutive monkeys remained healthy. The results of the study suggested that the burden of responsibility, including the need to maintain a high degree of vigilance and the pressure to make decisions, was the cause of the high level of stress resulting in death.

A follow-up study on rats conducted by Jay Weiss of Emory University provided additional information as to the demise of the executive monkeys.[112] One primary difference between the Weiss study and the Brady study was that Weiss used a warning tone to signal the imminent onset of electric current. Weiss showed that the executive animals were much more able to cope with responsibility and avoid ulcers if they were given feedback on their behavior. He did this by arranging conditions so that the lever, when operated, would prevent shock and would also turn off the warning tone that preceded the shock. This provided clear evidence to the executive animal, in the form of tone cessation, that shock could be avoided, whereas Brady's executive monkeys received no such assurances.

Weiss's animals learned through feedback that they could control their situation, whereas Brady's monkeys felt less control. The conclusion was that pressure to perform without feeling in control can result in health problems and even death. Weiss found that the responsibility of office was not the cause of debilitating stress, but the feeling of frustration and being out of control was.

A sense of powerlessness is a universal cause of stress, and it can have negative health consequences. Robert Karasek of Columbia University has found that people with little control over their jobs, such as assembly-line workers and cooks, have higher rates of heart disease than people who can choose the pace and method of their work. People who deal with the public but have little opportunity for independent decision making are those most negatively affected. The combination of high psychological demands and low personal control appears to raise the risk of heart disease by "about the same order of magnitude as smoking or having a high cholesterol level."[113]

If you are in a position to accept responsibility, be sure you have adequate power to influence the events for which you will be held responsible. In addition, as a leader, be sure to delegate to subordinates sufficient authority as well as responsibility to accomplish tasks. The following is a classic experiment demonstrating the importance of feeling in control—not only to manage stress, but to maximize job performance:

Adult subjects were given complex puzzles to solve and a proofreading chore. In the background was a loud, randomly occurring distracting noise; to be specific, it was a combination of two people speaking Spanish, one person speaking Armenian, a mimeograph machine running, a desk calculator, a typewriter, and street noise—producing a composite, nondistinguishable roar. The subjects were split into two groups. Individuals in one set were just told to work at the task. Individuals in the other were provided with a button to turn off the noise, a modern analog of control—the off switch. The group with the off switch solved five times the number of puzzles as their cohorts and made but a tiny fraction of the number of proofreading errors. Now for the kicker: . . . none of the subjects in the off switch group ever used the switch. The mere knowledge that one can exert control made the difference.[114]

Job Stress Interventions

The workplace is a recognized breeding ground for stress and associated mental and physical health disorders. Stress prevention can be achieved with various programs. Historically, three distinct approaches have been used as strategies for reducing or controlling stress. These approaches can be classified as primary, secondary, and tertiary prevention.[115]

Primary prevention seeks to correct the fundamental cause of stress by changing working conditions and the physical environment. Primary prevention strategies include occupational safety, physical work comfort, work design, and participative management initiatives.

Secondary prevention strives to reduce the severity of stress symptoms before they lead to serious health consequences. Stress education, health promotion, and wellness programs are examples of secondary prevention efforts.

Tertiary prevention involves the treatment of health conditions to lessen the impact on personal functioning, regardless of the source. Tertiary treatment is typically reactive to existing problems and is traditionally provided by medical personnel, often through an employee assistance program. An important example is treatment of post-traumatic stress syndrome.[116]

Wellness Programs

The workplace has become the home of many stress management and wellness programs. A dramatic example of the success of a wellness program is the one used by the New York Telephone Company that saved the organization $2.7 million in reduced absenteeism and treatment costs in one year alone.[117] In *Fortune* magazine's "One Hundred Best Companies to Work For," the most important criterion is the extent to which these companies are helping employees balance work and life issues. In 2008, Google emerged at the top for the second straight year. Google's benefits include on-site child care, subsidized fitness programs, and family-friendly work policies.[118] One of the national health objectives to be achieved by the year 2010 was to have at least 60 percent of American work sites employing 50 or more people provide programs to reduce employee stress.[119]

Wellness programs are implemented at three levels of intensity and depth.[120]

Level I programs include newsletters, health fairs, screening sessions, posters, flyers, and classes. These activities are useful in making people aware of the specific consequences of poor health habits.

Level II programs provide specific training, such as physical conditioning and proper methods of performing physically demanding tasks. The programs may last several months or may be available on an ongoing basis. Level II programs are aimed at helping people develop lifelong healthy habits, and may use behavior modification to achieve this goal.

Level III programs create an environment that helps people sustain healthy lifestyles and behaviors. A Level III program fosters participation by providing fitness center memberships and making healthy food available. Although a Level III program could be conducted independently, it is usually an outgrowth of ongoing Level I and Level II activities. The following describes a Level III program.[121]

Live for Life

In 1979, the Johnson & Johnson Company (J&J) began its Live for Life program for 28,000 employees in 50 plants. The name was changed to "Health and Wellness" in 1993. Today the program serves 120,000 employees worldwide. The goal of the program is to provide the means for Johnson & Johnson employees to become the healthiest in the world and to control the increasing illness and accident costs of the corporation. The program is free for employees.

The Johnson & Johnson program is a prototype of effective in-house wellness programs that reduce company costs by improving employee health. The J&J program incorporates the following basic elements:

1. Lifestyle assessment and health screening.

2. A lifestyle seminar that introduces employees to the basic concepts of wellness and the Live for Life (Health and Wellness) program.

3. Classes for smoking cessation, weight control, good nutrition, and stress management. The program also includes yoga classes, alcohol education, physical fitness classes, and work-life balance training.

4. Alteration of the work environment; that is, nutritious food in the cafeteria, rewards for nonsmokers, exercise facilities, car pools, flexible scheduling of work time, and training programs to improve employee–manager relations.

5. Feedback and follow-up. Each employee receives a summary of lifestyle points earned during a three-month period for lifestyle improvement and fitness achievement. Participants are contacted by letter or telephone for their reactions and progress in the program.

Kenneth Pelletier of Stanford's Center for Research in Disease Prevention has reviewed 48 studies of work-site health promotion programs published since 1980. The result: Every program but one has shown positive effects on workers' health, as measured by risk factors and by rates of actual illness. Of the 30 programs analyzed for cost-effectiveness, every one has saved money.[122]

Two examples of organizations with successful health promotion and employee wellness programs are the Cianbro Companies and The Jackson Laboratory, both in Maine. These are organizations with long histories of concern for employee well-being and good business practices.[123]

Important keys for success in implementing work-site health promotion programs include long-term commitment, top management support, employee involvement, professional leadership, clearly defined objectives, careful planning, and family involvement.[124]

The Role of the Family

Robert Haas, retired chairman of Levi Strauss, explains the relationship between home and work. Long hours, stressful jobs, and dual careers serve to compound problems.

We used to think we could separate the soft stuff from the hard stuff. The soft stuff was our commitment to the workforce, and the hard stuff—what really mattered—was getting pants out the door. No more. Now we know we can't get stuff out the door unless your employees are 100% committed and free of home life distractions. And the way you get them there is simple. You do everything you can to help them handle those home life issues, so work and family can coexist successfully.[125]

George Burns once said, "Happiness is having a large, close-knit family in another city." On a serious note, in different shapes and sizes, still the number-one source of satisfaction worldwide is having a family. Satisfaction with family relationships is a better predictor of overall life satisfaction than other key aspects of adult life, such as one's work. This is true even among highly educated people, for whom work commitment is typically high. In his autobiography, former Chrysler chairman Lee Iacocca makes this point: "Yes, I've had a wonderful and successful career. But next to my family, it really hasn't mattered at all." What does a family need to be effective? What qualities help its members deal with the stress of the external world as well as the demands of family life—disputes, disagreements, foibles, and finances? Author Jane Howard identifies eleven characteristics of effective families.

Complete Exercise 17–2 to evaluate a real-life family.

Exercise 17–2
Family Report Card[126]

Evaluate a real-life family on 11 key characteristics using the following guide: A = excellent; B = very good; C = average; D = needs improvement; F = dysfunctional.

1. *There is love;* that is, members show love and affection for one another. _____

2. *There is authority;* that is, there are parents who make final decisions. _____

3. *There is an anchor;* that is, there is someone who keeps track of what the others are doing. _____

4. *There is a place;* that is, there is a house or a town or some other place to which members feel connected. _____

5. *There is ritual;* that is, members celebrate holidays, grieve at funerals, and in other ways experience a sense of tradition. _____

6. *There is safety;* that is, members are secure in the knowledge others will provide comfort and protection. _____

7. *There is competence;* that is, when problems arise, they are dealt with quickly and effectively. _____

8. *There is continuity;* that is, members feel as though something came before them and something will continue after them to which they are linked. _____

9. *There is honor;* that is, all members are valued and cared for. Their experience and wisdom are respected. _____

10. *There is work;* that is, all lend a hand to do household chores, make a pleasant home, and provide economic security. _____

11. *There is talk;* that is, conversation is rich as members say what they think and listen to each other. _____

Scoring and Interpretation:

To determine a grade point, use the following code: A = 4; B = 3; C = 2; D = 1; F = 0. Add the points for the 11 items and divide by 11. The interpretation is: 3.5 − 4.0 = A, excellent; 2.5 − 3.4 = B, very good; 1.5 − 2.4 = C, average; 0.5 − 1.4 = D, needs improvement; 0.0 − 0.4 = F, dysfunctional.

Discussion:

If improvement is needed for family effectiveness, time should be taken to have a family conversation around six key questions: (1) What are the positive forces that are helping the family? (2) What are the negative forces that are hindering the family? (3) What should be done to reinforce family strengths? (4) What should be done to correct low areas? (5) What action steps should the family take? (6) How should we monitor progress? All family members should participate—as the saying goes, the person in the boat with you never bores a hole in it.

The Stress-Resistant Person

In *Crucibles of Leadership,* Warren Bennis and Robert Thomas identify a critical attribute of effective leaders—*adaptive capacity,* the ability to transcend adversity and emerge stronger than before. Like a phoenix, the Egyptian mythical bird that perished by fire and then rose from its ashes to live another life, leadership requires stress resistance, the ability to survive even the most negative experiences.[127]

Stress-resistant people are hardy individuals who are able to accomplish tremendous tasks and still remain healthy. They are comfortable in almost any situation. Their lives are full, yet unhurried. They are relaxed and confident, even when they are making critical decisions. Physically fit and seldom tired, they project a sense of control and strength.[128]

Personality factors influence the coping strategies one uses, which in turn influence the amount and type of stress one experiences. Certain characteristics of personality belong potentially to everyone, but hardy people have more of them than do nonhardy individuals. These characteristics are **personal commitment, sense of control, positive attitude, balanced perspective**, and **caring relationships.**

Complete Exercise 17–3 to determine your level of stress resistance.

**Exercise 17–3
Characteristics of a
Hardy Personality**

The following questionnaire features the five characteristics of a hardy personality. Rate yourself on each characteristic by circling the appropriate number on the scale below each description.

Commitment

The Scottish philosopher Thomas Carlyle believed: We don't fear extinction, we fear extinction without meaning.[129] This entails having a purpose in life and being true to one's values. The hardy personality thinks he knows what is important and that he is doing the right thing. This translates into *commitment* that gives tremendous strength to overcome obstacles and persevere in the face of adversity. The committed person is emotionally strong, and this emotional strength, like a wonder drug, results in physical strength as well. Where does commitment begin? It begins with choosing to be an active participant in life, not a bystander. With involvement comes understanding. Only when we understand will we care. Only when we care will we be committed. Only when we are committed will we make a difference in life. *Rate yourself on commitment.*

1	2	3	4	5	6	7	8	9	10	11	12	13	14	15	16	17	18	19	20
Low									Middle										High

Control

In *Don Juan in Hell,* George Bernard Shaw wrote, "Hell is to drift, heaven is to steer."[130] The hardy personality believes this idea fully, and seeks to *control* her own life. When asked the question, "Who is in charge, the world or you?" the hardy personality's answer is "I am." She sees herself as the master of her own destiny, the captain of her own ship, not the pawn of fate and not flotsam on the sea of life. What gives legitimacy to this feeling is the fact that the hardy personality has mastered and employs effective time management principles. She sets goals in line with her values, keeps a daily to-do list with priorities indicated, works on first things first, and checks off tasks as they are completed. The result is a feeling of accomplishment and satisfaction. *Rate yourself on sense of control and practicing effective time management principles.*

1	2	3	4	5	6	7	8	9	10	11	12	13	14	15	16	17	18	19	20
Low									Middle										High

Attitude

The hardy personality lives by William James's prescription: "Change your *attitude*—change your life."[131] Unlike the pessimist who builds dungeons in the air, the hardy personality accentuates the positive. He recognizes the influence of mind over matter and therefore chooses to think positive thoughts that elicit positive moods that result in positive actions.[132] This doesn't mean he denies reality; the opposite is true. He sees life as it is, both good and bad. Then, having seen both, he emphasizes possibilities over problems, strengths over weaknesses, and potentialities over deficiencies, both in the situation and in himself. In the area of attitude, the hardy personality practices three key habits—expect greatness, strive for the best, and appreciate any good that results. The hardy personality agrees with Hans Selye, who prescribed a technique for optimism—"Imitate the sundial's ways; count only the pleasant days." Because the hardy personality is an optimist, he is energized and focused; and with energy and focus, he indeed achieves his goals.[133] *Rate yourself on attitude.*

1	2	3	4	5	6	7	8	9	10	11	12	13	14	15	16	17	18	19	20
Low									Middle										High

Perspective

The hardy personality keeps life in *perspective* and doesn't get upset over small matters. She realizes, in the final analysis, most matters are small matters. Consequently, she doesn't develop a full-blown fight-or-flight response to every minor hassle, obstacle, or setback. In this way, she avoids unnecessary states of alarm and vigilance leading to exhaustion and breakdown. The hardy personality realizes there is a need for the hot-reacting linebacker in times of defense, but she prefers to remain the cool-thinking quarterback on offense.[134] One way she does this is to remember what is important (her hills worth dying on). All else is viewed with tolerance and patience as matters of style, taste, and individual differences that can enrich the world. *Rate yourself on keeping things in perspective.*

1	2	3	4	5	6	7	8	9	10	11	12	13	14	15	16	17	18	19	20
Low									Middle										High

Relationships

For most people most of the time, concern for others is the most important characteristic of a hardy personality. This person develops caring relationships in his home life, work life, and community at large. He gives tender loving care (TLC) to all creatures, great and small; and as he sows, so he reaps. The hardy personality gives love, and in turn is beloved.[135] In this process, physiological responses are generated that are life enhancing and life prolonging, helping to explain the hardy personality's ability to overcome germs and disease and maintain good health in spite of heavy responsibilities and demanding schedules. *Rate yourself on TLC.*

1	2	3	4	5	6	7	8	9	10	11	12	13	14	15	16	17	18	19	20
Low									Middle										High

Scoring:

Add your scores for each characteristic to obtain a total: _____

Score	Grade
90–100	A
80–89	B
70–79	C
60–69	D
59 and below	F

Interpretation:

A   You currently embody the characteristics of a hardy personality. You are doing all that you can do to succeed in life, plus live to enjoy it. You are a model for psychological strength and effective living.

B   This is a high score. Your life is characterized by an effective pattern of **personal commitment, sense of control, positive attitude, balanced perspective**, and **caring relationships**.

C   You do some things well but need to improve in others. To improve, focus on low spots and take positive steps to change yourself or the situation.

D   D stands for deficiencies. This means you must improve, not only to succeed in your life, but to live to enjoy it. Low scores for commitment, control, attitude, perspective, and relationships should be addressed.

F   F is for falling short. You should begin immediately to raise the quality of your life. Advice and support from others can be helpful. Attention and a sustained effort are required.

Discussion:

If you are currently low in one or more of the characteristics of a hardy personality, take concrete action to improve; in so doing, you will enhance your life. If you are high in an area, you should continue to capitalize on this strength and asset for effective living.

The five characteristics of a hardy personality are moving targets that you must keep your eye upon. This is a lifelong challenge, meaning that just because you have a high score today; it doesn't guarantee a high score tomorrow. Also, it is never too late to improve. Doing so at any point in time is worthwhile, resulting in a fuller and more satisfying life.

After heredity, the three most important influences in our lives are the people we are around, the messages we give ourselves, and the books we read. Along with religious and other inspirational books that mean so much to so many millions, there are five books that are particularly helpful in developing the characteristics of a **hardy personality:**

For commitment, read *Man's Search for Meaning* by Viktor Frankl.

For control, read *First Things First* by Stephen Covey.

For attitude, read *Learned Optimism* by Martin Seligman.

For perspective, read *Is It Worth Dying For?* by Robert Eliot.

For relationships, read *The Art of Loving* by Erich Fromm.

The Stress-Prone versus the Stress-Resistant Personality

Table 17–3 presents a day in the life of two individuals—one with a stress-prone personality and the other with a stress-resistant personality. Multiply this day by weeks, months, and years, and you can see the important influence personality patterns can have in determining the quality and length of your life.

Table 17–3 A Day in the Life of Mr. A and Mr. B	Time line	Mr. A's Stress-Prone Path	Time line	Mr. B's Stress-Resistant Path
	7:00 A.M. Alarm goes off.	*Thoughts:* The first thing he thinks of is last night's argument. The second is the battle ahead. He resolves to be vigilant.	7:00 A.M. Alarm goes off.	*Thoughts:* The first thing he thinks of is last night's get-together. Good times should be relished. His second thought is about the day ahead. He knows he will do his best.
		Action: He hurries through showering and dressing, and walks out the door, calling good-bye to his wife.		*Action:* He showers and dresses and takes time to have breakfast. He gives his wife an affectionate good-bye hug and kiss.
	8:15 A.M.	He sees snow on the car, and the roads are icy. He is furious, because he doesn't have a scraper.	8:15 A.M.	He sees snow on the car, and the streets are icy, but he is calm because he has a scraper and a shovel and is prepared for bad weather.
	8:30 A.M. Traffic is slow.	*Action:* He honks the horn, grips the wheel, gnashes his teeth, and yells at bad drivers.	8:30 A.M. Traffic is slow.	*Action:* He goes with the flow, realizing that getting upset will not change the conditions. He listens to the radio.
		Result: Blood pressure and pulse rate go up. He arrives at work angry and tense.		*Result:* He remains calm and relaxed and arrives at work fresh and alert.
	9:00 A.M.– 11:00 A.M.	*Events:* Unimportant meetings follow disorganized meetings, and frustration goes up. He becomes increasingly resentful, angry, and worried because of wasted time.	9:00 A.M.– 11:00 A.M.	*Events:* There is a sense of progress and satisfaction as well-run meetings support important goals.
	11:00 A.M.– 12:30 P.M.	Emotions heat up when a customer complains and an employee gets angry.	11:00 A.M.– 12:00 P.M.	When a customer and an employee fail to communicate, he remains calm.
		Reaction: If people don't like the way things are, they can go elsewhere. This is a free country. Besides, complaints and problems are hassles I don't need.		*Reaction:* When people complain or get upset, it gives me a chance to share information, learn something important, and try to improve things by developing a common ground.
		Action: He delegates the problem to a subordinate and gets into a shouting match with another customer.		*Action:* He meets with the customer and employee personally. He takes the time to listen and understand their concerns. He takes their grievances seriously and is responsive to their suggestions.
	12:30 P.M. Lunch break (Behind schedule)	*Action:* He eats at his desk with a telephone in one hand and a pencil, candy bar, and coffee sharing the other.	12:00 P.M.– Lunch break (On schedule)	*Action:* He escapes for a while by taking a walk in the park. He eats yogurt and a banana on a bench.
		Effect: Stress builds as he feels chained to his chair; indigestion sets in.		*Effect:* Exercise and nutrition are healthy, and getting away from the office helps put things in perspective.
	1:00 P.M. Board meeting starts.	*Mental State:* Coming off a working lunch, he feels fragmented and ill-prepared.	1:00 P.M. Board meeting starts.	*Mental State:* He returns from lunch energized and focused, ready to give his best to the important meeting ahead.
	2:30 P.M. Modest progress made.	*Thoughts:* This group couldn't change a lightbulb in a weekend. We aren't accomplishing a thing! If they don't get their act together, this company's going down the tube.	2:30 P.M. Modest progress made.	*Thoughts:* We were slow today, but we did make progress. We need to celebrate these victories and learn from our shortcomings. If we work together, I think we'll succeed.

4:00 P.M. Board meeting ends.	Action: He goes to the bar for a quick drink and to lament the wasted day. One drink leads to another as he tries to forget his problems.	4:00 P.M. Board meeting ends.	Action: He goes to his office to summarize thoughts while they are fresh and to return telephone calls in a timely manner. 5:30 P.M. finds him exercising (three times a week).
7:00 P.M. Arrives home.	Action: He has dinner with the family. Interaction goes from polite conversation to active argument. Effect: Stress goes up; tension leads to headache; indigestion develops.	7:00 P.M. Arrives home.	Action: He has dinner with the family. Interaction goes from discussion to dialogue. Effect: Happiness and a sense of well-being are experienced.
8:00 P.M.	Everyone watches television—alone. Result: Self-absorption develops and loneliness sets in.	8:00 P.M.	He helps his son make a kite and helps his daughter with her homework. Result: Responsibility is taught and relationships grow.
10:00 P.M. Disagree- ment occurs with teenage son.	He is tired and his patience is thin. He launches into an attack and "wins" by intimidation.	10:00 P.M. Disagree- ment occurs with teenage son.	He garners his energy and seeks the facts. He talks *with* his son, not *at* him, and gives reasons for his views. Father and son reach agreement together.
11:00 P.M. Goes to bed.	Action: Can't sleep; tosses and turns for two hours. Thoughts: What is wrong with everybody? Why can't things be smooth instead of a constant struggle? All I do is work and worry, work and worry. The truth is, I'm fed up. Result: Wakes up at 7:00 A.M. exhausted and depressed.	11:00 P.M. Goes to bed.	Action: Falls asleep quickly. Thoughts: This has been a good day. There is much to appreciate—family, good health, good job. Result: Wakes up at 7:00 A.M. refreshed and happy.

Developing Resilience

The following are two scenarios in the life of a leader and her company:

Good Times Your product is great, your service is fabulous, and you are the envy of your industry and market. You have a vision that energizes your people, a strategy to succeed, all resources are aligned, and (critically) your execution is flawless. Your leadership team masters complexity and your frontline employees respond positively to change in structure, tasks, technology, and people. The company has achieved remarkable success. On a personal plane, your home front is smooth and your happiness is high. The question on your mind is how do I keep this up?

Bad Times Your board is unhappy, your team is dysfunctional, your spouse is ill, and your son's school wants "a meeting." Hitler couldn't win a two-front war and you have four. On top of this, your customers are complaining, you have a cash-flow problem, IT systems have failed, and you are personally exhausted. You are in your middle years, disaster surrounds you, and the future looks dim. The question on your mind is how do I keep this up?

The answer to both scenarios is **resilience,** based on the five characteristics of a hardy personality.

Personal Commitment

Psychologist Abraham Maslow once remarked: "If you purposefully choose to be less than you can be, then you are surely doomed to be unhappy." As inspiration for living a purposeful and committed life, consider the words of Theodore Roosevelt:

> The credit goes to the man who is actually in the arena,
> Whose face is marred with sweat and dust and blood;
> Who strives valiantly; who errs and comes short again and again;
> Who knows the great enthusiasms, the great devotions,
> and spends himself in a worthy cause;
> Who at the best knows the triumph of high achievement;
> and who, if he fails, at least fails
> While daring greatly.
> Far better it is to dare mighty things, to win glorious triumphs,
> even though checkered by failure,
> Than to take rank with those cold and timid souls who live in
> the gray twilight that knows not victory or defeat.[136]

With fervor and eloquence, Roosevelt advocates a life of engagement and meaning. For the caring leader, this means personal commitment to accomplish a goal. The goal may be a one-time endeavor or a life's work. The goal may be a tangible product, such as the creation of a business, or it may be an idea or a cause, such as stamping out tyranny. In any case, the leader's commitment becomes contagious, igniting the emotions of all who are present.

Sense of Control

For sense of control, remember Benjamin Franklin's advice, "Dost thou love life? Then do not squander time, for it is the stuff that life is made of." If you waste time, you waste your life. If you master time, you master your life. For what purpose should time be used?

Take Time

> Take time to *think,*
> It is the source of power.
> Take time to *play,*
> It is the secret of youth.
> Take time to *read,*
> It is the basis of knowledge.
> Take time to *love,*
> It is the essence of life.
> Take time for *friends,*
> It is the road to happiness.
> Take time to *laugh,*
> It is the music of the soul.
> Take time to *give,*
> It is too short to be selfish.
> Take time to *work,*
> It is the price of success

Franklin was well known for his wise use of time. To keep himself on track, he would start each morning with the question, "What good shall I do today?" and he would end each day with the question, "What good have I done today?"[137]

Positive Attitude

William Shakespeare wrote in *Hamlet,* "There is nothing either good or bad, but thinking makes it so." The physical basis for Shakespeare's observation is the fact that the autonomic nervous system cannot differentiate between real and imagined experiences. It acts the same in either case, and this is the reason why voodoo, hypnosis, and other forms of "mind over body" work.

The following story shows how it helps to focus on the positive and natural things in life, however small:

The historian Will Durant described how he looked for happiness in knowledge, and found only disillusionment. He then sought happiness in travel, and found weariness; in wealth, he found worry and discord. He looked for happiness in his own writing, and was only fatigued. One day he saw a woman waiting in a tiny car with a sleeping child in her arms. A man descended from a train and came over and gently kissed the woman, and then the baby, very softly, so as not to waken him. The family drove off and left Durant with a stunning realization of the true nature of happiness. He relaxed and discovered, "every normal function of life holds some delight."[138]

When asked for advice, it is not unusual for those who have survived heart attacks or learned they have only a short time to live to say, "Take pleasure from the little things in life." Finding something that gives you pleasure may require a change in your environment. If so, take steps to make your work and living areas pleasant and satisfying. Surround yourself with people who give you happiness, and, every day, strive to do at least one activity that gives you peace of mind.

Balanced Perspective

Cardiologist Robert Eliot relates a personal account showing the importance of keeping things in perspective.

Wise men speak of the moment of clarity—that instant when absolute knowledge presents itself. My moment of clarity came as I was doubled up in a bathroom at a Nebraska community hospital 200 miles from home. Earlier that morning, after conducting grand rounds in the facility's coronary care unit, I had participated in a cardiology conference before my peers. My lecture had been on heart attacks and sudden death. I had experienced some discomfort during the program but dismissed it as indigestion—or, at worst, a bout with my gallbladder.

It had been a hectic week. The day before the conference, back at my own hospital, I had argued both vehemently and unsuccessfully with administrators over the budget, manpower, and timing regarding a planned cardiovascular center of my own. Two days before that I had flown back from an exhausting lecture series in New Orleans—where, once again, I had been the so-called expert on sudden cardiac death.

In that bathroom, the first symptom I noticed was intense pressure. It began near my breastbone; shot up into my shoulders, neck, and jaws; and surged down again through both of my arms. It was as if an elephant had plopped down on my chest. I could barely catch my breath. I started sweating. I began getting bowel cramps and then overwhelming nausea. Immediately I diagnosed my own condition: myocardial infarction. Later, as the nurses helped me into a hospital bed, I remember saying with astonishment, "I'm having a heart attack." I was 44 years old.

During my recovery I realized my professional life had become a joyless treadmill. I had worked tirelessly for acceptance within the medical community, and yet efforts to establish my own cardiovascular center had failed. This was a bitter pill for someone who had always defined life in terms of victory or defeat. My disillusionment was compounded by the knowledge that I had brought promising associates into this seemingly futile situation. I've since described my state of mind as invisible entrapment.

> I didn't like being on the wrong side of the sheets in a coronary care unit. Something had to change; and I asked myself, "Is any of this worth dying for?" Fortunately for me, my answer was "No!" I had looked into the abyss and decided to stop sweating the small stuff. Pretty soon, I saw that it was *all* small stuff.[139]

Caring Relationships

Scott Peck, author of *The Road Less Traveled,* describes the character of loving relationships. Such relationships are safe precisely because no one is attempting to heal or convert you, to fix you, to change you. Instead, you are accepted as you are. You are tolerated and your foibles are accepted. You are valued, not as an object or means to other ends, but as a precious thing in your own right. In loving relationships, you are free to be you. You are free to discard defenses, masks, and disguises; free to grow and achieve your full potential; free to become your whole and true self.

What about the benefits of positive relations for leaders? One of the best examples comes from the life of John D. Rockefeller. As a young man, Rockefeller entered the business world and drove himself so hard that by the age of 33 he had earned his first million dollars. Ten years later, he owned the world's largest business, Standard Oil. By the age of 53, he was the world's first billionaire. During the process, he had developed alopecia, a condition in which his hair fell out, his digestion was so poor that all he could eat was crackers and milk, and he was plagued by insomnia. His doctors agreed that he wouldn't live another year. Then, John D. Rockefeller changed. He began to think of and care about the welfare of others. He decided to use his wealth for the benefit of others. He founded hospitals and universities and a myriad of missions to help his fellow man. When Rockefeller began helping others he helped himself as well. For the first time in years, he was able to eat and sleep normally. He felt renewed. He lived to see not only his 54th birthday, but his 98th birthday, too, giving and caring for others.[140]

Part Eight Summary

After reading Part Eight, you should know the following key concepts, principles, and terms. Fill in the blanks from memory, or copy the answers listed below.

Many leaders view (a) _____ as the most rewarding of all their tasks. Types of leaders as teachers include shamans, priests, elected leaders, missionaries, and mystic healers. People grow best when there is a felt need, when they are encouraged by someone they respect, when their plans move from general goals to specific actions, when they move from a condition of lower to higher self-esteem, and when they move from external to internal commitment. These are (b) _____. One good way to learn leadership is by (c) _____ and learning from their examples. Good rules for succeeding in one's career include (d) _____, _____, _____, _____, and _____. What do employees want from their employers, and how do you keep good people? Six powerful answers are (e) _____, _____, _____, _____, _____, and _____. Types of change going on in the American workplace involve (f) _____, _____, _____, and _____. There are seven rules for guiding people through change: (g) _____, _____, _____, _____, _____, _____, and _____. Effective responses in dealing with change include (h) _____, _____, and _____, versus denial, resistance, and the attitude trough. Types of burnout victims include (i) _____, _____, _____, and _____. The formula for the burnout process is this: Too many demands on strength and resources + high expectations and deep personal involvement + too few actions to replenish the energy consumed = (j) _____. Strategies for dealing with burnout include (k) _____, such as deep breathing, positive self-talk, physical retreat; (l) _____, such as reducing workload, setting priorities, taking care of one's body; and (m) _____, such as clarifying values, making lifestyle changes, developing personal competencies. Five major forces or trends are sources of stress for increasing numbers of people: (n) _____, _____, _____, _____, and _____. The most stressful jobs have high-demand tasks with little relief, power, or pay. The combination of high demand with low personal control and small psychic or financial compensation is a formula for stress that the good leader can help prevent or solve. The five characteristics of a hardy personality are: (o) _____, _____, _____, _____, and _____.

Answer Key for Part Eight Summary

a. **developing others,** page 346

b. **personal conditions conducive to growth,** page 350

c. **studying the masters,** page 354

d. **put your best foot forward, deliver results, be considerate, be creative, have integrity,** pages 356–357

e. (any six) **clarity of work assignment, good work tools and supplies, challenge in one's area of expertise, recognition for one's accomplishments, opportunity to** grow, respect for one's opinions, a mission that motivates, feedback on performance, positive social interactions, and pride in one's group, page 357

f. structure, tasks, technology, people, page 360

g. have a good reason for making a change, personalize change, implement change thoughtfully, put a respected person in charge, tell the truth, wait patiently for results, acknowledge and reward people, page 362

h. exploration, responsibility, commitment, page 369

i. (any four) superpeople, workaholics, burned-out Samaritans, mismatched people, midcareer coasters, overstressed students, page 371

j. burnout, page 371

k. emergency aid, page 377

l. short-term actions, page 377

m. long-term solutions, page 377

n. new technology, workforce diversity, global competition, organizational restructure, changing work systems, page 379

o. personal commitment, sense of control, positive attitude, balanced perspective, caring relationships, page 389

Reflection Points—Personal Thoughts on the Leader as Coach, Helping People through Change, and Burnout Prevention

Complete the following questions and activities to personalize the content of Part Eight. Space is provided for writing your thoughts.

■ Discuss the vignette "Why Can't Roger Learn?" What could the teacher have done to keep Roger from failing?

_____

_____

■ What is your style of developing others? Are you a shaman, a priest, an elected leader, a missionary, or a mystic healer in your approach to teaching? How did you develop your style?

_____

_____

■ Apply conditions conducive to growth to your own development. What factors are present that will help you fulfill your potential?

_____

_____

■ Apply the attitude curve in dealing with change in your own work and career. Where are you now—denial, resistance, attitude trough, exploration, responsibility, or commitment?

_____

_____

■ Identify a change initiative in which you are either the owner or a principal player. Apply the seven rules for helping people through change to critique your efforts. Discuss success points and areas for improvement.

_____

_____

■ Discuss job stress and burnout prevention based on your own experiences. Discuss the role of the leader, as well as effective coping techniques.

Part Eight Video Case
Working Smart

The image of the American worker, putting in long hours at the office and at home and rarely taking time off, is one popularized by television programs and magazine columns. Is the overworked American an urban legend or a reality? It's a fact that 26 percent of Americans take no vacations at all; 13 percent of American companies don't even offer them. Some firms require employees to perform extra tasks before getting a vacation. Unlike other countries, the United States has no laws mandating companies to offer vacations. On average, workers in America take about 10 days of vacation a year, compared with 25 days in France, 20 in Italy and Great Britain, and 15 in China.

In much of the world, time off is a time for renewal. In the United States, taking time off can put people on a guilt trip, says author Jo Robinson. Without it, however, workers are more inclined to experience what Robinson calls vacation deficit disorder, the negative consequences of being overworked. Vacations serve the valuable function of interrupting job stress, which Robinson says is rampant among American workers. The Families and Work Institute states that an environment where workers don't take all of their vacation results in high stress rates and employee burnout.

Yet some experts believe that increased vacation for workers could bring more harm than good for the American workplace. Professor Brigitte Madison of the University of Chicago School of Business argues that more vacation time for Americans could mean lost jobs. "If employers can't pass the cost of vacation time on to workers in terms of lower wages," says Madison, "then we'll end up with reduced employment levels as well."

Besides forgoing vacations, many people never really leave their work on a day-to-day basis. Technology has linked people to their jobs even when they are out of their offices. E-mail, fax machines, cell phones, and laptop computers make workers more readily available day and night. Along with the time spent on the job, the nature of the work itself influences how employees feel. Demanding jobs that require a great degree of multitasking leave employees feeling more overwhelmed. Low-value work, which people complain about as a waste of time, increases the likelihood of feeling overworked.

One in three American employees is chronically overworked, according to Ellen Galinsky, the Families and Work Institute president who wrote a study called "Overworked in America." Galinsky looked at three different factors to determine whether someone is chronically overworked: Does a worker feel overworked? Is a worker overwhelmed by everything he or she has to do? Do workers have time to stop and think about what they are doing? The study showed that the percentage of overworked Americans goes up from 29 to 54 if you consider people who are overwhelmed by what they do. Only 29 percent of that study's respondents said they never feel overworked. Galinsky notes that while America's perspective on work and families is different from that of other countries, younger U.S. workers are more likely to put an equal emphasis on work and family. She attributes this attitude in part to the downsizing and the demanding jobs they have seen their parents experience.

Feeling overworked can influence not only job performance but also personal and family relationships and health. Galinsky reported that 20 percent of those feeling overworked make more mistakes, 39 percent feel angry with the employer, and 34 percent indicate being resentful of co-workers. In terms of personal outcomes, 36 percent report high levels of stress and 21 percent have symptoms of clinical depression. Additionally, those feeling overworked experience more work/life conflict, feel less successful in their personal relationships, are more likely to lose sleep because of work, and are less likely to report they are in good health.

Several strategies can be used to help prevent feeling overworked. On the job, workers can focus on the task at hand and the contribution they are making. Taking breaks during the day is also beneficial. Away from work, people are learning to create more boundaries between work and their personal lives. For instance, some workers simply refuse to work while on vacation. Finally, employees should take their full vacations and leave the job behind.

Questions for Discussion

1. Do you think Americans are overworked? Explain your opinion.

2. What do you do to maintain balance in your life and in your work? Are you *aging* at the rate you want and for the purpose(s) you want?

For more information, see www.familiesandwork.org and www.cdc.gov/niosh/docs/99-101/.

Action Assignment

As a bridge between learning and doing, complete the following action assignment.

1. What is the most important idea you have learned in Part Eight?
2. How can you apply what you have learned? What will you do, with whom, where, when, and, most important, why?

Part 9 Performance Management

18. **Managing Performance**
19. **Professional Performance and Sustaining Discipline**

YOU CANNOT BE DISCIPLINED in great things and undisciplined in small things. There is only one sort of discipline—*perfect* discipline. Discipline is based on pride as a soldier, on meticulous attention to detail, and on mutual respect and confidence. It can only be obtained when all officers are so imbued with the sense of their moral obligation to their men and their country that they cannot tolerate negligence.

—General George Patton

U.S. Army

Learning Objectives

After studying Part Nine, you will be able to:
- Master performance management as a leadership skill.
- Know how to set goals, provide feedback on progress, and correct performance problems.
- Know your level of performance in the areas of statesmanship, working through others; entrepreneurship, achieving results; and innovation, generating new ideas.
- Model and reinforce high standards of professional conduct, including upholding core values and using a caring confrontation when corrective action is necessary.
- Improve performance through behavior modification.
- Answer the question, Would you hire you, based on your current professional performance?

CHAPTER

18

Managing Performance

Performance management is at the heart of leadership success. It is important to have a vision; it is important to have values; it is important to have leadership qualities, such as vitality, persistence, and concern for others; it is important to have the power of leadership position. But all of these will result in little actual accomplishment without performance management skills. Effective leadership requires the art of clearly communicating goals, coaching others to succeed, and correcting poor performance.[1]

- **Performance planning** establishes direction and clarity of assignment. It provides the foundation on which individual and group performance can be developed and evaluated.
- **Performance coaching** involves the development and encouragement of people. The leader's challenge is to help individuals grow and fulfill their personal potential while advancing the organization's purpose.
- **Correcting poor performance** includes modifying and improving performance when mistakes are made.

Performance management seems reasonable and fairly simple to do, yet research shows that the majority of leaders fall short when it comes to clearly communicating goals, coaching others to succeed, and correcting poor performance.[2]

In their best-selling book on leadership, *The One Minute Manager,* Ken Blanchard and Spencer Johnson teach three secrets to leadership success that correspond with performance planning, coaching, and correcting. These are leadership techniques that work at all levels of leadership and in all work environments. The three secrets are as follows:

- One-minute goal setting for performance planning.
- One-minute praising for performance coaching.
- One-minute reprimand for correcting poor performance.[3]

These three secrets are drawn from the basic principles of behavioral psychology—the power of goals to focus and energize behavior; the need for feedback to reinforce or modify behavior; and the importance of praise as a recognition technique.[4]

One-minute goal setting. One-minute goal setting involves identifying three to five goals that are critical to success, and writing these on a single sheet of paper—in 250 or fewer words. It is important to include the individual in the goal-setting process, because there is a strong relationship between personal involvement and future success. The individual needs psychological investment, and participation in goal setting helps accomplish this purpose.

One-minute praising. One-minute praising involves showing appreciation for effort and accomplishments. It is based on two ideas: (1) People need feedback as a way of tracking and sustaining progress; and (2) what gets rewarded gets repeated. One-minute praising has four characteristics:

1. Praise is immediate.
2. Praise is specific.
3. Praise is sincere.
4. The individual is encouraged.

One-minute reprimand. The one-minute reprimand is saved for individuals who are trained and who know what to do, but make mistakes. The one-minute reprimand has four characteristics:

1. Correction is immediate.
2. Correction focuses on behavior, not on the character of the person.
3. Correction is sincere.
4. The individual is encouraged.

By mastering the three secrets of the one-minute manager, the effective leader can raise the productivity of individuals and groups. Use Exercise 18–1 to practice these secrets.

**Exercise 18–1
The Performance
Management Lab**

One-Minute Goal Setting

Use 250 or fewer words to identify the three to five most important goals of your job (or the job of another person). Include *what* the goals are, *why* they are important, and the *time frame* for action.

Goal 1: _____

_____

_____

_____

Goal 2: _____

_____

_____

_____

Goal 3: _____

_____

_____

_____

Goal 4: _____

_____

_____

_____

Goal 5: _____

_____

_____

_____

One-Minute Praising

Look for the opportunity to recognize and reinforce good performance. When you deliver praise, be *timely* (if you wait too long, you may lose goodwill); be *specific* (explain why the performance is good and what it means to others); be *sincere* (show that you care about the person and what has been done); and *encourage* the person (set the stage for future success).

One-Minute Reprimand

If attitudes or actions result in mistakes, correct performance in an effective way. Be *immediate* (don't store or save up punishment); be *specific* (let people know the impact of their behavior); be *sincere* (show how important good performance is to you; show your interest and show that you care); *encourage* the person (emphasize positive qualities and your confidence in him or her).

Taking Aim and Taking Stock

Effective job performance requires setting goods and measuring results, as the following story shows:

The famous industrialist Charles Schwab was visiting a steel mill that was producing far below its potential. The superintendent of the plant couldn't understand why—he had coaxed the employees, threatened them, sworn and cursed, but nothing seemed to work. Schwab asked the superintendent for a piece of chalk, and turning to the nearest worker, he asked, "How many heats did your shift make today?" "Six," was the answer. Without saying a word, Schwab drew a large "6" on the floor and walked away. When the night shift came in, they asked what the "6" meant. A day-shift worker said, "We made six heats today, and Schwab wrote it on the floor." The next morning, when Schwab walked through the mill, he saw "7" on the floor—the night shift had made seven heats. That evening, he returned to the plant and saw that the "7" had been erased, and in its place was an enormous "10." Within a short period of time, one of the lowest-producing plants was turning out more work than any other mill in the company. The employees had set performance goals, and they enjoyed recording the results.[5]

The power of goals to focus behavior and the importance of monitoring performance is well documented. Over a thousand research articles and reviews have been published on the subject over the past 30 years.[6]

Setting Performance Objectives

Management author Peter Drucker explains the importance of setting performance objectives:

Each person, from the highest level to the lowest level, should have clear objectives that support the success of the organization. As much as possible, lower-level employees should participate in the development of higher-level objectives as well as their own, thus enabling them to know and understand their supervisor's goals as well as their own place in the plan.[7]

Setting performance objectives is important in four major areas—quantity, quality, timeliness, and cost. One or more of these areas will fit every person's job:[8]

Quantity. The most common method of measuring performance depends to some degree on quantity. In one way or another, we tally number of sales made, dollar volume generated, number of hours billed, number of fenders painted, or any amount that may be processed or produced.

Quality. This is one of the most important areas for which standards apply. Measurements of quality include at least two factors: errors and appearance. *Errors* can include monitoring rejects, misfiles, safety records, customer complaints, miswelds, wrong diagnoses, and countless other areas. *Appearance* deals with items other than rejects or specific errors and is more subjective in judgment. It covers such areas as neatness, a person's manner in answering the telephone, a receptionist's greeting of visitors, or a service representative's explanation to a dissatisfied customer.

Timeliness. This area includes such time factors as meeting deadlines for on-time shipments, on-time departures and arrivals, and absenteeism. Timeliness can also involve the development of new and workable approaches. The most creative idea needs the right moment for its introduction.

Cost. Cost includes the four *M*'s of management: *m*anpower, *m*aterial, *m*achines, and *m*ethods. For example, is the person able to perform while controlling expenditures for labor, inventory, equipment, and corporate services? Can the person live within a reasonable budget?

Performance objectives should be measurable. A generalized objective, such as "improve customer service," provides insufficient guidelines for achieving success. When performance objectives are specific and measurable, the individual can know when, and to what extent, those objectives have been achieved. The following list consists of examples of measurable objectives for improving customer service:

1. Develop and implement a system that allows tracking, following up, and resolving customer complaints.

   The system should identify the number and types of complaints, actions taken by whom, and date of resolution.

   Maintain progress charts and graphs, and post them in places where employees can see them. This system is to be completed by January 1, 2013.

2. Achieve 98 percent on-time delivery by January 1, 2014.

3. Develop a blue-ribbon service system for our top 20 national accounts by January 1, 2015, by assigning one person to service each account.

Conducting Performance Reviews

After performance objectives have been established, progress should be reviewed to capitalize on strengths and improve weaknesses. Performance reviews keep communication lines open, help motivate employees, and give peace of mind to both employer and employee.[9]

Performance reviews should include three steps: preparation, implementation, and follow-up. Both the supervisor and the employee should be trained in carrying out each of these steps. Table 18–1 contains a performance review checklist for supervisors and employees.

**Table 18–1
Performance Review
Checklist**[10]

What to Do before the Performance Review

As an employee, you should

- Consider your strong points and formulate a plan to utilize them fully.
- Determine the areas in which you need to improve. Devise a plan to strengthen your performance in these areas.
- Think about what your supervisor can do to help you improve.

As a supervisor, you should

- Consider your employee's strong points and think about how you can reinforce or capitalize on these.
- Think about your employee's weak areas and consider actions for improvement.
- Think about what you can do to help your employee improve.
- Provide advance notice of the performance review; solicit employee input.

What to Do during the Performance Review

As an employee, you should

- Explain your strengths and weaknesses. Be thorough in expressing each one.
- Discuss issues that may not be apparent to the supervisor that hinder your performance.
- Present ideas to improve future performance; don't dwell on past mistakes, either to save face or to fix blame.
- Present what you think your supervisor can do to help you improve.
- Listen carefully to your supervisor's reactions; these are important indications of attitudes, priorities, and perceptions that will be useful in future dealings.
- Obtain final agreement on what each of you will do. Don't settle for "Let's discuss this again at a later date." Try to get as much commitment and agreement as possible.

As a supervisor, you should

- Create a positive climate—quiet, private, and free from interruptions.
- Tailor the conversation to suit the needs of your employee. Stop talking and listen. Have your employee begin by explaining each strength and weakness in his or her own words. Provide ample time for the full development of each point; avoid interrupting.
- Ask questions based on your prior preparation as well as on new information developed during the conversation. Encourage your employee to do the same.
- Be open and flexible to issues that may come up that you may not know about. Take a problem-solving versus problem-blaming approach.
- Ask how you can help your employee do a better job; listen carefully and take notes.
- Establish new performance objectives, standards, and completion dates. Make your expectations clear. Be direct and honest.
- Write down points of discussion and agreement. Review them so that both you and your employee have the same understanding.
- Remember that a performance review should involve two-way communication. Be prepared to compromise and be flexible. Remember also that you are the supervisor and, as such, are responsible for resolving differences.
- End the meeting on an upbeat, positive, and future-focused note.

What to Do after the Performance Review

As an employee, you should

- Keep your supervisor informed of progress toward meeting objectives.
- Discuss with your supervisor as soon as possible any changes that occur that affect your objectives.

As a supervisor, you should

- Develop a system of checks and reminders to be sure that performance objectives are being met.
- Show your employee that you want him or her to succeed. Provide positive reinforcement for progress made toward accomplishing objectives.

Multisource evaluations can be useful for improving performance. Approximately 90 percent of Fortune 1000 companies use some form of multisource assessment, including evaluations from supervisors, employees, peers, and customers. These assessments are called 360-degree feedback because the individual is rated by a whole circle of people.[11] Research shows improvement is most likely to occur when:

1. Behavior change is necessary.
2. Recipients believe change is possible.
3. Appropriate improvement goals are set.
4. Improvement is recognized and rewarded.[12]

At the core of using 360-degree feedback is the issue of trust. Using multisource evaluations confidentially for development purposes builds trust, while using them to make pay and personnel decisions reduces trust.[13] When coaching others for growth, use the following guidelines:

- Use feedback as soon as possible.
- Focus on behavior change not personality analysis.
- Link feedback to learning and performance goals.
- Align improvement goals with key results for the organization.
- Coach for improvement not just for final results.[14]

Studies show the evaluation of leaders by employees can be a valuable tool for improving leadership effectiveness. The questionnaire in Exercise 18–2 can be used to evaluate the performance of supervisors and managers.

Exercise 18–2
How Does Your
Supervisor Rate?[15]

Rate your supervisor on each criterion by circling the appropriate response.

Criteria	Responses		
Does the supervisor provide clarity of assignment?	Very well	Fairly well	Not very well
Are high standards of performance required?	Usually	Sometimes	Seldom
Is concern shown for employee needs and welfare?	Frequently	Sometimes	Rarely
Does the supervisor ensure that proper materials and equipment are available?	Very well	Fairly well	Not very well
Is favoritism shown in dealing with employees?	Never	Sometimes	Frequently
Do employees feel free to discuss job-related problems?	Whenever necessary	Sometimes	Seldom
Are employees given incomplete or confusing information?	Seldom	Sometimes	Almost always
Are all employees treated with equal respect?	Always	Sometimes	Rarely
Are employees recognized for good job performance?	Almost always	Sometimes	Seldom
Is the supervisor honest in all dealings with people?	Always	Sometimes	Almost never
Does the supervisor keep job knowledge current?	Very well	Fairly well	Not very well
Is the advice of employees sought in dealing with job-related problems?	Frequently	Sometimes	Seldom
Does the supervisor assign the right jobs to the right people?	Almost always	Sometimes	Rarely
Are employees criticized or otherwise belittled in the presence of others?	Never	Sometimes	Frequently
Are employees told in advance about changes that will affect them?	Almost always	Sometimes	Rarely
Does the supervisor encourage and support employee development?	Yes	Sometimes	No
Are employees kept waiting for decisions or information?	A short time	Varies	A long time
Are employee confidences kept?	Always	Sometimes	Seldom
Does the supervisor provide constructive feedback on employee performance?	Frequently	Sometimes	Rarely
Is blame shifted to employees for supervisory errors?	Never	Sometimes	Almost always

Scoring and Interpretation:

Count the number of items circled in the first column; then multiply that number by 3 and record the total:_____

Count the number of items circled in the second column; then multiply that number by 2 and record the total:_____

Count the number of items circled in the third column; record that number as the total:_____

Add the totals for the three columns to find the overall score:_____

Score	Evaluation
56–60	Excellent, outstanding
46–55	Very good, effective
35–45	Average; improvement encouraged
25–34	Poor; needs improvement
20–24	Failing; must change

Performance Management Strategies

Strategies for managing employee performance are presented in Figure 18–1. The effective leader takes action to be sure every employee performs good work and has a positive attitude. Good performance and attitude are rewarded; poor performance and attitude are addressed and corrected. In high-, middle-, and low-performer conversations, the goal is to move performance to the next level. The leader must:

1. Recognize and retain high performers.
2. Reinforce and develop the skills and attitudes of middle performers.
3. Confront and correct or dismiss low performers.[16]

Figure 18–1
Performance Management
Strategies[17]

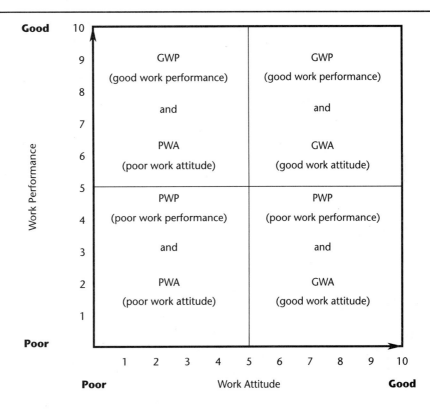

Using a scale of 1 to 10 (1 is low; 10 is high), evaluate each person reporting to you based on work performance and work attitude. Take action to be sure every employee performs good work and has a positive attitude. Use the following guide:

Assesment		Management Action
Poor work performance + poor work attitude (PWP + PWA)	=	**Dismiss** before completion of probation.
Good work performance + poor work attitude (GWP + PWA)	=	**Coach** to improve work attitude.
Poor work performance + good work attitude (PWP + GWA)	=	**Train** to improve work performance.
Good work performance + good work attitude (GWP + GWA)	=	**Reward** to show appreciation and reinforce morale and performance.

Followership—Would
You Hire You?

Good leaders and good followers have many qualities in common.[18] Exercise 18–3 looks at 15 qualities employers like to see in their personnel. They are important in all fields of work and all levels of responsibility.

**Exercise 18–3
Putting Your Best Foot
Forward**

Evaluate your current job performance by circling the appropriate number
(1 is low; 10 is high).

1. **Job knowledge.** Success at work begins with job knowledge. Make it your business
to know what to do, when to do it, and why you are doing it.

   1   2   3   4   5   6   7   8   9   10

2. **Dependability.** If your work requires being on time, be on time. You should be
10 minutes early for the workday if at all possible. Tardiness lowers your image (this
includes lunch and work breaks). Also, if you say you will do something, do it. Be
known as a person who can be counted on.

   1   2   3   4   5   6   7   8   9   10

3. **Cooperation.** Organizational citizenship involves various forms of cooperation and
helpfulness. Take interest in other people, and strive to be helpful. Everyone appreciates
someone who is willing to lend a hand. Show others you are interested in doing a good
job for them. Learn to understand and get along with all types of people.

   1   2   3   4   5   6   7   8   9   10

4. **Concentration.** There are three kinds of people: those who make things happen,
those who watch things happen, and those who have no idea what happened. You
don't want to be the third kind. Always pay attention to what is going on; that is how
you learn. You should try to learn something new every day. People are more
interested in those who show initiative and concentration. Don't sleepwalk through
your day; this is how accidents occur and opportunities are missed.

   1   2   3   4   5   6   7   8   9   10

5. **Initiative.** If you are not eager to do your job, either you are in the wrong line of
work or you have allowed yourself to become lazy. If it is the first, find another job; if
it is the second, overcome your laziness. It will pay off. Be a self-starter; don't wait for
others to generate a spark in you. It is your life, and you are in control. What you do
now will determine your future. Follow this motto: Seize the moment.

   1   2   3   4   5   6   7   8   9   10

6. **Communication.** No one likes excuses after the fact, even if they are legitimate. If
you can't accomplish a task as assigned, inform those who should know as soon as
possible. The more you communicate, the better your relationships will be.

   1   2   3   4   5   6   7   8   9   10

7. **Flexibility.** Don't be overly rigid. Most jobs require flexibility to get the best results.
Be open to changing your approach, your schedule, and even your goals if it will help
increase job performance.

   1   2   3   4   5   6   7   8   9   10

8. **Dedication.** You have to be dedicated to your job if you are to succeed. Don't automatically take the attitude that you are being exploited by others. A job is usually a
two-way street. You are helping your employer, but you are also acquiring knowledge
and experience that will benefit you; also, you are being paid. Most business owners
and managers work nearly 10 hours a day trying to keep their operations going, and
this creates jobs. Employee dedication is needed as well, and it is usually greatly
appreciated.

   1   2   3   4   5   6   7   8   9   10

9. **Conflict resolution.** Avoid arguments on the job. If you do become part of a conflict, try to solve the problem in private, as soon as possible, and without hurting anyone. Remember, seeing things from the other person's point of view helps resolve unnecessary conflict.

1	2	3	4	5	6	7	8	9	10

10. **Patience.** At times, you may feel dissatisfied with your job. If so, wait a reasonable period before deciding whether to change jobs. In the meantime, talking to the people with whom you work may help you feel like part of the group and may help you enjoy what you are doing.

1	2	3	4	5	6	7	8	9	10

11. **Personal appearance.** Impressions are important, so dress appropriately for work. Maintain excellent personal hygiene, and keep your clothes presentable.

1	2	3	4	5	6	7	8	9	10

12. **Conscientious use of time.** Avoid taking more break time than you truly need (including paid personal time). Would you like paying someone who is not working? Put yourself in the employer's position, and evaluate yourself. Are you giving a full day's work for a full day's pay?

1	2	3	4	5	6	7	8	9	10

13. **Gumption.** Always look for something to do. It costs money and time for one person to keep another person busy. If you cannot find something, ask. Never just sit or stand around. Remember, the difference between ordinary and extraordinary is the word *extra*.

1	2	3	4	5	6	7	8	9	10

14. **Excellence.** Study or practice your work so that you are truly good at it. This will boost your ego and make you more valuable to your employer, which will usually be reflected in your wages. Do not become complacent with current success. Remember, a professional in any field knows what it takes to perform well, but always strives to improve.

1	2	3	4	5	6	7	8	9	10

15. **Trustworthiness.** Be honest in all your dealings. Word travels quickly, and a poor reputation can be acquired faster than a good one. Always tell the truth as you believe it to be.

1	2	3	4	5	6	7	8	9	10

Scoring and Interpretation:

Add your scores from the 15 qualities, and record the total here: _____ Then read the evaluation and discussion that follow.

Score	Evaluation	Discussion
135–150	Outstanding	Extremely high performers receive these scores. These individuals produce top results.
105–134	Very good	Good performers receive these scores. They are solid producers in their organizations.
75–104	Ordinary	People who receive these scores are "doing their jobs"—no more and no less.
15–74	Below standard	These scores reflect problems with ability, experience, motivation, or attitude. Counseling and training should be sought.

Professional Performance and Sustaining Discipline

P erformance, as the following story shows, is important in all fields of work:

A mother was having a hard time getting her son to go to school one morning. "Nobody likes me at school," said the son. "The teachers don't and the kids don't. The superintendent wants to transfer me, the bus drivers hate me, the school board wants me to drop out, and the custodians have it in for me." "You've got to go," insisted the mother. "You're healthy. You have a lot to learn. You've got something to offer others. You're a leader. Besides, you're forty-nine years old, you're the principal, and you've got to go to school."[19]

The questionnaire in Exercise 19–1 evaluates job performance in three important areas—**statesmanship, entrepreneurship,** and **innovation.** Complete the questionnaire alone or with another person, such as a co-worker or supervisor. Points to remember are the following:

- Factors measured by the questionnaire are important for success in every field of work, from steel fabrication to public service. Every industry and profession requires statesmanship, the ability to work with and through other people; entrepreneurship, the ability to achieve results; and innovation, the ability to generate new and usable ideas.

- The questionnaire measures job behavior, not personal qualities. To increase objectivity, evaluation is based on actual rather than potential performance.

- Results on the questionnaire are based on a normative group. Scores show how you compare with individuals considered to be top producers and those considered to be poor producers in U.S. business and industry.

- How high or low you score is less important than what you do about your results. It is important to know where you stand to capitalize on strengths and improve weaknesses.

Exercise 19–1
The Performance Pyramid[20]

Read the following sets of statements. For each set, place a check mark next to the statement that is most like your behavior on the job at this time. Although it may be difficult to select one statement over the others, you must choose one statement in each set.

1. _____ a. You are interested in what will work, not what might work.
   _____ b. You are willing to listen to anyone's ideas.
   _____ c. You seek out the ideas and opinions of others.
   _____ d. You are tolerant of those whose ideas differ from yours.

2. _____ a. You rarely get worked up about things.
   _____ b. You measure up to what is expected of you in output.
   _____ c. You are one of the top producers of results.
   _____ d. You are busy with so many things that your output is affected.

3. _____ a. You avoid changing existing methods and procedures.
   _____ b. You continually search for better ways to do things.
   _____ c. Sometimes you think of things that could be improved.
   _____ d. You often make suggestions to improve things.

4. _____ a. You go out of your way to help others.
   _____ b. You rarely spend time on other people's problems.
   _____ c. Other people often come to you for help.
   _____ d. You lend a hand if others request your assistance.

5. _____ a. You have selected assignments that have had a good future.
   _____ b. Most jobs you have worked on have resulted in significant contributions.
   _____ c. You would be much further ahead if you had not been assigned so many things that turned out to be unimportant.
   _____ d. Some of your time has been wasted on things that you never should have undertaken.

6. _____ a. You have changed the whole approach to your work.
   _____ b. You have initiated many changes in the work you are doing.
   _____ c. From time to time, you have made a change in the way you do your work.
   _____ d. You go along with established ways of working, without upsetting things.

7. _____ a. You seek consensus in settling disagreements.
   _____ b. You do not concern yourself with the affairs of others.
   _____ c. You will yield a point rather than displease someone.
   _____ d. Once your mind is made up, you prefer not to change it.

8. _____ a. You follow the motto "better safe than sorry."
   _____ b. You avoid taking risks except under rare circumstances.
   _____ c. You will gamble on good odds any time.
   _____ d. You sometimes take risks when the odds are favorable.

9. _____ a. You are well known for your creativity.
   _____ b. You often think of new ways of doing things.
   _____ c. You are conservative and rarely experiment with new ideas.
   _____ d. From time to time, you introduce new ideas.

10. _____ a. You sometimes trust the wrong people.
    _____ b. Your judgment about people is usually correct.
    _____ c. You have as little to do with others as possible.
    _____ d. Your ability to work with people is outstanding.

423

11. _____ a. You prefer doing work yourself rather than planning work for others.

_____ b. You plan work and hold performance to schedule.

_____ c. You make plans, but adjust to day-to-day changes.

_____ d. You rarely make plans.

12. _____ a. Your ideas are almost always used.

_____ b. You frequently say to yourself, I wish I had thought of that.

_____ c. Your ideas are sometimes put into practice.

_____ d. Your ideas are often adopted.

13. _____ a. You consider alternatives before making decisions.

_____ b. You wait as long as possible before making decisions.

_____ c. You make decisions before weighing the consequences.

_____ d. You involve others in decisions that affect them.

14. _____ a. You rarely push to have your plans adopted.

_____ b. Inevitable roadblocks prevent you from accomplishing your goals.

_____ c. You are known for getting difficult jobs done.

_____ d. If you want something done, you find a way to get it done.

15. _____ a. You believe change should be gradual, if it should occur at all.

_____ b. You are open to change and new methods.

_____ c. You prefer traditional and established ways.

_____ d. You are innovative in your ideas and approach to work.

Scoring:

Follow the steps below to complete the scoring matrix and the Performance Pyramid.

Step 1:

In the Self-Evaluation columns of the scoring matrix, circle the number that corresponds to the lettered statement you checked in each set of statements in the questionnaire. For example, if you checked statement c. for item 1, you would circle 7 in the Self-Evaluation column.

Step 2:

If another person evaluated you, circle the appropriate numbers in the Partner's Evaluation columns. For example, if your partner checked statement b. for item 1, you would circle 5 in the Partner's Evaluation column.

Step 3:

Add the circled numbers in each column of the scoring matrix to find your total scores on statesmanship (A), entrepreneurship (B), and innovation (C). Record the totals in the appropriate spaces at the bottom of the columns.

Step 4:

Plot your results on the Performance Pyramid in Figure 19–1. (See the sample in Figure 19–2.) If there is a difference between your self-evaluation and your partner's evaluation, use either an average of the two scores or your self-evaluation scores. In general, you know your own performance best. Nevertheless, you should discuss points of agreement and disagreement with your partner; you may be doing an exceptional job and not communicating this to your partner.

Scoring Matrix

		Statesmanship				Entrepreneurship				Innovation	
		Self-Evaluation	Partner's Evaluation			Self-Evaluation	Partner's Evaluation			Self-Evaluation	Partner's Evaluation
1.	a.	1	1	**2.**	a.	1	1	**3.**	a.	1	1
	b.	5	5		b.	5	5		b.	7	7
	c.	7	7		c.	7	7		c.	3	3
	d.	3	3		d.	3	3		d.	5	5
4.	a.	7	7	**5.**	a.	5	5	**6.**	a.	7	7
	b.	1	1		b.	7	7		b.	5	5
	c.	5	5		c.	1	1		c.	3	3
	d.	3	3		d.	3	3		d.	1	1
7.	a.	7	7	**8.**	a.	1	1	**9.**	a.	7	7
	b.	1	1		b.	3	3		b.	5	5
	c.	3	3		c.	7	7		c.	1	1
	d.	5	5		d.	5	5		d.	3	3
10.	a.	3	3	**11.**	a.	3	3	**12.**	a.	7	7
	b.	5	5		b.	7	7		b.	1	1
	c.	1	1		c.	5	5		c.	3	3
	d.	7	7		d.	1	1		d.	5	5
13.	a.	5	5	**14.**	a.	3	3	**15.**	a.	3	3
	b.	1	1		b.	1	1		b.	5	5
	c.	3	3		c.	5	5		c.	1	1
	d.	7	7		d.	7	7		d.	7	7
		A _____	A _____			B _____	B _____			C _____	C _____

**Figure 19–1
Your Performance Pyramid**

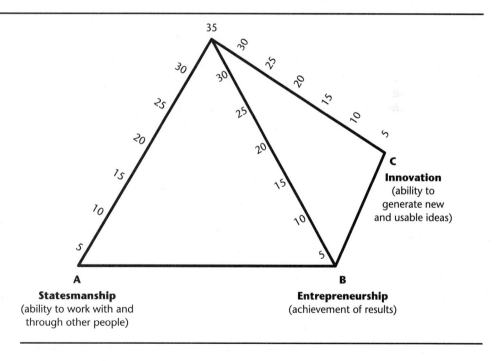

**Figure 19–2
Sample Performance
Pyramid**

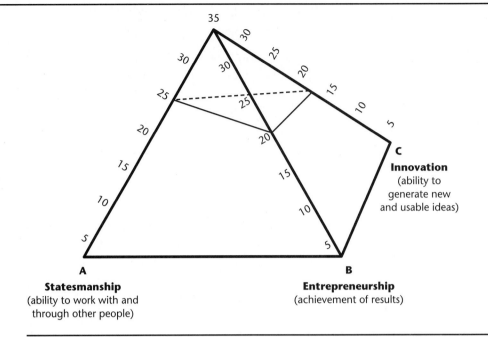

A
Statesmanship
(ability to work with and
through other people)

B
Entrepreneurship
(achievement of results)

C
Innovation
(ability to
generate new
and usable ideas)

Interpretation:

High scores represent strengths in job performance; low scores represent areas you should strive to improve. Use the following information to evaluate your scores:

Score	Evaluation
30–35	Extremely high performers receive these scores. As a result of ability, experience, motivation, and attitude, these individuals produce top results. If such a person were to leave, it is likely that the organization would suffer significantly.
20–29	Good performers receive these scores. They are pivotal people in their organizations and are solid producers. In college, these scores represent very good work.
15–19	People who receive these scores are doing their jobs. They are doing what is expected of individuals in their positions—no more and no less. Although these scores are acceptable, they are not extraordinary.
14 and below	People whose performance needs improvement receive these scores. Such scores reflect problems in ability, experience, motivation, or attitude. Counseling and training should be considered.

Improving Performance

What can you do to maintain high performance or to improve in the areas of statesmanship, entrepreneurship, and innovation?

- First, you have to want to perform at your best.
- Second, you have to know the essential behaviors that represent statesmanship, entrepreneurship, and innovation.
- Third, you have to apply principles and practices to perform those behaviors.

The following is a discussion of each performance area, including behaviors that reflect high performance, as well as principles and techniques that can be used to improve.

Statesmanship

Statesmanship is the ability to work with and through other people. A statesman is skillful in human relations and is able to multiply personal accomplishments through the efforts of others. The following describes the role of the statesman:

A statesman is not a dictator, but rather a developer of effective relationships. The statesman is one who guides rather than leads, helping others to make decisions rather than making decisions alone. The statesman believes that if everyone works together, more can be accomplished.[21]

Throughout his life, Abraham Lincoln was willing to teach others what he had learned himself. From childhood onward, he was the statesman—storyteller, speech maker, and always the ringleader. As one boyhood comrade relates:

When he [Lincoln] appeared, the boys would gather and cluster around him to hear him talk. . . . He argued much from analogy and explained things hard for us to understand by stories, maxims, tales, and figures. He would almost always paint his lesson or idea by some story that was plain and near to us, so that we might instantly see the force and bearing of what he said.[22]

Examine the following behaviors that represent a high level of statesmanship:

- You seek out the ideas and opinions of others.
- You go out of your way to help others.
- You seek consensus in settling disagreements.
- Your ability to work with people is outstanding.
- You involve others in decisions that affect them.

If you would like to increase your ability to work with and through others, develop good **human relations skills** and use the **four-step method** listed below to solve problems.

Develop Good Human Relations Skills

The following principles will help you accomplish this goal:

1. *Let people know where they stand.* You should communicate expectations and then keep people informed on how they are doing. If criticism is necessary, do it in private; if praise is in order, give it in public.

2. *Give credit where due.* Look for extra or unusual performance, and show appreciation as soon as possible. As psychologist Gordon Allport writes: "Not only does human learning proceed best when the incentive of praise and recognition is used, but the individual's capacity for learning actually expands under this condition."[23]

3. *Tell people as soon as possible about changes that will affect them.* Keep people informed, and tell them why change is necessary. Many people dislike change, and they especially dislike sudden changes.

4. *Make the best use of each person's ability.* Let each person shine as only that person can. Take the time to look for potential not now being used. Also, never stand in a person's way. To do so creates resentment, reduces morale, and ultimately results in reduced performance.

Use the Four-Step Method to Solve Problems

Peter Drucker is famous for his advice to leaders: "The problem you deny or will not address is the one that will do you in."[24] Statesmanship requires addressing problems and solving them effectively. The following four-step method can be used for solving any problem:

1. *Get the facts.* As Mark Twain advised: "Get the facts first; then you can distort them as much as you please."[25] You simply cannot solve a problem without first knowing the facts, so (a) review all records; (b) talk with the people concerned; (c) consider opinions and feelings; and (d) look at all sides. Abraham Lincoln tried to understand the views of both the North and the South when he said:

I have no prejudice against the Southern people. They are just what we would be in their situation. If slavery did not now exist among them, they would not introduce it. If it did now exist among us, we would not instantly give it up. This I believe of the masses of North and South.[26]

2. *Weigh and decide.* After getting all the facts, you must weigh each fact against the others, fit the pieces together, and consider alternatives. Consider the effects that different courses of action will have on individuals and groups. Sometimes it is a good idea to sleep on a problem so that you do not jump to conclusions or overreact.

3. *Take action.* After you have gathered the facts and determined a course of action, carry out your plan. Harry Truman realized the importance of this step when he said, "The buck stops here" and "If you can't stand the heat, get out of the kitchen." Many people occupy positions requiring statesmanship but are indecisive and fail to act. Consider what William James wrote: "There is no more miserable human being than one in whom nothing is habitual but indecision."[27]

The U.S Marine Corps provides a helpful formula—the 70 percent solution. If an officer has 70 percent of the information and has performed 70 percent of the analysis and feels 70 percent confident, he or she is instructed to *take action.*[28]

4. *Follow up.* Statesmanship requires asking, Did my action(s) help the quality of work or the quality of work life? If not, admit this fact and try to find a better solution. By taking time to follow up on actions and being willing to admit mistakes, the statesman achieves three important goals: (a) the respect of all who are watching; (b) another chance to solve the problem; and (c) the opportunity to set an example of honesty and thoroughness in problem solving.

Herb Kelleher, former CEO of Southwest Airlines, states:

One thing I knew was to admit mistakes. If I discovered a decision I made was a mistake, I would just stop it. You have to look at things the way a scientist would: this experiment didn't work out; it's over. You can't get emotional about it. That's the key so far as I'm concerned: there's no ego involved. You can't keep something on life support for years and years because you've let your self-esteem get tied up in things.[29]

Entrepreneurship

Entrepreneurship is the ability to achieve results, regardless of obstacles. It takes entrepreneurship to build a plant on time, to produce a quality product, and to close a sale. An entrepreneur is action-oriented, but knows that it is not just action, but achievement, that counts. Consider the story of entrepreneur Henry Ford, who founded and built the Ford Motor Company. Ford believed in honesty and hard work and lived by the principle—Did you ever see dishonest calluses on a man's hands?[30]

Profile of an Entrepreneur

How It Began

The young inventor was gone a long time, and came back pushing the contraption. A nut had come loose, with all the shaking. But he was exultant; in spite of bumpy cobblestones and muddy ruts, he had gone where he wished to go. "You're wet clear through," said his wife, as he let her lead him into the kitchen, take off his wet things, hang them up, and give him hot coffee. He was talking excitedly all the time. "I've got a horseless carriage that runs," said Henry Ford.

The Early Years

He examined materials, read contracts, discussed selling campaigns, and prepared advertisements shrewdly addressed to the mind of the average American, which he knew perfectly because he had been one for forty years. It was his doctrine that any man who wanted to succeed in business should never let it out of his mind; and he had practiced this half a lifetime before he began to preach it.

In the first year the sales of the Ford Motor Company brought Ford a million and a half dollars, nearly one-fourth of which was profit. From then on, all his life, Henry Ford had all the money he needed to carry out his ideas. He took care of his money, and used it for that purpose.

Mission Accomplished

Henry had a seemingly inexhaustible market for his cars. He was employing more than 200,000 men, paying wages of a quarter of a billion dollars a year. He had developed 53 different industries, beginning alphabetically with aeroplanes and ending with wood-distillation. He bought a broken-down railroad, and made it pay; he bought coal mines, and trebled their production. He perfected new processes—the very smoke that had once poured from his chimneys was now made into automobile parts.[31]

The following behaviors represent a high level of entrepreneurship:

- You are one of the top producers of results.
- Most jobs you have worked on have resulted in significant contributions.
- You will gamble on good odds anytime.
- You plan work and hold performance to schedule.
- If you want something done, you find a way to get it done.

Entrepreneurship in any field requires **good work habits, a belief in oneself,** and **the willingness to take risks.** The following action plan will help you maximize your entrepreneurial behavior.

*Exercise Good
Work Habits*

The achievement of results requires the ability to stick with a job until it is done. As a Polish proverb says, "If there is not enough wind, row." The following poem by Edgar Guest shows the kind of attitude that is necessary to accomplish difficult tasks:

> Some said it couldn't be done.
> But he, with a chuckle, replied
> That maybe it couldn't, but he would be one
> Who wouldn't say so until he tried.
>
> So he buckled right in with a bit of a grin,
> If he worried, he hid it.
> He started to sing, as he tackled the thing
> That couldn't be done—and he did it.[32]

The high performer goes the extra mile, living by the maxim that triumph is the "umph" added to "try." If you exercise good work habits, you will be rewarded both financially and personally as word gets out that you are a valuable asset.

Believe in Yourself

Eleanor Roosevelt once said, "No one can make you feel inferior without your consent."[33] The chronology of Abraham Lincoln's career shows the importance of belief in yourself and determined effort:

- In 1831, he failed in business.
- In 1832, he was defeated for the legislature.
- In 1833, he again failed in business.
- In 1836, he had a nervous breakdown.
- In 1843, he was defeated for Congress.
- In 1855, he was defeated for the Senate.
- In 1856, he lost the race for the vice presidency.
- In 1858, he was defeated for the Senate.
- In 1860, he was elected president of the United States.

Be Willing to Take Risks

Fear of failure can paralyze a person to the extent that opportunities are missed and achievement is reduced. As the following poem illustrates, courage is necessary to overcome self-doubt:

The Doubter

Edgar Guest

> He had his doubts when he began;
> The task had stopped another man;
> And he had heard it whispered low,
> How rough the road was he must go;
> But now on him the charge was laid,
> And of himself he was afraid.
>
> He wished he knew how it would end;
> He longed to see around the bend;
> He had his doubts that he had strength,
> Enough to go so far a length;
> And all the time the notion grew,
> That this was more than he could do.
>
> Of course, he failed. Whoever lives with doubt,
> Soon finds his courage giving out;
> They only win who face a task,
> And say the chance is all I ask;

They only rise who dare the grade,
And of themselves are not afraid.

There are no ogres up the slope;
It is only with human beings that man must cope;
Whoever fears the blow before it's struck,
Loses the fight for lack of pluck;
And only he the goal achieves,
Who truly in himself believes.[34]

In the final analysis, one must *execute* to succeed. As Henry Ford makes clear, you can't build a reputation on what you are going to do.

Innovation

Innovation is the ability to generate new and usable ideas. The innovator is not satisfied with the status quo, and therefore explores, questions, and studies new ways of doing things. Innovation accounts for advances in all fields of work, from agriculture to architecture. Important products we take for granted today are the result of yesterday's inventions—Thomas Edison's electric light, the Wright brothers' airplane, and Alexander Graham Bell's telephone are but a few examples. In the field of agriculture, George Washington Carver created more than 300 synthetic products from the peanut, more than 100 from the sweet potato, and more than 75 from the pecan.

The following behaviors represent a high level of creativity:

- you continually search for better ways to do things;
- you have changed the whole approach to your work.
- you are well known for your creativity.
- your ideas are almost always used.
- you are innovative in your ideas and approach to work.

How do you develop creativity and increase innovation? **Keep an open mind, have a questioning attitude,** and **use a new-ideas system.**

Keep an Open Mind

An essential quality of the innovator is openness to new experience. Charles F. Kettering, the famous inventor, emphasized the importance of keeping an open mind when he wrote:

The experienced man is always saying why something can't be done. The fellow who has not had any experience doesn't know a thing can't be done—and goes ahead and does it. . . . There exist limitless opportunities in any industry. Where there is an open mind, there will always be a frontier.[35]

Have a Questioning Attitude

Many people sleepwalk through their days, never stopping to ask themselves: Am I doing the right thing? Is there a better way to do it? For these individuals, creativity is reduced because new ideas are not considered. The following poem shows the importance of having a questioning attitude:

The Calf Path—The Beaten Path of Beaten Men

Samuel Foss

One day through an old-time wood,
A calf walked home, as good calves should;
But made a trail,
A crooked trail, as all calves do.
Since then three hundred years have fled,
And I infer the calf is dead.
But still, he left behind his trail,
And thereby hangs my mortal tale.

The trail was taken up the next day,
By a lone dog that passed that way.
And then a wise sheep,
Pursued the trail, over the steep,
And drew the flocks behind him too,
As all good sheep do.
And from that day, over hill and glade,
Through those old woods, a path was made.

This forest path became a lane,
That bent, and turned, and turned again.
This crooked lane became a road,
Where many a poor horse with his load,
Toiled on beneath the burning sun.
And thus a century and a half,
They followed the footsteps of that calf.

The years passed on in swiftness fleet,
And the road became a village street.
And this became a city's thoroughfare.
And soon the central street was a metropolis.
And men, two centuries and a half,
Followed the footsteps of that calf.

A moral lesson this tale might teach,
Were I ordained, and called to preach.
For men are prone to go it blind,
Along the calf paths of the mind;
And work away from sun to sun,
To do just what other men have done.
They follow in the beaten track,
And out, and in, and forth, and back;
And still their devious course pursue,
To keep the paths that others do.

They keep these paths as sacred grooves,
Along which all their lives they move.
But how the wise old wood gods laugh,
Who saw the first old-time calf.
Ah, many things this tale might teach,
But I am not ordained to preach.[36]

Use a New-Ideas System   Being open to change and having a questioning attitude are two ingredients of creativity; but a third element is necessary—a system is needed to generate new and usable ideas. One good system comes from the English writer Rudyard Kipling. Kipling, who was known for his creativity, was asked how he could come up with so many good ideas. His famous answer was:

I keep six honest serving-men;
They taught me all I knew;
Their names are What and Where and When,
And How and Why and Who.
I send them over land and sea;
I send them east and west;
But after they have worked for me,
I give them all a rest.
I let them rest from nine till five,
For I am busy then,
As well as breakfast, lunch, and tea,

> For they are hungry men:
> But different folk have different views:
> I know a person small—
> She keeps ten million serving-men,
> Who get no rest at all.
> She sends 'em abroad on her own affairs,
> From the second she opens her eyes—
> One million Hows, two million Wheres,
> And seven million Whys.[37]

By asking six simple questions—who, what, why, when, where, and how—and by constructively answering these, you can usually find new and workable solutions to any problem.

Portrait of an Innovator

Benjamin Franklin is perhaps the most remarkable figure in American history: the greatest statesman of his age and the most prominent celebrity of the eighteenth century. He was also a pioneering scientist. Franklin never stopped considering things he could not explain.

Franklin's study of the world's wonders extended to electricity. He began those experiments when he was 40. Ten years later, they made him famous throughout the world. The image of Franklin flying a kite in a thunderstorm is as familiar as the one of George Washington crossing the Delaware.[38]

You Can Improve if You Want To

It is possible to improve performance, and the rewards can be great. Consider the following story:

When Gene Malusko first went to work for his company, he was hired as a laborer. Before long, it was apparent that he would become either a union steward or a work group supervisor. Gene had the ability to work with and through other people. Gene could talk people into things; he was a statesman. Gene chose supervision because he had a family to raise and needed the money. For the next year, he was a successful foreman—he had good relations with his subordinates, and he had a good production record.

Then Gene became interested in advancement. As he considered those who had been promoted in the past, he realized that they had each excelled at obtaining results. The quality and efficiency of their production had stood out over that of the other supervisors. This convinced him to set forth on a self-improvement program to improve entrepreneurship, the delivery of results.

Thereafter, when Gene arrived at work, he began working immediately, and he worked diligently until the job was done. He developed a reputation for making his production quota each day, and he could be counted on to help out in emergencies. Gene was also willing to stick his neck out and take risks when the situation warranted it. He overcame self-doubt with the attitude "nothing ventured, nothing gained." With confidence in himself and good work habits, Gene developed a superb record of achievement. Gene exhibited entrepreneurship, and within two years, he was promoted to general foreman.

Gene performed well as a general foreman on the strength of his ability to work with people (statesmanship) and his ability to obtain results (entrepreneurship). After a mere three years in this capacity, he was selected as the youngest superintendent in the history of the company.

Two years later, Gene was talking with a friend about future plans when he stated that his goal was to be a general manager. He wondered aloud, "What do those people have that I don't?" The answer was creativity. A good general manager must work with and through others, which Gene did; must achieve results regardless of obstacles, which Gene did; and must come up with new and usable ideas, which Gene almost never did.

Gene's friend told him about the ideas of Charles Kettering and the importance of keeping an open mind; he gave him "The Calf Path—The Beaten Path of Beaten Men," emphasizing the need to question things; and finally, he told him about Rudyard Kipling's six honest serving-men, a system of constructive questioning.

Until this time, Gene had rarely questioned whether there was a better way to do something and he had never been given a system for generating new ideas. For Gene, a new dimension of work performance was unveiled, and he set about to improve his creativity.

Each day, Gene would go into his work area and ask six important questions—who, what, why, when, where, and how—to analyze the production bottlenecks and employee problems he encountered. He would ask: Who should do this work, the machine operator or the material handler? What work should be done, milling or planing? Why should this work be done, production or politics? Where should the work be done, in the office or the field? When should the work be done, on the first shift or the second? And how should the work be done, by person or by machine? And, like Kipling, Gene always found a better way.

Gene worked at constructive questioning until it became a habit, and he gained a reputation as a creative person. He added innovation to the qualities of statesmanship and entrepreneurship that he had already developed, and two years later, Gene Malusko was promoted to general manager.[39]

Gene's story is one of professionalism. He learned what was required to perform his job well; he performed good work; yet he constantly tried to improve. He was not complacent. As a result of professional development, Gene Malusko improved the performance of his company and achieved personal rewards as well.

Performance Success Story—A Case in Point

Sam Walton, founder of Walmart, was America's richest person, a multibillionaire, when he died, and he was beloved by all who knew him. His prescription for success, as detailed in *Sam Walton: Made in America, My Story,* has three key elements:

statesmanship, entrepreneurship, and innovation. Walton wrote that success came only through building a team, only after hard work, and only by breaking old rules.

Statesmanship—share the rewards. "If you treat people as your partners, they will perform beyond your wildest dreams." (In the effort to treat others as partners, Sam's reading of people wasn't always 100 percent. Once he attempted to thank big-city investors by taking them camping on the banks of Sugar Creek. A coyote started howling and a hoot owl hooted. Half the Back-East investors stayed up all night around the campfire because they couldn't sleep.)

Entrepreneurship—commit to your business. "I think I overcame every single one of my personal shortcomings by the sheer passion I brought to my work." (Hard work and risk have a price, as revealed by Sam's youngest child, Alice, when she once confided to a friend, "I don't know what we are going to do. My daddy owes so much money, and he won't quit opening stores.")

Innovation—be creative. "If everybody else is doing it one way, there's a good chance you can find your niche by going in a new direction. I guess in all of my years, what I heard more than anything else was: a town of less than 50,000 can't support a decent store." (Of course, some say this strategy stemmed from Sam's wife, Helen, who insisted on raising the Walton family in a town with fewer than 10,000 people.)[40]

The Role of Organizational Culture

Organizational culture is an important factor in professional development and performance. Some organizations are excellent in developing statesmanship, entrepreneurship, and innovation. This is done by modeling and rewarding desired behaviors. For example, 3M has a well-established history of developing successful new technologies. The case of Francis G. Okie shows how: Okie proposed using sandpaper instead of razor blades for shaving to reduce the risk of knicks. The idea failed, but instead of being punished for the failure, he was encouraged to develop other ideas, which included 3M's first big success: waterproof sandpaper. A culture that permits failure is crucial for fostering creative thinking and innovation. 3M uses six rules to keep new products coming:

1. *Set innovation goals.* Twenty-five percent of annual sales must come from new products less than five years old.
2. *Commit to research.* 3M invests in research at double the rate of the average U.S. company.
3. *Support new ideas.* $50,000 Genesis grants are awarded to develop brainstorms into new products.
4. *Facilitate flexibility.* Divisions are kept small to operate with independence and speed.
5. *Satisfy the customer.* 3M's definition of quality is to create a product that meets the customer's needs, not some arbitrary standard.
6. *Tolerate failure.* 3M knows learning and new ideas may come from what seems like failure at the moment.[41]

Five Levels of Performance Excellence

There are many models of performance excellence, none more interesting than the five-level hierarchy proposed by management author James Collins in his book *Good to Great*. Level 1 refers to highly capable individuals. Level 2 refers to contributing team members. Level 3 refers to competent managers. Level 4 refers to effective senior leaders. And Level 5 refers to the exceptional executive. See Figure 19–3.

Figure 19–3
The Five-Level Hierarchy[42]

Level 5: Exceptional Executive
Builds enduring greatness
through a paradoxical combination
of personal humility plus professional will

Level 4: Effective Senior Leader
Catalyzes commitment to and vigorous pursuit
of a clear and compelling vision; stimulates
group to high performance standards

Level 3: Competent Manager
Organizes people and resources toward the effective
and efficient pursuit of predetermined objectives

Level 2: Contributing Team Member
Contributes to the achievement of group
objectives; works effectively with others in a group setting

Level 1: Highly Capable Individual
Makes productive contributions through talent, knowledge,
skills, and good work habits

The Level 5 leader sits on top of a hierarchy of capabilities necessary for transforming an organization from good to great. What lies beneath are four other layers, each one appropriate in its own right, but none with the power of Level 5. Individuals do not need to proceed sequentially through each level of the hierarchy to reach the top, but to be a full-fledged Level 5 leader requires the capabilities of all the lower levels, plus the special characteristics of Level 5.

Exceptional leaders are masters of paradox. They are expert at managing the "and." The combination of **personal humility** "and" **professional will** makes a potent formula for the highest level of leadership success. Humility refers to consideration and service to others, and should not be confused with either submissiveness or introversion. Humility is not thinking less of yourself; it is thinking of yourself less. Professional will refers to conviction and fierce resolve, and should not be confused with either blind ambition or ruthlessness. The Level 5 leader values achievement of a worthy goal, not winning at any cost. See Table 19–1.

Table 19–1
The Paradox of Level 5
Leadership[43]

Personal Humility	Professional Will
The Leader	The Leader
Demonstrates a compelling modesty, shunning public adulation; is never boastful.	Creates superb results; is a clear catalyst in the transition from good to great.
Acts with deliberation and determination; relies principally on inspired standards to motivate.	Demonstrates an unwavering resolve to do whatever must be done to produce the best long-term results, no matter how difficult.
Channels ambition into group success, not the self; sets up successors for even more greatness in the next generation.	Sets the standard of building an enduring and great organization; will settle for nothing less.
Looks in the mirror to assign responsibility for poor results, never blaming other people, external factors, or bad luck.	Looks out the window to assign credit for success to other people, external factors, and good luck.

Procter & Gamble (P&G) CEO Alan G. Lafley is a good example of Level 5 leadership. His unassuming and humble demeanor belies his position. If there were 15 people sitting around a conference table, it wouldn't be obvious that he was the CEO. Yet this did not stop him from transforming P&G where more charismatic predecessors had failed. Lafley's consistent vision, strategic actions, personal humility and professional will moved P&G toward a more customer-friendly and innovative company. The result: P&G regained its stellar status for innovation, market share, profitability, stock value, and a great place to work.[44]

Collins concludes that the most effective executives possess a mixture of personal humility "and" professional will. They are both timid "and" ferocious. They are shy "and" fearless. They are rare "and" unstoppable. The triumph of humility "and" fierce resolve in the leader is instrumental in catapulting an organization from merely good to truly great.

Collins's good-to-great research is based on the business performance of private-sector organizations, but the case of Abraham Lincoln can be used to illustrate the Level 5 leader. Modest and willful, shy and determined, Lincoln never let his personal ego get in the way of his ambition to preserve an enduring nation. Described as a quiet, peaceful, and shy figure, Lincoln had a resolve that was unshakeable—to the scale of 258,000 Confederate and 364,511 Union lives, including Lincoln's own.

Organizational Performance

The tasks of leadership are to interpret conditions, establish direction, mobilize followers, and develop people—all for the purpose of achieving organizational success. The leader who wants to improve the performance of his or her work group or organization can use **benchmarking** as a job aid in the leadership process.[45]

Benchmarking is a careful search for excellence—taking the absolute best as a standard and trying to surpass that standard. Great leaders are constantly in search of excellence both personally and organizationally. Benchmarking begins with an objective evaluation of the organization against the very best. The goal is to determine what winners are doing, and then take steps to meet or exceed that high standard. To personalize the concept, complete Exercise 19–2.

Exercise 19–2
Benchmarking the Best[46]

Plot your organization (company, institution, etc.) on the performance graph below. Where are you today? Then plot your best competitors. Where are they? If your organization is not in the upper right corner, you are at risk. Your current performance is not satisfactory to the people who care about the work you do—customers, employees, owners, governing boards, and the like. What you must do is take action to improve your performance record. An interesting variation is to have others who know and care about your organization provide this evaluation. Note that product quality includes elements such as fit, finish, beauty, reliability, and most important, functionality. Service quality includes timely delivery, response to questions and problems, courteous treatment, and consideration of customers' needs.

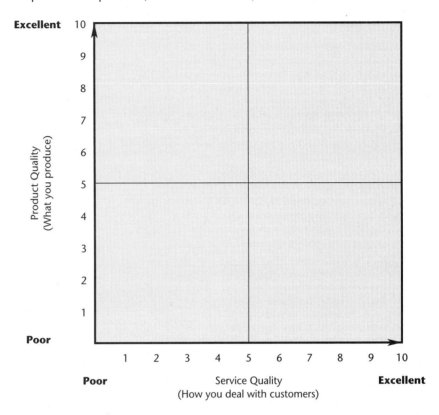

An interesting example of performance excellence is Toyota at its best. A philosophy of excellence is described in Toyota's *Basic Management Handbook:* "The only acceptable quality percentage is 100%. Every car must be manufactured exactly according to specifications. No Toyota vehicle should ever leave the factory without passing every quality test perfectly." One can see the positive attitude, high standards, and uncompromising commitment of a business winner in Toyota's mandate to leaders. Toyota believes the success of the company will be determined by constant adherence to this high standard of work performance and if the company strays from the standard, dire consequences will result.[47]

A good example of organizational success based on management commitment to be the best is Walmart. Between 1972 and 2006, Walmart went from $44 million in sales to $33 billion, powering past Sears and Kmart with faster growth, higher profits, and lower prices. How did Walmart achieve this record? Through focus, hard work, and innovation.

An example is cross-docking, in which goods delivered to a distribution center from suppliers are immediately transferred to trucks bound for stores, without ever being placed in storage. Cross-docking and other innovations have resulted in lower inventory levels and operating costs, which Walmart has used to lower prices for customers.

In evaluating your organization, what improvements can be made to become (or remain) the best in your industry or market? What innovations should you make in product quality (what you produce) and service quality (how you deal with customers)? Be specific: Who should do what, when, where, how, and why?[48]

Organizational Success—The Cianbro Story

There are many role models for organizational success. The Cianbro story is one to which everyone can relate.[49]

From Logging in the Woods to Taming the Ocean. Over 60 years ago, the Cianchette brothers—Carl, Bud, Ken, and Chuck—launched a company that was destined to become a legend in the construction industry. They were short on net worth, but long on hard work, as they plunged into the construction business and toiled mightily to succeed. From their first job loading hardwood pulp onto boxcars with their bare hands, they learned the hard lessons of the business world. Today Cianbro is one of the best heavy-construction companies on the Atlantic coast, building bridges, dams, and factories for public and industrial clients from Maine to the Carolinas to Florida. Annual revenues are over $450 million, with nearly 2,500 employees working as a team to bring their impressive projects to a timely and profitable completion. The Cianchettes developed a work culture with three characteristics: *a can-do attitude, a teamwork ethic,* and *caring leadership.*

A Can-Do Attitude: "Job Defies Impossible." It is not possible to do two years of work in less than a week. Or is it?

Holyoke is a textile town built around several canals. When the city decided to build an interceptor sewer system, part of the work included a contract to lay pipe across nine different areas of the canals. Cianbro was low bidder.

Cianbro's job would be to drive two walls of steel sheeting (a cofferdam) across each crossing, remove the water, excavate, lay pipe, backfill, and then pull the sheeting.

Yes, the workers would need to do that nine different times. It was a $1.3 million contract that was expected to take two years.

Then employees on the job learned that every year around the Fourth of July, the canals were drained for a week to allow the Holyoke industries to work on their canal gates. Someone suggested, "Why don't we do all nine areas at the same time, when the canals are drained during the shutdown week?"

With a can-do attitude, they formed nine teams and equipped each team with everything that would be required to do its crossing. They had all materials on-site. They counted every gasket and every bolt, and they triple-checked to be sure.

On the morning of the draining, they swung into action. They related it to a military operation, and the job was finished as planned—way, way under budget and way, way under deadline: two years of work in less than a week.

Impossible? Not at Cianbro. Someone wrote in the company newsletter: "The difficult can be done immediately, the impossible takes a little longer."

Teamwork Ethic: "Good People Enjoy Working with Good People." Chuck Cianchette explains the company's hiring policy: "We hire people with a good attitude. We want people who will do whatever is needed to get the job done and who are happy in their work." Bud Cianchette describes the relationship with the crews: "We work with them. If the work is in a ditch, we work with them in the ditch. We never ask anyone to do anything that we wouldn't do ourselves." Ken Cianchette cites a song:

> Give me some men who are stout-hearted men
> who will fight for the right they adore.
> Start me with ten who are stout-hearted men,
> and I'll soon give you ten thousand more.

"That is our basic philosophy. Good people enjoy working with good people, and together they can accomplish anything."

Caring Leadership: "Passing It On." The best advice the Cianchette brothers ever received was from their father, Ralph Cianchette, who said, "Be careful what you promise someone you will do. But once you say you will do it, make sure that you do." This principle has been instilled as gospel into every Cianbro supervisor, manager, and executive for over 60 years.

When the time came for someone other than a Cianchette to take over the leadership of the company, Pete Vigue was chosen to do the job. His co-workers tell why: "He had the most gumption, the most savvy. He will not accept the word 'no.' He will always find a way to be successful. He will not be defeated. Plus he makes sure everyone practices the five P's of success: Prior planning prevents poor performance."

Pete explains how leadership lessons were passed on to him as he absorbed everything he could from the brothers: "Carl taught integrity as he lived by the code of honesty. Bud always demanded excellence. I learned to set high goals from him. Ken taught me how to think because he always asked the tough questions. Chuck taught me how to work with people; how to give and take—especially to give. All of them taught humility. While they were willing to talk about the positive things in their lives, they were also willing to share the mistakes they made. That has helped us not make the same mistakes twice."

As Pete looks ahead, he feels the challenge is to perpetuate the organization. The key to this is to pass on the principles of caring leadership embodied by leaders of the past. To this end, new Cianbro leaders undergo leadership training that features not techniques, but the basic principles of dignity, honesty, and respect, and proven practices of keeping your word, setting high goals, thinking creatively, and working as a team. To these, Pete adds, "Take care of the people," and by this he means safety first. If you have four hours to spare, ask him about it.

Reaching the Summit

How do organizations achieve greatness? Organization development techniques include: Job enrichment, management by objectives, survey feedback, top grading, team building, total quality management, succession planning, gainsharing, reengineering, performance management, action research, appreciative inquiry, balanced scorecard, knowledge management, coaching, Six Sigma, employee engagement, and behavior modification etc.[50]

A study of 200 techniques employed by 160 companies over 10 years identified four success factors and management practices that lead to sustained and superior performance regardless of the techniques used.[51]

Factors	Management Practices
Strategy	Establish a direction, focus on customers, and communicate with employees.
Execution	Hire good people, delegate decision-making, and perform quality work.
Culture	Empower people, reward performance, and maintain strong core values.
Structure	Align resources, exchange information, and promote teamwork.

Organizational success is a never-ending challenge. It is a subject leaders must continually address. An excellent resource to help in this task is *Your Summit Awaits,* a video presentation by the Canadian mountain climber, Jamie Clark. Based on three attempts to climb Mt. Everest, five lessons are shared. These lessons apply to every organization or group striving to reach its summit, and they apply to leaders and followers, alike:

1. **Truth**–Care enough to confront; share the brutal truth.
2. **Perspective**–Know the difference between passion and obsession.
3. **Trust**–What matters are the promises we keep, not the promises we make.
4. **Focus**–Managing fear requires focusing on what is important.
5. **Humility**–It is important to appreciate the people who helped get you there.

The Kite and the String

"The kite and the string" is an important concept related to organizational performance. Just as a kite won't fly without a string and a string won't fly without a kite, it can be argued that full organizational success requires at least two individuals who are both competent and committed. Although a leader alone can achieve a degree of success

for a period of time, at least two dedicated people working together effectively are needed to achieve and sustain long-term success.

Improving Performance through Behavior Modification

During the early 1900s, Edward L. Thorndike formulated his famous law of effect, which says behavior with a favorable consequence tends to be repeated, while behavior with an unfavorable consequence tends to disappear. This was a dramatic departure from the prevailing notion that behavior was the product of inborn instincts.[52]

Behavior modification, established in the 1950s by B. F. Skinner, is a practical and effective way to apply the law of effect and improve human performance. Behavior modification today is based on the conceptual premises of classical behaviorists John Watson and Ivan Pavlov, reinforcement theorists C. B. Ferster and B. F. Skinner, and applied behaviorists Albert Bandura and Fred Luthans.[53] The application of behavior modification principles has been shown to have a positive impact on performance in a wide range of sales, service, manufacturing, and not-for-profit organizations in both Western and non-Western cultures. Meta-analysis shows that when desired behaviors are tied to contingent consequences, performance improvement is 17 percent.[54]

The central objective of behavior modification is to change behavior (B) by managing its antecedents (A) and consequences (C). The following example shows how behavior modification—**goal setting, feedback on performance,** and **positive reinforcement**—can be used to improve employee performance.[55]

Improving Employee Performance in the Transportation Industry

The purpose of a mass transit organization is to provide safe, dependable, efficient, and courteous transportation to the public. The performance of the operator is critical in meeting this mission because this is the person who deals directly with the passenger. To improve driver performance, one organization sponsored a six-hour passenger relations program. Participants learned human relations principles and were asked, "What are the day-to-day actions a driver should perform to provide the best possible service to the public?" Table 19–2 lists the performance objectives developed by the 250 participants.

For a period of three months after attending the training session, each operator completed a self-evaluation based on the list of performance objectives. At the end of each work shift, drivers checked off the behaviors they had performed and left blank those they had not. This paper-and-pencil checklist provided personal feedback on performance. At the end of every month for three months, each driver also met privately with the supervisor,

**Table 19–2
Operator Performance Objectives**

A Coach Operator Should

1. Start and stop smoothly.
2. Avoid smoking when carrying passengers.
3. Clean up trash around driver's quarters when leaving the bus.
4. Address adults by name if known and by "Sir" or "Ma'am" if name is not known. Never call a youngster by a nickname—Junior, Sonny, Peanut, Sister, and the like—unless requested.
5. Have exact working tools—transfers, punch, change, ticket refunds, and so on—when starting the job.
6. Greet all passengers in a friendly manner.
7. Try to solve problems that arise in carrying out the job. Do not complain to passengers about other employees.
8. Wave recognition to police officers, firefighters, school guards, and other uniformed public workers.
9. Always use hand and arm signals in traffic; say thank you in this manner whenever possible.
10. Wait for slow arrivers, making sure that all who want rides get them.
11. Never run ahead of schedule.
12. Pull to the curb if possible; avoid puddles.
13. Give clear, friendly, and sensible answers to the public.

who had been a fellow participant in the passenger relations program. The supervisor held these meetings to review performance checklists, discuss job problems, and express appreciation for employee participation in the program. These meetings emphasized the positive and ignored the negative. If a driver had a good performance record, this accomplishment was praised; if a driver had a poor record, he was thanked for keeping the checklist and encouraged to continue trying to implement the agreed-upon performance objectives; if a driver failed to keep records, this fact was ignored and a discussion was held reviewing and reaffirming the importance of the performance objectives.

The following were the results of the employee development program:

- Safety records showed substantial improvement, and there were significant financial savings.

- Passenger complaints decreased, and the organization's public image improved.

- The company set a national record for increased ridership.

- Employee morale and pride increased.

- Relations between managers and employees improved.

Reward systems can be counterproductive if negative behavior is rewarded while positive behavior is ignored or punished. This is called the folly of rewarding A while hoping for B. Examples are: hoping for high performance but rewarding mediocrity; hoping for teamwork but rewarding self-promotion; hoping for innovation but rewarding low risk taking; hoping for candor but rewarding silence; hoping for empowerment but rewarding tight control.[56]

How do leaders avoid this problem and capitalize on the positive potential of behavior modification? Three rules should guide:

1. Provide clarity of assignment and require high standards of behavior that support the purpose, values, and goals of the organization.

2. Give positive reinforcement through recognition of effort and reward for good performance.

3. Address or correct poor performance and do not reward negative attitudes or inappropriate behavior.

The Importance of Discipline

George Washington believed: Discipline is the soul of an army. It makes small numbers formidable, procures success to the weak, and esteem to all.[57] Three elements are important for effective **discipline:** (1) defined roles and responsibilities so that employees know what is expected; (2) clear rules and guidelines so that employees understand what is acceptable behavior; and (3) effective methods and procedures for taking corrective action. Discipline problems include permissiveness, rigidity, and inconsistency.[58]

Permissiveness results in an untrained, poorly organized, and unproductive workforce. People need to know that they are responsible for their actions. Performance problems that go unaddressed can reduce the morale of good employees and lower the performance of the entire work group.

Rigidity, on the other hand, may cause employees to fear or hate authority and to feel anxious or overly guilty about making mistakes. If people feel that conditions are too restrictive, counterproductive measures such as slowdowns, sabotage, and strikes may result.

Inconsistency should be avoided because it makes it difficult for employees to understand what behavior is appropriate and what is not allowed. When people are punished one time and ignored or even rewarded the next time for doing the same thing, they become confused. Inevitably, this confusion results in resentment, lowered morale, and reduced productivity.

Taking Corrective Action

The two central elements of caring leadership—caring about the work and caring about people—come together in the corrective action process. The effective leader knows that performance and behavior problems must be addressed. Taking corrective action can be unpleasant and unpopular, but it is necessary because people may make mistakes that should not be condoned. Examples include theft, equipment abuse, and safety violations. Use of the following principles will help provide effective discipline and corrective action and ensure a sense of organizational justice.[59]

■ *Establish just and reasonable rules based on core values.* Think of civil rules that are just, reasonable, and necessary, such as not driving through a red light or not stealing. Employees need similar guidelines for behavior on the job. If corrective action is necessary, it should take the form of a **caring confrontation** based on core values of the organization.

Work rules should be established in such areas as attendance, safety, security, language, dress, and personal conduct. When possible, employees should be involved in establishing rules based on the core values of the organization—honesty, respect for others, and the like. Committees on safety and quality of work life help serve this purpose.

■ *Communicate rules to all employees.* Rules should be thoroughly explained to new employees during orientation and should also be published in an employee handbook or posted on a bulletin board. As few rules as possible should be made, and these should be reviewed annually. Changes in rules should be communicated in writing, since people can be held responsible only for rules they know about.

■ *Provide immediate corrective action.* Some leaders postpone corrective action because carrying it out is uncomfortable or distasteful. The practice of storing up observations and complaints and then unloading on an employee in one angry session only alienates the subordinate. Immediate correction and penalties (if appropriate) are more acceptable to the offender, and thus more effective. If there is an association between misconduct and swift corrective action, repetition of the offense is less likely to occur.

■ *Create a system of progressive corrective measures for violation of rules.* Fairness requires a progression of penalties—oral warning, written warning, suspension from the job, and discharge. The leader should be sure that a final warning has been issued prior to actual discharge. This progression gives the leader a chance to help the employee improve. If a penalty is necessary, severity should depend on the offense, the employee's previous record, and the corrective value of the penalty. Theft may justify immediate suspension; tardiness may not.

■ *Provide an appeal process for corrective action.* An appeal process helps ensure fair treatment for employees. If a mistake is made during the corrective process, a procedure for review can help correct a wrongful disciplinary action.

■ *Preserve human dignity.* Corrective action should take place in private. This approach reduces defensiveness and the likelihood that other employees may become involved and create an even bigger problem. Meeting privately provides a better opportunity to discuss the problem and prevent it from happening again. *Never* reprimand an employee in public.

When meeting with an employee, allow time to explain fully. Be a good listener. Ask questions that help the employee clarify actions. Allow for honest mistakes. Everybody makes a mistake sometime. Strike a balance between correcting the problem and developing the employee. Criticize the act, not the employee as a person. Be sure to look at all sides of the problem. If you are in error, admit it. It is possible that the employee is innocent of intentional wrongdoing. If this is so, do not take punitive action, but provide training if appropriate. End corrective action on a positive note. Emphasize cooperation and optimism for future performance.

■ *Do not charge a rule violation without first knowing the facts.* In any situation involving disciplinary action, the burden of proof and fairness is on the accuser. Be sure that (1) the rule is enforced consistently and that this incident is not an isolated case; (2) the employee was informed of the rule; (3) the employee broke the rule; (4) it can be proved that the employee broke the rule; and (5) corrective measures are fair.

There is no substitute for good preparation prior to a meeting on discipline. However, even in cases where you think you have all the facts, you might find otherwise once you begin discussion with the employee. If something new comes to light that should be investigated, suspend the meeting so that the facts can be determined. On those occasions when something new is presented, take time to confirm the facts before acting. Some leaders think, Well, I've come this far. I don't like doing this anyway. I am just going to do what I planned from the beginning, regardless of these new facts. This approach is a mistake. Aside from taking action that may be wrong, you lose credibility with the employee and everyone else who knows the facts.

■ *Obtain agreement that a problem exists.* If you cannot get agreement that a problem exists, the answer is to inform the employee that it is not likely that the employment arrangement will continue. If the employee will not acknowledge that a problem exists, how can steps be taken to correct it? If the problem is not corrected, the employee must be reassigned or terminated.

■ *Avoid negative emotions.* Relax before meeting with your employee; remain calm. *Never* confront an employee in anger. It is difficult to think and to communicate clearly when you are upset or arguing. Never scold or talk down to the employee, and do not curse or strike the person. Once you have taken corrective action, start over with a clean slate. Do not hold grudges or stereotype the employee as a troublemaker.

■ *Remember the purpose of corrective action.* The purpose is to prevent future problems, not to punish or obtain revenge. Be sure the employee understands what is wrong and why it is wrong. Be sure the employee understands the rules and the reasons they exist. Be clear. Also be fair. Ask yourself, Is this disciplinary action too severe? If a lesser measure will accomplish the same purpose, use it. Also ask, Did I clarify the problem, or did I blame the employee? Finally, ask, Does this corrective action provide a way to avoid the same situation in the future?

■ *Avoid double standards.* Rules and standards of conduct should be the same for all people in the same occupation and organization, and they should be enforced equally. If this is not the case, disciplinary action is unfair, and when higher management, union arbitrators, or governmental agencies review the decision, the action taken probably will be reversed. Consider the following case:

> Sure, I had a crescent wrench in my lunch box, but I'm no thief. Everybody does it. I could give you dozens of examples, but I won't. One thing I will say is that taking company property is not restricted to hourly employees. Look at the way management uses company cars and gasoline for personal trips. And in the shops, we're always fixing something for management—using company labor, tools, and parts. I'm always hearing stories from the front office about how managers combine vacations and company-paid business trips, or use their expense accounts for personal entertainment. I'm willing to live by the same rules everybody else does, but I won't sit still for being singled out. Let's face it: the way most employees think is that as long as you don't overdo it, taking company property is a form of employee benefits—like vacations and insurance.[60]

■ *Enforce rules consistently and firmly.* Disciplinary measures should be taken only when they are fair, necessary, procedurally correct, immediate, and constructive. Once these conditions are met, if disciplinary action is in order, the leader should proceed with confidence and firmness and should stick to the decision. When a leader backs down on a rule violation, employees either think the rule is unimportant or is being applied unfairly. The only time backing down is advised is when a wrong decision has been made. If a mistake is made, the leader must correct the mistake.

■ *Follow the four-step method for solving performance problems.* See Figure 19–4. Note that step 4 accomplishes two important purposes: (1) ensuring the correction is made; and (2) building goodwill by recognizing improvement.

Figure 19–4
Four-Step Method for
Solving Performance
Problems[61]

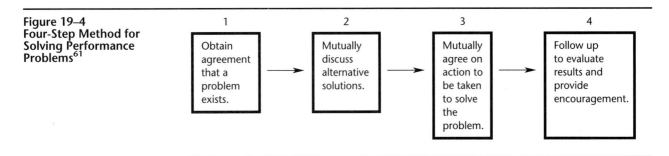

1	2	3	4
Obtain agreement that a problem exists.	Mutually discuss alternative solutions.	Mutually agree on action to be taken to solve the problem.	Follow up to evaluate results and provide encouragement.

In summary, employee discipline is an important ingredient for organizational success. Discipline in the form of a caring confrontation can be an effective leadership tool that helps employee development, keeps work morale high, and results in the best job performance.

Case Study

The Forklift Fiasco[62]

There are three forklift truck operators in the warehouse. Two of them are young employees who have both been warned twice (the second warning in writing) about careless operation of the trucks. Last week one of them (Jack) made a fast turn and spilled a shipment. The dropped cartons had to be opened and inspected and a number of damaged items sent back for repair.

The supervisor said it was inexcusable carelessness and gave him a three-day layoff. She warned all truck operators that any damage with trucks would be punished by layoff from here on.

Today Ray Harrison, the third truck operator, ran into a door frame overhead and spilled the entire load he was carrying. He had simply failed to lower the truck. He is a valued employee and has never had an accident or any disciplinary record in all his years on the job. He is a friend and neighbor of the supervisor, and they ride to work together. Everyone is watching to see what the supervisor is going to do.

Questions

1. If a supervisor makes a threat, is it necessary to carry it out?

   _____

   _____

   _____

2. Have you ever been punished for a mistake on the job? Was the action fair? Explain.

   _____

   _____

   _____

3. Discuss the issues and challenges of women leading men, especially in work settings traditionally dominated by men.

   _____

   _____

   _____

Part Nine Summary

After reading Part Nine, you should know the following key concepts, principles, and terms. Fill in the blanks from memory, or copy the answers listed below.

Performance management skills include (a) _____, _____, and _____. Management performance is important in three areas: (b) _____, the ability to work with and through other people; (c) _____, the ability to achieve results regardless of obstacles; and (d) _____, the ability to generate new and usable ideas. Statesmanship involves good (e) _____ and using the _____ to solve problems. Entrepreneurship requires (f) _____, _____, and _____. Developing creativity and increasing innovation is helped by (g) _____, _____, and _____. Level 5 leadership is required to help an organization go from good to great. The Level 5 leader builds enduring greatness through a combination of (h) _____ and _____. (i) _____ is a careful search for excellence—taking the absolute best as a standard and striving to surpass it. Behavior modification, a method of improving the performance of individuals and groups, involves three elements: (j) _____, _____, and _____. George Washington thought that (k) _____ is the soul of an army, making small numbers formidable, procuring success to the weak, and esteem to all. The three enemies of effective discipline are (l) _____, _____, and _____. Corrective action taken to support core values or principles can be termed a (m) _____.

Answer Key for Part Nine Summary

a. **performance planning, performance coaching, correcting poor performance,** page 406
b. **statesmanship,** page 421
c. **entrepreneurship,** page 421
d. **innovation,** page 421
e. **human relations skills, four-step method,** page 427
f. **good work habits, belief in oneself, willingness to take risks,** page 429
g. **keeping an open mind, having a questioning attitude, using a new-ideas system,** page 431
h. **personal humility, professional will,** page 436
i. **Benchmarking,** page 437
j. **goal setting, feedback on performance, positive reinforcement,** page 443
k. **discipline,** page 444
l. **permissiveness, rigidity, inconsistency,** page 444
m. **caring confrontation,** page 445

Reflection Points—Personal Thoughts on Managing Performance, Professional Performance, and Sustaining Discipline

Complete the following questions and activities to personalize the content of Part Nine. Space is provided for writing your thoughts.

- Discuss the importance of setting goals. Apply the concept of performance planning to your own job or career.

_____

_____

- Discuss the merits of performance appraisal. Cite true-life examples in which performance reviews helped or hurt job performance. What do's and don'ts can you recommend for evaluating employees?

_____

_____

- Discuss the idea of rating leaders. If you were a supervisor, manager, or executive, would you want to be evaluated by your employees? Explain.

_____

_____

- Discuss your performance in the areas of statesmanship, entrepreneurship, and innovation. What are your strengths? What areas do you need to improve? What actions will you take to improve?

_____

_____

- Discuss a Level 5 leader you know on the basis of personal humility and professional will. How does the leader demonstrate consideration and service as well as conviction and resolve?

_____

_____

- Evaluate an organization you know on the basis of product quality and service quality. Compare the results against those of its best competitors. Develop an action plan to stay excellent or improve.

_____

_____

- Develop a behavior modification program to improve performance in an existing group: (a) Identify a group with critical performance behaviors (examples—teachers, machine operators, police officers, food service employees, salespeople, nurses); (b) meet with members of the group to help them agree on critical performance behaviors; (c) prepare a checklist of critical performance behaviors (typically, 10 to 15 points); (d) enlist the cooperation of group members in monitoring their own performance and using the checklist to document behaviors exhibited (typically, daily); (e) review progress with group members (typically, weekly); (f) reward participation and progress (provide recognition and reinforcement). Discuss results.

_____

_____

- Discuss the concept of the caring confrontation in the context of effective discipline, employee development, work group morale, and job performance. Have you ever experienced a caring confrontation, either as a leader or a subordinate? Describe the situation and outcome.

_____

_____

Part Nine Video Case
Louisville Slugger—Hillerich & Bradsby

What do Babe Ruth's 60th home run, Joe DiMaggio's 56-game hitting streak, Ted Williams's .406 season, and Hank Aaron's record-breaking 715th home run have in common? They all were accomplished with Louisville Slugger bats manufactured on the Ohio River at Hillerich & Bradsby. The company makes about 300 models for major league baseball and has about 60 percent of the major league market. Best known for its wooden bats, the Louisville, Kentucky-based firm also manufactures a variety of baseball, golf, and hockey equipment for amateur and professional athletes.

The company was founded in 1857 as J.F. Hillerich & Son to manufacture butter churns. It entered the baseball market when one of Hillerich's sons, Bud, promised a star player he could make a bat for him. H&B began producing bats in 1928 and today relies on the wooden and aluminum bat business for nearly three-quarters of annual revenues.

The company remains family-run; John Hillerich IV is the fourth-generation CEO, taking over the private company from his father. He feels the pressure heading a successful company more than 120 years old, as competition in the industry has intensified as never before. The Louisville Slugger bat now competes with bats made by a host of others, ranging from carpenters to Amish craftsmen. To gain an advantage, H&B looked at its internal system in order to streamline operations. The company needed to address everything from order entry problems to production deficiencies to returns. The overview led to discussion of a new system to handle the flow of information.

H&B had a big decision to make: it could either reconfigure its information system or start over. A new system would need to streamline information flow in support of the sales operation and supply chain management, as well as accounting, finance, and marketing. Management realized it needed a new system to improve its dismal shipping record; about 40 percent of its orders were being shipped on time. They opted for the enterprise resource planning (ERP) system, designed to simplify all processes by storing all information in one common database and automatically updating the information in every stage of production.

Implementation of the new ERP system usually takes years, and the transition from the old system to the new one is difficult. Since the ERP system uses real-time information, the production department manufactures only the inventory that the sales department has requested, and the shipping department has the proper amount of inventory to send to customers. The benefits of ERP are bottom-line savings for the company and improved morale as frustration from repetitive tasks and missing information dissipates. H&B managers thought the cost of implementing the new system was worth the potential savings. Communication between production and sales had been inefficient, as well as that with management. Getting an answer to one simple question could take a week.

The first step in streamlining production was to identify problems and devise the needs of the new ERP system. Then, the German company SAP was chosen to provide the software. SAP is a system in which a common server holds all the company's information. Every personal computer (PC) is connected to the server. Once data is entered, it is stored on the server, where everyone can access it from a PC.

During the 18-month configuration process, morale sagged as longtime employees struggled to change the way they worked. Some employees left during training class, stress levels temporarily increased, and some production processes failed. H&B managers thought about halting the new system, but after struggling through implementation, the company began seeing benefits. It took five years to see quantifiable results. Now the company ships 85 percent of its orders complete and on time, compared with 40 percent before SAP. Top customers surveyed rate H&B in the 90–95 percent satisfaction category.

Questions for Discussion

1. What role does information technology play at Hillerich & Bradsby?

2. Discuss "best practices" in IT today.

For more information, see www.slugger.com.

Action Assignment

As a bridge between learning and doing, complete the following action assignment.

1. What is the most important idea you have learned in Part Nine?

2. How can you apply what you have learned? What will you do, with whom, where, when, and, most important, why?

The Road Ahead: Challenge and Charge

UPON THE PLAINS OF HESITATION bleach the bones of countless millions, who on the threshold of victory sat down to wait; and awaiting they died.

—Winston Churchill

The Road Ahead

Leadership has become an increasingly important and popular subject. The U.S. Library of Congress contains more than 9,000 books with the word *leadership* in the title. There are currently more than 6,200 English-language journals being published on the subject of leadership, and today almost every college and university in the United States (4,323) is teaching leadership in its curriculum. Eighty percent of Fortune 500 companies either have or are planning to implement a corporate university with leadership development as its primary purpose.[1]

Books, articles, seminars, and courses are flourishing. Instead of older models of command and control, newer models of commitment and consideration are needed to deal effectively with changing organizations, changing work, changing people, and a changing society. Instead of leadership by a few hierarchical, position-based leaders, leadership today is shared at all levels and in all walks of the organization.

It is no longer just "the boss" who leads; individuals up and down a far flatter organization provide leadership based on the task to be performed and the skills required to perform it. An individual may be a leader one day, a follower the next, and a co-leader the third. The trend toward team-based projects, virtual communities, and personal responsibility will only accelerate the move toward shared leadership and the need for leadership education.[2]

The Association to Advance Collegiate Schools of Business (AACSB) and the Conference Board, the research organization that studies trends and makes forecasts about management, have identified critical skills leaders need to be successful. Skills and related chapters of this book are as follows:

1. Cognitive ability and ethics; see Chapters 2, 3, 6, and 7.
2. Strategic thinking; see Chapters 3, 4, 5, 6, 7, 16, 17, 18, 19, and 20.
3. Analytical skills; see Chapters 3, 10, 11, 18, and 19.
4. Decision making; see Chapters 1, 9, 10, 11, and 18.
5. Communication skills; see Chapters 7, 8, 10, 12, 13, 15, and 16.

6. Team leadership; see Chapters 7, 8, 9, 10, 11, 12, 13, and 19.
7. Managing diversity; see Chapters 10, 13, and 15.
8. Delegation skills; see Chapters 14, 15, 16, and 18.
9. Coaching ability; see Chapters 1, 2, 3, 6, 8, 9, 10, 11, 12, 14, 15, 16, 17, 18, and 19.
10. Reflective thinking, self-management, and learning skills; see Chapters 6, 7, 12, 16, 17, 18, 19, and 20.

Bright new leaders of the future can draw on teachers from the past. In the first quarter of the past century, management author and business advisor Mary Parker Follett identified the challenge of leadership:

The leader must have an eye for change and a steadying hand to provide both vision and reassurance that change can be mastered, a voice that articulates the will of the group and shapes it to constructive ends, and an ability to inspire by force of personality while making others feel capable to increase and use their own abilities.[3]

In her book *Creative Experience,* first published in 1924, Follett writes: "Leadership is not defined by the exercise of power but by the capacity to increase the source of power among those who are led. The most important work of the leader is to create more leaders."[4]

The 21st century will be an exciting time, requiring leaders in the best sense of the word—people who care about others and who want to make a difference. It will be a time requiring leaders whose ideas and deeds will light the path, encourage the heart, and make the world a better place. It will be a time requiring *caring leadership.*

Nine Key Areas of Leadership

We have defined leadership, emphasized the need for caring leadership, and discussed the concepts, principles, and techniques of nine key areas of leadership success, which correspond to the nine parts of this book. The example of Abraham Lincoln, one of America's greatest leaders, shows the importance of leadership and the critical role of each of these areas:[5]

■ *Part 1—Leadership variables.* Lincoln's character (honesty and courage), the ability of his followers (Grant's determination and persistence), and the nature of the situation (the North's economic strength) combined, a civil war was waged, and America endured as one nation.

■ *Part 2—The power of vision.* With compassion for all people and dedication to preserving the Union, Lincoln delivered the Gettysburg Address, considered by historians the most powerful speech since the Sermon on the Mount. In so doing, Lincoln articulated a vision of a united America that would inspire and sustain his country through bitter civil war.

■ *Part 3—The importance of ethics.* To his vision of a united country and his concern for all people, Lincoln applied the bedrock character elements of honesty, courage, and hard work. He was devoted to goodness as he understood it to be, regardless of self-interest or the dictates of public opinion.

■ *Part 4—The empowerment of people.* Lincoln was a servant leader who used the office of president in an empowering way, saying, "Am I not helping people when I make friends of them? A drop of honey that catches a man's heart is the high road to his reason."

■ *Part 5—Leadership principles.* Lincoln's great competence as a leader was seen in his knowledge of history, law, and current conditions, which he used in addition to common sense and practical judgment in dealing with people.

■ *Part 6—Understanding people.* It was common to hear it said that Lincoln understood the American people better than they understood themselves, and he would tap the great fountains of humor and wit to make his points without rancor.

- *Part 7—Multiplying effectiveness.* This ability was seen best in the selection and support of Ulysses S. Grant as commander of the Union army. Lincoln was effective at achieving his goals through delegation, support, and encouragement of others.

- *Part 8—Developing others.* Lincoln was by nature a teacher—patient and encouraging in the development of others. Almost no situation could occur in which Lincoln could not apply the techniques of metaphor and example to instruct his audience and inspire them.

- *Part 9—Performance management.* Lincoln held the bar high for his war generals. He expected results and if they were not forthcoming, he replaced the generals, no matter how uncomfortable he personally felt. To victorious performers—Grant, Sherman, and Sheridan—he was grateful, and he credited the preservation of the Union to them.

Abraham Lincoln is acclaimed for leading America through the Civil War that preserved the Union and ended slavery. Ulysses Grant wrote of Lincoln: "I knew his goodness of heart, his generosity, his yielding disposition, his desire to have everybody happy, and above all his desire to see all the people of the United States enter again upon the full privileges of citizenship with equality among all."[6]

The nine key areas of leadership can be used to diagnose past leadership events, as well as to predict future leadership effectiveness. The ideas and deeds of one person or group will influence the behavior of others to the degree that the nine dimensions of leadership are present and in force. Deficiency in these areas leads to inaction, confusion, ethical drift, stagnation, low morale, lack of motivation, inefficiency, underachievement, and failure; whereas mastery in these areas leads to movement, focus, moral strength, commitment, high morale, motivation, effectiveness, fulfillment of potential, and performance excellence.

For a personal evaluation of the nine key areas of leadership, complete Exercise 20–1.

**Exercise 20–1
Personal Analysis
of Leadership**

Step 1:

Identify a true-life situation requiring leadership in your work, personal, or community life. Examples include creating a business, raising a family, and leading a task force or team.

Step 2:

Answer the following questions.

The Leadership Equation

Describe your leadership traits, behaviors, qualities, and style. Describe the characteristics of your followers. Describe the situation in terms of time and circumstances. Are the people and conditions right for you to provide leadership?

_____

_____

_____

The Power of Vision

What is your vision—what do you want to accomplish? Why would you provide leadership in this situation—for power, achievement, or affiliation? How strong is your interest in providing leadership?

_____

_____

_____

The Importance of Ethics

Do you base your actions on moral principles, regardless of personal loss or gain, and without regard to social influence? Describe your values in terms of honesty, respect, concern for others, and the like. Do you have conviction and courage so that others will follow you?

_____

_____

_____

The Empowerment of People

What authority do you have? Do you possess the power of position? Do you view leadership as the opportunity to serve others? What will you do to empower people? What steps will you take to develop a high-performance workplace?

_____

_____

_____

Leadership Principles

What principles of leadership will you practice that will help your followers be effective? What will you do to keep work morale high? What will you do to develop communication, teamwork, and a one-team attitude?

_____

_____

_____

Understanding People

Do you understand the nature and needs of the people you lead? What are their motivations? What are your own reasons for doing what you do? What will you say or do to persuade others to take action?

_____

_____

_____

Multiplying Effectiveness

How will you increase your leadership effectiveness? Are you willing to delegate duties and authority to others? Who will you assign to do what by when? Are you effective in meeting the needs of and achieving results with the different personalities reporting to you?

_____

_____

_____

Developing Others

What will you do to attract and keep good people? Do you have the ability to train and develop others? Do you have the ability to help people through change? Do you maintain a positive attitude of exploration, responsibility, and commitment?

_____

_____

_____

Performance Management

Do you set high goals, reinforce good performance, and correct performance problems? What are your strengths and weaknesses in the areas of statesmanship, entrepreneurship, and innovation? Do you have, or are you developing, the paradoxical qualities of personal humility and strong resolve?

_____

_____

_____

Step 3:

What is your prediction of the outcome? To what extent are the nine key dimensions of leadership present in this situation? Whether you would be hero, teacher, or ruler as a leader, how successful will you be in lighting the path and encouraging others to follow? Will your ideas and actions show the way and influence the behavior of others? Explain.

_____

_____

_____

Leaders Who Care

There are two principal aspects of successful leadership—commitment to a task and concern for others. Both are necessary for leadership success. The effective leader cares not only about the work but about people as well.[7] By caring so much, the leader focuses, energizes, and empowers others. In this sense, caring leadership is the universal key that unlocks success. The caring leader (1) aims higher than others think is practical; (2) gives more than others think is prudent; and (3) achieves more than others think is possible.

A concept in literature states: "No tears in the writer, no tears in the reader." The same concept can be applied to leadership—"No passion in the leader, no passion in the people." If the leader doesn't care, the people won't either. As Lee Iacocca said when he was the leader of Chrysler Corporation during a period of great uncertainty and struggle for survival, "The speed of the leader is the speed of the team." People will never care more or perform better than their leaders do.[8]

To understand the importance of leadership passion, consider the words of author and educator Price Pritchett.

People always look at the leader when they want to take the pulse of an organization. Example says a lot. Do they see a person they can believe in? Can they have faith in whom they follow? Does the fire inside the leader burn hot enough for them to warm from the heart of that flame?

Commitment climbs when people see passion in the person out front. They catch the feeling. Commitment, after all, is a highly contagious thing. It is a spirit that stirs others, that touches their souls, that inspires them to action. It carries a mental magnetism that captures the attention and enlists the energies of all who watch.

The more consuming your commitment, the more you will draw your people toward you, and toward the task to be done. Your intensity—your focus, drive, and dedication—carries maximum influence over the level of commitment you can expect from others.

Like it or not, you set the climate. People always take a reading on the person in charge. So when it comes to building commitment, you must lead by example, just as commanders must show courage if they want soldiers showing bravery on the battlefield.

If you provide lukewarm leadership, you will see the passion cool among your people. Commitment can't survive when the leader doesn't seem to care. So be obvious. Turn up the burner inside yourself. Let the heat of your commitment be strong enough to glow in the dark.[9]

To personalize the subject, consider how you rate on leadership commitment. Do you have self-drive and determination that ignites and energizes others? Does your intensity burn bright enough to glow in the dark? Does your passion stir others and inspire them to action?

The leader also must care about people. To understand the importance of concern for others, consider the words of leader and businessman Clarence Francis:

> You can buy a person's time. You can buy a person's presence at a given place. You can buy a measured number of skilled muscular motions per hour or day. But you cannot buy enthusiasm. You cannot buy initiative. You cannot buy loyalty. You cannot buy the devotion of hearts, minds, and souls. You have to earn these things. To do this the leader must believe that the greatest assets are human assets, and that the improvement of their value is both a matter of material advantage and moral obligation. The leader must believe that workers must be treated as honorable individuals, justly rewarded, encouraged in their own progress, fully informed, and properly assigned, and that their lives and work must be given meaning and dignity on and off the job. If a leader has supervision of so much as one person, the leader must honor these principles in practice.[10]

To personalize the subject, consider how you rate on concern for people. Do you care about the well-being of others? Do they know it? Does your consideration for others create support and loyalty to you and your goals?

Learning from Lincoln

Scholars unanimously acclaim Abraham Lincoln as a great leader. More books have been written about his life than any other U.S. president.[11] Lincoln shows that leaders are not either–or people; they are masters of paradox. They care about the mission, *and* they care about people. They focus on doing the right things *and* doing things right, not one without the other. They think and feel and act for the benefit of others, *and*, in so doing, are true to themselves. They pursue the large *and* attend to the small, knowing that both of these matter. This is the kind of leader the world needs and the kind of leader that Abraham Lincoln was.

> The people were divided and the nation was at war. Prejudice, cruelty, sickness, and death all waited at the door. In this hour, Abraham Lincoln called to Washington a soldier from the field. He wanted to talk with him about something important. The soldier was a good-hearted man, but he had neglected his mother. He had not written her for two years, and she believed him killed. She had asked the president if he could locate his grave.
>
> Lincoln talked with the young man sternly, but not unkindly. He told him that he must write his mother every week beginning now, or be court-martialed for a crime worse than treason: ingratitude. The record shows that one hour later, the young man left. About the time spent, Lincoln said, "It needed doing."[12]

Lincoln thought the nation should not be divided, and he thought the slaves should be freed. He was committed to these great goals. He also thought a mother should be spared unnecessary sorrow and grief, and that a son should be grateful and kind. He thought all these things needed doing and he did them because he cared. There may be no such thing as a perfect leader, but Lincoln was close. Those who would be effective leaders can learn from his good example.

Lincoln thought that what matters to people is not style, but substance; not the entrance, but the exit. By word or deed, the caring leader makes the world a better place.

Going Forward

The knowing–doing gap is an important concept that explains a great deal about human behavior. On the one hand, we are curious and we want to improve both our public and private lives, so we study and learn. On the other hand, we often fail to apply what we discover and fail to fulfill our potential. The solution is to close the gap between knowing and doing.

As you develop the characteristics of a caring leader and apply the nine keys to success, we hope you will keep this book handy and refer to it often in your leadership role. What are the qualities of effective leaders? See pages 30–33. Why would you want to be a leader? See pages 70–74. What is the importance of leadership character? See pages 89–136. How do you use and not abuse leadership authority? See pages 138–152. What are the principles of effective leadership? See pages 184–200. How do you build a high-performance team? See pages 214–241. How do you motivate people? See pages 249–264. What are the rules for effective delegation? See pages 302–308. How do you deal with different personalities? See pages 320–339. How do you help people develop and grow? See pages 346–359. How do you help people through change? See pages 361–399. How do you manage performance and sustain organizational success? See pages 405–447. We encourage you to use this book as a reference and learning guide.

Leadership is an important subject with enormous potential to help or harm. Consider your own experiences with the leaders you have known, and think how they have affected you. Now consider your own work and life and the occasions you may have to provide leadership to others, the opportunities you will have to light the way and influence others to action. During these times, remember to display the commitment to task and the support of people characteristic of caring leadership. Always keep in mind the nine key dimensions of leadership, and apply the concepts, principles, and techniques you have learned to *be the leader you have always wanted to have.*

People remember little about what they hear and see, and, for that matter, read. Mostly, they remember how they have been made to feel. The caring leader makes people feel worthy, empowered, and motivated to make a positive difference in the world, and that has been the goal of this book.

In appreciation of leaders both past and present, we end this book with a poem by James Autry, whose wise and wonderful book *Love and Profit* inspired this one.

Retirement

It is early—6:30. The building is quiet.
Soon the place will come to life as it always
does with the rush of people working.
These days, though, it's the smaller, slower things I notice;
the droning of the fans and compressors keeping us warm or cool,
the buzz of fluorescent lights, the burble of the big percolator and
the smell of coffee.
As the time here grows shorter, I find myself thinking of other
times when I could not wait for the day or the week to be over—
The times I strained for Christmas or vacation; I think of
meetings that would never end, of hours stuck on a taxi-way,
airliners lined up as far as I could see;
of those eternal minutes right before someone was to come into my
office to be fired.
I understand now why every writer who ever lived wrote about time
and its paradoxes, and everything they ever said about
how fast time passes is true.
But, they never told us how many slow days we would have
to endure before we realized
how fast they had gone.[13]

Endnotes

Chapter 1

1. S. Jamara, "How to Successfully On-board Executives," Society for Human Resource Management Annual Conference, Atlanta, GA, 2008; Einarsen et al., "Destructive Leadership Behavior," *Leadership Quarterly* 18 (2009): 207–216; and W. Bennis, "The Challenges of Leadership in the Modern World," *American Pschologist* (January 2007): 2–5.

2. J. Wren, *The Leader's Companion* (New York: Free Press, 1995); and J. Antonakis et al., "Leadership: Past, Present and Future," in J. Antonakis, A. Cianciola, and R. Sternberg, eds., *The Nature of Leadership* (Thousand Oaks, CA: Sage, 2004).

3. G. Ashe, *Camelot and the Vision of Albion* (London: Hinemann, 1977), 134.

4. R. Warner, *Greeks and Trojans* (London: MacGibbon & Kee, 1951), 136.

5. D. Phillips, *The Founding Fathers on Leadership* (Collingdale, PA: Diane, 2000).

6. C. Oman, *The Dark Ages: 476–918* (London: Rivingstons, 1962), 512.

7. K. Anthony, *Susan B. Anthony* (Garden City, NY: Doubleday, 1954), vi, viii.

8. U. Wikken, *Alexander the Great* (New York: Norton, 1967), 3.

9. R. Heilbroner, The Worldly Philosophers (London: Penguin, 2000).

10. J. Allen, *100 Great Lives* (New York: World, 1945); M. Hart, *The One Hundred* (New York: Beaufort Books, 1985); and M. Mumford, *Pathways to Outstanding Leadersip* (Mahwah, NJ: Lawrence Erlbaum, 2006).

11. G. Bellman, *Getting Things Done When You Are Not in Charge* (San Francisco: Berrett-Koehler, 2001); B. Kellerman, *Followership* (Boston: Harvard Business School Press, 2008); and B. Groysberg et al., "The Different Ways Military Experience Prepares Managers for Leadership," *Harvard Business Review* (November 2010): 81–86.

12. C. Wilson, *Rosa Parks: From the Back of the Bus to the Front of a Movement* (New York: Scholastic, 2001).

13. J. Burns, Leadership (New York: Harper & Row, 1978); and J. Burns, *Rethinking Leadership* (College Park, MD: James MacGregor Burns Academy of Leadership, 1998).

14. T. Carlyle, *On Heroes, Hero Worship and the Heroic in History* (London: Chapman & Hall, 1870).

15. R. Stogdill, *Handbook of Leadership,* rev. and exp., B. Bass (New York: Free Press, 1981), 81.

16. G. Lord and D. Brown, *Leadership Process and Follower Identity* (Mahwah, NJ: Erlbaum, 2004).

17. Stogdill, *Handbook of Leadership,* 5.

18. Stogdill, *Handbook of Leadership,* 5; and J. Chhokar et al., *Culture and Leadership Across the World: The GLOBE Book of In-depth Studies of 25 Societies* (Thousand Oaks, CA: Sage, 2007).

19. H. Levinson, *Executive* (Cambridge, MA: Harvard University Press, 1981); and D. Sobel, "Findings," *Harvard Magazine* 81, no. 3 (January–February 1979): 15.

20. J. Kouzes and B. Posner, *The Leadership Challenge,* 3rd ed. (San Francisco: Jossey-Bass, 2007).

21. W. Bennis and R. Thomas, "Crucibles of Leadership," in *Harvard Business Review on Developing Leaders* (Boston: Harvard Business School, 2004).

22. Kouzes and Posner, The Leadership Challenge; and D. May et al., "The Moral Component of Authentic Leadership," *Organizational Dynamics* 32 (August 2003): 247–260.

23. A. DuBrin, *Leadership: Research Findings, Practice, and Skills* (Boston: Houghton Mifflin, 1998).

24. DuBrin, *Leadership.*

25. T. Roosevelt, *The Strenuous Life* (New York: Bartleby.com: Great Books Online, 1999), retrieved August 13, 2005, from www.bartleby.com/index.html. Used by permission of Bartleby.com.

26. G. Fairholm, *Capturing the Heart of Leadership* (Westport, CT: Praeger, 1997); M. Mayeroff, *On Caring* (New York: Harper Perennial, 1990); and J. Dutton et al., "Leading in Times of Trauma," *Harvard Business Review* (January 2002): 54–61.

27. J. Carlzon, *Moments of Truth* (Cambridge, MA: Ballinger, 1987).

28. The poem "Threads" is excerpted from the book *Love & Profit* (Avon Books, 1991) by J. Autry and is reprinted by permission of the author.

29. J. Kotter, "What Leaders Really Do," *Harvard Business Review* 68, no. 3 (May–June 1990): 103–111; and J. Gardner, *Self-Renewal* (New York: Norton, 1995).

30. H. Fayol, *General and Industrial Management* (London: Pitman, 1916); H. Mintzberg, *The Nature of Managerial Work* (New York: Harper & Row, 1973); A. Zaleznik, "Managers and Leaders: Are They Different?" *Harvard Business Review* 70, no. 2 (March–April 1992): 126–135; and W. Bennis and B. Nanus, *Leaders* (New York: Harper & Row, 1985).

PART 1, Chapters 2–3

1. B. Bass and R. Stogdill, *Bass and Stogdill's Handbook of Leadership* (New York: Free Press, 1990); J. Rost, *Leadership for the 21st Century* (New York: Praeger, 1991); and G. Goethals et al., eds. *Encyclopedia of Leadership* (Thousand Oaks, CA: Sage, 2004).

2. F. Galton, *Hereditary Genius* (Bristol, UK: Thoemmes, 1869).

3. P. Northouse, *Leadership* (Thousand Oaks, CA: Sage, 2010); W. Wilhelm, "Learning from Past Leaders," in F. Hesselbein et al., eds., *The Leader of the Future* (San Francisco: Jossey-Bass, 1996); and S. Zaccaro, "Trait-Based Perspectives of Leadership," *American Psychologist* 62 (2007): 6–16.

4. E. Ghiselli, *Explorations in Management Talent* (Santa Monica, CA: Goodyear, 1971); and S. Zaccaro et al., "Leader Traits and Attributes," in J. Antonakis et al., eds, *The Nature of Leadership* (Thousand Oaks, CA: Sage, 2004).

5. H. Mann, "State of OKI," Ohio-Kentucky-Indiana Planning Conference, Cincinnati, Ohio, 1998.

6. K. Lewin et al., "Patterns of Aggressive Behavior in Experimentally Created Social Climates," *Journal of Social Psychology* 10 (1939): 271–299.

7. R. Stogdill and A. Coons, eds., *Leader Behavior* (Columbus: Ohio State University, Bureau of Business Research, 1957); and R. Stogdill, *Handbook of Leadership* (New York: Free Press, 1974).

8. R. Likert, *New Patterns of Management* (New York: McGraw-Hill, 1961); and R. Likert, *The Human Organization* (New York: McGraw-Hill, 1967).

9. R. Blake and J. Mouton, *The Managerial Grid* (Houston, TX: Gulf Publishing, 1964); R. Blake et al., *Leadership Dilemmas—Grid Solutions* (Houston: Gulf Publishing, 1991). Used by permission of Grid International.

10. M. Morrell, *Shackleton's Way* (New York: Viking Press, 2001).

11. F. Fiedler, *A Theory of Leadership Effectiveness* (New York: McGraw-Hill, 1967); A. Tannenbaum and W. Schmidt, "How to Choose a Leadership Pattern," *Harvard Business Review* 36 (March–April 1958): 95–101; R. Neustadt, *Presidential Power and the Modern Presidents* (New York: Macmillan, 1990); and G. Yukl, *Leadership in Organizations,* 6th ed. (Upper Saddle River, NJ: Prentice Hall, 2006).

12. A. Hadland, "Nelson Mandela," in K. Asmal et al., *Nelson Mandela in His Own Words* (New York: Little, Brown, 2003).

13. E. Jennings, *An Anatomy of Leadership* (New York: McGraw-Hill, 1960), 13.

14. W. Reddin, "The 3-D Management Style Theory," *Training and Development Journal* (April 1967): 8–17; P. Hersey, *The Situational Leader* (New York: Warner Books, 1985); and K. Blanchard and P. Hersey, "Great Ideas Revisited," *Training and Development* 50, no. 1 (January 1996): 42–47.

15. W. Clarnay and W. Berliner, *Management Training,* 5th ed. (Homewood, IL: Richard D. Irwin, Inc., 1970), 34–35. Reprinted with permission.

16. M. Weber, *The Theory of Social and Economic Organization,* trans. A. Henderson and T. Parsons, ed. T. Parsons (New York: Oxford University Press, 1947), 358.

17. R. House, "A Theory of Charismatic Leadership," in J. Hunt and L. Larson, eds., *Leadership* (Carbondale: Southern Illinois University Press, 1976), 189–207; and D. Mason, "Secrets of the Charismatic Leader," *Nonprofit World* 22, no. 4 (July–August 2004): 19–20.

18. D. McClelland, *Power* (New York: Irvington/Halstead Press, 1975).

19. J. Kramer, ed., *Lombardi* (New York: Crowell, 1976), 158, 160, 162.

20. J. Burns, *Leadership* (New York: Harper & Row, 1978), 9.

21. B. Avolio and F. Yammarino, eds., *Transformational and Charismatic Leadership* (Greenwich, CT: JAI Press, 2002); and B. Avolio, *Full Leadership Development* (Thousand Oaks, CA: Sage, 1999).

22. J. Downton, *Rebel Leadership* (New York: Free Press, 1973); and J. Burns, *Leadership.*

23. J. Hunt and J. Conger, "From Where We Sit," *Leadership Quarterly* 10, no. 3 (Fall 1999): 335–343; and B. Bass and R. Riggio, *Transformational Leadership* (Mahwah, NJ: Lawrence Erlbaum, 2006).

24. B. Aviola, *Full Leadership Development.*

25. Burns, *Leadership;* W. Edmondson, Island Creek Coal Company Leadership Conference, "Leadership in the Air Force,"

Maxwell Air Force Base, AL, October 1974; Yukl, *Leadership in Organizations*; K. Blanchard, *Leading at a Higher Level* (Upper Saddle River, NJ: Prentice Hall, 2007); and L. Braksick and J. Hillgren, *Preparing CEOs for Success* (Pittsburgh, PA: The Continuous Learning Group, 2010).

26. A. de Saint–Exupéry quotes retrieved August 13, 2005, from www.brainyquote.com/quotes/a/antoinedes161736.html.

27. M. Mumford et al., "Leadership Skills for a Changing World," *Leadership Quarterly* 11 (2000): 11–35.

28. H. Ferguson, *The Edge* (Fairview Park, OH: Ferguson, 1983), section 2.

29. Ferguson, *The Edge,* section 4.

30. N. Machiavelli, *The Prince,* trans. G. Bull (New York: Penguin, 1961).

31. G. Meir, *My Life,* reissued ed. (New York: Dell, 1976).

32. J. Kegan, *Winston Churchill* (New York: Viking, 2002); and C. Sandys, *We Shall Not Fail* (New York: Penguin, 2003).

33. F. McLynn, *Napoleon* (New York: Arcade, 2002).

34. Korn/Ferry International Consulting Firm, with University of California–Los Angeles, School of Management, "Leadership Study of Success," 2000.

35. J. Schroeder et al., *Life and Times of Washington* (Albany, NY: Washington Press, 1903).

36. J. Burns and S. Dunn, *George Washington* (New York: Times Books, 2004).

37. B. Kellerman, *Bad Leadership* (Boston: Harvard Business School Press, 2004); see also J. Zenger et al., *The Inspiring Leader* (New York: McGraw-Hill, 2009).

38. M. McCall and M. Lombardo, "Off the Track: Why and How Successful Executives Get Derailed" (Greensboro, NC: Center for Creative Leadership, January 1988), Technical Report nos. 21 and 34; see also J. Beeson, "Why You Didn't Get That Promotion," *Harvard Business Review* (January 2009): 101–105.

39. F. Fukuyama, *Trust* (New York: Free Press, 1995).

40. W. Menninger and H. Levinson, *Human Understanding in Industry* (Chicago: Science Research Associates, 1956), 6–7.

41. J. Jaworski, *Synchronicity* (San Francisco: Berrett-Koehler, 1996); and R. Kelley, *The Power of Followership* (New York: Doubleday, 1992).

42. R. Kelley, "In Praise of Followers," *Harvard Business Review* (1988): 142–148.

43. S. Levine and M. Crom, *The Leader in You* (New York: Pocket Books, 1995); and G. Goethals et al., *Encyclopedia of Leadership,* vol. 2 (Thousand Oaks, CA: Sage, 2004), 828–833.

44. "A Test: Are You a Machiavellian?" in R. Christie, "The Machiavellians among Us," *Psychology Today* (November 1970): 82–83, 85–86; and A. Drory and U. Gluskinos, "Machiavellianism and Leadership," *Journal of Applied Psychology* 65 (1980): 81–86.

45. I. de Sola Pool, "The Head of the Company," *Behavioral Science* 9, no. 2 (April 1964): 147–155.

46. Jennings, *An Anatomy of Leadership,* 13, 131–134.

47. C. Handy, *The Age of Unreason* (London: Arrow Business Books, 1995); and A. Davis-Blake et al., "Happy Together?" *Academy of Management Journal* 46 (2003): 475–485.

48. L. Stapley, *The Personality of the Organisation* (London: Free Association Books, 1996).

49. R. Cattell, "The Measurement of Adult Intelligence," *Psychological Bulletin* 40 (1943): 153–193; R. Cattell, *Abilities* (Boston: Houghton Mifflin, 1971); and R. Sternberg, "Culture and Intelligence," *American Psychologist* 59 (2004): 325–338.

50. S. Zaccaro et al., "Leader Traits and Attributes," in J. Antonakis et al., eds., *The Nature of Leadership* (Thousand Oaks, CA: Sage, 2004), 101–124; and T. Judge et al., "Intelligence and Leadership," *Journal of Applied Psychology* 89, no. 3 (2004): 542–552.

51. Adapted from J. Rogers, *The Rogers Indicator of Multiple Intelligences (RIMI)* (Provo, UT: Brigham Young University, 1995), used by permission of the author. H. Gardner, *Creating Minds* (New York: Basic Books, 1993), 338; R. Sternberg and D. Detterman, *What Is Intelligence?* (Norwood, NJ: Able X Publishing, 1986); see also H. Gardner, *Intelligence Reframed* (New York: Basic Books, 2002).

52. N. Miller, Northern Kentucky University, 1981, based on A. Uris, *Techniques of Leadership* (New York: McGraw-Hill, 1953), 49–52, 78–89; J. Lorsch, "A Contingency Theory of Leadership," in N. Nohria and R. Khurana, *Leadership Theory and Practice* (Boston: Harvard Business Press, 2010); and K. Kewin, "Patterns of Behavior," *Journal of Social Psychology* 10 (1939): 271–299.

53. Reprinted by permission of *Harvard Business Review* from "How to Choose a Leadership Pattern," by R. Tannenbaum and W. Schmidt, March–April 1958. Copyright © 1958 by the Harvard Business School Publishing Corporation; all rights reserved.

54. Based on J. Newstrom and K. Davis, *Organizational Behavior,* 11th ed. (New York: McGraw-Hill/Irwin, 2002).

55. P. Hersey and K. Blanchard, *Management of Organizational Behavior,* 6th ed. (Englewood Cliffs, NJ: Prentice Hall, 1993); R. Sparrowe and R. Liden, "Process and Structure in Leader–Member Exchange," *Academy of Management Review* 22, no. 2 (April 1997): 522–552; and D. Goleman, "Leadership That Gets Results," *Harvard Business Review* 78, no. 2 (March–April 2000): 78–79.

56. Ned Herrman Group, Leadership Kentucky, 2005.

57. D. McGregor, in J. Sargent, *What Every Executive Should Know about the Art of Leadership* (Chicago: Dartnell Corp., 1964), 13.

PART 2, Chapters 4–5

1. P. Drucker, *Managing in a Time of Great Change* (New York: Truman Talley Books, 1995).

2. H. Ford, *My Life and Work* (New York: Cosimo Classics, 1922); and T. Stewart et al., "The Businessman of the Century," *Fortune* 140, no. 10 (November 22, 1999): 108–128.

3. J. Newton, *Uncommon Friends* (New York: Harcourt, 1987).

4. R. Tedlow, "What Titans Can Teach Us," *Harvard Business Review* 79, no. 11 (December 2001): 70–79.

5. The Johnson & Johnson credo was written in 1943 by Robert Wood Johnson.

6. C. Huntington, Newport News Shipbuilding and Dry Dock Company, 1886; and Y. Kondo, "Customer Satisfaction," *Total Quality Management* 12, nos. 7 & 8 (2001): 867–872.

7. J. Getty, *As I See It,* rev. ed. (New York: J. Paul Getty Trust Publications, 2003).

8. Excerpted from M. L. King, Jr.'s speech at the Lincoln Memorial, Washington, DC, August 28, 1963. Reprinted by arrangement with the Estate of Martin Luther King, Jr., c/o Writers House as agent for the proprietor. New York, NY. Copyright 1963 Martin Luther King, Jr., copyright renewed 1991 Coretta Scott King.

9. W. Stavropolus, Marion Merrell Dow Chemical Co., 1993.

10. W. Bennis, *On Becoming a Leader* (Reading, MA: Addison-Wesley, 1989); and J. Livingston, *Founders at Work* (New York: Apress, 2007).

11. W. Bennis and R. Townsend, *Reinventing Leadership* (New York: William Morrow, 1995); and S. Zaccaro and D. Banks, "Leadership, Vision and Organizational Effectiveness," in S. Zaccaro and R. Klimoski, eds., *The Nature of Organizational Leadership* (San Francisco: Jossey-Bass, 2001), 181–218.

12. N. Tichy and M. DeVanna, *The Transformational Leader,* 2nd ed. (New York: Wiley, 1990).

13. Based on J. Humphrey, "Leadership: A Forum Issues Special Report," Forum Corporation, 1998. See also "All in a Day's Work," *Harvard Business Review* 79, no. 11 (December 2001): 55–66.

14. Adapted from Humphrey, "Leadership."

15. Adapted from Humphrey, "Leadership"; and G. Yukl, *Leadership in Organizations,* 6th ed. (Upper Saddle River, NJ: Pearson, 2006).

16. H. Thoreau, "Economy from Walden," in C. Boardman and A. Sandomir, eds., *Foundation of Business Thought,* 5th ed. (Boston: Pearson, 2002).

17. M. Weisbord, *Productive Workplaces* (San Francisco: Jossey-Bass, 1991).

18. R. Kaplan and D. Norton, *The Strategy-Focused Organization* (Cambridge, MA: Harvard Business School Press, 2000); and S. Covey and K. Gulledge, "Principle-Centered Leadership," *Journal for Quality and Participation* 17, no. 3 (March 1994): 12.

19. Kaplan and Norton, *The Strategy-Focused Organization;* and Covey and Gulledge, "Principle-Centered Leadership."

20. Based on J. Schermerhorn, *Management,* 9th ed. (New York: John Wiley & Sons, 2010). Reprinted with permission of John Wiley & Sons, Inc.

21. Covey and Gulledge, "Principle-Centered Leadership"; and Schermerhorn, *Management.*

22. G. Labovitz and V. Rosansky, *The Power of Alignment* (New York: Wiley, 1997); R. Kroc and R. Anderson, *Grinding It Out* (Chicago: Henry Regnery, 1977); and F. Smith, "Creating an Empowering Environment for All Employees," in P. Krass (ed.), *The Book of Leadership Wisdom* (New York: Wiley, 1998).

23. M. LeBoeuf, *Working Smart* (New York: McGraw-Hill, 1979), 52–54.

24. P. Drucker, "The New Society of Organizations," *Harvard Business Review* 70, no. 5 (September–October 1992): 95–104.

25. J. Collins and J. Porras, *Built to Last* (London: Random House Business, 2000).

26. J. Barker, *Future Edge* (New York: Morrow, 1992); and J. Barker, "The Power of Vision," video from *Discovering the Future* series, ChartHouse Learning Corp., 2000.

27. F. Polak, *The Image of the Future,* trans. from the Dutch and abridged by E. Boulding (Amsterdam: Elsevier Scientific, 1973).

28. B. Singer, "The Future-Focused Role Image," in A. Toffler, ed., *Learning for Tomorrow* (New York: Random House, 1974);

and B. Carson and C. Murphy, *Gifted Hands* (New York: Zondervan Publishing, 1996).

29. M. Edelman, *The Measure of Our Success* (Boston: Beacon Press, 1992).

30. O. Khayyám et al., *The Rubáiyát of Omar Khayyám* (New York: Classics Club/W. J. Black, 1942).

31. V. Frankl, *Man's Search for Meaning* (Boston: Beacon Press, 2000); and M. Scheler, *Man's Place in Nature,* H. Meyerhoff, trans. (New York: Noonday Press, 1961) (original work published 1928).

32. Barker, *Future Edge;* Barker, "The Power of Vision"; and J. Barker, "The Business of Paradigms," video from *Discovering the Future* series, ChartHouse Learning Corp., 2000.

33. C. Garfield, *Peak Performers* (New York: Morrow, 1986); and L. Kossoff, *Executive Thinking* (Palo Alto, CA: Davies-Black, 1999).

34. B. Nanus, *Visionary Leadership* (San Francisco: Jossey-Bass, 1992); and J. Kouzes and B. Posner, "To Lead, Create a Shared Vision," *Harvard Business Review* (January 2009): 20–21.

35. B. Davis, *Successful Manager's Handbook* (Minneapolis, MN: Personal Decisions International, 1996).

36. Frankl, *Man's Search for Meaning.*

37. A. Maslow, *Toward a Psychology of Being,* 3rd ed. (New York: Wiley, 1998).

38. Developed by J. Burleson, from S. Schacter, *The Psychology of Affiliation* (Stanford, CA: Stanford University Press, 1965); D. McClelland, *The Achieving Society* (Princeton, NJ: Van Nostrand, 1961); D. McClelland et al., *The Achievement Motive* (New York: Appleton-Century-Crofts, 1953); and D. McCelland and D. Burnham, "Power Is the Great Motivator," *Harvard Business Review* 73 (January–February 1995): 126–139.

39. S. McShane and M. Von Glinow, *Organizational Behavior,* 5th ed. (New York: McGraw-Hill, 2010).

40. B. Schneider, "The Psychological Life of Organizations," in N. Ashkanasy et al., eds., *Handbook of Organizational Culture and Climate* (Thousand Oaks, CA: Sage, (2000): xvii–xxi; C. Ostroff et al., "Organizational Culture and Climate," in W. Borman et al., eds., *Handbook of Psychology*, vol. 12 (Hoboken, NJ: John Wiley & Sons, 2008): 565–593; and C. O'Riley III et al., "People and Organizational Culture," *Academy of Management Journal* 34, no. 3 (1991): 487–518.

41. E. Fromm, *Escape from Freedom* (New York: Holt, 1993).

42. R. Likert, *New Patterns of Management* (New York: McGraw-Hill, 1961); R. Likert, *The Human Organization* (New York: McGraw-Hill, 1967); and G. Litwin and R. Stringer, *Motivation and Organizational Climate* (Boston: Harvard University, 1968).

43. Likert, *New Patterns of Management;* Likert, *The Human Organization;* and S. Moss et al., "Are Your Employees Avoiding You?" *Academy of Management Executive* 18, no. 1 (2004): 32–47.

44. Likert, *New Patterns of Management,* 222–236.

45. Adapted from Likert, *The Human Organization;* and R. Likert, *Likert's System 4: Organizational Dynamic Series* (New York: AMACOM, 1973), 3–19.

46. Likert, *New Patterns of Management,* 197–211; and C. Glover and S. Smethurst, "Creative License," *People Management* (March 20, 2003): 30–33.

47. Likert, *New Patterns of Management;* and R. Likert and J. Likert, *New Ways of Managing Conflict* (New York: McGraw–Hill, 1976), 52, 98.

48. R. Rosen, *The Healthy Company* (Los Angeles: Tarcher, 1991); J. O'Toole, *Leadership A to Z* (San Francisco: Jossey-Bass, 1999); and R. Stringer, *Leadership and Organizational Climate* (New Jersey: Prentice Hall, 2001).

49. J. Hoerr, "The Payoff from Teamwork," *BusinessWeek* (July 10, 1989): 56–62.

50. J. Campbell, *The Power of Myth* (New York: Anchor Books, 1991); and R. Coles, *The Call of Stories* (New York: Houghton Miflin, 1990).

51. K. Freiberg and J. Freiberg, *Nuts! Southwest Airlines' Crazy Recipe for Business and Personal Success* (New York: Bantam Doubleday Dell, 1998).

52. J. Gardner, "Building Community," prepared for the Leadership Studies Program of the Independent Sector (Washington, DC: American Institutes for Research, 1991); and J. Brown, "Corporation as Community," *New Directions* (Sandwich, MA, 1993).

53. J. Gardner, "Reinventing the Community," address to the Carnegie Council on Adolescent Development, Washington, DC, December 11, 1992.

54. T. Carlyle, *Past and Present* (New York: New York University Press, 1977; original work published 1843).

55. J. Gardner, "Building Community."

56. M. Weisbord, *Productive Workplaces* (San Francisco: Jossey-Bass, 1990).

57. R. Kreitner and A. Kinicki, *Organizational Behavior,* 7th ed. (New York: McGraw-Hill, 2007); and D. Packard, *The HP Way* (New York: HarperCollins, 1995).

58. M. Peck, *A World Waiting to Be Born* (New York: Bantam Press, 1993), 271–298; and J. Greenberg and R. Baron, *Behavior in Organizations* (Upper Saddle River, NJ: Pearson Prentice Hall, 2008). See also J. O'Toole and W. Bennis, "A Culture of Candor," *Harvard Business Review* (June 2009): 54–61.

59. J. Conger, "The Brave New World of Leadership Training," *Organizational Dynamics* (Winter 1993): 56.

60. *"Leading the Search for Tomorrow's Cures,"* The Jackson Laboratory Annual Report 2010. See also http://www.jak.org/ (accessed May 25, 2010).

61. H. Leavitt, *Top Down: Why Hierarchies Are Here to Stay* (Cambridge, MA: Harvard Business School Press, 2005).

62. P. Glader, "It's Not Easy Being Lean," *The Wall Street Journal* (June 19, 2006): B1; Nucor Corporation, "About Us," Charlotte, NC, 2008, www.nucor.com/indexinner.aspx?finpage=about us (accessed September 2, 2008).

63. T. Wall et al., "Empowerment, Performance, and Operational Uncertainty," *Applied Psychology: An International Review* 51 (2002): 146–169.

PART 3, Chapters 6–7

1. J. Ciulla, *The Ethics of Leadership* (Belmont, CA: Wadsworth/Thomson Learning, 2003); and M. Velasquez, *Business Ethics,* 5th ed. (Upper Saddle River, NJ: Prentice Hall, 2002).

2. R. Heifetz, *Leadership without Easy Answers* (Cambridge, MA: Harvard University Press, 1994); J. Burns, *Leadership* (New York:

Harper & Row, 1978); and R. Greenleaf, *Servant Leadership* (New York: Paulist, 2002).

3. H. Titus and M. Keeton, *Ethics for Today,* 5th ed. (New York: Van Nostrand, 1976).

4. M. de Cervantes Saavedra, *The History of Don Quixote de la Mancha,* trans. S. Putnam (Chicago: Encyclopaedia Britannica, 1990).

5. Titus and Keeton, *Ethics for Today;* and R. Soloman and K. Higgens, *A Short History of Philosophy* (England: Oxford University Press, 1996).

6. N. Berrill, *Man's Emerging Mind* (London: Oldburne, 1962); and E. Sinnott, *The Biology of the Spirit* (New York: Viking Press, 1955).

7. N. Tichy and W. Bennis, *Judgment* (New York: Penguin, 2007); and Soloman and Higgins, *A Short History of Philosophy;* and J. O'Toole, "The True Measure of a CEO," *Across The Board* (September/October 2005): 45–48.

8. Aristotle, *The Nicomachean Ethics,* book 10, chap. 5, trans. H. Apostle (Dordrecht, Netherlands: Reidel, 1975); see also J. O'Toole, *Creating the Good Life* (New York: Rodale, 2005).

9. V. Bourke, ed., *The Essential Augustine* (Indianapolis, IN: Hackett, 1964).

10. B. Russell, *Bertrand Russsell's Philosophy* (New York: Barnes & Noble Books, 1974).

11. D. Kennedy, *St. Thomas Aquinas and Medieval Philosophy* (New York: Encyclopedia Press, 1919).

12. G. Rogers, ed., *Benjamin Franklin's The Art of Virtue* (New York: Acorn, 1996).

13. Titus and Keeton, *Ethics for Today,* 39.

14. C. Darwin, *The Descent of Man* (London: J. Murray, 1871); C. Darwin, *The Origin of Species by Means of Natural Selection* (New York: Modern Library, 1936), 471.

15. J. Locke, "An Essay Concerning Human Understanding," 1690.

16. B. Franklin, *Poor Richard's Almanac* (New York: Ballantine Books, 1977).

17. L. Pojman, *Ethical Theory* (Belmont, CA: Wadsworth, 1995).

18. J. Piaget, *The Moral Judgment of the Child* (New York: Free Press, 1997); and J. Marx, *Season of Life* (New York: Simon and Schuster, 2004).

19. H. Thoreau, in C. Boardman and A. Sandomir, eds., *Economy from Walden,* 5th ed. (Boston: Pearson, 2002); and L. Festinger, *Theory of Cognitive Dissonance* (Evanston, IL: Harper & Row, 1957).

20. L. Kohlberg, "The Development of Children's Orientations toward a Moral Order," *Vita Humana* 6 (1963): 11–33; and L. Kohlberg, *The Philosophy of Moral Development* (New York: Harper & Row, 1984).

21. L. Kohlberg, "Cognitive-Development Approach to Moral Education," *The Humanist* (November–December 1972): 113–116; S. Milgram, *The Individual in a Social World* (Reading, MA: Addison-Wesley, 1977); and R. Hare, *Moral Thinking* (New York: Oxford Press, 1981).

22. Kohlberg, "The Development of Children's Orientation toward a Moral Order," 1, 18–19.

23. Kohlberg, "Cognitive-Development Approach to Moral Education," 13–16; and V. Grassian, *Moral Reasoning* (Englewood Cliffs, NJ: Prentice Hall, 1981).

24. Z. Rubin and E. McNeil, *The Psychology of Being Human,* 3rd ed. (New York: Harper & Row, 1981), 321–324.

25. Testimony of A. Eichmann (April 1961) at the Nuremberg War Trials, in Kohlberg, "The Cognitive-Development Approach to Socialization."

26. M. Gandhi in his defense against a charge of sedition, March 23, 1922, in Bartlett, *Famous Quotations,* retrieved August 13, 2005, from www.bartleby.com/99/ index.htm/.

27. Milgram, *The Individual in a Social World;* D. Kidder and N. Oppenheim, *The Intellectual Devotional* (New York: Rodale, 2006); and K. Peterson and C. Grossman, "Abuse Less Shocking in Light of History," *USA Today,* May 13, 2004.

28. Titus and Keeton, *Ethics for Today,* 42; and O. Ferrell and J. Fraedrich, *Business Ethics* (New York: Houghton Mifflin, 2006).

29. H. Hesse, *Siddhartha* (New York: Macmillan, 1962), 33–34.

30. Titus and Keeton, *Ethics for Today;* and Aristotle, *The Nicomachean Ethics,* trans. S. Broadie and C. Rose (Oxford: Oxford University Press, 2002).

31. L. Marinoff, *Plato, Not Prozac!* (New York: HarperCollins, 1999), 162–163.

32. J. Greenberg and R. Baron, *Behavior in Organizations* (Upper Saddle River, NJ: Pearson Prentice Hall, 2008); and D. Rhode, *Moral Leadership* (New York: Wiley & Sons, 2006).

33. E. Morgan, *Benjamin Franklin* (New Haven, CT: Yale University Press, 2002).

34. R. Kanter, "Values and Economics," Notes from the Editor, *Harvard Business Review* 68, no. 3 (May–June 1990): 4; and R. Brajen, "Building a Solid Foundation on Value-Driven Principles," *Business Leader* 14 (June 2003): 6.

35. K. Blanchard and M. O'Connor, *Managing by Values* (San Francisco: Berrett–Koehler, 1997).

36. L. Wieseltier, "Total Quality Meaning," *The New Republic* (July 19, 1993): 16–18, 20–22, 24–26.

37. P. Drucker, "The New Society of Organizations," *Harvard Business Review* 70, no. 5 (September–October 1992): 98.

38. T. Watson, *A Business and Its Beliefs* (New York: McGraw-Hill, 1963); and T. Watson, Jr., and P. Petre, *Father, Son and Company* (New York: Bantam Books, 1990).

39. J. Michelli, *The Starbucks Experience* (New York: McGraw-Hill, 2007).

40. R. May, *The Courage to Create* (New York: Norton, 1975), 3–5.

41. A. Whitehead, *Science and the Modern World,* Lowell Lectures, 1925 (New York: Macmillan, 1925), 124–125.

42. Solomon and Higgins, *A Short History of Philosophy.*

43. N. Machiavelli, *The Prince* (Chicago: University of Chicago Press, 1952).

44. F. Nietzsche, *Thus Spake Zarathrustra,* trans. T. Common (New York: Modern Library, 1917), prologue, no. 3 as found in Titus and Keeton, *Ethics for Today,* 178.

45. M. Heidegger, *Being and Time,* trans. J. Macquarrie and E. Robinson (New York: Harper & Row, 1962).

46. Titus and Keeton, *Ethics for Today,* 67.

47. H. Thoreau, *Walden* (New York: Potter/Crown, 1970).

48. *The Reflections and Maxims of Vauvenargues,* trans. F. Stevens and B. Rogers (London: Humphrey Milford, 1940), 121.

49. Titus and Keeton, *Ethics for Today,* 327.

50. *Holy Bible,* King James Version, Matthew 22:37–39.

51. R. Tsanoff, *The Great Philosophers,* 2nd ed. (New York: Harper & Row, 1953), 102–103.

52. *The Reflections and Maxims of Vauvenargues,* 115.

53. J. Bentham, *An Introduction to the Principles of Morals and Legislation,* chap. 10 (London: Oxford University Press, 1879); and J. Mill, *Utilitarianism* (New York: Dutton, 1910), 6.

54. Bentham, *An Introduction to the Principles of Morals and Legislation;* Mill, *Utilitarianism;* and A. Quinton, *Utilitarian Ethics* (New York: St. Martin's Press, 1973), 28.

55. Titus and Keeton, *Ethics for Today,* 142.

56. M. Syrkin, *Golda Meir* (London: Gollancze, 1964).

57. J. Dalla Costa, *The Ethical Imperative* (Reading, MA: Addison-Wesley, 1998); and G. Goethals et al., *Encyclopedia of Leadership,* vol. 2 (Thousand Oaks, CA: Sage, 2004), 496.

58. *Holy Bible,* King James Version, John 8:32.

59. W. Shakespeare, *Hamlet,* Act 3, Scene 1.

60. See A. Serwer, "Southwest Airlines: The Hottest Thing in the Sky," *Fortune* 145, no. 5 (2004): 86–88.

61. T. Brock, "Weather Any Storm with a Little Flexibility," *CyberSense,* June 26, 2000, retrieved August 13, 2005, from http://bizjournals.bcentral.com/extraedge/consultants/cybersense/2000/06/26/column205.html.

62. J. Dalla Costa, *The Ethical Imperative.*

63. J. Petrick and J. Quinn, *Management Ethics* (Thousand Oaks, CA: Sage, 1997).

64. Petrick and Quinn, *Management Ethics.*

65. Plato, *The Republic,* trans. A. Bloom (New York: Basic Books, 1968); and M. Cicero, *De Officiis* (Cambridge: Harvard University Press, 1961).

66. Plato, *The Republic.*

67. O. Kidder and H. Oppenheim, *The Intellectual Devotional* (New York: Rodale, 2006).

68. L. Van der Colff, "Leadership Lessons from the African Tree," *Management Decision* 41 (2003): 257–261.

69. G. Goethals et al., *Encyclopedia of Leadership,* vol. 2, 880–881.

70. Plato, *The Republic;* S. Wells, *From Sage to Artisan* (Palo Alto, CA: Davies-Black, 1997); and T. Peters, "Leadership," *Harvard Business Review* 79, no. 11 (December 2001): 121–128.

71. L. Paine, *Value Shift* (New York: McGraw-Hill, 2003); and J. Huntsman, *Winners Never Cheat* (Upper Saddle River, NJ: Pearson, 2008).

72. J. Podolny, "The Buck Stops (and Starts) at Business School," *Harvard Business Review* (June 2009): 62–67.

73. K. Albrecht, *The Northbound Train* (New York: AMACOM, 1994); A. Sagie and D. Elizur, "Work Values," *Journal of Organizational Behavior* 17 (1996): 503–514.

74. P. Schuman, "A Moral Framework for Human Resource Management Ethics," *Human Resource Management Review* 11 (2001): 93–111.

75. J. McCue and M. Bailey, Northern Kentucky University, 1983 (rev. 2010), based on E. Spranger, *Types of Men* (New York: Johnson Reprint, 1966); and G. Allport et al., *The Study of Values,* 3rd ed. (Boston: Houghton Mifflin, 1970).

76. G. Allport and P. Vernon, *A Study of Values,* rev. ed. (Boston: Houghton-Mifflin, 1931), retrieved August 13, 2005, from http://www.hfr.org.uk/ figures/spranger/html; also see J. Keats, "Ode on a Grecian Urn," 1819.

77. M. Massey, *The People Puzzle* (Reston, VA: Reston, 1979).

78. A. Van Vianen, "Person–Organization Fit," *Personnel Psychology* 53 (2000): 113–149; and H. Elfenbein and C. O'Reilly, "Fitting In," *Group and Organizational Management* (February 2007): 109–142.

79. *The Reflections and Maxims of Vauvenargues.*

80. M. Smith, *A Practical Guide to Value Clarification* (La Jolla, CA: University Associates, rev. ed., 2007).

81. J. Gardner, "Building Community," prepared for the Leadership Studies Program of the Independent Sector (Washington, DC: American Institutes for Research, 1991).

82. P. Drucker, *Management: Tasks, Responsibilities, Practices* (New York: Harper & Row, 1973), 645.

83. K. Dechant and B. Altman, "Environmental Leadership: From Compliance to Competitive Advantage," *The Academy of Management Executive* (August 1994): 10.

84. L. Wayne, "A Promise to be Ethical in an Era of Immorality," *New York Times* (May 30, 2009). Retrieved June 15, 2009, from http://www.nytimes.com/2009/05/30 business; and M. Bradford et al., "Beyond compliance: The value of SOX," *Strategic Finance* (May 2010): 48–53.

85. T. Hine LLP, "U.S. Sentencing Commission Announces Stiffened Organization Sentencing Guidelines in Response to the Sarbanes-Oxley Act," advisory bulletin, June 1, 2004, last modified August 31, 2006, http://www.thompsonhinecom.

86. J. O'Toole and W. Bennis, "A Culture of Candor," *Harvard Business Review* (June 2009): 54–61; and J. O'Toole, *Vanguard Management* (New York: Doubleday, 1985).

87. Rotary International, Evanston, IL.

88. R. Clement, "Just How Unethical Is American Business?" *Business Horizons* (July–August 2006): 313–327.

89. Paine, *Value Shift.*

90. Paine, *Value Shift;* and Walker Information Global Network and Hudson Institute, "Commitment in the Workplace: The 2000 Global Employee Relationship Report," Indianapolis, IN, October 18, 2000.

91. Paine, *Value Shift;* P. Block, *Stewardship* (San Francisco: Barrett-Koehler, 1993); and Avolio et al., "Leadership," *Annual Review of Psychology* 60 (2009): 421–449.

92. R. Hay and E. Gray, "Social Responsibilities of Business Managers," *Academy of Management Journal* 18, no. 1 (March 1974): 135–143.

93. J. Martin, *Organizational Culture* (Thousand Oaks, CA: Sage Publications, 2004) used by permission of SAGE Publications. See also T. Deal and A. Kennedy, *Corporate Culture* (Reading, MA: Addison-Wesley, 1985).

94. Ethics Resource Center, "Performance Reviews Often Skip Ethics," news release, June 12, 2008, http://www.ethics.org.

95. R. Cook, "Danger Signs of Unethical Behavior," *Journal of Business Ethics* (April 1991) 249–253.

96. B. Heineman Jr., "Avoiding Integrity Land Mines," *Harvard Business Review* (April 2007): 100–108.

97. H. Leavitt, *Corporate Pathfinders* (Homewood, IL: Dow Jones–Irwin, 1986); J. Margolis and J. Walsh, *People and Profits*

(Mahwah, NJ: Erlbaum, 2003); T. Morrison et al., *Dun and Bradstreet's Guide to Doing Business around the World* (Paramus, NJ: Prentice Hall, 2001); and "America's Most Admired Companies," *Fortune* (February 19, 2006), retrieved August 13, 2005, from http://money.cnn.com/magazines/fortune/mostadmired/.

98. A. Bernstein, "Too Much Corporate Power?" *BusinessWeek* (September 11, 2000): 149.

99. Paine, *Value Shift;* and J. Ciulla, *Ethics: The Heart of Leadership* (Westport, CT: Greenwood, 1998).

100. R. Tedlow, "James Burke: A Career in American Business," HBS Case No. 9-389-177 (Boston: Harvard Business School Press, 1989).

101. S. McShane and M. Von Glinow, *Organizational Behavior,* 5th ed., (New York: McGraw-Hill, 2010): 318–319.

102. C. Cooper, *Surviving at Work* (London: Health Education Authority, 1995); and J. Ciulla, *The Ethics of Leadership* (Belmont, CA: Wadsworth, 2003).

103. P. Sellers, "The Recruiter," *Fortune* (November 27, 2006): 87–88, 90.

PART 4, Chapters 8–9

1. S. McShane and M. Von Glinow, *Organizational Behavior,* 3rd ed. (New York: McGraw-Hill, 2009), 444–469.

2. A. Chandler, Jr., "Origins of the Organization Chart," *Harvard Business Review* 66, no. 2 (1998): 156–157.

3. G. Colvin, "Power: A Cooling Trend," *Fortune* (December 10, 2007): 113–114.

4. D. Wren and A. Bedeian, *The Evolution of Management Thought* (New York: Wiley, 2008).

5. C. Barnard, *The Functions of the Executive* (Cambridge, MA: Harvard University Press, 1938), 161–184.

6. D. McGregor, *The Human Side of Enterprise* (New York: McGraw-Hill, 1960), 23.

7. McShane and Von Glinow, *Organizational Behavior.*

8. S. Sendjaya and J. Sarros, "Servant Leadership," *Journal of Leadership and Organizational Studies* 9, no. 2 (2002): 57–64.

9. R. Greenleaf, *Servant Leadership* (New York: Paulist Press, 2002); and R. Greenleaf, *The Servant as Leader* (Newton Centre, MA: Robert K. Greenleaf Center, 1970).

10. L. Spears and M. Lawrence, eds., *Focus on Leadership* (New York: Wiley, 2002).

11. H. Hesse, *The Journey to the East* (New York: Noonday, 1968).

12. H. Levinson and C. Lang, *Executive* (Cambridge, MA: Harvard University Press, 1981), 187–189.

13. D. Tarrant, "The Leading Edge," *The Bulletin* (November 15, 2005); and "2006 Movers and Shakers," *Financial Planning* (January 2006): 1.

14. Q. Studer, *Hard Wiring Excellence* (Gulf Breeze, FL: Five Star Publications, 2005).

15. M. Wheatley, *Leadership and the New Science* (San Francisco: Berrett-Koehler, 1992); and E. Hallowell, "The Human Moment at Work," *Harvard Business Review* 77, no. 1 (January–February 1999): 58–65.

16. J. Hunter, *The Servant* (New York: Crown Business, 1998).

17. M. DePree, *Leadership Is an Art* (New York: Doubleday, 1989), 45–53.

18. B. George, *Authentic Leadership* (New York: John Wiley & Sons, 2003); B. George and P. Sims, *True North* (San Francisco: Jossey-Bass, 2007); F. Walumba et al., "Authentic Leadership," *Journal of Management* 34, no. 1 (2008); and N. Mandala, *Nelson Mandala Speaks* (Johannesburg, South Africa: David Philip, 1994).

19. G. Goethals et al., *Encyclopedia of Leadership,* vol. 3 (Thousand Oaks, CA: Sage, 2004), 1000–1010.

20. M. Imai, *Kaizen (Ky'zen)* (New York: Random House, 1986).

21. J. Case, *Open-Book Management* (New York: Harper Business, 1995).

22. T. Barton, W. Shenkir, and T. Tyson, *Open-Book Management* (Morristown, NJ: Financial Executives Research Foundation, 1998). Adapted from Donna Renn, "Open-Book Management 101," *Inc.* (2007).

23. J. Welch, *Jack: Straight from the Gut* (New York: Warner Books, 2001); and P. Slater and W. Bennis, "Democracy Is Inevitable," *Harvard Business Review* (March–April 1964): 51–53.

24. W. Lindsay et al., "A Participative Management Primer," *Journal for Quality and Participation* (June 1989): 78–84; and J. Mathieu et al., "Team Effectiveness," *Journal of Management* 34 (2008): 410–476.

25. M. Weisbord, *Productive Workplaces* (San Francisco: Jossey-Bass, 1990), 97.

26. H. Kelleher, as quoted in K. Brooker, "The Chairman of the Board Looks Back," *Fortune* (May 28, 2001): 62–70.

27. J. Humes, *The Wit and Wisdom of Abraham Lincoln* (New York: Gramerly, 1999).

28. A. Moody, *The Cambridge Companion to T. S. Eliot* (Cambridge, England: Cambridge University Press, 1994).

29. *Forum Issues Special Report,* 1996.

30. Lao Tzu and Lao Zi, trans. R. Blakney, *The Way of Life: Tao Te Ching* (New York: New American Library, 2001).

31. J. French, Jr., and B. Raven, "The Basis of Social Power," in D. Cartwright, ed., *Group Dynamics* (Evanston, IL: Row, Peterson, 1962), 607–613; P. Podaskoff and C. Schriesheim, "Field Studies of French and Raven's Bases of Power," *Psychological Bulletin* 97 (1985): 387–411; and J. Nye, "Power and Leadership," in N. Nohria and R. Khurana, eds., *Handbook of Leadership Theory and Practice* (Boston: Harvard Business Press, 2010).

32. G. Smith, "Here Comes Abby," *BusinessWeek* (July 2, 2002): 62.

33. S. Maitlis and T. Lawrence, "Triggers and Enablers of Sense-giving in Organizations," *Academy of Management Journal* 50, no. 1 (2007): 57–84.

34. T. Hinkin and C. Schriesheim, "Development and Application of New Scales to Measure the French and Raven (1959) Basis of Social Power," *Journal of Applied Psychology* 74 (1989): 74, 561–567.

35. H. Mintzberg, *Power In and Around Organizations* (Englewood Cliffs, NJ: Prentice Hall, 1983).

36. G. Reedy, *The Twilight of the Presidency* (New York: World, 1970), 11–15, 76–83.

37. A. Mehrabian, *Nonverbal Communication* (New York: Aldine Transactions, 2007); and J. Newstrom and K. Davis, *Organizational Behavior* (New York: McGraw-Hill/Irwin, 2002).

38. C. DeLoach, *The Quotable Shakespeare* (Jefferson, NC: McFarland, 1988), 1, 3, 68.

39. DeLoach, *The Quotable Shakespeare,* 1, 3, 59.

40. K. Nair, *A Higher Standard of Leadership* (San Francisco: Berrett–Koehler, 1997).

41. E. Lawler, *The Ultimate Advantage* (San Francisco: Jossey-Bass, 1992); and R. Forrester, "Empowerment," *Academy of Management Executive* 14 (August 2000): 67–90.

42. R. Frock, *Changing How the World Does Business* (San Francisco: Barrett-Kohler, 2006).

43. S. Suzawa, "How the Japanese Achieve Excellence," *Training and Development Journal* (May 1985): 114.

44. J. Cosco, "General Electric Works It All Out," *Journal of Business Strategy* 15, no. 3 (May–June 1994): 48–50; and J. Welch and S. Welch, *Winning* (New York: Harper Business, 2005).

45. R. Slater, *The GE Way Fieldbook* (New York: McGraw-Hill, 2000); and T. Bateman and S. Snell, *Management,* 9th ed. (New York: McGraw-Hill/Irwin, 2011), 658–659.

46. General Electric, "GE Shares Skills, Intellectual Capital with Commonbond Communities," news release, December 4, 2006, http://www.genewscenter.com.

47. R. Cole, "Employee Involvement in Japan," Center for Japanese Studies, University of Michigan, 2005.

48. M. Conner, Tastemaker International, Cincinnati, OH, 1997. See also M. Fulford and C. Enz, "The Impact of Empowerment for Service Employees," *Journal of Managerial Issues* 7, no. 2 (Summer 1995): 161–175.

49. Used with permission from *Organizational Behavior,* 3rd ed., S. McShane and M. Von Glinow. Copyright 2005 by McGraw-Hill. Citing D. Magee, *Turnaround: How Carlos Ghosn Rescued Nissan* (New York: HarperCollins, 2003); and *Bloomberg Business Week,* 2010.

50. S. Friedman, "Where Employees Go for Information," *Administrative Management* (September 1981): 72–73. See also "Survey Finds Good and Bad Points on Worker Attitudes," *Eastern Pennsylvania Business Journal* (May 5, 1997): 13.

51. B. Murray, "Agency Profile: Mother London," *I Have an Idea,* January 28, 2007, www.ihaveanidea.org.

52. A. Lashinsky, "Lights! Camera! Cue the CEO," *Fortune* (August 2, 2006): 27.

53. H. Movius, "Nonverbal Communication," Linkage Inc., 2004, retrieved August 13, 2005, from www.linkageinc.com/newsletter/archives/ leadership; and D. Cohen, "The Need to Know Gap," *Link&Learn* (March 2004): Accessed May 22, 2008, from http://www.Linkage.inc.com.

54. E. Harvey and A. Lucia, *144 Ways to Walk the Talk* (Dallas: Performance Publishing, 1997).

55. T. Peters and R. Waterman, Jr., *In Search of Excellence* (New York: Harper & Row, 1983), 16.

56. C. Powell and J. Persico, *My American Journey* (New York: Ballantine, 2003).

57. Greenleaf, *Servant Leadership;* W. Arnold and J. Plas, *The Human Touch* (New York: Wiley, 1993); and G. Spreitzer and R. Quinn, *A Company of Leaders* (San Francisco: Jossey-Bass, 2001).

58. J. Jablonski, *Implementing Total Quality Management* (San Diego: Pfeiffer, 1991), 41; and B. Creech, *The Five Pillars of TQM* (New York: Truman Talley, 1994).

59. Peters and Waterman, *In Search of Excellence,* 249–250.

60. R. Ford and C. Heaton, "Lessons from Hospitality That Can Serve Anyone," *Organizational Dynamics* (Summer 2001): 30–47.

61. D. Halberstam, *The Reckoning* (New York: Avon Books, 1987); and C. Byron, "How Japan Does It," *Time* (March 30, 1981): 57.

62. Halberstam, *The Reckoning;* L. Dobyns, "Ed Deming Wants Big Changes and He Wants Them Fast," *Smithsonian* 21, no. 5 (August 1990): 77.

63. W. Scherkenbach, *The Deming Route to Quality and Productivity* (Washington, DC: CEEPress Books, 1994).

64. From W. Deming, *Out of the Crisis* (Cambridge, MA: The MIT Press, 1982), 3. Copyright © 1982 the W. Edwards Deming Institute. Used by permission.

65. H. Neave, *The Deming Dimension* (Knoxville, TN: SPC Press, 1990).

66. D. Jones, "Teamwork Speeds Boeing Along," *USA Today* (November 18, 1998).

67. S. Konig, "The Challenge of Teams," *On Wall Street* (August 1, 2003), retrieved August 13, 2005, from www.thomsonmedia.com.

68. From W. Deming, *Out of the Crisis* (Cambridge, MA: The MIT Press, 1982), 23–24. Copyright © 1982 the W. Edwards Deming Institute. Used by permission.

69. F. Taylor, *Principles of Scientific Management* (New York: Harper, 1911); and R. Kanigel, *The One Best Way* (New York: Viking, 1997).

70. M. Weisbord, *Productive Workplaces* (San Francisco: Jossey-Bass, 1990), 69.

71. H. Kroos and C. Gilbert, *The Principles of Scientific Management* (New York: Harper & Row, 1911), and M. Weisbord, *Productive Workplaces.*

72. F. Roethlisberger and W. Dickson, *Management and the Worker* (Cambridge, MA: Harvard University Press, 1939).

73. O. Schisgall, *Eyes on Tomorrow* (Chicago: J.G. Ferguson, 1981); and T. Welsh, "Best and Worst Corporate Reputations," *Fortune* (February 7, 1994): 58–66.

74. S. Ingle, *Quality Circle Master Guide* (Englewood Cliffs, NJ: Prentice Hall, 1982), 170–181; and Spreitzer and Quinn, *A Company of Leaders.*

75. E. Lawler et al., *Employee Involvement and Total Quality Management* (San Francisco: Jossey-Bass, 1992).

76. *Management Practices* (Washington, DC: U.S. General Accounting Office, May 1991); and M. Vora, "Creating Employee Value in a Global Economy through Participation, Motivation and Development," *Total Quality Management and Business Excellence* 15, nos. 5–6 (July–August 2004): 793–806.

77. O. Port, "Innovations," *BusinessWeek* (September 7, 1998): 111–116.

78. D. Kinlaw, *Continuous Improvement and Measurement for Total Quality* (New York: Vision Books, 2007); and N. Tague, *Quality Toolbox* (Milwaukee: ASQ Quality Press, 2005).

79. J. O'Toole and E. Lawler, *The New American Workplace* (New York: Palgrave Macmillan, 2006): R. Kaplan and D. Norton, *The Balanced Scorecard* (Boston: Harvard Business School Press, 2000); and T. Kloppenberg and J. Petrick, *Managing Project Quality* (Washington, DC: Management Concepts, 2002).

80. K. Richardson, "The Six Sigma-Factor for Home Depot," *The Wall Street Journal* (January 4, 2007): http://online.wsj.com; and S. Minter, "Six Sigma's Growing Pains," *IndustryWeek* (May 2009): 34–36.

81. J. Liker and J. Morgan, "The Toyota Way in Services," *Academy of Management Perspectives* 20, no. 2 (May 2000): 5–20; and R. Delbridge, "Workers Under Lean Manufacturing," in D. Holman et al., *The New Workplace* (Chichester, UK: John Wiley, 2003), 19–36.

82. A. Gawande, *The Checklist Manifesto* (New York: Henry Holt and Company, 2009).

83. International Organization for Standardization, "ISO9000/ISO1400: Understand the Basics," http://www.iso.org, accessed May 7, 2007.

84. K. Auletta, *Googled: The End of The World as We Know It* (New York: Penguin Press, 2009); G. Gibson and J. Birkinshaw, "The Antecedents, Consequences, and Mediating Role of Organizational Ambidexterity," *Academy of Management Journal* 47 (2004): 209–226; and B. Hindo, "At 3M, A Struggle between Efficiency and Creativity," *BusinessWeek* (June 2007).

85. G. Hamel, "The Why, What, and How of Management Innovation," *Harvard Business Review* 84 (2006): 72–84.

86. J. Michelli, *The Starbucks Experience* (New York: McGraw-Hill, 2007); and "The Best Advice I Ever Got," *Fortune* (March 21, 2005): 98.

87. www.nist.gov/publicaffairs/factsheet/MBNGA.htm; and National Quality Program, "Criteria for Performance Excellence, 2007," National Institute of Standards and Technology (NIST), http://www.quality.nist.gov, accessed May 4, 2007.

PART 5, Chapters 10–11

1. W. Bennis, *On Becoming a Leader* (Reading, MA: Addison-Wesley, 1989).

2. P. Drucker, "Not Enough Generals Were Killed!" in C. Boardman and A. Sandomir, eds., *Foundations of Business Thought*, 5th ed. (Boston: Pearson, 2002).

3. F. Hesselbein, "Peter Drucker's Light Shines On," *Leader to Leader* 40 (Spring 2006): 4–7; and George Anders, "Drucker's Teachings Find Following in Asia," *The Wall Street Journal* (2008).

4. M. DePree, *Leadership Jazz* (New York: Doubleday, 1997); and J. Flaherty and P. Drucker, *Shaping the Managerial Mind* (San Francisco: Jossey-Bass, 1999).

5. S. McMillen and S. Martin, Northern Kentucky University, 1984, rev. 2010, based on D. Freedman, *Corps Business* (New York: Harper Business, 2000); K. Blanchard, *Leading at a Higher Level* (New York: FT Press, 2006); and B. Joiner and S. Josephs, *Leadership Agility* (San Francisco: Jossey-Bass, 2006).

6. R. Emerson, *Journals,* in B. Stevenson, ed., *Home Book of Quotations* (New York: Dodd, Mead, 1967), 338.

7. *Plutarch's Lives,* trans. J. Dryden and A. Clough (New York: Modern Library, 2001).

8. K. Menninger, as found in W. Brown, *13 Fatal Errors Managers Make and How to Avoid Them* (New York: Berkley Books, 1985).

9. M. Gregory, ed., *Bits and Pieces* (Fairfield, NJ: Economics Press, 1980), 16–17.

10. M. Miller, *Plain Speaking* (New York: Berkley Books, 1984).

11. B. Jonson, *Explorata: Consilia,* in B. Stevenson, *Home Book of Quotations* (New York: Dodd, Mead, 1967).

12. P. Drucker, *People and Performance* (New York: Harper's College Press, 1997).

13. N. Bonaparte, *How to Make War,* trans. K. Sanborn, ed. Y. Cloarec (New York: Ediciones la Calarera, 1998), retrieved from www.napoleonguide.com/maxim_war.html; and J. Markham, *Napoleon's Road to Glory* (London: Brassey's, 2003).

14. N. Podsakoff et al., "Turnover and Withdrawal Behavior: A Meta-Analysis," *Journal of Applied Psychology* (March 2007): 438–454; M. Riketta, "Organizational Commitment and Job Performance: A Meta-Analysis," *Journal of Organizational Behavior* (March 2002): 257–266; R. Griffeth et al., "A Meta-Analysis of Antecedents and Correlates of Employee Turnover," *Journal of Management* (2000): 463–488; B. Hoffman et al., "A Quantitative Review of the OCB Literature," *Journal of Applied Psychology* (March 2007): 555–566; and T. Judge et al., "The Job Satisfaction–Job Performance Relationship," *Journal of Applied Psychology* (February 2004): 165–177.

15. T. Cummings, "Analysis of Job Satisfaction Studies," Case Western Reserve University, Cleveland, OH, 1988; see also J. O'Toole and E. Lawler, *The New American Workplace,* Society for Human Resource Management (2006).

16. R. Levering, *A Great Place to Work* (New York: Random House, 1990); C. Cranny et al., *Job Satisfaction* (New York: Lexington, 1992); and J. Rentsch and R. Steel, "Construct and Concurrent Validation of the Andrews and Withey Job Satisfaction Questionnaire," *Educational and Psychological Measurement* 52 (1992): 357–367.

17. Levering, *A Great Place to Work;* and M. Kelly, *The Dream Manager* (New York: Hyperion, 2007).

18. R. Levering and M. Moskowitz, "The Best Companies List—Employees at Hundreds of Companies Cast Their Votes—and Southwest Airlines Came Up No. 1," *Fortune* 137, no. 1 (January 12, 1998): 84–95; and Southwest Airlines (2002), retrieved June 18, 2002, from www.southwest.com.

19. K. Freiberg and J. Freiberg, *Nuts!* (New York: Broadway Books, 1998).

20. K. Brooker and A. Wheat, "The Chairman of the Board Looks Back," *Fortune* 143, no. 11 (May 28, 2001): 62–70.

21. "The Greatest Briton in Management and Leadership," *Personnel Today* (February 18, 2003): 20.

22. P. Barger and A. Grandey, "Service With a Smile and Customer Satisfaction," *Academy of Management Journal* 49, no. 6 (2006): 1229–1238; and P. Guenzi and O. Pelloni, "The Impact of Customer Relations on Customer Loyalty," *International Journal of Service Industry Management* 15, no. 3–4 (2004): 365–384.

23. G. Spreitzer and R. Quinn, *A Company of Leaders* (San Francisco: Jossey-Bass, 2001); and W. Adamchik, *No Yelling* (New York: Firestarter Speaking and Consulting, 2006).

24. National Research Council, *The Changing Nature of Work* (Washington, DC: National Academy Press, 2007); and F. Landy and J. Conte, *Work in the 21st Century* (New York: Wiley, 2010).

25. H. Levinson, *Executive* (Cambridge, MA: Harvard University Press, 1981), 28.

26. M. Peterson, *Thomas Jefferson* (New York: Library of America, 1984), retrieved June 19, 2002, from www.braingquote.com/quotes/f/thomasjeff143405.

27. M. Csikszentmihalyi and I. Csikszentmihalyi, *Optimal Experience* (New York: Cambridge University Press, 1992).

28. M. Csikszentmihalyi, *The Evolving Self* (New York: HarperCollins, 1993); and M. Csikszentmihalyi, *Flow* (New York: Harper & Row, 1990).

29. P. Drucker, *The Effective Executive* (Oxford, UK: Butterworth-Heinemann, 2007), 22; and P. Drucker, "Managing Oneself," in *Leadership Fundamentals, Harvard Business Review* (January 2008).

30. M. Buckingham and D. Clifton, *Now, Discover Your Strengths* (New York: Free Press, 2001).

31. A. Smith, *An Inquiry into the Nature and Causes of the Wealth of Nations* (London: W. Strahan and T. Cadell, 1776); and C. Babbage, *On the Economy of Machinery and Manufacturers* (London: Knight, 1835).

32. O'Toole and Lawler, *The New American Workplace.*

33. J. Hackman and G. Oldham, *Work Design* (Reading, MA: Addison-Wesley, 1980); and J. Greenberg and R. Baron, *Behavior in Organizations* (Upper Saddle River, NJ: Pearson Prentice Hall, 2008).

34. J. Donne, *The Complete Poetry and Select Prose of John Donne* (New York: Random House, 1941), 332.

35. M. Peck, *The Different Drum* (New York: Simon & Schuster, 1987), 288.

36. W. Menninger and H. Levinson, *Human Understanding in Industry* (Chicago: Science Research Associates, 1956).

37. E. Mayo, *The Human Problems of an Industrial Organization* (New York: Macmillan, 1946), 56–59, 129–130; F. Roethlisberger and W. Dickson, *Management and the Worker* (Cambridge, MA: Harvard University Press, 1939); and Y. Hsueh, "The Hawthorne Experiments," *History of Psychology* 5 (2002): 163–189.

38. Mayo, *The Human Problems of an Industrial Organization;* and Roethlisberger and Dickson, *Management and the Worker.*

39. T. Peters, *Liberation Management* (New York: Knopf, 1992).

40. K. Macher, "The Politics of People," *Personnel Journal* (January 1986): 50.

41. J. Gardner, "Building Community," prepared for the Leadership Studies Program of the Independent Sector (Washington, DC: American Institutes for Research, 1991).

42. P. Levy, *Industrial Organizational Psychology* (New York: Worth Publishers, 2010); and T. Parker-Pope, "When the Bully Sits in the Next Cubicle," *New York Times* (March 25, 2008): D5.

43. F. Landy and J. Conte, *Work in the 21st Century* (New York: Wiley-Blackwell, 2009).

44. S. Armour, "Death in the Workplace," *USA Today* (July 16–18, 2004); U.S. Bureau of Labor Statistics (August 20, 2008), *Fatal Occupational Injuries by Event or Exposure, 2006–2007* [tables].

45. "Put Up Your Dukes," *The Wall Street Journal* (August 13, 1996): A1; Zogby International, *U.S. Workplace Bullying* (Bellingham, WA: The Workplace Bullying Institute, 2008); and R. Sutton, *The No Rule: Building a Civilized Workplace* (New York: Warner Business Books, 2007).

46. S. Robinson and A. O'Leary-Kelly, "Monkey See, Monkey Do," *Academy of Management Journal* 41 (1998): 658–672.

47. A. Garrett, "How to Cure Bullying at Work," *Management Today* (May 2003): 80; and H. Weeks, "Taking the Stress Out of Stressful Conversations," *Harvard Business Review* 79, no. 7 (July–August, 2001): 112–119.

48. J. Fitness, "Anger in the Workplace," *Journal of Organizational Behavior* 21 (2000): 147–162; and K. Zellars et al., "Abusive Supervision and Subordinate Organizational Citizenship Behavior," *Journal of Applied Psychology* 87 (2002): 1068–1076.

49. W. Leebov, *Effective Complaint Handling in Health Care* (Chicago: American Hospital Publishing, Inc., 1990).

50. J. Jones, in J. Pfeiffer and J. Jones, eds., *A Handbook of Structured Experiences for Human Relations Training* (San Diego: Jossey-Bass/Pfeiffer, 1985). Reprinted with permission of John Wiley & Sons, Inc.

51. B. Stevenson, *The Home Book of Proverbs, Maxims and Familiar Phrases,* 4th ed. (New York: MacMillan, 1961), 655-entry 8. Source attributes variations of their quote to Cicero, Socrates, Diogenes, and Epictitus.

52. C. Rogers and F. Roethlisberger, "Barriers and Gateways to Communication," *Harvard Business Review* (July–August 1952): 52.

53. J. Hasling, *Group Discussion and Decision Making* (New York: Thomas Crowell/Harper & Row, 1975), 55.

54. R. Nichols, *Are You Listening?* (New York: McGraw-Hill, 1967), 77–101, 128–140.

55. A. Wolvin and C. Coakley, *Listening,* 4th ed. (Dubuque, IA: Brown, 1992), 243.

56. A. Zimmerman, "We've Got to Keep Meeting Like This," *Communi-Care* (Winter 1991).

57. Hasling, *Group Discussion and Decision Making,* 55.

58. M. Goldsmith, *What Got You Here Won't Get You There* (New York: Hyperion, 2007).

59. D. McGregor, *The Human Side of Enterprise 25th Anniversary Edition* (New York: McGraw-Hill, 1985); republished 2006 with J. Cutcher-Gershenfeld.

60. D. McGregor, *The Human Side of Enterprise*; and D. McGregor, "The Human Side of Enterprise," *Management Review* (November 1957).

61. McGregor, *The Human Side of Enterprise.*

62. D. Jacobs, review of D. McGregor, *The Human Side of Enterprise*, in *Academy of Management Review* 29 (2004): 293–296.

63. W. Brown, *13 Fatal Errors Managers Make and How You Can Avoid Them* (Old Tappan, NJ: Revell, 1985); and J. Hall and S. Donnell, "Managerial Achievement," *Human Relations* 32 (1979): 77–101.

64. R. Semler, *Maverick* (New York: Warner Books, 1993).

65. M. Totty, "Rethinking the Inbox," *The Wall Street Journal* (March 26, 2007), http://onlinewsj.com.

66. A. Mehrabian, "Communication without Words," *Psychology Today* (September 1968): 52, cited in M. McCaskey, "The Hidden Message Managers Send," *Harvard Business Review* (November–December 1979): 135–148.

67. K. Lorenz, "WANT2CHAT? 10 Tips for IMing at Work," *AOL Jobs* (December 15, 2006), http://jobs.aol.com; T. Mackintosh, "Is This the Year You Move to a Virtual Office?" *Accounting Technology* (May 2007), http://find.galegroup.com; and D. Tapscott and A. Williams, *Wikinomics* (New York: Penguin, 2006).

68. M. Richtel, "Lost in E-mail, Tech Firms Face Self Made Beast," *New York Times* (June 14, 2008).

69. K. Byron and D. Baldridge, "Toward a Model of Nonverbal Cues and Emotion in E-mails," *Academy of Management,* OCIS

(2005): B1; B. Avolio et al., "E-leading in Organizations," *Leadership Quarterly* 11 (2000): 615–670; and W. Casio, "The Virtual Organization," in C. Cooper and W. Burke, eds., *The New World of Work* (Oxford, UK: Blackwell, 2002), 203–221.

70. Emile Durkheim, *Professional Ethics and Civic Morals,* trans. Cornelia Brookfield (New York: Routledge, 1992); Georg Simmel, *The Society of Georg Simmel,* trans. and ed., Kurt Wolff (Glencoe, IL: Free Press, 1950); and Max Weber, *Basic Concepts in Sociology,* trans. H. P. Secher (New York: Philosophical Library, 1962).

71. Bernard Berelson and Gary Steiner, *Human Behavior* (New York: Harcourt, Brace, and World, 1964).

72. G. Porter and M. Beyerlein, "Historical Roots of Team Theory and Practice," in M. Beyerlein, ed., *Work Teams* (Dordrecht, Netherlands: Kluwer, 2000), 3–24; C. Li and J. Bernoff, *Groundswell* (Boston: Harvard Business School Press, 2008); and K. Stagl et al., "Best Practices in Team Leadership," in J. Conger and R. Riggio, eds., *The Practice of Leadership.*

73. L. Berry, "The Collaborative Organization," *Organizational Dynamics* (August 2004): 228–241.

74. L. Tolstoy, *Great Works of Leo Tolstoy* (New York: Harper Perennial Modern Classics, 2004); and www.saidwhat.co.uk/quote2279.html.

75. T. Harris and J. Sherblom, *Small Group and Team Communication,* 4th ed. (Boston: Pearson, 2007).

76. S. Martin, Northern Kentucky University, rev. 2010, based on D. McGregor, *The Human Side of Enterprise,* 232–235; D. Forsyth, *Group Dynamics,* 5th ed. (Belmont, CA: Wadsworth, 2010); and J. Katzenbach and D. Smith, *The Wisdom of Teams* (Boston: Harvard Business School Press, 1993).

77. W. Stattler and N. Miller, *Discussion and Conference,* 2nd ed. (Englewood Cliffs, NJ: Prentice Hall, 1968).

78. B. Franklin and G. Rogers, *Benjamin Franklin's The Art of Virtue* (New York: Acorn Publishing, 1996); and www.famousquotes.me.uk/nursery_rhymes/for_want_of_a_nail.html.

79. Stattler and Miller, *Discussion and Conference,* 476–488.

80. H. Levinson, "The Abrasive Personality at the Office," *Psychology Today* (May 1978): 78–84.

81. P. Levy, *Individual Organizational Psychology* (New York: Worth Publishers, 2010).

82. E. Sunstrom et al., "Work Groups from the Hawthorne Studies to Work Teams Today," *Group Dynamics* 4 (2002): 44–67; and L. Hill et al., "Unlocking the Slices of Genius in Your Organization," in N. Nohria and R. Khurana, *Handbook of Leadership Theory and Practice* (Boston: Harvard Business Press, 2010).

83. A. Taylor and H. Greve, "Superman or The Fantastic Four?" *Academy of Management Journal* 49, no. 4 (2006): 723–740; and R. Levering and M. Moskowitz, "Top 50 Employers," *Fortune* (February 4, 2008).

84. B. Stockton et al., Northern Kentucky University, 1981, rev. 2010, based on "Learning and Problem-Solving," in J. Osland and D. Kolb, *Organizational Behavior,* 8th ed. (Englewood Cliffs, NJ: Prentice Hall, 2006), 37–53; see also D. Kolb et al., "Experiential Learning Theory," in R. Sternberg and L. Zhang, eds., *Perspectives on Thinking, Learning, and Cognitive Styles* (Mahwah, NJ: Erlbaum, 2001), 227–248.

85. C. Darwin, *On the Origin of Species* (London: J. Murray, 1859); and C. Darwin, *The Descent of Man and Selection in Relation to Sex* (New York: Burt, 1874).

86. A. Einstein, *The World As I See It* (New York: Citadel Press, 1993); and W. Isaacson, *Einstein: His Life and Universe* (New York: Simon and Schuster, 2007).

87. J. Allen, *100 Great Lives* (New York: Journal of Living, 1944), 20–22, 25.

88. M. Josephson, *Edison* (New York: Wiley, 1992); and J. Newton, *Uncommon Friends* (New York: Harcourt, 1987).

89. U. Sinclair, *The Flivver King* (New York: Phaedra, 1969).

90. Team-building story from the authors' files.

91. M. Jordan, *I Can't Accept Not Trying* (San Francisco: Harper, 1994), 20.

92. P. Lencioni, *The Five Dysfunctions of a Team* (San Francisco: Jossey-Bass, 2002); and D. Goodwin, *Team of Rivals* (New York: Simon and Schuster, 2005).

93. D. Patrick, "Summit Still Driven to Be Best," *USA Today* (March 15, 2005): 2C.

94. B. Smart, *Topgrading* (Paramus, NJ: Prentice Hall Press, 1999), l.

95. C. Hymowitz, "Ranking Systems Gain Popularity But Have Staffers Riled," *The Wall Street Journal* (May 15, 2001): B1.

96. S. Wuchty, "The Increasing Dominance of Teams in The Production of Knowledge," *SCIENCE* 316 (May 18, 2007): 1036–1039.

97. S. Beatty, "Boss Talk: Plotting Plaid's Future," *The Wall Street Journal* (September 9, 2004): B1.

98. L. LaFasto and C. Larson, *When Teams Work Best* (Thousand Oaks, CA: Sage, 2001); and C. Burke et al., "What Types of Leadership Behavior Are Functional in Teams? A Meta-Analysis," *Leadership Quarterly* 17 (2006).

99. J. Hackman, *Groups That Work* (San Francisco: Jossey-Bass, 1990); and E. Sundstrom, "Supporting Work Team Effectiveness," in E. Sundstrom, ed., *Supporting Work Effectivenss* (San Francisco: Jossey-Bass, 1999), 301–342.

100. K. Fisher and M. Fisher, *The Distance Manager* (New York: McGraw-Hill, 2000); and B. Bell and W. Kozlowski, "A Typology of Virtual Teams," *Group and Organization Management* 27 (March 2002): 14–49.

101. G. Buckler, "Staking One for the Team," *Computing Canada* (October 22, 2004): 16.

102. B. Hindo, "The Empire Strikes at Silos," *BusinessWeek* (August 20 and 27, 2007): 63; and S. Zaccaro et al., "Leadership in Virtual Teams," in D. Day et al., *Leader Development for Transforming Organizations* (Mahwah NJ: Lawrence Erlbaum, 2004).

103. G. Parker and R. Lacoursiere, *Team Players and Teamwork* (San Francisco: Jossey-Bass, 1990); B. Morgan et al., "An Analysis of Team Evolution and Maturation," *Journal of General Psychology* 120 (1993): 277–291; and B. Tuckman, "Developmental Sequence in Small Groups," *Psychological Bulletin* 63 (1965): 384–399.

104. B. Tuckman and M. Jensen, "Stages of Small-Group Development Revisited," *Group and Organizational Studies* 2, no. 4 (1977): 419–427; and S. Furst et al., "Managing the Life Cycle of Virtual Teams," *Academy of Management Executives* (May 2004): 6–20.

105. R. Daft, *Leadership Theory and Practice* (Orlando, FL: Dryden Press, 1999).

106. J. Harvey, *The Abilene Paradox and Other Meditations on Management* (San Francisco: Jossey-Bass, 1996); and I. Janis, "Groupthink," *Psychology Today* 5, no. 6 (1971): 43–46, 74–76.

107. I. Janis, *The Anatomy of Power* (New York: Houghton Mifflin, 1982); I. Janis, *Victims of Groupthink* (Boston: Houghton Mifflin, 1972); and W. Park, "Comprehensive Empirical Integration of the Relationship Among the Variables of the Groupthink Model," *Journal of Organizational Behavior* 21, no. 8 (December 2000).

108. I. Janis, *Groupthink,* 2nd ed. (Boston: Houghton Mifflin, 1982); and J. Esser and R. Ahlfinger, "Testing the Groupthink Model," *Social Behavior and Personality* 29, no. 1 (2001): 31–41.

109. Janis, *Groupthink;* and D. Henningsen, "Examine the Symptons of Groupthink and Retrospective Sensemaking," *Small Group Research* 37, no. 1 (February 2006): 36–64.

110. J. Jaworski, *Sychronicity* (San Francisco: Berrett–Koehler, 1996); and D. Bohm and L. Nichol, eds., *On Dialogue* (New York: Routledge, 1996).

111. E. Salas et al., "The Effect of Team Building on Performance," *Small Group Research* 30 (2007): 309–329; and W. Dyer et al., *Team Building,* 4th ed. (San Francisco: Jossey-Bass, 2007).

112. W. French and C. Bell, Jr., *Organization Development* (Upper Saddle River, NJ: Prentice Hall, 1999).

113. T. Egan and C. Lancaster, "Comparing Appreciative Inquiry to Action Research," *Organization Development Journal* (Summer 2005): 29–49.

114. J. Watkins and B. Mohr, *Appreciative Inquiry* (San Francisco: Jossey-Bass, 2001), 25, 42–45.

115. S. Berrisford, "Using Appreciative Inquiry to Drive Change at the BBC," *Strategic Communications Management* 9, no. 3 (2005): 22–25; and M-Y Cheung-Judge and E. Powley, "Innovation at the BBC," in *The Handbook of Large Group Methods,* eds. B. Bunker and B. Alban (New York: Wiley, 2006), 45–61.

116. Harris, "What Makes Teams Work," Forum Corporation (1995).

117. Harris, "What Makes Teams Work"; and S. Zaccaro et al., "Team Leadership," *Leadership Quarterly* 12 (2001): 451–483.

118. Harris, "What Makes Teams Work"; and F. LeFasto and C. Larson, *When Teams Work Best* (New York: Sage, 2001).

119. O. Marks, "From Command and Control to Collaboration and Teamwork," ZDnet.com, February 9, 2009, http://blogs.zdnet.com; B. Fryer, "Cisco CEO John Chambers on Teamwork and Collaboration," *Harvard Business Review* (October 24, 2008), http://www.discussionleader.hbsp.com; and C. Hymowitz, "Rewarding Competitors Over Collaborators No Longer Makes Sense," *The Wall Street Journal* (February 13, 2006): B1.

120. J. Collins, *How the Mighty Fall* (New York: HarperCollins, 2009).

PART 6, Chapters 12–13

1. B. Cummings, Organizational Psychology, Class paper, Northern Kentucky University, 1978; Michelangelo (1475–1564) is regarded as the greatest artist of the Italian Renaissance.

2. L. Iacocca, *Iacocca* (New York: Bantam Books, 1985); and M. McCormack, *What They Don't Teach You at Harvard Business School* (New York: Bantam Books, 1986), xiv.

3. A. Maslow, *Motivation and Personality* (New York: HarperCollins, 1987).

4. V. Frankl, *Man's Search for Meaning* (Boston: Beacon Press, 2000), 44–45.

5. A. Montagu and F. Matson, *The Human Connection* (New York: McGraw-Hill, 1979), 114, 116, 118.

6. W. James, *Principles of Psychology,* vols. 1, 2, and 3 (Cambridge, MA: Harvard University Press, 2003; original work published 1890).

7. J. Huxley, *Evolution in Action* (New York: Harper & Row, 1953), 162–163.

8. A. Maslow, *Toward a Psychology of Being* (New York: Wiley, 1998).

9. A. Maslow, *Maslow on Management* (New York: Wiley, 1998); and A. Maslow, *The Farther Reaches of Human Nature* (New York: Viking, 1971).

10. H. Munsterburg, *Psychology and Individual Efficiency* (Boston: Houghton-Mifflin, 1913); C. Pinder, *Work Motivation in Organizational Behavior* (Upper Saddle River, NJ: Psychology Press, 2008); and G. Latham, *Work Motivation* (Thousand Oaks, CA: Sage, 2007).

11. J. Simpson and E. Weiner, eds., *The Oxford English Dictionary,* 2nd ed., vol. 9 (Oxford: Clarendon Press, 1989), 1131.

12. "Valuing the Power of Praise and Reward," *Employee Benefits* (July 20, 2003); and K. Blanchard, *Whale Done!* (New York: Free Press, 2002).

13. Centaur Communications, Ltd., retrieved August 13, 2005, from www.employeebenefits.co.uk/archive/default.asp. Questionnaire based on Maslow and Frager, *Motivation and Personality* (New York: Addison-Wesley, 1987). Interpretation based on J. Hall, *Understanding Motivation at Work.*

14. J. Steinbeck, *The Grapes of Wrath* (New York: Viking Press, 1939), 124.

15. S. Terkel, *Working* (New York: Pantheon Books, 1974), xi.

16. Maslow, *Motivation and Personality;* and Pinder, *Work Motivation in Organizational Behavior;* and A. Maslow, "A Theory of Human Motivation," (*Psychological Review,* 50:4, 1943): 370–396.

17. J. Pfeffer, *The Human Equation* (Cambridge, MA: Harvard Business School Press, 1998).

18. M. Useem, *The Leadership Moment* (New York: Times Books, 1998), 117.

19. G. Flaubert and G. Wall, *Madame Bovary* (London: Penguin, 2001; original work published 1924).

20. M. Peck, *The Road Less Traveled* (New York: Walker, 1978); and S. Kopp, *If You Meet the Buddha on the Road, Kill Him!* (New York: Bantam Books, 1976).

21. D. Yankelovich, "Who Gets Ahead in America?" *Psychology Today* 13 (July 1979): 43.

22. D. Messick, "On the Psychological Exchange between Leaders and Followers," in D. Messick and R. Kramer, eds., *The Psychology of Leadership* (Mahwah, NJ: Erlbaum, 2005).

23. C. Argyris, *Integrating the Individual and the Organization* (New York: Wiley, 1964); and C. Argyris and D. Schön, *Organizational Learning* (Reading, MA: Addison-Wesley, 1996).

24. Interview with J. Pfeffer, "Leading with Values" (Linkage, Inc, 2004), retrieved August 13, 2005, from www.linkageinc.com/newsletter/archives/leadership.

25. *Human Capital* (Washington, DC: U.S. General Accounting Office, September 2001).

26. W. Macey and B. Schneider, "The Meaning of Employee Engagement," *Industrial and Organizational Psychology* 1 (2008): 3–33.

27. Gallup Study: "Feeling Good Matters in the Workplace," *Gallup Management Journal* 12 (January 2006); "Few Workers are 'Engaged' at Work," *Dow Jones Business News* (San Francisco) (October 22, 2007); and Blessing White, *The State of Employee Engagement, 2008: North American Overview* (Princeton, NJ: BlessingWhite, Inc., 2008), retrieved from http://www.blessingwhite.com/research.

28. Scottish Executive Social Research, *Employee Engagement in the Public Sector* (Edinburgh: Scottish Executive Social Research, May 2007); S. Edelson, "The Penney Program," *Women's Wear Daily* (February 12, 2007): 1; and J. Engen, "Are Your Employees Truly Engaged?" *Chief Executive* (March 2008): 42.

29. J. Haudan, *The Art of Engagement* (New York: McGraw-Hill, 2008); and A. Bakker and W. Schaufeli, "Positive Organizational Behavior: Engaged Employees in Flourishing Organizations," *Journal of Organizational Behavior* 29 (2008): 147–154.

30. F. Fiedler, *A Theory of Leadership Effectiveness* (New York: McGraw-Hill, 1967).

31. D. Goleman, *Working with Emotional Intelligence* (New York: Bantam Books, 2006); S. Côté and C. Miners, "Emotional Intelligence, Cognitive Intelligence, and Job Performance," *Administrative Science Quarterly* 51 (2006): 1–28; and S. Zaccaro, "Organizational Leadership and Social Intelligence," in R. Riggio, ed., *Multiple Intelligence and Leadership* (Mahwah, NJ: Lawrence Erlbaum, 2002).

32. H. Gardner, *Multiple Intelligences* (New York: Basic Books, 1993).

33. E. Thorndike, "Intelligence and Its Use," *Harper's Magazine* 140 (1920): 227–235.

34. R. Walker and J. Foley, "Social Intelligence and Its Measurement," *Psychological Reports* 33 (1973): 839–845.

35. M. Michalko, *Thinkertoys* (Berkeley, CA: Ten Speed Press, 1991).

36. A. DuBrin, *Leadership* (Boston: Houghton Mifflin, 1998).

37. DuBrin, *Leadership;* and L. Gerstner, Jr., *Who Says Elephants Can't Dance?* (New York: HarperCollins, 2002).

38. "Federal Express's Fred Smith," *INC* (October 1986): 38.

39. D. Goleman, *"Emotional Intelligence"* (New York: Bantam Publishing, 2006); and K. Webb, "Why Emotional Intelligence Should Matter to Management: A Survey of the Literature," *SAM Advanced Management Journal* (Spring 2009): 32–41.

40. D. Goleman, R. Boyatzis, and A. McKee, *Primal Leadership* (Boston: Harvard Business School Press, 2002).

41. A. Fisher, "Success Secret," *Fortune* 138, no. 8 (October 26, 1998): 293. © 1998 Time Inc. All rights reserved; see also M. Tapia, "Measuring Emotional Intelligence," *Psychological Reports* 88 (2001): 353–364; and J. Mayer et al., "Models of Emotional Intelligence," in R. Sternberg, *Handbook of Intelligence* (Cambridge: Cambridge University Press, 2000).

42. D. Goleman, *Social Intelligence* (New York: Bantam, 2006); and D. Goleman, "What Makes a Leader," *Harvard Business Review* (November–December 1998).

43. P. Lopes et al., "Emotional Intelligence and Social Interaction," *Personality and Social Psychology Bulletin* 30, no. 8 (August 2004): 1018–1034; and C. Daus and N. Ashkensky, "The Case for Ability-Based Models of Emotional Intelligence," *Journal of Organizational Behavior* 26 (2005): 453–466.

44. C. Fox, "Shifting Gears," *Australian Financial Review* 13 (August 2004): 28; and J. Thomson, "True Team Spirit," *Business Review Weekly* (March 18, 2004): 92.

45. *Bits & Pieces,* Lawrence Ragan Communications, Inc., 316 N. Michigan Avenue, Chicago, IL 60601.

46. V. Lombardi, Jr., *What It Takes to Be #1* (New York: McGraw-Hill, 2003).

47. D. Goodwin, *Lyndon Johnson and the American Dream* (New York: St. Martin's Press, 1991).

48. W. Churchill and G. Boas, *Winston S. Churchill* (London: Macmillan, 1952).

49. Churchill and Boas, *Winston S. Churchill.*

50. Churchill and Boas, *Winston S. Churchill.*

51. Speech by P. Henry, delivered at St. John's Church, Richmond, Virginia, March 23, 1775.

52. From LEADERSHIP MOMENT by M. Useem, copyright © 1998 by M. Useem. Used by permission of Times Books, a division of Random House, Inc.

53. M. Shaara, *The Killer Angels* (New York: Random House, 1974).

54. Malcolm X, *The Autobiography of Malcolm X* (New York: Random House, 1964).

55. J. Heindrichs, *Thank You for Arguing* (New York: Three River Press, 2007).

56. C. de Dreu and A. Van Vianen, "Managing Relationship Conflict and the Effectiveness of Organizational Teams," *Journal of Organizational Behavior* 22, no. 3 (2001): 309–339.

57. R. Lussier, *Human Relations in Organizations* (New York: McGraw-Hill, 2009).

58. K. Thomas, "Conflict and Conflict Management," in *Handbook of Industrial and Organizational Psychology*, M. Dunnette, ed. (Chicago: Rand McNally, 1976); and K. Thomas, "Conflict and Negotiation Processes in Organizations," in M. Dunette and L. Hough, eds., *Organizational Psychology,* 2nd ed., vol. 3 (Palo Alto, CA: Consulting Psychologists Press, 1992).

59. J. Schermerhorn, *Management,* 10th ed., 341–342. Reprinted with permission of John Wiley & Sons, Inc. See also C. de Dreu et al., "A Theory-Based Measure of Conflict Management Strategies in the Workplace," *Journal of Organizational Behavior* 22 (2001): 645–668.

60. A. Filley, *Interpersonal Conflict Resolution* (Glenview, IL: Scott, Foresman, 1975).

61. T. Kilmann, *Conflict Mode Instrument* (Tuxedo, NY: Xicom, 2007); and Schermerhorn, *Management.*

62. J. Arnold, *When the Sparks Fly* (New York: McGraw-Hill, 1993).

63. J. Conger, *Winning 'Em Over* (New York: Simon & Schuster, 1998).

64. G. Hofstede, *Culture's Consequences,* 2nd ed. (Thousand Oaks, CA: Sage, 2001); and R. House et al., "Understanding Cultures and Implicit Leadership Theories Across the Globe," *Journal of World Business* 37 (2002): 3–10.

65. D. Schultz and S. Schultz, *Psychology and Work Today,* 10th ed. (Upper Saddle River, NJ: Prentice Hall, 2009).

66. R. Kanter, "Leadership in a Globalizing World," in N. Nohria and R. Khurana, *Handbook of Leadership Theory and Practice* (Boston: Harvard Business Press, 2010); R. Thomas, Jr., and M. Woodruff, *Building a House for Diversity* (New York: AMACOM, 1999); R. House, and M. Javidan, "Overview of GLOBE," in R. House et al., eds., *Culture, Leadership, and Organizations* (Thousand Oaks, CA: Sage, 2004), 9–28; and M. Javidan, P. Dorfman, J. Howell, and P. Hanges, "Leadership and Cultural Context," in N. Hohria and R. Khurana, *Handbook of Leadership Theory and Practice* (Boston: Harvard Business Press, 2010).

67. S. Page, "Making the Difference: Applying a Logic of Diversity," *Academy of Management Perspectives* 21, no. 4 (2007): 6–20; and H. Adler and S. Bartholomew, "Managing Globally Competent People," *Academy of Management Executive* 6 (1992): 52–65.

68. C. Johnson, "Cultural Sensitivity Adds Up to Good Business Sense," *HR Magazine* (November 1995): 82–83. Reprinted with permission of *HR Magazine.* Published by the Society for Human Resource Management, Alexandria, VA.

69. T. Bateman and S. Snell, *Management,* 9th ed. (New York: McGraw-Hill/Irwin, 2011), 382–383.

70. M. Velasquez, *Business Ethics,* 5th ed. (Upper Saddle River, NJ: Prentice Hall, 2002); and E. Schultz, "Scudder Brings Lessons to the Navajo, Gets Some of Its Own," *The Wall Street Journal* (April 29, 1999): C12.

71. R. House et al., *Culture, Leadership, and Organizations;* S. Ronen and O. Shenkar, "Clustering Countries on Attitudional Dimensions," *Academy of Management Review* 10, no. 3 (1985): 435–454; and Chhokar et al., *Culture and Leadership Across the World* (Thousand Oaks, CA: Sage, 2007).

72. R. House et al., "Cross-Cultural Research on Organizational Leadership," in P. Early and M. Erez, eds., *New Perspectives on International Industrial and Organizational Psychology* (San Francisco: Jossey-Bass, 1997), 535–625; and M. Javidan et al., "In The Eye of the Beholder," *Academy of Management Perspectives* 20 (2006): 67–90.

73. M. Marger, *Race and Ethnic Relations,* 5th ed. (Belmont, CA: Wadsworth Thomson Learning, 2008); and C. Taulbert, *Eight Habits of the Heart* (New York: Viking/Dial Books, 1997).

74. L. Copeland, "Learning to Manage a Multicultural Workforce," *Training* (May 1988): 48–49, 51, 55–56.

75. G. Hofstede, "Cultural Constraints in Management Theories," *Academy of Management Executive* 7, no. 1 (1993): 81–94; and P. Dorfman et al., Leadership in Western Asian Countries," *Leadership Quarterly* 8, no. 3 (1997): 233–274.

76. P. Dorfman et al., "Leadership and Cultural Variation," in R. House et al., *Culture, Leadership, and Organizations.*

77. P. Harris and R. Moran, *Managing Cultural Differences* (Houston: Gulf, 1986); and M. Barak, *Managing Diversity* (New York: Sage, 2005).

78. *A Class Divided,* video, PBS, 1320 Braddock Place, Alexandria, VA 22314; *Valuing Diversity,* video, Copeland Griggs Productions, 311 Fifteenth Avenue, San Francisco, CA 94118; and telephone interview with Jane Elliot, Iowa, June 10, 2010.

79. A. Morrison, *The New Leaders* (San Francisco: Jossey-Bass, 1996); A. Kalev et al., "Best Practices or Best Guesses?" *American Sociological Review* 71 (2006): 589–617; and R. Anand and M. Winters, "A Retrospective Review of Corporate Diversity Training from 1964 to the Present," *Academy of Management Learning and Education* (2008): 356–372.

80. R. Wentling and N. Palma-Rivas, "Current Status of Diversity Initiatives in Selected Multinational Corporations," *Human Resource Development Quarterly* 11, no. 1 (2000): 35–60.

81. Verizon, *Doing the Work: 2007 Verizon Corporate Responsibility Report* (New York: Verizon, 2008).

82. J. Gilbert and J. Ivancevich, "Valuing Diversity," *Academy of Management Executive* 14, no. 1 (2000): 93–105; J. Walter, "Managing Differences," *Great American Insurance Group* (2010); C. Kulik and L. Roberson, *Diversity at Work* (Cambridge: Cambridge University Press, 2008); and S. Horwitz and I. Horwitz, "The Effects of Team Diversity on Team Outcomes," *Journal of Management* 33 (2009): 987–1015.

83. S. Thiederman, *Making Diversity Work* (New York: Kaplan Business Center, 2003); R. Thomas, *Building on the Promise of Diversity* (New York: AMACOM, 2005); and T. Bateman and S. Snell, *Management,* 9th ed. (New York: McGraw-Hill/Irwin, 2011), 407–409.

84. A. Poussaint, "A Negro Psychiatrist Explains the Negro Psyche," in *Confrontation,* Part 3 (New York: Random House, 1971), 183–184.

85. C. Barkley, *Who's Afraid of a Large Black Man?* (New York: Penguin Press, 2005).

86. A. Pope, *Poetry and Prose of Alexander Pope* (New York: Houghton Mifflin, 1969).

87. S. Terkel, *American Dreams* (New York: Pantheon Books, 1980). Reprinted by permission of Donadio & Olsen, Inc. Copyright © September 26, 2005, Studs Terkel.

88. U.S. Census Bureau, *Statistical Abstract of the United States: 2008* (Washington, DC: U.S. GPO 2008).

89. D. Tannen, *You Just Don't Understand* (New York: Quill, 2001), 216–221.

90. Tannen, *You Just Don't Understand.*

91. Tannen, *You Just Don't Understand;* and D. Tannen, *Talking from 9 to 5* (New York: Morrow, 1994).

92. Tannen, *You Just Don't Understand.*

93. Tannen, *You Just Don't Understand;* and M. Dainton and E. Zelley, *Applying Communication Theory for a Professional Life* (Thousand Oaks, CA: Sage, 2005).

94. Current Population Survey, annual averages: Household Data (U.S. Bureau of Labor Statistics, 2008a and 2008b); Catalyst, Statistical Overview of Women in the Workplace, retrieved May 27, 2009, from http://www.catalyst.org/file/172/qt_statistical_overview_of_women_in_the_workplace.pdf; and Center for Women's Business Research, "Key Facts About Women Owned Businesses 2008," retrieved May 29, 2009, from http://www.fwbo.org/facts/index.php.

95. Center for Women and Politics, "Women in elected office 2009," retrieved May 28, 2009, from www.cawp.rutgers.edu/facts/officeholders/cawpfs.html.

96. A. Morrison et al., *Breaking the Glass Ceiling* (Reading, MA: Addition-Wesley, 1987); Catalyst, *Women in U.S. Corporate*

Leadership (New York: Author, 2003); and A. Eagly and L. Carli, *Through the Labyrinth* (Boston: Harvard Business School Press, 2007).

97. A. Eagly and L. Carli, "The Female Leadership Advantage," *Leadership Quarterly* 14 (2003): 807–834; M. Van Engen et al., "Sex and Leadership Styles," *Psychological Reports* 94 (2004): 3–18; and C. Holt, "Women and Leadership," in P. Northouse, *Leadership Theory and Practice* (Los Angeles: Sage, 2010).

98. G. Dobbins and S. Platz, "Sex Differences in Leadership," *Academy of Management Review* 11 (1986): 118–127; and H. Bowles and K. McGinn, "Claiming Authority," in D. Messick, *The Psychology of Leadership* (Mahwah, NJ: Lawrence Erlbaum, 2005).

99. *Catalyst Board Directors of the Fortune 500* (New York: Author, 2006).

100. C. Hoyt, "Women and Leadership," in P. Northouse, *Leadership Theory and Practice* (Thousand Oaks, CA: Sage, 2010); and S. Helgesen, *The Female Advantage* (New York: Doubleday, 1995).

101. E. Ensher and S. Murphy, *Power Mentoring* (San Francisco: Jossey-Bass, 2005).

102. Catalyst, *Women in Corporate Leadership* (New York: Author, 2003); and E. Bell and S. Nkomo, *Our Separate Ways* (Boston: Harvard Business School Press, 2001).

103. L. Belkin, "The Opt-out Revolution," *New York Times* (October 26, 2003): 42; and S. Hewlett, *Creating a Life* (New York: Talk Miramax, 2006).

104. J. Oakley, "Gender-Based Barriers to Senior Management Positions," *Journal of Business Ethics* 27, no. 4 (2002): 321–334; and J. Fletcher, *Disappearing Acts* (Boston: MIT Press, 2001).

105. S. Bianchi et al., "Is Anyone Doing the Housework?" *Social Forces* 79 (2000): 191–228; D. Bielby and W. Bielby, "She Works Hard for the Money," *American Journal of Sociology* 93 (1988): 1031–1059.

106. M. Ryan and S. Haslam, "The Road to the Glass Cliff," *Leadership Quarterly* 19 (2008): 530–546; and Z. Kunda and S. Spencer, "When Do Stereotypes Come to Mind and When Do They Color Judgment?" *Psychological Bulletin* 129 (2003): 522–544.

107. C. Golden and C. Rouse, "Orchestrating Impartiality," *American Economic Review* 90, (no. 4) (2000): 715–741.

108. R. Ely and D. Rhode, "Women and Leadership: Defining the Challenges," in N. Nohria and R. Khurana, *Handbook of Leadership Theory and Practice* (Boston: Harvard Business Press, 2010).

109. R. Zemke et al., *Generations at Work* (New York: AMACOM, 2000); and B. Tulgan, "Managing in the New Workplace," *Financial Executive* (December 2009): 50–54.

110. J. Conger, "The Brave New World of Leadership Training," *Organizational Dynamics* 21, no. 3 (Winter 1993): 46–58.

111. M. Edelman, *The Measure of Our Success* (Boston: Beacon Press, 1992).

PART 7, Chapters 14–15

1. B. Gates et al., *Business @ the Speed of Thought* (Harlow, England: Pearson Education, 2001).

2. L. Jones, *Jesus CEO* (New York: Hyperion, 1995).

3. W. Brown, *13 Fatal Errors Managers Make and How You Can Avoid Them* (New York: Berkley, 1985).

4. J. Hann, "Why Entrepreneurs Don't Scale," in *Harvard Business Review on Developing Leaders* (Boston, MA: Harvard Business School, 2004).

5. J. Newton, *Uncommon Friends* (New York: Harcourt, 1987).

6. K. Brooker, "The Chairman of the Board Looks Back," *Fortune* (May 28, 2001): 62–70.

7. R. Heifetz, *Leadership without Easy Answers* (Cambridge, MA: Belknap Press of Harvard University Press, 1995).

8. G. Archbold and S. McMillen, based on *Delegation Concepts* (Grandville, MI: Time Management Center, 1977); and J. McKinney, *Time Management* (New York: Penton Learning, 1977, rev. 2008).

9. A. Carnegie, *The Autobiography of Andrew Carnegie,* reissued ed. (Boston: Northeastern University Press, 1986).

10. A. Uris, *The Executive Deskbook* (Florence, KY: Van Nostrand Reinhold, 1988); R. Hughes et al., *Leadership* (New York: McGraw-Hill, 2008).

11. N. Maier, *Psychology in Industrial Organizations,* 4th ed. (Boston: Houghton Mifflin, 1982), 437–438.

12. J. Lawrie, *You Can Lead! Essential Skills for the New or Prospective Manager* (New York: AMACOM, 1989); and P. Buhler, "Managing in the New Millennium," *Supervision* 65 (August 2004): 15–18.

13. N. Peterson et al., eds., *An Occupational Information System for the 21st Century: the Development of O*NET* (Washington, DC: American Psychological Association); and A. Kristof-Brown et al., "Consequences of Individuals' Fit at Work: A Meta-Analysis," *Personnel Psychology* (Summer 2005): 281–342.

14. W. Bridges, *Job Shift* (Reading, MA: Addison-Wesley Publishing, 1994).

15. J. Holland, *Making Vocational Choices: A Theory of Vocational Personalities and Work Environments* (Odessa, FL: Psychological Assessment Resources, 1997); and A. Furnham and R. Schaffer, "Person–Environmental Fit, Job Satisfaction, and Mental Health," *Journal of Occupational Psychology* 57 (1984): 295–307.

16. R. Bolles, *What Color Is Your Parachute?* (Berkeley, CA: Ten Speed Press, 2010).

17. R. Katz, "Skills of an Effective Administrator," *Harvard Business Review* 52, no. 5 (September–October 1974): 90–102; M. Mumford et al., "Leadership Skills," *Leadership Quarterly* 11, no. 1 (2002): 155–170; and R. Charan et al., *The Leadership Pipeline* (San Francisco: Jossey-Bass, 2001).

18. Katz, "Skills of an Effective Administrator," J. Schermerhorn, Jr., *Management,* 9th ed. (New York: Wiley, 2009); and M. Porter and N. Nohria, "What Is Leadership," in H. Nohria and R. Khurana, *Handbook of Leadership Theory and Practice* (Boston: Harvard Business Press, 2010).

19. H. Mintzberg, *The Nature of Managerial Work* (Englewood Cliffs, NJ: Prentice Hall, 1980); R. MacKenzie, "The Management Process in 3-D," *Harvard Business Review* 47 (November–December 1969): 80–87; G. Yukl, *Leadership in Organizations,* 7th ed. (Upper Saddle River, NJ: Prentice Hall, 2009); and, C. Boardman, "How Managers Spend Their Time," Slide #24, retrieved October 2, 2005, from http://home.business.utah.edu/~fincmb/day24/tsld024.htm.

20. J. Stafford, Special Topics Class Project, Psychology 495/595, Northern Kentucky University, 2009, based on M. Mumford et al.,

"Leadership Skills for a Changing World," *Leadership Quarterly* 11, no. 1 (2002): 11–35.

21. M. Broadwell and C. Ditrich, "Culture Clash," *Training* 437, no. 3 (March 2000): 34–36; and P. Glen and W. Bennis, *Leading Geeks* (New York: Jossey-Bass, 2002).

22. L. Peter and R. Hull, *The Peter Principle* (New York: Harper Business, 2009).

23. L. Steinmetz, *The Art and Skill of Delegation* (Reading, MA: Addison-Wesley, 1976), 46–63; and R. Charan, *Leaders at All Levels* (New York: Jossey-Bass, 2007).

24. W. Menninger and H. Levinson, *Human Understanding in Industry* (Chicago: Science Research Associates, 1956), 21.

25. B. Spinoza as quoted in Will Forpe and John McCollister, *The Sunshine Book: Expressions of Love, Hope, and Inspiration* (New York: Jonathan David Publishers, Inc., 1979), 41.

26. S. Kierkegaard in R. F. Gale, *Development Behavior* (New York: Macmillan, 1969), 25.

27. Shakespeare, *As You Like It,* 2.7.139.

28. J. Coleman, *Personality Dynamics and Effective Behavior* (Glenview, IL: Scott, Foresman and Company, 1960), 63–64.

29. J. Burger, *Personality* (New York: Wadsworth, 2007).

30. D. Schultz and S. Schultz, *Psychology and Work Today,* 10th ed. (Upper Saddle River, NJ: Prentice Hall, 2009).

31. T. Bier, "Contemporary Youth," Doctoral Dissertation, Case Western Reserve University, 1967, rev. 2010; D. Oyserman et al., "Rethinking Individualism and Collectivism," *Psychological Bulletin* 128 (2002): 3–72; and D. Matsumoto et al., "Context–Specific Measurement of Individualism-Collectivism on the Individual Level," *Journal of Cross-Cultural Psychology* 28, no. 6 (1997): 743–767.

32. C. Woodham-Smith, *Queen Victoria, from Her Birth to the Death of the Prince Consort* (New York: Knopf, 1972); and G. Coats, *Moses* (Sheffield, UK: JSOT Press, 1988).

33. D. Emblidge, *My Day* (New York: DeCapo Books, 2001).

34. E. Morgan, *Benjamin Franklin* (New Haven, CT: Yale University Press, 2002).

35. H. Thoreau, *Walden* (Chicago: Lakeside Press, 1930), 285–286.

36. R. Pernoud, *Joan of Arc* (New York: Stein & Day, 1969).

37. E. Hall, *Beyond Culture* (New York: Doubleday, 1976); and H. Triandis, "Vertical and Horizontal Individualization and Collectivism," in J. Cheng and R. Peterson, eds., *Advances in International and Comparative Management* (Greenwich, CT: IAI Press, 1998), 35.

38. G. Hofstede, *Culture's Consequences* (Thousand Oaks, CA: Sage, 2001); and T. Masuda et al., "Placing the Face in Context," *Journal of Personality and Social Psychology* 94, no. 3 (2008): 365–381.

39. Hofstede, *Culture's Consequences.*

40. C. Hui and M. Villareal, "Individualism–Collectivism and Psychological Needs," *Journal of Cross-Cultural Psychology* 20 (1989): 310–323; and G. Goethals, *Encyclopedia of Leadership,* vol. 1 (Thousand Oaks, CA: Sage, 2004), 256–259.

41. B. Schwartz, "The Creation and Destruction of Value," *American Psychologist* 45 (1990): 7–15.

42. S. Joseph, *The Me Nobody Knows* (New York: Avon, 1969).

43. E. Hertz, *Lincoln Talks—A Biography in Anecdotes* (New York: Viking Press, 1939), 367.

44. W. Shakespeare, *Hamlet,* Act I, Scene 3, lines 78–80.

45. R. Frost, *The Road Not Taken* (New York: Holt, Rinehart & Winston, 1985), stanza 4.

46. E. Markham, in R. Gale, *Developmental Behavior* (New York: Macmillan, 1969), 192.

47. S. Horwitz and I. Horwitz, "The Effects of Team Diversity on Team Outcomes," *Journal of Management* 33 (2009): 987–1015.

48. R. McCrae and P. Costa, Jr., "The Stability of Personality," *Current Directions in Psychological Science* (Cambridge, UK: Cambridge University Press, 1994); L. Hough and D. Ones, "The Structure, Measurement, Validity and Use of Personality Variables," in N. Anderson et al., eds., *Handbook of Industrial Work and Organizational Psychology,* Vol. 1 (London: Sage, 2001), 233–377; and F. Cheung et al., "Use of Western and Indigenously Developed Personality Tests in Asia," *Applied Psychology* 53 (2004): 173–191.

49. D. McClelland, "Is Personality Consistent?" in A. Rabin et al., eds., *Further Explorations in Personality* (New York: Wiley–Interscience, 1981), 87–113.

50. J. George and J. Zhou, "When Openness to Experience and Conscientiousness Are Related to Creative Behavior," *Journal of Applied Psychology* 86 (2001): 513–524.

51. L. Witt et al., "The Interactive Effects of Conscientiousness and Agreeableness on Job Performance," *Journal of Applied Psychology* 87 (2002): 164–169; and M. Barrick and M. Mount, "Yes, Personality Matters," *Human Performance* 18, no. 4 (2005): 359–372.

52. M. Barrick et al., "Personality and Job Performance," *Journal of Applied Psychology* 87 (2002): 43–51.

53. G. Neuman and J. Wright, "Team Effectiveness," *Journal of Applied Psychology* 54 (1999): 421–448.

54. R. Peterson et al., "The Impact of CEO Personality on Top Management Team Dynamics," *Journal of Applied Psychology* 88 (2003): 795–807.

55. J. Hogan and B. Holland, "Using Theory to Evaluate Personality and Job Performance Relations," *Journal of Applied Psychology* 88, no.1 (2003): 100–112.

56. T. Judge et al., "Personality and Leadership," *Journal of Applied Psychology* 87 (2002): 76–78.

57. F. Galton, "Measurement of Character," *Fortnightly Review* 36 (1884): 179–185.

58. G. Allport and H. Odbert, "Trait Names," *Psychological Monographs* 47, no. 211 (1936).

59. E. Tupes and R. Christal, "Recurrent Personality Factors Based on Trait Ratings," *Journal of Personality* 60 (1992): 225–251 (original work published in 1961).

60. L. Goldberg, "The Big Five Factor Structure," *Journal of Personality and Social Psychology* 59 (1990): 1216–1229; and P. Costa and R. McCrae, *Revised NEO Personality Inventory and Professional Manual* (Odessa, FL: Psychological Assessment Resources, 1992).

61. E. Diener, "Subjective Well-being," *American Psychologist* 55 (2000): 34–43.

62. B. Sarason et al., "Close Personal Relationships," in S. Duck, ed., *Handbook of Personal Relationships,* 2nd ed. (New York: Wiley, 1997), 547–573.

PART 8, Chapters 16–17

1. M. DePree, *Leadership Is an Art* (New York: Doubleday, 1989); and R. Pausch, *The Last Lecture* (New York: Hyperion, 2008).

2. W. Stewart, "Developing Others," Department of Adult Technical Education, University of California, 1980.

3. R. Rosenthal, *Pygmalion in the Classroom* (New York: Irvington, 1992).

4. M. Useem, *The Leadership Moment* (New York: Random House, 1998).

5. D. McNatt and T. Judge, "Boundary Conditions of the Galatea Effect," *Academy of Management Journal* (August 2004): 550–565.

6. D. McNatt, "Ancient Pygmalion Joins Contemporary Management," *Journal of Applied Psychology* 85 (2000): 314–322; and J. Livingston, "Pygmalion in Management," *Harvard Business Review* 47, no. 4 (1969): 81–90.

7. S. Oz and D. Eden, "Restraining the Golem," *Journal of Applied Psychology* 79 (1994): 744–754; and O. Davidson and D. Eden, "Remedial Self-Fulfilling Prophecy," *Journal of Applied Psychology* (June 2000): 386–398.

8. J. Gardner, *On Leadership* (New York: Free Press, 1990).

9. J. Walter, "GAI Leadership Development," Great American University, Cincinnati, OH, 2010; B. Martinuzzi, "We Are What We Think We Are," *Canadian HR Reporter* (February 6, 2007); D. Eden et al., "Implanting Pygmalion Leadership Style," *Leadership Quarterly* (Summer 2000): 171–210; and A. Lashinsky, "Search and Joy at Google," *Fortune* (January 22, 2007).

10. J. Wooden, *Wooden on Leadership* (New York: McGraw-Hill, 2005).

11. M. Lang and J. Kelly, *Homer: Printed Editions of the* Iliad *and* Odyssey *in Greek and in Translation, and Landmarks in Homeric Scholarship* (New York: Grolier Society, 2001); and T. Allen et al., "Career Benefits Associated with Mentoring for Protégés," *Journal of Applied Psychology* 89 (2004): 127–136.

12. H. Levinson, *Executive* (Cambridge, MA: Harvard University Press, 1981), 150.

13. E. Thorndike, *Human Learning* (New York: Century, 1931); and C. Argyris, "Teaching Smart People How to Learn," in *Harvard Business Review on Developing Leaders* (Boston: Harvard Business School, 2004).

14. P. Senge, *The Fifth Discipline* (New York: Currency/Doubleday, 2006).

15. N. Amand et al., "Knowledge-Based Innovation," *Academy of Management Journal* 50, no. 2 (2007), 406–428; D. Garvin et al., "Is Yours a Learning Organization?" *Harvard Business Review* 86, no. 3 (March 2008): 109–116; T. Bingham and P. Galagan, "Learning Is a Powerful Tool," *T&D* (January 2008); and P. Harris et al., "A Passion for Learning, ASTD Best," *T&D* (October 2008): 26–89.

16. See W. B. Yeats.

17. A. Zimmerman, *Commun–Care* (Prior Lake, MN: Zimmerman Newsletter, 1992).

18. T. Stewart, "The Businessman of the Century," *Fortune* 140 (November 22, 1999): 64–79. Copyright © 1999 Time, Inc. All rights reserved.

19. K. Kram, *Mentoring at Work* (Lanham, MD: University Press of America, 1988).

20. *The Sayings of Confucius,* trans. J. Ware (New York: New American Library, 1955); see also *Analects of Confucius.*

21. J. Pfeffer and R. Sutton, *The Knowing–Doing Gap* (Cambridge, MA: Harvard Business School Press, 2000); and H. Mintzberg, *Managers, Not MBAs* (San Francisco: Berrett-Koehler, 2004).

22. G. Hamel, *Leading the Revolution* (New York: Plume, 2002); R. Noe, *Employee Training and Development,* 4th ed. (New York: McGraw-Hill, 2008); and A. Paradise, "2008 ASTD State of the Industry Report," *T&D* (November 2008): 45–51.

23. J. O'Toole and E. Lawler, *The New American Workplace* (Society for Human Resource Management, 2006).

24. B. Sugrue, *State of the Industry* (Alexandria, VA: American Society for Training and Development, 2005); W. Arthur et al., "Effectiveness of Training in Organizations," *Journal of Applied Psychology* 88 (2003): 234–245; and Noe, *Employee Training and Development.*

25. M. Van Buren and S. King, "ASTD International Comparisons Report" (Alexandria, VA: American Society for Training and Development, 2000).

26. K. Kraiger, ed., *Creating, Implementing, and Managing Effective Training and Development* (San Francisco: Jossey-Bass, 2002).

27. J. Gordon, "Measuring the 'Goodness' of Training," *Training* (August 1991); and D. Kirkpatrick, *Evaluating Training Programs* (San Francisco: Barrett-Koehler, 1994).

28. G. Goethals et al., *Encyclopedia of Leadership,* Vol. 2, (Thousand Oaks, CA: Sage, 2004), 919.

29. P. Jackson and H. Delehanty, *Sacred Hoops* (New York: Hyperion, 1995).

30. R. Katz, *Skills of an Effective Administrator* (Boston: Harvard Business Review Reprint Service, 1974); and M. Allen, *The Next Generation of Corporate Universities* (San Francisco: Wiley, 2007).

31. Y. Berra, *When You Come to a Fork in the Road, Take It* (Waterville, ME: Thorndike Press, 2001).

32. C. Handy, *Myself and Other Matters* (New York: AMACOM, 2008).

33. C. Douglas, *Key Events and Lessons for Managers in a Diverse Workforce* (Greensboro, NC: Center for Creative Leadership, 2003).

34. M. Goldsmith, *What Got You Here Won't Get You There* (New York: Hyperion, 2008); and N. Klippert et al., "Maximizing Returns on Professional Executive Coaching," *Corporate Leadership Council* (New York: Corporate Executive Board, 2003).

35. B. Joiner and S. Josephs, *Leadership Agility* (San Francisco: Jossey-Bass, 2007).

36. D. Dunning, "The First Assistant," in *Effective Leader,* no. 2, Cynthia Jacobs, ed. (Seattle, WA: Corporate Leadership Consultants, 1996).

37. N. Tichy, *The Leadership Engine* (Dallas, TX: Pritchett, 1998); and C. McCauley and E. Van Velsor, eds., *The Center for Creative Leadership Handbook of Leadership Development* (San Francisco: Jossey-Bass, 2004).

38. J. Conger, "Leadership Development Interventions," in N. Nohria and R. Khurana, *Handbook of Leadership Theory and*

Practice (Boston: Harvard Business Press, 2010); and R. Hughes et al., *Leadership* (New York: McGraw-Hill, 2008).

39. Authors' files, Correction Corporation of America, 2010.

40. O'Toole and Lawler, *The New American Workplace;* and M. Arthur et al., *The New Careers* (London: Sage, 2007).

41. Goleman, *Working with Emotional Intelligence;* O'Toole and Lawler, *The New American Workplace;* and Arthur et al., *The New Careers.*

42. W. Bliss, "Cost of Employee Turnover," www.isquar.com/turnover.cfm, accessed April 15, 2008; see also "Calculate Your Turnover Cost," www.keepemployees.com/turnovercalc.htm, accessed April 15, 2005.

43. R. Sommer, *Retaining Intellectual Capital in the 21st Century* (Alexandria, VA: Society for Human Resource Management, 2007).

44. M. Buckingham, *First Break All the Rules* (New York: Simon & Schuster, 1999); and M. Buckingham and D. Clifton, *Now Discover Your Strengths* (New York: Free Press, 2001).

45. M. Buckingham, "What Great Managers Do," *Harvard Business Review* (March 2005): 70–79.

46. J. Hudnut, *Architecture and the Spirit of Man* (New York: Greenwood Press, 1949), 3.

47. H. Greenberg and P. Sweeney, *Succeed on Your Own Terms* (New York: McGraw-Hill, 2007).

48. R. Griffith, Health Alliance Management Presentation, Cincinatti, Ohio, 2006; and L. Holtz *Winning Every Day* (New York: Collins Business, 2005).

49. M. Korda, *Success!* (New York: Ballantine Books, 1978); and S. Smiles, *Self-Help* (New York: Waking Lion, 2006).

50. D. Conner, *Managing at the Speed of Change* (New York: Villand Books, 1993), 38; and G. Hamel, "Leadership: Making a Shift from Survival to Innovation," Linkage Inc., 2004, retrieved August 13, 2005, from www.linkageinc.com/newsletter/archives/leadership.

51. H. Leavitt, *Corporate Pathfinders* (Homewood, IL: Dow Jones–Irwin, 1986); and J. Greenberg and R. Baron, *Behavior in Organizations* (2008).

52. P. Pritchett, *Business as Unusual* (Dallas: Pritchett, 1994); and S. Johnson, *Who Moved My Cheese?* (New York: Vermillion, 2002).

53. B. Filipczak, "Weathering Change: Enough Already," *Training* 31, no. 9 (September 1994): 23. Used by permission of VNU Business Publications USA, via The Copyright Clearance Center.

54. C. Scott and D. Jaffe, *Managing Organizational Change* (Los Altos, CA: Crisp Publications, 1989); and M. Maccoby, "Learn Change Leadership From Two Great Teachers," *Research Technology Management* (March-April 2010): 68–69.

55. A. Benedict, *2007 Change Management Survey Report* (Alexandria, VA: Society for Human Resource Management, 2007) accessed at http://www.shrm.org.

56. C. Aiken and S. Keller, "The Irrational Side of Change Management," *McKinsey Quarterly* (April 2009), http://www.mckinseyquarterly.com.

57. K. Lewin, *A Dynamic Theory of Personality* (New York: McGraw-Hill, 1935); and R. Hughes, et al., *Leadership* (New York: McGraw-Hill, 2006).

58. Z. Kotter and D. Cohen, *The Heart of Change* (Boston: Harvard Business School Press, 2002).

59. J. Kotter, *Leading Change* (Boston: Harvard Business School Press, 1996), 21. Reprinted by permission of Harvard Business School Press; Copyright © 1996 by John P. Kotter; all rights reserved; and J. Kotter and H. Rathgeber, *Our Iceberg Is Melting* (New York: St. Martin's Press, 2008); see also J. Kotter, "A Sense of Urgency" (Boston: Harvard Business Press, 2008).

60. Kotter, *Leading Change,* 16; and E. Heffes, "You Need Urgency Now!" *Financial Executive* (January–February 2009), http://galenet.galegroup.com (interview with John Kotter).

61. C. Hymowitz, "In Deal Making Keep People in Mind," *The Wall Street Journal* (May 12, 2008).

62. D. Conner, *Leading at the Edge of Chaos* (New York: Wiley, 1998); D. Magee, *Turnaround* (New York: HarperCollins, 2003); and E. Schein, *Organizational Culture and Leadership* (San Francisco: Jossey-Bass, 1992).

63. Schein, *Organizational Culture and Leadership,* 115.

64. Conner, *Leading at the Edge of Chaos;* and C. Handy, *Age of Unreason* (Boston: Harvard Business School Press, 1990).

65. J. Naisbitt, *Megatrends* (New York: Grand Central Publishing, 1988); T. Friedman, *The Lexus and the Olive Tree* (New York: First Anchor Books/Random House, 2000); U.S. Census Bureau, *Statistical Abstract of the United States: 2008* (Washington, DC: U.S. GPO); M. Hitt, "The New Frontier," *Organizational Dynamics* 28, no. 3 (2009): 7–17; and Sony Executive Conference Video, 2008, accessed from http://www.youtube.com/watch?v=cl9wu2kwwsy; and M. Cetron and O. Davies, "Trends Shaping Tomorrow's World," *The Futurist (*May-June 2010).

66. Pritchett and Associates, *High-Velocity Culture Change* (Dallas: Pritchett, 1994); and A. Deutschman, *Change or Die* (Los Angeles: Regan, 2007), 164–178.

67. C. Darwin, *The Descent of Man and Selection in Relation to Sex* (New York: Burt, 1874).

68. K. Wexley and S. Silverman, *Working Scared* (San Francisco: Jossey-Bass, 1993).

69. C. Scott and D. Jaffe, *Managing Personal Change* (Los Altos, CA: Crisp Publications, 1989).

70. B. Davis, *Successful Manager's Handbook* (Minneapolis, MN: Personnel Decisions International, 2000).

71. J. Canfield and M. Hansen, *Chicken Soup for the Soul* (Deerfield Beach, FL: Health Communications, 1993), 72.

72. L. Fischer, ed., *The Essential Gandhi* (New York: Vintage, 2002).

73. S. Toppinen-Tanner et al., "The Process of Burnout in White-Collar and Blue-Collar Jobs," *Journal of Organizational Behavior* 23 (2002): 555–570; and H. Freudenberger, "Burn-Out," *Training and Development* 31, no. 7 (July 1977): 26–27.

74. Freudenberger, "Burn–Out"; and R. Cropanzano et al., "The Relationship of Emotional Exhaustion to Work Attitudes," *Journal of Applied Psychology* 88 (2003): 160–169.

75. C. Maslach et al., "Job Burnout," *Annual Review of Psychology* 52 (2007): 397–422.

76. M. Rosenthal, "How to Win the Burn-Out Game," *USA Today Magazine* (January 1991): 70–72.

77. *Cincinnati Enquirer* (January 20, 1980): F10.

78. C. Krucoff, "Careers," *The Washington Post* (August 5, 1980, health section), 5. Copyright © 1980. The Washington Post, reprinted with permission. See also C. Maslach and S. Jackson, *The Maslach Burnout Inventory* (Palo Alto, CA: Consulting Psychologists Press, 1986).

79. B. Bryson, *A Walk in the Woods* (New York: Anchor, 2006); W. Muller, *Sabbath* (New York: Bantam, 2005); and M. Gill, *How Starbucks Saved My Life* (New York: Penguin, 2007).

80. S. Sauter et al., "A National Strategy for the Prevention of Work-Related Psychological Disorders," *American Psychologist* 45 (1990): 1146–1158; and L. Lapierre and T. Allen, "Work and Family Supportive Supervision," *Journal of Occupational and Health Psychology* 11 (2009): 169–181.

81. M. Raber and G. Dyck, *Managing Stress for Mental Fitness* (Los Altos, CA: Crisp Publications, 1993).

82. E. Greenberg and C. Canzoneri, *Organizational Staffing and Disability Claims* (New York: American Management Association Report, 1996).

83. Marlin Company, *Attitudes in the American Workplace VII* (North Haven, CT: Marling Company, 2001); and M. Campbell et al., "The Stress of Leadership," Center for Creative Leadership, Chapel Hill, North Carolina.

84. M. Cavanaugh et al., "An Empirical Examination of Self-Reported Stress among U.S. Managers," *Journal of Applied Psychology* (2000): 65–74.

85. P. Cynkar, "Whole Workplace Health," *Monitor on Psychology* (March 2007): 28–32; and S. Miller, "CEO's Urged to Make Wellness a Strategy," *HR Magazine* (April 2007): 30–36.

86. R. Goetzel et al., "The Relationship between Modifiable Health Risks and Health Care Expenditures," *Journal of Occupational and Environmental Medicine* 40 (1998): 843–854.

87. C. Cooper et al., *Stress Prevention in the Workplace* (Dublin, Ireland: European Foundation for the Improvement of Living and Working Conditions 1996).

88. R. Lee and B. Ashforth, "A Meta-Analytic Examination of the Correlates of the Three Dimensions of Job Burnout," *Journal of Applied Psychology* 81 (1996): 123–133.

89. S. Sagerstrom and G. Miller, "Physiological Stress and the Human Immune System," *Psychological Bulletin* 130 (2004): 601–630.

90. R. Price et al., "Links in the Chain of Adversity Following Job Loss," *Journal of Occupational Health Psychology* 9, no. 4 (2002): 304–312.

91. M. Losey, "Managing Stress in the Workplace," *Managing Office Technology* (February 1991); G. Olson and J. Olson, "Human-Computer Interaction," *Annual Review of Psychology* 54 (2003): 491–516; and P. Hemp, "Death by Information Overload," *Harvard Business Review* (September 2009): 83–89.

92. "Who's Stressed Out at Work?" *BusinessWeek* (April 12, 1999): 26.

93. J. Schor, *The Overworked American* (New York: Basic Books, 1993).

94. B. Hunnicutt, *Kellogg's Six-Hour Day* (Philadelphia: Temple University Press, 1996); and E. Galinsky et al., *Overwork in America* (New York: Families and Work Institute, 2005).

95. R. Gephart, Jr., "Introduction to the Brave New Workplace," *Journal of Organizational Behavior* 23 (2002): 327–344.

96. W. Cascio, "Whither Industrial and Organizational Psychology in a Changing World of Work," *American Psychologist* 50, no. 11 (November 1995): 928–939.

97. D. Schultz and S. Schultz, *Psychology and Work Today,* 10th ed. (Upper Saddle River, NJ: Prentice Hall, 2009).

98. R. Walton, *Innovating to Compete* (San Francisco: Jossey-Bass, 1987).

99. S. Gwynne, "The Long Haul," *Time* (September 28, 1992): 34–38.

100. P. Lawrence and D. Ryer, *Renewing American Industry* (New York: Free Press, 1983).

101. W. Cascio, "What Do We Know? What Have We Learned?" *Academy of Management Executive* 7, no. 1 (February 1993): 95–104.

102. Cascio, "Whither Industrial and Organizational Psychology in a Changing World of Work"; and S. Dray, "From Tier to Peer," *Ergonomics* 31, no. 1 (1988): 721–725.

103. E. Curtis, "Surveillance of Psychological Disorders in the Workplace," in G. Keita and S. Sauter, eds., *Work and Well-Being* (Washington, DC: American Psychological Association, 1992): 97–99.

104. S. Sauter, "Introduction to the NIOSH National Strategy," in Keita and Sauter, eds., *Work and Well-Being.*

105. National Safety Council Report, *Stress Management* (Boston: Jones and Bartlett, 1995).

106. L. Levi and P. Lunde-Jensen, *A Model for Assessing the Costs of Stressors at National Level* (Dublin, Ireland: European Foundation for the Improvement of Living and Working Conditions, 1996); and G. Harnois and P. Gabriel, *Mental Health and Work* (Geneva, Switzerland: International Labour Organization, 2000).

107. D. Ibison, "Overwork Kills Record Number of Japanese," *Financial Times* (May 29, 2002): 12.

108. J. Loehr, *Toughness Training for Life* (New York: Plume, 1994).

109. A. Hochschild, *The Second Shift* (New York: Viking, 1989); and N. Rothbard and J. Edwards, "Investment in Work and Family Roles," *Personnel Psychology* 56 (2003): 699–736.

110. F. Crosby, *Spouse, Parent, Worker* (New Haven, CT: Yale University Press, 2002).

111. J. Brady, "Ulcers in Executive Monkeys," *Scientific American* 199, no. 4 (October 1958): 95–100.

112. J. Weiss, "Psychological Factors in Stress and Disease," *Scientific American* 226 (June 1972): 104–113.

113. R. Karasek and T. Theorell, *Healthy Work* (New York: Basic Books, 1990); and S. Ettner and J. Grzywacz, "Workers' Perceptions of How Jobs Affect Health," *Journal of Occupational Health Psychology* 6, no. 2 (2001): 101–113.

114. E. Demerouti, "The Job Demand-Resources Model: State of the Art," *Journal of Managerial Psychology* 22, no. 3 (2007): 309; and T. Peters and R. Waterman, Jr., *In Search of Excellence* (New York: Harper & Row, 1982), xxiii, xxiv.

115. J. Greenberg and R. Baron, *Behavior in Organizations* (Upper Saddle River, NJ: Pearson Prentice Hall, 2007).

116. J. Murphy et al., eds., *Job Stress Interventions* (Washington, DC: American Psychological Association, 1995), xi–xiii.

117. S. Cartwright et al., "Diagnosing a Healthy Organization," in Murphy et al., eds., *Job Stress Interventions,* 217–233.

118. "100 Best Companies to Work For," *Fortune* (August 2008).

119. Office of Disease Prevention and Health Promotion, *Healthy People 2010* (Washington, DC: Department of Health and Human Services, 2000).

120. J. Green and R. Shellenberger, *The Dynamics of Health and Wellness* (Ft. Worth, TX: Holt, Rinehart & Winston, 1991).

121. J. Bly et al., "Impact of Worksite Health Promotion on Health Care Costs and Utilization," *Journal of the American Medical Association* 256, no. 23 (1986): 3235–3240.

122. K. Pelletier, *Sound Mind, Sound Body* (New York: Fireside, 1995), 261–262.

123. See Cianbro.com; TheJacksonLaboratory.com.

124. "Public Policy, Work, and Families," *American Psychological Association* (2004); R. Ilies et al., "The Spillover of Daily Job Satisfaction into Employees' Family Lives," *Academy of Management Journal* (February 2009): 87–102.

125. R. MacGregor, "Work and Family Policies," Center for Corporate Leadership, Minneapolis, MN (1999); and L. Hammer et al., "The Longitudinal Effects of Work-Family Conflict," *Journal of Occupational Health Psychology* 10, no. 2 (2009): 138–154.

126. J. Howard, *Families* (New York: Simon & Schuster, 1978), 350.

127. W. Bennis and R. Thomas, "Crucibles of Leadership," in *Harvard Business Review on Developing Leaders* (Boston: Harvard Business School, 2004); G. Bonanno, "Loss, Trauma, Human Resilience," *American Psychologist* 59, no. 1 (2004): 20–28; and J. Sonnenfeld and A. Ward, "Firing Back After Career Disasters," *Harvard Business Review,* Special Issue: The Tests of a Leader (January 2007): 76–84.

128. M. Beasley et al., "Resilience in Response to Life Stress," *Personality and Individual Differences* 34, no. 1 (2003): 77–95; and G. Mangurian, "Realizing What You Are Made Of," *Harvard Business Review* (March 2007): 125–130.

129. T. Carlyle, *Past and Present,* R. Altick, ed. (New York: New York University Press, 1977).

130. G. Shaw, "Don Juan in Hell," in *Man Is Superman,* Act II. See also V. Florian et al., "Does Hardiness Contribute to Mental Health?," *Journal of Personality and Social Psychology* 68 (1995): 687–695.

131. W. James, *The Principles of Psychology* (New York: Holt, 1890).

132. M. Scheier and C. Carver, "On the Power of Positive Thinking," *Current Directions in Psychological Science* 2, no. 1 (February 1993): 26–30; and C. Peterson, "The Future of Optimism," *American Psychologist* 55 (2000): 44–55.

133. M. Seligman, *Learned Optimism* (New York: Knopf, 1991); see also D. Danner and W. Frieden, "Positive Emotions in Early Life and Longevity," *Journal of Personality and Social Psychology* 80 (2001): 804–813.

134. R. Eliot and D. Breo, *Is It Worth Dying For?* (New York: Bantam Books, 1989); see also S. Hemenover, "Mediators between Personality and Stress Appraisals," *Personality and Social Psychology Bulletin* 27 (2001): 387–394.

135. E. Fromm, *The Art of Loving* (New York: Bantam Books, 1963); see also R. Niaura et al., "Hostility, the Metabolic Syndrome and Incident Coronary Heart Disease," *Health Psychology* 21 (2002): 588–593.

136. Address at the Sorbonne in Paris, France, April 23, 1910; see *Works of Theodore Roosevelt*, vol. 13, "Strenuous Life," Ch 21, p. 510.

137. William Stewart, "The Life of Benjamin Franklin," address at the University of Cincinnati, May 1970.

138. W. Durant, "The One Sure Way to Happiness," in J. Callwood, *Love, Hate, Fear, Anger, and the Other Lively Emotions* (Hollywood: New Castle Publishing, 1964).

139. Eliot and Breo, *"Is It Worth Dying For?"*; and R. Eliot, *From Stress to Strength* (New York: Bantam Books, 1994), 9–10.

140. R. Chernow, *Titan: The Life of John D. Rockefeller, Sr.* (New York: Random House, 1998).

PART 9, Chapters 18–19

1. D. Ulrich et al., *Results-Based Leadership* (Boston: Harvard Business School Press, 1999); and J. Pfeffer, *Hard Facts* (Boston: Harvard Business School Press, 2006).

2. Z. Weatherly, "Performance Management," *HR Magazine* (March 2007): 1–11.

3. K. Blanchard and S. Johnson, *The One Minute Manager* (New York: Berkley Books, 1982).

4. P. Brown, *Managing Behavior on the Job* (Boston: Houghton Mifflin, 1982).

5. *Bits and Pieces,* Lawrence Ragan Communications Inc., 316 N. Michigan Ave., Chicago, IL 60601.

6. T. Mitchell et al., "Goal Setting," in C. Cooper and E. Locke, eds., *Industrial and Organizational Psychology* (Oxford, England: Blackwell, 2000): 216–249; and G. Latham and E. Locke, "Enhancing the Benefits of Goal Setting," *Organizational Dynamics* (November 2006): 332–340.

7. P. Drucker, *The Practice of Management* (New York: Harper & Row, 1954), 126–129.

8. W. Brown, *13 Fatal Errors Managers Make* (Old Tappan, NJ: Revell, 1985).

9. S. Martin, "Performance Appraisal—Employee Interview Checklist," Cincinnati, OH, 2010; and D. McGregor, "An Uneasy Look at Performance Appraisal," *Harvard Business Review* (May-June 1957): 89–94.

10. Martin, "Performance Appraisal"; see also R. Hughes et al., *Leadership* (New York: McGraw-Hill, 2008); and P. Levy, *Industrial Organizational Psychology* (New York: Worth Publishers, 2010), 126.

11. G. Toegel and J. Conger, "360-Degree Assessment," *Academy of Management Learning and Education* 2, no. 3 (2006): 279–311; and J. Maxwell., *The 360° Leader* (Nashville: Nelson, 2005).

12. J. Smither et al., "Does Performance Improve Following Multi-Source Feedback?" *Personnel Psychology* (Spring 2005): 33.

13. S. Wellner, "Everyone's a Critic," *Inc* (July 2004): 38, 41; and W. Byham, "Fixing the Instrument," *Training* (July 2004): 50.

14. J. Gordon, "The Coach Approach," *Training* (October 2006): 26–30.

15. B. Montgomery and J. Meeke, "Organizational Psychology," Northern Kentucky University, 2007; and R. Deems and T. Deems, *Leading in Tough Times* (Amherst, MA: HRD Press, 2003).

16. Q. Studer, *101 Answers* (Gulf Breeze, FL: Fire Starter Publishing, 2005).

17. B. Edwards, *Management Interview* (Cincinnati, OH: 2007); and Q. Studer, *Handwinning Excellence* (New York: Wiley, 2007).

18. J. Maxwell, *Leadership Gold* (Nashville: Thomas Nelson, 2008); L. Offermann, "When Followers Become Toxic," *Harvard Business Review* (January 2004): 54–60; J. LaPine et al., "The Nature and Dimensionality of Organizational Citizenship Behavior," *Journal of*

Applied Psychology 87 (February 2002): 52–65; and R. Dalal, "A Meta-Analysis of Organizational Citizenship Behavior," *Journal of Applied Psychology* 90 (2005): 1241–1255.

19. Source unknown.

20. P. Marvin, *The Right Man for the Right Job* (Homewood, IL: Dow Jones-Irwin, 1973); L. Bossidy and R. Charan, *Execution* (New York: Random House, 2002); D. Abrashoff, *It's Your Ship* (New York: Business Plus, 2002); and R. Charan and A. Lafley, *Game-Changer* (New York: Crown Business Books, 2008).

21. Marvin, *The Right Man for the Right Job.*

22. W. Forpe and J. McCollister, *The Sunshine Book* (Middle Village, NY: Jonathan David, 1979).

23. G. Allport, "The Ego in Contemporary Psychology," *Psychological Review* 50 (1943): 466.

24. P. Drucker, *People and Performance* (New York: Harpers College Press, 1977).

25. M. Twain, *The Wit and Wisdom of Mark Twain* (New York: Dover Publications, 1999).

26. A. Lincoln, *Selected Speeches and Writings* (New York: Vantage, 1992).

27. W. James, as quoted in J. Cohen and M. Cohen, *The Penguin Dictionary of Quotations* (London: Claremont Books, 1995).

28. M. Useem, "Decision Making as a Leadership Foundation," in N. Nohria and R. Khurana, *Handbook of Leadership Theory and Practice* (Boston: Harvard Business Press, 2010).

29. K. Brooker, "The Chairman of the Board Looks Back," *Fortune* (May 28, 2001): 62–70.

30. H. Ford and S. Crawther, *My Life and Work* (New York: Kessinger, 2003).

31. U. Sinclair, *The Flivver King* (New York: Phaedra, 1969): 6, 7, 19, 69, 70, 78; and H. Ford, *Today and Tomorrow* (New York: Productivity Press, 1926).

32. R. Marshall and E. Guest, *Edgar A. Guest* (Chicago: Reilly & Lee, 1920).

33. E. Roosevelt, *This Is My Story* (New York: Harper, 1936).

34. Marshall and Guest, *Edgar A. Guest.*

35. *The Reader's Digest Great Encyclopedic Dictionary* (Pleasantville, NY: Reader's Digest Association, 1966), 2039.

36. S. Foss, "The Calf Path," as found in P. Frost et al., *Organizational Reality,* 3rd ed. (Glenview, IL: Scott, Foresman, 1986), 486–487.

37. J. Beecroft, *Kipling* (Garden City, NY: Doubleday, 1956), 383–384.

38. E. Morgan, *Benjamin Franklin* (New Haven, CT: Yale University Press, 2002).

39. Case from the authors' files.

40. S. Walton, *Sam Walton, Made in America* (New York: Doubleday, 1992).

41. R. Mitchell, "Masters of Innovation: How 3M Keeps Its New Products Coming," *Business Week* (April 10, 1989): 58–63; T. Martin, "Ten Commandments for Managing Creative People," *Fortune* (January 16, 1995): 135–136; and P. Drucker, "The Discipline of Innovation," *Harvard Business Review* (August 2002): 95–98, 100, 102.

42. J. Collins, "Level 5 Leadership," *Harvard Business Review* 79, no. 1 (January 2001): 66–76. Reprinted by permission of *Harvard Business Review.* Copyright © 2001 by the Harvard Business School Publishing Corporation; all rights reserved.

43. Collins, "Level 5 Leadership"; see also K. Brooker and J. Schlosser, "The Un-CEO," *Fortune* (September 16, 2002): 88.

44. S. McShane and M. Von Glinow, *Organizational Behavior,* 5th ed. (New York: McGraw-Hill Irwin, 2010), 372; and A. Lafley, "What Only the CEO Can Do," *Harvard Business Review* (May 2009): 54–62.

45. R. Camp, *Benchmarking* (New York: Productivity Press, 2006); and "TR50 2010: The World's Most Innovative Companies," *Technology Review* (March-April 2010): 33–44.

46. T. Kinni, *America's Best* (New York: Wiley, 1996); and A. Grove, *Only the Paranoid Survive* (New York: Currency Doubleday, 1999).

47. J. Liker, *The Toyota Way* (New York: McGraw-Hill, 2003); and J. Liker, *Toyota Culture* (New York: McGraw-Hill, 2008).

48. M. Hammer, "Deep Change," *Harvard Business Review* (April 2004): 86; J. Michelli, *The Starbucks Experience* (New York: McGraw-Hill, 2006); and D. Vice and M. Malseed, *The Google Story* (New York: Delta, 2006).

49. A. McGowan, with foreword by T. Dailey, *Cianbro, The First 50 Years* (Pittsfield, ME: Cianbro Corporation, 2010 rev.).

50. P. Leary, *Industrial Organizational Psychology* (New York: Worth Publishing, 2010); F. Luthans and C. Yousef, "Emerging Positive Organizational Behavior," *Journal of Management* 33, no. 3 (June 2007): 321–349; and A. Brahamson and M. Eisenman, "Employee Management Techniques," *Administrative Science Quarterly* 53, no. 4 (2008): 719–744.

51. N. Nohria et al., "What Really Works," *Harvard Business Review* (July 2003): 42–52.

52. E. Thorndike, *Animal Intelligence* (New York: Macmillan, 1911); and E. Thorndike, *Educational Psychology* (New York: Columbia University Teachers College, 1913).

53. J. Watson, "Psychology as the Behaviorist Views It," *Psychological Review* 20 (1913): 158–177; I. Pavlov, *Conditioned Reflexes* (London: Oxford University Press, 1927); B. Skinner, *Science and Human Behavior* (New York: Free Press, 1953); C. Ferster and B. Skinner, *Schedules of Reinforcement* (New York: Appleton-Century-Crofts, 1957); A. Bandura, *Principles of Behavior Modification* (New York: Holt, Rinehart & Winston, 1969); F. Luthans and J. Schweizer, "How Behavior Modification Techniques Can Improve Total Organizational Performance," *Management Review* (September 1979): 43–50; and A. Stajkovic and F. Luthans, "Differential Effects of Incentive Motivators in Work Performance," *Academy of Management Journal* 44 (2001): 580–590.

54. A. Stajkovic and F. Luthans, "A Meta-Analysis of the Effects of Organizational Behavior Modification on TASK Performance, 1975–95," *Academy of Management Journal* 40, no. 5 (October 1997): 1122–1149; and F. Luthans and A. Stajkovic, "Reinforce for Performance," *Academy of Management Executive* 13 (May 1999): 49–57.

55. Authors' files, Transit Authority of Northern Kentucky (TANK); T. Connellan, *How to Improve Human Performance* (New York: Harper & Row, 1978); and R. Miltenberger, *Behavior Modification: Principles and Procedures* (Pacific Grove, CA: Brooks/Cole, 1997).

56. S. Kerr, "On the Folly of Rewarding A, While Hoping for B," *Academy of Management Executive* 9 (February 1995): 32–40.

57. E. Lengel, *General George Washington* (New York: Random House, 2005).

58. Y. Cohen-Charash and P. Spector, "The Role of Justice in Organizations," *Organizational Behavior and Human Decision Processes* 86 (November 2001): 278–321.

59. A. Uris, *The Executive Deskbook* (New York: Van Nostrand Reinhold, 1988); and J. Greenberg and E. Lind, "The Pursuit of Social Justice," in C. Cooper and E. Locke, eds., *Industrial and Organizational Psychology: Linking Theory with Practice* (London: Blackwell, 2000).

60. J. Williams, *Human Behavior in Organizations* (Cincinnati, OH: South-Western, 1986).

61. M. Hils and K. Shields, "Behavior Problem Flow Chart," Northern Kentucky University, 1999.

62. W. McLarney and W. Berliner, *Management Training,* 5th ed. (Homewood, Ill.: Richard D. Irwin, Inc., 1970), 599. Reprinted with permission.

Chapter 20

1. Library of Congress online catalog, retrieved May 25, 2010, from http://catalog.loc.gov/; General Education Online, retrieved May 25, 2010, from http://www.findaschool.org; and J. Burke, ed., 2010 *Higher Education Directory* (Falls Church, VA: Higher Education Publications, 2010).

2. D. Messick and R. Kramer, *The Psychology of Leadership* (Mahwah, NJ: Erlbaum, 2005); F. Hesselbein and M. Goldsmith, *The Leader of the Future 2* (New York: Wiley, 2006); and "Creativity and Innovation," *Workplace Visions,* no. 1, 2007.

3. M. Follett, *Dynamic Administration* (New York: Harper, 1949).

4. M. Follett, *Dynamic Administration.*

5. M. Kunkel, *Abraham Lincoln: Unforgettable American* (Charlotte, NC: Delmar, 1976); D. Phillips, *Lincoln on Leadership* (New York: Warner, 1992); and D. Donald, *Lincoln* (New York: Touchstone, 1996).

6. Phillips, *Lincoln on Leadership.*

7. M. Mayeroff, *On Caring* (New York: Harper & Row, 1971); and W. Bennis, "The Seven Ages of Leadership," in *Business Leadership,* J. Gallows, ed. (New York: Jossey-Bass, 2008).

8. P. Pitcher, *The Drama of Leadership* (New York: Wiley, 1997); J. Shaffer, *The Leadership Solution* (New York: McGraw-Hill, 2000); and L. Iacocca, *Iacocca* (New York: Bantam Books, 1986).

9. P. Pritchett, *Firing Up Commitment during Organizational Change* (Dallas, TX: Pritchett, 1996).

10. C. Francis, "Hippocratic Oath for Executives," in J. Sargent, *What Every Executive Should Know about the Art of Leadership* (Chicago: Dartnell, 1964), 24.

11. G. Goethals et al., *Encyclopedia of Leadership,* vol. 2 (Thousand Oaks, CA: Sage, 2004), 911–915; and D. Goodwin, *Team of Rivals* (New York: Simon & Schuster, 2006).

12. Phillips, *Lincoln on Leadership;* and Donald, *Lincoln.*

13. The poem "Retirement" is excerpted from the book *Life & Work* (Avon Books, 1994) by James A. Autry and is reprinted by permission of the author.

Glossary

A

ability innate and learned competency; talent required to perform a task; one's level of achievement based on skill, motivation, and expectation that one will succeed. The greater the ability, the greater the potential for leadership effectiveness. See *job knowledge.*

access a means of approach and interaction, both electronic as well as personal; an important commitment of the servant leader who satisfies the human need for face-to-face contact.

achievement accomplishment of a task; fulfillment; a social motive for assuming leadership responsibility.

action plan outlines the activities or tasks that need to be accomplished in order to obtain a goal.

aesthetic sensitive to art and beauty; pleasing to senses of sight, hearing, smell, taste, and touch; pertaining to a value orientation advancing form, harmony, and beauty as ideals.

affiliation the joining of people for mutual support; membership; a social motive for assuming leadership responsibility.

affirmative action employers are urged to hire groups of people based on their race, age, gender, or national origin to make up for historical discrimination.

alignment the arrangement and adjustment of parts, such as the alignment of people and resources to accomplish a goal; an essential leadership function.

art a skill acquired by experience or study; an endeavor requiring special knowledge and ability, such as the art of leadership.

assessment centers collections of instruments and exercises designed to diagnose individuals' development needs.

assigning work effectively deploying personnel, designating duties, and giving orders, following such proven principles as the following: know what you want to communicate before giving an order; ask rather than tell, but leave no doubt that you expect compliance; be considerate but never apologetic for asking someone to do a job; take responsibility for the orders you give; give people the opportunity to ask questions and express opinions; follow up to make sure assignments are being accomplished.

associations the company one keeps, as in family, friends, and other role models who help shape one's life; important determinants of individual character.

attitude a disposition or mood; the combination of thought and feeling that predisposes one to take action. Positive attitudes focus and energize people whereas negative attitudes depress people.

attitude survey a survey that focuses on employees' feelings and beliefs about their jobs and organizations.

authority the power or right to command, create, change, or otherwise act. The successful leader uses both formal and informal authority to accomplish goals.

autocratic pertaining to a form or style of leadership that is directive and leader-centered, and in which power is exercised by a dominant and dictatorial individual.

axiological arrest reduced level of morality that occurs if one fails to know, cherish, declare, act, and act habitually according to one's values. Axiology is the branch of philosophy concerned with the study of values.

B

behavior one's bearing, demeanor, and conduct. Behavior theory in leadership focuses on leadership style, such as autocratic, democratic, and laissez-faire, as well as leadership dimensions, such as initiating structure and showing consideration.

behavior modification an effective way to improve human performance, established in the 1950s and used in a wide variety of business, government, and nonprofit organizations. Elements include goal setting, feedback on performance, and positive reinforcement.

benchmarking in a search for excellence, taking the absolute best as a standard and trying to surpass it; objectively evaluating what an organization does compared with what its best competitors do and then taking steps to meet or exceed that high standard. Fundamental benchmark measures are product quality (what is produced) and service quality (how one deals with customers).

Big Five model of personality categorizes traits into dimensions of openness to experience, conscientiousness, extroversion, agreeableness, and neuroticism.

book a literary work, record, or account entailing many forms, such as volume, scroll, treatise, pamphlet, script; an important determinant of human character and leadership development.

bullying harassing, offending, or assigning humiliating tasks to a person of subordinate status.

burnout physical, psychological, and spiritual fatigue; inability to cope. Symptoms include lack of energy, low vitality, depression, loss of sharpness in thinking and feeling, lack of interest and meaning in life. Types of burnout victims include workaholics, burned-out Samaritans, mismatched people, and midcareer coasters. The formula for burnout is: Too many demands on strengths and resources, plus high expectations and deep personal involvement, plus too few actions taken to replenish the energy consumed, equals burnout.

burnout prevention strategies for dealing with inability to cope, including emergency aid, such as positive self-talk and physical retreat; short-term actions, such as reducing workload and setting priorities; and long-term solutions, such as clarifying values and making lifestyle changes.

C

care concern for the well-being of others and commitment to the accomplishment of a task. Caring is the emotional element required for successful leadership. See *concern* and *commitment.*

career success rules guidelines for succeeding in one's work, including exceeding expectations, delivering results, being considerate of others, being creative, and having integrity.

caring confrontation a corrective action that is taken to support core values, such as truth, trust, and respect, while simultaneously preserving human dignity.

caring leadership leadership marked by two principal aspects—commitment to a task and concern for people. The component of caring is the underlying requirement for successful leadership. See *commitment, concern,* and *Level 5 leadership.*

case study in-depth study of a single person, group, or organization.

change alteration and transformation; paradoxically, a constant in nature and life. Types of change in the workplace include structure, tasks, technology, and people. Effective responses in dealing with change include exploration, responsibility and commitment, versus denial, resistance, or an attitude trough characterized by resentment, anger, and worry.

charisma   a special charm or allure that inspires allegiance; an amalgam of inspirational traits or qualities of the leader, such as optimism, sense of adventure, and commitment to a cause. See *transformational leadership.*

code of conduct   a listing of rules to live by; the basis for determining whether an action is ethical. An example is the Rotary International code of conduct, which requires asking these questions: Is it the truth, is it fair to all concerned, will it build good will and better relationships, and will it be beneficial to all concerned?

cognitive dissonance   psychological discomfort experienced when attitudes and behavior are inconsistent.

collaboration   working together in pursuit of a common cause; cooperation in a joint effort.

collectivism   the belief that the values and goals of the group—whether extended family, ethnic group, or company—are primary.

collectivist culture   personal goals less important than community goals and interests.

commitment   a pledge or promise; an agreement that binds one with others or to a cause; the sense of duty one has to accomplish a task; an essential element of caring leadership. See *care* and *caring leadership.*

communication   the giving and receiving of information; the basis of constructive relationships; the essential requirement for both a humanistic and productive workplace. Types of communication ranked in order of importance to employees include immediate supervisor, small group meetings, information from top executives, policy handbooks, orientation programs, and member newsletters.

concern   consideration; regard for others; a demonstration of respect; the sense of responsibility one has for the well-being of others; an essential element of caring leadership. See *care* and *caring leadership.*

conditions conducive to growth   favorable conditions for personal development, including a felt need or desire to learn, encouragement by someone who is respected, movement from general goals to specific actions, movement from a state of lower to higher self-esteem, and movement from external to internal commitment.

contingency   contingency theory holds that multiple leadership variables determine the probability that leadership will occur, including qualities of leaders, characteristics of followers, and the nature of a situation.

core competency   a unique capability that creates high value and differentiates an organization from its competition.

counterproductive work behavior (CWB)   behavior that violates organizational norms and threatens the well-being of the organization, its members, or both.

courage   the ability to overcome fear and live (or die) by one's convictions, even in ambiguous, uncertain, and dangerous situations; the virtue that underlies and gives reality to all other values; the basis for moral worth and dignity.

creativity   innovation; the ability to use imagination and insight to produce new ideas, products, and processes; an important ability that can be enhanced by keeping an open mind, having a questioning attitude, and using a new-ideas system.

cross-cultural leadership   understanding and initiating behavioral patterns in different cultures.

cross-cultural training   structured experiences to help people adjust to a new culture/country.

cultural sensitivity   an awareness of and willingness to understand why people of another culture act as they do; a leadership quality requiring patience, willingness to learn, and flexibility, resulting in a bond of trust and respect among diverse people.

culture   societal forces affecting the values, beliefs, and actions of a distinct group of people.

culture shock   anxiety and doubt caused by an overload of new cultural expectations and cues.

D

deed   an act accomplished; a means of influence. A leader's deeds may inspire and mobilize people.

delegation   the act of assigning to another; authorization and entrustment of tasks; enlistment of the energy and talents of others to accomplish more than would be possible working alone; a leadership skill required for multiplying effectiveness, including the following rules: Don't delegate the bad jobs, saving the good ones for yourself; use delegation as a development tool; delegate work fairly among all employees; insist on clear communications; and learn to live with work styles that are not like your own.

democratic   pertaining to a form or style of leadership based on equality, shared power, group decision making, and the greatest good for the greatest number.

development   efforts to improve employees' abilities to handle a variety of assignments and to cultivate employees' capabilities beyond those required by the current job.

dilemma   any situation requiring a choice between alternatives; any serious problem or quandary, such as making difficult moral decisions.

direction   the point, objective, or targeted goal; the establishment of purpose as an essential leadership function. See *vision, commitment,* and *initiating structure.*

discipline   action that develops self-control, efficiency, and orderly conduct; regulation, training, and enforcement. Discipline problems include permissiveness, rigidity, and inconsistency. Elements of effective discipline include defined roles and responsibilities, clear rules and guidelines, and methods for taking corrective action.

distributive justice   the perceived fairness of how resources and rewards are distributed.

diversity challenge   the task of dealing with a wide variety of people and customs, including different genders, races, ages, religions, nationalities, and personalities; the goal of behaving in a way that creates mutual trust and interpersonal respect among people and gains benefits from their differences.

diversity practices   actions that can result in increased knowledge, skill, and creativity; better products and services provided to diverse populations; and the ability to recruit excellent talent from the entire labor pool. Such practices include top management's personal involvement, targeted recruitment, diversity education, network and support groups, and work and family policies that support diversity.

dyadic   refers to the relationship between two people.

E

economic   pertaining to the production, distribution, and consumption of products and services; the management of income and expenditures; a value system based on the satisfaction of material needs and the accumulation of wealth.

effective group   a work group with the following characteristics: a clear mission, an informal atmosphere, lots of discussion, active listening, trust and openness, acceptance of disagreement, issue-oriented (never personal) criticism, consensus as the norm, effective leadership, clarity of assignments, shared values and norms of behavior, and commitment.

effective leadership   leadership that is the result of getting the facts, creating a vision, motivating people, and empowering others. Effective leadership requires being oneself, hiring good people, treating others fairly, focusing on key objectives, listening well, calling the play, and encouraging others, as well as being enthusiastic, setting the example, showing support, and keeping promises. See *leadership.*

e-learning   use of the Internet or an organizational intranet to conduct training online.

emotional intelligence (EI)   the ability to understand and deal effectively with people; a type of intelligence possessed by successful leaders. Elements include self-awareness, impulse control, persistence, confidence, self-motivation, empathy, and social deftness, resulting in an overall characteristic of persuasiveness. See *persuasion.*

employee assistance program (EAP)   plan that provides counseling and other help to employees having emotional, physical, or other personal problems.

employee engagement   an individual's involvement, satisfaction, and enthusiasm for work.

empowerment   authorization and enablement; the awakening, liberation, and inspiration of people. Principles of empowerment include trust in people, investment in people, recognition of accomplishment, and decentralized decision making. Empowerment is closely associated with the concepts of democratic and participative leadership. See *democratic* and *participative leadership.*

energize   to activate and mobilize, as in empowering people to accomplish results, an essential leadership function. See *empowerment* and *motivation.*

energy   force of expression and capacity for action; vitality and stamina to initiate tasks and see them to completion; an important trait or quality for leadership success. See *vitality* and *stamina.*

enlightened leadership   highly effective leadership resulting from viewing human resources as an organization's greatest asset; treating every individual with dignity, warmth, and support; tapping the constructive power of groups through visioning and team building; and setting high performance goals at every level of the organization.

enthusiasm   intensity of interest; the passion one has for a purpose or task; a leadership quality that ignites the interest and energy of others. See *commitment.*

entrepreneurship   the ability to achieve results, based on demonstrating good work habits, believing in oneself, and having the courage to take risks; an important element of leadership performance.

environment   surroundings; conditions and circumstances including physical and social factors; climate, geography, habitat, and social custom.

equation   a statement that matches, links, or relates objects or quantities. A leadership equation relates qualities of leaders, characteristics of followers, and the nature of a situation to explain the occurrence of leadership.

ethics   the branch of philosophy concerned with the intent, means, and consequences of moral behavior; derived from the Greek word *ethos,* referring to a person's fundamental orientation toward life or inner character. See *moral.*

evidence-based management (EBM)   management decisions and organizational practices based on the best available scientific evidence.

example   a case, prototype, or illustration; a representative model or ideal, as in one who leads by personal example.

excellence   a state of exceptional merit or goodness; a performance ideal. See *quality.*

experience   the act of living through an event; that which is known through personal exposure or involvement, such as leadership skills learned through experience.

extrinsic rewards   financial, material, or social rewards from the environment.

F

feedback   objective information about performance.

flextime   scheduling arrangement in which employees work a set number of hours a day but vary starting and ending times.

flow   a satisfying psychological state resulting from the confluence of high challenge and high skill, in contrast to states of apathy, anxiety, and boredom. Dimensions of flow include a clear and present purpose, immediate feedback, supreme concentration, a sense of growth, and an altered sense of time.

followship   the behavior of followers that results from the leader–follower relationship.

full-swing values   a concept used to describe the strength of one's values; full-swing values are known, cherished, declared, acted upon, and acted upon habitually. See *values* and *axiological arrest.*

G

gainsharing   an incentive plan that engages employees in a common effort to achieve productivity objectives and share the gains.

Galatea effect   an individual's high self-expectations lead to high performance.

glass ceiling   a term used to describe the impediments women face as they seek top leadership positions, including lack of encouragement, closed corporate culture, and double standards of conduct and performance.

globalization   the tendency of firms to extend sales, ownership, and/or manufacturing to new markets abroad.

goals   enduring intentions to act; process or functional accomplishments that are targets of effort; the ends one strives to attain.

Golem effect   loss in performance due to low leader expectations.

grapevine   unofficial communication system of the informal organization.

group   two or more freely interacting people with shared norms and goals and a common identity.

group cohesiveness   a "we feeling" binding group members together.

groupthink   a mode of thinking that people engage in when they are deeply involved in a cohesive group, and when members striving for unanimity override their motivation to realistically appraise alternative courses of action; in contrast to group strength, groupthink results in mistakes and failure. Causes of groupthink include the illusion of invulnerability, belief in the inherent morality of the group, rationalization, stereotyping of out-groups, self-censorship, direct pressure, mindguards, and the illusion of unanimity.

H

hardy personality   having the characteristics of a stress-resistant person–personal commitment, sense of control, positive attitude, balanced perspective, and caring relationships; having the adaptive capacity to deal effectively with stress and change.

heart   that which is vital; the center or core of a person or thing. Expressing one's innermost thoughts and feelings is termed "speaking from the heart," and it is the basis of credibility and trust.

hero   one who inspires through manners and actions; an individual who leads through personal example and accomplishments requiring bravery, skill, determination, and other admirable qualities.

hierarchy of needs   proposes that people are motivated through five levels of needs—physiological, safety, belongingness, esteem, and self-actualization.

honesty   truthfulness; a quality of character necessary for trust, respect, and honor; a foundation value and fundamental requirement for successful leadership.

human capital   the collective value of the capabilities, knowledge, skills, life experiences, and motivation of an organizational workforce.

human relations movement   the results of the Hawthorne studies ushered in this movement, which focused on work attitudes and the newly discovered emotional world of the worker.

human side of enterprise   all aspects of an organization relating to people, including relationships, performance, morale, and leadership. *The Human Side of Enterprise* is the title of a book by Douglas McGregor emphasizing the human potential for growth, the importance of the individual in the organization, and enlightened leadership practices. See *enlightened leadership.*

I

idea   a thought, mental conception, or image; a means of influence, as when the leader's ideas influence the behavior of the people.

imperative   a necessary, urgent, and important command, such as a quality imperative dictated by customers in the marketplace.

income   earnings; material rewards received (usually money), such as in wages, rent, interest, dividends, commissions, royalties, profits.

individualism   the belief that the values and goals of the individual are primary.

individualistic   pertaining to a style of interpersonal relations characterized by a need for freedom. Individualists generate new ideas and creativity, challenge the system, and accentuate possibilities. Leadership needs of individualists include being treated as separate individuals and avoiding rigid controls and close supervision.

individualistic culture   primary emphasis on personal freedom and choice.

initiating structure   the process of defining relationships, assigning tasks, making decisions, and holding performance to schedules and standards; job-centered leadership; concern for production. See *direction* and *vision.*

innovation   generation of new and usable ideas; an important element of leadership performance. See *creativity.*

integrative   pertaining to an approach to leadership that brings different people together and develops a whole that is greater than the sum of its parts; a building-up versus a melting-down process that preserves the identity of the individual while this identity is simultaneously transcended and made greater.

integrity   completion, wholeness, and soundness; a quality of character requiring honesty and courage; a virtue necessary for trust; the most important quality desired in a leader. See *values, honesty,* and *courage.*

intelligence   the ability to understand and solve problems; an important leadership trait or quality involving discernment, comprehension, and judgment; capacity to understand information, formulate strategies, and make good decisions.

internal locus of control   attributing outcomes to one's own actions.

interpersonal   between persons; for example, interpersonal trust and respect.

interpersonal competence   includes social awareness and social skills such as the ability to resolve conflict and foster a spirit of cooperation.

interpersonal styles   a construct of personality that helps explain why people do what they do. Although no trait or concept can capture the full richness and uniqueness of a single human being, styles of interpersonal relations reflect general patterns of behavior and needs.

intrinsic rewards   self-granted, psychic rewards.

J

job aid   set of instructions, diagrams, or similar methods available to guide the worker.

job enrichment   building achievement, recognition, stimulating work, responsibility, and advancement into a job.

job families   distinct clusters of interests and aptitudes that separate people and help account for personal satisfaction and occupational success; examples are investigative, artistic, social, enterprising, conventional, and realistic.

job knowledge   mastery of essential theory and practical skills necessary to perform a function or task; a quality of leadership admired and deemed important by followers. See *ability.*

justice   the concept of fairness in human affairs; that which is good is good without regard to social, economic, and political consideration.

K

knowing–doing gap   knowing what to do, but failing to do it; a tendency to study and learn a concept, principle, practice, or skill, but neglect to use it in a practical way.

knowledge management   the way an organization identifies and leverages knowledge in order to be competitive.

L

laissez-faire   pertaining to a free-rein form or style of leadership characterized by minimum control and maximum individual freedom.

law of effect   behavior with favorable consequences is repeated; behavior with unfavorable consequences disappears.

leadership   social influence; showing the way or course of action; causing to follow by ideas and deeds; influencing through instruction, heroic feats, and force of will, magnified by the component of caring about the task to be done and the welfare of others; the functions or processes of establishing direction, aligning people and resources, and energizing people to accomplish results. See *effective leadership.*

leader trait   personal characteristic that differentiates leaders from followers.

lean production   method that focuses on reducing waste, including overproduction, lengthy waiting times for materials, excessive transportation costs, unnecessary stock, and defective products.

learning   acquisition of knowledge, skills, and attitudes; growth and development enhanced by attention, pace, relevance, value, participation, repetition, and application; developed through study and experience.

learning organization   proactively creates, acquires, and transfers knowledge throughout the organization.

Level 5 leadership   the paradoxical combination of personal humility and professional will that makes a potent formula for the highest level of leadership success. Personal humility refers to consideration and service to others; professional will refers to conviction and fierce resolve. Together, these define the caring leader who is able to catapult a group or an organization from merely good to truly great. See *caring leadership.*

listening   hearing and paying attention to another as an expression of respect; an effective means of raising the psychological size of others, liberating their energies, and leading them to higher levels of achievement.

loneliness   a state of detachment, separation, and isolation; a feeling of being friendless and forlorn.

M

management   the performance of four functions or processes— planning, including charting a direction, determining strategies to succeed, and making policy decisions; organizing, including aligning structure, people, and resources to achieve goals; directing, including supervising, facilitating, coaching, and developing people; and controlling, including tracking progress against plans and making corrections; an endeavor requiring technical, relational, and conceptual skills.

management by objectives   management system incorporating participation in decision making, goal setting, and feedback.

managerial grid   identifies five leadership styles: 1,1 impoverished; 9,1 sweatshop; 1,9 country club; 5,5 status quo; and 9,9 fully functioning.

managing change   helping people through change. Leaders should be guided by these seven rules: Have a good reason for making a change; personalize change; implement change thoughtfully; put a respected person in charge of coordinating change; tell the truth; wait patiently for results; acknowledge and reward people.

managing conflict   dealing effectively with conflicting purposes and personalities, and achieving solutions that benefit all parties; a social skill of the effective leader, involving a collaborative style, versus avoidance, accommodation, domination, and compromise.

mentor a term referring to the development of others; derived from *The Odyssey* in which Homer describes Ulysses as choosing his trusted friend, Mentor, to protect and teach his son, Telemachus, as Ulysses begins a 10-year journey from home.

mentoring a form of coaching in which a more-experienced person helps a less-experienced protégé.

meta-analysis statistical method for combining and analyzing the results from many studies to draw a general conclusion about relationships among variables.

methods of learning approaches to learning, including classroom instruction, performance coaching, action learning, field assignments, and studying the masters.

mission central purpose or reason for existence; a clear, compelling statement that provides focus and direction; an organization's answer to the question, Why do we exist?

moral referring to what is right and wrong, good and bad, with emphasis on overt behavior—acts, habits, and customs. Levels of moral reasoning include preconventional morality, based on avoiding punishment and striving for pleasure; conventional morality, based on pleasing others and doing one's duty as prescribed by authorities; and postconventional morality, based on mutual consent and personal conviction. See *ethics.*

morale mental and emotional condition with respect to satisfaction, confidence, and resolve; the attitude or spirit of an individual or group resulting in courage, dedication, and discipline; the level of satisfaction one has with intrinsic job factors, such as variety and challenge, feedback and learning, wholeness and meaning, and room to grow, as well as extrinsic conditions of employment, such as fair and adequate pay, job security, and health and safety. See *raising morale.*

motivation stimulation and inspiration to move; the leadership task of mobilizing people with different ideas, skills, and values to achieve a common mission; the experience of physical and emotional needs, progressing from basic needs for survival and security, to social needs for belonging and respect, to the complex need for fulfillment. See *energize* and *empowerment.*

motivation principles principles for understanding human behavior in the workplace, including the following: A satisfied need is not a motivator, employee motivation and company success are related, leadership is important in meeting employee needs, and the ideal is to align individual needs with organizational goals.

multiple intelligences different kinds of ability required to understand and solve problems; innate and learned competencies, including verbal–linguistic, musical–rhythmic, logical–mathematical, visual–spatial, bodily–kinesthetic, intrapersonal, and interpersonal.

N

negative group member roles group member roles that reduce effectiveness, including ego tripper, negative artist, above it all, aggressor, jokester, and avoider. See *effective group.*

negotiating a process in which two or more parties are in conflict and attempt to come to an agreement.

nonverbal communication messages sent without of the written or spoken word.

O

occupational information network (O*NET) collection of electronic databases, based on well-developed taxonomies, that has updated and replaced the Dictionary of Occupational Titles (DOT).

Ohio State University leadership model identifies leadership styles based on two dimensions: initiating structure and showing consideration.

ombudsperson a person entrusted with the responsibility of acting as the organization's conscience.

onboarding efforts aimed at helping employees integrate, assimilate, and transition to new jobs.

open book a management philosophy and practice emphasizing the sharing of information and employee involvement for organizational success.

organization any group or aggregation of individuals into a purposeful entity, such as those found in business and industry, government, and the social community; also, the process of aligning people and resources to accomplish tasks (visions, goals, initiatives, and the like).

organization chart a chart showing the organization-wide distribution of work, with titles of each position and interconnecting lines showing who reports to and communicates with whom.

organization development a set of techniques or tools used to implement organizational change.

organizational behavior interdisciplinary field dedicated to better understanding and managing people at work.

organizational citizenship behavior (OCB) employee behavior that meets or exceeds work-role requirements.

organizational climate the social and psychological work atmosphere, including reward systems, organizational clarity, standards of performance, warmth and support, and leadership practices; a range of organizational health from exploitation to enlightenment that influences both employee morale and organizational effectiveness.

organizational commitment the degree to which employees believe in and accept organizational goals and desire to remain with the organization.

organizational culture the shared values and beliefs in an organization and its workforce.

organizational justice type of justice that is composed of organizational procedures, outcomes, and interpersonal interactions.

P

participative pertaining to a style of interpersonal relations characterized by a need for human interaction and warm relationships. Participatives provide peace and harmony, give encouragement to others, and instill team spirit. Leadership needs include keeping human relations smooth and considering personal feelings.

participative leadership a philosophy of and approach to leadership that taps the constructive power of people, resulting in both a humanistic and productive workplace. The participative leader begins by involving people, which is necessary to achieve understanding, which is necessary to achieve commitment. See *democratic* and *empowerment.*

people-building skills the ability to teach, counsel, and otherwise develop others to higher levels of performance; a quality of leadership desired by followers. Developing others is a leadership function viewed by many leaders as the most rewarding of their tasks.

people, products, profit the focus of concern for effective business leaders; a formula for success identified by business leader Lee Iacocca.

performance management the heart and essence of leadership success; the process of performance planning, establishing direction and clarity of assignment; performance coaching, developing and encouraging others; and correcting poor performance, modifying and improving performance when mistakes are made.

performance review evaluation and discussion of work behavior, such as dependability, initiative, and cooperation, as well as achievement of results in the areas of quantity, quality, timeliness, and cost. Performance reviews are used to capitalize on strengths and improve weaknesses. The process includes preparation, implementation, and follow-up. Types of performance reviews include tell and sell, tell and listen, problem-solving, and multisource assessment from supervisors, employees, peers, and customers.

persistence constancy of purpose and unrelenting determination; a leadership quality required to persevere and prevail, even when others lose their strength and will.

personality   the sum total of an individual's character, resulting from biological, cultural, and psychological factors. Personality differences can account for frustrations and conflicts that lower performance and reduce opportunities, as well as satisfactions and accomplishments that enrich the human experience.

person–organization (P–O) fit   extent to which the values of an employee are consistent with the values held by most others in the organization.

person–position fit   the successful matching of personal qualities with job demands. The result is high morale and work performance.

persuasion   the act of influencing; the ability to get buy-in based on an understanding of people, the effective use of words, and the ability to manage conflict.

Peter Principle   a term coined by author Lawrence J. Peter describing the tendency to promote individuals to their levels of incompetence. The overpromotion syndrome harms the individual and the organization because it inevitably results in lowered morale and job performance.

political   of or concerned with governance and the expression of power; a value orientation prizing social influence and the exercise of authority.

positive group member roles   group member roles that enhance effectiveness, including encourager, clarifier, harmonizer, idea generator, ignition key, standard setter, and detail specialist. See *effective group.*

positive reinforcement   occurs when desired behavior is followed by a reward, which increases the probability that the behavior will be repeated.

power   vigor and strength; the force necessary to exert one's will; a social motive for assuming leadership responsibility. A leader with power has the ability to dominate and control people and events. Sources of power used by leaders include rewards, coercion, legitimacy, and information; types of power include expertise, reference, rational, and charisma.

pragmatism   a philosophical belief emphasizing the importance of concrete evidence and practical usefulness in all human endeavor—social, economic, political, aesthetic, religious, and theoretical.

prejudice   an adverse opinion without just cause about people who are different in terms of gender, race, ethnicity, or any other definable characteristic.

prestige   renown and influence; reputation based on position, achievement, and character.

principles   standards of ethical conduct; fundamental truths and proven rules, such as the principles of effective leadership. See *ethics.*

problem-solving styles   distinct approaches to problem solving resulting from different emphases in having experiences, reflecting on results, building theories, and taking action. Identifiable styles include those of Charles Darwin, Albert Einstein, Socrates, and Henry Ford, each with special strengths and potential weaknesses.

project team   created to solve a particular problem and disbanded after the problem is solved; also called ad hoc committee, task force, or cross-functional team.

psychological diversity   differences in underlying attributes such as skills, abilities, personality characteristics, attitudes, beliefs, and values; may also include differences in functional, occupational, and educational backgrounds.

psychological size   the perceived power one person has over another; the ability to make others feel weak and dependent; the ability to determine careers, decide wages, and make job assignments; an important concept for people in authority positions. The abuse of psychological size results in resentment and rebellion, or apathy and dependence, whereas the effective use of psychological size results in maximum morale and productivity.

Pygmalion effect   proposes that leaders' expectations of followers, and their treatment of them, explain and predict followers' behavior and performance.

Q

qualities   characteristic elements that make things what they are; attributes deemed desirable, such as the leadership qualities of integrity, job knowledge, and people-building skills.

quality   the degree of excellence of a thing; a virtue resulting from superior form, function, beauty, utility, fit, and other valuable attributes; the character of a person or thing that makes it desirable. See *excellence.*

quality circle   work group that typically involves 6 to 12 employees who meet regularly to identify work-related problems and generate ideas to increase productivity or product quality.

quality movement   the synthesis of "hard" efforts to improve work performance, such as scientific management and quantitative methods, with "soft" efforts, such as improving morale and building community. The quality movement, most associated with the work of W. Edwards Deming, typically involves participative leadership, continuous process improvement, and the use of groups.

R

raising morale   taking actions that have a positive impact on employee satisfaction and work performance, including introducing a group bonus, allowing job autonomy, providing training, assigning whole tasks, gaining direct feedback from users, and increasing group interaction. See *morale.*

reinforcement   based on the idea that people tend to repeat responses that give them some type of positive reward and avoid actions associated with negative consequences.

relational skill   the ability to work effectively with people, including the ability to motivate, coordinate, and advise other people; an important skill required at all levels of leadership—frontline supervisor, mid-level manager, and senior executive.

relationship management   relates to the ability to work well with others.

religious   pertaining to the belief in and worship of a god or gods, a specific system of belief and worship involving a code of ethics, a value orientation emphasizing spiritual peace.

resiliency   the ability to handle pressure and quickly bounce back from personal and career setbacks.

respect   honor and esteem for another; regard for others as demonstrated through listening and being responsive to their beliefs and needs whenever possible.

retention   avoidance of turnover and ability to keep good people, which requires knowing what makes them stay. Factors that are particularly important to talented and productive employees include letting people know what is expected of them, giving them materials and equipment to do their jobs right, giving them the chance to do what they do best every day, providing recognition and praise for good work, showing that you care about them as people, and encouraging their development.

rich job   a job that contains optimum variety and challenge, opportunity for decision making, feedback and learning; maximum support and respect, wholeness and meaning, and room to grow; as well as fair and adequate pay, job security, benefits, safety, health, and due process.

ruler   one who governs, determining policy and making decisions; a commander, such as a chief, king, or other authority figure, who leads through power and enforcement.

S

schema   mental picture of an event or object.

school   a place or process of learning with many varieties, including elementary, secondary, and high school; technical, professional, community college, and university; continuing education and graduate studies; an important factor in the development of character and leadership.

scientific management   using research and experimentation to find the most efficient way to perform a job.

secular   not religious; not connected with a church, synagogue, mosque, pagoda, temple, or other religious institution.

self-actualization   a state of psychological fulfillment, including acceptance of self and others, accurate perception of reality, close relationships, personal autonomy, goal directedness, naturalness, need for privacy, orientation toward growth, sense of unity with nature, sense of brotherhood with all people, democratic character, sense of justice, sense of humor, creativity, and personal integrity.

self-concept   a unifying construct of personality; the most important determinant of human behavior; the basis of present identity and future conduct; the primary factor in character formation.

self-confidence   a belief in oneself that gives inner strength to overcome difficult tasks; a leadership quality that raises the trust and confidence of followers and increases their ability to perform.

self-efficacy   belief in one's ability to do a task.

self-fulfilling prophecy   someone's high expectations for another person result in high performance.

self-management   relates to the ability to control disruptive emotions and impulses.

servant leader   a person devoted to others or to a cause or creed. A servant leader advances the interest of others, often at personal sacrifice. The essential component of servant leadership is the element of caring. See *concern, commitment,* and *care.*

service   aid and assistance provided to others; concern for the well-being and the best interest of another person or group.

showing consideration   developing relationships, providing support, and demonstrating kindness toward others; exhibiting employee-centered leadership, concern for people. See *concern* and *servant leader.*

situational factors   factors that influence the leadership process, including size of the organization, social and psychological climate, patterns of employment, and type, place, and purpose of the work performed.

Six Sigma systems   approach to quality management providing training for employees and managers in statistical analysis, project management, and problem-solving methods to reduce the defect rate of products.

social   of or having to do with other beings of one's kind; genial and companionable; a value orientation concerned with the well-being of others, typified by kindness, understanding, and helpfulness.

social awareness   relates to the ability to understand others.

social loafing   reduced motivation and performance in groups that occurs when there is a reduced feeling of individual accountability or a reduced opportunity for evaluation of individual performance.

social motive   cause of human interaction. Social motives for assuming leadership include power, the goal to influence people and events; achievement, the need to discover, create, and build; and affiliation, concern for others and their welfare.

stability   steadiness and firmness of purpose; a leadership quality required for making good judgments and generating the trust and confidence of others.

stages in the life of a group   the natural sequence of conditions in the life of a group, including forming, the start-up stage; storming, a period of polarization and conflict; norming, a shift to affiliation and agreement; and performing, a state of focus, energy, and high performance.

stakeholders   individuals and groups who may be affected by what an organization does or does not do. Stakeholders include owners, employees, customers, suppliers, and the general public.

stamina   resistance to fatigue and illness; vigor, strength, and endurance to continue even in the face of difficult and trying conditions; a leadership quality required to create, advance, and sustain a vision. See *energy* and *vitality.*

statesmanship   the ability to work with and through other people, based on mastery of human relations skills and use of the four-step method to solve problems; an important element of leadership performance.

status   the condition of a person or thing, a position in relation to others, as in a social system.

stewardship   employee-focused leadership that empowers followers to make decisions and have control over their jobs.

strategy   the science of planning; the process of giving definition to a vision, of focusing people and resources on specific objectives that can be measured; analysis of conditions and determination of initiatives; a requirement for successful leadership.

stress   physical and emotional wear and tear resulting from pressures, conflicts, and frustrations. Stress can be caused by self or others, work-related or personal, short-term or continuous. Sources of job stress for increasing numbers of people include new technology, workforce diversity, global competition, organizational restructure, and changing work systems.

succession planning   process of identifying a long-term plan for the orderly replacement of key employees.

support   care, encouragement, and help. The servant leader provides support to others through constructive feedback to reinforce and/or improve performance.

SWOT   an acronym standing for *S*trengths, *W*eaknesses, *O*pportunities, and *T*hreats. A SWOT analysis is a thorough and objective study of an organization's internal strengths and weaknesses and external opportunities and threats.

T

tactical   pertaining to the science of maneuvering, methods and techniques to achieve an end, projects and activities designed to implement strategy, the plays that drive the game to success.

talent management   concerned with enhancing the attraction, development, and retention of key human resources.

Taoism   an ancient spiritual tradition that is both a philosophy and a religion; Tao, or "the Way" is present in all that exists, and, through the complementary forces of yin and yang, is the source of endless change in the world.

teacher   one who provides knowledge, skill, and attitude development; a master or mentor who leads through insight, modeling, and the encouragement of others.

team   interdependent individuals who work together toward a common goal and who share responsibility for specific outcomes for their organizations.

team building   experiential learning aimed at better internal functioning of groups.

team concept   belief in the principle that together everyone can accomplish more than each could do working alone; tapping the constructive power of the group by having clear and elevating goals, a results-driven structure, competent team members, unified commitment, a collaborative climate, standards of excellence, external support and recognition, and principled leadership.

theoretical   that which is based on speculative thought and abstract reasoning; pertaining to a value orientation seeking universal principles and the discovery of truth.

theory X   negative assumptions about employees' values and intentions.

theory Y   positive assumptions about employees being responsible and creative.

360-degree feedback   process of collecting and providing feedback from many sources including supervisors, peers, subordinates, customers, and suppliers.

tolerance of differences   openmindedness; understanding, appreciation, and patience with different kinds of people, such as those with different styles of interpersonal relations, types of intelligences, value orientations, and problem-solving styles.

top grading   the staffing process of selecting and developing high-quality (A and B) performers, and reassigning lower-quality (C, D, and F) performers to more appropriate functions; a difficult but necessary task of the successful leader in a competitive environment.

total quality management   a management philosophy dedicated to employee training, continuous improvement, and customer satisfaction.

traditional   pertaining to a style of interpersonal relations characterized by a need for structure, order, and consistency. Traditionals provide stability and discipline, give attention to detail, and adhere to high standards. Leadership needs include respecting traditions and being clear and logical when giving orders.

trait   a distinguishing characteristic, such as a habit, manner, or peculiarity. Trait theory in leadership focuses on qualities that mark a leader, such as intelligence, integrity, and energy.

transactional leadership   focuses on clarifying employees' roles and providing rewards contingent on performance.

transformational leadership   the elevation of the potential of followers beyond previous expectations; the ability to raise aspirations and achievements to new levels of performance primarily as a result of the intelligence, charm, and talents of a charismatic leader. See *charisma*.

trust   a firm belief in the honesty and reliability of another; confidence developed by dealing openly with others, considering all points of view, keeping promises, and caring about people.

turnover   the process in which employees leave an organization and have to be replaced.

U

University of Michigan leadership model   identifies two leadership styles: job-centered and employee-centered.

V

value   the estimated worth of something. To be most valued, a person, object, or principle must be known, cherished, declared, supported, and supported habitually, even at personal sacrifice. The value-based leader demonstrates courage of conviction, an important leadership trait or quality. See *integrity* and *full-swing values*.

value system   the organization of one's beliefs about preferred ways of behaving and desired end-states.

virtual teams   groups that interact primarily through electronic means, with little, if any, in-person contact.

vision   a positive and future-focused image of what could and should be that focuses and energizes people; an essential requirement for effective leadership. A successful vision is leader-initiated, shared and supported by followers, comprehensive and detailed, and uplifting and inspiring.

vitality   the strength to live; a basic requirement for successful leaders who, through personal energy and stamina, breathe life into their visions and followers. See *energy* and *stamina*.

vital shift   a change in work responsibilities when one moves from doer to coordinator to thinker; a transition period requiring adjustment to different job demands.

W

wellness programs   programs designed to maintain or improve employee health before problems arise by encouraging self-directed lifestyle changes.

work   a thing made or done; a creation requiring effort; an endeavor that can be positive and ennobling or negative and unpleasant, depending on one's attitude.

Z

Zeigarnik effect   deterioration of morale and performance when tasks begun are not completed, which can be prevented by assigning whole tasks and allowing sufficient time for completion.

zeitgeist   trend of thought and feeling in a period of history, such as individual freedom, social responsibility, and love as an ideal—the spirit of a time.

Index